MW00635932

Reclaiming the Archive

CONTEMPORARY APPROACHES TO FILM AND TELEVISION SERIES

A complete listing of the books in this series can be found online at wsupress.wayne.edu

General Editor
Barry Keith Grant
Brock University

Advisory Editors
Patricia B. Erens
School of the Art Institute of Chicago

Lucy Fischer
University of Pittsburgh

Caren J. Deming
University of Arizona

Robert J. Burgoyne
Wayne State University

Tom Gunning
University of Chicago

Anna McCarthy
New York University

Peter X. Feng
University of Delaware

Lisa Parks
University of California–Santa Barbara

Frances Gateward
Ursinus College

Walter Metz
Montana State University

Thomas Leitch
University of Delaware

Reclaiming the Archive

FEMINISM AND FILM HISTORY

EDITED BY *Vicki Callahan*

WAYNE STATE UNIVERSITY PRESS DETROIT

© 2010 by Wayne State University Press, Detroit, Michigan 48201. All rights reserved. No part of this book may be reproduced without formal permission. Manufactured in the United States of America.

16 15 14 13 12   6 5 4 3 2

Library of Congress Cataloging-in-Publication Data

Reclaiming the archive : feminism and film history / edited by Vicki Callahan.
p. cm. — (Contemporary approaches to film and television series)
Includes bibliographical references and index.
ISBN 978-0-8143-3300-6 (pbk. : alk. paper)
1. Feminism and motion pictures. 2. Women in motion pictures. 3. Women in the motion picture industry. 4. Feminist film criticism. I. Callahan, Vicki.
PN1995.9.W6R445 2010
791.43'6522—dc22
2009041403

"Black and White: Mercedes de Acosta's Glorious Enthusiasms" by Patricia White originally appeared in a longer format in *Camera Obscura* 45, vol. 15.3 (2001). Reprinted by permission.

"On Cyberfeminism and Cyberwomanism: High-Tech Mediations of Feminism's Discontents" by Anna Everett is adapted from her essay "Double Click: The Million Woman March on Television and the Internet" in *Television after TV: Essays on a Medium in Transition,* ed. Lynn Spigel and Jan Olsson (Durham, NC: Duke University Press, 2004), 224–41; it also appears in *Digital Diaspora: A Race for Cyberspace,* by Anna Everett (New York: SUNY Press, 2009). Reprinted by permission.

An earlier version of "The Birth of the Local Feminist Sphere in the Global Era: *Yeoseongjang* and 'Trans-cinema'" by Soyoung Kim appeared in *Inter-Asia Cultural Studies* 4.1 (2003), 10–24. Reprinted by permission.

Typeset by Maya Rhodes
Composed in Adobe Garamond, Zapfino, and Myriad Pro

For John

Contents

I. Gazing Outward: The Spectrum of Feminist Reception History 9

CONTENTS

Acknowledgments

Reclaiming the Archive: Feminism and Film History is truly a collaborative work that would not have been completed without the efforts and support of many people. My desire to make the book as inclusive as possible produced issues of scope, size, and duration that required what seemed at times like an army of feminist volunteers to see it to completion. I am very grateful for the sustained help from a group of magnificent scholars who provided close readings, needed feedback and commentary, and especially enthusiasm and good cheer when at times the project seemed daunting and impossible.

Several people served in a coediting capacity on the book but the vicissitudes of life and academia called them elsewhere as the project's lifespan extended beyond the normal tour of duty. First and foremost, Alison McKee provided clarity, organization, and her incredible editing skills to the project when I was most in need of all three talents—simply put, this book would not have been completed without her labor and solid scholarship. Kelley Conway and Jennifer Holt both worked diligently in the early stages of the book to help map out the scope and define the parameters of the work. Jennifer's early enthusiasm for the project launched the enterprise and shaped the focus of the work particularly as a cross-generational venture.

I am also grateful to several scholars who generously took time out from their busy schedules to read essays and introductions at various stages and give needed expertise: Sumiko Higashi, Janet Staiger, and Gregory Jay all pitched in on short notice with their impeccable analysis and always honest and direct commentary. Sumiko and Janet have become for me especially wonderful and lively interlocutors on issues of feminism, media, and history, and I have enjoyed their friendship, intellectual rigor, and laughter over many meals (and in Janet's case, museum tours). Suzanne Leonard deserves a special shout-out for her ongoing interventions as skillful editor and postfeminist scholar extraordinaire. I also would like to thank a group of feminist scholars who provided input or made suggestions on the project over the years and have greatly influenced how I have understood and shaped the work: Jane Gaines, Janet Bergstrom, Diane Negra, Yvonne Welbon, Rachel Raimist, Britta Sjogren, Catherine Grant, Vivian Sobchack, Lisa Nakamura, Nam Lee, and Anne Friedberg especially provided important ideas and commentary that I found invaluable.

Although credited with the photos later in the book, a special thank-you goes to the Kobal Collection and Ricky Byrd, Shelley Stamp, Lynn Hershman Leeson, and Jeff Aldrich for their extra effort and generosity with the images they supplied.

I must also acknowledge my contributors, who have been overwhelmingly supportive and enthusiastic about this book; they have truly sustained and inspired me. My graduate students from assorted feminist film studies seminars over the years also deserve special acknowledgment. I have been very fortunate to work with some amazing young scholars at UCLA, UC-Irvine, and UWM interested in media and gender issues, many of whom are now well on their way to outstanding careers of their own.

Wayne State University Press has, as always, provided solid editorial support. Their commitment to this, at times, unwieldy and complicated project has been steadfast and spirited. Barry Keith Grant and assorted readers from the press gave incisive and crucial critical insights that ensured the book's integrity and quality of scholarship. Jane Hoehner and Annie Martin were both relentlessly resilient and helpful throughout this long endeavor. Annie Martin has been a particularly important force behind this project. I can say without exaggeration every conversation and e-mail I had with Annie left me energized and with a clear sense of direction about how best to proceed. Carrie Downes Teefey deserves particular credit for her meticulous care and concern in the final editing stages.

Lastly, I must thank my husband, John Callahan, who is probably upstairs right now formatting something or other for a project or class I am working on. He always identifies himself as the "sales guy" at parties, but he is undoubtedly one of best analytical readers I have encountered. John is also the center of calm and wisdom in the household and thus any bumps along the path of the book's completion were always put into his usual Zen-like perspective. His unwavering support, energy, and passionate belief in the project from the very beginning to the last footnote make him an important contributor to this collection.

Vicki Callahan

Introduction: Reclaiming the Archive
Archaeological Explorations toward a Feminism 3.0

This book was inspired by the graduate students in my feminism and film theory seminar at UCLA a few years ago. As we worked through an array of texts from nineteenth-century women's rights polemics to various 1970s manifestos to contemporary readings on the complexity of film spectatorship and commentaries on postfeminism, it became clear that feminist theory was still a vibrant area of study for young scholars and that its centrality to current cinema studies was self-evident once discussed in relation to its historical trajectory. A synchronous and chronological reading of feminist history and theory exposed distressingly repetitive issues and, most importantly, revealed to us a sense of the *generations* who have struggled to expand the possibilities for women's lives and identity. This generational insight and sense of debt to our feminist predecessors enabled the class to reevaluate and appreciate 1970s feminist film theory, which for many of them had been a moldy and isolated artifact of film studies, and to imagine the necessity for claiming and marking out a feminist future. B. Ruby Rich's *Chick Flicks: Theories and Memories of the Feminist Film Movement,* a parallel text read alongside canonical feminist works, emerged from the class, at least for me, as an innovative model for feminist history and theory. While some may take issue with whether Rich's entire chronicle was precisely reconstructed or even accurate, the ideas crucial for our purposes were an ongoing self-reflective turn and a sense of a dialogue between past and present.

Reclaiming the Archive: Feminism and Film History is expressly staged, then, as an ongoing intervention in the above two domains: film history and feminist studies (particularly feminist film theory). Moreover, this en-

1

deavor takes place during a time when the categories of cinema and feminism are problematized through the proliferation of media technologies and the phenomenon of postfeminism. Thus, implicitly framing the collection are two *theoretical* questions: what is cinema and what is feminism *today*?

Vivian Sobchack argues in a 2006 *Camera Obscura* essay that we cannot "engage in either the past or the future of feminism in relation to media unless we begin *in the present*."[1] While Sobchack is referencing a pedagogical context for this intersection of historical moments, her remarks are consistent with the deep-time possibilities emanating from the emergent field of media archaeology.[2] Here archeology is, as Michel Foucault notes within a separate but related context, not a "search for a beginning" but rather "designates the general theme of the already-said at the level of its existence: of the enunciative function that operates within it, of the discursive formation, and the general archive system to which it belongs."[3] Media archaeology's deep-time methodology opens the possibilities for film history and theory by envisioning temporality as a nonlinear, multidirectional flow of information rather than a singular reductive and evolutionary stream of apodictic data. We might even begin to think about deep time as a useful metaphorical and polemical structure for a renewed feminist film activism. While the notion of deep time might at first glance seem antithetical to a *historical* project given its absence of strict chronology, its multiple vectors through time are more consistent with *feminist* and *cinematic* topologies.

An explicit goal of this collection is to demonstrate the diversity of approaches possible within feminist film history: archival research, visual culture, ethnohistorical studies, critical race theory, biography, reception studies, historiography, cultural studies, poststructuralism, and textual analysis. Another crucial objective is to open the conversation on feminist film history to an international focus (included are essays by scholars working outside the usual Anglo-American context) across an expansive chronological terrain (from early cinema to postfeminist texts). Jennifer Bean and Diane Negra's *A Feminist Reader in Early Cinema* provided an exemplary model of historical research focused on the silent era,[4] and *Reclaiming the Archive* continues the debate initiated by their collection. The essays in this collection cross areas from early cinema to cyberspace and postfeminism in order to examine the complex symbiotic relationship between feminist historiographical and theoretical practice within cinema studies and to trace key social, political, and international implications for work within our field.

As Jane Gaines notes in *Cinema Journal,* the turn to history in feminist film studies is the product of debates both with earlier historical accounts of the cinema *and* with feminist film theory.[5] That is, much of the feminist work in the arena of film history functions as a double-edged sword: on one level reviewing received notions of what and who counts in film history (and why particular early women directors and stars are newly "discovered") and on a second level rethinking the ongoing tension in feminist film studies between cinema as a machine of pleasure and cinema as a machine of oppression. It could be argued that the increased interest in historical projects in cinema studies can be linked to a debate directly with and within feminist theory, particularly around the questions of audience, spectatorship, and reception. In this regard, we cannot overstate the impact of Laura Mulvey's seminal essay "Visual Pleasure and Narrative Cinema" on both feminist and cinema studies.[6] Her explicitly polemical account of woman's place in the cinema functions as a paradigmatic shift for both fields. Most important, as Janet Bergstrom and Mary Ann Doane argue, Mulvey's essay represented "the inaugural moment—the condition of possibility—of an extended theorization of the female spectator."[7] Ironically, this spectator's "'origin' is constituted by an absence."[8] Many scholars returned to the very materiality of cinema practice and experience in an effort to complicate our understanding of cinema as visually and politically monolithic. As Christine Gledhill argues in her classic essay "Recent Developments in Feminist Film Criticism," naive realism (e.g., "negative stereotypes of women") and antirealist epistemology (i.e., an exclusively psychoanalytic/semiotic approach) are equally detrimental to political action in that both ignore the complexities of audience across a dynamic of interlocking social relationships.[9] Gledhill's effort to address race and class questions particularly in this early essay are just as relevant today, and there is an ongoing debate whether contemporary feminist studies adequately examines these relations. "The Oppositional Gaze: Black Female Spectatorship," by bell hooks, remains the definitive critique of the essentially white perspective that frames much of feminist film studies. For hooks, feminist film theory's attention to sexual difference elides "any discussion of racial difference—of racialized sexual difference."[10] hooks's commentary is crucial both for her naming of the black female spectator as well as for her positioning of a gaze outside of psychoanalytic or patriarchal boundaries (i.e., an oppositional gaze that extends beyond the black male viewer).[11]

As Amelia Jones notes in her introduction to *The Feminism and Visual Culture Reader,* the constant thread in feminist work is not toward any essential definition of feminism (or, for that matter, of woman) but rather toward a commitment to questions of social justice. In short, Jones states, feminism is a *political* or *ethical* engagement with questions of culture.[12] However, it is precisely this political and ethical dimension that many scholars feel has been unfulfilled and is indeed missing in contemporary feminism. Thus, hooks's earlier critique remains largely unaddressed alongside other questions of heterosexism, classism, and ethnocentrism.

Yvonne Tasker and Diane Negra point out that the term "feminism" is conspicuously absent from popular usage while numerous political gains of the movement have been absorbed, assimilated, and woefully unacknowledged.[13] For example, while young women today would never knowingly accept a lower paycheck than their male counterparts for the same position, many women would still, maddeningly, begin a discussion of equal pay issues, with the all too familiar disavowal: "I am not a feminist, but . . ." On the academic side, a similar denial has occurred. Alexandra Juhasz contends the political goals of the feminist movement have now been replaced with professional ones. What is missing today, she argues, is our past commitment to theory/practice, which is "linked to real struggles and actions."[14] I would also argue that our turn to history represents a way out of this dilemma, since history gives us the practical and material information needed to inform our theory. When situated as a deep-time project, history becomes a discovery process with open-ended results and multiple points of entry. If we consider the convergence of technology and the expansion of the cinematic arts, the opportunity for new forms and new voices increases exponentially. Jackie Hatfield sees digital technology as a crucial venue for opening up the possibilities of "future histories" or "gardens of history" across a range of creative and critical practices (e.g., the capacity of an electronic database to store information and assemble and present multiple narratives based on different search criteria).[15]

I have structured this collection as a kind of extended conversation about the role of feminism *today,* as both a disciplinary tool and a larger cultural critique. In addition, the essays I solicited and chose to include, as well as the introductory editorial commentaries, historicize the question of where film history and feminist theory are at present and assert the continued influence of 1970s feminist film studies in relation to the current production of film history and feminist film theory. On one level, this collection is intended as a correction to a kind of historical amnesia *within our own history as feminist film scholars,* and so these essays are posited as a continuation of rather than a break with the feminist goals of the 1970s.

That is to say, the history that we present as feminists always implies a kind of reclaiming, rewriting, and recontextualization of materials. This self-critical turn is our central heritage from 1970s feminism, for it asks us what it means to write from a feminist perspective.

Reclaiming the Archive presents an ongoing engagement with two key questions: (1) What are the different models available to us in feminist film history? and (2) How might feminist strategies in film history serve as paradigmatic for other sites of feminist and related forms of progressive intervention? These issues are interrogated through a series of rewritings and revisions of fundamental categories in cinema studies. In many ways, the diversification of cinema studies to a variety of related technologies and the proliferation of methodological terrains undertaken in pursuit of various media have opened new venues for and added new voices to our disciplines. However, there is a sense, underscoring this interdisciplinary investigation, that a crisis of definition is ongoing within the field(s).[16] A significant heritage of film studies lies in the study of film *as* film and of feminism and feminist film theory. What the cinema and feminism represent *historically* are new ways of seeing and thinking about the world, and as such, the cinematic metaphor is a central one, I would argue, to a feminist agenda. It is precisely this dynamic that needs to be reinserted into the debate within our discipline regardless of whether the external veneer of feminism or cinema (or cinema studies) has changed. While the term "expanded cinema" has long designated cross-media and multimedia experimentation based on the developments of new technology,[17] perhaps it is time we think of "expanded cinema" writing not only with regard to methodology but also with respect to formats employed. Online archives, interactive media, and even improvisatory, live remixes of found footage are but some of the options available to us today, and each of these provides fresh opportunities to displace homogenous, linear histories. The last section of the collection notes particularly the role of new media in generating alternative and innovative paths for feminist engagement—we should remember that women artists and audiences played an important role in the emergent technology of cinema (and is perhaps why feminist film history often focuses on the early days of film).

It is my hope that the collection will invigorate the debate within film studies about the relationship between film history and feminist theory as well as highlight the rich and diverse histories within feminist film studies. The following essays bear witness that feminist theory, film history, and social practice are inevitably, ineluctably, and productively intertwined as related objects of influence and study, as we can see from Laura Mulvey's reconfirmation of the "gaze" to Soyoung Kim's exposition of activist transmedia interventions.

Lastly, if technology situates us today in what has been proclaimed as the world of Web 3.0—a supposedly seamless, smarter, and ubiquitously accessible database that facilitates the sharing of information[18]—then perhaps we might appropriate this technology/terminology as a useful metaphor in conjunction with the cinematic one referenced earlier. Thus, "Feminism 3.0" might be seen as a new network of collaboration, across generations as well as across other divides of sexuality, race, and ethnicity.[19] This is not a utopian erasure of differences but rather an open arena of communication that acknowledges, visualizes, and gives voices to the diversity of our experiences. The key components here are the database, capable of infinite permutations of assembly, and the search engine, which should produce unexpected relations, further research possibilities, and new knowledge formations. The archive becomes in this context not the last edifice standing in a received history, but a dynamic agent of change and a space of becoming.

Notes

1. Vivian Sobchack, "'Presentifying' Film and Media Feminism," *Camera Obscura* 21.1 61 (2006): 67. *Camera Obscura* ran a series titled "Archive of the Future" that included various short essays by scholars on state of feminist film studies over the course of 2006–7, beyond the issue noted above; see issues 21.2. 62 and 21.3 63 (both 2006); 22.1 64 and 22.3 66 (both 2007).

2. Media archaeology is a relatively new critical and creative field that interrogates relationships between media forms from a macro perspective exclusive of linear or evolutionary accounts of their development. I believe it is a methodology of rich potential for feminist scholars and artists. For more on this area of research, see especially Siegfried Zielinksi, *Deep Time of the Media: Toward an Archaeology of Hearing and Seeing by Technical Means,* trans. Gloria Custance (Cambridge: MIT Press, 2006), and Erkki Huhtamo, *From Kaleidoscomaniac to Cybernerd: Towards an Archeology of the Media,* http://www.debalie.nl/persoon.jsp;jsessionid=A58148B22 D5F01449D47A0A820BAA03E?personid=10226. I am particularly indebted to Erkki Huhtamo and Norman Klein for introducing me to this area of research and to their generous mentoring on this topic.

3. Michel Foucault, *The Archaeology of Knowledge,* trans. A. M. Sheridan Smith (New York: Pantheon, 1972), 131.

4. Jennifer M. Bean and Diane Negra, *A Feminist Reader in Early Cinema* (Durham, NC: Duke University Press, 2002).

5. Jane Gaines, "Film History and the Two Presents of Feminist Film Theory,"

Cinema Journal 44.1 (2004): 113–19.

6. Laura Mulvey, "Visual Pleasure and Narrative Cinema," *Screen* 16.3 (1975): 6–18.

7. Janet Bergstrom and Mary Anne Doane, "The Spectatrix," *Camera Obscura* (Special Issue) 20–21 (1989): 7.

8. Bergstrom and Doane, "Spectatrix," 7.

9. Christine Gledhill, "Recent Developments in Feminist Film Criticism," *Quarterly Review of Film Studies* 3.4 (1978): 457–83.

10. bell hooks, "The Oppositional Gaze: Black Female Spectators," in *Feminist Film Theory: A Classic Reader,* ed. Sue Thornham (New York: New York University Press, 1999), 314.

11. hooks, "Oppositional Gaze," 317.

12. Amelia Jones, "Introduction: Conceiving the Intersection of Feminism and Visual Culture," in *The Visual Culture Reader* (London: Routledge, 2003).

13. Yvonne Tasker and Diane Negra, "Postfeminism and the Archive for the Future," *Camera Obscura* 21.2 62 (2006): 171–74.

14. Alexandra Juhasz, "The Future Was Then: Reinvesting in Feminist Media Practice and Politics," *Camera Obscura* 21.1 61 (2006): 54, 56.

15. Jackie Hatfield, "Imagining Future Gardens of History," *Camera Obscura* 21.2 62 (2006): 185–89.

16. See *Cinema Journal* 43.3 (2004), special "In Focus" section, "What Is Cinema, What Is *Cinema Journal?*" edited by Frank Tomasulo.

17. Gene Youngblood, *Expanded Cinema* (New York: E. P. Dutton, 1970).

18. For an introduction to the concept of "Web 3.0" and how the term has been used, see John Markoff, "Entrepreneurs See a Web Guided by Common Sense," *New York Times,* November 12, 2006, http://www.nytimes.com/2006/11/12/business/12web.html; Victoria Shannon, "A More Revolutionary Web," *International Herald Tribune,* May 24, 2006, http://www.iht.com/articles/2006/05/23/business/web.php; Nova Spivak, "The Third Generation Web Is Coming," KurzweilAI.net, December 17, 2006, http://www.kurzweilai.net/meme/frame.html?main=/articles/art0689.html.

19. As noted in the text, my use of the term "Feminism 3.0" is as metaphor for a new networked, collaborative, and deep-time inflected phase of feminism. Given the rhetorical and historical baggage, not to mention the confusion surrounding the terms "postfeminism" and "Third Wave feminism," Feminism 3.0 is offered here as a "friendly amendment" to the current linguistic impasse.

Part 1

GAZING OUTWARD

The Spectrum of Feminist Reception History

In many ways, one might say that feminist film history begins in 1975 with Laura Mulvey's essay "Visual Pleasure and Narrative Cinema." Certainly, it could be argued the essay generated cinema/feminist studies' historical turn in *response to* Mulvey's focus on the "male gaze" and her declaration of visual pleasure as essentially masculine, thereby seemingly eliding or erasing women's actual *experience* in the movie theater. But I would argue Mulvey's essay was in itself *the* moment of a "turn" to history, at least within feminist film studies. While there had been other noteworthy examinations of the representation of women in film, especially Molly Haskell's *From Reverence to Rape* and Marjorie Rosen's *Popcorn Venus* (both published in 1974), the need for a historical approach, that is, an effort to *explain* as well as *describe* events[1] in cinema's development from a feminist critical perspective now became crystallized around Mulvey's essay. "Visual Pleasure and Narrative Cinema" adds gender to the idealized spectator of 1970s film theory, thereby immediately inserting the concept in a social/cultural context. Hence, I would argue that Mulvey's essay functions as a metahistory, but a history nonetheless, since it outlines a larger social/cultural category as the driving *internal* mechanism of cinema.

Whether or not we label this as history, Mulvey's close textual analysis of the politics of looking, which made women solely objects and never subjects of the gaze, generated a search for women's agency elsewhere than on the screen itself. Regardless of an individual film's narrative details, the look of the camera invariably seemed to reinforce women's secondary status, an effect seemingly out of sync with what women in the audience sometimes felt. Many feminists found this perspective far too limiting and

9

thus suggested that perhaps the gaze needed to be reconsidered or, at the very least, directed outward.[2] Even beyond such variable and difficult-to-measure emotive factors, there was, however, the material reality of cinema's production context and the explicit use of film to engage (and to construct) the modern woman as consumer. Miriam Hansen's work on Valentino pointed out not only his films' direct appeal to the female audience but also the complications added to a politics of vision when a male star serves as the erotic object on the screen.[3]

Mulvey's organization of the gaze around exclusively sexual difference also reinforced a range of binary logics around sexuality, with the cultural prescription toward heterosexuality especially unexamined and racial, ethnic, and class difference equally erased from the screen. For Manthia Diawara, the "color blind" approach offered by a gendered theory of the gaze did not account for the historical specificity of black men's experience, or their "resisting spectatorship" with regard to Hollywood cinema.[4] If black male spectatorship was misrepresented or framed by white privilege, then black female spectatorship was doubly oppressed by both patriarchal gendered looking (which black men did not completely "resist") as well as racism both on the screen and within feminist theory.[5] For bell hooks, neither Mulvey nor Diawara spoke to the possibility of a critical black female spectatorship and her "oppositional gaze," which chooses to identify neither with patriarchy nor white womanhood, marking a spectator who not only "resists" but "create(s) alternative texts" and "see(s) our history as a counter memory, using it as a way to know the present and invent the future."[6]

The focus on the cinema audience and the larger social conditions and discourses in which they were situated was vital to rethinking the dynamics of textual practices. While the relation between text and context might vary widely and feature any number of other methodologies in conjunction with the approach (e.g., besides feminism, critical race theory, Marxism, poststructuralism, queer theory), reception studies became an important component in feminist history. Janet Staiger's research and writings in this area have been exemplary both in defining and employing "reception studies" as a rich and diverse umbrella concept for film historiography.[7] As Staiger notes, reception studies encompasses a rather larger area of research, some of it rather uncomfortably or inappropriately fitting within our historical rubric but all potentially constructive to the task of thinking about where meaning is located and how to outline the parameters, fields, or boundaries of text and reader. Usefully, Staiger maps out reception studies into "text-activated," "reader-activated," and "context-activated" groups, all of which can be, though not necessarily so, historically grounded, the distinction among the categories being where the locus of meaning occurs.[8]

Many feminists have found the "reader-activated" approach a particularly important corrective to the "absent" female spectator in Mulvey's account of mainstream cinema. Jackie Stacey's ethnographic study *Star Gazing: Hollywood Cinema and Female Spectatorship* features a close examination of the responses by female film viewers to various classical-era cinema stars in an attempt to complicate our understanding of "identification" beyond the singular psychoanalytic account complicit with dominant ideology.[9] Stacey's explicitly sociological investigation provides some compelling testimony from women viewers and a complex account of the different *levels* of identification (both off screen and on, visually and at the level of narrative) with attention to the emotive power accompanying the women's commentary.[10]

The focus on women's voices and emotions is crucial to Annette Kuhn's advocacy of "memory work" as a historical method in her book *Family Secrets.* In this case, however, the viewer's recollection or memory does not represent apodictic evidence as much as provide access to "untold" and unofficial stories. Most important, unlike many feminist critics, Kuhn feels no compulsion in her analysis of remembrances to choose between psychoanalytic or sociological/cultural paths of investigation. As she notes, "Engaging as it does the psychic and the social, memory work bridges the divide between inner and outer worlds. It demonstrates that political action need not be undertaken at the cost of the inner life, nor that attention to matters of the psyche necessarily entails a retreat from the world of collective action."[11] Moreover, the language of Kuhn's memory work is not the immediately obvious, linear, and coherent speech associated with public or official discourse (and narrative) but rather discontinuous, fleeting, and fragmented.[12] The radicality of this method, for Kuhn, is not only in the identification of voices heretofore at the margins but also in the process of critical recollection itself, which becomes an act of writing ourselves into history.[13]

If these ethnographic or "reader-activated" efforts seem at times like different paths along a well-traveled "talking cure," we are reminded of the central role of language and discourse—alongside images and the gaze—in shaping sexual identity. For Judith Butler, identity is a performative "effect" that is not an essential quality or a momentary and completely willful "performance" but rather a *product* of reiterative discursive practices.[14] We

"understand," for example, gendered, lesbian, or heterosexual identity, because we *use* the terms in everyday speech and have an ongoing negotiation
of the boundaries of these terms in public and private contexts. However,
it is crucial to remember that Butler's understanding of identity is neither
relativist nor reductive, and that, following Michel Foucault, it points toward not *a* discourse of sex but a "multiplicity of discourses produced by
a whole series of mechanisms operating in different institutions."[15] These
multivalent factors on identity do not deny the possibility of agency, notes
Butler, but prevent a single space *outside* of language/discourse. "Agency"
or resistance to dominant discourse comes for Butler through a subversive
testing of the reiterative practices, a repetition of gender practices, as for
example in the case of drag, which foregrounds the practice itself as a performance rather than a truth or normative action.[16]

While some might see Butler's poststructuralist approach as antithetical to a historical project, some theorists argue for a necessary connection
between these two paths of analysis. For Geoff Bennington and Robert
Young, poststructuralism presents a thoroughgoing critique of all essential
or idealist categories, thus clearing the way for less totalizing and hegemonic accounts, whereby more marginalized histories might be heard.[17]
For Tony Bennett, poststructuralism and deconstruction provide a needed
self-critical tool for historical work in that they enable one to reveal the
"discursivity" or political consequences of any methodology regardless of
its relationship to our own preferred and seemingly transparent (i.e., objective) philosophy.[18]

The first section of the collection highlights the complicated interplay
between text and context, theory and history across this diverse spectrum
of reception. Laura Mulvey's essay, "Unmasking the Gaze," is not so much
a correction as a supplement to or recontextualization of her groundbreaking work on the gendered operations of the cinematic apparatus. As Mulvey points out, both the text *and* the theorist are therefore altered by the
economic, social, political, and technological conditions under which they
exist. Thus, history should not be seen as a static entity but rather a process or ongoing conversation with the materiality of the moment. While
Mulvey's analysis draws on historical research concerning consumerism,
the modern woman, and early female cinema audiences, her use of reception is in dynamic interplay with an array of textual and theoretical concerns. Mulvey presents us with temporally dispersed and differing formats
of *Gentleman Prefer Blondes* (from Loos's novel to 1950s film and today's
consumer electronic versions) to insert both the question of spectatorship

into feminist textual analysis and the varying conditions under which it should be considered. The gaze as originally defined in "Visual Pleasure and Narrative Cinema" is not in this case rejected or revised as much as written over, becoming a palimpsest with additional insights given the new information and circumstances.

In the next essay, Janet Staiger's examination of the femme fatale text and context intersect in a different domain. Here we might want to situate her analysis as weighted toward a "text-activated" reading as attention is given to multivalent narrative and narrational possibilities emerging from a broader cultural shift in representations of the "modern woman." Staiger's careful and comprehensive discussion produces a taxonomy of "aggressive fallen women" from cinema's late 1920s and early 1930s, which demonstrates an array of complex and competing discourses on femininity during the era.

Annette Kuhn's ethno-historiographical study "'I wanted life to be romatic, and I wanted to be thin'": Girls Growing Up with the Cinema in the 1930s" places us within the domain of "reader-activated" reception studies. In this essay, the dominant "text" is not so much the story or setting but rather the era's stars and the audience's appropriation of style and attitude into the textual dimensions of their daily life. Kuhn's essay underlines the centrality of stars to cinema history and especially to questions of spectatorship, given the vital role they play in personal and social identity. Like Jackie Stacey's work, Kuhn's essay adds to the discourse on stars by highlighting ordinary women's voices and their individual experiences of the cinema, designating a kind of "authorship" to their words and actions.

Suzanne Leonard's essay on the highly publicized romance of Elizabeth Taylor and Richard Burton illuminates related dynamics within the star text. In her case study of Taylor and Burton, the texts proliferate, including not only the immediate films and popular discourse (which includes gossip, publicity materials, studio memos, newspapers accounts, and first- and second-hand star anecdotes) that surround their "true love," but also the very performance of romance by the couple that blurs public and private worlds, text and context. As happens with Kuhn's cinema viewers, films become a "writerly text" freed of narrative constraints or boundaries and even indeed logic, which the audience (which in this case *includes* Burton and Taylor!) can insert themselves to "construct" their identity (and themselves as texts). Given her attention to multiple external spheres of influence on the text(s) and the ongoing slippage between the borders of text and context, Leonard's analysis could be situated within a "context-activated" reception studies. More specifically, the Taylor/Burton romance could be said to function as one of Butler's "subversive interventions" into heteronormativity given the sheer repetition of the couplings and uncouplings publically performed by the duo. Significantly, the archival data used by Leonard, whether studio production memoranda or newspaper and tabloid accounts, deals in the main with rumor and gossip, which, as Andrea Weiss notes in a related context, serves to foreground marginalized stories.[19] The site of repression in the Taylor/Burton affair(s) is the very discursivity that surrounds heterosexual romance and marriage, a self-evident or transparent "truth" or "essential nature" that is in this case completely exposed as dependent on its repeated *public* performance.

Finally, the writerly text and performance are center stage both on and off screen in Terri Simone Francis's essay, "'She Will Never Look': Film Spectatorship, Black Feminism, and Scary Subjectivities." Francis's essay returns us to our starting point, incorporating Mulvey, theories of the gaze, and women's—especially black women's—absence at both the level of the film and feminist criticism. Examining both the history of black women's literary and film criticism as well as the textual workings of both experimental and mainstream film that feature black women, Francis's essay constructs a place and a gaze for the black female spectator—which she defines as "scary." In effect, Francis's "scary subjectivity," which entails a *willful* turning back of the gaze onto patriarchy and white privilege, builds on hooks's oppositional gaze and Anna Everett's notion of "transcoding" or the process whereby black spectatorial pleasure is achieved through critical distancing.[20] Francis transforms the discussion from the critical eye to a creative and performative act, from a critical reading/distance to a critical writing, engagement, and authorship.

Notes

1. I am borrowing here Gomery and Allen's distinguishing characteristic of a historian's work as explanatory of change and stasis (and thus different if not distinct from criticism and theory) as seen in Robert C. Allen and Douglas Gomery, *Film History: Theory and Practice* (New York: Knopf, 1985), 5.

2. Perhaps the best place to see an overview of responses by a range of feminist scholars to questions of female spectatorship, and particularly the dilemma around this issue set in place by Mulvey's essay, is in the *Camera Obscura* 20–21 1989 special issue "The Spectatrix," edited and with an introduction by Janet Bergstrom and Mary Ann Doane. Also, see Judith Mayne's extremely useful book on this subject, *Cinema and Spectatorship* (New York: Routledge: 1993).

3. Miriam Hansen, "Pleasure, Ambivalence, Identification: Valentino and Female Spectatorship," *Cinema Journal* 25.4 (1986): 6–32.

4. Manthia Diawara, "Black Spectatorship: Problems of Identification and Resistance," in *Film Theory and Criticism*, 6th ed., ed. Leo Braudy and Marshall Cohen (New York: Oxford University Press, 2004), 892–93.

5. bell hooks, "The Oppositional Gaze: Black Female Spectators," in *Feminist Film Theory: A Classic Reader*, ed. Sue Thornham (New York: New York University Press, 1999), 307–20.

6. hooks, "Oppositional Gaze," 319.

7. See especially Janet Staiger's *Interpreting Film: Studies in the Historical Reception of American Cinema* (Princeton: Princeton University Press, 1992).

8. See chapter 2 of Staiger's *Intrepreting Film,* "Reception Studies in Other Disciplines" (pp.16–48), for a discussion of the complexity of possible intersections between texts, readers, and contexts in these three groups.

9. Jackie Stacey, *Star Gazing: Hollywood Cinema and Female Spectatorship* (London: Routledge, 1994), 170.

10. Ibid., 171.

11. Annette Kuhn, *Family Secrets: Acts of Memory and Imagination* (Verso: London, 1995), 8.

12. Ibid., 68–69.

13. Ibid., 38–39.

14. Judith Butler, *Gender Trouble: Feminism and the Subversion of Identity* (New York: Routledge, 1989): 147.

15. Michel Foucault, *History of Sexuality, Vol. 1, An Introduction* (New York: Vintage, 1990), 33.

16. Butler, *Gender Trouble,* 148.

17. Geoff Bennington and Robert Young, "Introduction: Posing the Question," in *Post-structuralism and the Question of History,* ed. Derek Attridge, Geoff Bennington, and Robert Young (Cambridge: Cambridge University Press, 1987), 7.

18. Tony Bennett, "Texts in History: The Determinations of Readings and their Texts," in Bennington and Young, *Post-structuralism and the Question of History,* 66–68.

19. Andrea Weiss, "'A Queer Feeling When I Look at You': Hollywood Stars and Lesbian Spectatorship in the 1930s," in *Multiple Voices in Feminist Film Criticism,* ed. Diane Carson, Linda Dittmar, and Janice Welsch (Minneapolis: University of Minnesota Press, 1994), 330–42.

20. Anna Everett, "Lester Walton's *Écriture Noir:* Black Spectatorial Transcodings of 'Cinematic Excess,'" *Cinema Journal* 39.3 (2000): 31.

Further Reading

Butler, Judith. "Imitation and Gender Insubordination." In *Inside/Out: Lesbian Theories, Gay Theories,* ed. Diana Fuss, 13–31. New York: Routledge, 1991.

Dyer, Richard. *Heavenly Bodies: Film Stars and Society.* London: Macmillan, 1987.

————. *Stars*. London: BFI, 1979.

Hansen, Miriam. *Babel and Babylon*. Cambridge: Harvard University Press, 1991.

Mulvey, Laura. *Visual and Other Pleasures*. Bloomington: Indiana University Press, 1989.

Staiger, Janet. *Bad Women: Regulating Sexuality in Early American Cinema*. University of Minnesota Press, 1995.

Unmasking the Gaze

Feminist Film Theory, History, and Film Studies

When I was thinking about the title I had chosen for this article, "Unmasking the Gaze," I found that, unexpectedly, one of the cinema's most famous images persistently came to my mind—the opening sequence of Buñuel/Dali's *Un chien andalou* (1928) in which a man's hand cuts open a woman's eye with a razor. My recollection of this image seemed unexpected because I am approaching my topic from the perspective of over nearly thirty years' involvement with feminist film theory—and that image has often been cited, rightly, by feminists, as one of sadism and misogyny. Nevertheless, the image persisted, and I realized that my recollection was, in a way, a semi-conscious appropriation. In *Un chien andalou,* the act of cutting is a figurative representation which implies a move away from a literal, external mode of perception to the irrational interiority of surrealism, but this figuration of a transformed way of seeing can be extended into a metaphor for the changing ways of seeing the cinema and understanding spectatorship within feminist film theory. The woman's eye then stands for the perception of the feminist film critic, not a single, stable way of seeing but one that must find ways of mutating. More particularly, it stands as a metaphor for feminist film theory's search for an analytical framework that goes beyond the question of the male gaze and its voyeurisms as such, to seeing with the mind's eye.

   In this essay I would like to discuss the relation between the aesthetics of film and film spectatorship and the historical context that they reflect and the effect that their position within an economy has on women's image and iconography. Within this perspective, not only does the surrounding cultural and economic context make an essential contribution to understanding a particular cinema but that particular cinema can also, in its turn, act as a document of a culture and an economy. To illustrate my argument I will occasionally invoke *Gentlemen Prefer Blondes*—the 1926 novel by Anita Loos as well as the 1952 film (dir. Howard Hawks; Twentieth Century Fox)—to discuss the relation between American consumer society, the cinema-going audience (in the United States and elsewhere), and the way the film and the book raise questions about gender and sexuality. Because the title itself links the 1920s and the 1950s, *Gentlemen Prefer Blondes* allows a shift to take place between both periods, although, as the 1928 film version (dir. Malcolm St.Clair; Paramount Famous Players) is lost, I will restrict my discussion of film texts to the 1950s version only. However, *Gentlemen Prefer Blondes* also allows me to reflect on the development of feminist film theory out of its first phase, in which "gaze" and "spectacle" construct its primary binary opposition, toward its more recent interest in the historical conditions that created and inscribed that binarism, using the novel and film as a metaphorical parable of that trajectory. In the course of my discussion of *Gentlemen Prefer Blondes* I will also pose a question about the relationship between Hollywood's image of woman, signifying sexuality and desirability on the screen, and the extent to which it bears witness, not only to male desire, but also to a masking of political conflicts, including those of race, within American society itself. Hollywood has come to stand not only for the film industry of the United States but also for the conventions and codes of cinema it generalized. However, a move away from analyzing cinema simply within its own aesthetic and psychoanalytic integrity involves approaching "Hollywood" from a different angle: as the specific cinema of the United States at a particular moment of its social and economic evolution. And the simplicity and satisfaction of that original theoretical binary opposition of "spectacle" and "gaze" then begins to break down.

Before I move forward, however, it may be useful to look back at how film studies and feminist film theory developed in Britain (that is, within my own background) with an orientation toward textual criticism. Here, the origins of feminist film theory coincided with the first wave of interest in establishing film studies in British universities during the 1970s; this establishment tended to take place under the auspices of other disciplines, for instance, departments of English, modern languages, and even linguistics. An early priority, therefore, for film studies was to establish the cinema's specificity and autonomy. This need for self-sufficiency is reflected in contemporary debates on film aesthetics, particularly the new emphasis on the specificity of the medium. While the term and concept "specificity" had emerged out of avant-garde theory and practice, it was also of use to those film critics and theorists who were struggling to free narrative cinema from the trappings of literary tradition and high cultural values that focused on, for instance, how cinema created meaning out of its own aesthetic possibilities, whether a language of cinema could exist in its own right, and where that language could be found. Out of these concerns, early film studies tended to give priority to the text and to textual analysis as the key methodology for both academic and critical practice. However, as archives and resources opened up and enabled more historically founded research, the concentration on specificity, language, and the text was rigorously challenged as film historians and film sociologists argued that both the industry itself and the social composition of audiences had been hitherto overlooked and undervalued by film studies. Feminist scholarship and research played an important role throughout these developments. For instance, when, under the influence of feminism, I began to use psychoanalytic theory to analyze Hollywood cinema, my focus was primarily textual. Subsequently, the question was asked, "what about the women in the audience?" which led in turn to questions about and research into the actual composition of an audience which modified the exclusively textual approach without necessarily invalidating it (writings by Christine Gledhill, B. Ruby Rich, and others made key contributions here). This process has continued to expand and broaden the scope of film studies so that a film may be understood, Janus-like, as both deeply imbricated with its surrounding context but also finding a formal visualization for that context through its own, specific, cinematic and dramatic form. To my mind the form in which a social context is translated into the language of cinema, the ways in which it finds its meanings and representation in images ordered and organized within a cinematic narrative, works in this double direction. While the cinema reflects the society that produces it, its mediating images, forms, and cinematic language contribute to the way a society understands and internalizes itself as image. Thus, how cinematic meaning is created still remains central to the analysis of film, but these images take film theorists and historians away from the screen and into the surrounding cultural context to which they refer and from which they emerge.

However, other considerations and complications arise in the case of Hollywood, which functions both as a national and transnational cinema. Many critics and theorists, myself included, have referred to Hollywood not just as the cinema of a particular country, the United States of America, but also as cinema as such. So often, when cinema and spectatorship were under debate, implicitly, the debates revolved around the conventions and structures of Hollywood cinema. There are, of course, well-known reasons for this. From the end of World War I, Hollywood, due to its domination of the world film market, became, de facto, an international cinema. Although the product of the social economy of one nation, films made in Hollywood addressed an international constituency. Hollywood not only represented American identity to its own people at home but also came to be the outstanding means for exporting *the idea of America* to audiences abroad. Miriam Hansen has pointed out that this "America" was, at the crucial moment of the mass diffusion of its cinema, also the purveyor and mediator of modernity. Its cinema "played a key role in mediating competing cultural discourses on modernity and modernization because it articulated, multiplied and globalized a particular historical experience."[1] But while that internationalism, and its ability to slide into the universal, might lead away from the United States as a nation into its cinema's popularity both at the world box office and with European cinephiliacs, those histories eventually return to the history of Hollywood and further to the cultural and economic relations between the United States and the world.

In "Visual Pleasure and Narrative Cinema," I argued that the eroticized cinematic look was constructed textually, inscribed on the screen through its cinematic organization, point of view, privileged screen space, and so on, and that this way of looking is understood as gendered "male," in keeping with Freud's naming of the pleasure of looking, voyeurism, as active and, therefore, metaphorically masculine. This masculinization of the look also responded to the feminization of spectacle, which had emerged with particular strength in mass entertainment and its commodification in the twentieth century. The male body, on the other hand, even when on display on the cinema screen, played down its spectacular attributes. I also argued that this gendered gaze produced contradictions, especially for the female spectator, whose position would be aligned with the male gaze or self-consciously detached from it or oscillating between both. It was this textual critical perspective that was challenged by a concern for the actual aspirations and anxieties that might accompany an audience into the cinema from the real world and through which they would "negotiate" with the pleasures offered by the movie on the screen.

The comedy in *Gentlemen Prefer Blonde*s revolves, at certain moments, around the male gaze so that the film gives an exaggerated, parodic version of the relation of looking between the figures on the screen, the spectators in the cinema, and the sources of visual pleasure. At an early point in the film, Jane Russell (as Dorothy) and Marilyn Monroe (as Lorelei) arrive at the New York dockside to board an ocean liner bound for Cherbourg, France. On the screen, they "make an entrance," with full (nondiegetic) orchestral accompaniment. Just as they had appeared on stage as showgirls performing for a nightclub audience, their entrance here is also staged as spectacle (and this "entrance as spectacle" recurs several times throughout the film). On the dock, waiting to board, is the U. S. Olympic Team and, individually and collectively, they become the spectators of the showgirls' spectacle, becoming screen surrogates for the visual pleasure of the spectators sitting in the darkened auditorium. As the camera registers pure gaze, the film gradually detaches itself from the surrogate males, offering appropriate closer reverse shots of Lorelei and Dorothy. As the image of female stars is constructed as "to be looked at," as the conventions of editing create the voyeuristic point of view and its object, then the women in the audience are necessarily drawn into a complicity with the film's own inscribed "gaze." Their relation to the screen is constructed by the formal organization of the screen space, what is shown, and the gender assumptions that are built into it.

However, as this sequence satirizes cinematic voyeurism, so the voyeuristic gaze becomes visible, uncomfortable, and comic. Ultimately, comedy subverts and overrides the conventions of "visual pleasure" by making its textual construction comically visible, and the spectator is unavoidably distanced by laughter. Later, during Dorothy's "Anyone Here for Love?" number, the Olympic Team is transformed into a dance troupe. They no longer provide a "relay" into the scene for the spectator but become themselves the object of the gaze, enacting the process of "feminization" that necessarily affects the exhibitionist figure on display, bringing into visibility the usual taboo on the male body as overt spectacle. In this sequence, the distanciation generated by comedy affects male visual pleasure, producing the instability characteristic of the self-conscious female spectator.

As illustrated by this exaggerated example, the static, textually orientated, psychoanalytically influenced concept of the gaze still has an obvious, common-sense validity to the extent that its conventions are satirized and thus "unmasked." However, to return to the original metaphor with which I began this essay, this "gaze" has been "unmasked" not only by comedy but also by two other significant factors. As cinema ages, not only does academic research enormously expand knowledge of its history but

21

films also seem to be more closely attached to their era and exemplify that history. Second, feminist film historians have made a particular contribution to the "theorization" of film history (or, perhaps, the "historicization" of film theory). Without losing sight of those issues of gender, spectacle, and so on that characterized the first wave of feminist film theory, they have built up a more nuanced and shifting concept of spectatorship that leads directly to the question of audience. The constitution of the audience in the 1920s, for instance, complicates the male gaze that I discussed in "Visual Pleasure and Narrative Cinema."

Historical research into the audience of the 1920s reveals it to have been considerably more a "female audience" than spectator theory from the 1970s could have imagined. And the industry itself, rather than presuming a male spectator and a traditional voyeuristic gaze, understood its audience to be predominantly female and young. Miriam Hansen's work on Rudolph Valentino's star persona and cult following made a key contribution to this shift from the concept of the spectator as such to a historically identifiable audience. Valentino's mass following was female, and Hansen indicates his iconography and emblematic attributes were designed for a female gaze. In addition to Hansen's work, feminist historians such as Lea Jacobs, Lauren Rabinovitz, and Gaylyn Studlar suggest that to understand Hollywood and its audience in the 1920s from the perspective of gender and sexuality, scholars must also take into account economic and social change. This was the crucial, formative period for both Hollywood and the modern United States. It is important to remember that, although the United States did not invent the relationship between femininity and consumer culture, it streamlined and politicized a "society of the spectacle."

During the 1920s, a new femininity, mass production, and mass entertainment emerged side by side, deeply imbricated with each other, with images of modernity, and, in the words of the pioneer advertiser Earnest Elmo Calkins, "beauty as a business tool." The American film industry grew alongside, and boomed alongside, an extended period of economic expansion lasting from the end of the depression of the 1890s until the crash of October 1929. This was the "second industrial revolution" during which young women went into new industries in large numbers and took advantage of the expanding credit market to go into debt to keep up with new fashions. While the boom may have created the modern woman as a social and economic phenomenon, Hollywood cinema made movies for her and turned her image into an iconography and her aspirations into narrative event.

Hollywood in the 1920s took on board the "New Woman" phenomenon not only iconographically but also industrially. As the number of women in the work force escalated, so did the market in female-orientated consumer goods. In the nineteenth century, department stores and advertisers had pioneered the elision of femininity, commodity, and desirability. But as the film industry consolidated in the post–World War I United States, a newly emerging "Hollywood" became the shop window of America. And the shop window offered itself to young women with spending power; since they also accounted for the majority of box-office returns, "photoplays" had to take them into account. Lary May summarizes Hollywood's response to this phenomenon:

Films that featured a New Woman were usually written by female scenarists and played by one of the large number of actresses under twenty five who worked in the Hollywood industry. The female heroine was generally found in contemporary urban society and whether she was an emancipated wife or a flapper played by Clara Bow, Mae Murray, Joan Crawford, Gloria Swanson or Norma or Constance Talmadge, she portrayed a restless young woman eager to escape from an ascetic home. Seeking a new role, she could take a job in search of freedom or money but these heroines find their true emancipation in short skirts, glamour and innocent sexuality.[2]

The conjuncture between glamour and the cinema screen had developed in the early, pre-Hollywood days of the film industry around the nascent star system. But in the late 1920s, the stars had to be believable and recognizable to appeal to their audience of young working women.

That the importance of the female audience was well understood at the time is born out by Iris Barry, writing in Britain in 1926, who says quite simply: "Now one thing never to be lost sight of in considering the cinema is that it exists for pleasuring women. Three out of four of all cinema audiences are women."[3] Antonia Lant and Ingrid Periz have collected commentaries and reminiscences in their study of the habits and preferences of women filmgoers. They note that the pre-talkie era had particular significance for their respondents:

The extraordinary novelty of moviegoing for women, and for those observing them, cannot be overestimated. Where before had droves of women been allowed, indeed invited, to amass, to stare, to assemble in darkness, to risk the chance encounter the jostling and throng of the crowd? Via cinema, they saw, alone or in groups, largely without censure, and publicly, images not slated for their gaze, as well as towering icons of femininity, and tales of female derring-do.[4]

While the New Woman and her new freedoms were celebrated on the screen, a question inevitably arose: how much freedom? Most particularly: how much sexual freedom? The implications of economic independence, and the social changes that went with it, provoked a backlash. The late 1920s engulfed the United States in a new moral panic. Hollywood had staved off church campaigns for greater censorship at the beginning of the decade, appointing Will Hays as president of the Motion Picture Producers and Distributors of America, Inc. (MPPDA) with responsibility for the industry's internal regulation, but battles over censorship returned to the center of the arena. Hollywood compromised. In image and iconography, the modernity of its "flapper" stars was preserved. In its narratives, Hollywood's young female characters exuded energy and initiative that reflected the aspirations of its young female audience. However, in the last resort, scripts had to balance these images with extreme care. Emblematic freedom and independence stayed ultimately within bounds, traditions of sexual morality were maintained, and endings could bring the heroine back to the tradition and stability of conventional marriage. Feminist film historians have pointed out that, in effect, Hollywood produced a double discourse, in which the culture of consumption played an important part. A "liberated" female sexuality was invested in image and fashion while any actual sexual involvement was postponed to the safety of The End. Lauren Rabinovitz has noted that this duality was essential to the process of both pleasing and containing the target audience for this kind of film: "This double edged process of subjectivity and objectivity was fundamental to recuperating female desire so that it functioned in the service of patriarchy."[5] That is, pre-Hays Hollywood movies had to acknowledge and address the New Woman but also defuse and contain her potential for social disruption. While the presence of an active, assertive female sexuality in culture and in everyday experience had to be acknowledged, the discourses surrounding it were contorted by hypocrisy and social anxiety. Female sexuality, once it had become linked to modern fashionability, could be channeled into commodification and negotiated into a more conventional relation to male money and power.

Anita Loos's 1926 novel *Gentlemen Prefer Blondes* makes use of this 1920s split between the New Woman's freedom, particularly in relation to sexuality, and its redirection toward consumption, glamour, and fashion. Loos's characterizations of Lorelei and Dorothy reflect this split in a satirical doubling. It is as though, in creating two central characters rather than one, Anita Loos has found a way to articulate and thus represent in caricature the dualisms of the 1920s, the balance between an excess of liberation and censorship. Two young modern women—"flappers" par excellence— Dorothy is interested in sex and not money; Lorelei is interested in money and not sex. Dorothy represents the sexual autonomy and independence of the New Woman. Lorelei represents the New Woman's investment of sexuality into commodification and exchange. The question of gender relations becomes satirically tied to questions of value: the young woman who controls her own sexual value in a free exchange for pleasure rather than profit is juxtaposed to the young woman who calculates her sexual value in a free exchange for profit rather than pleasure. In addition, the end of the novel sketches in the pressure for censorship in Hollywood. Lorelei decides to move to Hollywood and produce, and star in, her own movies, keeping Gus, the puritanical Philadelphia millionaire now her husband, happy by making him responsible for "senshuring."[6] The novel brings its characters "back home" from Europe to the United States, to the prevailing obsession with censorship combined with an equally obsessive preoccupation with sex. *Gentlemen Prefer Blondes* was an international smash hit as a novel, which Anita Loos then adapted as a Broadway play; it was made into the now-lost Paramount film in 1928 only two years after its publication.

There are a number of contradictions embedded in the emblem of the flapper and the debates that she generated. Women's political and economic freedoms made real advances, also promoting a discourse around sex, sexuality, and femininity that were crucial for women's liberation. At the same time, the popular culture of the United States mastered a discourse of sexuality and the new freedoms associated with "our modern maidens" while also promoting an identification of modernity with femininity and consumerism. From this perspective, women's liberation tended to be displaced into image rather than substance, and change could remain as ephemeral as the flapper fashions that faded when the financial bubble burst. But the "sexiness" of American femininity and its consumer culture played a key role in establishing American exports as desirable in world markets, and not even the depression could roll back the power of the American economy abroad. In this process, Hollywood consciously cooperated with the American government's export drive, and its cinema became quite literally a "shop window" for American goods of all kinds.

The projected image of America as a modern, affluent, freethinking, and progressive society drew international audiences into the cinema. While the liberated, modern stories and stars captured this image, giving it both substance and glamour, it was above all the image of new American femininity that captivated the international imagination. These stars, ordinary and extraordinary at the same time, could represent a point of resistance to local class oppressions and traditional sexual taboos, their appeal extending beyond the United States. Although the discourse of woman and sexuality in these iconographies and narratives were addressed primarily to a female audience, the address was also generalized, looking toward youth, consumption, and a celebration of the success of America, its freedom, and its classlessness.

Again, however, these economic and ideological issues cut both ways. The impact of modernity, even refracted in the ways that I have described, had important repercussions for women in Europe, but also, for instance, for women in Rio, Cairo, Shanghai, and Tokyo. We see here the "problem of America" as it offers an image of liberation and model of modernity on the one hand and domination and economic mastery on the other. But these movies also suggest another contradiction, this time at home rather than abroad: to what extent did Hollywood's erasure of difference and ethnicities create a cinema in which sex and glamour distracted from the underlying social divisions and struggles in the country as a whole? From this perspective, the image of woman, signifying sexuality and desirability on the screen, would refer, ultimately, not so much to male desire but to the conflicts within American society itself.

Both the 1920s and the 1950s were marked by economic prosperity in the United States, accompanied by a demand for consumer goods, luxuries, and fashion items that affected women in particular. However, the consumer of the 1920s, a young working woman with her own money to spend, mutated into the housewife consumer of the 1950s. Newly moved to the newly built suburbs, she was responsible for fueling the U.S. economy, buying a new generation of consumer goods: refrigerators, vacuum cleaners, and, of course, television sets. While the consumer boom of the 1950s had to do with staying in, the boom of the 1920s had to do with going out. The Hollywood of the 1920s had to appeal to the unmarried, fun-loving New Woman of the jazz age who was discovering cosmetics and new fashion styles. The top stars represented the cinema's audience to itself; the young women at the movies did not feel so far removed from, say, Clara Bow or Colleen Moore. And it was these stars and their image of energetic, self-sufficient, and liberated modernity who would, in turn, appeal to young women elsewhere in the world. By the 1950s, however, Hollywood's address had shifted and split: stars such as Marilyn Monroe and Jane Russell were not promoting domesticity or, indeed, consumer durables, but rather the glamour and desirability of the Hollywood perfected movie star, streamlined not so much for mystery or for classical beauty as exaggerated sexuality. This exaggeratedly eroticized femininity may well be characteristic of a time of war, addressing, in 1953, the American soldiers in Korea.

But there is another context that gives greater point to this iconography of female sexuality, that is, the cold war. Whereas Hollywood's glamour had functioned in the 1920s to showcase American products, in the 1950s glamour could also condense with cold war propaganda. Through Hollywood, the United States could present itself to the world as "the democracy of glamour"; the economics and politics of capitalism acquired the sheen of desirability and sexuality in contrast to the drab and not sexy image of Soviet communism. Capitalism signified the pleasure of consumption while communism represented the toil of production.

Viewed from this perspective, Hollywood's streamlining of the image of woman as spectacle, with the highly stylized and sexualized iconography of Jane Russell and Marilyn Monroe, might not be explained so much by the gendered nature of visual pleasure, or as an attribute of the spectacular potential of cinema as a medium. Rather, this iconography may represent, figuratively, American promotion of its own economy and society as essentially "desirable" in a cold war context. From this perspective, the "democracy of glamour" brings with it an iconography of women that can be rearticulated and reinserted into varying historical contexts with varying messages and modes of address. On the other hand, however, the spectacular potential of the cinema plays into Hollywood's easy translation of glamour into film language and its fluent adaptation of sex into highly stylized iconography.

The condensation of the showcasing of America abroad, the sexualized star, and the cinema itself slide easily into each other and find a logical expression in the 1953 film adaptation of Anita Loos's novel. While the original 1926 novel *Gentlemen Prefer Blondes* satirized the contradictory discourses of sexuality in the United States, most of its story is taken up with Dorothy and Lorelei's trip around Europe. Their journey and their many affairs represent the modernity, overt sexuality, desirability, and glamour of America and its women for impoverished Europeans, of all classes. However, in the 1953 film, adapted from a recent Broadway musical and updated to its own present, most of the story takes place on the ocean liner, in between the opening section in New York and the concluding section in Paris. Lorelei and Dorothy's journey may also be understood, metaphorically, to stand in for the United States' marketing of itself to Europe following the Second World War when and where most audiences would still be experiencing rationing and a general deprivation in which glamour and luxury were unknown.

The flapper in the Loos time frame had the streamlined, androgynous look associated nowadays with Louise Brooks and Clara Bow. By contrast, the 1952 *Gentlemen Prefer Blondes* launched Marilyn Monroe as the sex symbol of the epoch, building on the iconography of the post–World War II pinup and sweater girl and costarring Jane Russell, whose image had been established definitively with the bust-obsessed publicity for Howard Hughes's *The Outlaw* (finally released in 1948). Marilyn in particular represented a fusion of desires: desire for the blonde and desire for the commodities that produced her. In 1926, William Fox had said: "Trade follows the American motion picture, not the flag"; the slogan might have been reformulated in 1953, the era of the Korean War and the Marshall Plan as: "Resistance to communism follows Marilyn Monroe, not the Stars and Stripes."

It is important to note that in addition to promoting the United States abroad in the 1920s as well as in the 1950s, Hollywood constructed a homogeneous image that marked uncontroversial "American-ness" as a neutral white obscuring its heterogeneous, racially divided society. With the invention of glamour for the masses and "innocent sexuality" in the 1920s, Hollywood found a means of concealing, of "screening," rifts in society. Not only was "nativism" on the rise after World War I, leading to the end of free immigration in 1924, but the politics of racism and the struggle for civil rights were being clearly articulated during the same period as well. The image of female sexuality, reasonably safely contained and censored, could promote an ideology of liberation and modernity that was essentially white. At the same time, Hollywood continued to operate a near apartheid division of the races, and racial discrimination had not vanished by the 1950s and the cold war period. Indeed, race and labor struggles, still bitterly fought in both the 1920s and the 1950s, failed to find any widespread representation in mass entertainment or on the screen. Thus, Hollywood cinema contributed to constructing American identity with images of a by-and-large homogeneous nation that directly contradicted its historical reality. Hansen's research into the Valentino iconography, to which I referred earlier, has shown how far the industry resisted star images that had connotations of ethnicity or in any way evoked or represented America's massive immigrant population. The implication might then be that this repression of class, race, and ethnic difference was secured through the discourse of the liberated, "modern girl," rolling back, that is, one area of repression in the interests of maintaining another.

Liberation and consumerism are inextricably tied together through the changing nature of the United States and its relation to its internal and its external politics. In the last resort, women were only one element in the jigsaw, if significant and emblematic. The 1920s illuminate the particular place femininity came to occupy for American consumer capitalism, both at home and abroad, during a key formative period. Hollywood cinema is deeply involved in all the strands in which economics, culture, and ideology are woven together. Its cinema stands in a liminal space, between culture and economics, reflecting social conditions outside itself while also giving image and narrative, in imagination, to contradictions and difficulties that cannot find resolution in the real world.

In retrospect, it seems that the textual focus characteristic of "Visual Pleasure and Narrative Cinema" may have overinvested in the psychic structures of cinematic pleasure, especially the specificity of the male gaze. However, this theoretical perspective "unmasked" the central place of sex and sexuality, however censored, at the heart of studio system Hollywood. Feminist historians worked to transcend early feminism's generalized analysis of Hollywood cinema's preoccupation with sex and sexuality to locate the whys and wherefores behind this preoccupation. No longer is the focus on women and cinema as such, but on the significance of gender within the American cultural and economic history that formed and molded Hollywood. As Hollywood cinema came to be internationally dominant, exporting its discourse of (sanitized) sexuality, the appeal of "America" then had to be relocated again within the economic and political context of relations between the United States and the rest of the movie-going world. In the last resort, the concept of the "male gaze" leads away from the screen to "unmask" the way that Hollywood cinema created a lasting and visible monument to America's invention of itself in the twentieth century, its successful colonization of modernity, and its sexualization of everyday life.

Coda

As old films are reissued on video or DVD, the conditions of film viewing appropriate to the visual pleasures of voyeurism have declined while the spectator has acquired a new ability to manipulate the linearity and flow of film, allowing stillness to disrupt flow and repetition to fragment narrative linearity. As I have argued in my recent book, *Death Twenty-four Times a Second: Stillness and the Moving Image,* these new ways of consuming old films, particularly Hollywood films, have brought me to reconsider my 1970s theories of spectatorship. While the performance of the female star had, I argued in "Visual Pleasure and Narrative Cinema," always involved moments of pose, a display for the voyeuristic gaze, the delayed cinema flattens gender difference. The "pause" disturbs the flow of the narrative, upsets the male protagonist's control over the action, and allows the spectator to "possess" the star image, to hold it for contemplation and erotic enjoyment. But the moment of pause in the flow of film also allows the spectator to pause for thought. As passing time removes the contemporary spectator further from the cinema of the Hollywood studio system, the more the images on the screen seem to bear witness not only to its history but also to time itself fossilized in image. Quite apart from its ability to capture images aesthetically or store them historically, celluloid cinema, as a medium of duration created out of a sequence of still frames, has a complicated relation to temporality. While film as fossil of the past leads the cinema into the realms of culture and history, its own aesthetic attributes lead to consideration of time itself as the halted, slowed, or repeated image that in turn leads to the human mind's difficulty with time and its closeness to death, to the past as loss, as a jumbled accumulation of ruin and trace that survive the inexorable process of time's passing and human forgetting. Ultimately, of course, this line of reflection links to history as an attempt to address these problems, negotiating with human need and imagination, and offering a means of ordering and figuring time's passing. The cinema, combining its long celluloid memory with its new digital capacity, offers a means for negotiating and forging connections across the divide between the present and different moments within the past. As I have attempted to argue in this essay, the cinema leads its theorists back into history through the images it has recorded over the course of the twentieth century. As the cultures of modernity come to be rendered increasingly archaic, the accumulated body of film makes a crucial contribution, not only to preserving but also to visualizing the complex interweaving of femininity, America, and cinema itself.

Notes

This paper draws on material in Laura Mulvey, "Close-ups and Commodities" in *Fetishism and Curiosity* (Bloomington: Indiana University Press; London: British Film Institute, 1996) and prefigures some of the material developed in the second edition of *Visual and Other Pleasures* (New York: Palgrave Macmillan: 2009).

1. Miriam Hansen, "The Mass Production of the Senses: Classical Cinema as Vernacular Modernism," *Modernism/Modernity* 6.2 (1999): 68.

2. Lary May, *Screening Out the Past* (Oxford: Oxford University Press, 1980), 218.

3. Iris Barry, "The Public's Pleasure," in *Red Velvet Seat: Women's Writing on the First Fifty Years of Cinema,* ed. Antonia Lant, with Ingrid Periz (New York: Verso, 2006), 128.

4. Antonia Lant, "Part One: Introduction" in *Red Velvet Seat, 37.*

5. Lauren Rabinovitz, "Temptations of Pleasure: Nickelodeons, Amusement Parks and the Sights of Female Sexuality," *Camera Obscura* 23 (May 1990): 15.

6. See also the satire on censoring in Lloyd Bacon's *Footlight Parade* (Warner Brothers, 1933): Hugh Herbert plays Charlie Bowers ("It'll never do in Kalamazoo"), imposed on an unwilling Chester Kent.

Les Belles Dames sans Merci, Femmes Fatales,
Vampires, Vamps, and Gold Diggers:
The Transformation and Narrative Value
of Aggressive Fallen Women

This essay is about continuity and difference, about things remaining the same but also changing. It is about the appearance and reappearance of an aggressive woman, but it is likewise about historical transformations in that aggressive woman. That such continuity and difference exist—particularly over the past two hundred years—is easy to explain. Continuity persists at the epistemological level that Fernand Braudel might label the "longue durée"; difference appears at the "event" level of historical perspective.

The aggressive woman that I shall be considering is the femme fatale as she is depicted in early cinema (1905–33).[1] The femme fatale has been a persistent type and one of great interest to feminist and cultural scholars. In her influential discussion of masquerade, Mary Ann Doane suggests why the femme fatale is such a difficult image for some people. When Doane defines the concept of masquerade, she emphasizes the threat invoked by the intentional behavior of a woman becoming so attractive as to catch the eye of the man, the threat of a woman *masquerading* as a woman. She writes, "This type of masquerade, an excess of femininity, is . . . necessarily regarded by men as evil incarnate: 'It is this evil which scandalises whenever woman plays out her sex in order to evade the word and the law.'"[2] Doane's point is that the "masquerade confounds this masculine structure of the look" in which the male should be a voyeur with the woman unaware of her participation in the relation.

Indeed, what is at stake in the femme fatale image is the denaturalizing of the supposedly proper relation; the woman not only recognizes her value as an object but intentionally chooses to enter the exchange system and become the commodity. Rather than men operating as the only players in the property system, women now negotiate and, even more significantly, aggressively participate in the business.

This foregrounding of motivations and meta-commercialization of gender (and sexuality), however, is a historical phenomenon. While the femme fatale is an ancient figure, the dynamic I have just laid out is neither universal nor ahistorical. This dynamic is tied, I believe, to capitalism and modern representations of human agency. Moreover, the transition to this particular dynamic can be viewed through the representation of the femme fatale in early U.S. cinema, perhaps because the mass culture of movies so typify their cultural origins while also creating them. The femme fatale also initiates a narrative about masculinity in the face of a female's actions. What constitutes appropriate male behavior? The value of the femme fatale for the narrative revolves around masculinity as much as an evaluation of female agency.[3]

Film historians note that one of the earliest cinematic femmes fatales, the vampire as portrayed in *A Fool There Was* (1915), did not become a popular cinematic stereotype. In fact, Theda Bara, who played the vampire, rapidly dissociated herself from that role both in her screen characters and her star persona. Sumiko Higashi aptly points out that "during the twenties, the transition of the Vampire into a vamp meant the attrition of her strength and invulnerability"; this was due to "the film industry's increasing sophistication in portraying the vamp as a woman[, which] meant a process of humanization which left her less deadly and dangerous."[4]

Higashi's emphasis on the "humanization" of the vamp starts me on the way toward explaining what happens to the vampire. What I intend to accomplish here is a further description and analysis of this phenomenon. When looking back at U.S. cinema, we may understand its changes as attributable to "increasing sophistication"; yet such an explanation would not acknowledge that larger cultural contexts were changing how all women would be represented in fictional narratives both filmic and literary. Moreover, Higashi's discussion suggests a permanent and rather linear trajectory to the vamp image. What happens, I believe, is a major representational shift in the larger cultural context that then proliferates the vampire image into a variety of women—all less aggressive than the original vampire but capable in certain texts of reappearing in all the vampire's glorious forceful intent and consequential threat.

This is not an "image" study. I will be stressing narrative and narrational interactions with the figure of the woman. To move beyond the difficulties of labeling representations as one thing or another, I will pay attention to the character's position in the narrative, her agency and motivations, and the film's narrational voice. I will not argue that the narrative resolution provides any sort of "containment" of the image, since critical theory now respects the potential functions of the middles of text to be quite ideologically transgressive. While I cannot address spectacle adequately because of the scope of this essay, this too is a textual feature that may disrupt the main discourses of the text.

Both intersectionality theory and genre also matter in considering what happens. Recent feminist theory points out the pitfalls of assuming that one identity category suffices to account for analysis and has argued that this erases the structural inequities of other identity categories. For instance, not all women experience life the same; women of color are structurally subordinated, and multiple subordinations compound one another.[5] While the films that I will examine are typical of U.S. cinema in that they mostly tell stories about white women, often this cinema casts women of color into the figure of the femme fatale, and this should be noted for other sets of films. However, I will be pointing out that class identities matter in these stories. Similarly, genre does as well. So a single thesis about the femme fatale would fail to treat adequately concerns of contemporary feminist theory and critical cultural studies.

To carry out this argument, I will briefly examine the representational context in which the U.S. film industry begins and the case of *A Fool There Was* and then reconsider the representation of the vamp, the kept woman, and the gold digger at the end of the 1920s and start of the early 1930s. In looking extensively at the femme fatale of the 1927–33 era, I will argue for a quite plural and complex configuration to cinematic representations of this aggressive character.

Les Belles Dames sans Merci: *Contexts and Conflicts*

In Western representations of women up to around the 1970s, a woman who has sex but is unmarried or who is an adulteress is almost always defined as "fallen." Feminist and Marxist criticisms have linked this pattern to needs of patriarchy and capitalism. One analysis is Amanda Anderson's thesis in her *Tainted Souls and Painted Faces.* Anderson examines the rhetoric around the fallen woman in the 1800s and concludes that "fallen" implies not only a change in one's state of grace but also a loss of control. A fallen woman has "attenuated agency."[6]

Anderson's point might be expanded. Fallen women might have attenuated agency; they might, however, also have an *awesome agency.* That is, they may *will for themselves a condition at odds with normative social standards regarding women and women's sexuality.* Where traditional fallen women are excessively weak, their inversions, the femmes fatales, are excessively strong. Fallen, yes, but rather than being victims, they become victimizers. Their degraded nature pervades this representation, but the affect they invoke is closer to fear than pity. The aggressive femme fatale version of the fallen woman becomes scary within patriarchal society that fears the rising of the fallen women and an inversion of the normal sexual dominance. Moreover, because Western representations create homologies between sex relations and economic conditions, it has been common to find the femme fatale persistently represented as ruining men not only sexually but also economically.

In the 1800s, once virtuous but then fallen women abound in literature, poetry, drama, and sensationalized newspaper stories. Laura Hapke's study of the figure of the prostitute around 1900 indicates that a woman was "constantly threatened by entrapment, economic exploitation, and her own naiveté, and vulnerability."[7] Hapke argues that explaining how this could happen to a (presumably) naturally good individual required a narrative solution. That solution was to reduce "her complexity by removing her from the knowledge and often the consequences of carnal experience. She becomes in effect desexualized."[8]

However, David Graham Phillips's *Susan Lenox: Her Fall and Rise* (1917) provides a contradictory suggestion about the victimized heroine: agency to change the situation exists, and, in fact, Susan Lenox aggressively alters her own behavior. She is a fallen woman who is not rescued by others; instead, she rescues herself. Lenox shifts her behavior from earning just enough to remain in poverty to making overt choices that produce a better income. Moreover, she does this by making explicit the financial exchange to her male companions. Hapke's word choice is telling: Lenox becomes a "manly" heroine—something not recognized as normal.[9]

Lenox's combination of masculine and feminine attributes, however, is the early twentieth-century fallen woman who synthesizes the nineteenth-century victim and victimizer. During the 1800s, texts represented the forces producing fallen women sometimes as poverty, sometimes as sexual desire. The narrative outcome for the fallen woman who was not rescued by her family or society was death, either by her own hand or the hand of the trade in which she worked. Some fallen women, however, fought back. Narratives often depicted their response as personal revenge if a man seduced them.[10] The vengeful prostitute is part of a new, broader wave of representing some fallen women as victimizers. Patrick Bade argues that the second half of the 1800s witnessed an "extraordinary proliferation of femmes fatales."[11] Although acts by men created some femmes fatales, other femmes fatales had more mysterious origins. Occult or satanic explanations were easily within the range of explanations. John Keats's version of the *belle dame sans merci* (1819) presents no explanation for why the woman entraps and destroys the knight-at-arms, but Keats fills the poem with archetypal images—a woman with long hair and wild eyes who sings to the man and gives him food. And when he "shut her wild wild eyes with kisses four," she lulls him into a permanent sleep from which he awakes only as a pale ghost to wander the countryside.

Sandra Gilbert and Susan Gubar connect femmes fatales of the late 1800s with "an interest in Egypt and, more generally, a preoccupation with colonized countries and imperial decline; a fascination with spiritualism; and an obsession not just with the so-called New Woman but with striking new visions and re-visions of female power."[12] Their analysis of a homology of correspondences between fictional and real "othernesses"—race/ethnicity, nation, metaphysics, and gender behavior—concurs with Bade's view that the reappearance of the femme fatale image is a consequence of threats (real or imagined) about women's place in the social hierarchy. As Bade puts it, "castration fears and suspicion of feminine 'deviousness' are perhaps the price that men have paid for their continuing domination of the female sex."[13]

Bade believes that at least for artists, the image of the femme fatale was worn out by 1900. Indeed, something significant occurs around the turn of the century, altering the specific dynamics of the femme fatale and her narrative.[14] In the early years of American cinema, film representations of fallen women duplicated trends in literary and dramatic narratives, often because those narratives were sources for the movies. When self-regulation through the National Board of Censorship was instituted in 1909, movie manufacturers obeyed the norms of representation generally operating for drama, novels, and short stories. Creating a story that involved a fallen woman was possible, even commendable, provided the movie spectator learned the right moral lesson—one reinforcing the social norm promoting monogamous, heterosexual sex that was legally sanctioned through marriage.

To learn a moral lesson, however, the representational world has to provide characters with choice or agency. The spectator cannot learn a moral lesson if characters are under sway of fate, destiny, or an otherwise determined world. Since bourgeois culture was already representing causality as self-generated, education through movies fit well with bourgeois ideology. Moreover, in the best sort of narrative lesson, character choice might also motivate the *initiation* of the impropriety (where the characters went wrong in the first place was to be avoided to prevent the difficulties that follow from the wrong decision). In any case, choice definitely had to be involved in narrative *resolution*. Coincidence ruined the moral point. The ideological function of such a rule is obvious: both social science theories of the period and much religion placed moral agency within the realm of individual action. To be saved or condemned required personal intention. Willful characters had to be the cause of their own doing or undoing.

Ironically, this agency-driven narrative works well in a revitalized melodramatic aesthetics; it does not do so well in hard-core realism or naturalism that presents a vision of a fated world. While these literary movements differed from traditional melodrama in their deeper development of the internal psychology of individual characters and a more pessimistic view of the universe, realism and naturalism posed great structural barriers for the characters: economic or social environments might prevent even the most willful (and good) characters from achieving their goals. Two exemplary literary instances are *Maggie: A Girl of the Streets* (1893) and *Sister Carrie* (1900). In *Maggie,* the young woman is seduced and then abandoned; she dies in the trade. In *Sister Carrie,* the victim drifts into the status of being a kept woman of at least two men before becoming a success on Broadway. She does not die, but she is not happy. Both of these novels were considered indecent and had limited first printings. I believe a major part of these books' scandal was the weight placed on the immediate family as the cause of the young women's difficulties. This differs from the more traditional narrative in which external agencies (men, poverty, white slavers) are the cause of the fall and any subsequent prostitution.[15]

A compromise between the nineteenth-century melodrama and the challenges of realism and naturalism is the social melodrama. John G. Cawelti defines the social melodrama as combining traditional melodrama with "a detailed, intimate, and realistic analysis of major social or historical phenomena."[16] This formula permitted moral regeneration by errant characters and was handy for the social conditions of the New Woman. A female protagonist could have a degree of wildness (indicating her willful agency) as long as she remained sexually pure.

U.S. filmmakers adopt this general aesthetic and narrative formula as they move from early narrative representations into the cinema of the early 1910s. The ideological functioning of this narrative is important to stress; human agency and action must explain the outcome, for

morality is [socially acceptable] behavior *in the face of a non-moral universe.* Hence "bad" is re-defined as the failure to act in the right way upon recognizing the proper choice. . . . [Thus,] tremendous weight is given to character psychology and development—manifested either through external means [as occurs through exaggerated acting, mise-en-scène, and music in nineteenth-century melodrama] . . . or through internal ones [as happens through dialogue and narrational exposition in realist aesthetics].[17]

Both Gilfoyle and Hapke suggest that in the early 1910s the prostitute begins to take on new characteristics in fictional treatments, and Gilfoyle specifically argues that Lenox is the first prostitute to be treated "as a symbol of female power and independence."[18] The difference between *Susan Lenox* and *Maggie* or *Sister Carrie* is in how Phillips's novel represents Susan's response. Like Maggie and Carrie, Susan drifts along in the current of forces arrayed against her until "she had something to live for—something to fight for."[19] A former lover returns to her life and she attempts to reactivate their relationship. "In her eyes came a new light; into her soul came peace and strength. Something to live for—someone to redeem."[20] This plot device has strong resemblances to the maternal melodrama formula, with Susan's lover substituting as the woman's child. Although this turning point seems to be the crossroads in Susan's life, once her lover begins to be successful, he returns to having affairs with other women, and Susan looks for some way to find total economic independence from men. Eventually, she learns the trade of acting. Like Carrie, Susan ends up on the stage—independent but world-weary. Yet the narrational voice is consistently approving of Susan's will and sets out her actions as "good" and honorable. A nonmoral universe is neither help nor hindrance to her fate; she is its cause.

This major transformation in bourgeois representation of personal causality was already occurring as film took up this formula. Social science was challenging early nineteenth-century explanations for behavior. Theories of economic, social, and environmental (family) influences initiated intense investigation of human behavior as a complex psychological reaction to those influences. Although nineteenth-century discourses of human behavior continue today, they survive in less verisimilar (and often "lower") genres, particularly, for instance, in horror. However, in drama, providing character motivation and choice making is tantamount to writing a good novel or screenplay. This is called "humanization" of characters although it is a very particular ideological version of human behavior. That the femme fatale was already being "humanized" explains what happens. Still, all villains—both female and male—were being given more detailed motives and human agency. This transformation is neither more nor less a containment than any earlier (or later) representation of why people do what they do. This transformation has continuity in its fear of the aggressive femme fatale; now, however, motivations for her behavior are receiving modern treatment.[21]

Vampires: Fools and Fallen Men

The vampire of the 1914 film *A Fool There Was* follows in a long line of femmes fatales, or more particularly *belles dames sans merci*.[22] Keats's knight-at-arms met his belle dame in a mead; she was "a faery's child." Neither the Knight nor the poem's narrator explains (or even tries to motivate) the lady's behavior beyond this allusion to the existence of a metaphysical order of safe and dangerous beings. Perhaps the long-standing image of femmes fatales is sufficient, the intertextual connections adequate for the poetic meditation.

Even the more specific direct sources of the film *A Fool There Was* are opaque as to the woman's goals. Rudyard Kipling's 1897 poem "The Vampire," which starts with the line "a fool there was," suggests that the Vampire is not capable of understanding her own actions: "(And now we know that she never knew why) / And did not understand!" Kipling's narrator implies that the woman acts without perception and cognition, and, most certainly, without empathy toward the fool.

"The Vampire" became the source for Porter Emerson Browne's *A Fool There Was* (1909).[23] This novel shows signs of both nineteenth-century and modern treatments of characters. Although the story begins with the lineage of the fool-to-be John Schuyler, it alternates in chapter 2 to the birth of a baby girl. A French aristocrat, the presumed father, visits the unwed mother, who is dying in childbirth, but he seems unconcerned by the events. He suggests the baby be named "Rien" (nothing). The next time the narrative returns to Rien she is a young woman who, in approaching her father, backs him up until he falls off a cliff. She says "Bien." In the rest of the novel, Rien is only referred to as "The Woman." Her ensuing appearance is on the deck of a boat that will take John to Europe on a governmental mission. "Coming down the deck was a woman, a woman darkly beautiful, tall, lithe, sinuous. Great masses of dead black hair were coiled about her head. Her cheeks were white; her lips very red."[24] She is almost "hypnotic" and even reminds John's friend of Kipling's vampire. Eventually (of course!), John becomes the fool.

While nineteenth-century women vampires might be motivated to take revenge on their former lovers (or other males as substitutes), explaining a woman's *adult* behavior as due to her youthful rejection by, and actual patricide of, her father is more modern. Browne does little more with Rien's motivations because his concerns are really to use the vampire as a catalyst for a different issue. Browne's interest is in the possible redemption of the fool or, failing that (as in this case), in protecting the wronged wife and the family.[25]

Fox's film version of *A Fool There Was* goes even further than Browne's novel in providing a more modern motivation for the vampire's actions. In the opening scene of the movie, "The Vampire" (Theda Bara) wanders in the general area around where John Schuyler (Edward José) and his family are enjoying yachting. The Vampire does not immediately direct her attention toward John. Rather, she walks up to Kate Schuyler and her daughter, attempting to engage the child and presumably the mother in conversation. Kate pulls her child away and walks off. The Vampire warns, "Some day you will regret that."

This opening scene then explains the Vampire's attention to John. Noting his pending departure to Europe, she arranges to sail on the same boat, and eventually, she seduces him. Higashi emphasizes the apparent supernatural powers of this film's vampire,[26] and, indeed, one of the Vampire's victims cries, "You have ruined me, you devil, and now you discard me!" However, Higashi does not point out the motive of vengeance supplied to the Vampire. Here, moreover, the Vampire's revenge is not toward a male victimizer. She wishes to repay Kate for the social slight, and much of the dissatisfaction represented in the Vampire and John's subsequent relation has to do with the Vampire's anger that she is not being accepted into his social world so that she might succeed in her goal. An emphasis on her use of sexuality not just for money (an older goal of vampires and show girls) but for social mobility sets up what will become a very commonsensical explanation for women soon to be labeled gold diggers.

Although for a short period of time, publicity around the actress Bara suggested equivalency between her and the character she played, within months, this altered to stressing that Bara was a nice girl from Cleveland.[27] Important in this public dissociation is the humanization it provides both Bara and the vampire. If dominant cultural directions were to explain human behavior in modern terms, all stereotypes were to be recast. A *Photoplay* reporter writes as early as September 1915 that people at the Fox studios had "affectionately nicknamed [Bara], 'Vamp!'" and the verb "vamping" as it relates to her appears in headlines in 1916.[28] This diminution of the original vampire is suggestive. The textual attribution of psychological motivations for the vampire's behavior and willful agency as well as the creation of a complex but sympathetic star image of an early movie vampire set up the impetus for a trend of "humanized" representations. So even in the first major film image of a vampire, we are already meeting a vamp. Had the film been more about the Vampire and less about the fool and his family, the transformation might have been more obvious. Still, the Vampire is a continuation of the femme fatale even if she is now motivated in modern terms: she desires social mobility and is willfully using a foolish man to achieve her goal.

Femmes sans fatales: *Vamps and Gold Diggers*

Although Bara's vampire was a brunette, vamps and gold diggers of the late 1920s and early 1930s are usually blonde.[29] Perhaps because of the overuse of the late nineteenth-century vampire image, the modern femme fatale needed to look new, but she was new as well in being more closely and psychologically motivated in her behavior and more intimately analyzed in her path toward proper (socially or morally acceptable) behavior. Such an emphasis on motivation may have humanized her in the sense we understand that term, but humanizing a femme fatale does not necessarily make her less threatening. As I shall indicate, vamps, kept women, and gold diggers may seem less injurious, but that does not mean that all movie texts were asserting that such female behavior was desirable—although some texts suggested that fears of such women were misdirected and that men who fell for them were more foolish than the women were dangerous.

Many cinematic femmes fatales were fallen women. The explanations for the initiation of a woman's fall in the early twentieth century are the same as those of the late nineteenth century—seduction, poverty, family, or intention. In the first three cases, a fallen woman's reaction may be to remain a victim or to respond in some way. However, in the case of the fourth—direct intention—the woman actively chooses to use her sexual attraction and abilities for economic or social gain. Given either accidental or intentional "falls," a woman follows sexual initiation with a reaction in which she allows herself to be defined, or defines herself, as victim or agent. If she becomes (or tries to become) an agent, she may also appear to become a victimizer, depending on the actions she takes toward men.

Within these formulaic options are two complicating factors: (1) the initial class status of the woman (also complicated by ethnicity or race); and (2) the generic mode of the narrative—whether or not the story is a comedy.[30] Schemas are dangerous in implying too much uniformity and coverage of every case, but schemas also sometimes help in finding patterns. In table 1, I present an overall typology of "fallen women" based on cause of the fall and the women's reactions to their circumstances. Table 2 further expands these categories by introducing generic treatment as well as listing films produced between 1927 and 1933 that generally fit in the categories.[31]

The value of this schema is to illustrate that fallen women are represented as dangerous only when their intentional actions bring harm to good men. That is, women can be actively aggressive so long as they do not usurp the power of the prudent men naturally in charge. Men who are fools deserve their fate at the hands of femmes fatales; men who are not fools will either redeem themselves or not succumb in the first place. Thus, since many of these films are as much about fallen men as aggressive women,[32] the aggressive women are punished in relation to the errors of the men instead of according to inherent principles of justice. Important to remember is that although these films often seem to be about aggressive women, in actuality, men are the cultural center of attention. The narrative value of the aggressive fallen women is in reminding men of the importance of remaining in control.

The upper half of table 1 lists some of the variations in representations of fallen women in the nineteenth century, when religious or occult explanations predominated. These figures carry into the twentieth century in some texts, but in many others, twentieth-century "humanization" from secular explanations of behavior such as psychology, psychoanalysis, and sociology complicates the imagery. Beyond that general division and into the twentieth century, I have tried to sort out some of the formulaic options already suggested, noting how class and genre affect this. Table 2 presents six narrative options for stories with fallen women as protagonists,

TABLE I

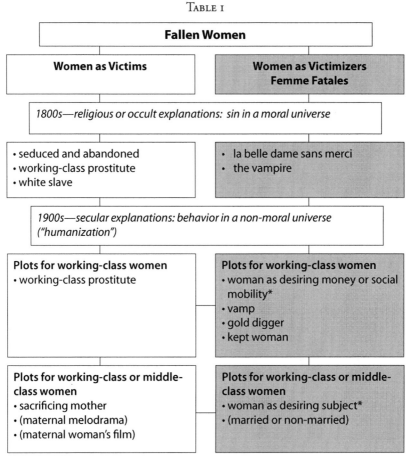

Fallen Women	
Women as Victims	**Women as Victimizers** **Femme Fatales**
1800s—religious or occult explanations: sin in a moral universe	
• seduced and abandoned • working-class prostitute • white slave	• la belle dame sans merci • the vampire
1900s—secular explanations: behavior in a non-moral universe *("humanization")*	
Plots for working-class women • working-class prostitute	**Plots for working-class women** • woman as desiring money or social mobility* • vamp • gold digger • kept woman
Plots for working-class or middle-class women • sacrificing mother • (maternal melodrama) • (maternal woman's film)	**Plots for working-class or middle-class women** • woman as desiring subject* • (married or non-married)

*In the comedy version, the woman may actually remain a virgin although she must appear to others to be fallen to be included in the category. Whether or not she is truly fallen is narratively significant.

four options of which involve fallen women who actively take up their role as agents in sexual exchanges (women as "victimizers"). These options seem primarily to serve as discursive warnings to men, although narrative complexity and spectacle can produce other sorts of ideological effects for both men and women.

The first option is the fallen woman who accepts her position as a "working girl" and remains in the victim, working-class category. An example would be Sadie Thompson (Joan Crawford) in *Rain* (1932). Sadie is (to

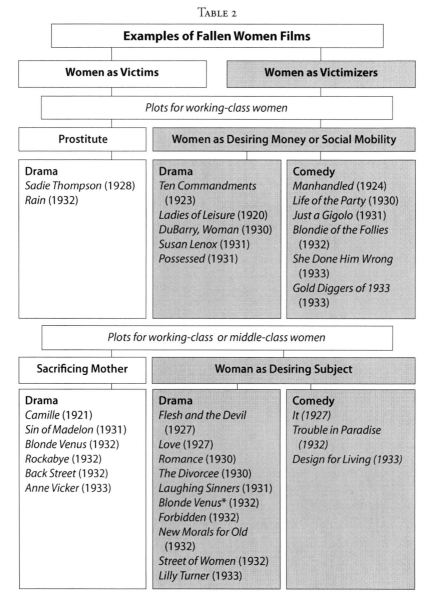

TABLE 2

Examples of Fallen Women Films

Women as Victims	Women as Victimizers	

Plots for working-class women

Prostitute	Women as Desiring Money or Social Mobility	
Drama *Sadie Thompson* (1928) *Rain* (1932)	**Drama** *Ten Commandments* (1923) *Ladies of Leisure* (1920) *DuBarry, Woman* (1930) *Susan Lenox* (1931) *Possessed* (1931)	**Comedy** *Manhandled* (1924) *Life of the Party* (1930) *Just a Gigolo* (1931) *Blondie of the Follies* (1932) *She Done Him Wrong* (1933) *Gold Diggers of 1933* (1933)

Plots for working-class or middle-class women

Sacrificing Mother	Woman as Desiring Subject	
Drama *Camille* (1921) *Sin of Madelon* (1931) *Blonde Venus* (1932) *Rockabye* (1932) *Back Street* (1932) *Anne Vicker* (1933)	**Drama** *Flesh and the Devil* (1927) *Love* (1927) *Romance* (1930) *The Divorcee* (1930) *Laughing Sinners* (1931) *Blonde Venus** (1932) *Forbidden* (1932) *New Morals for Old* (1932) *Street of Women* (1932) *Lilly Turner* (1933)	**Comedy** *It (1927)* *Trouble in Paradise* (1932) *Design for Living (1933)*

*Blonde Venus may fall into either category depending on the viewer's interpretation of the protagonist's motivations.

use a common adjective) loose[33] and seems to make her meandering way at the leisure of friendly men. She is not a vamp or gold digger, however, since she does not employ her sexual lures to trick or victimize men. In fact, the point of the story is her sincerity and honesty. All she wants to do is live her own life until Reverend Alfred Davidson (Walter Huston) places barriers in her way and then tries to "raise" her by converting her. Alfred's eventual rape of Sadie is the second turning point in the plot, but Sadie does not fight back. She accepts her situation, and upon hearing of Alfred's suicide, remarks, "Then I can forgive him. I thought that the joke was all on me." "I'm sorry for everyone in the world."

This dramatic examination of reformers was a common theme for the period and provides *Rain* with a critical edge that borders on resisting the dominant position if it were not for the fact that by 1932 reformers were a clichéd target. The examination does make *Rain* a fallen man story. While appearing to center on the problem of redeeming Sadie, Alfred's succumbing to his sexual desires for her—not even provoked by her—is the ultimate moral issue raised by the film. His actions provide the turning points to the narrative. Otherwise, Sadie's life would have continued as it were. Sadie is thus doubly the victim: as a woman, she exerts little or no agency in that she does not attempt to change her status in her working world (except once to try to repent with disastrous, if coincidental, consequences); moreover, she has no agency in the narrative because the plot positions her as a foil to the man's story. Since her agency does not directly cause the events, she deserves no particular punishment (the rape might suffice for that) but continued disillusionment in a nonmoral universe. Alfred's end is fully within the codes of compensating moral justice. *Rain* exists, thus, as an example of the narrative of a fallen woman as victim.

Opposed to the first option are the second and third options for the working-class fallen woman. These options exist when the desire for economic security or social mobility motivates the woman's behavior. She can refuse her status as (apparent) victim of her economic condition, take control of her situation (using men's interests in her sexual possibilities),[34] and, if successful enough at the expense of others, be a victimizer. These are many of the vamps, gold diggers, and kept women of the era.

In the second option, the narrative is played as a drama. Although numerous film examples exist in this period, three have gathered sufficient critical attention for a brief review here: *Possessed* (1931), *Red-Headed Woman* (1932), and *Baby Face* (1933). In *Possessed*, Marian (Joan Crawford) decides to escape the poverty of her childhood by traveling to New

York City and operating as a seductress of men. "My life belongs to me," she declares early in the film. This motivation is transformed when she falls in love with one of her victims, Mark Whitney (Clark Gable). As Higashi and Lea Jacobs note, fallen women can be socially and morally redeemed if they fall in love with men or, even better, sacrifice something they want for the men.[35] This surrender deflates the threat of their agency, making them "human" and transforming their power into a socially (rather than personally) constructive force. Ideologically, such a narrative has great value in bourgeois culture. In *Possessed,* Marian realizes that she might harm Mark's opportunities for a political career when her status as a kept woman becomes public in the campaign. She leaves him although he has offered her marriage, but when he realizes her motivations, he offers to sacrifice his career as well—if he wins, he will win with her. If he loses, they will still be together.[36]

The Red-Headed Woman is the closest example in option two to the older vampire formula in *A Fool There Was* and is also a fallen man narrative. Knowing that gentlemen prefer blondes,[37] Lillian Andrews (Jean Harlow) sets out deliberately to work her way up the social ladder by seducing men. While Lil declares that it is just as easy to fall in love with rich men, she gives no evidence of ever doing that. She does seduce Bill Lejenda (Chester Morris), who divorces his wife. Eventually, Bill catches on to Lil's primary interest in herself, and he returns, repentantly, to his former wife, who takes him back. Lil, however, receives no retribution, as the vampire in *A Fool There Was* also continued toward her next victim.

Because of films like *Red-Headed Woman,* social groups pressured the industry, and Warner Bros. rewrote into *Baby Face* the narrative resolution that had been used by *Possessed.*[38] Lily Powers (Barbara Stanwyck) also works her way up the corporate ladder until she encounters the playboy Courtland Trenholm (George Brent). Lily and Courtland marry. Then, in a crisis in which Lily must choose between her jewels and Courtland's honor over the failure of his bank, she eventually makes the right decision. She gives up her wealth to him, telling him, for the first time, that she loves him.

The films of option two start with the dramatic premise that women may seek economic independence and use men's gullibility about sex and women to succeed. Men may be somewhat suave and knowing about what is happening (for example, Mark in *Possessed* and Courtland in *Baby Face*) or rather foolish and stupid (Bill in *Red-Headed Woman*). The possibility of treating the potentially fallen man in a satirical and comedic way as occurs in option three has several psychological and ideological advantages.[39] Comedy can warn off an individual. It can also create the fool as an "other," distancing the threat implied to all men. That is, if only some men are so foolish, then smart men can laugh along with the powerful women who use the fools. If you can't beat the vamps, join them in laughing.

Often such a comedic process will produce "less" than masculine men as the victims-to-be.[40] For example, in a key text influencing this option, the novel *Gentlemen Prefer Blondes: The Illuminating Diary of a Professional Lady* (1925) by the screenwriter Anita Loos, the story is told from the first-person perspective of Lorelei Lee, our blonde diamond digger.[41] Lorelei and her friend Dorothy habitually manipulate men, but the victims are also represented as easily tricked because of their deficiencies in recognizing these women for what they are. The image is older than 1925. As Robert C. Allen suggests in *Horrible Prettiness,* among the dangers of the burlesque showgirl was her ability to lead silly men to ruin, and early cinema often used the type as a comedic plot.[42]

Three examples in option three are worth brief description. *Blondie of the Follies* (1932) is a Marion Davies vehicle, from a story by Frances Marion with dialogue by Loos. At moments the film is light comedy; at other times it is an unflattering investigation of female friendship. Exasperated by her restrictive parents, Blondie (Davies) decides to follow the example of her life-long friend Lottie (Billie Dove), and go into the theater. Unfortunately, Lottie's apartment and fine clothes have come partially from the financial support of her lover, Larry, who now finds Blondie more interesting. Through a series of misunderstandings and arguments over Larry, Blondie and Lottie are driven apart as friends. Blondie takes up with Mr. Murchison, whose support also provides Blondie with wealth. Elements of slapstick enter into the plot when Blondie and Lottie physically fight and fall overboard a ship. In retaliation or by accident, Lottie loses grip on Blondie's hand during a violent staged dance number, and Blondie breaks her leg. The leg is set badly, so it appears Blondie's career is over, and she heads back home to the working-class Upper East Side. Larry arrives with doctors who say the leg can be reset and heal properly; Larry and Blondie will be together.

Blondie of the Follies preserves Blondie's "goodness" by indicating her lack of viciousness in her gold digging—mostly by ellipsis through never showing her with Murchison. Moreover, the plot repeatedly characterizes Blondie as wanting to preserve her friendship with Lottie, even to forgoing the attentions of Larry despite Blondie's romantic interest in him. Finally,

Blondie's rise is rebuked with a literal fall into the orchestra pit, and her coupling with Larry is after an obviously permanent ending of her friendship with Lottie. This gold digger is by no means threatening, just occasionally fun at a party and really a good girl.

So are the gold diggers in *Gold Diggers of 1933* (1933), in which response to men's behavior, not avaricious intention, motivates the gold digging. Three show girls are excited when their neighbor Brad (Dick Powell) is able to find funds to finance a new show. Brad loves Polly (Ruby Keeler), but unbeknownst to the women, Brad is rich. So Brad's big brother Jay (Warren William) and his friend, Mr. Peabody (Guy Kibbee), come to town to break up Brad's relationship with Polly—whom they assume is a gold digger. Incensed by this presumption and aided by Trixie (Aline MacMahon), Carol (Joan Blondell) pretends to be Polly. Peabody is the classic "foolish man" in the comedic version of this. He remarks that all show girls are chiselers, parasites, and gold diggers: "I remember it well . . . I met this girl, we went to Rector's. She was Eunice, I was Fluffy."

Eventually, Jay and Peabody fall for Carol and Trixie, and the deception is made apparent so that Jay is pleased with Brad's marriage to Polly. Here the illusion of the women as gold diggers is part of the play and comedy, and the point of the narrative is to make fools of foolish men who assume stereotypes about women. Yet the film is hardly a progressive text. It reaffirms the value of sexual purity before marriage and the economic dependence of women on men because it does not challenge the assumption that truly "fallen" women are unacceptable. What if Polly had been having sexual intercourse with Brad rather than just "pettin' in the park"?

No doubt exists that Lou (Mae West) is more than pettin' with Chick (Owen Moore) and Gus (Noah Beery Sr.) in *She Done Him Wrong* (1933). As Lou remarks, "When women go wrong, men go right after them." Space constrains an analysis of this film. Its play with taste and class, its manipulation of well-wrought formulas about fallen women (including an amusing intertexuality with *Rain*), and its confrontation with bourgeois norms of heterosexual romance deserve extended discussion. Here I am interested only in emphasizing that *She Done Him Wrong* does not belittle the men who surround Lou, as often do other comedies of this option. Chick and Gus may be mistaken in where Lou's interests lie, but they are not made to look like fools or laughed at as happens to the men in *The Life of the Party* (1930) or *Gold Diggers of 1933*. Men may make errors, but the comedic assault is directed elsewhere—at institutions and stereotypes.

Options four, five, and six are fallen-women formulae available to either a working-class or middle-class woman. Here the cause for the woman's fall is not poverty or intention but seduction or, in the woman-as-agent form, woman as desiring subject. Economic hardship may complicate this seduction/desire, but the initial fall is connected to the woman's loss of control in maintaining the sanctity of marriage. Either she has sexual intercourse without marriage or with a man other than her husband. In the case of dramatic versions (options four and five), consequences of the act are not good. Something bad happens after the seduction or choice. It may be the appearance of a baby, the discovery of the affair, or the need to remain a "back street" woman. Then the woman's behavior as a reaction to that consequence is the focal point of the narrative's progress. In conservative approaches to this situation, the narrative considers whether the woman will compound the consequences of her first errant act or learn from it.[43] Here, paying back society in some way for the transgression can produce compensating moral justice.

What makes the films of the early 1930s so significant to feminist scholars is that some of these texts in options four and five, but particularly those in option six in the comedy genre, *do not assume that the first event/choice is a mistake,* and these narratives resist implying any fall has occurred. Such narratives seem critical of nineteenth-century versions of women's proper behavioral choices as desiring subjects and direct the focus toward society as creating the problems for the essentially good woman. Other films in these options, however, do take the older moral view.

Option four, generally labeled the sacrificing mother category, is a good example of the ambiguity of the larger category of the fallen woman as desiring subject. Here I am using "mother" in both a literal and metaphorical sense, since these narratives construct the event following the fall as requiring some sacrifice by the woman that relates to her (assumed) maternal characteristics. In *The Sin of Madelon Claudet* (1931) and *Blonde Venus* (1932), the protagonist must give up her child; in *Back Street* (1932), because a married man keeps the woman, she is prevented from having children; and in *Rockabye* (1932), the woman loses her adopted child because of her reputation and then also sacrifices her new lover back to his wife because the wife is pregnant. In her *Motherhood and Representation,* E. Ann Kaplan distinguishes between narratives about mothers that are complicit with hegemonic ideology (these she calls maternal melodramas) and those that resist dominant views (maternal women's films).[44] In my system, both would fit within this option of the sacrificing mother, with a specific film to be considered either a maternal melodrama or maternal women's film depending on its construction of agency and transgression.

One strikingly typical case is *The Sin of Madelon Claudet,* which won Helen Hayes an Academy Award for playing the lead role of a young French woman who ages into a haggard old mother. Madelon loves her American artist, but he leaves her unwed and, unknowingly, pregnant, to return to his family in the United States. Although she nearly puts up the child for adoption upon his birth, mother love takes over. To support the child, she becomes a kept woman until her protector is arrested for being a thief. Although she knew nothing of his crimes, Madelon is jailed for ten years, and her child is placed in a public school. When she is released, she considers reclaiming her son but chooses not to when she learns he might be able to become a doctor if she leaves him where he is. She turns to the streets to pay his tuition, eventually being reduced to nearly permanently entering a charity institution for old people. Her son's mentor saves her from this by moving her to a small home outside Paris.

Since the film is framed as a flashback in which the mentor is explaining to the wife of Madelon's son the value of sacrifices (the wife is about to leave the doctor because he works all of the time), the entire story is couched as an exemplar of right and wrong behavior, with Madelon exhibiting appropriate reactions of maternal nature and sacrifice once the pregnancy occurs. The irony, of course, is that to sacrifice she must "sin" according to normative moral views, in which case the problem of weighing moral values is really what the film proposes to its viewer. At the end of the story, the wife wants to tell Madelon's son about Madelon, but the mentor intervenes, declaring that Madelon is "too great a woman." Her sacrifice must remain private.

The Sin of Madelon Claudet presents a situation in which the fallen woman effectively remains a victim throughout the narrative. Although she has agency, in a convoluted way it is agency directed toward a larger social good (raising sons to be productive members of society at the expense of the woman). In fact, being a kept woman and then a prostitute and petty thief is praised as justified, but the system that would construct this as a viable choice for a woman is not criticized. *The Sin of Madelon Claudet* remains a maternal melodrama.

In option five, the woman as desiring subject has agency over her desires, perhaps even to the victimization of what might, according to hegemonic norms, be wiser for the men she desires.[45] An example of this narrative option is *Flesh and the Devil* (1927). As with options two and three, the fallen woman is a vamp or gold digger. In this film, Felicitas (Greta Garbo) desires and seduces Leo (John Gilbert). Only later does he realize that she is married. After a fatal duel with her husband, which Leo wins, Leo leaves the country until the scandal subsides. He places Felicitas in the care of his childhood friend, Ulric (Lars Hanson). Upon Leo's return, he discovers that Ulric and Felicitas have married. Doing the honorable thing, Leo avoids Felicitas, who clearly wishes to renew their previous relationship, again to be adulterous. Leo resists but eventually falls to her desires. Unlike *A Fool There Was,* however, Leo ultimately regains control, although a bit ambiguously. Leo and Ulric are about to duel, with Leo choosing not to shoot his friend (he has agency). Meanwhile, Felicitas is also making a right choice and a sacrifice. She runs to stop the duel, but as she crosses a frozen lake, the ice gives way and she falls in, drowning. Ulric feels a cosmic sense of release and lowers his gun. The boyhood friends embrace; the vamp's desires driving them apart are gone. Felicitas, as the instigator of the desire, pays the price.[46]

Option six also presents desiring kept women, vamps, and gold diggers, but in a comedic approach. *Design for Living* (1933), released some half year after public reactions against the representations in *Baby Face* and *She Done Him Wrong,* could probably never have been distributed if the film had been a drama or in the comedic tone of the Mae West vehicle. The film even foregrounds this at one point when a tiff between Gilda (Miriam Hopkins), George (Gary Cooper), and Thomas (Fredric March) becomes somewhat physical. As the dialogue puts it, if the fight had been played for slapstick, the scene would have been called burlesque; if it were serious, it would be labeled melodrama; but as it was, it had tone, and so was a high-class comedy.

A marvelously witty narrative of a woman who cannot decide between two men, both of whom she lives with and eventually has sex, drives the sequence of narrative events. Since *Design for Living* is a comedy, Gilda's desire and the men's desires for Gilda are treated as circumstances, but not as moral problems, for the narrative to resolve.[47] In fact, because of the difficulty in deciding between stars Fredric March and Gary Cooper, the narrative does not provide resolution. The last scene shows the trio returning to their ménage à trois but likely about to repeat the first mistake—thinking they could avoid sex!

It might be argued that it is illogical to place films of this type within the general subheading of women as victimizers, but it can also be argued that the men's troubles would not have existed had Gilda known which man she wanted. In that case, her agency of desire for *two* men (not a monogamous choice) creates the comedic difficulties for George and Tom. Happily, in *Design for Living,* unlike *Flesh and the Devil,* the conflict ceases (at least temporarily) without needing to kill off Gilda. Charles Musser has argued that the comedy of remarriage predates the mid-1930s series of films often examined as the start of the genre.[48] Certainly many "sex films" from the 1920s involve women's desire, including married women who become attracted to men other than their husbands. Such films might often fall in this option.

As I indicate in *Bad Women,* this proliferation of desire by women is part of the era's investigation of women and women's sexuality. Sometimes women act on their desires; sometimes they do not. Sometimes the narratives representing these actions consider them from a dramatic perspective, and sometimes from a comedic point of view. Sometimes the texts agree that fallen women are bad, and sometimes not; and sometimes, the representations create an image of that fallen woman as threatening when she has agency, although sometimes not.

I stress these options because the study of representations in texts is a very complicated critical and historical problem. In concluding this essay, I want to underline four points about what I have been doing here. For one thing, although I have started off with the stereotype of a fallen woman as potentially threatening when she becomes aggressive and a victimizer (the femme fatale), I have tried to indicate that given that basic condition, many optional characteristics in her behavior and her agency as well as the narrational voice of the text can greatly complicate the text and, consequently, its theoretical and ideological implications. What is important for critical practice is not to stop at the moment of the typing of the woman but to consider, among other things: (1) whether she is the protagonist or a foil (after all, most of these films might just as well be said to be as much discourse about masculinity as femininity); (2) whether her response is one of agency or mere reaction; (3) what motivations are supplied for her subsequent behavior; (4) what the narrational voice and the narrative resolution imply discursively about her behavior; and (5) where aspects of the text might produce transgressive currents.

The second point is that class, race, ethnicity, and sexual orientation may mediate representations and, certainly for intersectional analysis, require attention. As well, and very significantly, I believe, genre transforms the femme fatale's image—drama or comedy greatly inflect the potentially threatening nature of the fallen woman as victimizer and what discursive points are occurring. Third, I have not even touched here the implications of the reception of these images and narratives by real spectators. As cultural studies stresses, ideal readings need to be tested against empirical evidence regarding effect and affect, especially if we are asking questions about social consequences of representations.

Finally, I want to point out that all of the ideas just mentioned, along with the perspective of historical change, should caution us about assuming that what has occurred in the transformation of the *belle dame sans merci* into the vampire and then the vamp, kept woman, and gold digger is not a containment of one type of aggressive woman by a process of humanizing that image except insofar as every text can potentially function as a containment for any specific individual. Nor is the moderation of the dangerous aspects of this figure historically concluded. As I noted earlier, the more obviously threatening aspects of the vampire figure can, and have, returned at various times, but often alongside the less blatant instances of the woman as aggressive victimizer. In the late 1940s and early 1950s, the femme fatale of the film noir was not the only fallen woman in the cinema: gold diggers Lorelei Lee (Marilyn Monroe) and Dorothy (Jane Russell) are also resurrected in *Gentlemen Prefer Blondes* (1953). As scholars we want to observe what are dominant representations at any historical moment, but it is important to observe subordinated and continuing options also consistently present and available for being turned into a new screenplay. We will then be less tempted to make rash generalizations about what causes the continuation or existence of representations of aggressive women and be better able to figure out if anything is new.

What does seem to continue throughout these films, however, is the cultural focus on the effect of aggressive women on men. It seems that these women often function discursively to test men. Women can be assertive, but only insofar as they do not threaten "true" men. The femme fatale tests the self-control of the male and issues the threat of destabilizing who really runs the relation. The narrative's action decides the authenticity of the men as men—whether they can stand up to the woman's intentions. Thus, the narrative value of the femme fatale is determining masculinity in twentieth-century capitalism: not at all different from the femme fatale's ideological function in earlier centuries.

Notes

To Mary Desjardins, in thanks for being a good colleague. Thanks as well to Michael DeAngelis, Corey Creekmur, and Walter Metz for comments on earlier drafts of this essay.

1. I shall use the term "femme fatale" for the category of a dangerous woman able to seduce a person. The femme fatale has more specific versions—the *belle dame sans merci*, the vampire, the vamp, the gold digger, the femme fatale of film noir. Indeed, this paper will mostly be about the representation of the vamp and gold digger of the late 1920s and early 1930s. As an aside, the use of the term "gold diggers" for vamps occurs at least by 1919 in the play *The Gold Diggers*, a comedy written by Avery Hopwood and produced by David Belasco (New York, 1919).

2. Mary Ann Doane, "Film and the Masquerade: Theorising the Female Specta-tor," *Screen* 23.3–4 (1982): 82, quoting Michéle Montrelay, "Inquiry into Feminin-ity," *m/f* 1 (1978): 93.

3. To what degree this occurs in other cinemas is unknown to me. So not only am I historicizing this dynamic, I also only make claims regarding U.S.-dominant cinema. Initial study of U.S. exploitation movies and pornography suggests some-thing very transgressive may be occurring there, especially in comedy.

4. Sumiko Higashi, *Virgins, Vamps and Flappers: The American Silent Movie Her-oine* (St. Albans, VT: Eden Press Women's Publications, 1978), 71–72.

5. On intersectionality theory, see Norma Alarcón, "The Theoretical Subjects of *This Bridge Called My Back* and Anglo-American Feminism," in *Making Face, Making Soul, Haciendo Caras: Creative and Critical Perspectives by Women of Color*, ed. Gloria Anzaldúa (San Francisco: Aunt Lute, 1990), 356–69; Kimberlé Williams Crenshaw, "Beyond Racism and Misogyny: Black Feminism and 2 Live Crew," in *Words that Wound: Critical Race Theory, Assaultive Speech, and The First Amendment*, ed. Mari J. Matsuda, Charles R. Lawrence III, Richard Delgado, and Kimberlé Wil-liams Crenshaw (Boulder, CO: Westview Press, 1993), 111–32; Leslie McCall, "The Complexity of Intersectionality," *Signs* 30.3 (2005): 1771–1800.

6. Amanda Anderson, *Tainted Souls and Painted Faces: The Rhetoric of Fallenness in Victorian Culture* (Ithaca, NY: Cornell University Press, 1993), 15.

7. Laura Hapke, *Girls Who Went Wrong: Prostitutes in American Fiction, 1885–1917* (Bowling Green, OH: Bowling Green State University Popular Press, 1989), 2.

8. Hapke, *Girls Who Went Wrong*, 3.

9. I can only note this issue of transgendering and its threatening but logical consequences when a woman, instead of a man, acts with agency. See later for further discussion of this point.

10. Timothy Gilfoyle, *City of Eros: New York City, Prostitution, and the Commer-cialization of Sex, 1790–1920* (New York: W. W. Norton, 1992), 146–75. The ag-gressive femme fatale is an ancient image; see Patrick Bade, *Femme Fatale: Images of Evil and Fascinating Women* (London: Ash & Grant, 1979), 7.

11. Bade, *Femme Fatale*, 6. Also see Bram Dijkstra, *Idols of Perversity: Fantasies of Feminine Evil in Fin-de-Siècle Culture* (New York: Oxford University Press, 1986).

12. As Gilbert and Gubar note, the *belle dame sans merci* has many names, lives in

less accessible places, and has strange and deadly powers; see their "Heart of Darkness: The Agon of the Femme Fatale," in *No Man's Land: The Place of the Woman Writer in the Twentieth Century,* vol. 2 (New Haven, CT: Yale University Press, 1989), 26.

13. Bade, *Femme Fatale,* 9.

14. For extended discussion on these changes and the fallen man formula, see Janet Staiger, *Bad Women: Regulating Sexuality in Early American Cinema* (Minneapolis: University of Minnesota Press, 1995); Janet Staiger, "*Film Noir* as Male Melodrama: The Politics of Film Genre Labeling," in *The Shifting Definition of Genre: Essays on Labeling Films, Television Shows, and Media,* ed. Lincoln Geraghy and Mark Jancovich (Jefferson, NC: McFarland, 2008), 71–91.

15. Slow-witted women may also become prostitutes, but they are more secondary figures in these stories. After the turn of the century, texts represent white slavers as organized and increasingly of a minority ethnic, racial, or national origin. Also after 1900, women begin to be represented as directly interested in commercial products rather than in domestic security. Thus, their actions are represented as a wrong choice rather than as an effort to escape poverty. See Staiger, *Bad Women.*

16. John G. Cawelti, *Adventure, Mystery, and Romance: Formula Stories as Art and Popular Culture* (Chicago: University of Chicago Press, 1976), 261.

17. Staiger, *Bad Women,* 83.

18. Hapke, *Girls Who Went Wrong,* 135–38; Gilfoyle, *City of Eros,* 276–83, 276.

19. David Graham Phillips, *Susan Lenox, Her Fall and Rise,* vol. 2 (New York: D. Appleton and Company, 1917), 198.

20. Phillips, *Susan Lenox,* 198.

21. I do not have space here to go into the advantages of this in terms of consumer culture and capitalism; see Staiger, *Bad Women.*

22. *A Fool There Was* is not the first film version of the vampire story, but it is an early feature-length one and was certainly much more widely known and discussed than any earlier films. On the film history of the vampire story before this movie, see Staiger, *Bad Women* 151–52.

23. Porter Emerson Browne, *A Fool There Was* (New York: Grosset and Dunlap, 1909).

24. Browne, *A Fool There Was,* 111.

25. The novel advocates divorce through the counsel of the wife's sister. The same occurs in the film; see Staiger, *Bad Women* 147–62.

26. Higashi, *Virgins, Vamps and Flappers,* 58.

27. Janet Staiger, "Fashioning a Personality: Theda Bara and the Designs of Her Star Image" (paper presented at the Women and the Silent Screen Conference, Montreal, Canada, June 2–6, 2004).

28. Wallace Franklin, "Purgatory's Ivory Angel," *Photoplay* 8.4 (1915): 72; Rowland Thomas, "'Vamping' in Movies Suffices; This Star Prefers Normality in Real Life," *Cleveland Plain Dealer,* February 20, 1916 [n.p., New York Public Library clipping file].

29. In choosing a time frame for this discussion, I have skipped to the late 1920s and early 1930s for several reasons. One is that by that time period, the moderniza-

tion strategy had secured a mature cinematic and cultural representation. Additionally, during the late 1920s and early 1930s the major film studios were very tolerant of unconventional storytelling in terms of moral requisites, which potentially indicates the diversity of opinion circulating in American culture at that point. I use 1933 as an ending point because of the effect the Legend of Decency boycotts had on representations of fallen women. Not until after World War II and the decline of the strength of the Production Code does the complexity of the figure of the fallen woman have a renewed opportunity to appear.

Regarding my discussion of the blonde hair usually given to vamps and gold diggers, I wish to note that racism may also be a contributing factor, although I am not sure exactly how. Women with blonde hair may seem whiter, and thus more beautiful and tempting, than brunettes, yet brunettes' complexions may appear pale in contrast to their hair color. Some femmes fatale in cinema of the early and mid 1920s are women of color (see Anna May Wong, for instance); however, none appeared in the group of films I examined.

30. A third complicating factor is the time period being examined.

31. With more space, I could provide more extensive textual analyses, but this schema is more suggestive of how the aggressive fallen woman fits into other patterns. Schematizing in this manner, I hope to introduce some useful distinctions to Lea Jacobs's valuable start in defining these images. See her *The Wages of Sin: Censorship and the Fallen Woman Film, 1928–1942* (Madison: University of Wisconsin Press, 1991). I originally wrote this paper in 1994 and have presented portions of it between that time and this publication. In the interim Jacobs has published a descriptive essay discussing the dramatic versus comedic treatments, but she provides no explanation for these variants; see "The Seduction Plot: Comic and Dramatic Variants," *Film History* 13.4 (2001): 424–42.

32. Staiger, "*Film Noir* as Male Melodrama."

33. As Anderson would point out, the term "loose" reinforces the image of being out of control.

34. The close association between these women and the profession of show business as a liminal environment in which a woman might safely and properly employ her talents as spectacle has not yet been fully examined.

35. At least in this period of the films; less so after 1934. Higashi, *Virgins, Vamps and Flappers,* 79, 169; Jacobs, *Wages of Sin,* 41.

36. This story's underlying plot structure is extremely similar to the romance formula laid out by Janice Radway in her *Reading the Romance* and suggests potential threads to follow between these groups of stories. See *Reading the Romance: Women, Patriarchy, and Popular Literature* (Chapel Hill: University of North Carolina Press, 1984).

37. A knowing reference to Anita Loos's novel published in 1925 (to be discussed later in this chapter). This is equally amusing because Loos wrote the screenplay for this film.

38. Richard Maltby, "'Baby Face,' or How Joe Breen Made Barbara Stanwyck Atone for Causing the Wall Street Crash," *Screen* 27.2 (1986): 22–45; Jacobs, *Wages of Sin,* 59–66.

39. In *The Wages of Sin* (66–68), Jacobs notes the importance of the generic differ-ence but then does not pursue the ideological, psychoanalytical, or narrative implica-tions. Nor does she consider this in her "The Seduction Plot."

40. Obviously, this is a culturally constructed version of masculinity.

41. Anita Loos, *Gentlemen Prefer Blondes: The Illuminating Diary of a Professional Lady* (1925; repr., New York: Vintage, 1981).

42. Robert C. Allen, *Horrible Prettiness: Burlesque and American Culture* (Chapel Hill: University of North Carolina Press, 1991) 201–4. Allen notes that these bur-lesque show girls embodied a mixture of masculine and feminine attributes, and I have noted that Anderson describes Lenox as "manly." In August 1932, as enough fallen women films appeared that they seemed to be constituting a trend, *Photoplay* remarked about the "new 'shady Dames'": "The new cinema heroine can take care of herself, thank you, since she combines, with her mysterious allure, many of the hard-headed attributes and even some of the physical characteristics—the tall, nar-row-hipped, broad shouldered figure—of men." This mixture of apparently separate sexes, as so many scholars have already noted, is part of what makes these women not only fallen but occasionally scary. (Apparently, the actresses playing these roles were also wearing trousers in real life!) Ruth Biery, "The New 'Shady Dames' of the Screen," *Photoplay* 42.3 (1932): 8. Sara Ross notes that most of the 1920s flapper films are comedies: "'Good Little Bad Girls': Controversy and the Flapper Comedi-enne," *Film History* 13.4 (2001): 409–23.

43. Ross indicates that in the late 1910s and 1920s flappers as fallen women were either shown to have a tragic fate or reduced to the comedic formula in which they reject modern ways and suffer "recuperation into the family" ("'Good Little Bad Girls,'" 409.

44. E. Ann Kaplan, *Motherhood and Representation: The Mother in Popular Culture and Melodrama* (London: Routledge, 1992), 12–13.

45. What is wiser is according to patriarchy and capitalism.

46. *Flesh and the Devil* contrasts with *Blondie of the Follies*. In *Flesh and the Devil,* a homosocial bond between men is permitted, but in *Blondie of the Follies* a hetero-sexual coupling must result from the triad constructed around two women's desires. As usual, men achieve what they desire.

47. Indeed, it may be this distinction that separates the genres. Comedies may need to resolve circumstances, but their moral or social implications are negligible in the scheme of the narrational voice.

48. Charles Musser, "Divorce, DeMille and the Comedy of Remarriage," in *Clas-sical Hollywood Comedy,* ed. Kristine Brunovska Karnick and Henry Jenkins (New York: Routledge, 1995), 282–313.

"I wanted life to be romantic, and I wanted to be thin"

Girls Growing Up with Cinema in the 1930s

Popular memory as well as historical record have it that in Britain cinema began to enjoy its greatest popularity during the 1930s. It has been claimed that Britain had the highest annual per capita cinema attendance in the world, and it is certainly true that for considerable sectors of the population "the pictures" became an integral part of daily life during the decade. Cultural competences associated with cinemagoing—a taken-for-granted shared knowledge of (invariably Hollywood) films and stars—were widespread, to the extent even of being referenced within films themselves.

The popular singer, radio performer, and music hall artiste Gracie Fields was the highest grossing performer in British-made films for a good part of the 1930s. Fields's appeal, which lay in the down-to-earth quality of her star persona, stood in complete contrast to the more obvious appeal of Hollywood glamour. For certain class and regional fractions of the British cinema audience, "our Gracie" was "one of us," and like any demotic performer could be relied upon to give voice to the current concerns and preoccupations of "ordinary people."[1] This included "the pictures," and there are knowing references to Hollywood cinema in several of her films. In the gritty but upbeat *Sally in Our Alley* (1931), for example, the Fields character—the Sally of the title—rescues a motherless and delinquent young woman, Florrie, from a brutal father. Florrie finds escape from her joyless existence in Hollywood's fantasy world, spending the little cash she has on film magazines and going to the pictures, and then trying to imitate the makeup and hairstyles of her favorite stars. Florrie's eventual redemption through Sally's generosity and goodness involves the exorcism of her obsession with "the pictures" and an acceptance of the limitations—and of the less glamorous if more communitarian pleasures—of "real" life. This resolution is fully in keeping with the general tenor of attitudes toward cinema in Britain during the early 1930s. Opinions would soften later in the decade, though; and the 1934 Fields vehicle *Sing As We Go* is perhaps indicative of the start of what was to become a significant cultural shift. The film features, in a minor part, a teenage maid-of-all-work, Gladys, whose last act before settling down to sleep at night is to moon over portraits of her favorite film star. Gladys's starstruck behavior is regarded more indulgently than critically by the Fields character: "Come on, hurry up. Put that light out and take Clark Gable with you."

In both these films, a preoccupation with cinema and film stars figures is seen as silly, even as damaging; and in both, the foolishness of the starstruck girls is set against the no-nonsense big-sisterliness of "our Gracie." It is as if in the characters she plays, Gracie Fields the film star absolves herself from involvement in the peculiar fascinations cinema held for its— and her—fans; while the pitiable or slightly ridiculous figures of Florrie and Gladys stand as embodiments of a stereotypical contemporary film fan. But such images of solitary, starstruck girls fail to do justice either to the complexity of 1930s cinema culture or to the significance of films and cinema in the everyday lives of young women of the time. According to the editors of *Mass-Observation at the Movies*: "While a large proportion of the population at large went to the cinema occasionally, the enthusiasts were young, working class, urban, and more often female than male."[2]

The downtrodden girls of the popular imagination, then, translate as the young, urban, working-class females of the social historians' account. However characterized, though, all these young women are undergoing the passage from girlhood to womanhood. Like Florrie, they are experimenting with identities, with ways of being women. But alongside their dreams, they must negotiate family ties and obligations, school or work, friendships, and the anxieties and pleasures of consumerism and courtship. For these young filmgoers of the 1930s, adolescence is constrained and shaped in particular ways by circumstances of social class, gender relations, and economics.

At some level, we already know who the keenest cinemagoers of the 1930s were, and even something of their tastes and preferences. We can speculate, too, about what was at stake for them, affectively, in their enthusiasms. But even so, there is a very real sense in which we hardly know them at all. Their moment as fans lies within living memory; and yet as women, their voices remain largely unheard in historical record. As cultural icons, Florrie and Gladys might be noticeable enough, but as cultural producers, makers of meaning in their own right,[3] they remain more or less invisible.

What, then, did the typical young film fan of the 1930s bring to her cinemagoing? What did she take from it? How did it fit in with other aspects of her daily life—school, work, leisure, friendship, courtship? In what ways was she formed by all this—not simply in the activity of "going to the pictures," but through all the various cultural competences and social discourses surrounding, and at whatever remove hinging upon, that activity? Questions like these are, of course, considerably easier to ask than to answer, though asking them itself challenges both the silencing of "ordinary" women's voices in standard historical accounts and the virtual absence of the social audience (as against the implied spectator) from historical studies of film reception.

This essay ventures a response to these challenges by presenting some findings from an ethnohistorical investigation of cinema culture that looks at how films and cinemagoing figured in the everyday lives of people throughout Britain in the 1930s; and attempts to situate filmgoing and fandom in this period within their broader social, cultural, and discursive contexts.[4] "Cinema culture" is understood as including the contexts of reception of films and cinema as well as the films themselves; and the activity of consuming films is the starting point of an investigation that draws both on source materials from the 1930s (publications like film fan magazines and women's magazines as well as unpublished materials such as letters to film magazines, diaries, and suchlike); and also on recent testimonies, written and oral, of surviving cinemagoers of the 1930s. The concept of ethnohistory references the project's objective of investigating the ways in which cinema and filmgoing figured in people's daily lives in the 1930s. Such a project clearly raises significant questions of methodology, particularly where its more innovative "memory work" component is concerned. As such, it draws on—and indeed critiques and develops—some of the methods and objectives of contemporary media ethnography, concerning itself with the texture as well as with the contents of informants' own accounts.[5]

The project's findings can be mined for insights on the questions about femininity and cinema culture raised earlier; and in this regard Janet Staiger's manifesto for the historical study of film reception is apposite: "The reception studies I seek would be historical, would recognize the dialectics of evidence and theory, and would take up a critical distance on the *relations* between spectators and texts. It would not interpret texts but would attempt a historical *explanation* of the event of interpreting a text."[6]

A focus on cinema culture implies a concern with the reception of films; and indeed my premise is that, in the moment of reception, an array of social conditions and cultural competences is brought together with the identifications proposed in the organization of meanings and pleasures within film texts; and that all these discourses and practices are interconnected. At these levels, femininity figures as a site of negotiation, and sometimes of contradiction and struggle. How, then, was the typical young female cinemagoer of the 1930s positioned in relation to the various conditions, competences, and discourses mobilized in the activity of cinemagoing?

Such little contemporary data as exist on the tastes of 1930s British filmgoers reveal a distinctively national quality in their likes and dislikes, a distinctiveness that emerges with particular force in relation to the Hollywood films and stars that dominated British screens and British filmgoers' engagements with cinema culture. Box-office takings suggest that the British were particularly fond of musicals; and while the child star Shirley Temple topped the box office on both sides of the Atlantic for several consecutive years, other stars of Hollywood musicals (singers Jeanette MacDonald and Deanna Durbin among them) scored levels of consistent success in Britain that they did not enjoy in the United States or elsewhere. Unfortunately, however, because contemporary box-office data on audience preferences make no distinction between male and female cinemagoers, no conclusions can be drawn from them as regards gender-specific tastes and preferences.

Nevertheless, a very striking finding concerns paradigms of femininity embodied in the personae of Britain's favorite female stars, all of which are conspicuously lacking in attributes of overt, adult, sexuality. While the more glamorous Hollywood stars of the 1930s found little favor in Britain (according to some contemporary surveys, the raunchy Mae West was positively detested), female performers who were, or appeared to be, prepubescent were especially highly rated by British filmgoers. If Hollywood stars like Shirley Temple and Deanna Durbin are the most prominent examples of this tendency, there are many others: of stars of British-made films, for example, the juvenile Nova Pilbeam enjoyed a large following among some sections of the audience, as did Elisabeth Bergner, an actress adult in years but childlike in appearance and image. The persona of the popular song-and-dance star Jessie Matthews was markedly gamine, too—

though with a potentially disturbing undertow of sexual allure.[7] And while Gracie Fields can hardly be regarded as juvenile either in years or in image, her screen persona—the sensible big-sisterly figure who always loses the man to someone more glamorous—is arguably more asexual than Shirley Temple's.[8] The British cinemagoer evidently preferred femininity on the cinema screen to be outwardly innocent and asexual.

While these broad trends in cinemagoers' tastes run throughout the decade, a number of changes are observable after the mid 1930s, when a new trend in star preferences and a marked shift in the "structure of feeling" of British cinema culture becomes observable.[9] In particular, while the musical maintained its appeal, an entirely new generation of musical stars emerged. In 1938, the year in which George Formby ousted Gracie Fields from her long-held position as top money-making star of British-made films, the Canadian-born Hollywood singer/actress Deanna Durbin shot virtually overnight into the position of Britain's overall highest-grossing star. Another juvenile musical performer, Mickey Rooney, also entered the British ratings in the late 1930s and, along with Durbin, displaced Shirley Temple from her longstanding leading ranking.

But these changes are by no means confined to cinema culture: they coincide with significant shifts in broader cultural discourses around femininity. The enthusiasms of the fictional film fans Florrie and Gladys in *Sally in Our Alley* and *Sing As We Go* are referenced through intertexts in the films' fictional spaces: Florrie has her film magazines, Gladys her portrait of Clark Gable. These references within films to cinema fandom speak to certain cultural competences on the part of the (female) social audience. They assume prior knowledge about cinema, films, and stars, and about their place in the culture of the everyday; about stars currently in the ascendant; and about the character of the cinema culture itself. They also point to a cinema culture thriving beyond the cinema screen and outside the doors of the picture palace—in books and magazines about films and stars; in organizations like fan clubs; in newspapers and other media consumed by filmgoers but not concerned centrally with cinema; and perhaps above all in the routines, habits, and talk surrounding the very ordinary activity of "going to the pictures." How is the cinemagoer addressed and positioned in these intertexts? And, more specifically, to what degree and in what ways is the cinemagoer constructed in terms of gender?

The popular press of the 1930s—and film fan magazines and some women's magazines in particular—offers some answers to these questions. While one or two of the major film fan magazines appear to have been uncertain how—and indeed whether—to address their female readers, a degree of duplication in content between these and the women's magazines is apparent, suggesting a perceived overlap between their constituencies. However, a feminine cinemagoer/reader is openly constructed and addressed in a type of popular periodical that appears to be peculiar to the 1930s—an intriguing hybrid of women's magazine and film magazine. Among such titles are *Film Fashionland* and *Woman's Filmfair*.[10]

The popular women's press of the period provides some sense of the normative modes of femininity in circulation throughout the decade; but until the late 1930s, which saw the birth of the mass circulation woman's magazine, there is a notable dearth of models of femininity for the younger woman. Until then, Britain's weekly woman's magazine scene had been dominated by such titles as *Woman's Weekly*, in which femininity is constructed in terms of a comfortable, but far from affluent, domesticity. The implied reader is married and her main concerns are her husband and children in general, and their health in particular. If the unmarried woman is addressed at all here, it is assumed that she is in domestic service, or perhaps in office work: it is taken for granted that *married* women do not have jobs outside the home. The only references, explicit or otherwise, to cinema appear occasionally in advertisements, usually for products endorsed by film stars; and in small ads for film magazines and similar publications. The picture is of a mature domestic femininity that is incompatible with an enthusiasm for cinema: for the *Woman's Weekly* woman, as for Florrie and Gladys, adult womanhood and a passion for cinema are irreconcilable.

From around 1937, however, a marked shift in constructions of femininity becomes apparent. The summer of that year saw the launch of the weekly magazine *Woman,* and the beginning of a transformation of the women's popular periodical press. Produced with the aid of new print technology, which permitted rapid production of large runs of full-color magazines, *Woman* addressed itself to a readership younger ("in tune with the changed ides of the woman of TODAY") than that of the existing women's magazines, and soon achieved a circulation of unprecedented proportions.[11] *Woman* also foregrounded the contradictions of femininity in an almost overt manner. It advanced a heterosexual, rather than a domestic, ideal in which marriage is regarded as companionate, and in which family building is not necessarily a sine qua non; nor was it taken for granted that marriage in itself excludes paid employment. At the same time, variant models of femininity were constructed. By the end of 1939, by which time the magazine was throwing its weight fully behind the war effort, these new models of femininity are well established, so that in this context the wartime exhortation that "women must work" was by no means out of key with what had gone before. The Florries and Gladyses of the early 1930s begin to look decidedly old-fashioned.

Woman's modern woman is also unequivocally a cinemagoer. Aside from the ubiquitous advertisements for products endorsed by the stars (Jessie Matthews and Gracie Fields recommending face powder; Madeleine Carroll, Carole Lombard, Joan Crawford and many others featuring in advertisements for cosmetics), the reader's enthusiasm for cinema is solicited both explicitly and implicitly: explicitly, from late 1937 until the outbreak of World War II, in a regular column on films by an established female film critic and in occasional features on films and stars; implicitly, in an unspoken assumption that the reader was culturally competent in all matters cinematic. And so a column on ice skating could include, without comment, a photograph of the Hollywood skating actress Sonja Henie; and a knitting pattern for a hat and scarf could be headlined, in an allusion to Deanna Durbin's 1937 film hit *Three Smart Girls,* "Two smart bits of fluff."[12]

Indeed, Deanna Durbin is an excellent exemplar of this sea change. The Durbin star persona and the cult of fandom that surrounded her in the years immediately before and after the outbreak of World War II— unusually, she appears to have been equally popular with male and female filmgoers—condense key discourses around cinema culture and femininity in circulation during that period. Durbin stands at once for the consistent popularity of musical comedy films and stars with British cinemagoers, for the distinctiveness of British audiences' preferences among Hollywood stars and films, for an idiosyncratically British predilection for juvenile female stars, and for the "good taste" and "quality" demanded by the more vocal sections of the increasingly "respectable" British filmgoing public. At the same time, her rise to fame forms part of the broader shift in British filmgoers' tastes apparent after 1937. As an adolescent girl, Durbin also stands for a typical British cinemagoer of the period, while her unusual musical talent gestures toward a world distant from the one in which the average working-class and lower middle-class girl lived her daily life. Leaving behind the silly and pathetic Florries and the Gladyses of the earlier years of the decade, Durbin stands above all for the new femininities that entered cultural circulation in the late 1930s and that were to feed into wartime models of British womanhood.

Informative as they undoubtedly are, however, contemporary data are limited in what they reveal about the cinema audience in general and about the female filmgoer in particular. Above all, they offer no insight into cinemagoing and cinema culture as they might have been experienced by those concerned, no sense of what it actually felt like to be a young woman growing up in those years, or of the emotions and imaginings stirred by the very ordinary and yet utterly fantasy-laden activity of "going to the pictures."[13] For the "memory work" component of the present project, several hundred men and women living across Britain took part in a questionnaire survey, or agreed to be interviewed, about their youthful cinemagoing. These oral and written testimonies from the cinemagoers themselves lend valuable texture to the evidence from the 1930s. In-depth interviews with eighty or so surviving cinemagoers of the 1930s living in four UK locations were complemented by a postal questionnaire survey of 186 men and women living throughout the UK—and with their completed questionnaires, many respondents enclosed long letters and essays containing additional information about their early cinemagoing.[14]

For the majority of those who took part in the questionnaire survey, men as well as women, "going to the pictures" is remembered as an activity associated exclusively with their youth: having entered late childhood or adolescence by the latter part of the decade, most of them are very much part of the 1937 generation. At the same time, certain gender differences in cinemagoing habits and tastes are apparent. Women who took part in the questionnaire survey, for example, recall going to the cinema more frequently, and more often with family members, friends, or sweethearts, than their male counterparts. Women recall choosing films on the basis of who was starring in them, and are more likely than men to mention favorite stars by name (the women's favorite male star was Clark Gable; the men's, Gary Cooper; for both sexes, the preferred female star was Deanna Durbin). Relatively few respondents, male or female, however, name favorite films, or films that are remembered as making a particularly lasting impression. And while the majority recollect reading film magazines, only a handful says they collected star photographs or belonged to fan clubs.

Rather, going to the pictures, and even following the fortunes of favorite stars, are remembered alongside, and as part of, other social activities, hobbies, and leisure pursuits. For the group as a whole, then, cinemagoing was clearly less about particular films, or even films in general, than about "going to the pictures" and its place in interactions and activities shared with family and friends, and in people's comings and goings within and beyond their neighborhoods. That women represent themselves as more active and social than men in their cinemagoing habit simply suggests that their recollected cultural competences around cinema were all the more firmly embedded in the everyday social worlds of peer group, family, school, and work.

Interview material confirms this picture of cinema's integral part in the culture of everyday life, while adding considerable richness of detail and depth of understanding.[15] Nearly all interviewees were visited twice or more, and the men and women who gave interviews come into relief very much as individuals with their own stories to tell—though common threads and themes do emerge, often in unexpected places. Many of the women's accounts offer illuminating insights into the formation of the 1937 generation and the active role of cinema culture in this generation's coming of age as women. The most vivid impression of the cultural pervasiveness of cinema, of its very "everydayness," tends to emerge not from answers to questions, nor in response to memory prompts, but from "asides," notably those offered during the last minutes of the second or third interview, by which time rapport has been well established and informants feel that all of the "facts" they wish to convey have been recorded. Much is inadvertently revealed in these moments, above all in valedictory comments, made perhaps over a final cup of tea, when the informant feels that the interview is more or less at an end.

A close look at just a few of the female interviewees' testimonies highlights a set of issues relating to femininity, one that arises across all the women's accounts. The ways in which women talk about these issues—the content and the style of their "memory talk"—are extraordinarily revealing about the investments of emotion and fantasy at stake for themselves, and perhaps for an entire generation of women, in their immersion in cinema culture.

Sheila McWhinnie was born in 1919 in the Gorbals, Glasgow, her father a street sweeper and fish seller. She left school at the age of fourteen and took a number of jobs, first in factories and subsequently as a cinema usherette:

I got a black dress, well, and started wearing it, and got a collar from Woolworths, and we all got the same collar out of Woolworths. And, I would never have thought, from the Gorbals, of wearing a black dress, then I began to think, "Uhuh, it's very *smart*." Ever afterwards, know?

But, eh, it was funny that, they *did* influence a lot of what you wore and things like that. Both working and watching the screen, you know?[16]

Mickie Rivers, the daughter of a laborer, was born in Suffolk in 1922, left school at fourteen, and later worked in a variety of clerical jobs.

Because we had so *little*. I think I had *two* dresses. Maybe two or three skirts, no more and that was about everything. I know I didn't have very much compared to a lot of people but I was one of five. They couldn't afford it. I had to be taken away from grammar school because my mum couldn't afford a replacement uniform. Which was wrong. These days [pause; 2 seconds] I don't know what would've happened. They would have to have done it because everybody wears school uniform. But in those days you only wore uniform when you went to school after you'd passed your scholarship.

Or if you went to a private school. But *clothing* aspect, oh-h-h, you used to drool and think, I wonder if I could do that to my old dress. I could do that. You'd see them their dark dress and different colored [inaudible]. And you'd got about half a yard of [taffeta?]. And spend all night making a [sack?]. But, I mean, do a little bit a trimming somewhere else on the clothes. You'd pick it up. You know. [. . .]

Interviewer: [Laughs]. So even then you were good at making clothes and,

Oh yes. My mum used to go to jumble sales and come home with a dress, *outsize* dress and fit me out of it. *Had* to. Hadn't got the money. I used to earn, when I first went to work, I earned seven and sixpence. I had to pay my mother seven shillings a week and buy my stockings out of the sixpence. The cheapest stockings you could buy were *ninepence a pair*. And they were lisle stockings with an artificial silk covering. And of course you wanted a pair of *silk* stockings. You went up to one and nine, one and elevenpence.[17]

Born in London in 1921, Beatrice Cooper left school at sixteen to study at the Guildhall School of Drama. She worked as a secretary and a performer, and married a general practitioner.

Course Deanna Durbin was one that I was keen on.

Because em, because [laughs] funny! There she is. Because she was the same age as me and we both sang. And, of course I sang all the songs *she* sang [laughs]. As her films came out, I got the songs. And em, sang them. Eh, and eh, you know, and I *dressed* like her. I think a lot of kids of that age, you know, around 15, 16. Eh, because there were no fashions for children of that age. No teenagers. You either dressed as a very small child. Or you dressed as an adult. Sophisticated clothes. You know, there were no teenage clothes at that time. And she brought a new fashion.[18]

Helen Smeaton was born in Glasgow in 1917, had a college education, and became a secretary and later a college librarian.

You all wanted to be as thin as they were. I never thought of ever looking like them in a facial manner. Eh, and I liked to [?] smart or decent. But we all wanted to be thin. And they were all thin. I mean, even looking at them now, they're as thin as the other ones were nowadays and you used to read all these magazines, the *Filmgoer* [sic] magazine, what was the other one, oh, there was umpteen. And all my pocket money went on buying and reading all about these film stars. My mum used to say if I knew as much about my schoolwork as I knew about the film stars, I would pass every exam with flying colors. Cos I never forgot it. I'd read it, and read it, and read it.

But they were all, nearly all slim. There was a few that weren't. Em, what's her name? Wallace Beery. *Marie Dressler,* Marie Dressler. She was very plump. So, my mum was plump. And so, to me, plump people always represent somebody that's got a kind and affectionate and nice. And that's how Marie Dressler came over. But you never wanted to look like them. Although you thought they were great, you didn't really want to look like that at all. So, I think these were the only things that I wanted to imitate. I wanted life to be romantic and I wanted to be thin. [Laughs].[19]

A number of themes emerge from these testimonies, the most insistent being a scarcity/poverty topos apparent in allusions to getting by, or "making do," in circumstances of material deprivation. While the incidence of this theme correlates to some extent with speakers' class or socioeconomic backgrounds—here it is more prominent in Mrs. McWhinnie's and Mrs. Rivers's accounts than in the other two—it arises in some form or other in virtually all of the interviews, most frequently in accounts of childhood cinemagoing. These accounts characteristically feature more or less detailed recollections of the cost of admission to the cinema and ingenious ways of finding the money—or of getting in for nothing. For women interviewees, however, "getting by" is very often expressed also in memories centered around *clothes.* Mrs. McWhinnie bought the collar of her usherette's uniform in Woolworths—the implication that it was cheap being underscored by the reminder that she came "from the Gorbals," a famously deprived area of Glasgow—and then modeled her entire wardrobe on her "smart" working outfit. The memory of what she wore for her job as a cinema usherette is conflated in Mrs. McWhinnie's account not just with recollections of her own clothes but with the fashions in the films as well ("working and watching the screen"). In her memory talk, then, her own developing style of dress and everything associated, for her, with the cinema are condensed.

Mrs. Rivers's poignant account of "making do" might at first appear to have nothing to do with the cinema: it begins with a story heard often from working-class women (and indeed men) of her generation: she was unable to take advantage of a scholarship for secondary education because the uniform required by the "good" school was beyond the family's means. Mrs. Rivers's apparent divagation is prompted by looking at pictures of stars in a 1930s film annual, and it turns out not to be a divagation at all but a train of thought prompted by and leading back to the idea, or rather to the remembered feeling, of earnestly desiring something you know you cannot have. In Mrs. Rivers's account, cinema was more accommodating than the education system where clothes (and in this train of thought, aspirations) were concerned, in that the former allowed for a certain amount of successful "making do," for creating something desirable and even "smart" for oneself from the limited materials to hand—jumble sale castoffs, a bit of taffeta. The vividly remembered detail of the cost of a pair of stockings is extraordinarily revealing of the emotional investment in this yearning for something out of reach.[20]

For Mrs. Cooper and Mrs. Smeaton, on the other hand, memories of imitating the appearance of film stars, while still vivid, feel less emotionally laden. Mrs. Cooper is straightforward: "I dressed like [Deanna Durbin]"; Mrs. Smeaton remembers quite clearly what it was about the stars she wanted to emulate ("I never thought of looking like them in a facial manner"). Significantly, these informants distance themselves somewhat from their younger selves: Mrs. Cooper by making a comparison between past and present fashions for teenage girls; Mrs. Smeaton by speaking of her young self in the affectionate terms in which one might describe a starstruck granddaughter. In Mrs. Rivers's account, by contrast, the sense of missed opportunity saturates the story with a tangible affective texture, a sense of loss brought to life and relived in the telling.

On one level, these stories are at once commonplace and idiosyncratic. But from the detail of their contents and their telling emerges significant insight into the experience of being a young woman growing up in a particular time and place; and this is especially apparent where the interviewee's narration as it were reimmerses her in the events recalled: Mrs. McWhinnie and the cut of a dress collar, Mrs. Rivers and the price of a pair of silk stockings. Many of the interviewees, men as well as women, make explicit comments on the disparity between the luxurious fantasy-worlds of the films and picture houses, and the ordinariness, and often material poverty, of their own lives: indeed, such observations are very much a feature of all popular memories of cinemagoing and may be regarded as conventional in many cases.[21] Such comparisons are present in the extracts quoted earlier, too, though in less conventionalized—and consequently in more revealing—form. Mrs. Smeaton sets her recollection of her plump mother against the film-star slimness to which she herself aspired ("I wanted to be thin"). Mrs. McWhinnie and Mrs. Rivers offer stories of ingeniously produced inexpensive imitations of stylish screen fashions, making a positive virtue out of economic necessity. All are testaments to an active, affirming, and redemptive relationship between the inner world of fantasy and the outer world of everyday activity.

The word "smart" figures twice in the interview extracts and conveys much about the normative femininity of the 1930s, about 1930s cinema culture, and about the distinctive structures of feeling of both. In the popular idiom of the day, "smart," when associated with femininity, encompassed a particular set of meanings: taking care with one's appearance, neatness, trimness, a particular kind of understated style. These qualities were regarded as indicative of certain valued personal qualities: alertness, briskness, energy, and femininity of an innocent, optimistic variety, a fresh, uncalculating charm. Like Britain's favorite female film stars, the "smart" young woman of the late 1930s would not have dreamed of overtly flaunting sex appeal. Significantly, "smart" calls to mind Beatrice Cooper's favorite: the juvenile singing star Deanna Durbin, the ultimate "smart girl" who "brought a new fashion" to, and provided a role model for, the New Woman of the late 1930s. The deployment of the idiom in interviewees' memory talk suggests, if not a "regression" into the past as they tell their stories, some degree of reentry into that world, some reinhabiting of their adolescent fantasies and aspirations.

Women who entered adolescence between the mid-1930s and the start of World War II were very different from women of earlier generations; and cinema culture, figuring prominently as it did in their formation as women, played a large part in this difference. Regardless of social background, this generation of women enthusiastically embraced aspirations for lives very different from those of their mothers: Alison Light has noted "the buoyant sense of excitement and release which animates so many of the more broadly cultural activities which different groups of women enjoyed in the period."[22] These women's aspirations are informed by their dreams of a better, more beautiful self, dreams nourished and given expression through cinema culture. These women's growing up is imbued, in memory, with dreams of a new and different sort of womanhood, represented not just in the personae of the film stars they chose to emulate but more pervasively in the desires and wishes embodied within cinema culture.

For these women, wishes and aspirations are condensed in the nexus of personal appearance and clothes. Through work on her appearance, a young woman could enjoy "an imaginary identification with a graceful or beautiful self which both anticipated the woman she would like to become, and transcended the hard work and poverty around her."[23] The embrace of cinema culture by the young woman of the 1930s at once sets her apart from the older generation and offers her the alluring prospect of entirely new ways of being a woman.

Notes

1. Jeffrey Richards, "Gracie Fields: The Lancashire Britannia (part 1)," *Focus on Film* 33 (1979): 27–35; Jeffrey Richards, "Gracie Fields: The Lancashire Britannia (part 2)," *Focus on Film* 34 (1979): 23–38.

2. Jeffrey Richards and Dorothy Sheridan, eds., *Mass-Observation at the Movies* (London: Routledge and Kegan Paul, 1987) 41. For further discussion of cinemagoing in Britain in the 1930s, see Jeffrey Richards, *The Age of the Dream Palace: Cinema and Society in Britain, 1930–1939* (London: Routledge and Kegan Paul, 1984). Contemporary evidence suggests that cinemagoing was in fact more than "occasional" for the majority of the population—two-thirds of which went to the cinema once a week or more. See Simon Rowson, *The Social and Political Aspects of Films* (London: British Kinematograph Society, 1939).

3. On fandom as a form of cultural production, see John Fiske, "The Cultural Economy of Fandom," in *The Adoring Audience: Fan Culture and the Popular Media*, ed. Lisa A. Lewis (London: Routledge, 1992), 30–49.

4. "Cinema Culture in 1930s Britain: Ethnohistory of a Popular Cultural Practice," Economic and Social Research Council Project R000 23 5385 (hereafter CCINTB).

5. See, for example, James Lull, "An Emerging Tradition: Ethnographic Research on Television Audiences," *Inside Family Viewing: Ethnographic Research on Television's Audiences* (London: Routledge, 1990), 1–27; James Clifford, "On Ethnographic Au-

thority," *The Predicament of Culture: Twentieth-Century Ethnography, Literature, and Art* (Cambridge, MA: Harvard University Press): 21–54. For a fuller discussion of these issues, including methodological questions around memory work, in relation to the CCINTB project as a whole, see Annette Kuhn, *An Everyday Magic: Cinema and Cultural Memory* (London: I. B. Tauris, 2002), 7–12 [published in the United States as *Dreaming of Fred and Ginger: Cinema and Cultural Memory* (New York: New York University Press, 2002)]..

6. Janet Staiger, *Interpreting Films: Studies in the Historical Reception of American Cinema* (Princeton, NJ: Princeton University Press, 1992), 81.

7. On the British audience's ambivalence toward Jessie Matthews, see Annette Kuhn, "Film Stars in 1930s Britain: A Case Study in Modernity and Feminity," in *Stellar Encounters: Stardom in Popular European Cinema,* ed. Tytti Soila (New Barnet, Herts, UK: John Libbey, 2009), 180–94.

8. In the magazine *Night and Day,* Graham Greene suggested that the child star's infancy was actually a disguise for a "more secret and more adult" appeal (October 28, 1937: 3).

9. These findings are derived from contemporary box-office figures and star popularity polls: for details of sources, see Annette Kuhn, "Cinema Culture and Femininity in the 1930s," in *Nationalising Femininity,* ed. Christine Gledhill and Gillian Swanson (Manchester: Manchester University Press, 1996), 177–92. They are confirmed, using a new method of analyzing contemporary box-office figures, in Nicholas Hiley, "'Let's go to the pictures': The British Cinema Audience in the 1920s and 1930s," *Journal of Popular British Cinema* 2 (1999): 29–53.

10. For further details, see Kuhn, "Cinema Culture and Femininity in the 1930s."

11. On the launch of *Woman,* see Cynthia L. White, *Women's Magazines, 1693–1968* (London: Michael Joseph, 1970). White cites an average weekly circulation for *Woman* of 750,000 for the years 1938–45.

12. *Woman,* October 23, 1937, and May 27, 1939. "'Bit of fluff' is also 1930s slang, referring to an attractive young woman."

13. J. P. Mayer's extraordinary testimonies, gathered from cinemagoers during the 1940s, are an exception; see his *Sociology of Film: Studies and Documents* (London: Faber and Faber, 1946) and *British Cinemas and Their Audiences: Sociological Studies* (London: Dennis Dobson Ltd, 1948).

14. Annette Kuhn, "Cinemagoing in Britain in the 1930s: Report of a Questionnaire Survey," *Historical Journal of Film, Radio and Television* 19.4 (1999): 531–43.

15. For details of research design, see Kuhn, *An Everyday Magic* 240–47.

16. Valentina Bold, interview of Sheila McWhinnie, Glasgow, December 12, 1994, CCINTB T94–20. All interviews quoted from were conducted by Bold and transcribed by Valentina Bold and Joan Simpson.

17. Mickie Rivers interview, Needham Market, Suffolk, November 8, 1995, CCINTB T95–130.

18. Beatrice Cooper interview, Harrow, Middlesex, November 27, 1995, CCINTB T95–153.

19. Helen Smeaton interview, Jordanhill, Glasgow, June 28, 1995, CCINTB T95–72.

20. On the significance of clothes in working-class women's memories, see Carolyn Steedman, *Landscape for a Good Woman* (London: Virago, 1986); in relation to cinema, see Joanne Lacey, "Seeing through Happiness: Hollywood Musicals and the Construction of the American Dream in Liverpool in the 1950s," *Journal of Popular British Cinema* 2 (1999): 54–65. In her oral historical essay "Becoming a Woman in London in the 1920s and 1930s," in *Metropolis-London: Histories and Representations,* ed. David Feldman and Gareth Stedman Jones (London: Routledge, 1989), Sally Alexander notes that "via the high street or the sewing machine, the mantle of glamour passed from the aristocrat and courtesan to the shop, office or factory girl via the film star" (264).

21. For some examples, and further discussion, see Kuhn, *An Everyday Magic,* 219–22.

22. Alison Light, *Forever England: Femininity, Literature and Conservatism between the Wars* (London: Routledge, 1991), 9.

23. Alexander, "Becoming a Woman," 257.

The "True Love" of Elizabeth Taylor and Richard Burton

> The most difficult problem for any actress is knowing the difference between reality and non-reality. Now Richard has given me a sense of reality. With Richard, as with Mike (Todd), I'm above and beyond anything else, a woman. That's infinitely more fascinating than being an actress, if you ask me.
>
> —Elizabeth Taylor, *Los Angeles Herald Examiner,* July 30, 1968

Elizabeth Taylor's invocation of the reality of her romantic relation with the actor Richard Burton, as well as her and Burton's repeated public declarations that they would die without the other, helped to secure for the pair permanent placement in the annals of Hollywood's most celebrated loves. In 1996, *People* magazine featured Taylor and Burton in their special double issue, "The Greatest Love Stories of the Century," and claimed, "through two marriages and 23 years, the lustiest of couples couldn't live with—or without—each other."[1] Such language evidences the degree to which Taylor and Burton's romance, which began as an adulterous affair on the set of *Cleopatra* in 1962, continued to be accorded epic status even some forty-odd years after its inception. That this relationship remains recognizable and even idolized in the twenty-first century might be attributed to its having so closely approximated itself to a script recognizable as that of a once-in-a-lifetime romance—the Burtons were described as utterly dependent on one another and passionately in love, even after years of marriage. Moreover, the pair had a penchant for showcasing their celebrated romance in the multiple films they made together, and especially for accepting roles so nearly aligned with their star persona that they were often considered to be playing themselves on screen.[2]

In addition to having repeatedly appeared on screen as a couple, Taylor and Burton were a consistent feature in the tabloid press. Gossip magazines charted the pair's every emotional upheaval and pursued the couple with such zeal that their spats literally made international headlines. Not ones to reject this constant commodification, Taylor and Burton also seemed eager to stage the spectacle of their relationship for the press, their public, and even each other—the pair made a habit out of discussing and performing their notorious bouts, seemingly as much for the edification of their followers as for their own pleasure. Taylor and Burton thus consistently appeared both on screen and in their personal lives to be performing, and quite convincingly at that, the role of great lovers.

Borrowing from a postmodern logic, we might say that Taylor and Burton's love was created through the act of incessantly citing that love on screen and in star discourse, rather than existing in any way outside the

Taylor and Burton's legendary passion finds expression in *The Comedians* (1967).

realm of performativity. Indeed, it is the argument of this article that the films in which Taylor and Burton appear together as well as the hyperbolic discourses that surrounded them in the form of advertisements, gossip columns, publicity materials, and magazine articles were constitutive of their "true love." Specifically, this investigation will call on the tenets of star studies, postmodernism, and the burgeoning field of sexuality studies in order to unpack the mechanisms of the couple's image construction, in an effort to illustrate their romance's discursivity. At the same time, the project has within its purview the larger aim of demystifying the heterosexual contract. The cultural theorists Lauren Berlant and Michael Warner have usefully defined the term "heteronormativity" to describe how scenes of intimacy, coupling, and kinship become associated with the forms and arrangements of social life. As they argue, in American culture "a whole field of social relations becomes intelligible as heterosexuality, and this privatized sexual culture bestows on its sexual practices a sense of rightness and normalcy."[3] Star discourses, I argue, participate in this process because they reify certain notions of heteronormativity, notions that are in turn codified across a wide social spectrum. While feminism has consistently been critical of the process of romantic mystification and also heterosexual marriage (at the risk, at times, of accusing women of false consciousness), the more recent theoretical tendency to think about the interrelationship between constructions of romance and the heterosexual imperative unveils the power of heterosexuality to delimit acceptable parameters for sexual behavior, divisions of labor, patterns of economic interest, regulations of space, and everyday practices.

Unpacking the so-called true love of Richard Burton and Elizabeth Taylor, as I will do here, represents a wider attempt to continue a feminist legacy that has always interrogated romance and marriage, while at the same time it brings contemporary models of heteronormativity to bear on the construction of a couple whose behaviors set the standard for staging romance, associating it with a strict set of ideological, aesthetic, and emotional parameters. The Burtons are a particularly fascinating case study in this regard because in high postmodern fashion, their star image worked at cross purposes. That is, at the same time that the couple appeared as a paragon of classical romance, the discourses surrounding them betrayed the highly unnatural and often irrational machinations required to create the appearance of an identity that was supposedly authentic. As this article will quantify, Taylor and Burton's star image adhered to an inverse formula whereby the more excessively unrealistic the couple's performances became, the more strongly did their relation guarantee its status as an iconic love.

The Cleopatra "Affair"

In a much-publicized act of adultery that was also linked to one of the biggest economic fiascoes in cinema history, Elizabeth Taylor and Richard Burton's romantic relationship began in 1962 on the set of the epic *Cleopatra*. The affair scandalized international audiences and became increasingly significant thanks to its association with the bankrupting of Twentieth Century Fox—after taking over three years and forty million dollars to produce, *Cleopatra* earned notoriety as the picture that brought down a studio. Ironically, that the four-hour film was at all profitable was due largely to the onscreen/offscreen relationship between Taylor and Burton, since film audiences flooded the theaters to get a glimpse of the couple whose sexual transgressions had for years captivated an international audience.

Notably, Taylor's relationship with Burton caused her to be branded for the second time in her young life a "scarlet woman," since she stole Burton from his then-wife Sybil and cuckolded her husband, Eddie Fisher, whom she had a mere three years earlier lured from Debbie Reynolds in an infamous scandal that would prefigure the later Taylor-Burton affair. As Burton and Taylor alternately flaunted and denied their illicit liaison, the *Cleopatra* scandal reverberated on both the national and international stage. In May 1962, U.S. Congresswoman Iris Blitch urged the Attorney General to deny Taylor and Burton reentry into the United States because Taylor's adulterous behavior had "lowered the prestige of American women abroad" and damaged foreign relations with Italy.[4] Legislators like Blitch also suggested that the affair was a publicity stunt designed to raise the profile of the film, which, in fact, it did. Twentieth Century Fox denied having any part in encouraging the affair, however, and in 1964 the studio sued Taylor and Burton for a fifty-million-dollar breach of contract, alleging that the couple had depreciated the commercial value of *Cleopatra* by holding themselves and the film up to "public scorn and ridicule." According to the lawsuit, their behavior was offensive to good tastes and morals because "each was to the public knowledge at these times married to another."[5]

The salacious nature of this adulterous spectacle was magnified by the equally if not more satisfying rumor that Taylor and Burton's affair had caught them both by surprise, a quality of feeling that came to circumscribe their star image. The film scholar Aida Hozić, for example, identifies Taylor and Burton's affair as signaling the end of an era in that it represented "an element of unscripted reality that burst into the tightly controlled environment of the Hollywood studio system." Hozić adds that the relation was "an act of emotional emancipation," both for audiences and for the actors.[6] Clearly, this figuring of the affair as an "unscripted reality" owes much to a classic romantic lexicon since it imagines Taylor and Burton as a loving and courageous pair who simply could not deny their feelings for one another.[7]

Taylor and Burton's relationship transitioned from an immoral sexual dalliance to a great love affair thanks in part to such attributions of authenticity. As well, the presence of their supposedly unfettered passion relied heavily on the crossover between Taylor and Burton's real life and their onscreen appearance as Marc Antony and Cleopatra, since the real-life lovers were playing a world-renowned couple whose affair had ostensibly changed the course of history. The two relationships existed in dialectical relation to one another: Taylor and Burton lent verisimilitude to the historical romance; likewise, Antony and Cleopatra's fated relation gave credence to the affair between the two stars. That Burton and Taylor were easily constructed in real life as possessing the same emotional intensity as their film counterparts was in turn confirmed by the gossip surrounding the affair, which frequently referenced the fact that contemporary life seemed to be taking its cues from Roman history. The film's director Joseph Mankiewicz reportedly confided to the producer Walter Wanger, "They are not just *playing* Antony and Cleopatra!" as if to suggest that in the process of acting *as* Antony and Cleopatra, the pair were beginning to turn into them or, more specifically, to reenact Antony and Cleopatra's epic romance.[8] Wanger also comments on the scene in which Cleopatra, lamenting Antony's imminent departure to Rome, tells him, "Love can stab at the heart." Wanger remarks, "It was hard to tell whether Liz and Burton were reading lines or living the parts."[9] The public construction of Taylor and Burton's affair (even by those who knew them best) was thus consistently filtered through the narrative of *Cleopatra,* and the actors' relationship to the film script was always already a cornerstone of their star image as a couple.

The fascination of both the press and the public with the Taylor-Burton affair can largely be credited to this slippage between Taylor and Burton's film roles and their lived ones. More directly, one might say that the film roles and the life roles each gained traction and legitimacy from the other, so that not only did the lived reality lend credibility to the film, but the film also lent credibility to the "real" life. Consider this section of Wanger's diary, kept during the filming, which he later published as *My Life with Cleopatra*:

March 8. The papers today had a story that Burton would never marry Liz. He was quoted as saying he has no intention of divorcing Sybil. The timing was perfect—we were filming the scene in which Cleopatra finds that Antony has deserted her. She enters his bedroom, takes a dagger, and rips all his clothes. Then she slashes the draperies. She ends up cutting the bed to ribbons and collapses on it, sobbing. It was a difficult strenuous scene, but Liz did it all in a few takes. She really went wild, lashing out in such a frenzy that she banged her hand. We had to send for Dr. Pennington.[10]

Certainly, it was the crossover between the filmed scene and what were reputedly Taylor's actual emotions at the time that made this scene fodder for the gossip mills—especially memorable is the image of Taylor lashing out in a wild frenzy when faced with the prospect that she will be cast off by Burton. Moreover, the film text lends authenticity to Taylor's star image in that Taylor's torment over Burton's reported denial is more believable precisely because it shows up in the film version of *Cleopatra*. In this sense, the film becomes a living record of what appear to be actual experiences, emotions, and events that took place between the actors. (Apparently, this hysterical performance also continued beyond the film set—newspapers reported that Taylor attempted suicide when Burton said he would not leave Sybil.)

The extent to which Taylor's and Burton's performances register as real or true depended on the degree to which their film roles were tied to their publicized romantic escapades, and vice versa. As Richard Dyer writes, "The criteria governing performance have shifted from whether the performance is well done to whether it is truthful, that is, true to the 'true' personality of the performer . . . Every truth is a peculiar criterion—we no longer ask if someone performs well or according to certain moral precepts but whether what they perform is truthful, with the referent of truthfulness not being falsifiable statements but the person's 'person.'"[11] Since Taylor had been so frequently constructed as one who regarded her romantic affairs as matters of international importance (and certainly the press treated them as such), her screen appearances paradoxically accrued legitimacy the more hyperbolic they became. That is, because her screen behavior was so closely aligned with what was considered her real-life personality, Taylor's exposition of overblown sentiments made her performances appear all the more authentic.

That the supposed cinematic urgency of the real life spilled over onto the film screen was a boon for Fox as well; the studio's and couple's fortunes were so interdependent that the studio openly admitted that it hoped to capitalize on scenes rumored to be consistent with the actors' real life. Assistant publicity manager Jake Brodsky describes "a Burton solo that is so magnificent, and inspired by Elizabeth at his feet (out of camera range). The best of it, in these scenes, parallels Sybil (Rome) and Cleo (Egypt) . . . Audiences will flip. And on the set where Liz must do an Oedipus-scream of discovery, what do you think it is she screams? She screams Sybil!"[12] Brodsky's sense that "audiences will flip" over this dramatization was wholly prescient, precisely because the most suggestive moments in *Cleopatra* are those in which the film invites the interpretation that Taylor and Burton were speaking to one another *as* one another. In one of their initial meetings, Antony says, "Don't ask me to be clear about my feelings right now; I'm tired, and with you, even at my best, it's not easy to say my meaning," which arguably represents an ambivalent answer to the question everyone believed Taylor was asking of her lover: what exactly were his intentions? Would the infamous womanizer actually leave his wife? One headline from the *Daily News* claimed, "Burt Kisses Wife, Dashes to Liz."[13] Moreover, Cleopatra's sweet-sounding supplication to a departing Antony, "You take so much away with you . . . Remember, remember, they'll want you to forget," echoed stories in the news reporting that Taylor was pleading with Burton to take her, and their affair, seriously. (In the film, Antony divorced his wife Octavia to be with Cleopatra, and conquer the world in her name.) That art was so perfectly imitating life seems not to have escaped Taylor either—her voice breaks when, as Cleopatra, she urges that Antony never forget her.

Cleopatra thereby positioned itself as a film that teased audiences with what was at best a barely concealed notion that it contained the "truth" of the romance between Taylor and Burton. In fact, the chance to learn about Taylor and Burton as a real-life couple was much of the reason audiences so eagerly awaited the opening of *Cleopatra* and patiently withstood the viewing of this otherwise rather laborious film. Fox also attempted to profit from this public pursuit as quickly as possible—once filming was done, it refused to allow Mankiewicz to edit the material into two films as he had planned because the studio hoped to release *Cleopatra* quickly, before, as was feared, Taylor and Burton broke up.

Perhaps because the film script dovetailed so neatly with Taylor and Burton's real-life affair, *Cleopatra* introduced qualities of affect that would be aligned with the real-life couple for the duration of their alliance. Both onscreen and off, the couple participated directly in the widespread romantic ideal that love is best made legible by extreme displays of emotions or heartbreak. For instance, the pair frequently discusses the ramifications of making love their "master"; Cleopatra notes, in a somewhat tongue-and-cheek fashion, that in doing so, people tend to forget who they are and what they want. She later forgets this cautionary tone, however, and while contemplating Antony's removal from Egypt to Rome asks in a tortured voice, "Antony, how will I live?" As if taking a cue from Antony and Cleopatra's obsessive devotion, Taylor and Burton frequently insisted that they refused to be parted for even the briefest of moments. In a *Look* article in 1965, for example, Burton allegedly remarked of their relationship, which was at this time over three years old, "We tried to be apart for an hour and a half once, but it didn't work."[14] A *Coronet* article also quotes Taylor as saying that "to exist without Richard is unthinkable," while Burton comments, "Elizabeth is my everything, my breath, my blood, my mind, and my imagination. If anything happened to her, I would die."[15]

Cleopatra also showcased some of the less obviously mythologized but equally metonymic aspects of the couple's affair: Antony's excessive drinking gestured toward Burton's chronic alcoholism, and Cleopatra's fluctuations between devotion and wrath were suggestive of Taylor's penchant for performing, at alternate turns, haughty dignity, wounded pride, and calculated vulnerability. The film also served as a thinly veiled expose of what were reported to be Taylor and Burton's darker sides: Cleopatra's magnificent anger when Antony marries Octavia mimicked Taylor's own rage at being relegated to the position of the other women; at one point, Cleopatra proclaims with seedy innuendo that she knows others think of her as "an Egyptian harlot." Jealousy over Sybil's status as Burton's wife also seems to inform Taylor's sneering description of Antony's wife as "so softly spoken, so virtuous . . . she sleeps, I hear, fully clothed." Certainly, such scenes construct Taylor and Burton as a couple with a passion so boundless that it precludes the possibility of emotional restraint.[16] These scenes also set forth the affective parameters for how the Burton/Taylor affair would be constructed by the press, and reports of the couple consistently commented on their tempestuous natures, petty jealousies, and roaring disagreements.

At the same time, *Cleopatra* inadvertently reveals the degree to which coupling is premised on falsifying one's intentions—Cleopatra's designs on Antony frequently appear motivated more by calculating ambition than serious devotion. While vehemently proclaimed, her love for him at times wanes, and this ambivalence is punctuated by her decision to leave Antony, who is locked in a spectacular naval battle, after being given an obviously unreliable message that he has died. Taylor's cold demeanor in this sequence raises the question, both textually and extratextually, of whether Antony/Burton was merely a means to an end. For Cleopatra, he provided the access to ruling the world, whereas for Taylor domesticating this famous womanizer would allow her to be crowned one of the most desirable women alive. The suspicion of Taylor's motivations, in fact, formed a cornerstone of the public critique of her adultery. The usual cries of immorality were joined by the accusation that Taylor was merely going after Burton for the thrill of the chase, as she had done with Eddie Fisher. One commentator laments, for example, that Taylor's first marriage to Nicky Hilton, who ignored her on their honeymoon, resulted in such humiliation for the actress that it "compelled her to triumph in her romances at all cost—as if, over and over, she must prove her attraction for men to herself and to the world."[17] Identifying Taylor's motivations and even speculating over the lengths she would go to in order to disguise those motivations became a constant public preoccupation. Like Cleopatra, Taylor reportedly stopped at nothing to secure her romantic future: the woman who loved being lavished with diamonds from Burton, including the famous sixty-nine-carat Cartier ring, once reportedly told him while they were beginning their relationship that she would live in a cold-water flat in England if that meant they could be together.[18]

That the couple was able to smooth over such contradictions and emerge as a still-memorable contender for the designation of "great lovers" is due, I suspect, to the fact that the discourses surrounding them coalesced in such a way as to comply with the romantic ideal that as partners all they wanted out of life was each other. This sentiment is perfectly encapsulated by the tagline to a story in *Movie Mirror* in July 1965: "When Richard Touches Me Nothing Else Matters!"[19] Yet, in this hall of mirrors, these designations of true love are notably all manufactured: Taylor and Burton's love was first authenticated by the great lovers they played in *Cleopatra,* the publicity discourses about them (produced in part by a studio with an eco-

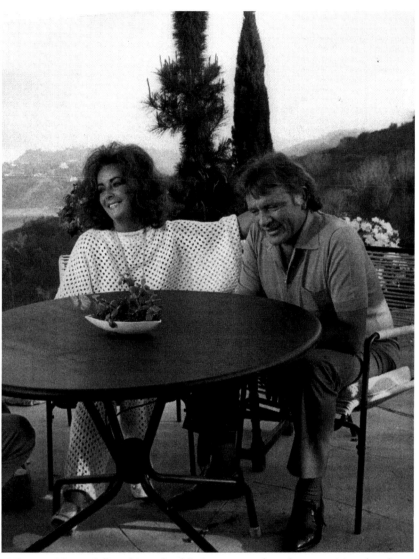

The couple's carefully cultivated public image turned on the recognition that they were domestically—and sexually—satisfied.

nomic interest in their affair), and the couple's willingness to accord their relationship epic significance. The couple achieved notoriety as great lovers as a result of their public existences, all the while paradoxically convincing audiences that what was at stake in their affair were the most personal of emotions. Publicity materials, for example, repeatedly described how "alone" the couple was, and commented on how they liked spending time away from the public, reading and talking to one another. Despite the fact that both Burton and Taylor had children from earlier marriages, these children largely drop out of their press coverage. On March 9, 1965, *Look* reported, "Do they seem to have any close friends they *really* want to see? No. Does he seem to like anybody? Oh, her. Does *she*? Only him. They don't even seem to go to the theater or the cinema, or have the curiosity to."[20] One of the world's most public couples nevertheless was constructed as if their relationship occurred purely in private.

Taylor and Burton's classification as great lovers might also appear surprising since their adulterous affair was at first so widely condemned. Yet, as will be explained in the next section, the key to securing public absolution for their adulterous acts came in part from Taylor and Burton's willingness to grant their affair institutional legitimacy by becoming man and wife.

Marriage, or The Adulterer's Redemption

The narrative of how Taylor and Burton achieved forgiveness for the *Cleopatra* scandal suggests that it relies heavily on a public reinterpretation of the affair as motivated by destiny rather than whim. This narrative also offers interesting insight into the legitimating discourses of heterosexual marriage, since it was thanks to Taylor and Burton's widely publicized nuptials that a repeatedly unfaithful woman was able to become one of the most adored lovers of the twentieth century.[21]

Taylor's pardon for her public acts of indecency was aided by her apparent willingness to engage in dialogue with those constructing her transgression. In an interview in *Look* magazine in May 1963, Taylor admitted she was hurt by the press reports condemning her behavior but said that she was prepared to lead her own life regardless of what they said. She commented that her male secretary kept the most vitriolic newspaper clippings away from her, which she called the "scorchers," because he loved her too much to let them hurt her. As she told the magazine, although such reports suggested that she was so scarlet she might seem "almost purple," she countered with, "Why get a heart attack over them? . . . I'm a human being, and I do make mistakes like all human beings."[22] Here, Taylor appears simultaneously repentant and headstrong; in fact, her comments were so easily available for multiple interpretations that twin accounts of the same interview, in articles that carried almost identical text, appeared in competing newspapers on the same day. The *Los Angeles Herald Examiner* summed up the interview with the headline "Liz Scolds Critics of Burton Romance," while the *Los Angeles Times* proclaimed, "Liz Says She Doesn't Mind Nasty Opinions."[23] As these competing discourses confirm, Taylor's star image was available for construction as defiant *or* repentant and was often malleable enough to suggest both.

Taylor and Burton's most public act of redemption, of course, was to legally marry, and after securing divorces from their respective spouses, the pair wed in Canada on March 15, 1964. In yet another tacit admission that the requirements of performance inflected virtually every aspect of this relation, Taylor's gown was designed by the woman who created her costumes for *Cleopatra* with the inspiration for the dress reportedly coming from the one she wore on the set the first time she met Burton.[24] Testifying further to the theatricality of this connubial event, Burton played Hamlet the night following their nuptials, and after his sixth curtain call borrowed a line from the production and told the audience, as Hamlet does in the first scene of act three, "We will have no more marriages."[25] (This statement, incidentally, turned out not to be true. The couple divorced in 1974, remarried in 1975, and then divorced again almost a year later, this time for good.)

The public persona of Taylor in the period where she and Burton slowly achieved legitimacy testifies to the legitimating power of institutional marriage, as well as affirms the stronghold this relationship retains in the cultural imaginary. Following Taylor and Burton's marriage, the press did an abrupt about-face and began to present her as a faithful and devoted wife.[26] In this refashioning, Taylor was granted not only public absolution but also sympathy for her trials. *Movie Mirror* christened her a martyr for love, noting that she had "endured almost unbearable world-wide scorn" solely for the chance to love Burton publicly. Forgetting perhaps the press's commanding role in propagating Taylor's vilification, the article continues, "It was for love of him that she heard herself called scarlet woman and home-wrecker and then they were married and no one called them names anymore."[27]

While a fickle press bears much responsibility for this rapid turnabout,

Taylor's path from cunning seductress to faithful wife nevertheless took a notable detour through a third figure—the childish schoolgirl whose wrongdoings are forgivable because she falls in love without the thought of consequences. Describing Taylor in *The Cleopatra Papers,* Nathan Weiss writes of how he and Wanger decided that Elizabeth was "one of the least promiscuous of women, because she intends to marry each man she falls in love with—and does. Each, for the time, is Prince Charming. It's very schoolgirlish, actually, to pledge undying love to each candidate."[28] Likewise, an article in *Pageant* magazine proclaimed, "Elizabeth's changing tastes can be compared with a schoolgirl's crush. An undying love of the lower grades is often viewed with amused dismay by the time a girl is a high school sophomore."[29] Apparently forgetting that Taylor was over thirty years old and four times married by the time of her affair with Burton, this rhetorical construction suggests that the threat posed by female promiscuity might be contained if any formulation of female sexuality that does not conform to classical notions is positioned as simply naïve or immature. Thus, it is "schoolgirlish" of Taylor to keep having affairs and sleeping with other women's husbands, but it is not wholly immoral because she sincerely wants to marry all the men she sleeps with, and usually does. The article continues, "Elizabeth, friends say, is old-fashioned enough to believe that she should marry her love . . . this is her code. Her ethic. And she is honest enough to live by it."[30] While Susan McLeland has argued that Taylor's image was constructed during a period when the values of femininity were in transition, and that Taylor became a poster girl for the "new morality" of the 1960s because she coupled marriage with eroticism and maternity with glamour,[31] Taylor's discursive construction as a girl seems to me to harken back to an older, more antiquated model of femininity, one that patronizes sexual women as "not knowing any better." Calling Taylor a foolish *girl* swiftly diffuses the threat she posed to patriarchal culture as an adulterous *woman* in that it removes from her any intentionality or autonomous sexual desire. In turn, casting extramarital sex as being driven by marital intentions inoculates such potentially transgressive behavior from challenging ideological norms or threatening heterosexual organizations. In a larger sense, this example reveals a patriarchal order willing to forgive transgression *if* the deviant can somehow be recuperated by the world order that she has betrayed, and confirms that the best way to effect such a rehabilitation is to recommit oneself to the sanctified institution of marriage.

In keeping with a patriarchal logic willing to ignore female misbehavior if accompanied by a recommitment to monogamy and, in turn, heteronormative ideals, Taylor's adulterous ways were framed as further pardonable thanks to her public assurance that she would now uphold conventional gender roles. Although Taylor was initially positioned as a power-hungry seductress who stole Burton from Sybil, once she and Burton were married, the press reported that she was eager to let *him* dominate the relationship. Taylor reportedly told *Look* magazine, "All women are really fighting only to be women, not to be superior to men. Women want to be dominated by men, not to dominate them. This applied even to Cleopatra."[32] After her marriage to Burton, Taylor insisted on being called Mrs. Burton, and the July 1965 issue of *Movie Mirror* quoted her as saying that Richard "wears the pants in this family."[33] Burton also confirmed his superior status, writing in a self-authored piece in *Life:* "We never had any question of who was the boss. She always realized I was to run the show. I do this by talking, talking, talking. My little shrew is inevitably tamed after a little bit of talking."[34] That this comment bears resemblance to the narrative of *The Taming of the Shrew* is not incidental—the article was published around the time of the film's release, which starred Taylor as the vitriolic Kate and Burton as her controlling Petruchio.

In spite of the predictability of Burton and Taylor's traditionalist rhetoric and the fact that it was clearly being used to generate publicity for films like *The Taming of the Shrew,* attempts in the popular press to depict Taylor as subservient to her husband nevertheless frequently deconstructed themselves. The article "How Liz Made Burton Her Love Slave," for example, positions Taylor's pliability as a posture designed to woo Burton. The article reports that she appealed to Burton through "not her intelligence, talent or fame—but her helplessness, her need for him, her desire to please him, an attraction that promised to grow into a deep, passionate love."[35] Yet these were apparently calculated moves, intended to "make life for him without her impossible."[36] At the same time, the article suggests that Taylor was in fact learning how to submit to Burton in a manner not unlike *The Taming of the Shrew*'s Kate. Taylor's image in the "Love Slave" article functions to reveal and simultaneously contain the lie that Taylor was a subservient woman. As a historical document, the twisted, inconsistent logic in this piece also inadvertently unveils the ideological back flips it takes to secure heterosexuality's place as a normative ideal, since Taylor emerges as happily compliant yet at the same time cunningly manipulative. In this way, the iteration confirms the opposite of what it intends;

while romantic love is supposed to arise organically between two people, the article confirms that one partner must be unrelentingly strategic to ensure that it actually happens.[37]

Examining the various inconsistent discourses necessary to laminate Taylor and Burton's love offers valuable insight into the fact that what we have come to name "true love" is in fact an unstable category containing so many contradictions that it threatens to deconstruct at any moment. In turn, the hyperbolic discourses that surrounded Taylor and Burton have a wider applicability to the study of sexual norms because they reveal that the heady rhetoric of romance is empirically at odds with the stabilizing logic of marriage. If the allure of romance is the "thrill of the chase" and marriage resolves that pursuit, star discourses surrounding Taylor and Burton negotiated this difficulty by persisting in manufacturing threats to the couple's continued happiness. The Burtons kept narrative momentum alive by continually showcasing the obstacles to their relationship, interventions that in effect constituted the relationship at the same time that they purported to disrupt it. Gossip magazines, for instance, frequently discussed the challenges facing Taylor and Burton's marriage, specifically Burton's drinking and his notorious wandering eye. In April 1964, *Photoplay* ran a story with the headline "How Long Can Burton Hold Liz—and His Liquor Too?" Likewise, in May 1964 *TV and Movie Screen* asked, "Can Liz Keep Burton Away from Other Women?"

Because such reports manufactured a threat to Taylor and Burton's love but then showcased the remaking and reconstituting of this romantic relation, Taylor and Burton were repeatedly positioned as a couple capable of reintroducing desire into the space of marriage. Such constructions confirm the extent to which their relation participated in a wider project of delimiting fixed parameters for romantic mythology.[38] As David R. Shumway has argued, the paradox of marriage in the twentieth century is that marriage supposedly represents the culmination of romance, and yet romance is identified with brief, intense affairs rather than lasting commitments. Because published reports were fond of recounting their blazing fights and passionate reconciliations, Taylor and Burton's relation sustained the appearance of romantic intensity by continuing to borrow from the rhetoric of extramarital sexuality even after they were married. In this way, the stars' modus operandi is not unlike the one Shumway claims for the screwball comedy, in that their tempestuous relations fueled a romantic mystification of marriage in order "to make it seem to be what it cannot be, an affair."[39]

Taylor and Burton's positioning as still-desiring marital subjects rested heavily on the suggestion that because they faced down the threat of romantic competition and survived public battles, they bravely silenced critics who doubted the legitimacy of their union. On their seventh wedding anniversary, Burton was reported as saying, "They would love to see us break up. They are disappointed that our marriage has lasted so long. It would give them so much pleasure to be able to say, 'I told you so.'"[40] In this construction, Taylor and Burton are framed as heroic for making their marriage work, a discursive positioning that confirms the extent to which the image of great love is manufactured by the invention of both public and private opposition to it. The aggregation of discourses of emotional insecurity coalesce in such a way as to suggest that the marital contract becomes desirable only when faced with the threat of its own dissolution.

Theaters of Marital Cruelty: Spectacles of Performance in Who's Afraid of Virginia Woolf

If the logic of romance depends paradoxically on obstacles to attain its realization, the couple's most famous iteration of such a principle came in the form of their starring roles as the feuding couple George and Martha in *Who's Afraid of Virginia Woolf.* Taylor and Burton's star image so well informed the film's enunciative capacity because, like their on-screen counterparts, the real couple also reportedly delighted in arguing. Taylor once said in an interview, "We adore fighting. Richard is like a well, there's no plumbing that depth. You can't describe an erupting volcano."[41] Furthermore, also like George and Martha, Taylor and Burton frequently made a habit of forcing others to watch the spectacle of their wildly angry bouts. A reporter from *Screen Stars* once described being in a hotel room with the couple and having Burton pick up a lamp and throw it at the television when Taylor asked him to be quiet.[42] Despite the seeming spontaneity of such events, the couple countered that their quarrels were enacted in large part for the edification of their public. Burton was recorded as saying: "The truth is that we live out, for the benefit of the mob, the sort of idiocies they've come to expect. We will often battle purely for the exercise."[43] Such comments suggest that Taylor and Burton did not expect their fights to be taken seriously, although audiences were presumably not always in on the joke.[44]

Taylor and Burton's fights were also described as a way of adding spontaneity and intensity to their marriage; the *National Tattler* quoted Taylor

Seen here in *Who's Afraid of Virginia Woolf* (1966), the couple was notorious for their battles, both onscreen and off. As Taylor once told a reporter, "Terrible fights we have. Sometimes they are public and we hear whispers of 'that marriage won't last.' But we know better."

as saying, "If you're really sure of yourself in your love—then having an out-an-out outrageous ridiculous fight is one of the greatest exercises in marital togetherness."[45] Clearly, *Who's Afraid of Virginia Woolf* capitalized on the couple's public persona as a pair who produced conflict simply for sport—in one pivotal moment, when George tells Martha that he can no longer stand her ceaseless humiliation of him, she baits him with the statement that not only can he stand it, but he married her *for* it.

According to the lexicon of *Who's Afraid of Virginia Woolf,* performance sustains marriage—and George and Martha's adherence to this organizing principle is evidenced specifically by the fact that each plays a number of different "roles" during the film's diegesis. Perhaps their most flagrant fictionalization is to identify themselves as parents, a characterization dependant on their invention of an imaginary child whom they bring into being through discursive repetition. The film progresses through a circular interplay of lies, invented identities, and confused attributions, all of which keep doubling back on themselves. Indeed, it is difficult, if not impossible, to discern if there are any moments in the film where George and Martha are *not* acting. Although the citational and performative practices of the film are sufficient to warrant extended discussion, I will name just a few examples. First, the film opens with Taylor performing the line "What a dump," and asking George what film the line comes from, which ignites a discussion of cinematic references. From the film's inception, George and Martha therefore exist in dialectical relation to film discourse and film characterizations, which is not unlike the ways in which Taylor and Burton's star image borrowed from the identities of other great lovers, most notably Antony and Cleopatra. This interplay of identity, and the confusion over whose identity is whose, in fact informs much of the discussion between George and Martha and between them and their guests, Nick and Honey. For example, George may or may not be the boy he describes to Nick, who inadvertently kills both his parents in separate accidents, and this boy may or may not be the subject of the unpublished novel George has written, if he has indeed written a novel. Likewise, George and Martha continually question whether Nick is in the math department or the biology department, and while talking to Nick, George deliberately confuses Martha with Honey and vice versa. (The rhetorical wife swapping later becomes literal when Martha and Nick attempt conjugal relations offscreen.)

Further, the stakes in this game of identity confusion get increasingly higher; George and Martha vow to battle to the bitter end, and during their verbal sparring, Martha speculates that George may not be the father of her "son," while she also makes George pointedly aware that she has attempted to bed Nick, thereby swapping George for a younger version. Despite the fact that George and Martha's acts of fictionalization would seem to threaten their relationship, their game sustains and even revitalizes their marriage. In fact, the brief moments in which the characters are forced to acknowledge the singularity of their own identities may be more threatening than the game itself. For example, George becomes furious when Martha suggests that the story of the murdering boy is in fact a story of his life; Honey vomits as much from inebriation as from humiliation when George tells her the story of her own hysterical pregnancy, which Nick has told to him; and Martha is eventually beaten at her own game when George "kills" their fictional son. Thus, the drama suggests that blurring the distinction between truth and illusion may in fact be preferable to hearing the truth about yourself, since the truth is often more grotesque than any fiction.

The film consistently collapses the boundary between truth and illusion, as if to suggest that marital intrigue is sustained precisely through such fictionalized exhibitions. Indeed, *Who's Afraid of Virginia Woolf* affirms that excitement can best be manufactured in marriage by stringing together a series of dissonant performances intended to surprise, and thus one-up, one's spouse. Not coincidentally, this strategy is not unlike the one Taylor and Burton claim to have deployed in their own marriage. Taylor once said in an interview, "The key to a perfect marriage is unpredictability,"[46] as if to confirm that for the fiction of love to be maintained, all action related to it must be a drama, a performance, or a theatrical event. According to this logic, one cannot create passion through regularity but must instead rely on tension, intrigue, conflict, and then reconciliation— or at the least, the performance of these.

Who's Afraid of Virginia Woolf functions according to a multilayering of performance, whereby Taylor and Burton, the real couple with a habit of performing for their public, also perform in the film as Martha and George, who then perform for Nick and Honey. Yet in true postmodern fashion, all this performing only makes the couple's relation seem more real, so that the end result is the appearance or effect of originality. That such repetition ensures the appearance of authenticity was even evidenced in the published responses to Taylor's acting in the film, since, thanks to her performance as Martha, Taylor garnered new respect as an actress capable of emotional depth. While Taylor's career had been circumscribed by the perception that she was beautiful but not necessarily gifted, the Oscar she won for *Virginia Woolf* was considered to have been duly earned because she made Martha seem so real.[47] Moreover, the Production Code refused to censor *Virginia Woolf's* foul language precisely because the film did such a good job of reflecting "the tragic realism of life."[48] Given this veritable hall of mirrors, it is perhaps not surprising that a film that blatantly acknowledges the performative nature of marriage is also assumed to be the most accurate depiction of the real-life couple's actual relation. Burton and Taylor were paradoxically the most convincing as *actors and as lovers* when they appeared in a film that not only admits to the performative nature of marriage but also confirms that performance sustains the fiction of marital unity. This layering upon layering of performance might thus be said to constitute an act of performativity, whereby the performance is so good at mimicking what we think of as reality that reality gets constituted in the process.

In closing, the excessive performances that underpin the entire Taylor-Burton relation destabilize the true love designation at the same time that they reify it, a statement that provides valuable insight into how the discourses of heterosexual romance can be overblown to the point of parody, and yet at the same time retain a pervasive ideological stronghold. While Taylor and Burton promulgated fantastic visions of love and devotion, their image as a couple nevertheless had great fun with—and made great fun of—the institution of heterosexual marriage. (It is worth remembering that Taylor has been married a total of eight times, and only two of those marriages were to Burton. For his part, Burton married twice after Taylor.) Thus, at the same time that Taylor and Burton have been memorialized as great lovers, by virtue of the sheer compulsion with which the pair approached their relation, they have also parodied it to the point of masquerade. If, as Mary Ann Doane claims, "masquerade, in flaunting femininity, holds it at a distance,"[49] we might say that in flaunting their involvement with the institution of marriage, the couple also holds it and the heterosexual paradigm at a distance. Likewise, this strategy of distanciation is in some ways inadvertently progressive, in that it reveals the imitative qualities of the heterosexual matrix and unmasks some of its fictions.

In fact, despite the authentication that their relationship would later receive, Taylor and Burton's star image often made a mockery out of the notion of monogamy: the pair cheated on their respective spouses in order to begin their relationship, often played adulterers in their joint films, and were at various time reputed to have cheated on each other. During the summer and fall of 1972 there were numerous allegations that Burton was having an affair with the French actress Nathalie Delon, while Taylor was reportedly spending time in Italy with the millionaire Aristotle Onassis. Moreover, even the dalliances Taylor and Burton supposedly had with others testify to the regularity with which their real life was used to generate publicity for their work, since the timing of these "affairs" corresponded quite neatly with Taylor and Burton's then-current acting project, *Divorce His, Divorce Hers,* a made-for-television movie that offered a husband's and a wife's version of the story of their failed marriage. Taylor and Burton's official separation was announced in July 1973, merely a few months after the premiere of *Divorce His, Divorce Hers,* which aired in February 1973.[50] Even in their relationship's last days, the requirements of performance never quite absented the couple: when the pair officially separated, Taylor wrote a letter to the press about their breakup which said, "Maybe we have loved each other too much (not that I ever believed such a thing was possible)."[51]

The irony of the Taylor-Burton love affair may be that the more excessively performative the couple became, the more deeply their image as great lovers was etched into the collective romantic unconscious. Burton and Taylor therefore reveal the extent to which one must reperform heterosexual love in order to constitute the originary status this identity claims to already have, such that their position as great lovers arose from the fact of their having played the role of great lovers so repeatedly, both in life and on film. In postmodern terms, their citational practices functioned so effectively in service of producing the "real" precisely because the entire specter of their relationship played out in the public eye and was subject to narrative requirements at every turn. Had Taylor and Burton not performed their marriage, and had they not fought and reconciled under the gaze of the public eye, they would likely not have been accorded the status of epic lovers. Thus, it would seem that the act of performing love, even in the most hyperbolic and parodic of ways, is what calls a designation of "true love" into being, such that this love can be said to have been constituted by, and thus did not preexist, the performance of it. Finally, because as Judith Butler writes, the repetition of play establishes the "instability of the very category that it constitutes,"[52] one might also understand Taylor and Burton's relation to reveal the extent to which heterosexuality is an identity at risk, in that it requires a repeated and multilayering string of performances, and an imitation of its own idealizations, to constitute the effect of its originality. Thus, one might demystify Taylor and Burton's epic relation with the statement that because their true love existed as a copy without an original, it registered as truer and more real than any real-life love ever could.

Notes

1. "Richard Burton and Elizabeth Taylor," Special Double Issue: The Greatest Love Stories of the Century, *People*, February 12, 1996, 62–65.

2. Examples of the incessant crisscrossing between film, fiction, and life include their appearances in *Cleopatra* (1963); *The Sandpiper* (1965); *Who's Afraid of Virginia Woolf* (1966); *The Taming of the Shrew* (1967); *The Comedians* (1967); *Boom!* (1968); and *Hammersmith Is Out* (1972). Taylor and Burton also appeared as themselves in a now-famous 1970 episode of *Here's Lucy*. In the skit, Lucy mistakes Burton, the accomplished Shakespearean actor, for a plumber, and gets Taylor's famous sixty-nine-carat Cartier diamond stuck on her finger. Taylor and Burton also had roles in

Dr. Faustus (1968) and *Under Milk Wood* (1972), although their romantic relation is somewhat downplayed in both films.

3. Lauren Berlant and Michael Warner, "Sex in Public," *Critical Inquiry* 24.2 (1998): 554.

4. Qtd. in Dick Sheppard, *Elizabeth: The Life and Career of Elizabeth Taylor* (Garden City, NY: Doubleday, 1974), 317.

5. "Liz, Burton Sued by Fox: $50 Million, 'Cleo' Conduct Is Basis," *Los Angeles Herald Examiner,* April 22, 1964. At the time of *Cleopatra*'s release in 1963, however, Fox had no problem capitalizing on Taylor and Burton's affair. Using the relationship as inspiration for a promotional device that they claimed was the first of its kind, the studio produced a poster for the film that consisted of an artistic rendering of Taylor and Burton lying in each other's arms in their Roman costumes. The poster deliberately failed to include the title of the film or the names of its stars. (Rex Harrison's image was added only after the studio realized it was liable for the omission.) That *Cleopatra* was able to sell itself on image recognition alone was said to be a reflection of the "global penetration achieved by the film to date," according to *Motion Picture Exhibitor* (February 13, 1963). Executives were clearly banking on the fact that the image of a half-clothed Taylor lying beside Burton would also suggest penetration of a different kind.

6. Aida A. Hozić, "Hollywood Goes on Sale; or, What Do the Violet Eyes of Elizabeth Taylor Have to Do with the 'Cinema of Attractions'?" in *Hollywood Goes Shopping,* ed. David Desser and Garth S. Jowett (Minneapolis: University of Minnesota Press, 2000), 217.

7. While this connotation of the affair as a spontaneous eruption had some basis in actual events, other discursive high jinks surrounding the Taylor/Burton romance strained credulity, especially as the couple labored to retrospectively rewrite their past relations. Although Taylor and Burton kindled their affair in Italy in 1962, in 1966 Burton published an account of a much earlier meeting between the pair, when Taylor was only nineteen. In *Meeting Mrs. Jenkins* (New York: William Morrow, 1966) Burton, whose original surname was Jenkins, recollected how, during his initial meeting with Taylor, he found her to be "the most astonishingly self-contained, pulchritudinous, remote, removed, inaccessible woman I had ever seen" (5). That the title of the novella refers to Taylor as "Mrs. Jenkins," even though Taylor would not become Burton's wife until more than ten years *after this meeting* and would never actually be known as Mrs. Jenkins, suggests how the narratives of the couple's meetings were, ex post facto, lent the weight of predestination. The framing of Burton's remembrance suggests that even with at least three other marriages yet to come before she would wed Burton, Taylor was somehow *already* Burton's wife.

8. Walter Wanger and Joe Hyams, "Cleopatra: The Trials and Tribulations of an Epic Film," *Saturday Evening Post,* June 1, 1963, 44.

9. Ibid., 47.

10. Ibid., 47.

11. Dyer, "*A Star Is Born* and the Construction of Authenticity," in *Stardom: Industry of Desire,* ed. Christine Gledhill (London: Routledge, 1991), 133.

12. Jack Brodsky and Nathan Weiss, "The Cleopatra Papers," *Esquire,* August

1963, 40.

13. Reynolds Packard, "Burt Kisses Wife, Dashes to Liz," *Daily News,* May 3, 1962.

14. Qtd. in Jack Hamilton, "King and Queen," *Look*, March 9, 1965, 32.

15. Qtd. in Ruth Waterbury, "Why Liz Taylor Needs Love More than Most Women," *Coronet,* July 1969, 24.

16. Susan McLeland has argued that although the press tried deliberately to construct a rivalry between Taylor and Sybil Burton, Sybil's refusal to engage in a catfight significantly stymied this attempt. "Elizabeth Taylor: Hollywood's Lost Glamour Girl," in *Swinging Singles: Representing Sexuality in the 1960's,* ed. Hilary Radner and Moya Luckett (Minneapolis: University of Minnesota Press, 1999), 245. Taylor's behavior in *Cleopatra,* however, aptly fueled speculation that she was as vindictive as the press wanted her to be.

17. Adele Whitely Fletcher, "Where Did Elizabeth Taylor Go?" *Family Weekly,* January 27, 1963, 11.

18. Brodsky and Weiss, "Cleopatra Papers," 36.

19. Constance Arthur, "Is Liz Taylor Legally Wed?" *Movie Mirror,* July 1965, 16.

20. Hamilton, "King and Queen," 31.

21. My focus in this section will remain largely on Taylor, for the figure of the adulterous woman is far more culturally threatening than is the married male womanizer.

22. Jack Hamilton, "Elizabeth Taylor Talks about Cleopatra," *Look,* May 7, 1963, 50.

23. "Liz Scolds Critics of Burton Romance," *Los Angeles Herald Examiner* April 23, 1963; "Liz Says She Doesn't Mind Nasty Opinions," *Los Angeles Times* April 23, 1963.

24. Martha Greene, "Liz Taylor's Wedding," *Motion Picture,* June 1964.

25. Greene, "Liz Taylor's Wedding."

26. I do not, of course, wish to overstate the ease of Taylor and Burton's transition into respectability. In fact, gossip magazines were still censuring the couple in December 1964 for having made a "joke" out of their adultery ("How Liz and Burton Make a Joke of Adultery *Every Day*," *Motion Picture,* December 1964.) Likewise, *Modern Screen* waited until August 1965 to proclaim that the couple's "long ordeal of scandal and heartbreak" was over, even though Burton and Taylor had by this time been married for more than a year ("Liz and Burton—It's Almost Over," *Modern Screen*, August 1965).

27. Arthur, "Is Liz Taylor Legally Wed?" 61.

28. Brodsky and Weiss, "Cleopatra Papers," 37.

29. Elaine Shepard, "This Is a Story that Tells What's Good about Elizabeth Taylor," *Pageant,* September 1964, 156.

30. Shepard, "This Is a Story," 154.

31. McLeland, "Elizabeth Taylor," 248.

32. Hamilton, "Elizabeth Taylor Talks," 50.

33. Arthur, "Is Liz Taylor Legally Wed?"

34. Richard Burton, "His Liz: 'A Scheming Charmer,'" *Life,* February 24, 1967.

35. "How Liz Made Burton Her Love Slave," *Modern Screen Yearbook,* July 1964, 46.

36. Ibid.

37. Ibid. That this narrative bears resemblance to Ellen Fein and Sherry Schneider's backlash phenomena *The Rules: Time-Tested Secrets for Capturing the Heart of Mr. Right* (New York: Warner, 1995), wherein women are encouraged to use calculated autonomy in order to secure a husband on whom they can eventually be utterly dependent, is both noteworthy and unsettling.

38. That the threat to the relation is actually what constitutes the relation is a trope that was actively reflected in Taylor and Burton's film roles during this time. Taylor commits adultery in *The VIPs* (1964) and *The Comedians* (1967), and a married Burton cheats on his wife with Taylor in *The Sandpiper* (1965).

39. David R. Shumway, *Modern Love: Romance, Intimacy, and the Marriage Crisis* (New York: New York University Press, 2003), 82.

40. Qtd. in Romany Bain, "Our Marriage after Seven Years: Richard Burton Talks about Elizabeth Taylor," *Ladies Home Journal,* April 1971, 89.

41. Liz Smith, "Elizabeth Taylor: A Frank Interview," *Cosmopolitan,* July 1973, 145.

42. Sara Murray, "Liz's Shocking Marriage Secrets," *Screen Stars,* July 1971, 86.

43. Doug Laurie, "Richard Burton Spends 46th Birthday Talking about His Deep Love for Elizabeth Taylor," *National Enquirer,* February 13, 1972.

44. The reporter's position in the hotel is thus not unlike that of the academic couple in the film, Nick and Honey, who are made to witness George and Martha's bitter and vituperative display.

45. John Marshall, "Liz: How She Keeps Zip in Her Marriage," *National Tattler,* May 9, 1971.

46. Ibid.

47. According to Foster Hirsch, *Virginia Woolf* helped Taylor "discover new ways to relate to her audience," and helped to transition her career so that afterward she could play older and more interesting characters.

48. Brenda Maddox, *Who's Afraid of Elizabeth Taylor?* (New York: M. Evans, 1977), 194.

49. Mary Anne Doane, *Femmes Fatales: Feminism, Film Theory and Psychoanalysis* (New York: Routledge, 1991), 25.

50. *Divorce His, Divorce Hers* was not the couple's last joint venture. In 1983, the pair once again attempted to synergize their real-life relation with an acting project by starring as still emotionally attached divorcés in a Broadway production of Noel Coward's *Private Lives.* Their performance in the play, however, received terrible reviews.

51. Qtd. in "Elizabeth and Richard Go Phfft," *Los Angeles Times,* July 4, 1973, 5.

52. Judith Butler, *Gender Trouble: Feminism and the Subversion of Identity* (New York: Routledge, 1990), 18.

Terri Simone Francis   Chapter 5

"She Will Never Look"
Film Spectatorship, Black Feminism, and Scary Subjectivities

In a 1966 *Negro Digest* article, the actress Ruby Dee laments the ways in which she and other black women actors face "double discrimination—that of sex and that of race."[1] Moreover, Dee goes on to say that a dearth of rewarding artistic material leaves the artists mere "tattered queens" who tend to retire too early or simply disappear from public life without explanation or much notice, "haunted by an aura of tragedy, failure and defeat."[2] Dee stresses the urgency of producing material for a range of black women actresses inasmuch as it would reflect and encourage diversity within the black community. She writes that because "art not only reflects life but also influences it, we must dedicate ourselves to the improvement of life and its truths—about women, about Negroes."[3] Despite the ways in which such "truths" may be complicated and shifting rather than essential and universal, as Dee implies, the spirit of her comments is well understood: social activism, aided by artistic intervention, would help to vindicate and validate black women as cultural producers.

Rather than disappearing politely into an invisibility that might be socially acceptable in the American racist and sexist symbolic order, black women, in a revised system, would insist on being seen, perhaps even in terms of their own visions. Dee experienced a measure of liberation intellectually. Writing that while she often felt isolated within her professional success, the actress found "a continuity of experience" through studying books that documented an earlier generation of entertainers; this knowledge helped to contextualize her own career. For Dee, the issue of black women's representation is best framed as a compound concept: race-and-

98

gender, or, as she put it, "about women, about Negroes." This intersectional way of thinking is foundational in black feminist thought and complicates the use of "woman" in mainstream or white feminist discourse.

My citation of Dee's essay and *Black Feminist Cultural Criticism,* the anthology in which it is reprinted, indicates the subjects of this essay: race/ethnicity, women, and African American film culture. My intervention is directed toward an overwhelmingly whiteness-dominated feminist film criticism: I explore theories of black women's spectatorship and the problem of cinematic subjectivity. In the spirit of creative and constructive incoherence, I define (and deny) the idea of black female "scary" subjectivity on the one hand, while on the other I provide a historical overview of black women's commentary on the cinema through writing, filmmaking, and performance. My essay's title is a phrase heard on the soundtrack of the film *Reckless Eyeballing,* discussed later; I use it, with Dee's article, to address issues of who can look and how the cinematic gaze is constructed or disallowed in particular films along racial and gendered lines.

I imagine that black feminist film theory would do more than illuminate the conditions of black women; it should address the receptivity and articulation of a black female psychic and social space in cinema, and do so in a way that is responsive to the idea of black women as both consumers and producers of cultural texts. An ideal black feminist film theory therefore shifts our emphasis from manifest images or the icons of black womanhood, and places greater attention on the mysterious give-and-take between images and viewers, the variation and unpredictability involved in spectatorship that takes place in the dark, collective privacy of the cinema. An ideal black feminist film theory also would open up more ways to think about how films address and affect spectators, and serve as a tool of self-fashioning. And it would account for cinematic pleasure—the attractions, fulfillments, and expectations of watching movies for black people. With regard to spectators, black feminist film theory would avoid prescriptive readings of black womanhood, and would shed light on the ways spectators shift, expand, or escape their subject positions and identify with film characters across gendered and racialized similarities or differences. It would consider the authorship of black women filmmakers in tandem with black women spectators in such a way that theories of shifting subjectivity and aesthetics rather than biology would frame the discussion. A black feminist film theory is not necessarily about literal black women. Black feminist film theory should help us imagine people who are not black women identifying with black women screen characters and would examine the complex relationships between the gaze, desire, and both gendered and racial difference, and how they signify.

In this essay, I address issues of a cinematic gaze and black feminism by examining what I call a "scary subjectivity" in spectatorship and in representations of black womanhood with reference to a selection of films that feature black woman actors in variations on this role. My concept of scary subjectivity has much in common with Kathleen Rowe's "unruly woman" as well as Andrea Elizabeth Shaw's concept of "black women's unruly political bodies."[4] Like Rowe, I wish to move beyond feminist film theory's emphasis on tears, victimization, fragility, and emotional repression to the extent that these hallmarks of melodrama point to, as she says, a preoccupation with "strategies of purity" and perhaps ideals of sincerity and honesty as well.[5] Her assertion that comedy, "with its exaggerations, hyperbole, and assault on the rational, depicts [strategies] of danger" resonates with my concept of black female performance.

First, black women performers tend to take on personas that manage (or encourage) pre-existing notions of unassimilated (physical and/or behavioral) blackness as dangerous and threatening, even if they present a "dangerous" erotic pleasure for audiences. They then turn the threat around. Moments in the careers of performers such as Bessie Smith, Josephine Baker, Pam Grier, and a range of recent figures associated with music, politics, and other public spheres, such as Queen Latifah, Oprah Winfrey, and Michelle Obama, offer differing examples of unruly political bodies. Further, in taking on the socially dangerous mask "that grins and lies,"[6] the performer, public figure, or fictional character who embodies a scary subjectivity rejects the terms of her oppression as not just wrong or unjust but as absurd, ridiculous, and stupid; she protects her vulnerability and subjectivity while rejecting her opponent's terms. The scary subject is not just rebellious against the received social order; rather, she seems to reject it, opt out of it, and operate instead according to her own values. "Scary" not only describes an individual image but is a give-and-take relationship between the black woman as viewer and as image. Shaw's perceptive study addresses the contradictions in black women's performances, such as "ghetto fabulousness." She says this style, which features bright colors, erotic clothing, and prominent jewelry, "suggests an excess of the femininity that those styles represent."[7] In other words, it is a kind of overcompensation for being aware that they are seen as unfeminine because they may not have any of the characteristics that mark mainstream style and fashion or white feminine acceptability.

Scary subjectivity refers to black female spectators or other wielders of the cinematic gaze who may be unruly in ways that are similar to Rowe's white feminist or other oppositional viewerships but whose unruly behavior, specifically through humor and the use of absurdity, has particular meanings and implications within the film culture of African Americans. Black women, as Shaw points out, must devise strategies of confrontation and visibility that counter what she calls "racial erasure."[8] Shaw explains that this erasure can take the form of subordinating typically black characteristics in favor of the appearance of physiological or behavioral assimilation, or it could be the hyperembodiment of black women through a visibility limited to sexualized objectification. Racial erasure is not merely invisibility or unacceptability, however; performance and exaggeration are key components of this process. While Shaw's argument seems to depend problematically on a unified notion of authentic and thus endangered black womanhood, what I find compelling is her idea that some black women's unassimilated bodies are already transgressive by their presence in public cultures, if those bodies are loud, fat, or dark-skinned. Moreover, qualities such as being taller than the average white woman, being verbally in command of one's thoughts, and making clothing choices that enhance physicality, such as suits that are cut with the body's lines, jewel tones, and sleeveless tops, tend to be controversial as well. If the mere visibility of women with these traits makes them disobedient affronts to the racial and gendered orders that inhere to the mainstream symbolic world, and if they choose to acknowledge criticism at all, is not the scariest and most dangerous response to the agents of that order to unmask it through irony and mockery rather than submit to it through sincerity, tears, and self-revelation? But this strategy does not mean that the scary subject is not vulnerable. In a situation where she is the underdog (and the black woman and other women of color are statistically the most underprivileged in terms of health, income, and education disparities, not to mention their exclusions from middlebrow notions of beauty and acceptability), the scary black woman subject risks ridicule and censure to speak her mind; she makes a spectacle of herself and her power to do so—even to *think* she can do so—makes her a potential threat.

Yet the scary subjectivity is different from both "the unruly woman" and "the unruly political body" because my terms encompass a wider range of particularly cinematic emotional responses and exchanges between black women and patriarchy, white feminism, and whiteness, as I will demonstrate. In a recently published study of what she called "black power action films," Stephanie Dunn writes, "We must recognize that various real viewers may see the films in far more diverse ways than those intended by filmmakers and marketers. The crucial feat is not to view the texts as having complete or dominant control over viewing positions, though the film controllers may have in mind a target audience and their expectations. We must also avoid the other extreme of viewing movies as only offering positions created by viewers."[9] Thus, scary subjectivity has less to do with the biology or appearance of a black woman than with what black women do and how they respond to the world of images in whose circulation they contradictorily participate. While Dunn is referring to real black women, it is also true that real black women share symbolic space in the public sphere with fictional characters. Overall in this essay, I am talking about constructions of black womanhood, which actual women may embody or engage in various ways through cultural practices that involve the movies.

Scary subjectivity is defined, in part, as an unruly spectator: someone whose behavior does not conform to established norms for watching movies, thus making of him- or herself a spectacle in the movie theater. Further, this subjectivity is an element of a given film's reflexivity and is manifest by a specific film's character who reads the movies or a particular film within the film in terms of his/her own racial and gendered identity. The scary character foregrounds the cinematic practices of racism, sexism, and its attendant reproduction of racialized sexual ideologies through their actions and speech at the movies. She splinters the audience along social lines, which in turn can disrupt the seamless enjoyment of the film for at least some viewers. The sequences from Wes Craven and Keenan Ivory Wayans's films that I discuss later illustrate the way that a scary spectator threatens the classical cinema's illusionist values of visual and narrative seamlessness and audience absorption.

To elucidate the scary subject, I include close readings of scenes from a cohort of films that cross diverse eras, genres, and even perhaps, to some extent, challenge scholarly decorum. All the films contain key moments in which expectations of cinematic spectatorship and subjectivity are questioned in particularly illuminating ways: *Uncle Josh at the Moving Picture Show* (dir. Edwin S. Porter, 1902), *Le Pompier des Folies Bergère* (1928), *Zou Zou* (dir. Marc Allégret, 1934), *Strands* (dir. Lorna Ann Johnson, 1996), *Reckless Eyeballing* (dir. Christopher Harris, 2004) as well as *Scream*

2 (dir. Wes Craven, 1997) and *Scary Movie* (dir. Keenan Ivory Wayans, 2000).[10] The selection of the last two films in particular is somewhat provocative on my part, given their seeming "lowbrow" parody. But they are instructive for the ways in which their parodic structure scratches away the cinema's sheen of preciousness through reflexivity. In them the figure of "Uncle Josh" from Porter's film is recast with a theoretical black woman film viewer. The fictional viewers I discuss are the movie characters Maureen and Brenda from *Scream 2* and *Scary Movie,* respectively, and they are parodies or a straight manifestation, depending on one's point of view, of the stereotypical "bitch." Patricia Hill Collins sheds light on this term, writing, "Depicting African American women as bitches . . . obscure[s] the closing door of racial opportunity in the post-Civil Rights era."[11] Such images of the bitchy black woman spectator perform a backlash, an explicit punishment for the tremendous influence that black women intellectuals gained as scholars, artists, and media makers during the 1990s.

In the films I examine here, black women characters use various strategies to interrupt the normal, expected entrancement of a movie audience. The black woman character becomes a "scary" viewer when she either addresses the camera or fellow audience members. By implication, she threatens the racialized symbolic order in the cinema, as well as the order of critical approaches in traditional feminist and film scholarship, and the limited roles deemed possible for black women's life beyond the screen, which, as Dee points out, is tied in complex ways to screen constructions of black womanhood. Throughout this essay, I presume a general fear/fascination/allure of black woman's ultimate otherness, which is condensed in the figure of the not so much naïve, but willfully *inassimilable* and, thus, scary, film viewer.[12] Perhaps more important is that while these figures seem to be aware of their outsider status, they are not necessarily asking to be let in to the mainstream; nor do they seem to regret their inability to become absorbed into the movies in the "right" ways.

Addressing the cinematic reproduction or representation of black womanhood means more than cataloguing the pictorial representations and "controlling images" of a recognizable or typical black woman.[13] We need to examine the representations and the ideologies about black women that circulate through cinematic images and the ways in which motion pictures uniquely frame them. The need for a black feminist theory of film production and reception warrants my focusing on the invisibility of black women, not only as actors, which Dee addresses above, but also as critics and historians of film. History forms the bedrock of black feminist theory, even if, as indicated by film scholar Mark Reid, one of its goals is an abstraction of black women's varied and shifting identities, rather than an overreliance on fixed social categories.[14] Applying Mary Ann Doane's concept of the woman spectator to the problematic of black women's spectatorship, Reid writes:

The concept of black womanist spectatorship should not be taken "to refer directly to the [black] woman who buys her ticket and enters the movie theater as the member of an audience, sharing a social identity but retaining a unique psychical history. Frequently, [it] do[es] not even refer to the spectator as a social subject but, rather, as a psychical subject, as the effect of signifying structures." Black womanist spectatorship, then, is a socio-psychical process, not a biological trait. It cannot totally exclude or include its audience based on race or gender.[15]

But the question of the image of black women, whether positive or negative, and what black women think about it, remains absolutely crucial. In the cinema, black womanhood is controlled by "mainstream cultural representations of black women . . . [as]: the sexual siren; the rotund, full-bosomed nurturing mother figure; the dominating matriarch incarnate; eternally ill-tempered wenches; and wretched victims."[16] Yet feminist film history and criticism, whose interventions transformed the study of film by addressing the multivalent discourses that inhere to screen womanhood, consistently neglect considerations of race and racial ideologies that would bring needed attention to the presence and meaning of black women characters or the absence thereof. However, black women cultural and literary critics have richly theorized representations of black womanhood.

In the 1970s, black women intellectuals established a critical publishing community in several edited anthologies that brought together diverse voices and literary forms. The publication of Toni Cade Bambara's *The Black Woman: An Anthology* (1970), followed by Mary Helen Washington's *Black-eyed Susans: Classic Stories by and about Black Women* (1975), built upon Anna Julia Cooper's work, *A Voice from the South by A Black Woman of the South* (1892). These anthologies ushered in a modern era of philosophy on black womanhood in light of the 1970s feminist movement and the movements for black power and civil rights. Both of these political movements gave limited consideration to the particularities of black women's experiences. In many ways, it was the project of these anthologies to show a range of contemporary black women's writings and experiences in order to complicate one-sided images of the black woman. Especially because of the breadth of activity in a variety of forms that the anthology represented, including poems, one-act plays, short stories, criticism, and mémoire, it served rhetorically and literally to establish black womanhood as a scholarly subject apart from white articulations of womanhood and apart from the patriarchal purchase black men have traditionally claimed on blackness.

However, while the 1970s scholarship on and by black women was concerned with "the image" of black womanhood, targeted analyses of films and film history came later. For example, Bambara's *Black Woman* includes an essay that references *The Battle of Algiers,* which is viewed as "the movie counterpart" to Frantz Fanon's *The Wretched of the Earth.* The author does not break down scenes from the movie or consider it in relation to film history but rather uses it as an unmediated window on the Algerian war.[17] Two other significant anthologies about black women, *All the Women Are White, All the Blacks Are Men, But Some of Us Are Brave: Black Women's Studies* (1982) and *Home Girls: A Black Feminist Anthology* (1983), announce their scholarly interventions by their titles. The editors of these works conceptualized a space for studying black women and representation as discrete subjects. Yet again, while the social image of black womanhood was addressed, sustained disciplinary attention to race and gender in the cinematic image was left out of these works. Certainly, black film criticism can be found embedded in newspapers and magazines that address African American publics throughout the twentieth century.[18] As Dee composed her article, for example, an important midcentury piece, she was doubtless in dialogue with film critics at *Ebony, The Chicago Defender, The Amsterdam News,* and more. Such writing formed a basis for the concepts and standards of black female cinematic subjectivity that would emerge later. The 1990s, however, would bring a watershed era in black feminist cultural criticism and black film criticism.[19] In 1995 the feminist film journal *Camera Obscura* published a special issue on black women spectators, which intersected with the heyday of publications on black women writers and black filmmakers, and gave overdue theoretical analysis to the relationship between black women and film. According to the issue editor Deborah Grayson, "The essays in this special issue of *Camera Obscura* on black women, spectatorship, and visual culture speak to the importance of naming and politicizing representations of black women in visual culture."[20]

Grayson's work considers the interplay of film in a larger media landscape, with the influence of home VCR viewing and video games. A "media" model in which the screen is part of the life of a home as well as the flows of the public sphere is closer to the reality of today's film consumption and conforms to a social and aesthetic model that a black feminist film theory is particularly positioned to engage. In other words, black feminist criticism asks what is cinema, situated among other cultural institutions (family, notions of beauty, politics) but not necessarily as an articulation of a particular nation or culture.[21] Accordingly, Grayson's article defines representation broadly, beyond cinema and television, so that a variety of texts and contexts can be addressed in the subsequent essays. Moreover, her specific focus on hair and beauty goes to the heart of "the relations of power working obscurely and not so obscurely" on black women through pressure to make their hair and hairstyles conform to social expectations.[22] Here, Grayson addresses black women's embodiment through "difference." The attention to hair may at first seem to have nothing to do with film, and may strike some readers as superficial besides, but hair texture has long been a cultural site as complex as skin color, although it is more easily refashioned through use of chemicals, applied heat, and other processes, to suit systems of taste and acceptance, particularly in an integrated world. Therefore, hair is uniquely reflective of deep-seated cultural norms and expectations. As we move toward considering the cinema as a performative space—both the acting on screen and the unintentional or intentional displays people make in the theater, all aspects of bodily preparation and presentation are crucial to interpret. More significantly, Grayson's framework reflects the ways in which black women's representation participates in an "intertextual coherence" or a shared discourse among black women writers that is thoughtful and deliberate as they draw on each other's work to address shared concerns and crises.[23]

Lorna Johnson's experimental short-essay film *Strands* (1995) exemplifies this shared and cross-disciplinary discourse but focuses on filmmaking as a cultural practice and personal expression. It resonates with black women's intellectual traditions of investigating new languages in order to address the gap between feminism and African American studies. In the film we see somewhat randomly arranged footage of various and unidentified locations. A woman talks about her hopes to make a new kind of film and to be a new kind of person/filmmaker. She describes her willingness to resist the pressure to follow what seems to be an inherited script of linear narrative progression within what she seems to feel are narrowly defined criteria of cinematic mastery and of womanhood without explicitly stating what exactly she is resisting. In this work, Johnson works in a random format, following multiple ideas in contrast to the classical paradigm of linearity and a united, single perspective. *Strands'* explicit search for a film-making model outside established norms and its use of both personal and multiple narrative voices places it on my continuum of scary subjectivity, between the extremes of hostile and bitchy, directly confrontational figures, on the one hand, and, on the other hand, to unpredictable or illegible ones, who opt out of the available categories. In this short essay film, Johnson's narrator seems to seek legibility, although on terms she must invent. The film expresses her negotiations with limitations of self as well as with her family and artistic community.

Strands' narrator describes her self-doubt as a filmmaker and the criticisms that her peers and advisors have made about her selection of subjects for filming—namely, hair—while images of a black woman in various settings as well as discontinuous sequences that show beads, family pictures, hair straightening products, passports, and houses in indeterminate locations play across the screen. These disparate images suggest broad if vague contexts for the narrator's dilemmas. Structured on the interconnectedness of personal voice, cinematic expression, and a critique of wider beauty culture, *Strands* is a dialogic text that addresses sexist, racist, and professional expectations of the self and of society. The title refers to strands of hair, but also to the interwoven strands of ideas that Johnson addresses in the film, particularly her concerns with the internalized agendas and standards inherited from the movies, family, and the university. Johnson implicitly wonders how to hear one's own voice amid this cacophony of internalized institutional talk. In black feminist writing on literature, there is a significant body of thought that addresses the need for a new kind of literary voice, one that examines black women's unique social position. The poet and essayist Elizabeth Alexander writes, "The great utility of so much black feminist theory was the guiding truism that black women have blazed alternative routes to making sense of the world, that regardless of our differing circumstances, we have had to look from the outside to make sense of a world that has not endeavored to include us among its intellectuals."[24] These "alternative routes" required alternative written expressions and intergeneric textual strategies such as Johnson uses in this film.

But Johnson's personal narrative is driven as much by a filmmaker's search for suitable aesthetic concepts as by touches of psychodrama. In the film, negotiating questions of personal identity is collapsed into questions of artistic practice: the narrator says, "Hair, like film, is about illusions. We use both to create fantasies of our lives." In this comment, we see that the film shifts roughly when it elliptically connects aesthetic concepts to identity, to hair, to fantasies, to self, and to artistic voices and family relationships. Each of these terms is loaded and complex, but in the film they are bundled and articulated together, not in a sequence of cause and effect, but in a stream of consciousness. However, certain moments in the film stand out and help us to untangle Johnson's ideas.

At one such point, Johnson shifts attention away from motion pictures of unidentified people and places toward a sequence of family photographs. Johnson contrasts the sensual density, the zigzag confusion of a carnival parade, with the understated order of the family photo album. These images are further contextualized by passport photos, which function as the visual cornerstone of modern public identity for many people. These shorter strands of images within the larger piece question formations of identity, whether they are self-fashioned or received, scripted or improvised, unofficial or official. Generally, family photographs are both private and public, inscribing a narrative of how subjects wish to be perceived. In this film, such pictures are evoked with a sense of irony. During this sequence, Johnson's narrator describes her mother's aspirations to a Jackie Kennedy–inspired model of womanhood, which she seems to reject while leaving the question of an alternative open. The film is in many ways about that search. Within the photo album sequence is a series of shots of Cyrille Phipps (herself a filmmaker) holding up a picture of her mother. It is a somewhat comic scene where Phipps affectionately compares herself to the photo, but the differences in style, communicated primarily through differences in hair texture, are clear. Phipps wears short dreadlocks, which are associated with resistance and Afrocentric aesthetics, while her mother wears a straightened style, which is associated with assimilation and black versions of white standards of beauty. When Phipps covers her face with the photo and then looks at the photo and then back at the camera, the moment effectively illustrates cheerful discontinuity with revisions of self from one generation to another. In the case of *Strands,* the characters are scary not because they are tough, hostile, or defiant but because they directly locate and lay bare the social and aesthetic norms that they do not wish to follow; they create alternate logics of their own.

Strands was not included in Grayson's project, as it was being made at the time the *Camera Obscura* special issue was put together, but both projects were doubtless informed by the wave of public attention black women writers such as Alice Walker were receiving, particularly that era's validation of personal voice motivated by a sense of history and politics. The ways in which *Strands* engages the regimes of beauty culture and fam-

Filmmaker Cyrille Phipps with a photo of her mom (Lorna Johnson, *Strands*, 1995).

ily expectations do not exclude or contradict the desires of Johnson's narrator to be desirable and to feel beautiful. But she also wants to look—to wield her gaze rather than remain a captive of the image. In this way, *Strands* helps us to envision what is at stake in black feminist film theory: who looks? What are the possibilities for subjectivity—for the spectator, the author, and the mediating characters on the screen? Feminist film theory is almost exclusively engaged with the opposition of femininity and masculinity, with other gendered options including forms of transvestitism or masochism. Whiteness, privileged and invisible within feminist film theory, erases black women's subjectivity. A black feminist film theory intervenes to impart intellectual history and conceptual frameworks to address such lacunae in the archive of feminist film studies.

Besides controlling images, black women's traumatic collective history in the United States, from slavery to persistent economic and political inequalities today, together with the legacies of near-crushing pressures to form new identities on the other sides of Emancipation and the civil rights movement, constitute the background to black women writers' and media artists' aesthetics. To be aware of this history is to feel its burdens—to be pressed into consciousness of oneself through the skewed views of a contemptuous, oppressive white social eye. Against the crushing weight of what it means to inherit the history of black womanhood, many black women filmmakers and writers position a fragile, fierce cosmology articulated through a deceptively simple first-person voice. Such a projected self, an example of which we see and hear in *Strands,* calls directly to the viewer. This statement of presence, "I'm here," serves as the framework, the point of departure for, and actually the whole point of black women's filmmaking and writing historically as well as in the contemporary moment. While African Americans are bombarded with images of themselves refracted through the vision of the wider society, they are not mere consumers.

Strands and Chris Harris's *Reckless Eyeballing* (2004) both offer narratives of critically reflexive spectatorship in African American film culture. They address the question of a scary black look in direct though complex ways. Where *Strands* concerns artistic aims, personal history, and mythologies, *Reckless* is about fundamental techniques of continuity editing, film history, and classical myth. Harris remixes or re-views and denaturalizes the classical expectation of seamless eyeline matching by having his characters *almost* appear to look at each other while they are pictured in obviously unrelated spaces. In terms of the content, Harris appropriates the Medusa story in which a woman's gaze threatens to turn a man into stone and remakes it with excerpts from *Foxy Brown* (dir. Jack Hill, 1974) and *Birth of a Nation* (dir. D. W. Griffith, 1915). The black action film figure Foxy Brown (Pam Grier) is in the Medusa role, while Griffith's Gus the Renegade (a supposedly lusty black man played by the white actor Walter Long in blackface) is the threatened, desirous man. *Reckless*'s unconventional use of sight lines and eyeline matches adds to the film's remix aesthetic and logic of discontinuity.

In the original *Birth,* Gus pursues Flora through the woods after she rejects his romantic intimations toward her. Then she eventually seems to jump from a cliff rather than succumb to his advances. In his remix of this sequence, Harris replaces Flora's image with Foxy's. Quoting these seemingly unrelated texts alters the way all three of these characters signify; however, Foxy is the primary, scary character. She is a looker in two senses: she wields her gaze (as well as a gun), and she attracts the gazes of others because of her appearance and exhibitionism. Through Harris's editing,

Foxy and Gus appear to look at or just beyond each other at some moments, while at others, their gazes seem to share similar sight lines but different physical spaces. Gus's facial expression looks both desirous and afraid. The images are layered with a voiceover that repeats phrases such as "She will never look," and "Don't look at her, you will turn to stone!" These lines refer directly (though not exclusively) to Foxy's image and gaze, thus representing a more general fear of the black woman's gaze. Foxy's pattern of looks includes a direct address and a sight line connecting her gaze to offscreen space or characters. Harris thus ties together Foxy's fearsome gaze, enhanced when she points a gun at offscreen space (not directly at the camera), with Gus's desire. Foxy's desirability, combined with her capacity to look back, makes the frankness of her gaze scary even without the gun, as reflected in reaction shots that Harris edits into this exchange between Gus and Foxy. But there is another scary exchange as well. Harris replaces Flora, the paragon of white female purity-as-vulnerability and victimhood, with an icon of black female desirability and physicality. Thus, in its revisions, *Reckless* unmasks and upsets the understructure of white female desirability that is as fundamental to classical narrative continuity as the eyeline match.

The scholar Jacqueline Stewart views cinema as one among many key spaces of African American participation in public spheres that include church, public transportation, and the workplace.[25] As she writes, "the status of the black body within the social space of the cinema, and the degree to which viewers assert and/or sublimate this black body, is of particular importance when imagining the social, psychological, and political valences of black spectatorship."[26] Stewart's statement raises the question: given the regimes of surveillance under which it is observed, regulated, and defined—that is, principles of "reckless eyeballing"—can or how does the spectating black body look with self-defining and self-expressing powers? Stewart offers "an alternative conception of black viewing practices," which she refers to as "reconstructive spectatorship, a formulation that seeks to account for the range of ways in which black viewers attempted to reconstitute and assert themselves in relation to the classical cinema's racist social and textual operations."[27] Explains Stewart, "by charting black spectatorship in relation to the negative and 'negating' representational politics of individual film texts, scholars have made a variety of claims about how black viewers have worked to subvert an otherwise degrading viewing experience."[28] Jacqueline Bobo and James Snead, using the words "negotiated" and "fluidity," have placed emphasis on the give-and-take between films and viewers, which Stewart picks up on in her definition of black spectatorship as "the creation of literal and symbolic spaces in which African Americans reconstructed their individual and collective identities in response to the classical system's moves toward narrative integration and in the wake of migration's fragmenting effects."[29] These ideas help us to visualize how the social circumstances that pressure black spectatorship fracture the presumed cohesion of film spectatorship in the classical cinema—that is, the absorption and identification with the diegetic screen world and the audience bonds of shared experiences. Nonetheless, spectators rework their experiences to create unexpected if impermanent cohesion.

As Stewart points out, black film spectatorship has been "documented" scarcely if ever in historical writing, but illuminating fictional accounts exist, significantly, in seminal novels such as *Native Son* (Richard Wright, 1940), *The Bluest Eye* (Toni Morrison, 1970) and *The Harder They Come* (Michael Thelwell, 1980).[30] Coming from different aesthetic traditions within African American and Diaspora literature, each one uses encounters with the cinema as points of departure for exploring characters' psychology and culture. Moreover, in these novels, scenes of cinema spectatorship are embedded in explorations of wider cultural processes, such as segregation and migration. Very few films show black people actually going to the movies, but the few that do are striking in that they often represent a profound lack of cohesion between themselves and other audience members of the film within the film.[31] Two of the rare examples come from the lowbrow comedies *Scary Movie* and *Scream 2*. Both films, which feature black women spectators, suggest moreover that black spectatorship may be motivated less by the particulars of the images on the screen than by the spectacle of the screen itself and cinema as a social event in which black folk can pleasurably occupy public space. The lights, the audience, getting dressed to go, and the building itself all constitute the occasion. The fact that the rare meditations on black film viewers I discuss feature black women necessitates a return to earlier film history and African American culture theory to expand our understanding of the relationship between cinema and spectatorship and between race and visual culture.

Although he does not address women directly, W. E. B. Du Bois's notion of double-consciousness helps to account for the complex subjectivity of the theoretical black woman spectator because of the emphasis he places on the gaze and performance in black subjectivity. In *The Souls of Black Folk*, Du Bois famously defines the burdens of black representations as follows: "It is a peculiar sensation, this double-consciousness, this sense of always looking at one's self through the eyes of others, of measuring one's soul by the tape of a world that looks on in amused contempt and pity."[32] Double-consciousness refers also to the bicultural origins of black Americans, but this meaning should not overshadow the aesthetic and performative implications of Du Bois's formulation for African art and its audiences. The black condition, as Du Bois would have it, is to be in perpetual performance. And as performance always implies a viewer, it mobilizes a double-consciousness involving two subjectivities or consciousnesses, the viewer and the performer, in which both perspectives are maintained or internalized. If black folks' subjectivity is characterized by double-consciousness, then what does it mean to be a spectating subject whose personhood is defined as a self-perceived object? How would he or she respond? How the object of the gaze can reclaim the gaze is a fundamental question that needs to be addressed in any useful black feminist film theory. My notion of the scary spectator begins to deal with this issue in that at its core is a returned gaze, as in the Medusa story retold in *Reckless Eyeballing*.

Josephine Baker's late 1920s and mid-1930s films abound with scenes in which double-consciousness as a feature of identity meshes with the inherent intersubjectivity of a performance. A phenomenon unto itself, Baker's Parisian career was shaped by the overall *tumulte noir,* or surge of commercially successful black creativity in France and in the United States. Cinematic representations of the spectacle Baker made around difference, both racial and sexual, provide a number of subtle starting points from which to consider black women's spectatorship, performance, and subjectivity. One particularly striking example of Baker's performative double-consciousness occurs in *Le Pompier des Folies Bergère* (*The Fireman of the Folies Bergère,* 1928).

In the short film, a white French fireman is both psychologically intoxicated with what he sees in the music hall and physically inebriated by a few glasses of wine. He stumbles about Paris, hallucinating naked white women. He eventually descends into a subway, perhaps a metaphor of his deeper subconscious, and there on the platform he meets the Folies Bergère star Josephine Baker dressed in the guise of a subway attendant. Then, through an editing trick, it appears that the fireman transforms the civil servant into a glamorous, primitivist dancing girl re-dressed in the pastiche costuming of the colonial imagination: dangling earrings, raffia skirt, tap shoes, and bangles. Baker is, then, positioned as a figment of the fireman's imagination. Yet while the fireman authors the sequence in a way, Baker is clearly the occasion for this scene. His point of view is established, but

Baker is filmed theatrically, straight on, so that the spectatorial point of view would be from a different angle than where the fireman is positioned. In fact, the point of view privileges the film's viewing audience, with the fireman serving as a surrogate for viewers. Baker is an object of desire here; however, the way in which her performance is directed toward the theatrical viewer, contradicting the fireman's point of view, complicates any notion of her as a passive object. Instead, she is scarily self-directed and self-contained on a platform she turns into a stage for her own exhibition.

Pompier compares interestingly with a sequence from the later feature film *Zou Zou*, in which Baker plays a laundress who accepts the lead role in a music hall show when the original lead actress runs off to Brazil and at the same time she finds herself needing to make money quickly. But before she decides to take the stage, her talents are discovered against her will in a key moment: Zou Zou, wearing a sequined bodice, walks on to the stage so that Jean, her love interest (played by Jean Gabin), can admire her. As Jean, a lighting technician, shines the spotlight on her, Zou Zou dances, creates shadows, and makes herself into a spectacle of motion, light, and shadow. However, unbeknownst to Zou Zou, Jean raises the curtain, and others in the theater, including the production team, gather to watch her. Zou Zou, lost in her dance, thinks that her performance is intimate and for Jean alone. When she realizes that it is public—that her subjectivity has been objectified—she stops abruptly and escapes the scene.

Both *Pompier* and *Zou Zou* contain sequences in which an onlooker initiates or partially occasions Baker's performance through his willful imagination. At the same time, Baker is the aesthetic dominant of these scenes, and the camera frames her apart from the unique vantage point of her diegetic audience. Thus, her performances enact a kind of double-consciousness in which the viewer, both onscreen and off, plays an authoring role and seems to create the scene with Baker. In neither of these sequences does Baker's character look back at the camera or seem to critique the narrative system in which they are placed. Rather, Baker's characters assimilate even if, as in *Zou Zou,* she resists her role at first by fleeing the scene. In that film she actually courts a desiring, objectifying gaze: she makes herself up, creating illusions with cosmetics and costuming meant to please Jean. In these cases, Baker's beauty accords her characters a measure of control (to attract attention), but they cannot entirely overcome the isolation that frames the characters she creates. Contained and defined mostly by the gazes of others, Baker's characters, like Baker the actress, do not look, but are looked upon. Nevertheless, I would argue that Baker represents a "scary" subjectivity because of the combination of her racialized and gendered difference and the way in which she uses the projections of her audiences in her own processes of self-creating.

In both *Pompier* and *Zou Zou*, Baker, through her characters, expresses herself within the scope of that Du Boisean white eye. Here, it is admiring rather than overtly contemptuous, but still invasive. In other words, the all-consuming and all-defining nature of the white admiring gaze that is figured in the film tampers with Baker's characters' capacity to reverse their gazes since they are almost entirely the product of the diegetic viewer's fantasy. Both the white fireman and the white Frenchman Jean presume and intrude upon the privacy and creativity of Baker's characters—although this is complicated because the purpose of these films is to showcase Baker the performer. But if publicizing Baker is their raison d'être, what does it mean, in an African American cultural context, that she is made public by playing characters wished and wrenched into the spotlight by others?

The narratives of these films, as well as those of *Siren of the Tropics* (dir. Henri Étiévant, 1927), *Princess Tam Tam* (dir. Edmond T. Gréville, 1935), and *Fausse Alerte* (dir. Jacques de Baroncelli, 1945), tend to plot Baker's characters as isolated and excluded from the romance that frames the story. Her characters reach toward the psychological romance of fulfilled subjectivity within the domestic, intimate sphere with a white male character only to be returned to the stage where she is instead consigned to the public romance of celebrity. In these scenarios Baker's characters function as "scary" in the sense that they threaten the formation of white couples. Zou Zou, Princess Tam Tam and Papitou can be understood through Shaw's concept of "racial erasure" as ultimately they are not acceptable as marriage partners compared with the white women who eventually are united with their love interests. Nonetheless, is Baker subversively scary in playing these roles?

As the world's richest and most desirable black woman of her era, Baker risked ridicule by playing roles in which she was far from the richest and her desirability was limited onscreen to on-stage adoration with merely affectionate but platonic off-stage friendships. Her characters seem ambivalent, certainly mourning the lost love but reveling in the attention of adoring audiences. In *Zou Zou*, Baker's character actually seems to be a victim of her success, and we see her running past publicity posters for her show with tears in her eyes after she has witnessed her Jean kissing her best friend Claire. While these films offer little payoff by way of confrontation scenes in which Baker's characters compete with a white woman or reject a gentleman friend for overlooking her, they do offer something else perhaps just as remarkable. Baker the international star allowed herself to be portrayed as an underdog, as the woman not chosen. By playing such characters, she risked exposing her vulnerability to the need for love and belonging—she shows tears—but she still maintains her success as a mask, emerging more complex and desirable for having done so. By repeatedly appearing in romantic scenarios in which she is not chosen, she exposes the narrow parameters of white family formation and the confines of professional success. Again, as I have discussed with earlier examples, the "scary" subjects and spectators are defined by their capacity for unmasking and self-containment. The presence of a scary, participatory black woman spectator/performer in a film introduces a self-reflexive dimension.

The scary subject/spectator notion, which I am saying brings reflexivity to film analysis and to certain films through black women characters who are always already outsider and unruly, dates back to the pre-Hollywood cinema, when filmmaking was necessarily experimental and reflexive. In a classic example, *Uncle Josh at the Moving Picture Show* features a figure Judith Mayne calls a "naïve spectator, unable to distinguish between the image and reality."[33] The fairly basic story is that Uncle Josh goes to the movies and sees three films. Uninitiated in film spectatorship conventions, he thinks that what he sees on screen is real. The climactic moment occurs when, distressed with what he sees in the third movie, *A Country Couple,* Uncle Josh tears down the screen, making himself the spectacle as he destroys the show for others in the audience. Mayne rightly points out that Uncle Josh's naïveté is more complex than it first appears because it "reflects a fundamental truth of the cinema," which, for her purposes, is that the woman's image exists for Uncle Josh to consume. She goes on to explain the ways in which the paradigmatic male gaze predates classical Hollywood cinema. We can see a similar dynamic at work in both *Zou Zou* and *Pompier* where Baker's characters are staged for consumption. Still, perhaps the scene with Uncle Josh reveals, too, an even more basic reality: the cinema is constructed and its power to persuade resides partly, if not mostly, with the viewer's willingness to accept and identify with the screen characters and their actions. When he or she does not identify in the "right ways," the show is over.

Uncle Josh is an example of cinematic reflexivity that provides some historical context for the moments of scary spectatorship already discussed. Like the scary subjects/spectators in these works, Uncle Josh's reaction to what he sees on screen is both naïve and resistant in complicated ways. On the one hand, he shows a lack of sophistication with cinematic norms when he responds to the screen narrative with a physical manifestation of emotion; literally attacking a character in the story, he ends up merely attacking the screen. On the other hand, his ignorance of the cinema's illusionism is, ironically, what permits him to expose it. He uncovers spectacle by making himself the spectacle. First, *Uncle Josh* shows how the cinema depends on fragile illusions that are wrought by the strategic use of light projected on a screen and images enlarged and projected at a certain speed, giving the images the appearance of true-to-life dimension and motion. The attentive audience in turn buttresses these elements; thus, even just one inattentive audience member undoes or at least threatens these processes. Second, and perhaps most important for my purposes, Uncle Josh models cinematic reckless eyeballing. The film sheds light on a potentially critical, performative spectatorship in which misrepresented or underrepresented viewers claim powers of looking back and recalibrating norms of cinematic desire to their own advantage.[34] In other words, the naïve spectator may have the capacity to become an insurgent, scary one. Despite the ways in which, as a white man, Uncle Josh may be assumed to be the master of the cinematic gaze, his so-called naïveté and unfamiliarity with or rejection of the codes of film viewing mark him as unruly. However, I see Uncle Josh as a critical, reflexive cinematic figure whose attack on the screen serves as a template for what I call "scary subjectivity." Unexpectedly, a representation of failed white male spectatorship in the early days of cinema is rearticulated through recent representations of black female critical spectatorship. Such links may be the ultimate threats to the social, technical, and visual relationships through which gendered and racial hierarchies in the cinema and histories of the cinema are projected and sustained.

Consider, for example, *Scary Movie,* a parody of the *Scream* series of films, which is itself a parody of teen horror films. Each movie features a black woman film viewer who carves out her own viewing position in the theater. In *Scream 2,* Maureen (Jada Pinkett) and Phil (Omar Epps) go to the Rialto cinema to see a slasher film called, bluntly, *Stab*. Phil seems ready to play along with the film's spectatorial genre expectations, while Maureen is a skeptical critic from the ticket line to her seat. For instance, while waiting in line, Maureen describes the movie they are about to see, saying it's a "dumb-ass white movie about some dumb-ass white girls getting their white asses cut the fuck up." Somewhat taken aback but amused by her hostility and profanity, Phil sarcastically suggests seeing a Sandra Bullock film instead. Maureen responds, "I'm just saying that the horror movie genre is historical for excluding the African American element." The implication is that Maureen is an informed spectator on the question of black representation and that there is nothing for us, as black people, in the movie.

Then comes the punch line in their discussion, as Phil asks, "Where did you get your PhD in [b]lack cinema, Sista Souljah?" to which Maureen responds, "Listen, I read my *Entertainment Weekly* so I know my shit." Phil's linkage of a PhD in black cinema with the rapper Sista Souljah, whose controversial writings brought her critical attention in the early 1990s, points toward exactly what the "scary subject" is: a critical, knowing cultural observer. Invoking Sista Souljah's intimidating intellect, which is signified by her name, which sonically recasts "soldier" with a West Indian accent while also referring to the soul and the Rastafarian word for God, "Jah," qualifies the idea of a black and female PhD as nonconformist and threatening and reflects back on how Maureen's attitude threatens the tranquility and seamlessness of her date with Phil. Further, Maureen's reference to the popular periodical *Entertainment Weekly* represents her intellectual inclinations but perhaps mocks her limited horizons. While Phil is just looking for entertainment, Maureen's historical awareness of the horror genre makes her an unwilling or resistant participant in the film's spectatorship because she will not be passive, as convention requires. Scary subjectivity plays out in her role as critic. First, Maureen frames the film in terms of race and gender, and as she does, it becomes apparent that as a black woman she feels excluded from identifying with the film's content. Although Phil quips to the ticket seller that they would like to see "a black film with a black cast," Maureen's commentary is clearly focused on the fact that horror movies are about the fates of white girls. Later, when *Stab* begins, its first few moments show a naked white woman getting into the shower. The spectacle of nakedness pleases Phil but alienates Maureen; she makes a critical comment easily heard by other audience members: "What does that have to do with the plot?" As no one offers a reply, Maureen's subjectivity as a spectator is shown as isolated. Phil's reference to a PhD in black cinema is a backhanded compliment. He acknowledges Maureen's insight, but he is also annoyed that her critical distance will prevent them both from being entertained by and absorbed in the movie. This raises the question of whether an ideal black spectatorship is necessarily a resistant one.

Maureen combines aspects of a naïve spectator and a critical spectator in ways that are similar to Uncle Josh. The best example of Maureen's critically resistant spectatorship comes early in the sequence when the couple is handed costumes to be worn during the screening. Maureen is skeptical while Phil takes the package with an obliging smile. The masks were probably sent by the studio as a promotional gimmick to enhance viewer identification with the film and to blur the space that normally separates the screen world from that of the spectator. Phil willingly identifies with the screen, but Maureen does not. Not only does she not play along with spectatorial expectations, she appears to be actively against them. Yet her response is complex, for when the movie starts, she becomes engrossed, advising the characters on the screen with loud comments. In the movie theater in the film, many audience members wear the mask, which we soon see is the same one the killer wears in the slasher movie. A turning point in *Scream 2* comes when a real masked killer stabs Maureen, pursuing her to the stage. Thus, she becomes part of a dual spectacle when, standing in front of the screen where the movie continues to play, she screams and bleeds to death. Maureen, a black woman, tragically enters the horror movie genre and is now an honorary horror movie white girl, having been turned into an object, a corpse, as punishment for her scary resistant spectatorship.

In the *Scary Movie* sequence that spoofs *Scream 2,* Brenda (Regina Hall) and Ray (Shawn Wayans) both go to the movies to see *Shakespeare in Love* (1998). The feature has not yet begun and a pre-show assortment of previews and commercials are playing. Ray leaves Brenda in the theater. Meanwhile, Brenda settles in, taking out of her bag packages of homemade cooked food, including chicken, and unwraps them noisily. The other patrons gesture for her silence and then shout at her, becoming increasingly more aggressive and eventually assaulting her. Unlike *Scream 2,* in the metaparody *Scary Movie,* Brenda's murder is motivated by the disgust she incites in fellow audience members. If *Scary Movie* is a comment or riff on *Scream 2,* then the way that Brenda is targeted for being a threatening, annoying spectator must show by exaggeration that Maureen was targeted for the critical comments she made earlier. *Scary Movie* takes the already extreme *Scream 2* to a ridiculous level of caricature, yet in both cases, the scary spectator has to be expunged. In the slasher film, the overly naïve or promiscuous white girl is punished with death, but here it is the "bitch" that is killed off. Defending herself, Brenda threatens the other moviegoers with her power to record them: in a reversal of gazes, Brenda, like Medusa/Pam Grier in *Reckless Eyeballing,* takes out a video camera and turns it on the other audience members, threatening them with her gaze as she declares, "I've got you. I've got you on camera. You're on *Candid Camera* now." It is a crucial point in the film and in film culture generally where a black woman explicitly takes on a knowing critical gaze. At this point, Brenda, as the scary spectator, reclaims the gaze with her performative deployment of the camera. Recalling with irony *Reckless Eyeballing*'s refrain "she will never look," Brenda does look back and challenge those looking at her.

Within the diegesis, Brenda violates several rules of film etiquette that are established by pre-show announcements seen by both the diegetic audience and real viewers. However, when the diegetic film, *Shakespeare in Love*, starts, Brenda talks to the screen. When her cell phone rings, she answers it and proceeds to talk loud enough for those around her to hear the conversation. When other patrons protest, she addresses them by saying, "I don't know why you all is acting like this. My girlfriend has already seen the movie and she said they don't even stay together in the end." Brenda gives away the ending, spoiling the suspense for others. Meanwhile, the patrons' scolding comments escalate to physical violence. They stab Brenda repeatedly with gusto, using expressions such as "your ass is grass." Screaming, Brenda flees her seat, but her attackers pursue her as she runs toward the screen, just as the killer chased Maureen in *Scream 2*. The image of Brenda clutching her chest and flailing in front of a movie screen is etched in my mind, symbolizing the complex relationships among performance, spectatorship, and the gaze in the context of black women's relationship to film culture. For me, it is an emotional imprint of the contradictions that surround Brenda and the figure of the critical black woman spectator. For example, she makes herself at home in the theater but is also ill at ease because, almost immediately, she is made to defend both her presence there and her responses to the movie: "I paid my money like everybody else up in here," she says while pointing a finger at her hostile fellow viewers in the audience. The theater is integrated and the majority of patrons violently police the established norms for viewing films. Although Brenda is not representative of all or perhaps even any actual black women, from the point of view of the white theater patrons, her character mobilizes controlling images about poor film-viewing etiquette. She is the working-class black woman whose behavior is at odds with mainstream values—pretensions to cultural capital, actually—as represented perhaps by *Shakespeare in Love*. Further, Brenda privatizes the public space by bringing her own food and talking on the phone. By making her theater seat into her home movie seat, Brenda violates film culture viewing etiquette, which, as everyone knows from theater pre-show announcements, requires silence, neatness, and deference toward one's neighbors. Rather than making herself small, she actually expands her presence to the point where she defines the experiences of others and becomes a greater spectacle than the movie screen. Brenda's actions reveal and mock their pretensions, which make her the object of spectacle although she is far from an object of desire. Instead, she is an object, rather a target, of disgust, that the audience attacks and purges from the movie theater.

Clearly, the presence of an unruly spectator distracts from others' immersion in the illusion of the film while she also marks a space of critique and reflexivity for examining the nature of film in a fundamental way. Scary spectators can be scary or unruly in different ways. Uncle Josh over-invests in the reality effect of the diegesis but is confronted with the physical elements of the illusion. Maureen, armed with historical and ideological awareness, is a resistant spectator, but her resistance means that she takes film in general seriously. She resists internalizing the implications that may arise from the horror genre's concern with white girls. By contrast, Brenda dismisses the conventions of viewer immersion on which Uncle Josh's and Maureen's spectatorship rely. She watches film through distraction, not absorption. For Brenda, a movie is one among many products to be used and consumed, rather than internalized. When a scary spectator over-believes or under-believes in the illusion that is taking place on the screen, she can ruin the immersive fantasy for others who have a different relationship to it. Scary spectators typically talk to the screen and react to the characters as though they were real people, collapsing the boundary between the spectator and the screen, the screen and the real world. The outward expression of their immersion or lack thereof actually disrupts the borders of the internalized imaginative space that the movie would otherwise occupy in the minds of the other viewers. The scary spectator mocks, repurposes, or misuses the suspension of belief that typically characterizes the audience's enjoyment.

Brenda exemplifies the viewer who assimilates neither to the norms of public space (a movie theater) nor to the private (varied, unpredictable) identification with the characters and story on screen. According to the film, the norms of the movie theater seem to require private enjoyment. The sequence is less about the image of black womanhood than it is a question of whiteness. How does majority or white mainstream culture react to or manage the presence of the outsider black woman or any outsider? Brenda is just one figure, while the audience that attacks her is composed of white characters of different ages and genders. What they have in common is a shared disgust with the way Brenda takes up space and makes herself at home at the movies—even daring to recklessly eyeball them when she takes up the amateur's video camera and aims it at her attackers. Effectively, Brenda is expunged for violating the rules of integrated film culture, where lines of insiders and outsiders are maintained. Earlier, I referred to Stewart's formulation of reconstructed spectatorship. In many ways it is meant to be a public performance of a self that is specifically outfitted for public consumption, and the concept depends, to some degree, on a segregated theater audience. Brenda was a stranger when she walked into the theater—both naïve and aggressive—and she became scary when she stepped out of her place, splintering seamless cinematic enjoyment within the illusion of a cohesive, integrated audience.

Finally, when Brenda says "This movie's good" as she records and watches it through her camera, she could be referring to the quality of her own video recording (which itself is a sign of film's commercial/aesthetic value). As her camera, a super eye, brings the film within the film closer, framed by her viewfinder, she is able to see it more closely, hence more clearly, although not "correctly." Brenda is scary because in many ways, she is paying closer attention to the film as film and as a product for a wider market beyond the movie theater than is the norm. She dismisses aspects of the experience that are crucial for others while layering her own recording and commentary onto the film.

Brenda and Maureen, who are both unassimilated spectators who disturb the illusions of others, highlight by opposition the role of the passive viewer in maintaining the illusions up on the screen. But what does it mean for a movie to include an unruly spectator among its characters when the unruly becomes scary? "Scary subjectivity" emphasizes the ways in which unruly spectators threaten or dismantle the conditions for passive acceptance of the narrative illusions offered in mainstream movies. The scary subject's role as a spectator is similar to a critic's role, distanced and seemingly "knowing." The scary subject in a film, a combination of naïveté, vulnerability, and resistance, combines both roles, positioned as participant and distanced critic. Scary subjectivities simultaneously undo cinematic illusion by revealing its constructed nature and also criticize if not subvert the visual power structures that govern these illusions and the worldviews they help to maintain. Ultimately, the notion of black women as scary spectators has less to do with biology tied to a certain perspective on the cinema than with unpacking the representational position, the looks, of black women in the movies as performers and as viewers. Wielding their unwillingness to distinguish between reality and the image in conventional ways, unruly, rather scary spectators target the actual site of cinema's illusion, which is the imagination, and expose the act of cinema as mere shadow.[35]

Notes

1. Ruby Dee, "Some Reflections on the Negro Actress: The Tattered Queens," *Negro Digest,* April 15, 1966, 32–36; rpt. in *Black Feminist Cultural Criticism,* ed. Jacqueline Bobo (Malden, MA: Blackwell, 2001), 59–62.

2. Dee, "Some Reflections," 62.

3. Ibid.

4. Kathleen Rowe, *The Unruly Woman: Gender and the Genres of Laughter* (Austin: University of Texas Press, 1995); Andrea Elizabeth Shaw, *The Embodiment of Disobedience: Fat Black Women's Unruly Political Bodies* (Lanham, MD: Lexington Books, 2006).

5. Rowe, *Unruly Woman,* 5.

6. Paul Laurence Dunbar, "We Wear the Mask," in *Lyrics of a Lowly Life* (1896). The first two lines are "We wear the mask that grins and lies / It hides our cheeks and shades our eyes." The complete poem is available online at http://www.potw.org/archive/potw8.html.

7. Shaw, *Embodiment of Disobedience,* 24.

8. Ibid., 3.

9. Stephanie Dunn, *"Baad Bitches" and Sassy Supermamas: Black Power Action Films* (Chicago: University of Illinois Press, 2008), 16.

10. Scholars such as bell hooks, Michele Wallace, and Toni Cade Bambara have debated the social and aesthetic implications of Spike Lee's *She's Gotta Have It* (1986). In the film, the protagonist, Nola Darling (Tracy Camilla Johns), addresses the camera directly. Lee's use of direct address engages the audience in a near-confrontational way, and Nola's self-assertion is framed by numerous other perspectives of her, primarily those of her three lovers. Discussion of the film deserves an article of its own because of the depth of film scholarship on Lee as well as the portrayal of women in other Lee films. It is a rare, nearly one-woman show in which a black woman is the protagonist in a reflexive film. It is about her moral character as well as the process of her cinematic characterization. In this essay, I opted to address a broader group of more marginal works in order to raise a wider and more abstract range of issues that could be applied generally rather than to one specific film.

11. Patricia Hill Collins, *Black Sexual Politics: Africans, Gender, and the New Racism* (New York: Routledge, 2005), 137.

12. My work is in dialogue with an archive of black feminist scholarship such as Lola Young's *Fear of the Dark: Race, Gender and Sexuality in the Cinema* (London: Routledge, 1996), Tracey Sharpley-Whiting's *Black Venus: Sexualized Savages, Primal Fears, and Primitive Narratives in French* (Durham, NC: Duke University Press,

1999), and Fatima Tobing Rony's *The Third Eye: Race, Cinema, and the Ethnographic Spectacle* (Durham, NC: Duke University Press, 1996). Jacqueline Bobo has been at the forefront of black feminist film history and theory, defining the field through her study of black women spectators in *Black Women as Cultural Readers* (New York: Columbia University Press, 1995) and her anthologies *Black Women Film and Video Artists* (New York: Routledge, 1998) and *Black Feminist Cultural Criticism* (Malden, MA: Blackwell, 2001). K. Sue Jewell's *From Mammy to Miss America and Beyond: Cultural Images and the Shaping of U.S. Social Policy* (New York: Routledge, 1993) tracks changes in social policies and their relationship to concurrent controlling images. Ann Kaplan's *Looking for the Other: Feminism, Film, and the Imperial Gaze* (New York: Routledge, 1997) concerns women of color internationally, and Gwendolyn Audrey Foster's *Women Filmmakers of the African and Asian Diaspora: Decolonizing the Gaze, Locating Subjectivity* (Carbondale: Southern Illinois University Press, 1997) is an essential reader on concepts of black womanist/feminist film production and scholarship. See also Kara Keeling, *The Witch's Flight: The Cinematic, the Black Femme, and the Image of Common Sense* (Durham, NC: Duke University Press, 2007), Janell Hobson, *Venus in the Dark: Blackness and Beauty in Popular Culture* (New York: Routledge, 2005), and Valerie Smith, *Not Just Race, Not Just Gender: Black Feminist Readings* (New York: Routledge, 1998). For an early perspective on the intersection of blackness and womanhood, see Marita Bonner, "On Being Young—a Woman—and Colored," *The Crisis*, December 1925, 65. For early black women's filmmaking, see Gloria J. Gibson, "Cinematic Foremothers: Zora Neale Hurston and Eloyce King Patrick Gist," in *Oscar Micheaux and His Circle. African-American Filmmaking and Race Cinema of the Silent Era,* ed. Pearl Bowser, Jane Gaines, and Charles Musser (Bloomington: Indiana University Press, 2001).

13. Hill Collins, *Black Sexual Politics,* 350

14. Mark Reid, "Dialogic Modes Representing Africa(s): Womanist Film," *Black American Literature Forum* 25.2 (1991): 375–88.

15. Ibid., 377.

16. Bobo, "Overview: The Moving Image," in Black Feminist Cultural Criticism, ed. Jacqueline Bobo (Malden, MA: Blackwell, 2001), 56.

17. Francee Covington, "Are the Revolutionary Techniques Employed in *The Battle of Algiers* Applicable to Harlem?" in *The Black Woman: An Anthology,* ed. Toni Cade Bambara (New York: Washington Square Press, 1970), 313.

18. See Anna Everett, *Returning the Gaze: A Genealogy of Black Film Criticism, 1909–1949* (Durham, NC: Duke University Press, 2001).

19. *Black Film Review* devoted a section of its summer 1986 issue to black women filmmakers. Occasioned by a daylong seminar, "Sexual Difference: Women Look At/Show Themselves," held at the Atlanta Third World Film Festival (March 2–29, 1986), the special issue contained articles by bell hooks and David Nicholson, among others. Three special issues of journals stand out for bringing concentrated attention to black film criticism: *Screen* 29.4 (1988); *Black Literature Forum* 25.2 (1991); and *Camera Obscura* 36 (1995).

20. Deborah Grayson, "Introduction," *Camera Obscura* 36 (1995): 7.

21. Reference to André Bazin, *What Is Cinema?* ed. and trans. Hugh Gray (Berke-

ley: University of California Press, 2004).

22. Grayson, "Introduction," 25.

23. Hazel Carby, *Reconstructing Womanhood: The Emergence of the Afro-American Woman Novelist* (New York: Oxford University Press, 1987), 160–69.

24. Elizabeth Alexander, *Power and Possibility: Essays, Reviews, and Interviews* (Ann Arbor: University of Michigan Press, 2007), 3.

25. Jacqueline Stewart, "Negroes Laughing at Themselves? Black Spectatorship and the Performance of Urban Modernity," *Critical Inquiry* 29.4 (2003): 650–77.

26. Ibid., 666.

27. Ibid., 653.

28. Ibid., 658. Her article further highlights significant concepts of black spectatorship, citing Manthia Diawara's reading of "resistant spectatorship" in "Black Spectatorship: Problems of Identification and Resistance," in *Black American Cinema,* ed. Diawara (New York: Routledge, 1993), 211–20; Jacqueline Bobo's "negotiated reception" from her *Black Women as Cultural Readers* (New York: Columbia University Press, 1995); bell hooks's "oppositional gaze" in "The Oppositional Gaze: Black Female Spectators," in *Black American Cinema,* 288–302; and James Snead's treatment of "spectatorial fluidity" in his book *White Images, Black Images: Hollywood from the Dark Side* (New York: Routledge, 1994).

29. Stewart, "Negroes Laughing at Themselves?" 653.

30. Set in Chicago, *Native Son* is social realist novel about the psychological (de)formation of a young man named Bigger Thomas by racism. *The Bluest Eye* takes up themes of rejection, self-hatred, and beauty. *The Harder They Come* is an adaptation of Perry Henzell's 1973 film of the same name. In the novel, Thelwell represents the cinema as a hub for Jamaican-based negotiations of city life, postcoloniality, and authenticity.

31. For a representation of silent-era film viewing within the currents of African American migration, see *Compensation* (dir. Zeinabu Irene Davis, 1999), available from Women Make Movies. There is a brief sequence in a movie theater twenty-seven minutes into the film.

32. W. E. B. Du Bois, "The Forethought," in *The Souls of Black Folk,* by Du Bois, ed. Henry Louis Gates (New York: Bantam, 1989), 3.

33. Judith Mayne, "Uncovering the Female Body," in *Before Hollywood: Turn-of-the-Century Film from American Archives,* eds. Jay Leyda and Charles Musser (New York: American Federation of Arts, 1986), 66.

34. Mayne, "Uncovering the Female Body," 63–67. Mayne discusses the film *What Happened in the Tunnel* (dir. Edwin S. Porter, 1903), in which a man sees a white woman and a black woman traveling in the train. When the train passes through a tunnel, he attempts to kiss the white woman but kisses the black woman instead. Both women laugh at him.

35. The sentence plays on the title of Ralph Ellison's collection of cultural criticism, *Shadow and Act* (New York: Random House, 1964). The title essay concerns African Americans and the movies.

Part 2

REWRITING AUTHORSHIP

Many feminist scholars have addressed the question of film authorship from a seemingly oblique perspective, in effect setting aside an understanding of the auteur as a direct transmittal between author and text via an intentional or ideological causal chain and instead focusing on the process of "rewriting." That is to say, regardless of whether the director is male or female, industrially or experimentally situated, the attention for much feminist film scholarship has been on finding alternatives paths of entry into the codes of cinematic enunciation. Women's "voices" are then found in stars, audiences, and formal strategies rather than in the individual humanist author so prominent in most directorial studies. Early investigations into this area by Claire Johnston and Annette Kuhn emphasized a move away from particular film content or authorial identity and emphasized the formal structures; it is clear in both these arguments that being a woman filmmaker was not sufficient cause for celebration.[1] While Johnston and Kuhn both focus on stylistic issues, the problem of history is not absent in their accounts since these formal patterns are indicative of larger ideological formations in which the texts are situated. Indeed, it is important to remember that much film theory of the 1970s and 1980s was not ahistorical, since the structures under study were seen as the signifying practices of a particular social structure. Within feminist theory especially, there were debates about the weight of cultural and social factors, since "real women" often seemed to be absent from the screen. But here again, as Johnston has argued, it was precisely the depiction of any "reality" as an ideological free zone that was suspect, making any sociological approach (as opposed to "historical") inappropriate for her project.[2]

These debates on film language and female "voice" drew attention to female-specific modes of address, a search for a "feminine aesthetic" or a distinctive women's "writing" in film. Sylvia Bovenshen's call for a counteraesthetic rejected an "inversion" or simple reversal of patriarchal forms and instead pointed to the need for a language in line with the "specifically feminine modes of perception."[3] Bovenshen's remarks were useful in thinking beyond both established formal practices and areas of study (i.e., her attention to Marlene Dietrich's subversive performance in *Morocco* offering a new site of "authorship"), but as might be expected were critiqued as operating within ahistorical and essentialist terrain. As Teresa de Lauretis argued, the notion of "sexual difference" was far too limiting. Rather, the focus should be on *differences* among women and on the "heterogeneity of address" required of a "counter-cinema," which could in turn create multiple and diverse perspectives onto our readings of cinema.[4]

Perhaps nowhere was the need for a more diverse approach to theory/ history more evident than in studies of Dorothy Arzner, one of the few Hollywood directors investigated by feminists with any kind of authorial scrutiny. Here much ink was spilled precisely over the possibilities of an alternative cinema language offered by Arzner's films (whether through subversive moments or structured contradictions within the patriarchal form), but astoundingly, none of the early work on Arzner considered an important biographical detail—that she had a long-term personal and professional relationship with a woman, Marion Morgan.[5] Judith Mayne's *Directed by Dorothy Arzner* not only corrected this erasure of lesbian voice(s) and vision(s) in classical-era Hollywood but also underlined how the addition of this crucial historical detail worked to rewrite the very ways in which we read a range of discourses within and surrounding the director's films.

In this section of the collection, the commitment to a rewriting of film history and authorship is clear. Whether starting from the path of the director, star, or "audience," all the essays here are efforts to foreground women's enunciative roles, in all their heterogeneous forms, in the cinema process. Tasker, Sellier, and Saito all ask us explicitly about received notions of authorship (whether in rethinking the centrality of the director's role in writing, as do Tasker and Saito; or in reevaluating the grand auteurs of the *Nouvelle Vague*, as does Sellier). For her part, Stamp complicates the ways in which directors are written into film history: her essay asks us to consider the boundaries we impose on female directors, even on those directors that film history has deigned to recognize as worthwhile. Stamp examines the language surrounding the famed silent film–era director Lois Weber in established and official histories of the period and in contemporary historical accounts as a point of departure for thinking through larger questions regarding feminist historiography. That is to say, the following question is evoked: does essentialist language serve to contain female authorship even with directors, like Weber, who are recognized and indeed hailed in both mainstream and feminist accounts?

As Victoria Duckett's essay on the actress Sarah Bernhardt makes clear, it is not only the definition of film authorship but also our definitions of the cinema itself that serve to erase the traces of female "voice." Examining Bernhardt's *Hamlet,* one of the earliest synchronized sound films, Duckett rewrites the received view that the film was but a failed effort at canned theater, arguing instead that the Bernhardt film was an exemplary and early example of cinema as an "integrative technology," which can in turn be seen as an "interval" that blurred the boundaries between two presentation forms (e.g., stage and cinema). Most importantly, this "interval" constructs a domain centered on performance, foregrounding the star's enunciative role in cinema.

The question of "authorship" is extended in Patricia White's essay outside the limits of the film text and into letters, photographs, assorted memorabilia, biographical, and autobiographical materials surrounding Greta Garbo, Marlene Dietrich, and their rumored shared lover, Mercedes de Acosta. White's essay is noteworthy, not only for the archival "truths" it reveals regarding the two film icons' personal lives and their relationship with de Acosta, but perhaps more significantly for its creation of an imaginary historical space of intersection vital to lesbian and nonheterosexist spectatorship. White's essay is equal parts de Acosta, audience, and scholar's fantasy—a commentary on all of our critical passion in and attachment to the archival treasure hunt. What we are looking for is clearly no less than ourselves or the part of ourselves that history has left unsaid. With this section, then, we might say the author is not so much dead as dispersed across an array of subject positions and sites of production/consumption.

Notes

1. Claire Johnston, "Women's Cinema as Counter-Cinema," in *Notes on Women's Cinema* (London: Society for Education in Film and Television, 1975); Annette Kuhn, *Women's Pictures: Feminism and Cinema* (London: Routledge, 1982).
2. Johnston, "Women's Cinema," 215.
3. Sylvia Bovenshen, "Is There a Feminist Aesthetic?" trans. Beth Weckmueller,

New German Critique 10 (Winter 1977): 124.

4. Teresa de Lauretis, "Rethinking Women's Cinema: Aesthetics and Feminist Theory," in *Issues in Feminist Film Criticism,* ed. Patricia Eren (Bloomington: Indiana University Press, 1990), 148.

5. Constance Penley's collection *Feminism and Film Theory* (New York: Routledge, 1988) has a good selection of the early writings about Arzner's films. Judith Mayne's *Directed by Dorothy Arzner* (Bloomington: Indiana University Press, 1994) is the first work to address her films with regard to the question of lesbian "authorship."

Further Reading

Dyer, Richard. *Stars.* London: British Film Institute, 1979.

Gerstner, David, and Janet Staiger, eds. *Authorship and Film.* London: Routledge, 2002.

Mayne, Judith. *Cinema and Spectatorship.* London: Routledge, 1993.

Wollen, Peter. *Signs and Meanings in the Cinema.* Bloomington: Indiana University Press, 1973.

Wexman, Virginia Wright. *Film and Authorship.* Piscataway, NJ: Rutgers, 2002.

Lois Weber, Star Maker

Historians often lament the fact that Lois Weber, the silent era's premiere female filmmaker, did not leave a memoir or autobiography for us to study, especially when so many of her contemporaries wrote memorably of their time in early Hollywood. Alice Guy-Blaché, Nell Shipman, Frances Marion, Mary Pickford, and Anita Loos, among a host of others, all published memoirs now actively mined by scholars.[1] Our curiosity is stoked further by Anthony Slide's report that a manuscript of Weber's memoirs, titled "End of the Circle," was stolen from her sister, Ethel Howland, in 1970, after Howland had tried for years to get the work published.[2] If such a manuscript did exist (or does in fact still exist somewhere), it suggests that at the time of her death in 1939, Weber, by then relegated to Hollywood's margins, nursed a genuine investment in making her mark on film history. In lieu of such a memoir, however, we are left to chart her legacy through the traces others left behind and to imagine, as historians, how she might have written herself into history.

Weber's obituaries, insofar as they represent early attempts to sketch her place in cinema's chronology, stress one singular aspect of her career—her role as "star maker" for the young female performers whose talents she helped to foster, best exemplified in the headline, "Lois Weber, Movie-Star Maker."[3] Indeed, several actresses became celebrated performers under Weber's tutelage in the late 1910s and early 1920s, among them Mary MacLaren, Mildred Harris, Claire Windsor, and Billie Dove. Her "discovery" of these stars became established facets of their own publicity bios and eventually their obituaries as well.[4] What are we to make of the fact that Weber, among the most-respected and highest-paid director-screenwriters in early Hollywood, a filmmaker whose name was frequently mentioned alongside D. W. Griffith and Cecil B. DeMille as those at the forefront of the industry, was remembered upon her death chiefly for making other, younger women famous celebrities?

Though it became a key focus of her obituaries, Weber's reputation as a star maker was initially cultivated during her years of active filmmaking, first when she worked under contract at Universal Pictures in the mid-1910s, then later when she left the studio to form her own company, Lois Weber Productions, in 1917. By 1921 profiles regularly touted this aspect of her renown, with *Moving Picture World* declaring that Weber had "been a star maker for years."[5] The filmmaker had "one hobby," noted another observer, "finding new photoplay stars."[6] Weber, fans were told, was "gifted with an acumen or instinct which enables her to fairly 'sense' talent and screen ability."[7] One profile simply cast her as a "film astronomer," so accurate were her celestial predictions.[8] Weber's reputation for discovering and nurturing young talent thus colored her association with many actresses over more than a decade. Marshaled at different junctures in her career, the potent star-maker mythos often became a means of accounting for her stature within the industry. Though Weber's status as "Hollywood's most powerful woman director" remains a constant theme of her publicity during these years, it is almost always linked to her reputation as a star maker.

Weber's first notable "discovery" was the actress Mary MacLaren, whom she reportedly first encountered on the Universal lot during the period of her greatest renown at the studio. "There's the girl for me," Weber was said to remark. "I'll make a star of her."[9] After a small part in *Where Are My Children?* the actress starred in five films with Weber released in 1916 and 1917: *Shoes, Wanted: A Home, Saving the Family Name, Idle Wives,* and *The Mysterious Mrs. M.* "Her talents so quickly developed under the tuition of Lois Weber that her future was assured," trumpeted Universal publicity.[10] Weber, who had formerly served as mayor of Universal City, was at that point the studio's highest-paid director, and MacLaren remembered the tremendous respect Weber commanded on the lot.[11] After a string of successful films for Universal, the filmmaker renewed her contract with the studio under terms that made her the best-compensated director in the industry.[12] Early the next year, she was the guest of honor at the first dinner of the Motion Picture Director's Association, inducted as its only female member.[13]

When Weber left Universal to form her own company, Lois Weber Productions, in 1917, Mildred Harris was the first actress she signed after negotiating a lucrative distribution contract with her former studio. It was the first time in her career that Weber had not worked with either a stock company or roster of studio actors and instead created projects exclusively for a single performer. As Weber explained then, "Mildred Harris is really my 'company' and we carry no stock, but engaged a new lead to play opposite her each time and selected all the others to dovetail around her personality and the play's demands."[14] Publicity at the time played up similarities between Weber's earlier "discovery" of a young MacLaren and her contract with Harris, then only seventeen, and, as we shall see, significantly downplayed Harris's long list of previous screen credits. "Miss Harris declares herself delighted to work under the guidance of the woman 'discoverer' of Mary MacLaren and other well known screen players," one piece announced.[15] Weber was, according to another publicity notice, "responsible for Miss Harris's entry as a star," having made the young woman "a star almost overnight," according to another."[16] Praising Harris's performance in her first film with Weber, *The Doctor and the Woman, Variety* observed that the director deserved "much credit for having discovered and developed the ability of this young woman."[17] Harris, for her part, was cast as the "erstwhile starlet for Lois Weber," further cementing the association.[18] That Harris married Charlie Chaplin in the midst of her work with Weber only added to her renown, of course. Ultimately, Harris starred in six films with Weber—*The Doctor and the Woman, For Husbands Only, When a Girl Loves,* and *Borrowed Clothes,* all released in 1918, and *Home* and *Forbidden,* which were released the following year—then signed a contract with Louis B. Mayer the following year.[19]

So serious was Weber's investment in her star-maker image by the early 1920s that she signed a contract with the actress Ola Cronk, vowing "to endeavor to cause her to become known as a star in motion picture work."[20] Cronk was better known as Claire Windsor, a name Weber herself chose to emphasize the young woman's "English type of beauty."[21] With the contract Weber retained exclusive rights to Windsor's services for one year, with an option to renew for a second year. Weber, at the height of her power after having signed a new, lucrative distribution contract with Famous Players-Lasky, was here promoting not only her ability to recognize and discover "natural" talent but her capacity to *create* stardom for someone like Windsor with virtually no experience. By this point the director's reputation was well established, with Windsor deemed "worthy of joining the distinguished ranks of Lois Weber discoveries."[22] Articles introducing Windsor cast her as Weber's "protégé" or Weber's "brightest star," her "latest discovery."[23] Windsor's performances in four Weber films, *What's Worth While, Too Wise Wives, The Blot,* and *What Do Men Want?* all released in 1921, did indeed make her a star. In the end, Windsor did not stay with Weber for long, signing with Goldwyn in July of 1922, just a year and a half after her initial contract with Weber, then signing on with MGM three years later.[24]

Following the release of Weber's last feature with Windsor, the director's career suffered a serious decline: she released only one film, 1923's *A Chapter in Her Life,* in the next four years. But early in 1926 she signed a new distribution contract with Universal, making her one of the highest-paid women in the business.[25] New contract in hand, Weber signed the actress Billie Dove, then only a contract player, to appear in two films, *The Marriage Clause* (1926) and *Sensation Seekers* (1927). Critics at the time noted Weber's reemergence as a director, with one arguing that *The Marriage Clause* "demonstrates that her art has broadened during her absence."[26] *Moving Picture World* declared the picture Weber's "triumphal return" to the screen after an absence of many years.[27] Universal, welcoming Weber back into its ranks after nearly a decade, gave *The Marriage Clause* a big push, releasing it as one of the leadoff pictures for the 1926–27 season under the banner of its "Greater Movie List."[28] Dove's performances in the film elevated her reputation in the industry considerably and helped her achieve the stardom she had been seeking. After its release Dove received offers from "every studio in the business," according to her. In fact, before filming on *Sensation Seekers* was complete, the actress signed a five-year contract with First National to star in a series of star vehicles.[29]

Whether at the height of her studio career, her first foray into independent production, or her return to filmmaking after a marked absence, it was Weber's ability to discover and nurture the talents of younger women that became the marker of her stature within the industry, not the salaries she commanded, the contracts she negotiated, or her own considerable creative accomplishments as screenwriter and director. Indeed, when she was hired to interview and test potential actresses for Universal in 1933, long after the active phase of her career had ended, it was, once again, this facet of her reputation that was played up in press reports. Readers were reminded, for instance, that Weber had been "the canny person who gave Claire Windsor her professional name when the blonde beauty tried to crash the gates under the name of Ola Cronk."[30] Even then, just six years after she made her last film, Weber's ability to make other women famous was quickly becoming the sole feature of her standing within the industry.

What then were the consequences of framing Weber's career so insistently within the rubric of star making?

Perhaps most strikingly, the moniker "star maker" focused attention on Weber's working relationships with other women, rather than her partnership with her husband Phillips Smalley, with whom she collaborated on virtually all of her projects from the early 1910s until their divorce in 1922. Working under the trade name "The Smalleys" for much of their initial career, the couple marketed themselves as a creative team who shared the responsibilities of filmmaking equally, and frequently used their status as a married, middle-class couple to enhance the cultural cachet attached to their upscale productions, first at Universal when they were put in charge of the Rex brand, then again in 1914 when they began making quality features for Bosworth Pictures.[31] Decentering Weber's collaboration with Smalley, the star-maker narrative instead celebrated the female-centered creative environment Weber evidently fostered, recognizing supportive working relationships among women in a notoriously competitive business. "One word spells the success of this woman—Women," one commentator declared. "Miss Weber studies women. Her photoplays are cross-sections of a woman's soul. They have a feminine touch lacking in most man-made films."[32]

It was no accident, many critics noted, that it had been a female director-screenwriter who had successfully transported notable young performers from the ranks of pretty starlets to distinguished thespians. Billie Dove, for instance, had been playing leading roles in Hollywood for four years with little impact before she began working with Weber in 1926. Reviewers at the time credited her success to Weber's direction of *The Marriage Clause,* saying it marked a new stage in the actress's career and noting that it had taken "a woman to bring out in celluloid the full talent of an actress who heretofore has been more or less purely decorative." With her performance in Weber's film Dove had become "virtually overnight an actress of the first rank."[33] Noting "Weber will amaze you," *Motion Picture Director* declared *The Marriage Clause* "the year's sensation." Dove, "by this one performance has made a place for herself in the photoplay."[34] The *Picture Play* writer Myrtle Gebhart also observed the new tenor of Dove's roles— "interesting, womanly characters"—in parts Weber had written for her in both *The Marriage Clause* and *Sensation Seekers.* Gebhart surmised that "the sympathetic understanding of the women director, Lois Weber, made [Dove] feel more at home, at ease, in her work than ever before."[35] Indeed, Carl Laemmle, head of Universal during Weber's several different engagements with the studio, felt "her greatest success has been in developing young actresses," a skill he related to her gender: "A woman can develop an actress just rising to stardom as no man can. Women understand women and respond to them. . . . Girls love her."[36]

Many of the actresses, in fact, reported how happy they were to be working with a female director and how different their interactions with her were when compared with those they'd had with male directors. Late in life Billie Dove remembered Weber as "the best director I ever had . . . If I'd had anything to say about it, I would have had her direct all my pictures. I had a lot of men directors that I liked too, but she understood women."[37] For her part, Weber cheered the particular strengths that women brought to filmmaking, saying, "I like to direct because I believe a woman, more or less intuitively, brings out many of the emotions that are rarely expressed on the screen. I may miss what some of the men get, but I will get other effects that they never thought of."[38]

Even as they celebrated Weber's working relationships with other women, such narratives also insisted, rather forcefully, that stardom was

Weber and Billie Dove on the set of *The Marriage Clause* (1926). Courtesy Kobal Collection.

136

the ultimate—oftentimes the *only*—goal for women in early Hollywood. In doing so, they reasserted highly conventional ideas about femininity in the face of Weber's powerful stature within the industry. Stories of Weber "discovering" young talents almost by accident, and elevating them to the ranks of superstardom seemingly overnight, only perpetuated this displacement, for they cast the actresses in wholly passive roles, simply waiting to be noticed and appreciated, and largely obscured the labor and training involved in acting for the screen.

The narrative of Weber's "discovery" of Mary MacLaren, for instance, emphasized MacLaren's passive investment in being noticed and admired, and reduced Weber's directorial role simply to an ability to recognize MacLaren's "natural" gifts. According to a tale spun in promotional literature, one bright day MacLaren's face "arrested" Weber's attention when the director happened to spot the young starlet in a long line of hopefuls gathered at Universal gates. Tired of being approached by aspiring actresses, Weber had adopted the habit of burying her face in a book or a script as she passed this parade every morning, but on this particular day, the story goes, she happened to look up from her work: "It was one of those trifles which so often affect the whole course of life," *Green Book* pronounced. Weber "looked directly into the eyes of a girl whose face attracted and held her attention. There were other girls there, a bevy of them; but she saw only the one girl. In her face was 'something' magnetic. 'Are you looking for work?' the woman director asked the girl."[39]

"Mary MacLaren is Lois Weber's discovery," *Moving Picture Weekly* proclaimed, "and it is entirely due to her chance meeting with the totally inexperienced girl that a new screen star has risen in the photoplay firmament. The story reads like a fairy tale, and in itself would make an extremely interested photoplay if Lois Weber should ever be at a loss for a striking plot."[40] Another piece compared MacLaren's "fairy tale" rise to fame with that of Cinderella, casting Weber in the role of fairy godmother who "brought happiness to Cinderella through the wave of her magic wand."[41] "From Extra to Stardom," *Motion Picture Magazine* blared in its profile of the actress.[42]

In Claire Windsor's case, the moment of discovery was set in the Paramount cafeteria instead of outside the Universal gates, but otherwise the ingredients remained largely the same. Shortly after having signed a lucrative four-picture deal with the studio, Weber lost her lead actress. "I'll not stop at this last minute to spend several days or weeks hunting for another," the director reportedly announced. "I'm going to comb this lot and

Supplement to Cinema Chat

Trans-atlantic

Mary MacLaren

Mary MacLaren. Collection of Shelley Stamp.

find one ready to work."[43] Weber promptly spotted Windsor, still known as Ola Cronk, in the lunch line at the studio's cafeteria and, according to one profile, the actress "forthwith became a leading player."[44] It was a story that "should fill any ambitious young actress with hope," according to one writer.[45]

Veritably cinematic, these encounters each culminate in a dramatic, silent exchange of glances between filmmaker and would-be star. And while they emphasize the passive beauty of these young actresses, they also dramatize Weber's command of whichever studio lot she happened to be working at. But as does much of the star-maker rhetoric, these tales circumscribe her stature within very strict parameters, limiting her power largely to an appreciation of beauty.

In contrast, MacLaren's own later recollection of meeting Weber stressed her ambition and drive as an experienced young actress, not the street waif persona played up in Universal publicity. Weber and Smalley had seen her perform on stage in San Francisco, MacLaren remembered, and then had arranged for her to meet with Weber in Los Angeles at the director's Universal offices.[46] Similarly, Weber's recollection of her first meeting with Windsor diverges sharply from the account that emerged in publicity discourse, for the director remembered that she had been introduced to Windsor by a friend who thought she might be interested in the type.[47]

These myths of discovery and overnight stardom not only cast actresses in passive roles where they merely waited to be caught by the director's gaze, they also diminished Weber's considerable creative role as screenwriter and director—reduced it to the task of merely noticing "natural" talent on display outside studio gates or in cafeteria lines. In distinct contrast, reviewers at the time extolled Weber's casting, writing, and directing abilities. Praising *What Do Men Want?* Windsor's second picture with Weber, the *New York Times* singled out Weber's ability "to select a cast of players capable of approaching something like an intelligent interpretation of their roles."[48] Of *Too Wise Wives*, *Motion Picture News* declared, "Lois Weber proves here once more that she is capable of drawing the characters of screen husbands and wives with remarkable skill."[49] *The Blot* represented "a splendid example of the powers of her direction," according to *Motion Picture News*.[50]

This was typical of the acclaim Weber usually received, particularly for bringing out singular performances from her cast. Mildred Harris's fourth feature with Weber, *Borrowed Clothes*, provided "the best opportunity she has yet had to demonstrate her abilities at emotional acting," *Moving Picture World* declared in an assessment that strongly contrasted this performance with the mere "passing personal charm" Harris had exhibited in earlier offerings.[51] Just a few years later, when Harris began receiving less-than-enthusiastic reviews, *Variety* paid an oblique tribute to Weber, noting that "it was direction that made [Harris] stand out in a couple of the big features that she did in the more recent past."[52] Admiring Weber's direction of *The Marriage Clause, Moving Picture World* argued that neither of the film's two male stars, Francis X. Bushman and Warner Oland, had ever given better performances than those Weber had elicited.[53] Of *Sensation Seekers,* the *New York Times* noted that Weber "tells her story with creditable sincerity and restraint," creating an atmosphere "so natural that many other directors would do well to study Miss Weber's style."[54]

Firsthand accounts of Weber's directorial style underscore the on-screen evidence noticed by reviewers. A reporter visiting the set of Weber's 1914 production, *Hypocrites,* observed her directing a large crowd scene with hundreds of extras and noted, "her commands were few, incisive and very direct."[55] Filming *The Dumb Girl of Portici* on location in Chicago in 1916, Weber remained at the center of all activity, "wanted here, there and everywhere," according to the *Chicago Herald,* as "Phillips Smalley came to her for advice upon every question that presented itself."[56] Another profile praised her "natural gift of leadership" on the lot, noting how she constantly fielded questions from all manner of personnel, from wardrobe assistants to performers and studio officials.[57] Mary MacLaren, for instance, remembered the enormous "popularity and respect" that Weber commanded from everyone at Universal.[58] She was an exacting filmmaker, according to another observer: "There are times when everything has to be changed over and over before Miss Weber is satisfied."[59]

Indeed, both Weber and the performers under her charge described her forceful directorial presence. "All of us in the Weber studio avoid all semblance of acting," Claire Windsor stated.

Miss Weber insists above all else on naturalness. She is never cross when she directs, but I always know when a scene is not going well, for then she walks up and down the set instead of sitting in her easy chair. While working in a picture I keep my eyes constantly on her. I try to read her thoughts, to anticipate what she wants me to do. My aim is to be as plastic as possible in her hands, and that is not difficult, because Miss Weber literally takes one's personality away from one.[60]

Weber herself declared, "I must have players who will let me lead them; I go so fast they must put their hands in mine and run with me. Both Claire [Windsor] and Louis [Calhern] do this and we work beautifully together."[61]

To reduce Weber's directorial acumen to that of simply discovering "natural" talents also obscured the considerable role she played in encouraging the participation of seasoned performers on film. Weber, whose own background was in the theater, was one of only a few directors in the 1910s to press strongly for trained actors on screen. Saying she preferred "stage people of training and experience who can really act," Weber argued that "the introduction of actors of reputation into the photoplay raises the class, both of the screen actors and of the audience which go to see them. Seeing men and women of real acting ability on the screen accustoms the picture-public to seeing something besides flurry-haired girls and handsome boys of no ability."[62]

Ultimately, Weber was described as a filmmaker involved in every detail of her productions, from wardrobe decisions and location scouting in the preproduction phase to editing and marketing in the final stages: "As a director she attends not only to the details of productions, but personally goes over every inch of films, scrutinizing each tiny detail closely, keen to detect . . . any false trick of the camera or error of the actor," one newspaper profile reported.[63] Even by the standards of the early industry, Weber exerted a tremendous amount of control over her productions and enjoyed an unusual degree of independence. Noting her accustomed practice of working independently, one 1926 profile marveled that "in her long and varied motion picture career, she has practically never worked under the direction of anyone but herself."[64]

Perhaps the best indication of Weber's reputation as a director and screenwriter was the respect she commanded from her peers. By 1916 she was included in the *New York Dramatic Mirror*'s list of "prominent directors," and she was described by the movie trade *Wid's Daily* as "one of our foremost directors" in 1921.[65] Exactly at the time she was celebrated for making other women famous, Weber was mayor of Universal City, the highest-paid director in Hollywood, the first (and only) woman in the Motion Picture Director's Association (a precursor to the Director's Guild), and one of the earliest director-screenwriters of either gender to run an independent production company. She was regularly cited, along with D. W. Griffith and Cecil B. DeMille, as one of the top visionaries in the industry.

If the star-maker label occults Weber's substantial professional résumé, it also ignores her own celebrity, which was considerable in the late teens and early 1920s, when she was arguably the country's most-profiled film-maker. Beyond her regular appearance in movie fan magazines, Weber was often featured in general-interest publications: *Sunset* magazine introduced Weber in its "Interesting Westerners" column in 1914, and *Overland Monthly's* 1916 profile cast her as "one of the big personalities in the photo-play world."[66] Newspaper articles published throughout the country described Weber in various hyperbolic alliterative configurations as the "wonder woman of the films," the "super-woman of the silent drama," and "the director deluxe of filmdom"—all suggesting a celebrity status reaching far beyond the confines of movie buffs, and certainly eclipsing that of any other director or screenwriter at the time.[67] To celebrate her achievements only as "star maker" is thus to rewrite Weber's career trajectory along lines more consistent with women's status in the industry after 1922, when she, like so many other women, experienced a marked downward mobility.

When we remember that "star maker" was also a label frequently used to describe Dorothy Arzner's associations with the women she directed, as Judith Mayne has pointed out, it becomes apparent that women powerful in the early industry were often depicted in the role of helpmate to beautiful stars in order to downplay their own authority. Such characterizations also helped gloss over more complex aspects of the women's interactions, which, in Arzner's case, involved same-sex attraction and flirtation.[68] That D. W. Griffith has never, to my knowledge, been described as Lillian Gish's star maker further underscores this gendered division of labor, for Gish, working solely under Griffith's direction for many years, achieved much greater fame than any actress directed by Weber. Even more so, collaborations between Erich von Stroheim and Gloria Swanson, around whom Svengali metaphors invariably circulate, are usually presented through narratives that forcibly assert a director's dominance over performers in his or her charge. The particularly gendered implications of the star-maker persona also become obvious when we consider the case of Louis Calhern, Claire Windsor's costar in three Weber pictures, *What's Worth While? Too Wise Wives,* and *The Blot.* As was the case with Windsor, these were Calhern's first starring roles, and like Windsor, he received considerable praise for these early performances; yet nowhere was Weber ever credited with "discovering" or "creating" Calhern, who had a long and respected acting career after his early association with Weber; nor was he ever described as Weber's "protégé" or "latest star."

In addition to sidelining Weber's considerable directing talents, profiles of the young women she "discovered" also tended to minimize their own considerable professional training and accentuate their youth. A *Photoplay* profile of Mildred Harris, called "Stage Experience? None!" emphasized the actress's lack of theatrical training, adding, "it seems like yesterday that *Photoplay* was running a picture of Mildred in short frocks and long hair."[69] On the contrary, though only seventeen years old, Harris already had a sizable acting résumé before she signed with Weber, having been a member of Thomas Ince's stock company for three years, where she played principal roles, then at Fine Arts, where she had been featured in several D. W. Griffith films.[70] According to *Moving Picture World*, the notice she finally achieved starring in Weber's films represented "six years of good solid effort."[71] In what sense, then, did the director "discover" Harris at all?

Indeed, many performers, like Mary MacLaren, sought to reclaim the talent and training hidden under myths of instant discovery by actively countering publicity accounts of their rise to fame. In an article titled "How I Happened," published just a year after she became famous in Weber's films, MacLaren rejected the ingénue guise that had been cast for her, emphasizing instead her own agency in the drive for professional success and her long years of training and experience, insisting that her acting talents be valued over the ability of others merely to recognize her

Mildred Harris Chaplin in *Home* (1918). Collection of Shelley Stamp.

skills. Working hard at Universal under Lois Weber's tutelage, MacLaren recalled, "[I] soon realized that I had 'found myself' at last."[72]

Like her predecessor, Claire Windsor frequently countered publicity stories of her "discovery" by calling attention to her own ambition and talent: "I worked very hard and don't want any one to believe that I merely fell into good fortune," she declared in 1921. "I like to feel that I am really deserving of my success."[73] Nor should Windsor's own considerable efforts to fabricate a legendary persona be underestimated. During the first year she signed on with Weber, Windsor engineered her own "disappearance," had a rumored engagement to Charlie Chaplin, was mentioned as a possible suspect in the murder of Screen Directors' Guild president William Desmond Taylor, and became the target of an alleged kidnapping scheme involving her son—stories, needless to say, that kept her name in newspaper headlines throughout most of 1921.[74] In perhaps the most pointed reassertion of their autonomy, both MacLaren and Mildred Harris later sought to be released from studio contracts they had signed as minors, contracts they claimed were exploitive.[75] MacLaren found herself in the ironic position of suing to retain control over the "Mary MacLaren" ingénue persona that Weber had fashioned for her at Universal, even as her aggressive legal stance verily shattered that persona.[76]

Alongside actresses painted within the confines of such narratives, there were others in early Hollywood who remained distinctly skeptical about persistent myths of instant stardom. In a 1922 article, ironically accompanying a contest for new screen personalities, novelist Mary Roberts Rinehart decried the "frenzy for novelty" and "wasteful demand for the new" that drove the industry's star system. Such folly had "placed on our silver sheets today so many pretty, vacuous faces, new and young and therefore appealing at first, but as cloying as a milk diet after a time," insisting that "no art thrives on immaturity and newness."[77] With great prescience Rinehart hit upon one of the enduring contradictions of the star system: its reliance, on the one hand, upon established, bankable personalities and, on the other, upon a desire for novelty and an investment in the idea that anyone can be plucked from the realm of ordinariness and elevated to stardom. Skepticism about the industry's appetite for new talent also began to fuel the scandals of the 1920s, particularly Theodore Dreiser's influential report from Hollywood in 1921, and Adela Rogers St. Johns's notorious characterization of Hollywood as "the port of missing girls" in 1927.[78]

In addition to stressing the passivity and naïveté of female performers, stories of their tutelage under Weber's watchful eye also framed Weber's relation to them as largely maternal rather than authorial or directorial. The director, for instance, was described as MacLaren's second mother in a profile titled "The Girl with Two Mothers," which assigned her a position as "mother of the *actress*" alongside MacLaren's biological mother.[79] To be sure, Weber's own characterizations of the young women she worked with also accentuated the maternal tenor of her dealings with them. "She's only sixteen and beautiful," Weber said of MacLaren, "but, more than that, she is the most sensitive and intelligent girl I ever directed."[80] Indeed, MacLaren later remembered that Weber took an altogether motherly interest in protecting her at Universal, even advising the aspiring actress not to let men kiss her. "My goodness," MacLaren recalled, "she had very strict ideas about morality and everything, and she wanted to preserve me as I was."[81] When Weber signed seventeen-year-old Mildred Harris to Lois Weber Productions, she described the young actress as "the dearest little thing" who spent her idle hours tidying up around the studio, as if she were a daughter rather than a fellow artist.[82]

Still, Weber evidently took great pride in the support she lent to other women in the industry, recounting, for instance, that she "had under [her] care many of the girls who are now famous in the writing field, notably Frances Marion . . . one of the very brightest girls writing today, and my close friend."[83] Though Marion was only nine years younger than Weber, the tenor of the director's commentary asserted her seniority within the profession and her maternal role. Indeed, Marion recalled that at their first meeting Weber tried to sign her to an acting contract, saying, "I have a broad wing, would you like to come under its protection?"[84] When Marion protested, citing her considerable experience in journalism, Weber encouraged her to sign an acting contract anyway, assuring her visitor that she could find other jobs within the studio until she made her way. And when Marion explained that she was not the young girl Weber had assumed her to be, that she was in fact twenty-six years old, the director advised her never to reveal her age, stipulating in Marion's contract that she was only nineteen. That Weber herself was only thirty-five at the time suggests her own investment in fashioning a quasi-maternal relationship with young women in the industry.

Weber's maternal presence in Hollywood was also foregrounded in the active role she took with younger performers and would-be starlets flocking to Los Angeles in the late 1910s and early 1920s, a flood of "movie-struck girls" causing considerable alarm.[85] Weber addressed the Los Angeles Women's Club on the fate of Hollywood's young women in 1917 and was a major early supporter of the Hollywood Studio Club, a residence for young actresses sponsored by the Los Angeles YWCA, giving an address to residents there that same year.[86] "Miss Weber is noted for the interest she takes in the younger members of the acting faces at Universal City," the studio's trade paper proudly proclaimed.[87] Later at her own studio Weber operated a school for "young actor folks" on the premises. An article on the studio included a photograph showing the director leaning over a boy's shoulder to correct his homework, her other arm encircling his shoulders in a nurturing posture.[88] In 1921, in the wake of some of the early star scandals, Weber spearheaded a campaign to have women's clubs, female newspaper editors, and businesswomen defend the safety of Hollywood, a stance that only underscored her matronly role within the industry.[89] While all of these activities certainly assert Weber's leadership within the industry, and define her primary alliances to be with women (whether naïve starlets or bourgeois clubwomen), they circumscribe this leadership within familiar tropes of maternal caregiving.

An emphasis on Weber's protective relationships with younger women and would-be stars not only displaces her directing talents, it also ignores the many associations she nurtured with female *peers*. Her longstanding friendship with Frances Marion, however much colored by Weber's early guidance of her colleague's career, endured at a time when both could easily be counted among the most powerful figures in Hollywood and stood as a testament to the alliances Weber fostered with other creative women.[90] Certainly the best example of this teamwork remains her collaboration with the world-renowned dancer Anna Pavlova on the 1916 film *The Dumb Girl of Portici,* a project celebrated at the time for bringing together Weber's "native ingenuity and Pavlova's theatric sense."[91] Pavlova, among the most notable artists of her time, had declined many other opportunities to work in film but finally signed with Universal after the studio agreed to commit considerable resources to the project, including assigning one of their top production teams, Lois Weber and Phillips Smalley, to the venture. Shot over two months in Chicago and in Los Angeles at Universal City, the film was an ambitious feature-length spectacle, compared upon its release to the era's other most notable films, *Cabiria, The Birth of a Nation* and Thomas Ince's *Civilization.*[92] Photos taken on the set show Weber and Pavlova working togethert, with Phillips Smalley noticeably disengaged on the sidelines. Indeed, the writer H. H. Van Loan informed *Motion Picture Magazine* readers that several of the director's projects, including *The Dumb Girl of Portici,* might very well be considered "suffraget [*sic*] propaganda," given that so many of the central creative positions were held by women.[93]

Alongside such high-profile collaborations, it is also likely that Weber helped foster the careers of other early women directors, for many of the actresses who first worked under her direction at Universal later went on to successful directing careers at the studio, among them Cleo Madison, Elsie Jane Wilson, and Lule Warrenton. It is reasonable to surmise that Weber, the highest-profile filmmaker on the lot, played a substantial role in encouraging and supporting these women's artistic aspirations. That Universal had the highest concentration of female directors and screenwriters of any studio during this era—a lineup that also included Ida May Park, Grace Cunard, Ruth Stonehouse, and Dorothy Davenport Reid—must in some respects be attributable to Weber's stature and influence.[94] And this is not to mention Weber's early influence upon renowned *male* filmmakers: Rupert Julian acted under Weber's direction at Universal before becoming a filmmaker himself; and Anthony Slide reports that both John Ford and Henry Hathaway worked as prop boys for Weber at the studio.[95]

After she left Universal and formed Lois Weber Productions, Weber continued her professional collaborations with other women, adapting the work of celebrated female writers of her era, including Mary Roberts Rinehart, whose novel *K* became the basis for Weber's script for *The Doctor and the Woman*. Rinehart, who had refused previous offers for rights to the novel, was happy to learn of Weber's interest in adapting the work: "I just shouted for joy, because I knew that *K* would receive the most artistic and truthful presentation possible at her hands."[96]

Weber's partnerships also extended beyond Hollywood, where she fostered extensive associations with women's clubs, the premiere activist organizations for middle-class women of her era. Weber addressed the Women's City Club of Los Angeles several times on matters such as improving motion picture quality and the safety of young women emigrating to Los Angeles in search of movie work.[97] She reportedly conceived the idea for *What Do Men Want?* (1921) after meeting with members of the Federated Clubwomen of America and agreeing to make a picture under their auspices in order to "offset as far as possible the spirit of unrest so dominant in the lives of many of the younger men of the present generation."[98]

Hence, while profiles that focused on Weber's star-making abilities drew attention to her many collaborations with other women, they did so at the expense of portraying her as a motherly helpmate to would-be starlets, and in doing so obscured the rich texture of her creative associations with many eminent women both within the film industry and beyond it. They obscured her considerable creative acumen as writer and director in favor of her ability to "discover" "natural" talent, while at the same time fuelling an impression that acting and fame were women's sole ambitions within the early industry. Even as it acknowledged Weber's influential stature within the early industry, the title "star-maker," reiterated at so many different junctures in Weber's career—repeated so often, in fact, that it became the singular note of her obituaries—ultimately cast her authority in considerably diminished terms.

If Weber's role as star maker colored much of the publicity during her lifetime, and dominated early eulogies of her career, it is strikingly absent from later attempts by the historians Richard Koszarski and Anthony Slide to reframe her place in film history. The first to write about Weber in the 1970s, Koszarski and Slide emphasized instead the degree to which Weber had been misplaced in histories of the medium. She had been "forgotten with a vengeance," Koszarski declared in a *Village Voice* piece titled "The Years Have Not Been Kind to Lois Weber."[99] Slide opened his essay by quoting ironically from a 1921 profile, noting its confident appraisal that Weber would "occupy a unique position" in histories of the early cinema— true only if "unique" is synonymous with "marginalized."[100] The subtitle of Slide's later book on the filmmaker dubbed her "The Director Who Lost Her Way in History." In these early chronicles, both scholars sidestepped mention of Weber's influence on the careers of movie stars, concentrating instead on her writing and directing accomplishments. In doing so they shaped Weber's career along lines suitable to a feminist era: it was her substantial body of creative work, the lucrative salaries and contracts she negotiated, the recognition she received within the industry that became factors worthy of celebration.

Analyzing Weber's reputation as a star maker, I do not set out to correct inaccuracies contained in her obituaries with the "truth" about her actual accomplishments; nor do I seek to ascertain the "real" value of her contributions to early filmmaking. Rather, I am interested in assessing how her authorial persona was produced through publicity discourses during the most active phase of her career and immediately upon her death. Investigating Weber's legacy in this manner allows us to interrogate the ways that women have been written into history generally, and into film history in particular. And it allows us to consider, in the end, the historian's own role as "star maker" of another sort.

148

Notes

I must thank Amelie Hastie for her contributions to this article. A conversation with her about the contract Claire Windsor signed with Weber sparked my thinking in this area, and her work on the historiographic projects of silent screen stars and directors remains a model for the field. Thanks also to Sirida Srisombati, research assistant extraordinaire, for her help in gathering many of the materials used in the essay.

1. Alice Guy Blaché, *The Memoirs of Alice Guy Blaché,* trans. Roberta and Simone Blaché, ed. Anthony Slide (Lanham, MD: Scarecrow Press, 1996); Nell Shipman, *The Silent Screen and My Talking Heart,* ed. Tom Trusky (Boise, ID: Boise State University Press, 1987); Frances Marion, *Off With Their Heads! A Serio-Comic Tale of Hollywood* (New York: MacMillan, 1972); Mary Pickford, *Sunshine and Shadow* (New York: Doubleday, 1955); and Anita Loos, *A Girl Like I* (New York: Viking, 1966). Amelie Hastie examines how such writings inscribe a place for their authors in film history; see her "Louise Brooks, Star Witness," *Cinema Journal* 36.3 (1997): 3–24; "Circuits of Memory and History: *The Memoirs of Alice Guy-Blaché,*" in *The Feminist Reader in Early Cinema,* ed. Jennifer Bean and Diane Negra (Durham, NC: Duke University Press, 2002), 29–59; and *Cupboards of Curiosity: Women, Recollection, and Film History* (Durham, NC: Duke University Press, 2007).

2. Anthony Slide, *Lois Weber: The Director Who Lost Her Way in Film History* (Westwood, CT: Greenwood Press, 1996), 151.

3. The headline appears in "Lois Weber Movie Star-Maker," unidentified newspaper clipping, n.d., n.p., clipping files, Billy Rose Theater Collection, New York Public Library for the Performing Arts (hereafter BRTC). See also the *New York Times,* November 14, 1939, n.p., BRTC; and "Lois Weber, First Woman Director, Dies," *Los Angeles Examiner,* November 14, 1939, n.p., *Los Angeles Examiner* Clipping Files, Special Collections, University of Southern California.

4. For instance, Weber's "discovery" of Claire Windsor is featured prominently in the actress's obituaries. See *New York Times,* October 25, 1972, n.p.; *Variety,* November 1, 1972, n.p.; and *London Times,* October 26, 1972, n.p., BRTC.

5. "Lois Weber Sails for Europe; Plans Production of Big Films," *Moving Picture World,* October 8, 1921, 676.

6. Unidentified newspaper item, vol. 2, Claire Windsor Scrapbook Collection, Cinema-Television Library, University of Southern California (hereafter CWSBC).

7. "Rialto," unidentified 1921 newspaper article, vol. 2, CWSBC.

8. "Claire Windsor Started Career as Film Extra," unidentified 1921 newspaper article, vol. 2, CWSBC.

9. "Saving the Family Name—Bluebird," *Moving Picture Weekly,* September 2, 1916, 16.

10. Ibid., 16–17.

11. Quoted in Richard Koszarski, "Truth or Reality? A Few Thoughts on Mary MacLaren's *Shoes,*" *Griffithiana* 40–42 (1991): 82. Koszarski conducted his interview with MacLaren in 1973.

12. *Photoplay,* March 1917, 87.

13. *Motion Picture News,* March 24, 1917, n.p. Reprinted in *Taylorology* 95,

http://silent-movies.com/Taylorology/Taylor95.txt.

14. *Motion Picture Classic,* May 1918, n.p., envelope 621, Robinson Locke Collection, New York Public Library for the Performing Arts (hereafter RLC).

15. "Mildred Harris with Lois Weber," *Moving Picture World,* October 27, 1917, 511.

16. *Motion Picture News,* August 30, 1919, 1873; and "Mildred Harris in 'Home,'" *Toledo Blade,* December 7, 1919, n.p., env. 621, RLC.

17. "Among the Women," *Variety,* May 3, 1918, 44.

18. *Photoplay,* March 1918, n.p., env. 621, RLC.

19. "Louis B. Mayer Signs Mildred Harris," *Moving Picture World,* June 28, 1919, 1948.

20. Signed contract between Lois Weber and Ola Cronk, January 12, 1921, vol. 2, CWSBC. Windsor had already appeared in one film directed by Weber before the contract was signed: *To Please One Woman,* released in December 1920.

21. Maude Cheatham, "The Heroine," *Motion Picture Classic,* April 1922, n.p., oversize scrapbook, CWSBC.

22. Helen Rockwell, "The Girl You Never Know," unidentified 1921 magazine article, vol. 1, CWSBC.

23. "Olga [*sic*] Cronk in the Movies Is Protégé of Lois Weber," unidentified 1921 magazine article, vol. 1, CWSBC; "A Very Real Message Conveyed in 'The Blot,'" unidentified 1921 newspaper article, vol. 2, CWSBC; and "'The Blot' Great American Drama of Today," unidentified 1921 magazine article, vol. 2, CWSBC.

24. "Goldwyn Signs Claire Windsor," *Moving Picture World,* July 15, 1922, 216; and "Signs New Contract," *Moving Picture World,* July 11, 1925, 196.

25. "The Screen's First Woman Director," *Motion Picture Director,* January 1926, 60.

26. "The Marriage Clause," unidentified magazine article, vol. 8, CWSBC.

27. "'The Marriage Clause'—Universal," *Moving Picture World,* July 3, 1926, 39.

28. "Billie Dove Signs with Lois Weber," *Moving Picture World,* August 7, 1926, 339; and "'The Marriage Clause' Premiere in West," *Moving Picture World,* September 4, 1926, 36.

29. William M. Drew, *At the Center of the Frame: Leading Ladies of the Twenties and Thirties* (New York: Vestal Press, 1999) 11, 33–34.

30. *(New York?) Daily News,* February 3, 1933, n.p., clipping File, BRTC.

31. See, for example, Minerva Martin, "A Versatile Couple," *Photoplay,* April 1914, 83–85; "Bosworth Stars a Talented Couple," *Motion Picture News,* November 21, 1914, 36; "Smalleys Are Most Unusually Gifted Pair in Pictures," *New York Telegraph,* December 6, 1914, n.p., env. 2117, RLC; and Richard Willis, "Lois Weber and Phillips Smalley—A Practical and Gifted Pair with High Ideals," *Movie Pictorial,* May 1915, n.p. Reprinted in *Taylorology* 59, http://silent-movies.com/Taylorology/Taylor59.txt. I analyze contemporary profiles of Weber and Smalley's creative partnership further in "Presenting the Smalleys: 'Collaborators in Authorship and Direction,'" Film History 18.2 (2006): 119–28.

32. "Lois Weber Is Whole Show in Her Company," unidentified 1921 newspaper article, vol. 2, CWSBC.

33. Unidentified magazine article, vol. 8, Chamberlin Scrapbooks, Margaret Herrick Library, Academy of Motion Picture Arts and Sciences.

34. "The Year's Sensation," *Motion Picture Director* 3.1 (1926): 33.

35. Myrtle Gebhart, "A Pot of Gold for Billie Dove," *Picture Play,* April 1927, 71. Quoted in Drew, *At the Center of the Frame,* 11.

36. Laemmle is quoted in Charles S. Dunning, "The Gate Women Don't Crash," *Liberty* 4.2 (1927): 31. Reprinted in Slide, *Lois Weber,* 137–38.

37. Quoted in Drew, *At the Center of the Frame,* 32.

38. L. H. Johnson, "A Lady General of the Picture Army," *Photoplay,* June 1915, 42.

39. "Discovering Mary McLaren [*sic*]. How One Girl Got Her First Big Chance," *Green Book,* March 1917, 404–5, env. 1280, RLC.

40. "The Strange Case of Mary MacLaren," *Moving Picture Weekly,* June 24, 1916, 9.

41. Unidentified article, *Theatre Magazine,* April 1919, n.p., env. 1280, RLC.

42. "From Extra to Stardom," *Motion Picture Magazine,* September 1917, 39.

43. "Why Be an Extra? Claire Windsor, She Waited—And Worried—And Won!" unidentified 1921 magazine article, vol. 1, CWSBC.

44. Unidentified 1921 photo caption, vol. 1, CWSBC.

45. Frances Deaner, "Happiness Hunt Is Revealed in Weber Film," unidentified 1921 newspaper article, vol. 2, CWSBC.

46. MacLaren's comments appear in Koszarski, "Truth or Reality?" 82.

47. Aline Carter, "The Muse of the Reel," *Motion Picture Magazine,* March 1921, 126.

48. *New York Times,* November 14, 1921, 18. Lillian R. Gale makes a similar point in her review in the *Motion Picture News,* November 26, 1921, 2811.

49. "Two [*sic*] Wise Wives," *Motion Picture News,* June 4, 1921, 348.

50. "The Blot," *Motion Picture News,* August 27, 1921, 1138.

51. "Borrowed Clothes," *Moving Picture World,* December 7, 1918, 1115.

52. Review of *The First Woman, Variety,* April 28, 1922. *Variety Film Reviews.*

53. "'The Marriage Clause'—Universal," *Moving Picture World,* July 3, 1926, 39.

54. *New York Times,* March 16, 1927, 28.

55. Johnson, "Lady General of the Picture Army," 42.

56. Unidentified newspaper clipping, *Chicago Herald* (1916), n.p., RLC.

57. Bertha H. Smith, "A Perpetual Leading Lady," *Sunset* 32.3 (1914): 636.

58. Quoted in Koszarski, "Truth or Reality?" 82.

59. Elizabeth Peltret, "On the Lot with Lois Weber," *Photoplay,* October 1917, 90.

60. Rockwell, "The Girl You Never Know."

61. Carter, "The Muse of the Reel," 126.

62. Mlle. Chic, "The Greatest Woman Director in the World," *Moving Picture Weekly,* May 20, 1916, 24.

63. Unidentified newspaper clipping, *Ohio State Journal,* n.p., env. 2518, RLC.

64. "The Screen's First Woman Director," *Motion Picture Director* 2.6 (1926): 60.

65. *New York Dramatic Mirror,* July 15, 1916, n.p.; and "Biographies of Impor-

tant Directors," *Wid's Daily,* April 24, 1921, 112. Weber was one of only four women listed in *Wid's* survey of close to 250 "important directors" in Hollywood. (Alice Guy-Blaché, Frances Marion, and Mrs. Sidney Drew were the others.)

66. Smith, "A Perpetual Leading Lady"; and Ernestine Black, "Lois Weber Smalley," *Overland Monthly,* September 1916, 198–200.

67. "Lois Weber, Film Genius, Has Spectacular Rise to Fame," unidentified newspaper clipping, n.d., n.p., env. 2518, RLC; "'Scandal' Terrific Denunciation of the Gossiping Evil, Seen at Orpheum Today," *Fort Wayne Journal Gazette,* n.d., ca. 1915, env. 2518, RLC; and Florence Lawrence, "Lois Weber in Studio De Luxe," *Los Angeles Examiner,* June 6, 1917, n.p., env. 2518, RLC. I analyze Weber's fame further in my article "Lois Weber and the Celebrity of Matronly Respectability," in *Looking Past the Screen: Case Studies in American Film History and Method,* ed. Jon Lewis and Eric Smoodin (Durham, NC: Duke University Press, 2007), 89–116.

68. See Judith Mayne, *Directed by Dorothy Arzner* (Bloomington: Indiana University Press, 1994), 45–49.

69. "Stage Experience? None!" *Photoplay,* October 1918, 43.

70. "Mildred Harris," *Moving Picture World,* November 7, 1914, 768; "Mildred Harris with Griffith Mutual," *Moving Picture World,* February 20, 1915, 1127; and "Mildred Harris with Lois Weber," *Moving Picture World,* October 27, 1917, 511.

71. "Mildred Harris with Lois Weber," 511.

72. Mary MacLaren, "How I Happened," *Moving Picture World,* July 21, 1917, 427.

73. Rockwell, "The Girl You Never Know."

74. "Hunt Actress by Plane. Chaplin Offers $1,000 Reward," *Los Angeles Record* (ca. July 1921), n.p., vol. 1, CWSBC; "May Be Next Mrs. Charlie Chaplin," *Toledo Blade,* October 26, 1921, n.p., env. 2626, RLC; "Clues Point to Director and Actress," *Toledo Blade,* February 4, 1922, n.p., env. 2626, RLC; "Claire Windsor's Son Foils Kidnapping Plot," *Los Angeles Examiner* (ca. October 1921), n.p., oversize scrapbook, CWSBC.

75. "Mrs. Chaplin Free Agent," *Variety,* July 27, 1919, n.p., env. 621, RLC.

76. "Actress Says Her Youth Was Sold for $50 a Week," unidentified newspaper clipping, March 9, 1917, n.p., env. 1280, RLC; *Photoplay,* May 1917, n.p., env. 1280, RLC; *Photoplay,* August 1917, n.p., env. 1280, RLC; and "MacLaren Returns to the Universal," *Moving Picture World,* February 16, 1918, 972. MacLaren eventually returned to Universal under undisclosed terms.

77. Mary Roberts Reinhart, "Faces and Brains," *Photoplay* (February 1922), 47–48, 107. Reprinted in *They Also Wrote for the Fan Magazines: Film Articles by Literary Giants from e.e. cummings to Eleanor Roosevelt, 1920–1939,* ed. Anthony Slide (Jefferson, NC: McFarland, 1992), 123–28.

78. Theodore Dreiser, "Hollywood: Its Morals and Manners," *Shadowland,* November 1921, n.p. Reprinted in *Taylorology* 41, http://silent-movies.com/Taylorology/Taylor41.txt. St. John's articles appeared in *Photoplay* from February to July 1927.

79. "The Girl with Two Mothers," *Moving Picture Weekly,* January 27, 1917, 19.

80. "Lois Weber Talks Shop," *Moving Picture World,* May 27, 1916, 1493.

81. Quoted in Koszarski, "Truth or Reality?" 81.

82. Fritzi Remont, "The Lady behind the Lens," *Motion Picture Magazine,* May 1918, 61.

83. Ibid., 60.

84. Marion, *Off With Their Heads!* 11–13.

85. I analyze this phenomenon in more detail in my article " 'It's a Long Way to Filmland': Starlets, Screen Hopefuls, and Extras in Early Hollywood," in *American Cinema's Transitional Era: Audiences, Institutions, Practices,* ed. Charlie Keil and Shelley Stamp (Berkeley: University of California Press, 2004), 332–52. Also see Heidi Kenaga " 'Making the Studio Girl': The Hollywood Studio Club and Industry Regulation of Female Labor," *Film History* 18.2 (2006), 129–39.

86. "Lois Weber Club Women's Hostess," *Moving Picture Weekly,* January 7, 1917, n.p., env. 2518, RLC; and "In the Capital of Movie-Land," *Literary Digest* 55 (November 10, 1917), 86.

87. "Lois Weber Club Women's Hostess."

88. Remont, "Lady behind the Lens," 61.

89. "Stars Defend Hollywood," unidentified 1921 newspaper item, vol. 2, CWSBC.

90. Cari Beauchamp details the women's friendship in *Without Lying Down: Frances Marion and the Powerful Women of Early Hollywood* (New York: Scribner, 1997); see especially 51, 282 and 346.

91. Julian Johnson, "*The Dumb Girl of Portici,*" *Photoplay,* April 1916, 102.

92. "Mme. Pavlowa [*sic*] with Universal," *Motography,* June 26, 1915, 1046; "Pavlowa [*sic*] in 'The Dumb Girl of Portici,' " *Motography,* July 10, 1915, 60; "Pavlowa [*sic*] Enthusiastic Worker in Universal Feature Studio," *Motography,* July 31, 1915, 192–93; H. H. Van Loan, "Pavlowa's [*sic*] 'The Dumb Girl of Portici,' " *Motography,* October 16, 1915, 801–2; and *New York Dramatic Mirror,* July 15, 1916, n.p. Cited in Slide, *Lois Weber,* 101.

93. H. H. Van Loan, "Lois, the Wizard," *Motion Picture Magazine,* July 1916, 44.

94. Anthony Slide provides an informative overview of this impressive group in the chapter "Universal Women" in his *The Silent Feminists: America's First Women Directors* (Lanham, MD: Scarecrow Press, 1996), 41–60. See also Frances Denton, "Lights! Camera! Quiet! Ready! Shoot!" *Photoplay,* February 1918, 48–50, env. 2518, RLC.

95. Slide, *Lois Weber,* 152.

96. "Lois Weber to Film 'K,' " *Moving Picture World,* July 21, 1917, 478.

97. *Photoplay,* September 1913, 73; and "Lois Weber Club Women's Hostess."

98. "What Do Men Want?" unidentified 1921 magazine article, vol. 2, CWSBC.

99. Richard Koszarski, "The Years Have Not Been Kind to Lois Weber," *Village Voice,* November 10, 1975, 40. Reprinted in *Women and the Cinema: A Critical Anthology,* ed. Karyn Kay and Gerald Peary (New York: E. P. Dutton, 1977), 147.

100. Anthony Slide, "Lois Weber," in *Early Women Directors* (New York: A. S. Barnes, 1977), 34.

Reading as a Woman
The Collaboration of Ayako Wakao and Yasuzo Masumura

"It was a kind of battle, after all. Well, ploys and gambits, on the front line. And that's why, when I showed even an inkling of being lost or insecure, [Masumura] would in no time push me. I always had to be ready for anything, so I wouldn't be caught off-guard."

—Ayako Wakao, interview by Sadao Yamane

Reading as a Woman

My own experience as a spectator of the films of Ayako Wakao, the actress most representative of Yasuzo Masumura's unique depictions of women, has been one fraught with ambivalence and inner contradiction. Indeed, Wakao, with her singular voice and aura of eroticism, attracted not only men during her tenure as a Daiei studio's leading star, and later as a television and stage actress, but fascinated and captivated women as well.[1]

Watching Wakao at work in a Masumura film, one is first struck by her distinctive beauty. Time and again, Wakao has been noted for her skill in evoking the sensuality of women. Her body—whose beauty is exposed to the men she loves as the incarnation of love—is presented, first and foremost, as an object of male desire. This sensuality and eroticism seems, at first glance, positioned as an exaggerated or excessive female sexuality within the confines of patriarchal notions of female sexuality. That is, she appears to be the very definition of a sexually regulated woman. It is for this reason that I experience an initial resistance to her films, and yet she fascinates me at the same time. I look at the actress and find *something attractive* there, which moves me.

154

What, then, is that *something* that attracts female spectators to Wakao? Premised on Laura Mulvey's feminist critique that asserts that the basic structure of mainstream film caters to male spectators, my question implies the necessity of acknowledging the presence of female spectators and considering their own practices of spectatorship. Mulveyan film theorists acknowledge the importance of analyzing images of women as objects of male desire, but they have less successfully addressed the question that Gertrud Koch has posed: "Why do women go to men's films?"[2] Koch's question points to the fact that feminist criticism has yet to engage with the historical presence of women's enjoyment of images of women as defined by the male gaze.

According to Koch, female spectators do not simply identify with the male gaze but are themselves desirous of the female image. Images of women are not simply superimposed on the mother, the object of a pre-oedipal desire; nor do female spectators merely objectify women through a masculine gaze. Indeed, images of women embodied by stars (Dietrich or Garbo, for example) have been meant for male and female consumption alike. Clearly, there is a need to examine the fact of female spectators' desire as well. In addition, Koch argues that an image does not bear just one meaning, but that, depending on the position of its interlocutor, it potentially embodies multiple readings. What much research in this vein reveals is not a "preferred reading" of film texts—that is, a dominant reading—but the ways in which this dominant reading is negotiated and new meanings emerge from potentially oppositional readings embedded in the text.

My objective, then, in this essay is to read, as a woman, the Wakao of Yasuzo Masumura's films. By *reading as a woman,* I designate a practice of reading advanced by Shoshana Felman which she describes as an act of "conjugating literature, theory, and autobiography, together through the act of reading and by reading, thus, into the texts of culture, at once our sexual difference and our autobiography as missing."[3] However, I wish to avoid the equation of this act of reading as a woman with a privileged notion of female reading that is both monolithic and deterministically different from that of men.[4] Rather, this essay attempts to shift the playing ground upon which reading practices occur, creating a strategy for the superposition of female spectators' desire and those subtle tremors, or hidden traces, of desire existing within the text.

My endeavor to read as a woman the Wakao of Masumura's films is threefold. First, I wish to uncover the meanings that lie in the traces of resistance revealed by the body of a woman appropriated by a male film-maker and the desires of male spectators—specifically, those meanings for female spectators excluded from the geography of desire of the film text. Second, through the reading of this resistance, I hope to bring to the surface those voices that have been "dominated, displaced or silenced" at the level of production, revealing the moment at which a film deviates from the dominant ideology of the community that controls it.[5] Third, since critical writings about the actress in the Japanese context have been written by predominantly male writers, my reading attempts to reappropriate and dislocate Wakao from the dominant male discourses. Thus, what I propose is not a theoretical, objectively analyzable "object" comprising Wakao's portrayals of Masumurian heroines. Nor do I intend to close off consideration of the text as a wholly autonomous system, or indulge in uncritical reflection on the desires of spectators, rewriting the text to complement readers' arbitrary interpretations. Rather, I will attempt a reading of the moment in which Wakao endows her heroines with body and voice, returning to that unsettling moment confronting "you," the spectator, and as Felman puts it, "tun[ing] into the forms of resistance present in the text."[6]

Masumurian Heroine

Born in 1933, Ayako Wakao entered the Acting Institute of Daiei Film Studios in 1951, making her official debut in the 1952 film *Shi no machi o nogarete* (Escaping a city of death) and continuing her career until her final appearance on the screen in her 160th film, *Haru no Yuki* (Spring snow), which was released in 2005 and marked her return to film after an absence of eighteen years. In the year following her debut, she appeared in eight films, attracting attention for her appealingly ordinary features and gaining popularity following her performance as a "young high school girl in the throes of sexual awakening" in the 1953 film *Judai no seiten* (A textbook on sex for teenagers).[7] From 1954 to 1962, she averaged over ten films a year (fourteen films in 1956), and even in other years before 1966 she managed roughly seven films a year. Daiei's bankruptcy in 1971 precipitated her move to television and theater, after which she appeared in only three films. In the eighteen-year period between 1952 and 1969 when her film career was in full bloom, she completed over 150 films, in most of which she played major, if not always leading, roles. Averaged across this time period, this translates to nine films a year—truly an impressive output. Moreover, as the representative star of Daiei Studios, Wakao performed in no more than four films for other studios. She was a true daughter of the Japanese studio star system.

Having begun his career in early 1950s as an assistant director for Kenji Mizoguchi, Masumura, like Wakao, also enjoyed a long tenure with Daiei and, in his capacity as a studio director, worked in a variety of genres and with both male and female actors. Yet, for many critics, the study of Masumura as an auteur is synonymous with a consideration of Masumura's women, and, in particular, Wakao. For example, in his auteur study of Masumura, Sadao Yamane formulates his discussion around the central question, "What is it that drove Ayako Wakao?" Yamane even categorizes certain of Masumura's films as "woman's films," regardless of whether there are melodramatic tendencies in them, to highlight the fact that impressive Masumura films are those that center on their lead actress.[8] In Masumura's case, the term owes unmistakably to the strong presence of the distinctive actresses they feature, beginning with Wakao and continuing with Ruriko Asaoka, Michiyo Yasuda, Mako Midori, and Meiko Kaji, as well as the strong characters they portray. Nonetheless, as in the collaboration between von Sternberg and Dietrich, only Wakao is indispensable to Masumura's films. Conversely, it is also true that it was Masumura's films that created Wakao the actor; she was not content to remain a mere star.[9] In essence, the "women's film" genre within Masumura's work is characterized not so much by an adherence to a conventional narrative pattern but rather an adherence to and invocation of a specific persona, most clearly embodied by Wakao.

Just what kind of woman did Wakao portray in Masumura's films? His heroines are very determined and egoistic women, made up not with concepts but flesh and blood, strong and self-assertive in love, who discover the road to self-realization only *through* love. However, they are not the classical heroines of Japanese film who live and suffer for love, unhappy women typified in such characters as "the mother who trusts in her son and endures a life of hardship," or the wife who "sacrifices everything for the sake of her faith in her husband," a kind of female representation typical of *shinpa* drama.[10] For female characters of the classical model, it is the erasure of self that is proof of their love, and through self-denial they become heroines, as exemplified in the heroine, Shiraito, in Kenji Mizoguchi's *Taki no Shiraito* (The water magician, 1933). As a famous critic Tadao Sato observes, this "self-sacrificing type" of heroine emerges from a masculine "cult of female worship" in which the heroine constitutes a "painful reminder of female pathos"; that is, this "tradition of the cult of female worship" is interpreted by Sato as one of "Japanese film feminism" in which "one woman's unhappiness" becomes a "censure of masculine oppression."[11] Accordingly, the classical "unhappy woman" is unhappy *for men* and *because of men;* her unhappiness exists for the purpose of upholding and valorizing the morals of men. The proposal of this kind of heroine as a male moral dilemma is made possible by a certain *martyred* nature given to women's suffering within patriarchal society.

The Masumurian heroine is the antithesis of this classical heroine. Far from self-sacrificing, she single-mindedly pursues love as a means of achieving self-emancipation and self-realization. However, for her the pursuit of love is not necessarily synonymous with the pursuit of a man. She destroys not only men but also herself. She obstinately wants the object of her love to love her as much as—or even more than—she loves herself. For many of Masumura's heroines, "sexual love" presents an "opportunity for awakening to an ego," a process by which "women look through the small window of antisocial, individual desire to confront a wider world."[12] In contrast to the kind of masochistic pleasure found in classical heroines' self-sacrificing pursuit of men, Masumura's heroines are unwilling to surrender themselves to the goals of masculine social advancement or love, instead achieving love through their refusal to subscribe to the classical heroine's virtues.

In many Masumura films, Wakao characteristically plays the heroine who is first characterized by her loneliness, and, as if intent on burying this solitude, she battles to the death to win the sense of self and love that physical love has awakened. She is almost egotistical in her faithfulness to her own desires and in her attempt to achieve self-actualization through the pursuit of love. While it cannot be denied that this kind of sexually defined heroine is the incarnation of that femininity assigned to women by patriarchal society, her intense self-assertion marks a complete departure from codified notions of womanliness.

As many critics have observed, and as Masumura himself stated on more than one occasion, such a characterization of the typical Masumurian heroine certainly owes much to Masumura's attempts to portray people *as individual human beings.* While identifying with the postwar generation of Japanese filmmakers, and criticized by Nagisa Oshima for being "modernist," Masumura engaged in pointed criticism of Japanese film traditions—as well as in the cultural and social climate that gave rise to such traditions—through creating works that defied the conventions that had heretofore constrained Japanese film. Soon after the end of the U.S. occupation of Japan, he studied in Italy at the Centro Sperimentale della

Cinematografia for two years (1953–54), and, as he later wrote, he returned to Japan with his mind set on "portraying people as, first and foremost, 'individuals' with strong instincts and solid logic."[13] For Masumura, Japanese society was made up of formal communities based on premodern organizations that failed to recognize the radical concept of the individual. Masumura became strongly aware in Italy that, in the wake of Japan's wartime defeat, it was necessary for the nation to establish a concept of self in order to survive and overcome the defeat, and that Japan was incapable of rejecting a modernity it had never achieved (i.e., because it was a modernity forced by the American occupation, it was often regarded as false). Thus, Masumura's films consistently wrestled with the problem of how war-defeated Japanese could live as real *individuals* within the various institutional and cultural settings of a nation founded on community and organizational belonging that define and confine them. As though confronting this problem with the audience, Masumura focused on the direct, dynamic depiction of human instinct, passion, and violence, all of which have negative connotations and thus are rejected within the Japanese cultural climate. Masumura's heroines insist on a "murderous egoism," revolting against the "illogical and anti-individual, local and undifferentiated" cultural climate of Japan and trying to escape through the assumption of an "individual" identity.[14]

Woman as Metaphor

Masumura's criticisms of traditional Japanese cinema were deeply colored by his views on gender, which were evident in his own writings. In the paper "Nihon eigashi" (Japanese film history), originally written in 1954 for *Bianco e Nero* in Italy, Masumura not only equates "Japaneseness" with "womanliness," but he also asserts that Japanese film traditions such as the *shinpa* dramas bear this "femininity," criticizing the lack of "masculine power" in Japanese cinema.[15] Masumura's conception of Japanese culture as such relied heavily on metaphors of gender, placing masculine values over feminine values. For Masumura, who was trying to grapple with the war defeat and postwar reality, traditional Japanese masculine attributes such as "virtue, loyalty, endurance, effort, and harmony are basically feminine," and men are less "fierce wolves" than "mild-mannered sheep" because they are so tamed by organizational rules and regulations, that is, they are too institutionalized to express human nature.[16] Moreover, by evoking Renaissance art as an ideal art form and identifying it as fundamentally "masculine," Masumura criticizes the "lack of masculinity"—that is, the "feminine"—in Japanese traditional aesthetics. He exposes his own highly orthodox masculinist gender values that lie at the heart of his definitions of femininity. Masumura associates such terms as passivity, motherhood, nature, self-restraint, mystery, illogical passion, indirectness, and escapism entirely with femininity; at the same time, these culturally determined associations form an essentialist idea of femininity. Masumura thus contrasts Japan and Europe through an oppositional and dichotomous framework, overlaid by sexual and gender differences. Here, "woman" is considered the opposite of "man"; that is, his *other,* or *that which he is not.*

Consequently, the portrayal of women in Masumura's films is premised on, first, woman as symbolic representation. Striving for what he considered a European-style masculine art and rejecting Asian communality in order to illuminate the problems in postwar contemporary Japan, Masumura attempts to portray the self as individual by using women to symbolize the contradictions between Japanese society and Japanese cinema; yet, as women are the means of recovering a lost masculine art, his heroines must denounce feminine Japanese men. This denunciation alerts audiences to the lack of essential masculinity within Japanese society. However, in his films, Masumura utterly refused to imbue his portrayals of women with traditionally melodramatic feminine characteristics, instead depicting women as a negative mirror image of masculinity in his pursuit of an original masculine art. In this sense, Masumura's depictions of women are complicated, at once occupying a heretical place within feminine Japanese culture and, at the same time, lacking that feminine virtue Japanese culture regulated.[17]

Considered from *Masumura*'s perspective, then, Wakao was certainly faithful to his vision of the heroines she portrayed. Indeed, Masumura defines the actress primarily as "*miko,*" or oracle, a role he wished his actresses to perform; his heroines existed first and foremost to "become oracles, acting as the mouthpiece of the god (director) and preaching truth to humanity."[18] Naturally, within existing critical discourse, Wakao is thought to have been the Masumurian heroine who most faithfully incarnated this role. The desires of the women Wakao plays are such that they seem "utterly *possessed* by something."[19] While this evaluation clearly indicates the high level of tension in Wakao's superlative performances, it also reveals that Wakao's portrayals of women are the key to understanding of the tense action that characterizes Masumura's films.

However, even more telling than Yamane's question about what drove Wakao is his acknowledgment that Wakao *is* driven by something,—that is, that *something* makes Wakao act. For Yamane, Wakao is not the subject of her own self-assertion; instead, *something* causes her to act, and his interest in that *thing* stems not from an awareness of the heroines Wakao portrayed but of the man behind the scenes, Masumura.

Interestingly, in her own implicit attempt to present a reading different from the dominant male critical discourse, Midori Yajima too reads Masumura's heroines as consistent with the director's aims, labeling them "Masumura's earnest oracles."[20] They are "faithful to the commands of the director," not only "restricted to the task of revolting against society and wringing the proof of life from sexual love," as dictated by the director, but expressing the belief that, "sex is a place of discipline leading to an awareness of eros."[21] Thus, they meticulously play the kinds of heroines Masumura *intended to portray*, and whom he "mobilized in the pursuit of life, that their senses might bring about self-realization."[22] However, Yajima wonders if these women, "despite their fierce countenances, are immersed in true pleasure?" She argues that all Masumurian heroines, "in a uniform expression of anger . . . dive right in" to adultery, but that "they certainly do not go beyond those roles that Masumura plans, losing themselves in a darkness of timeless pleasure."[23] Yajima concludes that Masumura's heroines are all the same, decidedly "not resisting the commands of the director" and instead "functioning" as mere formalities in their roles as "oracles" whose "sexual love" and "selves" exist to convey Masumura's myth. Her reservations concerning Masumura's women surface not because they are the subjects of pleasure but because Masumura constructs them for the purpose of transmitting his own ideas. Though Yajima recognizes Wakao's contributions to Masumura's films, for her Wakao remains at best a faithful collaborator who portrayed the heroine who would give everything, even her *jouissance,* for men. While traditional heroines raise a moral quandary for men through their self-sacrifice, Masumurian heroines exist as sexual beings with their own desires; and the moral problem they raise is sexual in nature. Yet both have in common the fact that they exist *for men*. In this sense, Wakao, who portrayed these heroines, remains an oracle for Masumura.

However, is this a complete picture? Is Masumura's intention all that counts? Perhaps there was something that even Yajima, let alone Yamane, failed to discern inscribed in the film text, in part because they were paying too much attention to the director's conception of woman, that is, the functions and characterizations of the *Masumurian* heroine herself. I argue, rather, that Wakao was able to act as Masumura's "oracle" by, paradoxically, working *against* his expectations. While she was faithful to his conception of characters, it is the hidden resistance in her performance that is the source of the overwhelming force and tension of their films together.

Woman in Battle

Wakao's resistance—whether conscious or unconscious acts of rebellion— can be said to have begun with the film that gave birth to the Masumura heroine, *Tsuma wa kokuhaku suru* (A wife confesses), made in 1961. According to Masumura himself, "this was the first of my works to depict women."[24] Its narrative follows a pattern of ruination involving a wife who is neglected by her selfish husband, a marriage that has become loveless and physically exploitative, and a heroine who has awakened to desire and dives single-mindedly into love; this narrative pattern is fundamental in later collaborations between Masumura and Wakao as well.

In *Tsuma wa kokuhaku suru,* Wakao portrays a young married woman, Ayako Takigawa (in order to avoid confusion, hereafter Ayako designates the female protagonist of the film and Wakao, the actress). The story revolves around her, her husband, and her young lover, Koda, culminating in a mountain accident causing the husband's death. Ayako is prosecuted for killing her husband to save herself and her lover and to obtain her husband's life insurance.

If we read *Tsuma wa kokuhaku suru* according to Masumura's schema, marriage is seen as a Japanese-style institution that restricts the once-free individual. The three men in the film—Takigawa, the husband who robs Ayako of her freedom in order to possess and control her; Sugiyama, the prosecutor who condemns her for not following her husband in death in a mountain-climbing expedition; and Koda, the young man whom Ayako loves and who is unable to stray from the prescribed common knowledge and morals of society and love Ayako independently—all function as social, legal, and moral agents. Takigawa's position as a university professor and the legal authority of the prosecutor represent the symbolic institution of law, and Koda, in the name of common knowledge, falls under the influence of a community that identifies with these institutions. Ayako's lawyer operates as the conscience of the film in his attempts to uncover the truth, which is that Ayako cut the rope from which her husband hung in order to save the man she loves, Koda, on the mountainside.

Ayako is a *victim* of the institution of marriage and in attempting to change her situation, she chooses love instead, making enemies of both institution and the law. Not only in this film, but also in *Otto ga mita* (The husband witnesses) and *Seisaku no tsuma* (Wife of Seisaku), Masumura's heroine is alone from the outset, and the impetus for her escape from her circumstances is the discovery of a love object. However, this love is not conceived of as simply spiritual. It is always a sexual love or desire as well. For Masumura, "Love is the perfect satisfaction of desires emerging in the meeting of one body and soul and the body and soul of another," and "genuine love" is "selfish" and "decidedly physical, something that cannot exist without the body"; he sees its "murderous egoism" as something inconsistent with those elements of "compromise," "surrender," and "collectivity" that characterize Japanese human relations.[25]

On the one hand, Masumura depicts the possessiveness of Ayako's oppressor, her husband, as egoism; on the other hand, in representing Ayako's love for Koda as a warped version of sincere love to the extent that it appears egoistic, he emphasizes the double-edged nature of love. In this sense, Ayako and her husband exist as each other's doppelgängers. What is particularly interesting here is that the egoistic ownership and desire that Ayako's husband bears for her are, at a certain level, a grotesque negative image of the self-centered love that Ayako has for Koda. Through the destruction of her own negative mirror image, ironically, Ayako is freed to pursue pure love.

Interestingly enough, while Masumura applies his equation of man = reason, woman = love to Koda and Ayako, the active agent of love is the latter, and Koda remains the passive recipient; in contrast to Koda's *inability* to discern the difference between love and sympathy (which marks his love as essentially conceptual), Ayako's love is nothing if not actualized. This is a reversal of the more or less common pattern of the dominant Japanese melodramas in which male protagonists are liberated by the destruction of women as the negative of the masculine. Moreover, Ayako usurps the kind of physical love usually associated with and reserved for men, while Koda's pity for and charity toward the possessed woman reveal a more spiritual love. Because of this reversal, there exists a latent potential for the disruption of that conflict between physical and spiritual love surrounding traditional symbolic representations of conventional gender roles. Despite Masumura's orthodox views of gender, one characteristic of the Masumura/Wakao collaborations is this kind of latent subversion of gender codes in Japanese cinematic conventions.

Subversion does not always result in victory, however. Ayako defiantly tries to live for love, is rejected, and finally commits suicide. Ironically, in attempting to live out the rhetoric that is utilized in the valorization of femininity—the woman who loves with all her being—Ayako approaches madness. Her love for Koda, which originally had a reason, becomes the antithesis of reason and drives her mad; that is, she is consigned to the periphery of femininity ("madness is precisely what makes a woman *not* a woman," to borrow Felman's insightful phrase[26]). Just as Ayako has abandoned her "other self" (i.e., her husband), she is driven to destroy herself, and through this act, *Tsuma wa kokuhaku suru* rejects that affective logic of love by which Ayako resists the symbolic law of reason. In fact, even though Ayako's absolution means a triumph of the logic of affectivity over symbolic law, in the end her defeated suicide reverses this triumph. Ayako paradoxically loses her own womanhood through her enactment of the rhetoric of femininity, approaching madness. Because of this, she is restored to the position of *woman,* the countercategory of masculinity; that is, she becomes the other that exists outside the realm of patriarchal language. In this way, Ayako's suicide not only robs her of woman's resistance, the basis of her subjectivity, but it also reduces her to an image of woman.

The problem, then, is not that Ayako as an individual is defeated by an institution but that culturally constructed woman, stripped of her womanliness, peripheralizes herself; she is made into a mere signifier. Of course, Ayako's suicide is a patriarchal punishment for her transgression in assuming a masculine position. However, even here the contradictions characteristic of Masumura/Wakao depictions of women are exposed. Structurally speaking, only one character moves freely between the two competing worlds of the symbolic law of the father and the logic of affectivity: namely, Rie, Koda's fiancée, in whose pronouncement "as she was a murderer, so are you" ultimately offers little defense of Ayako's affective logic. Even if we perceive Rie as passing from the law of the father to that of affectivity as the story concludes, femininity is nonetheless defeated at the end of the film.

In the final analysis, Ayako's logic—meant as an indictment of an institutional society itself—is rejected; as such, we can say that the heart of *Tsuma wa kokuhaku suru* consists of scenes leading to her suicide. Ayako begs Koda, "You can get married. Please, just see me even once every half-month . . . once a year . . . once every two years . . . once every three years." Wakao's cries seem imploring, and her body, consumed by this one thing, radiates a dark passion and energy. She is drenched in rain, and her hair and kimono are disheveled; she looks like a ghost, and her unearthly pres-

Wet and ghostly, Ayako desperately visits Koda at his office to plead for his mercy and love in *Tsuma wa kokuhaku suru* (A Wife Confesses/The Wife's Confession, 1961). Courtesy Kadokawa Pictures, Inc.

ence brings the film to a momentary halt. A tension—like that of a horror film based on the curse of a woman—hangs in the air, and the scene stands out for its ability to take away the breath of its viewers.

Essentialist, Too Essentialist

One novelist describes in a contemporary review Ayako's rain-soaked ghostly figure, noting, "I saw a vivid 'woman' exposed to the world there."[27] He continues, "in one shot, the naked body of woman as such moves with an intense eroticism. The woman we see is vibrant and beautiful enough to take my breath away," and he even goes so far as to declare that "Ayako is a complete woman; no, more than a woman. Madame Beauvoir's assertion that 'woman are not born but made' is actually mistaken."[28] Although his words may suggest that there is actual nudity in the film—and in fact there is none—he means to suggest a kind of raw femininity that Ayako embodies. This essential "woman" he finds in Wakao here testifies that only the woman as pure image can extract the essence of womanhood, the very legitimacy of woman-as-signifier defined by patriarchal law.

This novelist is Masao Yamakawa, and his statement, part of an intriguing criticism that became famous within studies on Masumura, is a characteristically revealing example of the discourse surrounding Wakao. His point of departure is the question "Why is [. . .] Wakao, in *Tsuma wa kokuhaku suru,* that beautiful?" and the answer that satisfies him is that, more than the star's own beauty, there is an "eternal woman" inhabiting her body (he notes that the heroine Ayako is unmistakably "abnormal" in her madness, yet "in her, I saw the semblance of one kind of 'perfect woman'"[29]); that the thing which (in his estimation) makes a woman a woman is her femininity. In other words, Wakao's incarnation of Ayako becomes a symbol of femininity, and it is because she is rendered symbolic that her beauty strikes Yamakawa.

Let us assume that Yamakawa's reading is not incorrect. As we have seen up to now, he has discovered the latent existence of an "essential woman" in Wakao's embodiment of Ayako and, focusing on this, he overlays his reading with his own desire. In his own reading of Ayako's death scene, he offers an impressive outline of the characteristics of the "symbolic woman":

One by one, as if removing her clothes, the human semblance is stripped from the object, and at last [Mr Masumura] plunges the human into a body. Ayako is governed by an independent physiology, living in her own world. . . . Presently, as "her own world" is being destroyed, she loses that balance heretofore struck between reality and physiology, and she first attempts to live through clinging to an other, Koda. Now, Ayako lives only for one purpose. That is, she has since lost herself and has become a living ghost. However, because of the illusion that she cannot accomplish her love, she turns to poison. In other words, she dies by the illusion she had first obtained. Her profile shines brightly in death. She is completed when her loneliness is *objectified. Objectified* people are obscene and grotesque. However, the intense eroticism and beauty of Wakao, who has been *objectified,* stabs at our hearts. Here, she is a perfected "woman"; no, she is a completed human being. . . . I applaud Mr. Masumura's originality here.[30]

Yamakawa's position is clearly masculine, and the eroticism of the objectified dead Ayako is the necrophiliac love for a woman's body. That Yamakawa finds in the dead Ayako the womanly "beauty" and "perfection" is because for him, there is something essential about the "objectified human," and he discerns Masumura's "empty self" in this depiction. But in the end all he sees in the form of Ayako at the end is "loss."[31] However, as I have discussed, Ayako's suicide is the *result* of the rejection of her final resistance, and for her it constitutes a fundamental defeat. For Yamakawa, however, this defeat is one kind of "consummation," which he understands as the return of Ayako, heretofore "governed by an independent physiology," to her essential state. Even so, suicide is most decidedly not a consummation for Ayako (or for those who identify with her). Instead, through her suicide, not only is Ayako recognized and condemned as a challenger of and traitor to institutions, but she is also made to function as little more than an indictment of Koda.

It is important to note, as Yamakawa does not, that before she visits Koda, Ayako is not someone who "has . . . lost herself." With his rejection of her, Ayako realizes that Koda cannot comprehend the meaning of resistance and loses all hope. The dead Ayako not only becomes a signifier of the masculine other but she also represents Koda's castration by social institutions. What is at stake here, however, is that she *has resisted* until the very end being made a signifier of the other.

Let me turn not to a consideration of Ayako's dead face in the last scene but rather to the scene in which, after imploring Koda to accept her and staging her final resistance, that resistance is broken and she stands in front of the mirror in the lavatory just before taking her life. She catches sight of Rie and realizes that her potential for life has been severed; entering the bathroom, she stares vacantly at her reflection in the mirror as if all energy has left her.[32] Wakao's body is not the essence of woman that Yamakawa sees. Rather, it is the body of a woman who has failed at love, a woman who has become a shadow of her former self. Wakao's whole form radiates sadness. Yet, from the position of those who have objectified and consigned her to madness, all that is reflected here is an *objectified* Ayako.

Wakao Confesses

As an interview with Sadao Yamane reveals, Wakao considered working with Masumura a "a kind of battle."[33] She explained that the actor is in no position to tell a director, "I think you've got it wrong." "Indeed," she observed, "we are wholeheartedly devoted to doing things as the director has asked, no matter what." Nevertheless, Wakao reported that she had read thoroughly the script of *Tsuma wa kokuhaku suru* in advance and had considered "from the beginning, what I could bring to the [suicide] scene, what kind of tone I should strive for, especially because the character was to die in the next sequence," adding that "quite a bit of it was myself." The suicide scene was shot on the first day of filming, and Wakao chose a slow tempo for her acting during the scene, observing, "I just thought I might as well do it my way. There was no way of telling the director what you'd think. The alternative was to present your own performance. If I tried it, he might go ahead and use my version." And in fact, although Masumura asked her to repeat the scene and speed up her performance, he ultimately did use Wakao's slower paced interpretation instead. Wakao observed, not without pleasure, "I thought I won."[34] Indeed, the quick tempo of performances characteristic of Masumura's early films began to show a general slowing tendency from around the time of *Tsuma wa kokuhaku suru*. Considered from the perspective of Wakao's statements, this film can be understood as one impetus for this unexpected change in the director's career and Wakao herself as one of its sources. On that first day of shooting, Masumura chose Wakao's version of the scene, and he also chose Wakao's interpretation of the heroine, Ayako, and that choice, to a greater or lesser extent, determined the way in which all of the heroines that Wakao played subsequently were depicted in Masumura's films. Wakao's powerful performance and her reading of the script from the female character's point of view played a determining role in the overall tone and pace of the film.

Let me be clear about this. The heroines of Masumura/Wakao films were, from the first, collaborations, or to be more precise, they emerged from a dynamic tension between the director and the actress, from a quiet "battle" to borrow Wakao's expression.[35] At that time, the conceptual symbolic woman that Masumura intended as the opposite of men was given life by the flesh-and-blood Wakao. Thanks to Wakao's secret battles with Masumura, in which she challenged the cinematic institution of directorial authority, Masumura's direction of Ayako's mad passion is tempered by Wakao's own performance, which imbues the character with humanity and authenticity that is palpable to the viewer.

Moreover, Wakao was not unconscious of the masculine position of the camera's gaze. In the scene in which Ayako appears unannounced at Koda's office, soaked from the rain, the camera pans down her body in a close-up. When it reaches her feet, Ayako draws her foot back slightly—an action born of Wakao's "feeling that the camera was equivalent to being looked at by a man," and the "natural" action of hiding her soiled *tabi* (Japanese sock).[36] In equating the camera's gaze with that of a man, Wakao uses this awareness to evoke in Ayako "a double movement of exhibition and of chaste retreat."[37] She recognizes that the camera's gaze coincides with that of the male filmmaker and is channeled through the male character, and, as the institutions and controlling gaze that close in on Ayako are identified as male, so is the masculine position of that gaze being evoked for the audience. Ayako, who up to this point has demonstrated a paradoxically performative flattery, demanding the love of Koda in an almost unnaturally perseverant way—in a sense, *performing the role of a woman* while assuming a masculine position—now reveals an instant of hesitation. She takes on a heretofore-absent passive attitude, simultaneously losing the masculinity of her position and becoming feminine.

Wakao was painfully aware that the heroine Ayako was not "a typical Japanese woman," and she understood that women like Ayako "do not exist in reality."[38] She recalls that Ayako's actions had to bear a certain "propriety," that there was a need to convince the audience that, "whatever else, this is not an inconceivable story for this woman."[39] In this sense, it is Ayako's desperation—evident in her defiant refusal to show weakness and confess a sense of wrongdoing in court, and in her battle against institutionally sanctioned "wifely self-immolation"—that marks this presuicide bathroom scene as key in avoiding the reduction of Ayako to a mere madwoman, something that Wakao, who had grappled with the script, through her own reading as a woman, fully understood.

Made at a time when adultery melodramas were all the rage, it is not difficult to imagine that *Tsuma wa kokuhaku suru* was Masumura's attempt to respond to the demands of his studio for melodrama with a level of social commentary in his depiction of "a victim of the rigid Japanese marriage institution," that is, "a person who, even as she tries to protect her own pureness as a human, is left in a state of near madness through her restraint by an immutable marriage institution."[40] Through her thorough adherence to Masumura's designs, Wakao gave flesh and blood to the character of Ayako. It is precisely because of this sort of double layered textual signification in the film that a contradiction of femininity emerges. This contradiction is embodied in Ayako and surely results from her having been created from a masculine logic. The greatest problem posed by Ayako is that of her femininity: her contradiction is that, on the one hand, because she goes against social law (i.e., the law of the symbolic), in speaking a language of love or affect that does not belong to the language of the symbolic, she approaches madness, but on the other, owing to that very madness she violates that womanliness regulated by social gender codes, and thus winds up being defined as an "absence of womanhood." Ayako reveals the paradox of femininity within patriarchal law; that is, a woman is defined precisely by what she is not. Yamane expresses this contradiction clearly when he observes that "the bulk of Masumura's films are clearly women's films, yet at the same time, because of this, they are not women's films."[41] However, this contradiction is less one of women themselves, than one of the representation of women held by men. Complicating this further is the fact that women have internalized this paradox and reproduced it. As discussed at the beginning of this essay, the ambivalent experience that assaults the female audience of Masumura/Wakao films is one that cannot be understood without confronting this contradiction.

There is little likelihood that Wakao was unaware of the contradiction surrounding the heroine of *Tsuma wa kokuhaku suru,* as her interview suggests. By the time she assumed the role of Ayako, Wakao not only keenly perceived the problems surrounding Masumurian heroines—namely, the paradox of femininity as defined by men—but she also secretly inscribed in her performance her own resistance against presenting Ayako totally lost in erotic pleasure, that is, *jouissance,* buried in total surrender, even if she allowed the heroine to be exposed to the male gaze asking desperately for love. The secret battle that Wakao waged against Masumura's conceptual woman was waged in her resistance, the assertion of Wakao's own subjectivity as an individual and performer, and her own creative and authorial voice. In particular, if we consider Wakao's sense of being "looked down upon" by the decidedly patriarchal filmmaker, to the extent that she spoke casually of her own "low position," her battle can be perceived partly as one waged by a woman approaching her thirties against male authority itself.[42] She did not simply enact heroines who were self-assertive and fought, she herself fought. Of what value are studies of Masumura/Wakao collaborations that focus solely on Masumura?

This Isn't All a Woman Is

Masumurian heroines share certain characteristics, but when Yamane asked Wakao, "Is this the kind of woman Masumura trusted *you* to perform?" Wakao had this to say:

I think so, yes. Even if there were other ways to perform her, in the end none of them worked. I'd admit that's partly just my lack of acting ability. Still, the image of woman Masumura sought to represent was unyielding—as if bound by a heavy rope. But, if you think about it from my perspective, there was also the fact that this couldn't be all there is. *That this isn't all a woman is.* But, there was nothing I could do about it. You know, in the case of a film, the director is always the most powerful person" (emphasis mine).[43]

In believing that "this isn't all a woman is," Wakao, who had "worked for the sake of hearing 'ok' from Masumura,"[44] reveals that her "secret battle and resistance" continued from *Tsuma wa kokuhaku suru* (A wife confesses) through Masumura's subsequent noted works, *Otto ga mita* (The husband witnessed) and *Seisaku no tsuma* (Wife of Seisaku). In 1963, between *Tadare* (Indulgence) and *Otto ga mita*, Wakao married for the first time, later divorcing in 1968. She herself passed through the marriage institution that so constrained Masumurian heroines. Without the personal experience of that first marriage and subsequent divorce, she might not have been able to breathe life into such heroines as Namiko in *Otto ga mita*, or Okane in *Seisaku no tsuma*. Nor would she have been able to overcome the problems of portraying the essence of femininity as a conceptual woman surmounting the problem of reality and unreality and coaxing the existence of a woman out of her heroines. Yet, as "the distance between the women Wakao portrayed and Wakao herself gradually grew closer" in Masumura/Wakao collaborations, surely it was a process of the fusing together of the Masumurian heroine and Wakao herself.[45] Considered in this way, Wakao's resistance is nothing less than the friction, the dislocation of the text.

Whether the viewer can discern such friction in the text, can hear her own "voice" behind her performative body depends on the position of the spectator. In previous critical writings about Yasuzo Masumura, one of the most self-conscious, critically minded studio directors in the 1950s and 1960s, the significance of Ayako Wakao has always been pointed out. However, virtually no attention has been paid to what the actress actually had to say; her words are read as evidence of the director's will, not as the product of her own thought. Despite her rather explicit statement "*that this isn't all a woman is*," Wakao herself as the actor remained outside the critical discourse surrounding her; what remained is only the symbolically elaborated image of feminine beauty, or the desiring gaze of the male critic objectifying her body.

The Wakao conundrum I have outlined is a question of the reading of a film text; it poses a reading that does not exclude the dynamic relationship between the director and the actor in the filmic text. I have no intention of arguing that Wakao was consciously fighting with the director with a feminist perspective (in fact, her interviews imply otherwise); she is no feminist as might be defined by the second wave of the women's movement in the West.[46] Rather, at issue in my reading of the Masumura/Wakao film collaborations is an exploration of the ways to "tune into the forms of resistance present in the text" without reducing the text to either an auteurist invention or a biographical element of a star. To consider an actual site of production is to historicize a process of production, to analyze a dynamic tension between mise-en-scène and performative body in the text, as my analysis attempts to demonstrate. It is also an attempt to deconstruct the image of Wakao constructed by predominantly male critical discourses in Japan and to retrieve her own performative discourse in the process of production as well as of the reading of a text. To reconfigure Wakao's body as a critical element of determining textual movement is to reconsider the relationship among the spectatorial, performative, and directorial positions. Wakao's secret battle with Masumura in both acting and interpreting of the (female) character cannot be understood merely as a power relationship between director and actor; instead, it has to be read in the context of gender dynamics and structure. It is in the resistance of the heroine Wakao plays and of Wakao herself as an actor that a site of negotiation resides in which the female spectator's desire is inscribed in the text. Wakao's resistance has never been acknowledged by previous male critics, but her comment was always there waiting to be heard. Probably, it required a female critic with the feminist eye to discern the actress's secret resistance in the text.

I hope my reading as a woman of Ayako Wakao in Masumura's films will indicate a methodological possibility for feminist film analysis of Japanese cinema, whose critical discourses still need feminist exploration from both historical and theoretical perspectives. In the predominantly male Japanese studio system, an actress may be merely an oracle to deliver the director's messages, as Masumura once claimed. But there is always something more to it; that isn't all she is. Her body, her voice, her performance, and her very presence deliver more, often leaving traces of resistance in the text waiting to be found. We still have to listen more carefully to those distant voices. And this is just a beginning.

Notes

This article is based on an English translation by Lori Hitchcock Morimoto of a longer Japanese original paper. (A further expanded version of my discussion appears in a book dedicated to Ayako Wakao, *Eiga Joyu Wakao Ayako* [Film actress, Ayako Wakao], by Yomota Inuhiko and Ayako Saito [Tokyo: Misuzu Shobo, 2003].) I thank Lori for her excellent job. I also owe special thanks to Alison McKee, my dearest friend, who helped me revise the English version, for her intellectual insight as a gifted reader and editor.

1. In 1956, the greatest point of Wakao's popularity, an analysis of her fan letters was conducted. Wakao's fans were predominantly those who were teens and in their twenties; the research points out that "there's a tendency that indicates a slight predominance, among teenager fans, of female fans over male ones," and that "generally speaking, women fans tend more than male counterparts to write fan letters, but in Wakao's case, this tendency is particularly conspicuous." See Shakaishinri Kenkyujo, "*Fanretaa no kenkyu: Wakao Ayako no baai*" (Institute of Social Psychology, "An analysis of fan letters: A case of Ayako Wakao"), *Kinema junpo* 141 (March 15, 1956): 105–8. After 1960, when Wakao began to present a more mature, sexual image of femininity, her image appeared to cater more to men than to women.

2. Gertrud Koch, "Why Women Go to Men's Films," in *Feminist Aesthetics,* ed. Gisela Ecker (Boston: Beacon, 1985), 108–19. I should add, however, that there is now a significant body of studies on female audiences' attraction to female stars, let alone those on female spectatorship: for example, see Jackie Stacey's *Star Gazing: Hollywood Cinema and Female Spectatorship* (New York: Routledge, 1994) and Christine Gledhill, ed., *Stardom: Industry of Desire* (New York: Routledge, 1991).

3. Shoshana Felman, *What Does a Woman Want? Reading and Sexual Difference* (Baltimore: John Hopkins University Press, 1993), 14.

4. Certainly, doubts have arisen in post-1980s feminism about the use of such essential gender/sexual categories as "woman." I am aware that my own invocation of practices of "female reading" could be problematic. However, as little research has been done on either sexuality or gender criticism in film studies in Japan, this essay is premised on the need to consider these issues before reacting to them as essentialist.

5. The quote "dominated, displaced or silenced" is from Edward Said, *The World, the Text, and the Critic* (Cambridge: Harvard University Press, 1983), 53.

6. Felman, *What Does a Woman Want?* 6.

7. Tadao Sato and Chieo Yoshida, *Nihon eiga joyushi* (A History of Japanese Film Actresses) (Tokyo: Haga shoten, 1992), 217.

8. Sadao Yamane, *Masumura Yasuzo—ishi toshite no erosu* (Yasuzo Masumura: Eros as will) (Tokyo: Chikuma shobo, 1992), 59. The term "Onna no eiga" (women's film) here is evoked by Yamane to imply a certain tradition of melodrama in Japanese film that links Masumura to his mentor, Mizoguchi, whose films were often called woman's films; therefore, it is not related to the specific context of 1940s and 1950s Hollywood women's film.

9. However, Wakao gave luminous performances under the direction of Yuzo Kawashima, a contemporary of Masumura who was as brilliant and experimental as the latter but whose work remains unfortunately unknown to non-Japanese audiences. Had he not died so early in 1963, after having directed such films as *Onna wa nido umareru* (A woman is born twice, 1961), *Gan no tera* (The temple of the wild geese, 1962), and *Shitoyakana kedamono* (The graceful beast, 1962), Wakao's career might have taken a very different turn.

10. Tadao Sato, *Nihon eiga shisoshi* (A history of ideas in Japanese cinema) (Tokyo:

Sannichi shobo, 1970), 15. Derived from the traditional *kabuki* theater, *shinpa* (new school) theater (or drama) is a drama school developed in the nineteenth century as an attempt to depict the manners and customs of contemporary Japan, and in contrast to the traditional school of *kabuki,* which continued to present plays set in an earlier period. *Shinpa* is characterized by a more naturalistic style than *kabuki* and the coexistence of *oyama* and actresses; it is significant in that it featured the melodramatic narratives that would later provide a basic framework for early cinematic melodramas.

11. Ibid., 18.

12. Midori Yajima, "Kinben na miko-tachi" (Earnest oracles), *Deai no enkinho* (Perspectives for encounters) (Tokyo: Ushio shuppansha, 1979), 43.

13. Yasuzo Masumura, "Itaria de hakken shita kojin" (Individuality which I discovered in Italy), in *Eiga kantoku—Masumura Yasuzo no sekai "eizo no maesutoro" eiga to no kakuto no kiroku, 1947–1986* (Film director—the world of Yasuzo Masumura, 1947–1986) (cited hereafter as *Eiga kantoku*), ed. Hiroaki Fujii (Tokyo: Waizu shuppan, 1999), 61. Most of Masumura's essays listed below were originally published in the mid-1960s.

14. On "murderous egoism," see Masumura, "Ningen to wa nani ka—*Otto ga mita* de kakitakatta koto" (What is a human being? What I wanted to depict in *The Husband Witnessed*), *Eiga kantoku,* 413. Japan's "illogical and anti-individual, local and undifferentiated" cultural climate is discussed in Masumura, "Tanizaki no sekai to Girishia-teki na ronrisei—*Manji* ni tsuite" (The world of Tanizaki Junichiro and the Greek logic: About Manji), *Eiga kantoku,* 417.

15. Masumura, "Nihon eigashi" (Japanese film history), *Eiga kantoku,* 72–94.

16. Masumura, "Mizoguchi Kenji no riarizumu" (Kenji Mizoguchi's realism), *Eiga kantoku,* 50.

17. Ironically, it is this complexity that suggests the potential for the disruption of gender codes in Masumura/Wakao films. Within his project of exorcising such generic characteristics as sentiment and emotion from his works, the films of Masumura hold a potential for the freeing of women from gender codes that were entrenched in depictions of femininity in romantic melodramas aimed at a presumed audience of female viewers. However, at the same time, the contemporary masculinization of film audiences hastened the tendency toward the objectifying and symbolizing of women between both the filmmaker and his audience. That is, during this time (i.e., from the late 1950s to the 1960s) Japanese film began to discount its female audience at a structural level.

18. Masumura, "Joyu=miko ni naru tame no joken wa" (What are the requisites for being an actress/oracle?), *Eiga kantoku,* 151–52.

19. Yamane, *Msumura Yasuzo,* 133. Yamane goes as far to say that Masumura's heroines are nearly insane.

20. Yajima, "Kinben na miko-tachi," 47. Yajima, one of the few female critics actively writing in the late 1960s and 1970s for scholarly cinema journals that were predominantly controlled by men, presented different (not necessarily feminist in the contemporary theoretical context) critical points of view that often challenged dominant male discourses.

21. Ibid., 44.

22. Ibid., 33.

23. Ibid., 44.

24. Masumura, "Enshutsu ito" (My directorial intensions), *Eiga kantoku,* 423.

25. Masumura, "Ningen to wa nani ka," *Eiga kantoku,* 413.

26. Felman, *What Does a Woman Want?* 34.

27. Masao Yamakawa, "Masumura Yasuzo-shi no kosei to erotishizumu" (Mr Yasuzo Masumura's personal color and eroticism), *Yamakawa Masao zenshu* (Tokyo: Tokisha, 1970), 307 (first published in 1962).

28. Ibid., 307, 308.

29. Ibid., 311.

30. Ibid., 313 (emphasis in original).

31. Ibid., 315.

32. Looking at her own image in the mirror, she mumbles to herself sadly, "This is a face of a murderer," and takes poison.

33. Ayako Wakao, "Masumura Yasuzo kantoku to no shigoto" (Working with director Yasuzo Masumura), interview by Yamane, in Masamura Yasuzo, 217. (The epigraph beginning this essay is also quoted from this interview.)

34. All quotes in this paragraph are from Wakao, interview by Yamane, 217–33.

35. No writings and statements of Masumura indicate that he was aware of Wakao's description of her work with him as a kind of "battle." This kind of difference in power structure is all the more important when we try to read "traces" of production emerging from the text itself.

36. Ayako Wakao, interview by Takashi Ito, in *Masumura Yasuzo Retrospective* catalogue (Tokyo: Petit Grand Publishing, 2000), 14.

37. Luce Irigaray, *This Sex Which Is Not One,* trans. Catherine Porter (Ithaca, NY: Cornell University Press, 1985), 25–26.

3841. Ayako Wakao, interview by Fujii et. al., in *Eiga kantoku,* 245.

39. Ibid., 246.

40. Masumura, "Jisaku o kataru" (Talk about my own work), *Eiga kantoku,* 411.

41. Yamane, *Masumura Yasuzo,* 71.

42. Wakao, interview by Yamane, 222.

43. Ibid., 216.

44. Ibid., 218.

45. The quote is from Mika Tomita, "Mada mada mitai Wakao Ayako" (Still want to see more of Ayako Wakao), *Image Forum* (November 1992): 114.

46. On many occasions, she described herself as rather old-fashioned, respecting traditional female virtues and values as many women of her generation (born in the 1930s) would do.

Women in the *Nouvelle Vague*

The Lost Continent?

The cinema is a privileged terrain in which to study the construction of gender identities and of representations of gender relations, because the majority of fiction films focus on individual relations between men and women or between people of the same sex. And yet, "gender studies," widespread in Britain and the United States today, where they have more than proven their productivity within film studies, are still largely taboo in France across the cultural landscape, for reasons that can be attributed in part to our country's attachment to a culture of elites in which the ideal of universalism carefully masks masculine hegemony.

The *Nouvelle Vague* (New Wave) is without a doubt *the* major development of postwar French cinema history, but it is also the movement that scholars are most reluctant to study from a sociocultural viewpoint, given the extent to which its mythical dimension as an aesthetic revolution has obscured, within the *cinéphile* orthodoxy that reigns in France both in intellectual circles and the academy, the historical sense of the phenomenon.[1] This also explains the absence of any studies on cinematic representations in the Nouvelle Vague, despite some initial attempts undertaken by contemporary sociologists at the time of the phenomenon's emergence.[2] The study of representations of gender identities and relations as they operate within a cinema movement that prides itself, in a highly French tradition, for artistic creation with a universalist vocation (despite or even because it is essentially masculine), would seem particularly iconoclastic. We will nevertheless try to demonstrate here that placing the Nouvelle Vague in context once again, as well as analyzing the representations of women within that movement, offers a greater understanding of the stakes, and how they relate to the current French cinema that is its direct heir.

176

The Emergence of a New Generation of Male Filmmakers

Nearly 150 filmmakers made a commercially distributed first film between 1957 and 1962 (an average of thirty per year, compared to fifteen per year in the previous years); among them, not a single woman (Agnès Varda released her first feature-length film, *La Pointe courte,* in 1954), which gives an interesting indication of the noncoincidence (if not outright contradiction), in France at least, at the time, between modernization, creative renewal, and the emergence of women. The fact that the majority of these young directors were from middle- and upper middle-class milieus, their denial of any political activism (on the Left)[3]—deemed incompatible with their creative freedom—their fascination with American cinema and their refusal to participate in domestic ideological debates, is both the breeding ground and the outward manifestation of their profound implication in this phase of modernization, which seeks to bury the highly conflicted society that emerged after the Liberation.

An investigation led by sociologists in 1962 on "the conditions of the emergence of the *Nouvelle Vague*" comparing two contemporary French film corpuses between 1956 and 1961, one popular and commercial, the other a "New Wave," reveals the significant strains that distinguish the two.[4] Indeed, the Nouvelle Vague films set all their narratives in the immediate present, privileging the sphere of the personal and private, as well as geographic proximity, limiting action to a brief time period, often portraying characters stripped of any past, without memory, without plans; they were films that disregarded the notion of hero as defined by popular literature and taken up by commercial cinema.

The division of gender is less inequitable than in traditional cinema, even if women remain in the minority and more often serve as partner than protagonist in their own right. These films focus on the sexual problems of their characters, who are clearly much younger than those in the traditional cinema. This is a world of antiheroes, whose problems are purely personal, in a stable social order, and no effort is made to render them especially sympathetic. The spectator is asked to participate solely at the level of empathy, without an ethical frame of reference.

From a sociological standpoint, the heroes of the Nouvelle Vague belong to the privileged classes to the same extent as was true in the "*cinéma de papa*" [literally, "daddy's cinema"—Trans.], but their attitude toward money is marked by indifference, without rendering the poor any more sympathetic. The professional problems of the protagonists play a slighter role than in traditional cinema, in a context in which work is devalued with respect to leisure. But this idleness is often experienced with a tragic overtone, while investment in one's work serves as a dramatic foil. Professional success is inversely proportional to romantic success. The characters' rejection of social institutions is apolitical; social values are a matter of indifference. The notion of responsibility is inexistent. The heroes live in an absurd daily routine lifted directly from Camus's *L'Etranger* [*The Stranger*]; a universe characterized by nihilism and a lack of altruism. Communal values have no currency.

The family as a social unit is dead. Familial and conjugal relations are in a state of perpetual crisis. Infidelity is the rule, within marriage and without. The majority of romantic relations occur outside of marriage, and outside of any matrimonial prospects. The (male) hero of the Nouvelle Vague is characterized by his solitary pride. One notes also the nearly total sexualization of the male roles, in that the films emphasize the sexual dimension of their behavior, and sexual activity is clearly indicated in most of the films and, in most instances, the evoked activity represents the first such occurrence between the two partners. Passion is always recent, and transient. The irruption of love is seen as threatening attachment, causing the hero to lose his availability. Even so, it is precisely that vulnerability that elicits the spectator's empathy.

Nearly all Nouvelle Vague films revolve around the theme of love as the ultimate threat—a Romantic affirmation of the transcendental value of passion—while in fact the hero's daily life routinely involves an accommodation of mediocrity. The films often end with a "meaningless death" striking down the hero. A majority of these endings are pessimistic, suggesting the hero's failure. At times we get an open ending, without the patently "happy end," because the future is unpredictable and destiny whimsical, despite the social structure having been appeased; the individual, depending only on himself, is overwhelmed by an excess of personal liberty.

The Romantic and Modernist Legacy

The Nouvelle Vague figures in French cultural history as a key moment in the legitimization of a new means of artistic expression: despite a mode of production and consumption that aligns with an industry, the cinema officially attained the status, confirmed by the establishment of quality subsidies and advances on receipts, of an art unto itself. Young artists succeeded in bending this instrument to the demands of individual freedom, which since the Romantic era has been a necessary if not sufficient condition for recognition of this status. The Nouvelle Vague emerges as a revolt of "Young Turks" against the French "tradition of quality," that is, against a mass culture that "apes" intellectual culture on behalf of an innovative creative capacity with no interest in academic rules. It sought instead the legitimacy of a singular masculine point of view over the communal patriarchal authority that underlay the cinema as mass culture.

This new generation of films is in fact distinguished from the "working-class" cinema of the period by the presence of a masculine character around whom the dominant point of view in the film is constructed. As in the Romantic tradition of the apprenticeship novel, this generally involves a young man, as an alter ego of the author, with whom the spectator will establish an empathetic connection. Michelle Coquillat has written that Romanticism trafficked, since the time of its best-known precursor, the author of *La Nouvelle Héloïse* (Jean-Jacques Rousseau, 1761), in the claiming by artists of a kind of self-fathering that combines ontological creation and masculinity, while women are defined in terms of contingency, nature, and reproduction.[5] The artisan humbly adheres to the rules of Beauty, cedes his place to the inspired thinker, to the solitary prophet, who accepts no other social bond than the fraternity of artists. This valorization of individual singularity with respect to social hierarchies and the communal environment is expressed in most of the great Romantic texts through the articulation between the male hero's tragic destiny and his "entrapment" in the love of a woman, which causes him to lose his creative capacities or, more broadly, his capacity to be himself, in the absolute autonomy of a personality that fathers itself.[6] Michelle Coquillat identified the matrix of this Romantic schema in *The Sorrows of Young Werther,* which would become the obligatory reference for French writers at the start of the nineteenth century. Two abysses open before the young poet: his own passivity as a sensitive being, which renders him androgynous, and the passivity of the woman who comes between him and his creative desires. He will have to conquer them or die of them. Coquillat shows that behind the argument of a frustrated love is the hero's creative capacity, which is threatened by his encounter with Charlotte: Werther does not die so much from his inability to marry the young girl he loves, as from the dissolution of his vital energies in this love, which rendered him dependent on others, when male identity must in fact not be constructed outside of splendid isolation. The figure of the Romantic hero is one of a creator (of himself or his work) who aspires to complete autonomy, in contrast to the woman, who needs others to exist and who threatens to draw him toward that contingency. Nineteenth-century French literature expanded on this schema from Rousseau through Baudelaire, who marked the transition from Romanticism to Modernism by exaggerating the relationship between woman and death. This "ontologically" misogynist dimension to Romanticism (which is paradoxically expressed through intensely poignant female characters) establishes an exclusionary relationship between the construction of male identity and a romantic relationship with a woman, and is found in most of the Nouvelle Vague films, with the same tragic tonality that proffers this exclusion as a fatality.

But to cast greater light on the cultural tradition in which the Nouvelle Vague aligns itself, one must also refer to the manner in which the space of artistic creation has been structured in France since the mid-nineteenth century. Andreas Huyssen notes, with respect to Flaubert's invention of literary Modernism, that this new creative posture tends to oppose the "bad object" of mass culture consumed by women to the "good object" of "authentic" culture created by male artists.[7] Take, for instance, Emma Bovary's penchant for what we would today call "airport novels": "It was nothing but loves, lovers, mistresses, persecuted women fainting in lonely manors, messengers killed at every stage-post, horses run ragged on every page, dark forests, heartaches, oaths, sobs, tears and kisses, skiffs in the moonlight, nightingales in the groves, gentlemen as brave as lions, sweet as lambs, impossibly virtuous, always well-dressed and weeping like fountains."[8] This ironic description irresistibly evokes the popular cinema before the Nouvelle Vague, and more particularly to those genres aimed primarily at a female audience: melodramas and romantic comedies, or American "women's films."

In the new cinema's "first-person masculine singular," the imbrication between social, cultural, and sexual dimensions in the claiming of creative freedom has an effect on the representation of gender relations and identities, and in particular on images of women.[9] We can distinguish between two highly schematic tendencies. Most frequently, the images of women are the fantasmatic concretization of a male conscience torn between its desire for autonomy and its fascination for the female Other. Women are mysterious and troubling, objects of both desire and mistrust, if not fear, who must often be eliminated in order for the male to survive, if they do not ultimately succeed in destroying the hero, wittingly or not. They are Jeanne Moreau, the adulterous woman in *Ascenseur pour l'échafaud [Elevator to the Gallows]* (Louis Malle, 1957), Juliette Mayniel, as Florence in *Cousins* (Claude Chabrol, 1959), Jean Seberg as Patricia in *A bout de souffle [Breathless]* (Jean-Luc Godard, 1959), or Anouk Aimée, Lola in the eponymous film by Jacques Demy (1961). Similarly, it is the twin gazes of Jules and Jim in the film of the same name that serve as a filter to construct the character of Catherine, the dazzling and fatal woman Jeanne Moreau personified for François Truffaut in 1962.

There exists, however, another vein, in the minority, in which women are the primary protagonists of the story: the author's view in this case is that of a "sociologist" who describes, with more or less pity and distance, the social and sexual alienation of the female character, on the unsurpassable model of *Madame Bovary.* Louis Malle aligned her with a scandalous eroticism in *Les Amants* [*The Lovers*] (1958) and an alienated mass culture in *Vie privée* [*A Very Private Affair*] (1962). Jean-Luc Godard successively constructed a Romantic and austere version in *Vivre sa vie* [*My Life to Live*] (1962), then a flamboyant and modernist version in *Le Mépris* [*Contempt*] (1963). Only Agnès Varda and Alain Resnais (with Marguerite Duras) succeed in constructing female protagonists as the subjects of their own stories.

Ambivalence in Godard's Images of Women

It is possible to analyze the hero of Godard's first film, *A bout de souffle* (from a scenario by Truffaut) as a male figure inherited from Romanticism, beyond the modernist effects of writing frequently privileged by critics. The female partner of Jean-Paul Belmondo, Jean Seberg, was a young American actress basking in the glow of the international success of Otto Preminger's *Bonjour Tristesse* (1958), adapted from the first novel and best seller by Françoise Sagan (1954). Her American accent and her status as a Hollywood star confer on Patricia's character an aura that Godard deploys with ambivalence. As a symbol of the *Cahiers du cinéma*'s Young Turk fascination for Hollywood cinema, she portrays a young student torn between career and love, without allowing the spectator any access to her interiority. Her "foreignness," in both the literal and figurative sense, evokes a typically male fantasy of woman as desirable because mysterious, incomprehensible, and, for these reasons, threatening (the film's ending makes this abundantly clear: she "gives" her lover to the police).

The long and much-vaunted scene between Patricia and Michel in the young woman's hotel room is a good example of the film's ambivalence. Godard oscillates between fetishistic close shots, in which he films the face and female body as objects of desire, and a more distanced framing that attempts to document the relations between the two characters. The latter emphasizes the autonomy, the difference and the isolation of each, while at the same time conveying the contrapuntal impulses of their attempts to connect. Nevertheless, the film establishes, on multiple occasions, a kind of complicity between the male character and the spectator, at the expense of the female character. Several moments after she slaps him for lifting her skirt, he then caresses her bottom with no reaction from her as she hangs a Renoir poster in the bathroom. The shot first frames the character from the waist up, before tilting lightly down to reveal Michel's hand on Patricia's bottom, thus soliciting the spectator as Michel's accomplice.

Furthermore, the female character is the one who possesses "legitimate" culture (as defined by Pierre Bourdieu[10]): she speaks of Renoir, Bach, Faulkner, Dylan Thomas, and so on, and each time, Michel rudely rebuffs her or assuredly contradicts her, to such an extent that the young woman's knowledge seems more of a social veneer than a vital and internalized component, as is the case for male characters in other Godard films—Bruno in *Le petit soldat* or Ferdinand in *Pierrot le fou,* for example. In spite of its disjointed appearance, the scene is structured around Michel's desire to sleep with Patricia, and the resistance she offers before giving in. The spectator will learn nothing more of the reasons for her resistance, nor for her relenting. We are confronted with the old stereotype of women as incapable of knowing or accepting their desire. The novelty lies no doubt in Godard's treatment: Patricia is not revealed to us as tease but rather as a young woman with contradictory ambitions and desires. In this scene, the film notes her hesitation, her fears (she's afraid of becoming pregnant), and her aspirations, but this is no longer the case in the following scene. When she takes part, as a journalist, in an interview with the writer Parvulesco (Jean-Pierre Melville), the film is happy to deride her professional ambitions in order to reduce her once again to a pretty face, all smiling complicity. The ending, in fact, goes even further, tipping her over into the male fantasy of the *femme fatale.*

A bout de souffle is thus fairly representative of Nouvelle Vague cinema in terms of its representations of gender relations and identities: the majority of these films are constructed around the point of view of a male character, more or less the author's alter ego, through whose eyes we discover the female character(s) as "other." This alterity is for the most part ambivalent, that is to say, alternately fascinating and threatening. But the status of the female character in the filmic story is that of an object (of the gaze, of male desire), not of a subject (of her own story).

Truffaut's Fascinating and Terrifying Woman

Released in January 1962, François Truffaut's *Jules et Jim* [*Jules and Jim*] represented a high point in Jeanne Moreau's career, as it did for the film-maker. Centered (despite its title) on the character of Catherine, portrayed by the actress, the film is also the most fully-realized manifestation of Truffaut's artistic mastery; it was his third film, and for many of today's *cinéphiles,* his masterpiece. The film would receive multiple awards and enjoy a respectable commercial success, despite its eighteen-and-older audience restriction for "indecency." The press received the performance of the actress with some ambivalence. The film is often described as a "festival" of Jeanne Moreau, intended more often as criticism than compliment.

Adopting the same self-reflexive posture as Louis Malle had done in *Les Amants,* Truffaut uses *Jules et Jim* to depict the construction of Jeanne Moreau's image, specifically through the scene with the ancient statue. Jules and Jim are lost in contemplation before a photo of a stone statue, and decide to set off in search of the original on an Adriatic isle. The camera revolves around the stone head, as though it too were fascinated by the figure. From that moment, the two friends are in quest of the woman with the same smile as the statue. They find her in the character of Catherine, and their life then begins to revolve around this woman-goddess. But if the film operates in such a manner as to share Jules's and Jim's fascination for Catherine with the spectator, this deification of the woman transforms gradually into a demonization, since she ultimately destroys the one who would not be subjected to her will. Her character combines the modernity of modern romantic behavior with the most archaic traits of the *femme fatale.* With no clear social function or role, she seems primarily occupied by the task of conquering the men around her, as suggested cheerfully in the song "*Tourbillon de la vie*" [whirlwind of life], before the film's ending reveals a more deadly connotation (i.e., a whirlpool).

And yet the extraordinary vitality that radiates from her character, sweeping up everything in its path, makes this film a key moment in the construction of the image of modern femininity, as something in motion. If the female readers of *Cinémonde* preferred Annie Girardot over Moreau by 1962, she would nevertheless become for an entire generation of educated, middle-class women the personification of female romantic freedom. In June 1962, her recording of the song "*Le Tourbillon*" from the soundtrack of *Jules et Jim* would beat all records for French album sales. This is an interesting indication of the public's desire to privilege the sunny, jubilant side of the character, since the song resolutely rejects the more troublesome aspects of Catherine's character in the film.

Chabrol, a Flaubertian Look at Women

Given a view of women that is to a large degree the legacy of Romanticism, it is appropriately symmetric that within the Nouvelle Vague, we can identify a more "Flaubertian" strain, of which Claude Chabrol's fourth film, *Les Bonnes femmes* [*The Good Girls*] (1960), is no doubt the most successful example. Presented by its author as a materialist look at female alienation, the film was somewhat poorly received on its release, because it broke with the romantic subjectivism that had largely characterized films made by the young filmmakers associated with the Nouvelle Vague (and Chabrol himself). Chabrol's look at four shopgirls in a Parisian appliance store is completely stripped of any reassuring populist illusions. Like Flaubert with *Madame Bovary,* he assumes an entomologist's perspective to describe the various guises taken by the alienation of young untrained women in contemporary Paris. An insistence on grotesque characters and derisive situations is evident throughout the film, which follows the four young women at work and at leisure, during a period of no more than two days. After showing an interminable day of work in the boredom of the shop, the portrayal of an evening at a music hall, and another at a swimming pool, allows him to sketch out the derisory limits of their world.

If the filmmaker assigns the harshest traits to the men, to whom these young girls inevitably fall victim, each in their own way, either by marrying, agreeing to sleep with or being strangled by them, their total lack of even the most fleeting consciousness of their situations invariably places the spectator in a position of superiority. And the fact of limiting their choice to either pathetic Don Juans, a reincarnation of Flaubert's Monsieur Homais, or a psychopath testifies to the manipulative aspect of the film. Like Flaubert, Chabrol adopts a different tone depending on the degree to which his young "heroes" are more or less his alter ego, likely to elicit the spectator's empathy, as in *Le Beau Serge* or *Les Cousins,* his first two films; if they are female characters, they lose all individuality, becoming the "good women" that he constructs, under the pretext of describing a certain social alienation, as "Others" radically stripped of consciousness.

A masterfully controlled film both in structure and tone, *Les Bonnes femmes* repeatedly posits as an "objective" fact the equivalence between woman and alienation, within a cultural tradition that has been particularly enduring in France since the mid-nineteenth century.

Rozier's Sociological Look at the New Mass Culture

Adieu Philippine (1960–62) by Jacques Rozier is told in a quasi-documentary style, with nonprofessional actors and narrative events reduced to the minimum, recounting several months in the life of a young draftee before his departure for Algeria: the film first shows him in his job as a stagehand for television, and this is followed by his vacation in Corsica with two girlfriends who vie for his favors.

The film adopts an ironic point of view toward its working-or middle-class characters, the polar opposite of the idealized populism of 1930s cinema. The machismo of the male character around whom the narrative is structured is shown to be derisory, every bit as much as the superficial trendiness of the two "city swinger" women who undertake to seduce him. Yet in this distanciated regard that seems to lump all the film's characters into a single sociological category, the balance is not as even as it might appear. The main character, the young Michel, is unique, compared to his two conquests, Juliette and Liliane, depicted as interchangeable (particularly given their resemblance and inseparability). What is more, Michel has found real paid employment in television, even if only as a grip, whereas the girls are incapable of bringing their professional goals to fruition, with the film complacently emphasizing their complete incompetence.

The "ontological" differentiation between the masculine and the feminine, however, is achieved above all through the use of the Algerian war: Rozier's film, completed between 1960 and 1962, at a time when no one could be unaware of the mortal danger faced by the draftee contingent thrown for twenty-seven months into a "dirty war" that dare not say its name, establishes from the story's outset a sword of Damocles hanging over the male character's head. The Algerian war is not evoked here from a political perspective, but rather it is implemented as a decisive means of distinguishing male from female, out of reach of any common claim to working-class origins.

Brigitte Bardot, the Incarnation of Alienated Mass Culture

It is in their relation to actresses, and more particularly to the most popular among them, that the filmmakers of the Nouvelle Vague most clearly reveal the sexualized dimension of the new creative posture. While an Anna Karina or a Jeanne Moreau may function in the films of Louis Malle, François Truffaut, or Jean-Luc Godard as a "creation" of the author and his eroticized projection within the text, Brigitte Bardot, the first star of the

185

mass-media era, was from the outset a foreign "object" within auteur films.

If Louis Malle and his scenarist on *Vie privée,* Jean-Paul Rappeneau, have said that they wrote their scenario based on documentation of the "BB phenomenon," adapting certain autobiographical elements provided by the star herself, a comparison of the scenario with different biographical and autobiographical sources reveals an effort at reconstruction underpinned by the opposition (entirely absent from the source material) between the elite culture, as embodied in the figure of the art publisher Fabio Rinaldi, played by Marcello Mastroianni, the film's co-star, and the passive and alienated mass culture, to which the character Jill, played by Bardot, is most frequently reduced.[11] The construction of the female character as an object rather than a subject is reinforced by the omnipresent male voice-over (the voice of the supposed-subject-of-knowledge) that comments on her deeds and gestures, and allows us access to her thoughts in the Balzacian style of the omniscient narrator.

When a filmmaker (or, rather, an "authorless" camera) identifies the photogenic aspect of this young girl from a good family, Jill's career is launched, but with complete passivity: she is an instrument in the hands of clever marketers who manufacture her celebrity. The entire first half of the film, marked by rapid editing of elliptical scenes, something that prevents any identification of the spectator with the heroine, adopts without the slightest nuance every cliché about mass culture—a product manufactured by the dominant class to reap profits from the dominated classes. Jill is merely merchandise, conscious of neither her beauty nor her eventual talent (which the film carefully insists on denying), or of the manipulations to which she is victim. The only expression of her liberty in the first half is her use of young men as sexual objects, which she changes as frequently as her clothes. Here another stereotype emerges, the association of the female to sexuality as primary identity (whereas the male characters in the film have a social and professional identity, or even artistic talent, as with Mastroianni).

The second half of the film is constructed around the opposition between the autonomy of the male creator and the emotional dependence of the woman associated with mass culture. Fabio Rinaldi (Mastroianni) is mounting a production of Heinrich von Kleist's *Katherine de Heilbronn,* the quintessence of elite culture, and here functions as the alter ego of the authors (Malle and Kleist, but also Fellini—Mastroianni, in 1961, basked in the glow of the success of *La Dolce Vita*). Jill, reduced to the role of inactive spectator, is killed falling from the rooftops during the first performance of the play, during an attempt to watch the production without being seen by the "paparazzi" tracking her. Her descent into the void is filmed in slow motion, as though she were gliding, against an aural background of Verdi's *Requiem,* and so the film ends on this suspension of meaning, as if the filmmaker could only grant her a shred of artistic dignity at the moment of her death.

The film suffers from the contradictory nature of its project: the principal female character, Jill, is constantly depicted as uninteresting, without autonomy, without plans, without consciousness of her situation (a cinematic *Madame Bovary,* but without the austere "perfection" of Flaubertian writing!). Fabio, however, the true alter ego of the author, is highly valorized by the film, even if it is not his story that is told. In *Vie privée* (as was the case a year later in *Le Mépris*), the character played by Bardot, reduced to a sexualized femininity, is excluded from the circle of male creativity. As Andreas Huyssen notes, "modernism hides its jealousy over the popularity of mass culture behind a screen of condescension and contempt."[12] It is hardly surprising, then, that both of these films, *Vie privée* and *Le Mépris,* kill off the female lead, as if the popular star could only fall victim to her image. In fact the "real" Bardot would impart throughout the 1960s the image of a woman laying claim to her economic, professional, and romantic independence, an image that had a tremendous impact on the young women of that generation.

The Alternative of a Woman's Vision: Agnès Varda

In this first-person cinema, it's perhaps no accident that the only films that construct female characters as conscious beings are the work of female filmmakers, in the larger sense of the word, since Marguerite Duras, after all, was technically the scenarist for Alain Resnais's films.

Agnès Varda does not in the strictest sense belong to this new generation of filmmakers who emerged at the end of the 1950s, since she made her first feature film, *La Pointe courte,* in 1954, after some prior experience as a set photographer for Jean Vilar's Théâtre National Populaire (TNP). But the highly personal nature of this first film, both a poetic meditation on the couple and a documentary on a fishing village, as well as the circumstances of its production on the fringes of commercial circles, make it a typical *auteur* film. *Cléo de 5 à 7* [*Cléo from 5 to 7*], produced seven years later, in 1961, confirmed that Agnès Varda had found a unique place for herself within this new way of making movies, if only because she is and will remain the only woman in the Nouvelle Vague. This cultural difference is constructed here within a completely uneven power balance, reinforced by a French creative tradition that excludes women to a great extent, as demonstrated convincingly in Michelle Coquillat's *La Poétique du male*.[13]

Cléo de 5 à 7 depicts, in nearly "real time," two hours in the life of a woman, a variety singer who is waiting to learn whether or not she has cancer. Sandy Flitterman-Lewis offers a remarkable analysis of the innovative nature of this film, which tells with perpetually jubilant, yet never gratuitous formal liberty the trajectory of this woman who journeys from being the object of the gaze to subject of that gaze, and of her own consciousness.[14]

The film is structured into two dramaturgically opposed halves: in the first part, we see Cléo suffer her fears and withstand her life without managing to master either, other than through the expression of her "capricious" mode (so labeled by her housekeeper, Angèle, and by her musical accompanist, played by the cinematic composer Michel Legrand). After rehearsing a song that repeatedly evokes woman's utter dependence on love (*"I am an empty house, without you. . . . Alone, ugly, pale, without you . . ."* [*Je suis une maison vide, sans toi . . . Seule, laide, livide, sans toi . . .*]), the camera indicates her dawning consciousness by a slow zoom forward focusing on her heartbroken expression as she sings; the lens pulls back abruptly as Cléo cries out in revolt against this image of woman alienated from love and beauty in which others have imprisoned her. She tears off her wig and her feather negligee, symbols of her masquerade of femininity, and departs, dressed in black, alone for the first time.

From that moment, the film's tone changes; the female character becomes an instance of consciousness: she looks at the world around her, discovering first that her fame as a singer is relative (in the café where she plays her song on the jukebox, the other customers do not even lift their heads to listen). At the same time, she rediscovers her friend, a studio model in a sculptor's atelier, who greets her warmly, listens to her while she discusses her illness, then helps her to forget about it by showing her a short slapstick film. After, she goes for a stroll in the Parc Montsouris, where she allows herself to be approached by a pleasantly chatty soldier on leave (Antoine Bourseiller) who accompanies her to the hospital where she is to learn of her medical prognosis. The film ends on the two young people smiling at each other, face to face, despite the threat of cancer, which has just been confirmed by the doctor, or that of the war in Algeria, for which the young man departs that very evening.

These stories of "dis-alienation," which to a certain extent evokes the tradition of Hollywood melodrama, nevertheless displace the problematic of alienation from the terrain of gender relations to that of sociocultural relations.[15] Superstition becomes, through the figures of Cléo and Angèle, a veritable leitmotif linking popular culture, femininity, and alienation in the purest modernist tradition.[16] Cléo initially identifies completely with the beautiful image of woman reflected by her mirror, one who flatters her rushed lover (José Luis de Villalonga). Her accompanist (Michel Legrand) suggests that she sing love songs (mass culture) that construct an image of woman entirely reduced to her sexual identity. In contrast, the alternative models offered in the second half of the film associate "real" sentiment with "real" culture, that of her model friend who shares her film-projectionist lover's taste for the Nouvelle Vague's distanciated slapstick; later on, that of the cultivated soldier on leave who gives her back her "real" name, Florence, by revealing to her its meaning.

This masking of alienation/sexual oppression with sociocultural alienation bears witness to the contradictory posture of Agnès Varda as filmmaker, who sees relations based on gender domination only in the context of mass culture, from which she resolutely distances herself through her artistically innovative project. Her problematic affiliation (as a woman) in an artistic milieu in which creativity is "naturally" associated with masculinity leads her to obscure these contradictions in order to offer an idealized image of gender relations in that milieu.

Cléo de 5 à 7 thus reveals the inevitably contradictory place of a creative woman in the domain restricted by/to the male universal that is the Nouvelle Vague.

An Example of Creative Parity: Resnais/Duras

Hiroshima mon amour, Alain Resnais's first feature-length film, also represents a break with the dominant representations of the Nouvelle Vague, not only because the political and professional trajectory of this committed leftist filmmaker is fundamentally different from those of the young people who gravitated to the *Cahiers du cinéma*, but more particularly because his films ascribe to a different logic than that of the dominant current I have attempted to define in the preceding pages. There is no trace in his work of the Romantic posture so dear to the Nouvelle Vague, neither in his cinematic vision nor in the construction of the characters. Creativity is conceived in nonsubjective terms, since for his first two films he turns to innovative contemporary writers (Marguerite Duras, then Alain Robbe-Grillet), with whom he maintained surprisingly "egalitarian" relations. Last but not least, he makes his first feature-length fiction film with a woman writer, centered on the point of view of a female character. All of these elements make *Hiroshima mon amour* a sort of in vivo alternative to the choices that operate in the Nouvelle Vague.

Resnais's first full-length film runs counter to the dominant tendencies of the Nouvelle Vague on more than one level. He deploys a woman as the structuring principle of the narrative, and establishes her as an instance of consciousness: the story unfolds from her point of view, doubly so, we could say, since her amorous encounter with a Japanese man becomes the occasion for her (and for us as spectators) to relive a previous encounter with a German lover during the war. The film's writing is almost entirely structured as an attempt to record the flow of her consciousness. Furthermore, Duras and Resnais, by choosing to recount a story of "horizontal collaboration" from the point of view of the woman shamed by having her head shaved after the Liberation, inscribe the legitimacy of a female point of view within an extremely controversial historic context, that of the shameful "unspoken" in the official history.[17] *Hiroshima mon amour* takes this "dime-store novel" story of a young French girl in love with a German soldier completely seriously, by giving an extraordinary lyrical aspect to its evocation, as much through the choice of images, which are entirely stripped of the picturesque, as through the musical theme, which transcends the distinction between popular and "high-brow" music. Finally, the choice of a highly transgressive writing style with respect to the dominant codes of cinema, associated with a female consciousness, forges an organic link, both valorizing and heretofore unknown in French culture, between creativity and femininity.

Yet the voyage taken by the heroine (Emanuelle Riva) through her own memory, which is the subject of the film, is from start to finish solicited, stimulated, triggered, and decoded by her male partner, the Japanese lover (Eiji Okada), who initially denies the validity of her conscientious "tourist's" view of Hiroshima (as in his opening litany, "You saw nothing in Hiroshima . . ." [Tu n'as rien vu à Hiroshima . . .]), before drawing out her traumatic memories of 1944, as a therapist would. We can clearly see the critical distance that has been taken, with respect to the discourse of official history, in favor of a history/memory that comes via the individual's lived experience. Yet it's the male character who instigates this critique and this substitution. He himself is not implicated as a character but as an instance of legitimacy: whence the abstraction of his character, he is gradually revealed as a body that awakens sensation/memory, a questioning look, a projection space, a sympathetic ear. The triumphant cry he emits when she confesses that she has never spoken of the past to anyone else, not even to her husband, gives a fair indication of the feeling of potency provoked by the success of this "forceps delivery."

The final exchange, in which the two lovers, before parting company, give meaning to their encounter by naming each other ("Nevers" and "Hiroshima"), restores to them reciprocity. Yet we can see in the narrative and enunciative roles of each of the two protagonists an expression within the story of the unequal roles of the film's two authors, confirmed in the mainstream, to the extent that it recognizes the film's director as the sole veritable author of the film, despite the collaborative nature of cinematic creation.

Thus, even within films that break with dominant representations of gender identities and relations, the Nouvelle Vague cinema reveals the articulation that functions in the French tradition of an elite culture, between artistic creation and a male conception of identity associated with domination. With respect to frequently conservative social stereotypes of the popular cinema of the period, the Nouvelle Vague films offered images of women that were, of course, more modern and more complex; they were nevertheless more often (for obvious reasons) male fantasmatic constructions than new explorations of relations between men and women. For the latter, we had to wait until the first wave of women's film that accompanied and followed the feminist movement of the 1970s.

Notes

This essay has been translated from the French original by David Gardner.

1. Jean Douchet, *Nouvelle Vague* (Paris: Cinémathèque française/Hazan, 1998); Michel Marie, *La Nouvelle Vague, une école artistique* (Paris: Nathan Université, collection 128, 1998).

2. Edgar Morin, "Conditions d'apparition de la Nouvelle Vague" (intro) and Claude Bremont, Evelyne Sullerot, and Simone Berton, "Les héros des films dits de la Nouvelle Vague" (essay) in "Enquêtes et analyses," special focus area of *Communications* 1 (1961), 139–77.

3. With the notable exception of the "Left Bank" group (Resnais, Marker, Varda,

Franju, Demy), to which we will return—and not by accident—with respect to "alternative" female figures. However, the close links between the young filmmakers who emerged from *Cahiers* and the literary Right, more specifically through their regular collaboration on the journal *Arts,* edited by Jacques Laurent, is not seen by them as political engagement but rather as a "natural" alliance between intellectuals and artists. Indeed, anarchism of the Right has been the "spontaneous" ideology of many French writers and filmmakers since the 1930s. See Pascal Ory, *L'anarchisme de droite* (Paris: Grasset, 1985).

4. Morin et al., "Conditions d'apparition" and "Les héros des films," 139–77.

5. Michelle Coquillat, *La Poétique du male* (Paris: Gallimard, 1982).

6. This dynamic appears in texts such as *Le Rouge et le noir* [The Red and the Black] (Stendhal, 1830), *Le Lys dans la vallée* [The Lily of the Valley] (Honoré de Balzac, 1836), *La Confession d'un enfant du siècle* [Confessions of a Child of the Century] (Alfred de Musset, 1836), *Ruy Blas* (Victor Hugo, 1838), and *La Maison du berger* [The Shepherd's Hut] (Alfred de Vigny, 1843).

7. Andreas Huyssen, *After the Great Divide: Modernism, Mass Culture, Postmodernism* (Bloomington: Indiana University Press, 1980).

8. Gustave Flaubert, *Madame Bovary* (Paris: Garnier-Flammarion, 1966), 71. [Passage translated by David Gardner.]

9. On the "first-person masculine singular," see Geneviève Sellier, *La Nouvelle Vague, un cinéma au masculin singulier* (Paris: CNRS éditions, 2005).

10. Pierre Bourdieu, *La Distinction* (Paris: Éditions de Minuit, 1979).

11. Biographical and autobiographical sources on Bardot include Brigitte Bardot, *Initiales BB* (Paris: Bernard Grasset, 1997); Catherine Rihoit, *Brigitte Bardot, un mythe français* (Paris: Olivier Orban, 1986).

12. Huyssen, *After the Great Divide,* 17.

13. Coquillat, *Poétique du male.*

14. Sandy Flitterman-Lewis, *To Desire Differently, Feminism and the French Cinema* (New York: Columbia University Press, 1996).

15. Christine Gledhill, ed., *Home Is Where the Heart Is: Studies in Melodrama and the Woman's Film* (London: BFI, 1985).

16. Huyssen, *After the Great Divide.*

17. It was not until 1991, and the publication of the philosopher Alain Brossat's work, that this inglorious side of the Liberation, which largely affected women of modest social backgrounds, first became the subject of academic research. See Alain Brossat, *Les Tondues, un carnaval moche* (Paris: Manya, 1991).

Investigating an Interval

Sarah Bernhardt, *Hamlet,* and the Paris Exposition of 1900

In 1900 film was a nascent medium. The academic scholarship that would, some fifty years later, validate the distinction between film and the other arts (particularly film and the theater) was clearly not yet part of how film was imagined, publicized, and exhibited. Indeed, the idea that film offered a vision of a transparent and natural world, that it was a self-sustaining and independent art form, and that it (among all the arts) was uniquely "popular" had therefore yet to be circulated and promoted as accepted fact. What I think an investigation of film in 1900 can accordingly reveal are the possibilities the medium once suggested and the challenges it once enabled. Instead of going back to find proof of film's early ability to relay narrative or to shock us with its capacity to move and have things move, I therefore want to explore the ways in which film was an integrative technology that projected different ways of looking at and thinking about the world. To do this I will turn to Sarah Bernhardt, a figure usually sidelined as "too theatrical" in film history, and her short film *Hamlet* made for Paul Decauville's "Phono-Cinéma-Théâtre" at the Paris Exposition of 1900.

As just one film presented in a program that featured other stage stars in famous roles—Coquelin the Elder in *Cyrano de Bergerac* and Felicity Mallet in *L'Enfant prodigue,* for example—*Hamlet* is not a film that has been addressed in any depth by film scholars. It is the "Phono-Cinéma-Théâtre" itself that has received some attention and which is today understood to be an early yet failed effort to join recorded sound to film. What I want to return to in this essay, however, is the idea that these short films were experimental in nature, presenting known stage stars in new and challenging contexts. My aim is not to argue that Bernhardt's *Hamlet* has therefore been wrongly overlooked in film history, nor is it to centralize a production that featured little more than the reenactment of the fencing duel between Hamlet and Laertes. Instead, I want to demonstrate the challenges Bernhardt brought to traditional adaptations of Shakespeare, and the ways in which her cross-dressed performance might have been interpreted by a contemporary audience. Moreover, I want underline the fact that Bernhardt was conscious, even at this very early point, that film was different from the theater and adapted her stage work for the screen accordingly. She was also a savvy businesswoman, aware that theater and spectacle could entice an audience to film. While my remarks are restricted to Bernhardt's appearance in *Hamlet,* my aim is very broad. What I want to suggest is that the theatrical film—and particularly the theatrical film that drew upon the female star of the late nineteenth-century stage—was less a foreign anomaly imported belatedly into the industry than an ongoing and calculated response to the new medium and its public.

That Bernhardt began her involvement in film with the experiment of the Phono-Cinéma-Théâtre is significant. It draws attention away from the idea that she was a stage actress who belatedly (and mistakenly) came to film with the making of *La Dame aux Camélias* in 1911 and *Queen Elizabeth* in 1912. It also draws attention back to a transitory moment that bridged the nineteenth and twentieth centuries. As the official guide for the Exposition would explain, the Exposition was both "the synthesis of the century that has finished, [and] the beacon of the dawn of the twentieth century."[1] That cinema was part of this vision of a possible future (and was therefore still very much an experimental undertaking), indicates the extent to which Bernhardt engaged with new cultural and technological developments. As Emmanuelle Toulet explains in her article "Cinema at the Universal Exposition, Paris, 1900," the Phono-Cinéma-Théâtre joined other experiments in film: the panoramic views projected in Raoul Grimoin-Samson's "Cinéorama," the Lumière Giant Cinématographe, and Gaston Manceaux-Duchemin's "Animated Voyages." Although these undertakings met with little success when compared to the success of other spectacles at the Exposition—Decauville's receipts did not, for example, cover costs, while The Hall of Illusions (in which a play of light was reflected in a huge hexagonal room) was visited by 2,772,600 people[2]—the appearance of film at the Exposition was nevertheless important. Characterizing its appearance as a "parenthesis without immediate consequence, an episode both glorious and marginal," Toulet explains,

It was glorious because of the official recognition that it brought to the role of the Lumière brothers and their invention; because of the individual spectacles, new and varied, that appeared there; and because of the vast and varied public that it attracted. Nevertheless, at the same time, it was marginal. After the event had run its course, the palace and pavilions were, for the most part, destroyed and the center of a momentarily transfigured Paris was returned to its previous state.[3]

Returning to Bernhardt's *Hamlet* and the Phono-Cinéma-Théâtre, it can be suggested that this is Toulet's parenthesis in microcosm; that this was an episode without immediate consequence, yet an episode that was both glorious and marginal. It was glorious because it formed part of the first major "publicization" of a nascent art form that would, in its later development, join sound with action, performance with technology, and the star with an international audience. It was marginal because it was a program appendage that did not boast huge crowds and that would later be characterized as a failed experiment in recorded and synchronized sound.[4]

The Phono-Cinéma-Théâtre's slippage between terms—marginality and centrality, the past and the future, a local and an international audience—is linked also to the fact that it was Clément Maurice, the projectionist of the first public Lumière showings at the Grand Café in 1896, who served as projectionist for the program. As an individual who is famously associated with film "proper," yet who was nevertheless involved in a project that drew upon the renown of the stage star, Maurice makes explicit the early and productive exchange between theater and film. It is in the spirit of this exchange that *Hamlet* represents an interval—a break or intermission—that joins the image of the past (the legitimate stage of the nineteenth century) to the conjecture of what it might become (the cinema). The cinema that *Hamlet* anticipates is, I would argue, a cinema that celebrates performance and derives obvious pleasure from the blurring of disciplinary boundaries.

This emphasis on the blurring of boundaries was implicit in the posters used to advertise the Phono-Cinéma-Théâtre. In these, a woman stands facing forward, her right hand pointing a cane diagonally downward and her left hand holding aloft an unfurled banner that lists the featured attractions. In one poster (reproduced on the cover of David Robinson's *Music of the Shadows: The Use of Musical Accompaniment with Silent Films* and in Toulet's article), the woman leans on a cinématographe and the cane points down to a phonograph that rests besides her feet. Bernhardt is the opening attraction, followed by the likes of M. COQUELIN Aîne, M. Victor MAUREL *de l'Opéra Comique,* Mme, REICHENBERG *de la Comédie Française,* M. Louis MUREL *de la Scala,* and Mme RÉJANE.[5] As the names and titles suggest, this program not only joined the stage star to the reproductive media of film and phonograph but also drew on the range of theater available to a contemporary audience (the boulevard theater, the classical theater, the variety theater, and opera). In another poster, reproduced in Georges Sadoul's *Histoire générale du cinéma,* the phonograph and cinématographe are absent and the woman leans instead against a wooden sideboard. Again, she points, cane in hand, to a list of feature attractions. Bernhardt is here listed in bold, providing a final climax to FOOTIT et CHOCOLAT, COSSIRA, Melle. Félicia MALLET, LITTLE TICH, PO-LIN and COQUELIN AîNE.[6] In both posters, the woman, costume, and cane remain identical.

Sarah Bernhardt as Tosca advertising herself in *Hamlet* for the Phono-Cinéma-Théâtre. Courtesy David Robinson.

196

While these advertisements foreground Bernhardt's participation in the Phono-Cinéma-Théâtre, it is the woman depicted on the poster who best illustrates Bernhardt's importance to the program. The image of this woman, with her pointed black shoes, yellow dress, rounded feathered hat, and diagonally held cane is almost identical to François Flameng's *Portrait of Sarah Bernhardt as Tosca.* Reproduced in Sotheby's 1995 *Arcade Auction Catalogue of Old Master and 19th Century European Painting, Drawing and Sculpture,* Flameng's image has been dated 1908.[7] Whether this has been wrongly dated or is a later reproduction that capitalizes on an earlier image is unclear. What is certain, however, is that contemporary audiences, familiar with the visual cues of Bernhardt's *Tosca,* would have identified the actress and the role. As Gerda Taranow explains in *Sarah Bernhardt: The Art within the Legend,* Tosca was the first role in which Bernhardt used a cane.[8] This prop was, accordingly, foregrounded in sketches and paintings of the actress.[9] Bernhardt's pointed shoes and dress in the advertisement similarly coincide with descriptions of her appearance in *Tosca:* "From her head to her toes, it is a century that, on the stage, walks before us. There is no detail that is indifferent and the shoes are as important as the costume. . . . Everything, from the pointed Empire shoes in green satin embroidered by palm leaves to the mix of black Peking satin and yellow is impeccably authentic."[10]

That it was specifically Bernhardt who was used to publicize the "talking cinema" at the Exposition reveals the way in which she was seen as a mediator between the old and the new, the past and the present, and the nineteenth and twentieth centuries. As an actress in a role that had very recently been brought by Puccini to the operatic stage (Puccini's *Tosca* debuted in January 1900), Bernhardt also highlights an exchange between the performative arts. What is significant here is the fact that, from any number of roles, Bernhardt is depicted as Floria Tosca. Tosca, an Italian opera singer, was a figure created by playwright Georges Sardou in a work expressly written for Bernhardt and first performed in November 1887. With her identity associated with an art form (the opera) that encouraged spectacular display and that enabled Sardou to indulge his penchant for dramatic action, his Tosca is an excessive woman whose identity is inseparable from that of performance. This emphasis on spectacle suggests that the films, like Bernhardt's *Tosca* beforehand, would appeal and be legible to a broad and international audience. Sliding between categories—Tosca was Italian but performed by a French actress, an opera diva characterized in terms of dramatic gesture, and a figure from the eighteenth century introduced to the nineteenth century—Tosca brings her mediation of the phonograph, cinematograph, and live performance to other terms and categories. As a play whose climax is the moment in which Tosca watches her lover die, unwittingly believing that his death is being staged, *Tosca* similarly indicates the possibility of an exchange between the real and the represented, the event and the performance. This, in turn, suggests that the films presented by the Phono-Cinéma-Théâtre might be equivalent (if not more spectacular) to the theatrical productions of the plays themselves.

This slippage between terms and emphasis on the spectacular and performative nature of film is highlighted, quite obviously, by the fact that the poster presents Bernhardt as an Italian diva introducing herself cross-dressed as Hamlet, the Danish Prince. This was not *Lorenzaccio,* the Florentine Hamlet of Alfred de Musset, where Bernhardt initiated the new acting category of the *premier travesti rôle.*[11] Nor, too, was it *l'Aiglon,* the "white Hamlet" of Edmond Rostand, which was enjoying enormous success after its debut on March 15, 1900. Instead, it was the "black Hamlet" of William Shakespeare. Opening at the Théâtre Sarah Bernhardt on May 20, 1899, and commissioned by Bernhardt herself, this play demonstrates the control Bernhardt held as manager, producer, and actress in her own theater. As Taranow relays:

In her capacity as producer, Bernhardt requested Marcel Schwob and Eugène Morand to prepare a new translation of the play. When she performed the Schwob-Morand text, she was the first in the French theatre ever to have offered the public a translation rather than an adaptation of Shakespeare's tragedy . . . Gone were the rhyming alexandrine couplets used in the stage adaptations that preceded the Bernhardt Hamlet, and gone were the alterations in plot that had characterized theatrical adaptations of Hamlet since 1879. In place of previous adaptations was a prose translation based upon scholarly sources in English, French, and German, and presented with so few excisions that the performed text was fuller than any of those used by then contemporary English Hamlets.[12]

It is interesting to note that the Ghost, the gravediggers, the players, and the fencing match had appeared in French versions of *Hamlet* only within the preceding fifty years, and that it was not until 1886 that Hamlet would first die on the French stage.[13] What must be taken into consideration, therefore, is the very originality of Bernhardt's commission. Not dictated by questions of decorum and sensibility (which had seen the exclusion of these scenes), and based on an unadapted English text, Bernhardt's *Hamlet* is best conceived of as an intervention, if not a challenge, to French classical drama. Evidently, while Bernhardt as Tosca was endorsing a spectacular and performative cinema, she was conscious of the polemical and political nature of spectacle and performance.

Although the phonographic cylinders for the Phono-Cinéma-Théâtre's *Hamlet* are no longer extant (and while they apparently only consisted of the clashing of swords), it is significant that Decauville's program challenged the sounding of film in much the same manner that Bernhardt's staged *Hamlet* challenged the "sounding" of the stage. A dual challenge might therefore be heard: on the one hand, there was a disavowal of the silence of silent film, on the other, a refusal of the traditional form of the dodecasyllabic couplet. It is therefore fitting that it is Bernhardt as Tosca, an excessive and expressive opera singer, who introduces herself as Hamlet in the Phono-Cinéma-Théâtre's program, since this was a forum in which sound did indeed begin to challenge the traditional limits of a text.

In his introduction to *Hamlet,* Schwob would explain that his aim was to capture the flavor and imagery of Shakespeare's language and that his removal of the rhyming alexandrine couplets was based on linguistic criteria and textual analysis alone. Schwob's discussion contained, however, evidence of another theatrical challenge: surveying the pre-Shakespearian accounts of the play, he argued that Shakespeare used a 1570 French translation by Françoise de Belleforest of a thirteenth-century Saxo Grammaticus chronicle as inspiration for his *Hamlet.* As Romy Heylen notes in *Translation, Poetics, and the Stage: Six French Hamlets,* this positing of Old French literary models and practices as antecedents to Shakespeare's text was an attempt to reclaim *Hamlet* not only philologically but culturally as well. In an effort to preserve meaning and form, Schwob and Morand also translated *Hamlet* into the language of the period corresponding to the source text—they provided, in effect, a historical French equivalent of Elizabethan English. They inserted into this allusions to late fifteenth and sixteenth, and early seventeenth-century French literature and thus "seemed to be attempting to reappropriate (at least in part) *La Tragique Histoire d'Hamlet* back into the native, oral tradition whence they believed it came. . . . Although they 'historicized' the linguistic and textual/narrative material of the source text, they decided to 'naturalize' all space and culture-bound elements in Shakespeare's dramatic text, thus striking a blow for French literary imperialism."[14]

It is within the context of these claims that the reception of Bernhardt's *Hamlet* abroad might be situated. While advance tickets of the production would sell so rapidly in London that the number of performances jumped from eight to sixteen, and while the prices at the Adelphi Theatre (and later in New York) would—and could—be unusually high, criticisms were nevertheless directed at the French prose.[15] Exemplary of these is a review in the *London Times* which, while recognizing that Schwob and Morand had provided Bernhardt with an "entirely new version of the play," noted that "Of course their prose sounds bald after the magic phrasing and the musical glamour of Shakespeare's lines. There is even a touch of the ludicrous to the English ears in such a matter-of-fact rendering."[16] An instance of this "touch of the ludicrous" is the Wormwood/Absinthe translation. As *The Times* would again note: "It has a very curious effect . . . to find Hamlet's exclamation in the play scene ("Wormwood! Wormwood!") turned into "Absinthe! Absinthe!" with its inevitable suggestion of the *café*."[17] John Hansen, writing in the American *National Magazine,* would levy the same criticism:

To an English ear accustomed to the flow of Shakespeare's verse the prose version sounds rough, unadorned and insufficient, not to say ridiculous, in spots where the rendering is particularly matter-of-fact, as, for example, "The funeral baked meats did solidly furnish forth the marriage tables," converted into "Le roti des funerailles a été servi froid aux tables de noces." But the expression, bordering upon farce comedy, is born where Hamlet exclaims in the play scene: "Wormwood! Wormwood!" which the Frenchman turned into a cry of "Absinthe! Absinthe!"[18]

Schwob and Morand were not ignorant of this question of cultural context. Predicting such a response, they explained that:

We translated *old mole* by *vieille taupe* and *wormwood* by *absinthe.* To the English imagination, these words conjure up the Boulevard, its cafés, and its passers-by. But in French literature, thank God, a mole remains a mole and *absinthe* a bitter herb. . . . In a few years when apéritifs will no longer be fashionable and when our argot will have changed, even in England, *taupe* and *absinthe* will accurately convey what they are supposed to represent *sub specie aeternitatis.*[19]

Such fidelity to the original text resulted, clearly, in an extremely long play. Indeed, the French première was to last for over five hours. While 885 lines and three tableaux were cut for the London production, reviewers would still relay how "the wag in the gallery who whistled 'We won't go home till morning' during the last *entr'acte* was felt to have neatly expressed the feeling of the house."[20] This length would enable the inclusion of scenes never before seen on the French stage (i.e., the dumb show[21]) while it also attested to the time it took to arrange the elaborate scenography. Such a production, best characterized in terms of operatic opulence, "required more shifts of scenery than any of the elaborately designed spectacles that Sardou had written for Sarah Bernhardt."[22]

The length of Bernhardt's production and, of course, evidence of most of this elaborate scenography, is absent from the Phono-Cinéma-Théâtre's *Hamlet.* In this context, Bernhardt's film is indeed a veritable interval: at once part of a series of short films, it is also section to its larger, staged "whole." Perhaps more importantly, the film presents—in compressed form—visible evidence of the challenge Bernhardt's *Hamlet* levied at the traditional performance of the play. Relevant here is the fact that Bernhardt's film not only staged Hamlet's death but provided document to Bernhardt's introduction of the standing death.[23] This death, itself vignette to that which had been elaborated on the Boulevard stage, was later featured in Bernhardt's longer running narrative films *La Dame aux Camélias* (1911) and *Queen Elizabeth.* Here the Phono-Cinéma-Théâtre was again poised between past and future: allusion to a projected cinema, it was also witness to that which Bernhardt had already performed on the popular stage.

It is within this context of *Hamlet* providing introduction to a spectacularly conceived narrative cinema that the filming of the duel scene might be considered. This scene, it should be remembered, contains both the sword fight and Hamlet's death. Taranow contextualizes:

[Bernhardt] approached Hamlet from a background of two traditions—classicism and the Boulevard—and undoubtedly recognized that although Shakespeare's dramaturgy had points of contact with both, it had greater affinities with the popular tradition of the Boulevard. While the soliloquies of the Prince of Denmark could satisfy any classicist who savoured the tirades of Corneille and Racine, the Ghost, the mad scene, the grave yard scene, the fencing match, and the death scene must have seemed like indigenous fare to audiences at the Théâter Historique where the Dumas-Meurice Hamlet was performed in 1847 and to those at the Porte Saint-Martin where the Cressonnois-Samson Hamlet was performed in 1886.[24]

Like her standing death, Bernhardt's performance of this "indigenous fare" stood in contrast to the customs of the legitimate stage. Struck by the venom on Laertes's sword, Bernhardt relays the physical effect of her wound with her back to the camera/audience. Bernhardt's turn from classical tradition (where performers were traditionally told to face the audience) is thus given a visible inscription.[25] This "turn" from tradition is evident, also, in Bernhardt's eschewal of Hamlet's traditional hat and plume. While in the stage production Bernhardt was still costumed in a hat and a blonde Fechterian wig, it is the continued absence of the black plume that warrants attention. As Taranow, again describing the stage production, explains:

The most significant aspect of the hat was that it lacked, intentionally, that signature of Hamletism which was inextricably associated with the graveyard scene: the black plume. Sarah Bernhardt's entire production can be regarded as a repudiation of the hamletic Prince of Delacroix, Manet, Baudelaire, Laforgue, Mallarmé, and Mounet-Sully, the absence of the black plume represented a literary and theatrical statement. The unadorned hat announced boldly that this Hamlet was liberated from the delicacy, pallor, pessimism, and irresolution which characterized the young Prince of Hamletism.[26]

Here it can be suggested that the absence of the plumed hat in the film represents a negation of the romantic Hamlet's possible presence. In other words, Bernhardt's Hamlet is unable even to carry the plume: his turn from tradition is resolute, final.

This liberation of Hamlet from his traditional characterization as an irresolute, melancholy prince saw the physicalization of that which was contained in the Schwob-Morand text: Bernhardt's performance was translative, it challenged what had been traditionally presented on the stage, and its difference was ascribed national characteristics. For some, this represented a change for the better. Clement Scott, drama critic for the *Daily Telegraph,* would therefore describe Bernhardt's Hamlet as one of the "best" (with the Briton, Charles Fletcher) since he displayed "that dominant note of comedy, that rare vein of humour, that eccentric capriciousness which are in the very veins of Hamlet." Scott continued: "I begin to think, on the whole, that the French temperament is better for the play of Hamlet as acted by an audience than the philosophical German, the passionate Italian, the alert American, or the phlegmatic Englishman."[27] The French *Annales du Théâtre* would similarly speak of Bernhardt's performance in terms of a "tour de force."[28] In England, however, Bernhardt's Hamlet would be regarded as "little less than an invasion of national property," a "gain for the French stage—not English," and it was suggested that "the ardent, ambitious, and marvellous artist may be congratulated on her energy and her pluck, and upon the financial result of an experiment in trading upon English sheepishness and ignorance of and contempt for art."[29] John Hansen would contextualize:

As Paris differs from London so does Madame Bernhardt's Hamlet differ from Shakespeare's as it is understood by the English mind . . . The chief point of attack in Madam Bernhardt's performance, judged by British standards, is a lack of proper philosophical melancholy, the critic forgetting that whereas the northman would say "To be or not to be" with tears in his voice, the southman utters the same sentiment with the same wondering heartache, but with a smile on his lips. Few outside France understand the French smile or French philosophy, and certainly one could hardly expect a Londoner to comprehend a Hamlet brooding over the why and wherefore of creation unless he punctuated his reflections with lugubrious tears and sighs. Therefore, the British critics while admitting Bernhardt's poetic, forceful, magnetic impersonation accuse her of frivolity in her conception of the part, of creating "a pleasant, humorous, very gay prince, who in happier circumstances would have been the life and soul of the court," to quote one high dramatic authority present at that important first night in London.[30]

Like Schwob and Morand before her, Bernhardt would find it necessary to defend and rationalize the changes she introduced to the production. In a letter to the editor of the *Daily Telegraph* on June 16, 1899, she would respond

I am reproached for being too lively . . . I know that Hamlet is a scholar . . . I am reproached for not being stunned and frightened enough when I see the ghost; but Hamlet went expressly to see the ghost, he went looking for it . . . I am reproached for not being courteous enough to Polonius; but Shakespeare makes Hamlet say all sorts of stupidities to Polonius . . . I am reproached for getting too close to the king in the chapel scene; but if Hamlet wishes to kill the king, it would be necessary for him to get close to him.[31]

Anglo Saxon critics, castigating Bernhardt for her lack of restraint, tied this to her "southern origins." They also suggested that Bernhardt, as the star performer, was unable to relay properly the subtlety of Hamlet's character. Referring to the attention Bernhardt drew upon herself as Hamlet,

Hansen would note that "Ophelia flits in and out of Hamlet's life a pathetic shadow—no more; in fact all the other people are reduced to subsidiary themes woven about the grand motive of a star part."[32] Somewhat more vitriolically, the *Atheneum* would comment, "it is a French euphemism, which we have to a certain extent localized, to speak of an actor as 'creating' a role. A juster or apter term would be manufacturing."[33] As would be done by those critics who later dismissed *Queen Elizabeth* as "filmed theatre," Bernhardt's performative excess here is cast as a foreign (and female) intrusion into the bounds of an established art form. Implicit in the criticism of this excess is the idea that the actress, in her encroaching age and narcissistic infirmity, was unable to appreciate what was appropriate to the stage and screen. That this excess was an interpretative tool used by Bernhardt to render dramatic character and to justify narrative development is therefore overlooked. That Bernhardt (as the producer, principal director, and performer of Hamlet) was also representative of a nascent twentieth-century feminism that would go on to claim the right to self-representation and the right to interpret things "differently" is similarly overlooked. Hence, just as Bernhardt has been largely excluded from film history, so too has performative excess been denied its productive meanings.

Bernhardt's decision to stage and film a play, which, evidently, boasted a long and productive history, indicates the extent to which she was prepared to take on the role of female antagonist. Even her choice of theatrical role (she chose, for instance, to perform Hamlet and not Ophelia) demonstrates Bernhardt's awareness that she was at once producer, director, and actor, and so very much involved in the interpretation and presentation of a spectacle. As Silvia Bigliazzi explains, "Hamlet is both actor and director, he is the first stage presence with an acute awareness of what it means to be staged."[34] This awareness was articulated in the scene Bernhardt chose to record on film. Hamlet's fight with Laertes is, after all, a staged and performed fight, one that differs from Shakespeare's other duels—Edgar and Edmund in *King Lear,* Roderigo and Cassio in *Othello,* and Macduff and Macbeth in *Macbeth.* The bout is therefore introduced in the following manner: "His Majesty . . . sends to know *if your pleasure hold to play* with Laertes"; "the queen desires you to use some gentle courtesy to Laertes before you fall to a *play*"; "I . . . will this brother's wager frankly *play.*"[35] Even when the duel threatens to become "real" (i.e. Hamlet realizes the sword is poisoned), the tragedy is still contained within reference to its spectacular and dramatic nature: "give order that these bodies / *High on a stage be placed to the view,*" "Bear Hamlet like a soldier *to the stage.*"[36] As Lisa Hopkins explains, "One of the primary effects of this insistent emphasis is to link this exhibition of fencing skills less with the anger-driven fights of the other tragedies than with the play-within-the-play of Hamlet itself . . . the staged rather than impromptu quality of the duel underscores a motif already very markedly present in the play: of the fragility of the line separating illusion from reality."[37]

This interconnection between illusion and reality is also implicit in the film's status as excerpt to a longer play and document to a live performance. As a film that features a fencing duel, *Hamlet* similarly oscillates between narrative performance and sporting display. Hopkins, addressing the status of the fencing duel on the stage, notes it is "specifically conceived of as a largely academic exercise of skill, designed to test the combatants and, incidentally, to provide a show of spectacular entertainment suitable for the amusement of the courtly audience (and, by implication, for the real one too)."[38] Since the film does not include any other scenes and the Queen and King (Hamlet's attendant audience) are absent from view, *Hamlet's* duel presumes the engagement of a watching public. This focus on the fencing match, particularly in the context of a female protagonist, indicates the extent to which Bernhardt engaged in (and predicted) contemporary social trends.

By the mid-1880s in Paris, the display of fencing skills was a fashionable undertaking. Or, rather, fencing was fashionable for those "belles mondaines" with the money and leisure to pursue it. An article in *La Vie Parisienne* in 1884 that detailed the sport's burgeoning popularity explained that fencing reduced weight while it also provided a form of emancipation from traditional "feminine" pursuits:

The practice of different sports each day becomes more of a female Parisian custom. Their physique and their self-esteem are equally accounted for; the habit of exercise, especially masculine exercise, helps to put them in "good form," to make them more seductive. It is, at the same time, for them a sort of emancipation.

Of all the sports, the most favoured by our *belle mondaines* after horse riding is fencing. Nothing, in effect, is more efficient in combating this modern sickness of neurosis that they all more or less suffer, for accentuating the elegance of a slender waist, or for reducing the exaggerated opulence of the bodice. And then there is the vest, this provocative vest, a delicious cross-dress which is a thousand times more varied in cut and more becoming that the abominable "tank tops" of the beach, its tightness allowing the pretty woman to effortlessly appear in all her serpentine grace while she fences with agility.[39]

What is interesting to note here is the attention being paid the female figure. Hence, while Bernhardt's thinness had earlier prompted caustic comment (an 1880 publication was titled, for example, *"Too Thin"; or Skeleton Sara*[40]), by 1900 it was harbinger to a movement that would see increased attention paid to the smallness and suppleness of the female body. That Bernhardt would wear a mid-thigh length tunic in the film—and Pierre Magnier, as Laertes, a knee-length coat—is illustrative of this shift in the conception of the female figure. At a time when female costumes were, however, still often ankle-length, the exposure of Bernhardt's legs was hardly innocent. As Taranow remarks: "Bernhardt's costume appears to have remained the same throughout the play, with the length of her tunic extending only to mid-thigh so that her figure would seem elongated by the exposure of her legs."[41]

What is also interesting is that the article in *La Vie Parisienne* finds "serpentine grace" desirable and *travesti* dress "delicious." Again, this indicates changes in the approach to the female form. It also positions the actress as an anticipator of female trends. Explaining that fencing was first introduced via the actress on the stage, the actress becomes representative of a fashionable avant-garde.[42] That Bernhardt was clearly part of this avant-garde—she was famous for her thinness, posed on the stage and in photographs with her body twisted into the tendrillic curves of the art nouveau, and had long fenced on the stage—is often overlooked. Particularly in film history, where she is characterized as a theatrical anachronism, Bernhardt's challenge to the nineteenth century remains absent from discussion.

By the turn of the century (and thus in conjunction with *Hamlet's* appearance), popular women's presses would be detailing the availability of fencing classes in Paris. Fencing was also available, by this point, to working-class women. This fact parallels the idea that the staging of Hamlet's duel and subsequent death was "indigenous fare." The popular French journal *Femina* discussed the joining of fencing classes with the dance and music classes offered at "Mimi Pinson's School" in Paris:

Everyone now knows the Charity of Mimi Pinson. Founded in 1900 thanks to the initiative and tenacity of M. Gustave Charpentier, the famous composer of music, this initially proposed to offer theater seats to the female workers of

Paris thanks to some particular donations and to the graciousness of the theater directors. But since this, the aim has been enlarged, and M. Charpentier has founded for the young female workers of our great Paris popular classes in music and dance to which, two months ago, was added fencing lessons. . . . He had first dreamt of gymnastics, but the delicate body of the female does not generally accommodate its brusque and uncoordinated movements well. These violent and strong exercises tend not only to deform women's slender proportions, but also provoke all sorts of physical disorders, dizziness, flutters of the heart, etc.[43]

This practice of female fencing—and its accompanying rhetoric—was not unique to Paris. As an article in *Harper's Bazaar* would explain:

Time was when this most graceful and healthful of exercises was confined entirely to the sterner sex. Now all this has changed. The fashionable woman of today is quite as expert with foils as is her brother or husband . . . A man is usually satisfied to do one thing well: not so a woman. She must have various accomplishments. Its main value is in charm of person and grace of motion . . . Fencing gives a natural poise and grace to the body . . . It makes the body supple and sinuous . . . So important is good judgment that fencing by experts has often been claimed to be more the work of the head than of the hands.[44]

While stressing the body's sinuous charm, the notion that fencing is as much an activity of the mind as it is of the body provides echo to Bernhardt's characterization of Hamlet as an active yet reflective youth.

Crossing the boundaries between the play and female "play" would not, however, be received favorably in the press. In criticism of Bernhardt's apparent inability to sustain her performance of masculinity on the stage, the *North American Review* would state: "There is not a moment in the drama when the spectator is not fully and calmly conscious that the hero is a woman masquerading, or is jarred into sharp realization of the fact by her doing something that is very like a man. It is a case where every approach to success is merely another insistence on failure."[45] Almost but not quite: Max Beerbohm—the drama critic of the *Saturday Review*—would accordingly entitle his review of the play "Hamlet: Princess of Denmark," while *The Atheneum* would explain that "It is a full-blown truism to say that where everything is necessarily wrong nothing can possibly be right. Madame Bernhardt's Hamlet has not even the negative advantage of showing us what to avoid . . . The suggestion of *Punch*-offered, of course, as badinage—that Sir Henry Irving shall play Ophelia to the new Hamlet, seems, beside the present experiment, not wholly outrageous."[46]

What such reviews clearly ignore is the idea that Bernhardt might have actually sought to keep her gender visible to the watching public. What they also elide is the fact that, in emphasizing the performativity of gender, Bernhardt was also associating herself with a long and productive history of the theatrical stage. From the ancient Greek theater and the public theater of the English Renaissance through to the roles essayed by such women as Charlotte Cushman in the mid-nineteenth century, cross-dressing was an integral part of the theatrical stage. The very visibility of this custom—the fact that gender, as a social and cultural norm, was unsettled in so public and open a manner—highlights the challenge that the theater brought to its audience. Although entertaining and providing popular relief from quotidian life, the theater also undercut and disrupted the categories that structured normative reality. The theater's status as an art form that dealt with the problem of representation and reenactment was therefore joined to a critique of the constructed and artificial nature of reality. Bernhardt's "failed" *Hamlet,* introduced by a loud and self-publicizing Tosca, works to unsettle the natural transparency of social and cultural categories.

The criticisms of Bernhardt's performance of masculinity were carried into her performance of youth. John Hansen reviewed *Hamlet* in *The National Magazine* in 1899:

Physically Bernhardt's unusual lines of figure proved of assistance in rendering her impersonation sexless if not altogether masculine. Even now, with a contour rounded out considerably since the days when the supreme dramatic genius of our times was better known to the American public, Bernhardt, costumed in the traditional sables of the Dane, does not belie the part by strong suggestion of femininity except facially; there she comes up against a stumbling block—that elderly unique face, haunting at any time, becomes a nightmare, a specter in opposition to her faithful simulation of a youth's body.[47]

The insistence with which criticism was levied at Bernhardt's Hamlet was met by her own ongoing explanations of why and how she essayed the role. In an article published in *Harper's Bazaar* titled "Men's Roles as Played by Women," Bernhardt would contend that male roles were more difficult to perform than female roles and that it was this challenge which prompted her to perform *l'Aiglon* and *Hamlet.* Going on to argue that performativity is not a specifically female prerogative, she reminded her public of the constructed nature of both genders:

Much of the success of the usual woman's role lies in the feminine charm and magnetism with which the actress is capable of investing the part. It is contended that in assuming a man's role she is obliged to part with her strongest weapons, and that therefore more skill is required to achieve success. This is only partially true. Skill is undoubtedly demanded, but it is the skill which can assume and depict the masculine charm and magnetism which exists just as surely as does the feminine. It is not sufficient to look the man, to move like a man, and to speak like a man. The actress must think and feel like a man, to receive impressions as a man, and to exert that innate something which, for want of a better word, we call magnetism, just as a man unconsciously exerts it.[48]

As Bernhardt's demand for intellectual challenge makes clear, her performance of Hamlet levied a broad critique at the roles that were available for women to play on the stage. In stating "Most women's parts are mere play. The characters are required to look pretty, to move gracefully, and to portray emotions natural to the average woman," Bernhardt makes clear the changes and challenges she was introducing to the stage.[49] That these changes and challenges would, after the turn of the century, be incorporated into the demands of an emergent feminism, reveals the importance a performer such as Bernhardt played in the development and formation of twentieth-century feminist thought. As Susan A. Glenn explains,

As a figure of transition between traditional and modern values, Bernhardt constitutes . . . a perfect starting point for understanding how the theatre helped Americans explore and redefine femininity in the years between 1880 and 1910. At a time when actresses and female performers exhibited the unorthodox and increasingly fashionable qualities that would come to be associated with women's revolt against tradition, Bernhardt proved to be a highly elastic symbol of female irreverence. Because of that, she became a touchstone for a number of ambitious American women in as well as outside the theatre: from female comics in vaudeville to activists in the woman suffrage movement.[50]

While Glenn restricts her comments to the stage and an American public, it is evident that the effects of Bernhardt's transgressions were felt across the arts and before a broad and international audience. What needs to be emphasized, therefore, is that Bernhardt's *Hamlet* was part of the Exposition of 1900. An international event that suggested some of the possible futures for film, it was also a forum that enabled and encouraged experimentation. Film, yet to make a claim to its uniqueness and separation from other media and art forms, was still very much a new technology, which incorporated and projected different ways of looking at and thinking about the world. The legitimate theater, directly involved in the marketing and production of film, was still to be separated out as an art form whose established traditions retarded or at least suspended the "natural" development of the medium. The phonograph, only just beginning to be sold for use as a leisure pursuit, was not yet part of the history of private entertainment. In other words, Bernhardt's vision of a challenging and spectacularly conceived cinema had not yet been marginalized as a theatrical and mistaken intrusion into the development of film history. My task as a feminist film historian is not only, therefore, to recover and recuperate Bernhardt's contribution to film history: it is to ask whether we are still able to locate and appreciate the liberties that the cinema once offered.

Notes

1. Emmanuelle Toulet, "Cinema at the Universal Exposition, Paris, 1900," trans. Tom Gunning, *Persistence of Vision* 9 (1991): 10.

2. Ibid., 26.

3. Ibid., 33.

4. Georges Sadoul, *Histoire General du cinéma: Les Pionniers du cinéma, 1897–1909* (Paris: Denoël, 1948), 104.

5. David Robinson, *Music of the Shadows: The Use of Musical Accompaniment with Silent Films* (Pordenone: Le Giornate del Cinema Muto, 1990); Toulet, "Cinema at the Universal Exposition," 24.

6. Sadoul, *Histoire General,* 101.

7. *Arcade Auction Catalogue of Old Master and 19th Century European Painting, Drawing and Sculpture,* London, July 20, 1995. I would like to thank Susan Dalton for being so helpful during my research at the National Portrait Gallery, London.

8. Gerda Taranow, *Sarah Bernhardt: The Art within the Legend* (New Jersey: Princeton University Press, 1972), 128.

9. See, for example, the steel engraving of Bernhardt as Tosca—the cane "centering" her body and gesture—by Florian (after a picture by Jan Van Beers) reproduced in *Revue Illustré,* National Portrait Gallery, n.d., Negative number 31594.

10. Translation my own. "La soirée théâtrale, La Tosca," *Le Figaro,* November 25, 1887, Bibliothèque national, Rondel collection, RT 5884 (2), n.p.

11. Gerda Taranow, *The Bernhardt Hamlet: Culture and Context* (New York: Peter Lang, 1996), 17. "Beginning with Lorenzaccio, Bernhardt took principal or *premier,*

roles written for actors and transformed them into *travestis.* The first role in her *Hamlet* cycle, *Lorenzaccio,* represented a new acting category which she initiated: the *premier travesti rôle.*"

12. Ibid., xvii–xviii.

13. Ibid., 4–5.

14. On Schwob's introduction and the staging and history of *Hamlet* as discussed in this paragraph, see Romy Heylen, *Translation, Poetics, and the Stage: Six French Hamlets* (London: Routledge, 1993), 63, 54, 64. The quote with which the paragraph ends is from pages 75–76.

15. On ticket sales, see Taranow, *Bernhardt Hamlet,* 105–6.

16. "Madame Bernhardt's Hamlet," *London Times,* July 13, 1899, 12.

17. Ibid., 12.

18. John Hansen, "Sarah Bernhardt as Hamlet," *The National Magazine,* August 1899, 470.

19. Taranow, *Bernhardt Hamlet,* 36.

20. "Madame Bernhardt's Hamlet."

21. Taranow, *Bernhardt Hamlet,* 156.

22. Ibid., 48.

23. See Taranow's comment in relation to this: "It is a matter of no small significance that Bernhardt's Hamlet was the first Prince of Denmark to die standing. Writing of the Hamlet tradition and referring to the production in which he was directed by Guthrie McClintic, John Gielgud mentions that McClintic 'invented' for him the device of a standing death . . . John Gielgud's success with the use of the standing death is now well-known. What is not known is that the innovation actually took place thirty seven years prior to the performance of the great English actor." *Bernhardt Hamlet,* 186.

24. Ibid., 70.

25. See Bernhardt's *Ma Double Vie: Mémoires de Sarah Bernhardt* (trans.) (London: Arrow Books, 1984), 139–140, in which she explains, for example, how her performances at the Odeon theater in the early 1870s would upset the older members of the audience habituated to a more traditional and classical style of performance.

26. Taranow, *Bernhardt Hamlet,* 175.

27. Clement Scott, *Some Notable Hamlets of the Present Time* [1900] (New York: Benjamin Blom, 1969), 45–46, 51.

28. Edmond Stoullig, *Les Annales du théâtre et de la musique* (Paris: Librairie Paul Ollendorff, 1899) 169–70.

29. The comment about the production being "little less than an invasion" appears in Taranow, *Bernhardt Hamlet* (109), although she does not specify her source. The comments on the production being a gain for the French rather than the English stage, and about the "ignorance" of the English audience are from "The Week: Adelphi Performance of Madame Bernhardt's Hamlet, in innumerable Acts," *The Atheneum* 3738, June 17, 1899, 764.

30. Hansen, "Sarah Bernhardt as Hamlet," 469.

31. The criticism about Bernhardt's Hamlet and the ghost went as follows: "He

did not take the apparition for a ghost who might fade into formless shadow at any moment. He advertised to us his entire confidence that, when he chose to turn around again, the spectre king would be obligingly waiting there until he could secure his son's attention . . . the ghostliness of the scene had somehow evaporated." (Elizabeth Robins, "On Seeing Madame Bernhardt's Hamlet," *North American Review,* December 1900, 911. Bernhardt's letter appeared in the *Daily Telegraph,* June 16, 1899, 10.

32. Hansen, "Sarah Bernhardt as Hamlet," 470.

33. "The Week," 667.

34. Silvia Bigliazzi, *"Hamlet* on Screen and the Crystal Image," *Hamlet Studies: An International Journal of Research* 18 (Summer/Winter 1996): 107.

35. *Hamlet,* ed. Harold Jenkins (London: Methuen, 1982), 5.2.194–95, 5.2.203, 5.2.249. (References are to act, scene, and line.)

36. Ibid., 5.2.383, 5.2.401. (Emphasis added.)

37. Lisa Hopkins, "Playing at Bouts: Hamlet and the Use of the Culminating Duel," *Hamlet Studies: An International Journal of Research* 18 (Summer/Winter 1996): 131–32.

38. Ibid., 130.

39. Emile Blavet, "Les Femmes et l'escrime," *La Vie Parisienne: La Vie et le théâtre* 316 (January 14, 1884): 31–32. Translation my own.

40. Isaac George Reed, *"Too Thin;" or Skeleton Sara* (New York: Evans & Kelly, 1880).

41. Taranow, *Bernhardt Hamlet,* 177. See also page 83: "Masculine costume . . . exposed the actresses' legs, an effect not invariably emphasized, but one that was by no means ignored at a time when women's costumes were ankle-length."

42. Blavet, "Les Femmes et l'escrime," 33–34.

43. Max Rivière, "Mimi Pinson Escrimeuse," *Femina* 56 (May 15, 1903): 538–39. Translation my own.

44. "Fencing as an Exercise for Women," *Harper's Bazaar,* December 1899, 16.

45. Robins, "On Seeing Madame Bernhardt's Hamlet," 908.

46. The *Saturday Review* quotation is cited in Marjorie Garber, *Vested Interests: Cross-Dressing and Cultural Anxiety* (New York: Routledge, 1992), 40. The comments of the *Atheneum* appear in "The Week," 764.

47. Hansen, "Sarah Bernhardt as Hamlet," 469.

48. Sarah Bernhardt, "Men's Roles as Played by Women," *Harper's Bazaar,* December 15, 1900, 2113–15. The quote is from page 2114.

49. Ibid., 2114.

50. Susan A. Glenn, *Female Spectacle: The Theatrical Roots of Modern Feminism* (Cambridge: Harvard University Press, 2000), 11. I would like to thank Richard Abel for bringing this book to my attention.

Vision and Visibility

Women Filmmakers, Contemporary Authorship, and Feminist Film Studies

In her exploration of two Kathryn Bigelow films, *Near Dark* (1987) and *Blue Steel* (1990), Anna Powell observes in passing that auteurism "has a particular resonance within feminism."[1] While I agree absolutely that women filmmakers matter for a feminist cultural politics, it can be difficult to establish precisely why, not least since authorship is often regarded as a methodology that film studies has in many ways moved beyond. At worst reductive, at best naïve, auteurism privileges the authored text over the complexities of context. At the same time, the work of feminist film historians in documenting the contribution of women to the film industry represents not only an important attempt to write women's history but a rejection of the claims made by, or more typically on behalf of, one person—the male director—to have priority over the text. Although women have only recently been working as directors in the U.S. film industry in any numbers, writers and researchers, including Lizzie Francke, Gwendolyn Audrey Foster, and Ally Acker, have worked to foreground the contribution that women have made to the cinema across a range of other roles.[2]

And yet the figure of the filmmaker (typically, but not exclusively, the director) has rarely been so central to popular film culture as it is today.[3] Moreover, at the start of the twenty-first century, women are now working in the American film industry as directors, producers, and even cinematographers, as well as in the more established female roles of screenwriter and performer, on an unprecedented scale. Even so, the position of women filmmakers is typically both marginal and precarious. Clearly, this stems in part from the structure and character of the film industry itself. I'd also like to suggest here that, given the significance of the figure of the filmmaker within contemporary film culture, there is a crucial question of the *visibility* of women filmmakers to be addressed.

My argument focuses on contemporary filmmakers and film culture, considering the particular issues posed for women filmmakers within an era in which the visibility of the filmmaker, whether as personality or as auteur, is regularly foregrounded. The promotion of celebrity filmmakers is hardly new: in 1975 Victor Perkins talked in the British journal *Movie* of "the evasions and the image-mongering of the director, the whole projection business."[4] Of course there are very different issues at stake for men and women in this business. And although these differences might seem superficial rather than substantive, it is my contention that they are nonetheless quite significant.

In short, I wish to make a case here for a sustained consideration of female filmmakers and their work. I acknowledge the irony of a situation in which the achievement of some measure of visibility for women directors dovetails so neatly with the falling out of favor of authorship criticism.[5] And yet I would still insist that the female filmmaker remains a potent figure whose iconic presence has to do with the very possibility of a distinct women's cinema. She is significant in terms of her visibility within a field that remains male dominated. Of course this point could equally be made in relation to other fields of professional practice, whether within the media more broadly or outside it in areas such as politics, law, medicine, and business. The filmmaker is only a special case in this context to the extent that she is a public figure of a quite particular type, both creative and commercial. That is to say, the emergence and success or failure of women filmmakers is also a question of women who visibly, publicly appropriate titles perceived as male.

My concern here is less with authorship as a methodology or critical practice than with authorship as a discourse, a discourse within which women filmmakers have been marginalized. I discuss four American women filmmakers who have entered this discourse, taking up distinct positions within it: directors Allison Anders and Kathryn Bigelow, and cinematographers Ellen Kuras and Maryse Alberti.[6] These four filmmakers operate within and across the sectors (which are in any case difficult to truly separate) of U.S. mainstream and independent production. Bigelow and Anders are distinct in almost every way imaginable: sector, budget, visual scope, genre, and theme, not to mention background and persona. Promotional images of these filmmakers demonstrate their distinct articulation of the (still atypical) agency of women filmmakers with respect to discourses of femininity and creativity (compare images of Alberti and Kuras at work with the more obviously posed shots of Anders and Bigelow in circulation through the 1990s and since).[7]

As noted, authorship approaches tend to focus on the director, potentially erasing the part played by other contributors. It is also the case that the sort of visibility associated with the director is rather different from that developed in relation to the cinematographer, although a rhetoric of vision is central to both. The image of the director as industry celebrity is distributed fairly widely and is increasingly tied into the marketing of individual films. By contrast, the cinematographer is celebrated in rather different terms. She is much more likely to be represented within the trade press, for instance. In thinking about the careers, profiles, and different sorts of visibility at stake for and attained by these women, the "whole projection business" is very much at issue.

Sometimes visibility is a quite literal issue. How often and in what kinds of places do we see images of women filmmakers/women making films? What sort of profile do women filmmakers have within entertainment journalism, and in particular within the middle-market magazines that cater to the interested cinema-going general public? One way to access this issue is to look at the front cover of such magazines. The long-established British film magazine *Sight and Sound* relaunched in 1991 with an image of Jodie Foster in *The Silence of the Lambs*. The cover style that has subsequently evolved typically features a performer or (less frequently) a filmmaker. In the ten years that followed its relaunch, only one female filmmaker appeared on the cover of *Sight and Sound:* Jodie Foster, with the accompanying title "Why Jodie Foster Matters" (with a B. Ruby Rich essay on the director/actress).[8] The stylish black-and-white cover portrait features Foster looking directly out at the reader, head angled to emphasize the contours of face and neck, an image that echoes both the glamorous portraits of Hollywood's female stars through the years and the more cerebral associations of director portraits (the filmmaker caught in an intense or thoughtful pose). In the same ten-year period the U.S. movie magazine *Film Comment* also featured only one female filmmaker on its cover. Once again this was Foster, here promoting her directorial debut, *Little Man Tate* (a film in which she also starred and that was widely read as implicitly autobiographical).[9] Without in any way undermining her achievements, we can note that Foster is much better known as a performer—even a movie star—than as a director. Indeed, her developing reputation as a serious adult performer in this period gives her precisely the sort of visibility, the *profile,* that many other women filmmakers seemed to lack.

That the October 1999 issue of *Sight and Sound* illustrated its "Women Directors Special" with a head shot of Kate Winslet in Jane Campion's *Holy Smoke* suggests perhaps that visualizing the woman director remained a problem for what we can term mainstream, middle-market film criticism.[10] Yet how to talk about the work of women filmmakers, while avoiding unthinking celebration, or assuming that the issue of gender is simply irrelevant? Judith Mayne makes clear that authorship means something different when applied to the woman filmmaker; in the process she casts light on the extent to which the auteur was always understood as male. Thus, she suggests, "it can be argued that the privileging of female authorship risks appropriating, for women, an extremely patriarchal notion of cinematic creation."[11] Put simply, it's difficult to inscribe women in terms of the language and perspective of either traditional auteurism or a contemporary cinema culture, which has been so forcibly shaped by its legacy.

Authorship and Contemporary Film Culture

Auteurism has always been about cultural capital, staking a claim for cinema's status as art. Though the "politique des auteurs" was in part concerned with the achievements of those working within an often despised commercial (Hollywood) cinema, there was nonetheless, as Dudley Andrew emphasizes, an "aura of elitism" in evidence. For Andrew this was bound up with festivals "where auteurs were annually inducted and honored as individuals with strong (invariably masculine) personalities producing art capable of transcending its conditions of production and reception."[12] To some extent an insistence on transcendence is part of film studies discourse much more generally.[13] Popular culture still becomes critically acceptable largely to the extent that it can be framed as either aesthetically challenging, politically transgressive, or both. Within this mode women filmmakers such as Penny Marshall or Nancy Myers are found wanting in their ability to challenge or innovate.

The marketing of directors in commercial cinema along the lines established within art cinema is a marked feature of the New Hollywood.[14] While the figure of the director as either "auteur" or potentially marketable commodity has penetrated commercial cinema culture, it is, I would argue, much more clearly central to an independent distribution and exhibition circuit. This circuit is in turn linked to festivals and the prizes they bestow, sites of exhibition and debate that function as an important showcase for new work by an independent filmmaker like Allison Anders.[15]

From a feminist perspective, critical constructions of the New Hollywood are not so new. We are also familiar with the reciprocal patterns of influence between the French *Nouvelle Vague* and the Hollywood "renaissance" of the 1970s, though the names cited rarely include Agnes Varda. In Geoff Andrew's *Stranger than Paradise: Maverick Filmmakers in Recent American Cinema,* an author-led study of contemporary American independent cinema, various women are name-checked but none has a sole chapter devoted to her work. Why might this be the case? For a start, women find it tougher to make films—and, crucially, to make more than one film—than men. This is the case in the commercial cinema, where a track record of achievement matters a great deal, and in the seemingly relentlessly author-led independent sector. As Andrew puts it, "All too often either women directors have managed to make just one feature, or their follow-ups have been promoted so poorly that they remain best known for one film only."[16] Interviewed by Rose Troche while promoting her 1996 independent hit *I Shot Andy Warhol,* director Mary Harron talked of the movie she was developing at the time around Bettie Page. However, aside from work on the hard-hitting television series *Oz* the following year, Harron's next completed project as director turned out to be *American Psycho* (2000).[17] Of course, many projects are developed and do not make it to the screen. However, for women filmmakers this issue seems particularly acute.

While continuity of work is clearly an issue for women filmmakers, establishing a significant number of feature films is no longer a prerequisite to visibility of the kind associated with authorship criticism. Filmmakers such as Steven Soderbergh, Richard Linklater, Neil LaBute, Kevin Smith, or even David Fincher first attracted critical and commercial interest on the basis of relatively few features or even a sole success. Soderbergh in particular might function as testament to the truism that men have repeated opportunities to recover from the commercial (and even critical) failures that can seriously hamper a woman's career.[18] Though I don't agree with Geoff Andrew's assessment of Allison Anders's work—he sees the follow-ups to her 1992 *Gas Food Lodging* as either "disappointing" or "likeable but minor"—authorship criticism is, after all, largely a matter of taste. (This was one obvious reason for its decline during the scientistic structuralism of the 1970s.) To that extent, its judgments can be refuted fairly easily. Yet Andrew is right to identify promotion and marketing as issues. The achievement of the status associated with interviews, awards, and, crucially, further opportunities to make films is not unconnected with the wider questions of visibility with which I am concerned here. Both the awards they have received and their association with prestigious, award-winning projects has surely assisted both Kuras and Alberti to progress in a traditionally male field of endeavor. Moreover, it is apparent that criticism—including feminist criticism—has a role to play in this process.

Picturing the Woman Filmmaker

The work and careers of the directors Kathryn Bigelow and Allison Anders testify in different ways to the significance of these questions of visibility. Each has a relatively small but well-regarded body of films to their credit, although their respective personas and their relative positions within the U.S. film industry are very different. While Bigelow has been associated with sensational cinema through her work in a range of action-oriented genres (thrillers, westerns, horror, science fiction), Anders is associated with what can be very broadly termed the contemporary woman's picture. While her work inhabits a more conventionally "feminine" terrain in which women's lives and relationships are explored, Anders films have not commanded either the budgets or the visibility of Bigelow's work (the two factors are not unrelated, of course). Although she has directed a significant studio picture—the 1996 *Grace of My Heart* (which she also wrote) for Universal, with Martin Scorsese operating as executive producer—Anders began her career, and has largely remained within, independent production. Bigelow too began working outside the parameters of mainstream cinema (her background as a painter regularly features in profiles). Nonetheless, a productive use of genre defines the work of both filmmakers.

Bigelow crystallizes a series of issues to do with the visibility of the female filmmaker that are in turn centered on an idea of the appropriate: what is appropriate for the woman director, and for female celebrities more generally. Both she and her work have been read as inappropriate, with Bigelow occupying a long-standing and—as profiles repeatedly tell us—almost unique position as a woman directing action-oriented pictures. As a 1997 feature put it: "Her decidedly unladylike work has cast her as a maverick, a reputation that perplexes the fortyish director."[19] Overall, this is a celebratory portrait of Bigelow, emphasizing her talent and integrity (the time she takes to develop her own projects, for instance). In this context both the coy reference to the director's age and the comic uneasiness surrounding the invocation of gender conveyed by the anachronistic language (unladylike) seems particularly striking.

Whether in gendered or feminist terms, uncertain or celebratory, critics are often, or so it seems, responding to an inappropriate presence. To some extent Bigelow's comments seem to invite such an interpretation, as in the following thoughts on *Blue Steel:* "it occurred to me that it would take a certain personality to choose to be a cop . . . I mean you have to kind of suppress your femaleness on the job. I mean, obviously, the uniform is highly unflattering. You've got all this equipment. You need to be very, very practical. You can't think emotionally or in any other way than—completely about: you're focused on survival."[20] The suppression of both femaleness and femininity so that one can function in tough situations might well be taken as a simulation—albeit exaggerated—of the woman filmmaker's position. And yet the very visibility of Bigelow's persona, and the form that visibility takes, suggests something rather different. If her films are "unladylike," portraits that parade a sultry if not aggressive "femininity" invariably accompany profiles of the filmmaker. (The 1997 feature cited earlier is no exception, although it opens with Bigelow saying of being photographed: "I hate this . . . I'd rather be right there," i.e., behind the camera). For Christina Lane, such visibility is ultimately ironic since "the very press accounts which function as a recuperation of her femininity also increase her circulation as a star and serve to enhance her depiction as a notable director, possibly even an *auteur*."[21]

Claims to authorship, we might add, are typically enhanced by the idea of a maverick sensibility, by qualities that oppose the individual filmmaker to the supposed banalities of commercial cinema culture. In Bigelow's case this maverick image is never fully detached from an idea of gender rebellion that requires some comment on the part of interviewers and critics. Ultimately, we are led to understand, there remains something attractive but implicitly unfeminine about the whole business. As shown earlier, Andrew sees the strong personality of the auteur as "invariably masculine," a feature exemplified by the following extract from a 1962 *Movie* editorial (an issue devoted to the work of Howard Hawks):

When one talks about the heroes of *Red River,* or *Rio Bravo,* or *Hatari!* one is talking about Hawks himself. The professionalism of his heroes is shared by the director. They get on with the job without any unnecessary nonsense. So does Hawks. He can say what he wants to through actions, because his is a cinema of action. No need, then, to start playing hide-and-seek with the camera, which is there to capture the actions, not to interpret them. Hawks uses his camera simply to do a job, just as his heroes would use a gun or a lasso. . . . In the absence of planned effects in the Hitchcock manner, he communicates very directly through his personality. Finally everything that can be said in presenting Hawks boils down to one simple statement: here is a man.[22]

The strong individual is clearly marked as masculine, emphasizing qualities of simplicity and directness: here is a man indeed. Camera, gun, and lasso are drawn together in a notion of the right tools for the right purpose, each without fussiness or frills. Though Hawks worked across many genres, and notably in comedy, the emphasis here falls on his association with action genres and his status as a man of action. Though profiles of Bigelow do not construct her as a woman of action in the manner of Hawks, her incursion into such genres has been particularly symbolic in gendered terms.

Bigelow shakes up generic and gendered conventions—on this most critics agree (although they may differ as to the ultimate success or worth of her projects). Together with the image of the "woman in a man's world," her use of genre is one of the most frequent starting points for critical discussions of her work. The manipulation of genre provides a way of understanding her work and—ironically perhaps—branding her as a strong personality along conventional auteurist lines, an individual able to impose her interpretation on a commercial, generic system of film production. Bigelow endorses this view, saying: "I know that I'm fascinated by genre. I think that what's interesting is to try and redefine it even on maybe a microscopic level. To utilise it, invert it, subvert it."[23] Yet must this type of strong personality necessarily be imagined as masculine? Interviewed for a 1995 documentary on women filmmakers, Allison Anders contests this view, saying of Bigelow: "*Kathryn* came along and was just like, y'know, this is how I'm going to tell *my* stories. . . . I still think that her stuff is uniquely female but that she totally uses that structure and is able to, yeah, completely kick ass with what's already been set up. And I think that it is really subversive as a result, 'cos there's still a very feminine quality to it."[24] In emphasizing femininity Anders, it should be said, is exceptional in her take on Bigelow's work. Indeed, part of the problem of the inappropriate in relation to Bigelow stems, it seems, from an assumption that women will work best with emotionally led material, a category understood as fundamentally opposed to action-oriented films and genres. Thus Pauline Kael expresses surprise about Bigelow's directorial style: "She's the only woman director I know of who's really gifted at action yet not particularly gifted at character, story or emotions. There's an exuberance in the way she approaches action. It's not the usual approach. Her action is visually a little off-centre, yet it's central to her movies—it's what brings them to life."[25] Here Kael puts into play expectations to do with the areas in which a female director is likely to excel—character, story, and emotions rather than action. While this is of course stereotypical, we are nonetheless dealing with powerful cultural assumptions—a set of expectations that, as Rachel Williams has shown in relation to Mimi Leder, can also be exploited in the marketing of mainstream movies directed by women.[26]

Yet of course, we are not simply dealing here with an expectation that movies directed by women are more likely to operate primarily on an emotional level. It is also a question of the kind of emotional stories women are expected to tell as opposed to those that attract status and critical interest. After all, the telling of elaborate stories of the tortured male psyche; complex rites of passage; male bonding in the context of fear and violence; or melodramas of masculine transformation are rarely regarded as either uncommercial or even unmasculine. While there may be an expectation about the kind of stories women directors might (even should) be interested in, we should not downplay the sheer difficulty of getting stories told from a woman's point of view at all. Anders observes of her experiences at film school: "You watched a lot of people make movies before you. [For women, it] took longer, especially if you have projects that were from a woman's point of view."[27] Maitland McDonagh's comment in a 1994 profile encapsulates the particular kind of visibility Anders had attained at that point: "Penny Marshall, Martha Coolidge and Penelope Spheeris notwithstanding, times haven't changed so much that female directors are unremarkable in Hollywood, and Anders—a lavishly tattooed and pierced high-school-dropout single mother of two who went from white-trash welfare to UCLA film school—would stand out even if they were."[28]

Of course such a strongly visible persona has a downside, as Manohla Dargis comments: "Interviews seem less interested in ideas than body art and the fact that this 37-year-old mother of two has been on welfare." Yet, Dargis continues, in an appeal to the authenticity of the Anders persona: "For her part, Anders doesn't peddle hard times as sensational copy, it's just the stuff of life. This is one director you don't have to scratch too deep to find out what makes her tick."[29] The notion of a personal cinema is of course central not only to models of authorship but also to ideas of women's cultural production. It is interesting in this context to note that *Gas Food Lodging* in particular was understood and to some extent promoted as Anders's story, as very much informed by her life.[30] One report suggests, for instance, that it is "hard to find a dividing line between Allison Anders's life and work."[31] Promotional material for *Gas Food Lodging* plays on this blurring too: "the story of *Gas Food Lodging* cuts deeply with the authenticity of her [Anders's] own past, present and future." Promoting the film, Anders seemed to encourage such a reading as in the following interview extract: "A lot of the film is autobiographical," she explains, "from the single mother environment that I grew up in, the poverty and growing up with sisters. And now I'm a single mother myself, with two teenage daughters, so the set up was very, very close to me and so much like the reality that I grew up and raised my children in."[32]

Authorship criticism is potentially at its most reductive when it is biographical, and critics have been rightly skeptical of any desire to read the personality of the filmmaker from the text. Yet how might we think about both the use of Anders's life-experience in the promotion of *Gas Food Lodging* and the filmmaker's own seeming willingness to engage during interviews with this dimension of her work? The incorporation of biography, whether in criticism or promotion, involves the production of a version of events in which patterns of influence, early interests, and so on acquire a new significance. For women filmmakers—by virtue of their relative rarity—such an interest can often end up centering on the question of how they managed to get to the position they are in at all. Predictably, there seems to be a particular interest in the part played by men in their careers. Media commentary, for example, associates both Bigelow and Anders with male filmmakers in potentially problematic ways. Lane discusses Bigelow's collaboration with James Cameron and the need to acknowledge the importance of such relationships while avoiding assumptions of gendered mentoring.[33] Anders also gets linked to male friends professionally—to Tarantino around the promotion of the collaborative *Four Rooms,* and to Kurt Voss, with whom she codirected both her first Cylena feature, *Border Town* and the more recent *Sugar Town* (Voss also cowrote 2001's *Things behind the Sun.*)[34] While a *Daily Telegraph* profile of Anders informs us that she "has no need to trade on links with Tarantino," it nonetheless opens with reference to their relationship, the link clearly worth a mention at a time when the filmmaker was a hot property.[35] By contrast, although the cinematographers Ellen Kuras and Maryse Alberti have developed important relationships with male directors (Spike Lee, Todd Haynes), the language used to describe their collaborations is largely free from any suggestion that the female filmmaker is in some way indebted to the male.[36]

Ironically some critics are uncomfortable with Anders's work because her fondness for tales of romantic love is read as naïve ("an almost atavistic interest in the opposite sex," says Dargis of *Gas Food Lodging*),[37] while her use of her own experience has been read as narcissistic. For Fregoso indeed it works to marginalize and trivialize her ostensible subject: "*Mi Vida Loca* is as much about Anders as it is about Chicana gangs. She's a filmmaker who lets her own life experiences guide her narrative choices."[38] However, in a mid-1990s *Sight and Sound* profile, B. Ruby Rich celebrates Anders's unconventional persona:

She's an anomaly among today's independent US film-makers; a mature woman, not a twentysomething prodigy. In a time of aerobicised bodies, she eats as she pleases. In the heyday of Armani chic, she dresses how she likes and happily shows off her tattoos and her children. She's a single mother in a Hollywood obsessed with photo-op matrimony. She's a feminist eternally on the look-out for a man, who complains she's not successful because she still can't get laid. No less an authority than Matt Dillon once told her she was "kind of boy crazy." In the heyday of victimhood, she believes in neither blame nor regret. She lives in Los Angeles not New York but she behaves like an East Coaster. She writes her own scripts and cultivates her own tastes.[39]

For Rich, Anders is an important creative figure and a strong individual—a strong woman—whose seeming refusal of the whole projection business allows her to forge a precarious position within contemporary film culture. In terms of my concern here with authorship and the visibility of the woman filmmaker, Anders's persona suggests a different strategy by which women might manipulate the exclusionary language of authorship.

There is no doubt that the numbers of women directing features in the United States has increased significantly over the last thirty years. The New Hollywood has also seen significant change for other women in the industry. In a *Film and Video* cover feature celebrating the work of women cinematographers, David Heuring links the growing numbers of such women to the changes in the industry that saw the development of new routes into key roles, enabling those in the business to potentially bypass the long-established system of apprenticeship within a studio system: "More cinematographers started coming out of film schools, and many began careers shooting documentaries and low-budget features."[40] In turn, Heuring links this shift to the entrance of women into the field, reporting that between 1986 and 1996, numbers of camerawomen in the union had gone from 56 to 424, "including operators, still photographers, assistants, loaders and operators."[41] In a 1995 profile of Ellen Kuras, Cylena Simonds also discusses the significance of independent production, noting: "Women are becoming increasingly visible in key below-the-line positions in independent film. Cinematography, once a strictly male club, now has a female member who is gaining a remarkably high profile."[42] Similarly, an *American Cinematographer* editorial tied to the cover feature on *Velvet Goldmine* underlined the wider professional significance of Maryse Alberti's achievements: "Alberti has demonstrated that women clearly can hold their own behind the camera. Here's hoping that more and more industry executives will recognize the artistic merits of an egalitarian landscape."[43] I'd like to briefly consider here the work and careers of these two cinematographers, neither of whom had formal apprenticeships, instead developing their careers within documentary and what can broadly be termed the independent sector.

The involvement of women in cinematography suggests a different take on the question of visibility and the female filmmaker. In contrast to editing, cinematography—and the role of director of photography (DP) in particular—has long been a traditionally male-dominated aspect of film production.[44] Alexis Krasilovsky opens her collection on camerawomen with the bald statement: "Most film books refer to cameramen."[45] Yet, as her book testifies, a growing number of women have gained new visibility within the field. Clearly, this is a different kind of visibility to that surrounding either the performer or the director. Most profiles of DPs, for example, are to be found in specialist or trade magazines such as *American Cinematographer, Screen International,* or the *Hollywood Reporter* as well as in occasional publications such as the regular *Premiere* special issues celebrating women in film.

Both Kuras and Alberti were associated with the New Queer Cinema of the early 1990s.[46] Coming from a documentary background, Kuras gained widespread recognition (and an Excellence in Cinematography Award at Sundance) for her work on *Swoon* (1992).[47] Subsequently, she has worked with Spike Lee, on the documentaries *Four Little Girls* (1997, for which she was nominated for an Emmy), *Jim Brown All American* (2002), and two features, *Summer of Sam* (1999) and *Bamboozled* (2000). She has also shot a series of high-profile and award-winning films including the feature-length documentary *Unzipped* (1995), *Angela* (1995), and *I Shot Andy Warhol* (1996) as well as studio pictures including *The Mod Squad*

(1999), *Analyze That* (2002), and *Eternal Sunshine of the Spotless Mind* (2004).

Having worked on a range of projects, including Jennie Livingston's documentary *Paris Is Burning* (1990), Alberti collaborated with the director Todd Haynes on three films, *Poison* (1991), the 1993 short *Dottie Gets Spanked,* and *Velvet Goldmine* (1998), winning an Independent Spirit Award for the latter. She has also shot well-regarded independent films, including *Happiness* (1998) and the documentaries *Crumb* (1994) and *When We Were Kings* (1996), with *Crumb* gaining her an Excellence in Cinematography Award at Sundance in 1995, as well as more conventional mainstream features, including the teen movie *Get Over It* (2001).

The visibility that a filmmaker like Kuras has achieved is testament not only to her qualities as a cinematographer but to the opportunities afforded to women by the continued vibrancy of an independent sector of U.S. film production, however skeptically we might treat such a concept. This works in two obvious ways: first and most fundamentally, in providing the opportunity for women to work in DP roles. Second, in the commitment (however superficial that might seem in many instances) to a form of filmmaking frequently characterized by visual experiment, independent production draws attention to the work of the cinematographer.

Swoon was discussed as a Kalin film, it is true, but Christine Vachon's role as producer was also interestingly foregrounded[48]: "Innovative and stylish, Kalin and Vachon's film uses dramatic reconstruction, archive footage, anachronistic décor and 'monochromatic melodrama' to illuminate Nathan Leopold and Richard Loeb's lives."[49] *Gay Times* called it "hauntingly beautiful," while Sheila Johnstone wrote: "The film looks elegant—it's shot in swish black and white and is complex in its concerns."[50] In a piece reviewing the Sundance successes *Swoon* and *Gas Food Lodging* together, we learn: "Tom Kalin's roots in art video are evident throughout this self-conscious and highly stylized feature film debut that deservedly walked away with the cinematography award at this year's Sundance festival"[51] (the award of course went to Kuras). Writing in *Premiere,* J. Hoberman credited Kuras's work on *Swoon:* "The film is stunningly photographed by documentarian Ellen Kuras in rich black and white."[52] The trade journal *Variety* also noted her input: "Other notable aspect is the pic's look, and Ellen Kuras." In 1996 the *Hollywood Reporter* featured Kuras under "emerging talent," dubbing her "one of the most remarkable young cinematographers working today."[53] It is clear that *Swoon's* success brought Kuras a much-enhanced critical visibility: reviews of the documentaries *Romance de Valentia* and *Roy Cohn/Jack Smith* mention her contribution (the former is called "an impressionistic view, stunningly photographed by Ellen Kuras" according to the *New York Times*, while *Variety* notes her "sharp, elegant lensing"[54] on the latter). By the time of the documentary feature *Unzipped* (1995) and the biopic *I Shot Andy Warhol* (1996), Kuras's contribution is regularly discussed in reviews. (Hoberman, for instance, describes her as "brilliant."[55])

In the cover story for the March 2003 issue of the *Independent* (which, as has been mentioned, pictures Maryse Alberti on the set of *The Guys*), Ann Lewinson writes: "It shouldn't be news in 2003 that women are making movies—gorgeous, stunning, provocative movies—and with Ellen Kuras shooting big-budget Hollywood films like *Analyze That,* can anyone still argue that the gaze is male?"[56] Yet Lewinson's analysis suggests that independent film and documentary rather than studio work remain the primary areas in which women have thrived as cinematographers. The issues of difficulty she identifies are not only to do with getting started, in which the greater flexibility of independent production has aided women, but also include long-standing problems involved in managing DP work and family commitments. Here biographical detail functions in a quite different way than it does in the discussion of Anders discussed earlier, in which an emphasis on maternity feeds the picture of a strong, maverick woman. For instance, we are told "Alberti turned down *Boys Don't Cry* to spend more time with her son." Alberti herself comments: "This business is really not conducive to having a family first . . . I'm really going to try very hard to make the right choices to keep on having an interesting career. In order to be a good mother, I need to be a cinematographer—that's part of me; that always gives me life and passion. But my son will always come first."[57] Confirming this very difficulty in an interview focused on *Safe,* Todd Haynes raves about Alberti's work but notes that her pregnancy prevented them from working together on the film.[58]

Conclusion: The Vision Thing

Authorship criticism found romanticized personal vision within the constraints of commercial cinema, doing much to shape contemporary mainstream cinema criticism. Today the constraints are also to do with the appropriation and marketing of the idea of the director as auteur, someone with vision, style, and a story to tell. It is a contradictory process whereby women filmmakers are inscribed within popular discourses of authorship that are romantic, masculine, even elitist. I'm not suggesting that we should accept these terms uncritically and champion a new feminist auteurism. Indeed, one obvious danger of this strategy is that it could result in the neglect of women filmmakers working in roles other than director. However, in a context where, as Christina Lane writes, "the boundaries between independent companies and studios become more indefinite [and] the division between film criticism and film promotion also becomes less certain,"[59] we should be more aware that feminist film criticism itself has an important role to play in this process.

Notes

This research was supported by a grant from the UK's Arts and Humanities Research Board.

1. Anna Powell, "Blood on the Borders—*Near Dark* and *Blue Steel*," *Screen* 35.2 (1994): 136–56, 136.

2. Ally Acker, *Reel Women: Pioneers of the Cinema, 1896 to the Present* (London: Batsford, 1991); Lizzie Francke, *Script Girls: Women Screenwriters in Hollywood* (London: BFI, 1994); Amy L. Unterburger, ed., *Women Filmmakers and Their Films* (Detroit: St. James Press, 1998); Gwendolyn Audrey Foster, *Women Film Directors: An International Bio-Critical Dictionary* (Westport, CT: Greenwood Press, 1995).

3. Some film historians have reconciled this apparent contradiction by arguing for an attention to the postmodern marketing of star filmmakers in the postwar American cinema in a process that amounts to a critical and commercial contextualization of the auteur.

4. Victor Perkins, interview, *Movie* 20 (Spring 1975), reproduced in John Caughie, ed., *Theories of Authorship* (London: BFI, 1981), 59.

5. In her 1990 study of feminism and female authorship, Judith Mayne writes, "Surprisingly little . . . attention has been paid . . . to the function and position of the woman director," *The Woman at the Keyhole: Feminism and Women's Cinema* (Bloomington: Indiana University Press, 1990), 98. Mayne attributes the feminist neglect of female authorship in part to a critical determination to avoid essentialism. Since both essentialism and auteurism suggest a problematic understanding of both cinema and identity (one that is "untheoretical," or perhaps simply employs unfashionable theories), the topic of female authorship continues to be an awkward one. More than a decade later, there has been an increased interest in the work of women filmmakers and in the many complex questions that Mayne poses. See, for instance, Christina Lane, *Feminist Hollywood: From* Born in Flames *to* Point Break (Detroit: Wayne State University Press, 2000). Studies such as Lane's indicate the development of feminist critical work on women filmmakers working within the Hollywood cinema, in part a response to what seems to be a general shift on the part of feminist filmmaking toward narrative, if not necessarily commercial, cinema.

6. Both Anders and Bigelow also have writer and producer credits, the former typically writing her own projects, the latter developing them in collaboration with others.

7. This isn't to imply that we don't see plenty of shots of Anders and Bigelow on set or that there are no set portraits of Kuras and Alberti in circulation.

8. B. Ruby Rich, "Nobody's Handmaid," *Sight and Sound* 1.8 (1991): 7–10. For Rich, Foster "matters" in a variety of ways, not least for how she "came to suggest a different kind of filmmaking" and to "represent a different kind of woman" (7).

9. Robert Horton, "Life Upside Down," *Film Comment* 27.1 (1991), 38–39.

10. In October 2002 Lynne Ramsey appeared on the *Sight and Sound* cover with Mike Leigh and Marc Evans, together representing "The Confident New Face of British Cinema."

11. Mayne, *Woman at the Keyhole,* 94–95.

12. Dudley Andrew, "The Unauthorised Auteur Today," in *Film Theory Goes to the Movies*, ed. Jim Collins, Hilary Radner, and Ava Preacher Collins (London: Routledge, 1993), 77–78.

13. Though Douglas Sirk, declared an auteur in writings of the 1970s, worked with melodrama and the woman's picture, he could be seen to transcend the limits of this generic/feminized material somehow. See Barbara Klinger, *Melodrama and Meaning: History, Culture, and the Films of Douglas Sirk* (Bloomington: Indiana University Press, 1994).

14. To the extent that, as Richard Maltby notes, "by the 1980s, authorship in Hollywood had become a commercially beneficial fiction, indicated by the opening credits of movies that declared themselves to be 'a Taylor Hackford film' or 'a Robert Zemeckis film.'" See Maltby's *Hollywood Cinema: An Introduction* (Malden, MA: Blackwell, 1995), 33.

15. Of course the category of independent film is not uncontroversial, with the term used as often to refer to an edgy tone and challenging subject matter as to the logistics of film production and distribution. On this question, see Chris Holmlund and Justin Wyatt, eds., *Contemporary American Independent Film: From the Margins to the Mainstream* (New York: Routledge, 2005). Christina Lane's essay in that collection, "Just Another Girl Outside the Neo-indie" (193–210), is particularly relevant to my argument.

16. Geoff Andrew, *Stranger than Paradise: Maverick Filmmakers in Recent American Cinema* (London: Prion, 1998), 343.

17. "Rose Troche Yaks with *I Shot Andy Warhol* director Mary Harron" (interview), *Filmmaker* (Spring 1996): 43–45, 57–59. Harron's *The Notorious Bettie Page* (2005) has thus far received only a limited release. Troche has also had a mixed career, with both women working as much in television as film.

18. Barbara K. Quart makes this point in relation to Elaine May and Susan Seidelman, suggesting that remaining within smaller-scale, independent projects might have served the filmmakers better. Quart, *Women Directors: The Emergence of a New Cinema* (New York: Praeger, 1998), 50.

19. Torene Svitil, "Kathryn Bigelow: Director," in "Women in Film," special issue, *Premiere,* (1997), 88.

20. Kathryn Bigelow interview, *Cinefile: Reel Women* (dir. Chris Rodley), Broadcast Channel 4 (UK), February 19, 1995.

21. Christina Lane, "From 'The Loveless to Point Break': Kathryn Bigelow's Trajectory in Action," *Cinema Journal* 37.4 (1998): 62–63.

22. Geoff Andrew, editorial on Hawks, *Movie* 5 (December 1962): 7.

23. Qtd. in Acker, *Reel Women.*

24. Ibid.

25. Pauline Kael, *Modern Review,* December–January 1994/5, 6.

26. See Rachel Williams, "'They call me action woman': The Marketing of Mimi Leder as a New Concept in the High Concept 'Action' Film," in *Action and Adventure Cinema,* ed. Yvonne Tasker (London: Routledge, 2004), 385–97, and an earlier version of the essay, "'It's Like Painting Toys Blue and Pink': Marketing and the Female-Directed Hollywood Film," in *Scope: An Online Journal of Film Studies,* December 2000, http://www.nottingham.ac.uk/film/journal/articles/it's-like-painting.htm.

27. *Cinefile: Reel Women.*

28. Maitland McDonagh, "Sad Girls," *Film Comment* 30.5 (1994): 75–78.

29. Manohla Dargis, "Giving Directions," *Village Voice,* August 18, 1992, 60.

30. Anders's screenplay was actually an adaptation of a novel by Richard Peck.

31. *Time Out,* September 30, 1992, 6.

32. Anders interview by Anwar Brett, "Food for Thought," *What's On in London,* September 30, 1992, 44.

33. Lane, "From 'The Loveless to Point Break,'" 63.

34. Of course the fact that Anders's profile is higher than that of her collaborator Voss renders the association rather different.

35. Alice Cross, "Gas Food Lodging," *Daily Telegraph,* March 25, 1995, 16.

36. Kuras has also worked regularly with the director Rebecca Miller.

37. Alice Cross also regrets that "unfortunately, happiness for these women is defined entirely in terms of men," Review of *Gas Food Lodging, Cineaste* 20.2 (1993): 55.

38. Rosa Linda Fregoso, "Hanging Out with the Homegirls? Allison Anders's *Mi Vida Loca,*" *Cineaste* 21.3 (1995): 36.

39. B. Ruby Rich, "Slugging It Out for Survival," *Sight and Sound* 5.4 (1995): 15. Polemic, impassioned, and insightful, Rich's writing demonstrates the importance and the value of a feminist presence in cinema journalism and criticism. See her *Chick Flicks: Theories and Memories of the Feminist Film Movement* (Durham, NC: Duke University Press, 1998).

40. David Hearing, "Visionary Women," *Film and Video,* February 1996, 44.

41. Ibid.

42. Cylena Simons, "Ellen Kuras: Cinematographer," *Independent,* May 1995, 13.

43. Stephen Lizella, Editorial, *American Cinematographer,* November 1998.

44. Brianna Murphy was the first female member of the American Society of Cinematographers—she was admitted in 1973. Murphy was awarded the Crystal Award from the nonprofit organization Women in Film in May 1984 (see *American*

Cinematographer editorial, May 1984); Kuras later received a Vision Award from Women in Film in 1999.

45. Alexis Krasilovsky, ed. *Women behind the Camera: Conversations with Camerawomen* (Westport, CT: Praeger, 1997), xvii.

46. The term was coined by B. Ruby Rich in her essay "The New Queer Cinema," *Sight and Sound* 2.5 (1992): 30–35.

47. Kuras took the same award in 1995 for *Angela* and in 2002 for *Personal Velocity: Three Portraits,* both directed by Rebecca Miller.

48. For a useful discussion of Vachon and the producer as auteur, see Ros Jennings "Making Movies that Matter: Christine Vachon, Independent Film Producer," in *Fifty Contemporary Filmmakers,* ed. Yvonne Tasker (London: Routledge, 2002), 353–61.

49. *Weekend Guardian,* August 16, 1992, 19.

50. *Gay Times,* September 1992, 72–73; Sheila Johnstone, *Independent,* September 25, 1992, 20.

51. *Screen International* 844 (February 14, 1992): 20.

52. J. Hoberman, "Out and Inner Mongolia," *Premiere,* October 1992, 31.

53. *The Hollywood Reporter,* 1996 Crafts Series, March 19, 1996, 8.

54. *New York Times,* August 31, 1994. The *Daily News* review also refers to the film on the same date as "beautifully photographed by Ellen Kuras"; *Variety,* September 26, 1994, 62.

55. J. Hoberman, "Cult of Personality," *Premiere,* July 1995, 50.

56. Ann Lewinson, "The Women behind the Camera," *Independent,* March 2003, 45. Her reference to the male gaze explicitly evokes and questions debates within feminist film scholarship.

57. Ibid., 48.

58. Larry Gross, "Larry Gross Talks with *Safe's* Todd Haynes," *Filmmaker* (Summer 1995): 40.

59. Lane, *Feminist Hollywood,* 34.

Patricia White   *Chapter 11*

Black and White

Mercedes de Acosta's Glorious Enthusiasms

A June 1934 *Vanity Fair* item highlighted for its readers the latest roles of movie royalty Greta Garbo and Marlene Dietrich as Queen Christina and Catherine the Great, respectively, with "a composite photograph by Edward Steichen," "ingeniously constructed by superimposing two separate pictures . . . [of] those rival Nordic deities of Hollywood."[1] The image doubles up on all the sensual conventions of black-and-white studio-era glamour portrait photography. Garbo is in passionate profile at the bottom right, wearing black, her head thrown back, fingers spread, eyes half-closed. Dietrich's face is in the top left of the image, her white blouse open at the neck, but her eyes don't meet our gaze; heavy-lidded, she looks down and to the side. The stars look for all the world as if they are about to kiss.

In her 1991 videotape *Meeting of Two Queens* the Spanish video artist Cecilia Barriga manipulates clips of Garbo in *Queen Christina* (dir. Rouben Mamoulian, 1933, MGM) and Dietrich as Catherine the Great in *The Scarlett Empress* (dir. Josef von Sternberg, 1934, Paramount), as well as excerpts from these two stars' other films in a fashion strikingly similar to the 1934 magazine illustration.[2] Why was a Garbo/Dietrich meeting a still-potent fantasy in the 1990s? For a few years at the beginning of the 1930s, the Hollywood publicity machine exploited the stars' rivalry and elaborated their similar iconic status: European, arty, mysterious, and androgynous. Barriga's tape may be the product of a moment of unprecedented lesbian visibility, but it renders homage to an earlier Hollywood vision.

A genealogy of lesbian chic leads back to another woman who shared Barriga's investment in Hollywood. She clipped out *Vanity Fair*'s "composite photograph" and carefully saved it in her files. One wonders that

231

she needed such mass-marketed keepsakes, for Mercedes de Acosta, a New York writer of Spanish descent, dandy, dyke, and spiritually enlightened socialite, was intimate with both stars in the early 1930s; indeed she is the only woman lover they are believed to have shared. "You can't dismiss Mercedes lightly," wrote Alice B. Toklas to Anita Loos in 1960 after reading de Acosta's autobiography *Here Lies the Heart:* "She has had the two most important women in the United States."[3] Mercedes de Acosta briefly triangulated the Hollywood-manufactured Garbo-Dietrich rivalry. The stars came together by playing a role in *her* story; similarly, each of us fans is the imaginary intersection of eroticized fragments of mass culture—such as those Barriga reanimates in her tape—fragments that come together nowhere else. It is a story stranger than fiction: Mercedes, Blonde Venus, and Swedish Sphinx.

Mercedes de Acosta had a look; she was known for it. She may have pursued icons, but she also made *herself* iconic. Her flamboyance is a gift to anyone writing about the lives and times she passed through. In contrast—and perhaps in tribute—to her beloved elder sister Rita Lydig, a famous society clotheshorse, Mercedes was a dandy. Drawing on this gay male trope, she made her sexual identity uniquely visible. Almost every description of Mercedes emphasizes the distinctiveness and consistency of her wardrobe; she dressed all in black or all in white, she looked dramatic, she looked "Spanish." As early as 1928 a newspaper profile describes her thus: "She wears peculiarly characteristic clothes, and contends that she has succeeded in reducing the dress problem to a fine art," and it goes on to enumerate the items of her wardrobe. A similar litany is repeated in almost all print references to de Acosta:[4] highwayman's coats; tricorn hats (or cossack caps); pointed, buckled shoes; and much later, an eye-patch (though worn for health reasons, it was not inconsistent with her overall effect of "Cuban pirate elegance"[5]). At once typecast and unique, she called attention to ordinary butchness by going over the top, for instance by exaggerating the usually understated sartorial practice of having several versions of the same wardrobe item (leather jacket, jeans). Mercedes's coif was similarly dashing; she wore her black hair slicked straight back. Like anyone who dresses with the courage to convey a sexual persona, she was sometimes mocked. Perhaps her height—5'3"—was a liability in someone who pursued larger than life figures such as Greta Garbo. (Tallulah Bankhead is said to have called her, wickedly, "a mouse in a top coat!"[6]) It was Garbo who gave her her most charming and evocative nickname, one that others in their circle picked up: "Black and White" referred to Mercedes's exclusive palette, but the phrase captured her studiedly romantic nature, her mood swings, and a moment in Hollywood's aesthetics of glamour.

From childhood, Mercedes was both theatrical and a lover of actresses. Her Hollywood period came after achieving modest success as a playwright and poet, and acquiring a large acquaintanceship among the cultured and famous, in New York and in Europe.[7] Although none of her screenplays was ever produced, and although she seemed to have a rather snobbish attitude toward movies not starring her European friends, her romance with Hollywood is key to her significance. She mediated between "literate" and popular culture, she was a prism through which a joint project of high modernism and mass culture—creating new styles of femininity and sexuality—was refracted. Though behind the scenes and largely forgotten, de Acosta achieved a paradoxical visibility: the tabloids conveyed her "artistic" temperament, her Spanishness, her mannishness. She was famous for being a lesbian, when famousness and lesbianism were being redefined by Hollywood cinema. Arguably, her style left a trace in the movies. Take a look at another 1934 twist on the Hollywood studio portrait: Mercedes as shot by her friend Cecil Beaton. The intersection of a mass-marketed glamour aesthetic and legible lesbianism is all there, in black and white.

Since "lesbian chic" was declared a trend in the early 1990s, there's been a market for writing on Hollywood lesbians. De Acosta's book attracted some attention when it appeared in 1960, and it has remained an indispensable underground reference, but she didn't make a penny, dying poor in 1968. Today crass commercialism gives us ill-researched, opportunistic retellings of Mercedes's story such as Axel Madsen's *The Sewing Circle.* But "lesbian chic" also reflects a genuine sea change, allowing the contributions of queer women to be acknowledged in mainstream culture, and Mercedes's book can be seen as an advance indicator of the shift in current. The affective and sexual relationships that a number of major female screen and stage stars enjoyed with women—often, indeed, with Mercedes herself—have been given thorough and often thoughtful treatment in a number of important biographies.[8] And the academic meeting of cultural studies and queer theory has started to transform performing and screen arts history. Not interested simply in "outing" erstwhile representatives of chic, today we begin to analyze how "chicness" itself—notably the glamorous style that Hollywood disseminated worldwide—is connected to homoeroticism and to the historical formation of contemporary homosexual identities.

"Mercedes de Acosta, 1934 by Cecil Beaton." Courtesy Mercedes de Acosta Collection, Rosenbach Museum and Library, Philadelphia.

In the Garbo Archive

Various tawdry and worthy dimensions of the lesbian chic phenomenon fueled the publicity flurry surrounding April 15, 2000. On that date, the tenth anniversary of Greta Garbo's death at age eighty-four, fifty-five letters from the star to Mercedes de Acosta, together with seventeen cards, fifteen telegrams, a number of photographs, and a few miscellaneous items, were unsealed at the Rosenbach Museum and Library in Philadelphia. Acosta had given the cherished papers to the library, an elegant repository of modernist manuscripts and cultural artifacts, under condition that they remain sealed until ten years after the death of the longer-surviving correspondent. The unveiling took place amid much speculation, scholarly and sensational, that the sexual or romantic nature of the women's relationship might be revealed in the star's own words. It wasn't. But as Garbo's biographer Karen Swenson commented to the press, "for anyone to have expected she would say anything explicitly was contrary to Garbo's character."[9] It is what is implicit in the correspondence, the coverage of its opening, and the public and private relationship it indexes that is interesting.

The Garbo estate has vigorously dismissed the suggestion that the women ever were lovers, regarding Mercedes as an unreliable source. "Prior to the unveiling . . . I was asked many times if I thought the rumors of an affair between de Acosta and Garbo were true. The answer is no," said Garbo's grandniece Gray Horan at a press conference at the Rosenbach after the unsealing on April 18. "What I know of her personally (and what is publicly known about her amorous history) consists exclusively of men," she stated, with an emphatic gesture of "inning": what one knows of Garbo "consists of men." Yet the estate's prohibition against quoting from the letters adds to the uncertain status of the denial. Horan remarks, "Anyone determined to classify Garbo as one of de Acosta's lesbian lovers will certainly be disappointed with the contents of these letters." But the language of determination and certainty go against the grain of queer signification—and of Garbo's appeal. The point is not to out Garbo but to begin the historical and cultural analysis of what and how a connoted "lesbianism" might mean.

In fact disappointment pervades the correspondence itself, which extends from 1931, the year Mercedes met Garbo at the emigrée screenwriter Salka Viertel's Santa Monica home, to 1958, just a few years before de Acosta published her memoir and Garbo broke off contact. They are missives from an indecisive and dissatisfied woman—one who could also be wistful and funny—and from a reluctant correspondent. Written, sometimes printed, in blunt pencil on notebook paper, addressed playfully to "Black and white," "Boy," even "Honeychild" or "Sweetie," Garbo's letters seem warmest on gloomy topics. She is empathetic with Mercedes's health and housing problems and shares her own cares. She does send greetings to Mercedes's "friend" (her lover Maria Annunziata "Poppy" Kirk) and mentions the prospect of the latter's becoming jealous if Garbo were to visit Mercedes in Paris again, but these are the only indicators of a sapphic lifestyle—and that is Mercedes's, not Greta's.[10]

If the women had a romantic affair in the 1930s, Garbo for one had moved on. She wrote infrequently, sometimes answering Mercedes in exasperation and sometimes, it seems clear, not at all. There are no letters or telegrams or flower cards from 1941 to 1946. Besides this period (which coincides with Garbo's retiring from the screen), there were other breaks in the friendship, and Garbo expressed ambivalence about de Acosta's persistence in letters to their mutual friends Viertel and Beaton. Yet precisely because de Acosta *never* moved on, Garbo could count on her. By the 1950s there's a fairly regular flow of holiday and birthday flowers and cards, and a degree of responsiveness to what were evidently Mercedes's inquiries about travel schedules and meeting plans. Garbo's pain, bluntness, and humor are genuine. As the estate has habitually refused permission to quote from Garbo's letters, this new cache is unlikely to see print anytime soon. So as Horan's statement concluded, and her words signify perhaps more than she intends: "Garbo's mystery remains intact."

But the correspondence is now accessible at the Rosenbach, the piece de resistance of the collection Mercedes de Acosta deposited after she had published *Here Lies the Heart*.[11] Though at least one reader of the memoir is said to have quipped, "Here lies the heart—and lies and lies and lies,"[12] the more than five thousand items among de Acosta's papers at the Rosenbach collection include plenty of material to back up her accounts. As Beaton put it when he met de Acosta in 1928: "She has glorious enthusiasms, glorious friendships."[13] There is voluminous correspondence from her famous lovers, especially from the Broadway star Eva Le Gallienne, and lusty poetry from Isadora Duncan. There are letters from an assortment of modernist celebrities, including Beaton (the topic was most often their mutual obsession Garbo, but sometimes shoes) and Toklas, Stravinksy, and even fellow tricorn hat fancier Marianne Moore (whose papers are among the Rosenbach's treasures). Especially interesting for comparison is a delicious bunch of Dietrich's love letters, some of which had been under seal until her death in 1992. The collection also includes wonderful photographs and some intriguing miscellany, including "a single stocking" from Dietrich and an outline of Garbo's foot (so Mercedes could fetch her some slippers).

As Lisa Cohen has wittily noted, "If de Acosta is remembered at all today, it's still for *whom* rather than what she did."[14] Straddling public and private realms, the Garbo/Dietrich/Mercedes triangle illuminates how the stars' celebrity became bound up with lesbianism in a way that intimately influenced twentieth-century visual and sexual discourses. As Ann Cvetkovich notes, "The stock in trade of the gay and lesbian archive is ephemera."[15] The contrasting footwear mementos that de Acosta archived from each star show differences in their sensibilities, in their relationships with de Acosta, and indeed in their public star personae. Dietrich's stocking suggests a striptease in progress. Connoting the famous legs, it operates as a genuine, classic fetish. As one among many gifts sent to de Acosta, it signifies the star's generosity. Garbo traced her foot, allowing Mercedes access to the truth behind phallic, inflated rumors of its size. The tracing is more like an impression than an accessory, something essential rather than ephemeral. The care Garbo took in defining the slipper-buying errand reminds us of her fastidious frugality (another of her notes to Mercedes accompanies a pair of old socks—not preserved in the archive). The two stars' converging and contrasting—perhaps complementary—sexual and gender personae are constructed through films, promotion, publicity, and private lives, and de Acosta's own style and presence were part of this construction.

> Tra le la le la Triangle. My life's in such a tangle!
>
> —Patsy Cline

Over a brief period in the early 1930s, the Garbo–de Acosta and Dietrich–de Acosta relationships overlapped. Dietrich's liaison with de Acosta was brief and full-bodied. In her letters to Mercedes, many of them accompanying gifts, Dietrich luxuriates in memories of the "exquisite moments when I was in your arms that afternoon" and salutes Mercedes's "*mains sacrées.*"[16] She also writes poignantly of other things—signs of fascism's rise, of her sense of homelessness, and of "the Child" (her daughter Maria Riva, about eight years old at the time)—but these short letters and telegrams are primarily flirtatious. Most date from the beginning of their affair—several from its first week. Letters are addressed to "*Mon grand amour,*" or "*Femme adorée,*" and telegrams are to Raffael de Acosta, which was to have been Mercedes's name had she been born a boy.[17] (According to Riva's book on her mother, "White Prince" was another of Dietrich's masculine appellations for de Acosta.[18]) They are charming artifacts, often written in French—"because it is so hard to speak to you of love in English"[19]—in green ink on silvery-grey stationery, occasionally sealed with green wax and featuring Dietrich's monogram or her Paramount studio address. She sends a typed, self-translated quotation from Rilke, song lyrics they'd been trying to remember, the latest European sleeping potion, buttons, apologies. When Dietrich traveled to Europe to do publicity for her first film made independently of von Sternberg, *Song of Songs,* she sent back postcards—even Maria sent one to "My Prince"—plus a cigarette case from Vienna, snapshots, and press clippings (although she was busy with several famous male lovers on the trip). And Mercedes shared news of Garbo: she cabled that the director of *Song of Songs* was being considered for *Queen Christina.* Dietrich answered: "am happy about Scandinavian child I am sure she will like Mamoulian."[20]

Until Dietrich's death in 1992, many of these letters shared "Box 12: Restricted" at the Rosenbach with the sealed Garbo correspondence. Rosenbach librarian Elizabeth Fuller recalls simply reading the star's obituary and opening the box, not really considering publicizing the event. The unsealing certainly received nothing like the attention of the Garbo letters. This may be a measure of how much the tide of interest in things lesbian rose during the 1990s, or of de Acosta's importance in Garbo's story and status as amusing episode in Dietrich's. But it also measures a difference in the stars' images and in their afterlives. Dietrich artifacts do not suffer from the same economy of scarcity as Garbo's. The Marlene Dietrich Collection–Berlin includes about 300,000 leaves of correspondence—not to mention 440 pairs of shoes. Thousands of items of its memorabilia were in Dietrich's own possession at the time of her death. Her lovers also represent an embarrassment of riches, and Mercedes isn't the only woman among them—although she was one of the few "out" lesbians in the round-up. Dietrich's daughter reminisces: "I was accustomed to my mother always having someone around. I never questioned their gender or what they were actually there for. . . . I would have hated her habits more had she been motivated by sexual appetite. But all Dietrich ever wanted, needed, desired, was Romance with every capital R available, declarations of utter devotion, lyrical passion."[21] Adept at romance, Dietrich was a witty, sensual correspondent.

Garbo demanded a very different, less discursive sort of devotion. Though romantic in its way, the Garbo correspondence attests to an em-

bodiment less connected with lyrical passion than with the flesh's susceptibility to chest colds and assorted other ailments. Yet however terse or
banal Garbo's letters are, they are expected to reveal some inner truth. De
Acosta lucked into her affair with Dietrich; the star's interest was piqued by
Mercedes's association with Garbo just as was that of fan magazine readers
in the 1930s and again in 2000. De Acosta's relationship with Garbo was,
in contrast, utterly premeditated. Just how was it that Mercedes de Acosta
came to stand at the intersection of these stars' lives, to accumulate the
contents of Box 12?

Mercedes had moved to Hollywood in 1931 to write for another famous exotic European star, Pola Negri. Her itinerary connected the movie
colony quite directly with European dyke modernist literary circles and
the New York dyke theater world. Beaton notes that Mercedes "managed
not only to make a beeline for all the women who interested her, but by
some fluke—or some genius gift of her own, became intimate friends."[22]
In *Here Lies the Heart,* de Acosta piles up portents of her destined meeting
with Garbo.[23] Mercedes claims her wish came true on her third day in Hollywood (even if it took two months, as Karen Swenson thinks, this is still
respectable for a fan),[24] but an even more improbable fantasy was fulfilled
shortly thereafter.

Garbo had just finished shooting *Susan Lenox: Her Fall and Rise* (dir.
Robert Z. Leonard, 1931), and she departed for an isolated cabin in the
Sierra Nevadas for a much needed rest. But as soon as her chauffeur had
reached the end of the long drive to the mountain retreat, Garbo turned
right around and came back for her new friend Mercedes: "I could not be
such a pig as to enjoy all that beauty alone," Mercedes tells us she said.[25]
The pair may not have spent six harmonious weeks on that island in the
middle of isolated Silver Lake as Mercedes claimed—from consulting
MGM's records Swenson believes Garbo was gone at best for two.[26] But
photos in this wild setting of an Amazonian Garbo, topless with a sweater
tied strategically around her neck, have sparked the imagination of readers of Mercedes's memoir since its publication. The Rosenbach's unsealed
records yielded several snapshots from the trip, but an infamous shot from
the series of Garbo *sans* sweater was missing.[27] Gray Horan made no direct
comment on the Silver Lake vacation when reassuring the press, "There is
no concrete evidence that any sexual relationship between these two wom-
en ever existed." Of the topless photos, she aptly reminds us that her great
aunt was, after all, a Scandinavian!

Garbo sailed home to Sweden in 1932, and Anita Loos reported to

Cecil Beaton on the bumpy parting between the writer and the star: "The Garbo-Mercedes business has been too amazing. They had terrific battles, and Garbo left without saying good bye. . . . The story is as long as the dictionary—but much more amazing—so will hope you get together with Mercedes one day and hear it from her lips."[28] Mercedes does not let us hear the story from her pen, but *Here Lies the Heart* tells the equally too-amazing story of being courted by Dietrich on the rebound. Riva quotes her mother's version, from a letter to her father Rudi Sieber: "I am sorry for Mercedes. Her face was white and thin and she seemed sad and lonely—as I am—and not well. I was attracted to her and brought an armful of tuberoses to her house. I told her I would cook marvelous things for her and get her well and strong."[29] Mercedes made the embarrassing misstep of not recovering from Garbo fast enough. Riva includes Mercedes's lengthy attempt to explain:

Golden One, . . . To try and explain my real feeling for Greta would be impossible since I really do not understand myself. I do know that I have built up in my emotions a person that does not exist. My mind sees the real person—a Swedish servant girl with a face touched by God—only interested in money, her health, sex, food, and sleep. And yet her face tricks my mind and my spirit builds her up into something that fights with my brain. I do love her but I only love the person I have created and not the person who is real. . . . Until I was seventeen I was a real religious fanatic. Then I met Duse and until I met Greta, gave her the same fanaticism until I transferred it to Greta. And during those periods of fanaticism they have not prevented me from being in love with other people—which seems to take another side of my nature. It was so with you. I was passionately in love with you. I could still be if I allowed myself.[30]

While this is a valuable account of what Mercedes saw in Garbo, by any standard it is very insensitive as a love letter. Riva has her mother pausing while reading to exclaim aloud to Sieber: "De Acosta is too vain for words!" We're nearing the end of the affair, the inevitable moment when, as Riva puts it, "the one-time courted, the adored, the essential being would overstep. . . . and bang! That private door to Dietrich slammed shut. Everyone faced this future eventually. Now the White Prince's time was near. My mother had had enough of 'Greta this' and 'Greta that.'"[31] Riva vividly captures a sense of Dietrich's exasperation at all this butch earnestness. But the correspondence does not chronicle the wind-down. Instead it stands as an eloquent *recognition* of de Acosta in her identity as a lover: "I kiss your face and the scars particuly [*sic*]," wrote Marlene to Mercedes from Antibes.[32]

And so collapsed the glamorous triangle onto de Acosta's ongoing and one-sided devotion to Garbo. Her self-described fanaticism was a "side of her nature" no less Sapphic but certainly more tragic. As Mercedes continued in her letter to Dietrich quoted earlier: "But if I do get over [this insanity] what then shall I pray to? And what will then turn this gray life into starlight?"[33] A revealing artifact in her collection at the Rosenbach testifies to what extent de Acosta linked religious devotion to fandom. The inside cover of her personal Bible is pasted up with six small Garbo portraits. De Acosta's cut-outs resemble those used to compose the *Vanity Fair* composite or the sequences of *Meeting of Two Queens* in which Barriga renders her stars in the same frame. What should we make of the uniqueness (only Garbo) and multiplicity (six!) of the icon here? (There are other personal photographs affixed elsewhere in the Bible, another Garbo pin-up on the facing page.) We see the compulsiveness of the collector—we need multiple poses (and Mercedes had plenty in her files to choose among), or, in Barriga's tape, dozens of clips from many films—to begin to render homage. But the gesture of consecration is also one of desacralization and diffusion. Multiple Garbos afford an unconscious recognition of her image's indebtedness to mechanical reproducibility; the fan's icon is not unique the way a god is. Unfortunately, Mercedes wasn't able to live this understanding of the star's multiple faces in any other way but as a masochistic repetition of the same rejection scenario. Knowing the Divine Garbo in the flesh by no means deflated aura.

Mercedes continued to pray for the transformation of "this gray life" through contact with Garbo, her formulation strikingly reminiscent of the promise of cinema itself. Before Garbo left MGM, de Acosta elaborated her religious fantasy by adapting her play *Jehanne d'Arc* as a script for the star; devastatingly, Garbo rejected the project. Mercedes wrote to Beaton, she consulted her spiritual advisors—"Greta this," "Greta that"—and then heedlessly rushed in every time there was a small opening in Garbo's defenses. Remarkably, though, she remained in contact with Garbo during the 1940s and 1950s after the star's retirement. Beaton even acknowledged to Mercedes, "I've always thought that the two of you would end your days together."[34] De Acosta's at once thwarted and privileged access to Garbo allegorizes that of the public—and, perhaps even more specifically, of the lesbian viewer.

Epistemologies of the Celluloid Closet

The Garbo estate's reluctance to expose Garbo's letters demonstrates fierce protectionism toward a star who employed everyone around her for that purpose while she was alive; fear of publicity seems to run in the family. But like any prohibition, it has the effect of confirming what it means to deny. Though the worry around publicity is by no means entirely tied to worry about questions of Garbo's sexuality, the connection between secrecy and homosexuality so effectively documented and theorized by Eve Sedgwick in *The Epistemology of the Closet* is nevertheless strikingly reinforced. Arguably, the peculiarities of Garbo's star image implicate her in this drama of desire and disclosure more than any other star, Dietrich included. Sedgwick argues that the link between representations of knowledge/ignorance (and related questions of publicity/privacy) and the crisis of homo/heterosexual definition is central to modern culture. Sedgwick herself explores that culture mostly through its canonical (male-authored) literature (about men), so the epistemological nexus she has identified appears "indicatively male." I believe that the visual and celebrity culture so characteristic of the twentieth century—and so extensively characterized by female hypervisibility—is also fraught with dramas of sex and knowledge, dramas that implicate female homoeroticism far more extensively than has been acknowledged. But I would venture to say that in the case of the epistemology of Garbo's closet—especially insofar as her knowing de Acosta informs this discourse—Sedgwick's generalization holds. Garbo's secret's connection with the question of homosexuality *is* "indicatively male," or at least butch, or, in the parlance of the time, "mannish."

Garbo's "masculinity" connects her to ontological definitions of homosexuality (qua inversion) as something one *is* rather than something one does—even if *she wasn't one.* Commentators on her persona contributed to this construction of Garbo's "authentic" gender. As Parker Tyler writes: "Garbo 'got in drag' whenever she took some heavy glamour part, whenever she melted in or out of a man's arms, whenever she simply let that heavenly-flexed neck—what a magnificent line it makes: like a goose's rather than a swan's—bear the weight of her thrown-back head."[35] Moreover, the epistemological drama of knowing—is she or isn't she?—which is so pronounced in Garbo's case is attached to the acquaintanceship drama of knowing Mercedes. Mercedes's known-to-be lesbian "boyishness" puts the epistemological and erotic implications of the well-known star persona with whom she's associated into historical relief.

242

In contrast, seduction, which one might consider to be Dietrich's version of lesbianism by metonymy, though it includes the act, does not implicate the star in a discourse of essence. Having had an affair with Mercedes, or with Edith Piaf, made her less an ontological lesbian than a lesbian icon. Though Dietrich's suits were mannish, she wasn't. Dietrich's persona in pants was that of a sexual tease. And though Dietrich was mysterious, no one kept a secret like Garbo. Roland Barthes famously describes Garbo's face as "almost sexually undefined, without however leaving one in doubt," ultimately leaving sexual definition in doubt and implying that this constitutes her image.[36] The drama of knowledge is not nearly as pronounced in Dietrich's case because there isn't the same surface/depth tension; public and private can be seen as equally performative. Perhaps this is why the Dietrich persona feels more current, ripe for appropriation by Madonna and other wannabes. Garbo's image is pervaded with nostalgia, which might be thought of as a kind of lost heroic butchness. Today when the specific components of Garbo's persona may themselves be lost to contemporary audiences more likely to have encountered lesbian films than any of the star's on television, she belongs as much to the archeology of homosexuality as she does to that of Hollywood. Swenson describes the approach some scholars might take toward the correspondence with de Acosta: "If they feel the need to see lesbianism, they'll see it."[37] If lesbianism is connoted everywhere one looks in the Garbo archive, it is not because of tunnel vision or voluntarism on the part of fanatics driven by identity-politics. It is what history has taught us to look for.

Trouser Roles

Mercedes not only wore pants, she proselytized them. When she "went to Pickfair dressed in a white sweater and white trousers," on her second day in Hollywood, she reports, she was pulled aside and told, "'You'll get a bad reputation if you dress this way out here.'"[38] Mercedes was clearly *cultivating* a reputation, and she continues covertly to connect lesbianism to advanced ideas about clothing throughout her memoir. She can come right out and claim to have got both Garbo and Dietrich into pants. "When I had known Greta a little while I got her to exchange her sailor pants for slacks,"[39] she writes, and a few chapters later she's taking the topic up with Dietrich.

I told her she looked so well in *Morocco* in the sequence where she wore them that I thought she should wear them all the time. She was delighted at the suggestion. The next day I took her to my tailor in Hollywood and in true Dietrich fashion she ordered not one pair but many more, and jackets to go with them. Of course she looked superb in all of them. When they were finished she appeared at the Paramount studio one day dressed in one of them. The following day newspapers throughout the whole country carried photographs of her. From that second on, women all over the world leapt into slacks.[40]

While Mercedes exaggerates her taste-making role, her claims remind us that the memorable cross-dressing performances of both stars onscreen were accountable to offscreen lesbian looks and practices of the period.[41] In the historic sequence from *Morocco* (dir. von Sternberg, 1930) that Mercedes refers to so casually, Dietrich, in top hat and tails, had kissed a woman on the mouth. And *Queen Christina,* with its scenes of Garbo kissing her lady-in-waiting, and a barmaid coming on to the star (who is passing as a man in the fiction,) was in the works at this time. In a widely reported anecdote, the latter film's writer Salka Viertel recalls being "pleasantly surprised" when the producer Irving B. Thalberg encouraged her to put something of the flavor of *Mädchen in Uniform* in the screenplay.[42] One movie magazine feature among de Acosta's clippings asks, "Do you know about the NEW Garbo?" and answers with a focus on Garbo's "closest friends today"—de Acosta and Viertel. The article's description of Queen Christina as someone "enormously individualized and slightly bizarre who insisted upon carrying the title of king and wearing mannish garb for many years" might have characterized not only the queen's impersonator Garbo, whose affinity with the role of the Swedish monarch was overdetermined, but also Mercedes.[43] If Mercedes did not dress these screen icons in pants (though she claims to have influenced Adrian's designs for Garbo[44]), in her own trousers, she's living proof of the lesbian world their performances encoded and transmitted. Generations of lesbian and gay viewers, and indeed most sentient ones, have decoded some of the signs.

Because the images in *Meeting of Two Queens* are drawn entirely from the stars' films, it is an extraordinary example of such spectatorial decoding. It also *recodes* contemporary lesbian representation via its Hollywood antecedents. The by now somewhat flat iconicity of those few fetishized kissing and cross-dressing scenes is given nuance and depth in the context of the many other aspects of star performance on display in other sequences and in the context of the tape's own alternative narrative. The contrast between the stars' images emerges both aesthetically and affectively. It is precisely this internal difference that indexes a historical reality—returning us to lesbian lives through 1930s representational codes.

Let's entertain parallel pants histories for a moment. It was before her affair with de Acosta had entirely exhausted itself that Dietrich made headlines and courted arrest for appearing publicly in Paris in men's clothes. (She sent back a gorgeous studio portrait of herself in a black suit inscribed "für Mercedes.") Riva thinks the threat of arrest was partly a publicity stunt, and laws restricting the number of items of male clothing a biological female can wear have long been selectively enforced.[45] While Garbo never encountered the kind of police harassment that subjected mid-century butches to strip-searches, she was aggressively scrutinized by the press—not least on the idiosyncrasies of her wardrobe. Pants for glamour are different from pants for gender authenticity, and Garbo wore them for the latter reason, evoking, as I've argued elsewhere, the "mythic mannish" iconic style made famous by Stephen Gordon, the hero/ine of Radclyffe Hall's 1928 novel *The Well of Loneliness.*[46] Even Mercedes, who, in an early draft of her memoir, claims to have shared Stephen's biographical peculiarity of being raised as a boy, did not grow up to be as "mannish" as Garbo—perhaps because she did not grow up to be as big. Bringing Mercedes out from her place behind the screen dissolves a contrast between the realm of representation and that of reality, as far as tropes of gender authenticity are concerned, since the "real" dyke got herself up as elaborately as any movie star might. Her *style* was "authentic."

There is a fair amount of sartorial preoccupation within the de Acosta correspondence: Dietrich sends de Acosta a dressing gown and a handkerchief to match—"*also* from the *men's* department!" she emphasizes gleefully.[47] Garbo fusses about matching a particular shade of dark blue, and there's the foot tracing. In the visual archive, the idiom in which all three women communicated best, trouser styles are much in evidence. The unsealed Garbo box contains 1932 snapshots of an unsmiling star in tennis whites. A more forthcoming series from the height of the affair with Dietrich shows the star at the beach house she'd rented from Marion Davies. Both sets of images—plus the Amazonian Silver Lake series of Garbo—are indelibly marked by de Acosta's gaze behind the camera. We look with her desire, although her image is absent.

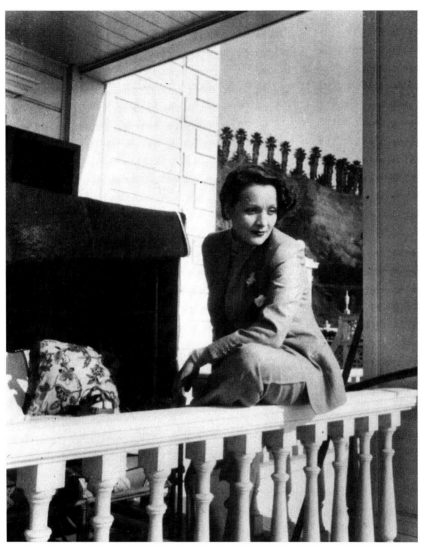

"Marlene Dietrich." Courtesy Mercedes de Acosta Collection, Rosenbach Museum and Library, Philadelphia.

"Greta Garbo ephemera." Courtesy Mercedes de Acosta Collection, Rosenbach Museum and Library, Philadelphia.

Walking with Garbo

In one of its several incarnations, a 1934 photograph of Mercedes and Greta together is shamelessly captioned: "An unauthorized shot of the elusive Swedish star, taken by a cameraman who had waited for three hours on the running board of a car parked on Hollywood's main boulevard. He just managed to snap the Garbo as she came out of her tailor's with her friend, Miss de Costa [*sic*]." The image is "well-contrasted," we're told, with a shot of Garbo in a nunlike habit from her upcoming film. The headline trumpets: "The Garbo in 'The Painted Veil' and in Corduroy Trews," and indeed some notion of veiling is dramatically invoked by the costume's contrast with the offscreen yet indisputable tactility of an everyday menswear fabric.[48]

I would like to suggest that this signature image of the friends, which Mercedes includes among the illustrations in her book, invites a different kind of lesbian speculation than the composite pairing of Steichen's star portraits with which I opened; indeed, I think it invited this speculation from the general audience to which both articles were initially addressed. The superimposed stars suggested a romantic couple, but the paparazzi snap of Garbo and de Acosta in synchronous strides—though just as treasured an image in the lesbian archive—suggests fellow travelers more than lovers. Mercedes herself discusses the photograph, rendering the newspaper caption a little more hyperbolically: "GARBO IN PANTS! *Innocent bystanders gasped in amazement to see Mercedes de Acosta and Greta Garbo striding swiftly along Hollywood Boulevard dressed in men's clothes.*"[49] The image is a rich negotiation of butchness on the line between public and private.

In her letters, Garbo often addresses Mercedes as Boy. She famously referred to herself using masculine pronouns. In the 1934 photograph the two were not courting; according to the tabloid, they were shopping—they'd been to the tailor's, the Ur-site of butch self-creation. Here's my borrowed literary caption:

She would go . . . that very afternoon and order a new flannel suit at her tailor's. The suit should be grey with a little white pin stripe, and the jacket, she decided, must have a breast pocket. She would wear a black tie—no, better a grey one to match the new suit with the little white pin stripe. She ordered not one new suit but three, and she also ordered a pair of brown shoes; indeed she spent most of the afternoon in ordering things for her personal adornment. She heard herself being ridiculously fussy about details, disputing with her tailor over buttons; disputing with her bootmaker over the shoes, their thickness of sole, their amount of broguing; disputing regarding the match of her ties with the young man who sold her handkerchiefs and neckties—for such trifles had assumed an enormous importance; she had, in fact, grown quite longwinded about them.[50]

Having grown quite longwinded herself in this passage from *The Well of Loneliness,* Radclyffe Hall implicates her literary taste for detail with her hero/ine's fuss over masculine accessories (the scene is set just after Stephen's first fallen in love). In *Female Masculinity,* Judith Halberstam observes that in Hall's crucial text of modern lesbian identity, "Stephen positively *wears* her sexuality . . . a sartorial semiotic provides this novel with its system of knowing and unknowing, concealment and disclosure."[51] The sartorial semiotics of Garbo's stardom was elaborated at a contemporaneous historical moment. The magazine photo of Garbo and her lesbian friend cuts across the long windedness of the novel with visual immediacy, giving us two versions of fastidiousness in the dandy and the picky-about-the-basics (later to be eccentrically so) dresser.

The mannish pair promenades with confidence. Mercedes is the more chic, certainly the more accessorized: gloves, cloak, and skullcap—no corduroy here—are shown off by her bantam posture. But Garbo has the longer stride. Her rush of movement conveys self-assured flânerie perhaps—but also the wish to escape. Garbo's hand shields her face from the intrusive camera. The elegant profile of a pair on parade exposes at the same time a vulnerable flank. The star is running from the press, the public gaze, and she is also outstepping, eluding Mercedes, in whose pace there is just the hint of a scurry. Another, overhead paparazzi photo has Garbo entering her car "followed by her one close friend, Mercedes D'Acosta" [sic]; in another caption, "the camera snaps as she makes for the car, Mercedes right behind."[52] In this unwanted (by Garbo, at least) documentation, a quality characteristic of her dynamic with Mercedes is captured. Even accompanied, Garbo must walk *alone* (a dominant trope of early to mid-twentieth century lesbianism). Though she might look like she's chasing her, Mercedes is better thought of as Garbo's lesbian shadow, metonymically connecting Garbo's very uniqueness and singularity to lesbian community style.

For Mercedes dressed to be seen, to be identified in the papers. Her own struggle for visibility was at war with her respect for Garbo's privacy; this troubled her in the publication of the memoir and in the disposition of her letters. Mercedes's visibility may have been self-dramatizing, it may have backfired, perhaps because of homophobia (none of her collection of nicknames—Gray Horan says their whole family, following Garbo, called her *krken,* the Swedish word for "crow," and Maria Riva likened her to a Spanish Dracula—was particularly flattering), but it bespoke her desire to have her sexual and gender identity recognized, to wear her desire on her sleeve. Inevitably, there was sapphic slippage when the tabloids talked about trousers. The double-butch two-shot gave Garbo a new kind of visibility.

As much as Garbo tried to save a "private" face from public viewing, her onscreen persona insistently enacted the drama of being seen as revelation of self—hence the emphasis on her eroticized visage and gaze. Interestingly, Garbo begged for onscreen trouser roles. Thalberg rejected, because of its cross-dressing scene, a script he'd asked Mercedes to write for Garbo titled *Desperate.*[53] So many of Garbo's "comeback" projects, documented, rumored, or fantasized—from Dorian Gray to Hamlet to St Francis of Assisi (Mercedes's idea) to Mademoiselle de Maupin (Parker Tyler's) to Georges Sand—were men's or cross-dressing parts. While she was still making films, Garbo wrote to Viertel from Sweden suggesting she "put in a little sequence with the trousers" in the film she was writing about Napoleon's mistress, released in 1937 as *Conquest* (dir. Clarence Brown). "I have a great longing for trousers," Garbo wrote.

I am sorry, not to contribute anything more, but it is merely to remind you about the trousers—
trousers, girls in trousers, pressed trousers, girls, trousers, trousers.
By G. Stein.[54]

This divine doggerel is as close as Garbo gets to the modernist lesbian set on whose periphery Mercedes moved, though her art pursued many of its visions by other means. The language of "great longing" shades into the representational mode of her films, though it is a male costume rather than a costar that she suffers for.

Girls. Trousers, trousers. The tabloid shot of Mercedes and Greta on Hollywood Boulevard, though not a "composite photograph" like *Vanity Fair's* image of Dietrich and Garbo or Barriga's fantasized "meeting of two queens" also depicts an impossible couple: impossible in the sense that Hollywood wasn't ready for a major female star to be involved with a woman, and perhaps impossible biographically. But finally, impossible as a couple because the mythic mannish lesbian type is ontologically lonely or at least a loner; two girls in trousers walk alone together, hinting more at a subculture than a romance. This is the mythic, anachronistic lesbian persona that resonates so strongly with Garbo's tragic onscreen characters, her many martyrs to impossible love. Regardless of her actual sexual choices, Garbo contributed enormously to one key historical figuration of what I have referred to as lesbian "representability"—the conditions under which lesbianism comes to be encoded and decoded in representations, whether movies or modes of dress.

In Garbo's shadow, de Acosta's own negotiation of visibility is a precedent, a condition, of ours today. Her being seen as a lesbian depended not only on her dress but also on the fact that she was an admirer, a suitor of women—in their most transparent and accessible and paradoxically unavailable form, that of female stars. She became the fan whose gaze was returned, reflecting the homoeroticism at the core of fandom and of chic. If she was forgotten in any number of contexts—her work was mediocre, Dietrich tired of her earnestness and her obsession with her rival, Garbo was selfish and suspicious—she has made a comeback in a moment when lesbian history finally has evidentiary status. Garbo is in the news for knowing *her*. When Mercedes died in May 1968, on the verge of a new cultural era, Beaton expressed his admiration for her: "She was one of the most rebellious & brazen of Lesbians." He was "just sorry she was not more fulfilled as a character."[55] Here too there's a shadow of Garbo; on- as well as offscreen, her legacy was that of the unfulfilled character, whether defined by tragic loss in film after film or by early, and fairly empty, retirement from the cinema. Only history can fulfill the promise of "the lesbian" as character, and only through recognition of the complexity of that designation that has only recently been possible in public.

Vulgar Eyes

If she craved being seen, Mercedes was more careful about what she said than she is given credit for. She wrote a name-dropping memoir, but for a work attacked for exaggeration, it barely alludes to homosexuality. When she told the story of her life, Mercedes worried most about what the private, mercurial, and just plain odd Garbo, with whom she was in regular but precarious contact in the late 1950s, would think, and she jeopardized her access to Garbo by publishing the book. When de Acosta negotiated the sale of her papers to the Rosenbach, she arranged to give the Garbo materials as a gift, stipulating the period of time that they should remain

sealed, even forbidding the curator, her friend Bill McCarthy, from reading them. She was impoverished at the time of the sale, and though it has
been unkindly rumored that she had intended to blackmail Garbo with the
letters, she reports having declined lucrative offers to sell them off to other
parties. This rumor is an inevitable corollary of the public/private epistemology of the closet, through which unread letters accrue more value.
Mercedes knew what wasn't there, of course. But she did not think in terms
of "in" and "out."

Her feelings about the letters' exposure were elaborated a few years
later, on October 31, 1964, in a letter to McCarthy:

I never get over the feeling that one should never give away or show letters
which, at the time, have meant much to one and are so very personal. And yet
I would not have had the heart or the courage to have burned these letters. I
mean, of course, Eva's, Greta's and Marlene's—who were lovers. So it seemed a
God-sent moment when you took them. I only hope, as the years go on, and
you are no longer there that they will be *respected* and *protected* from the eyes of
vulgar people.[56]

When the ten-year posthumous seal on the Garbo gift ran out on April
15, 2000, interest in the personal letters' content echoed that of the public
who had avidly consumed the tidbits about de Acosta and Garbo in movie
magazines in the 1930s, justifying to some degree the Garbo estate's protectionism. Yet the guardians of the star's legacy may have seen as vulgar a
curiosity more akin to respect—for the unique cultural and historical role
played by de Acosta.

The eyes that read letters to de Acosta in the Rosenbach collection
are not those for whom they are intended. One is easily interpellated—as
Dietrich's lover, as Garbo's confidante, then, almost as easily, as someone
pestering the star—but also kept in the dark. Mercedes's own letters are not
available. If we don't know *what* she wrote to her correspondents, we do
know *how* she wrote. Her handwriting was dramatic. She sometimes used
purple ink. A collection of poems to Garbo that was unsealed with the letters dips deeply into the well of loneliness:

I will go back to my own land.
Land of Spain.
Sad, tragic land. . . .
But at the End,

Cold lands swept by wind and snows
Is where my heart will
die, I know.
—Hollywood 1933.

But the addressee of this astounding, irreproducible body of correspondence may be most knowable as the collector who clipped and pasted from
mass-market magazines, who, in the same spirit, got these famous people
to write to her. Cohen characterizes her legacy thus: "The poetry for which
de Acosta should be remembered is composed of the fugitive lines of a fan's
devotion as well as of an archivist's commitment to preserving a material
sense of her times."[57]

After her detailed inventory of the illustrious correspondents encompassed in her donation to the Rosenbach, Mercedes adds a note to McCarthy: "P.S. I forgot to tell you that I have many photographs of Greta in a
trunk and a *great* many magazines—American, French, English and Swedish in which articles and photographs appeared of her from 1930 until
today."[58] Mercedes's cache of fan magazine and newspaper clippings—any
fan could have had one like it, my own crumpled obituaries of Garbo and
Dietrich fell out of my picture books when I began this essay—is archived
alongside her wonderful collection of letters from her wonderful collection
of women. Mercedes's glorious enthusiasm for Garbo may not have extended to the movies in general. But for me the vibrant colors on the covers
of *Photoplay* and *Modern Screen* burn through the black-and-white posing
and the melancholy. If these frankly very American publications do not
approach the high modernism fashioned by expatriate lesbian editors and
writers, they are artifacts of a movie modernism that has had just as great
an influence on twentieth-century culture, especially on the formation of
new sexual identities such as those alluded to by the term "lesbian chic."
And though Mercedes tended to disavow her American identity in her
persona and in her pursuit of European Golden Ones, she was a perhaps
unwitting apologist for Hollywood's American modernism.[59] What else is
Vanity Fair's "composite photograph" of "Garbo and Dietrich—the Northern Lights" if not an attempt at popular taste-making, queerness in the
dream language of fans? If the movies and the ephemeral visual culture surrounding them invited the eyes of vulgar people, they also made it possible
for some of us to look differently. For example, working in late-twentieth-
century Spain, Cecilia Barriga revisits in her video the same mise-en-scène
of lesbian celebrity that de Acosta experienced; she enriches our reading

of the contents of "Box 12: Restricted" at the Rosenbach. *Meeting of Two Queens'* fleeting, fragile, late twentieth-century fan's homage testifies to the historical and transnational reach of these Hollywood icons. Mercedes would have been enthusiastic. She would have saved a copy.

Notes

This is a somewhat shorter version of the essay that originally appeared in *Camera Obscura* 45, vol. 15.3 (2001), 226–65.

1. Maddy Vegtel, "Blonde Venus and Swedish Sphinx," *Vanity Fair*, June 1934, 28, 66.

2. I discuss Barriga's tape, and the differences and similarities between the Garbo and Dietrich star images, more fully in *Uninvited: Classical Hollywood Cinema and Lesbian Representability* (Bloomington: Indiana University Press, 1999), 53–58. See also Mary Desjardins's "Meeting Two Queens: Feminist Filmmaking, Identity Politics, and the Melodramatic Fantasy," *Film Quarterly* 48:3 (1995): 26–33. *Meeting of Two Queens* is distributed by Women Make Movies (wmm.com).

3. Alice B. Toklas to Anita Loos, May 8, 1960, *Staying on Alone: Letters of Alice B. Toklas,* ed. Edward Burns (London: Liveright, 1973). Quoted in Diana Souhami, *Greta and Cecil* (San Francisco: Harper, 1994), ix. Martha Gever discusses various versions of Toklas's comment, and its implications, in her chapter on de Acosta in *Entertaining Lesbians: Celebrity, Sexuality, and Self-Invention* (New York: Routledge, 2003), 149. Gever's excellent study appeared after this article's initial publication.

4. "Daily Sketch," April 27, 1928, London, n.p. Newspaper and magazine quotations from the ephemera files, Mercedes de Acosta collection, Rosenbach Museum and Library, unless otherwise noted.

5. Sybille Bedford to Hugo Vickers, September 16, 1992, quoted in Hugo Vickers, *Loving Garbo: The Story of Greta Garbo, Cecil Beaton, and Mercedes de Acosta* (New York: Random House, 1994), 155.

6. Brendan Gill, *Tallulah* (New York: Harper & Row, 1972), 52. Quoted in Barry Paris, *Garbo: A Biography (*New York: Knopf, 1995), 264.

7. Richard A. Schanke has recently published the first full-length biography of de Acosta as well as an edition of her plays. See *"That Furious Lesbian": The Story of Mercedes de Acosta,* and *Women in Turmoil: Six Plays by Mercedes de Acosta,* both (Carbondale: Southern Illinois University Press, 2003).

8. Axel Madsen, *The Sewing Circle: Hollywood's Greatest Secret; Female Stars Who Loved Other Women* (New York: Birch Lane Press, 1995). Besides the biographies of Garbo by Paris (*Garbo: A Biography)* and Karen Swenson (*Greta Garbo: A Life Apart* [New York: Scribner, 1997]), and of Dietrich by Stephen Bach (*Marlene Dietrich: Life and Legend* [New York: William Morrow, 1992]) and Donald Spoto (*Blue Angel: The Life of Marlene Dietrich* [New York: Doubleday, 1992]), Gavin Lambert's *Nazimova* (New York: Knopf, 1997) and Helen Sheehy's *Eva Le Gallienne: A Biography* (New York: Knopf, 1996) treat their subjects' relationships with de Acosta.

9. Quoted in Meki Cox, "Garbo's Secret Still a Secret," *San Francisco Chronicle,* April 18, 2000.

10. Mercedes lived in New York and in Paris with Kirk. During the time of her most consistent correspondence with de Acosta—the late 1940s and 1950s—Garbo's primary companion was George Schlee, who was married to the dress designer Valentina, with whom he lived in an apartment downstairs from Garbo's.

11. Mercedes de Acosta, *Here Lies the Heart: A Tale of My Life* (New York: Reynal, 1960). De Acosta's book is an odd combination of tell-all and discretion. The underground cachet of Mercedes's memoir, and its value as a work of queer history from a female "participant observer" perspective is considerable, despite its lack of explicitness. Most mentions of homosexuality were revised out of the book, though even widely quoted passages from the early drafts, available for consultataion at the de Acosta collection at the Rosenbach, on her own early masculine identification, her belief that one's love object should not be restricted by gender, and the gay subcultures of the 1920s are not all that extensive or revealing. Her accounts of her love affairs feature flowers and mementos shared, and the literary equivalent of the fade-to-black; the long-term relationships are illustrated with shared apartments and travels, but there are no kisses, no caresses.

12. Quoted in Vickers, *Loving Garbo,* 254, attributed to a friend. The quote is attributed to Salka Viertel by Jack Larson in a letter to Barry Paris, July 26, 1991, quoted in Paris, *Garbo: A Biography,* 264.

13. Quoted in Vickers, *Loving Garbo,* 40.

14. Lisa Cohen, "Fame Fatale," *Out,* October 1999, 76. Cohen's book about de Acosta, Madge Garland, and Esther Murphy (forthcoming from Farrar, Straus and Giroux) is a study of fandom, fashion, and failure in twentieth-century lesbian modernism.

15. Ann Cvetkovich, "In the Archives of Lesbian Feeling: Documentary and Popular Culture," *Camera Obscura* 49 (2002): 107–47.

16. Dietrich to de Acosta, October 10, 1932, de Acosta Collection, Rosenbach Museum and Library, my translation from French. Unless otherwise indicated, all subsequent Dietrich letters to de Acosta are from this collection.

17. De Acosta, Second draft, *Here Lies the Heart,* MS 70, de Acosta Collection.

18. Maria Riva, *Marlene Dietrich* (New York: Knopf, 1992), 254.

19. Dietrich to de Acosta, September 19, 1932. My translation.

20. Dietrich to de Acosta, May 17, 1933.

21. Riva, *Marlene Dietrich,* 164–65.

22. Vickers, *Loving Garbo,* 281.

23. De Acosta, *Here Lies the Heart,* 142, 162, 208.

24. Swenson, *Greta Garbo: A Life Apart,* 252. Swenson has corrected Mercedes's hindsight and several of her wish-fulfilling errors—such as her claim to have spotted Garbo on the streets of Constantinople although she wasn't there at the same time. Swenson nevertheless takes Mercedes seriously as a source and as an influence in Garbo's life.

25. De Acosta, *Here Lies the Heart,* 223.

26. Swenson, *Greta Garbo: A Life Apart,* 256.

27. In the sequel of *Hollywood Babylon*—a pair of volumes that might be considered Mercedes's memoir's evil-twin document in its name-dropping, queer perspective on movie stars—Kenneth Anger printed snapshots of Garbo from this trip without the sweater without mention of the image's provenance (a practice that defines his use of visual material). Nor does he mention Mercedes's presence behind the camera. The photo exists forever underground, a sublime signifier of Mercedes's marginal role in Hollywood history rendered slightly sordid. *Hollywood Babylon II* (New York: Dutton, 1984), 274.

28. Anita Loos to Cecil Beaton, September 29, 1932, in Vickers, *Loving Garbo*, 4. Beaton doubtless did hear it from Mercedes's own lips, since they stayed friends, and compared notes on Garbo, for decades. Hugo Vickers, Beaton's literary executor, opens his book on the relationship between the three of them with this memorable letter.

29. Riva, *Marlene Dietrich*, 154.

30. Mercedes de Acosta to Marlene Dietrich, n.d. Quoted in Riva, *Marlene Dietrich*, 168.

31. Riva, *Marlene Dietrich*, 168.

32. Dietrich to de Acosta, July 23, 1933. Despite the throwaway nature of her letters, Dietrich was much more in control of and verbal about her work. With this letter she sends her recordings she'd done on the trip, telling Mercedes not to play them too loud. Granted, Garbo had retired by the time her correspondence with de Acosta picked up in earnest, but, always an intuitive artist, she says nothing about her work life except for how it exhausts her and that she would like to be, well, left alone.

33. Riva, *Marlene Dietrich*, 168.

34. Cecil Beaton to Mercedes de Acosta. Quoted in Vickers, *Loving Garbo*, 210.

35. Parker Tyler, "The Garbo Image," in *The Films of Greta Garbo*, compiled by Michael Conway, Dion McGregor, and Mark Ricci (New York: Citadel, 1968), 12 and 15.

36. Roland Barthes, "The Face of Garbo," reprinted in *Film Theory and Criticism: Introductory Readings*, 6th ed., ed. Leo Braudy and Marshall Cohen (London: Oxford University Press, 2004), 589–91.

37. Quoted in Cox, "Garbo's Secret Still a Secret."

38. De Acosta, *Here Lies the Heart*, 212.

39. Ibid., 228–29.

40. Ibid., 243.

41. See Andrea Weiss, "'A Queer Feeling When I Look at You': Female Stars and Lesbian Spectatorship in the 1930s," in *Stardom: Industry of Desire*, ed. Christine Gledhill (London: Routledge, 1991), 283–99.

42. Salka Viertel, *The Kindness of Strangers* (New York: Holt Reinhart, 1969), 175.

43. Elza Schallert, "Do You Know the NEW Garbo?" *Movie Classic*, n.d., 19.

44. De Acosta, *Here Lies the Heart*, 230.

45. Riva, *Marlene Dietrich*, 206.

46. Esther Newton, "The Mythic Mannish Lesbian," *Signs* 9:4 (1984): 557–75.

For the comparison between Garbo's persona in Queen Christina and Stephen Gordon, see White, *Uninvited,* 13–14.

47. Dietrich to Acosta, November 6, 1932.

48. "The Sketch," November 7, 1934, 265.

49. De Acosta, *Here Lies the Heart,* 229. The fact that Mercedes's caption differs from those in her clippings files doesn't necessarily mean she paraphrased or quoted it from memory. Note, though, that she puts her name first, and of course spells it correctly. Another time the photo appeared, the caption was just as sartorially obsessed: "Corduroy slacks, jersey sweater, and oxfords—Greta returns from a long walk with Mercedes de Acosta." "It's No Snap to Snap Garbo," *Movie Mirror,* n.d., 20.

50. Radclyffe Hall, *The Well of Loneliness* (Garden City, NY: Sun Dial Press, 1928), 151.

51. Judith Halberstam, *Female Masculinity* (Durham, NC: Duke University Press, 1998), 99. My emphasis.

52. *Screen Book Magazine,* n.d., 29; "It's No Snap to Snap Garbo!" 20.

53. De Acosta, *Here Lies the Heart,* 233.

54. Greta Garbo to Salka Viertel, July 10, 1935, quoted in Swenson, *Garbo: A Life Apart,* 341.

55. Vickers, *Loving Garbo,* 281.

56. Mercedes de Acosta to William McCarthy, October 31, 1964, Rosenbach Museum and Library, De Acosta collection, box 7, item 1, quoted with permission, emphasis in original.

57. Cohen, "Fame Fatale."

58. Acosta to McCarthy, July 25, 196?, emphasis in original.

59. For Mercedes, Greta was a refined taste: "What relation had Mrs. America to a Viking's daughter whose soul was swept by wind and snow?" (*Here Lies the Heart,* 314). Beaton pays tribute to Mercedes's own ethnic mapping of her romantic persona: "She had excellent, severe Spanish taste—in her furnishing & in her interiors using only black & white—& was never willing to accept the vulgarity of so many American standards. She was strikingly un-American in her black tricorn & buckled shoes, highwayman coat & jet black dyed hair." Quoted in Vickers, *Loving Garbo,* 281. On the juncture of European modernism and Hollywood, see Miriam Hansen, "The Mass Production of the Senses: Classical Cinema as Vernacular Modernism," in *Reinventing Film Studies,* ed. Christine Gledhill and Linda Williams (London: Arnold, 2000), 332–50.

Part 3

EXCAVATING EARLY CINEMA

The early years of cinema history have proven to be a particularly rich area for feminist study both in regard to the amount of research undertaken by scholars in this domain and in the diversity of methodologies implemented, from archival and biographical accounts, cultural and reception studies, to poetic and interpretive readings of historical materials. This impressive body of work speaks to the interrogation of and fascination with an era and an emerging creative form that posed incredible opportunities for women in a pivotal artistic, cultural, and industrial space, and women's participation in early filmmaking can be found across a range of activities: they were directors, stars, screenwriters, editors, and producers. Moreover, as we know from a variety of research, notably Miriam Hansen's *Babel and Babylon: Spectatorship in American Silent Film* and Shelley Stamp's *Movie-Struck Girls,* women were a significant presence in the early cinema audience.[1]

Of course, as Jane Gaines and Giuliana Bruno have noted, the employment openings for women were owing in no small part to the cinema's lowly or at least unfamiliar status,[2] and certainly the allure of Alice Guy-Blaché's role as the "first woman director" is a bit diminished when we know it was approved by Léon Gaumont on the condition that it did not interfere with her secretarial duties. Nevertheless, as Cari Beauchamp's important book, *Without Lying Down: Francis Marion and the Powerful Women of Early Hollywood,* makes clear, the impact of women during the early years was neither short lived nor trivial.[3] While it might be stated that the influence of women within the Hollywood context diminishes with the coming of sound—although that in itself is a comment that re-

quires much more historiographical and theoretical exploration since it is
dependent upon how and where we define the site(s) of influence—it is,
at this point, undeniable that the cultural and economic power of women
during the silent era was extraordinary. Indeed, it is perhaps not an exaggeration to say that the larger field of "cinema," including both filmmaking
and audience practices of the time, functioned as kind of community for
women.

It is important to note here that early cinema emerged as a vital area
for feminist investigation, not only because of the quantitative increase in
filmmaking or viewing by women at that time, but for a range of questions
evoked by this line of inquiry, in part due to film's emerging forms—economic, cultural, and aesthetic. Miriam Hansen points to silent cinema's
part in breaking down formerly rigid distinctions between public and private as gendered domains. Moreover, "moving pictures" operated in concert with a range of other commercial and entertainment forms such as advertising, amusement parks, vaudeville, and department stores to produce
the "modern woman" as a key component and performer in consumer
culture.[4] While some argue that the early films carry the nascent codes
of classical patriarchal cinema, the very notion of the "modern woman"
troubles these homogenized models. Jennifer Bean's work on Pearl White
and my study of Musidora both propose the body of the female star during
this time as a site that demonstrates modernity's destabilization of "fixed"
codes of sexuality and identity.[5] For Anne Friedberg, the fluidity of identity
is not limited to the screen but also to the spectator and, again, is part of
this larger cultural mosaic driven by new ways of seeing primed by new
commercial and entertainment forms.[6]

At the textual level, Judith Mayne argues that many of the early films
uncover the contradictions at the heart of gendered vision through their
very unfamiliarity and strangeness—and thereby suggest an object lesson
for our understanding of its later more seemingly hegemonic form (i.e.,
classical cinema).[7] To put this another way, early films both foreground and
undermine a rigid application of the mantra "woman as spectacle," since
spectacle in this context is clearly extended outside its assumed gendered
"home" and can no longer only be read as an exploited, passive, and "feminine" state.[8]

In this section of essays, it is clear that the "modern woman" and
notions of spectacle are crucial to understanding early cinema. Sumiko
Higashi's "Vitagraph Stardom: Constructing Personalities for 'New' Middle-Class Consumption" provides important groundwork for our under-

standing of the rise of consumer culture during this time and the vital role of stars in the redefinitions of self in line with that ethos. Higashi's examination of early trade journals and fan magazines notes the transformation of such stars as Maurice Costello and Florence Turner into a highly specific commodity form that facilitates a parallel cultural makeover—one that privileges a notion of self as European, middle-class, and heterosexual (with the stars' lives literally being rescripted in line with these traits.)

Like stars, Hollywood screenwriters—who were predominantly female—also played a formative role in the cultural landscape of this era. Giuliana Muscio's essay, "Clara, Ouida, Beulah, et. al.: Women Screenwriters in American Silent Cinema," makes a point to see these women not as exceptional "authors" but as a collective group, a historical framing that enables us to understand their construction of and their own construct as "this modern female of the species."[9] Muscio's research also underlines other studies on the power and influence of the women screenwriter at this time in Hollywood. What becomes clear, though, in this essay is how common the phenomenon was—that is, this was not a few extraordinary individuals who accidentally or heroically forged ahead, but rather a significant group indicative of women's changing role in the U.S. culture of modernity.

Amy Shore's essay in this collection, "Making More than a Spectacle of Themselves: Creating the Militant Suffragette in *Votes for Women,*" speaks to another variant of the modern American woman, the suffragette. For Shore, the women's suffrage movement skillfully utilized diverse components of visual culture, from public demonstrations to a kinetophone experimental sound film (*Votes for Women,* 1913), to reshape the political and social landscape for women. More specifically, the suffragette's public display and voicing of female political desire in effect worked toward rewriting the notion of female spectacle as solely a silent and passive enterprise at the service of male spectatorial pleasure. While both the cinema and female desire (and the female voice) were soon to be recuperated within patriarchal discourse, Shore argues that our "recovery" of this rarely examined moment in women and film's history allows us to reshape not just our understanding of the past but also the potential of visual culture as an organizing tool.

The modern woman is also the central focus of Joanne Hershfield's essay, "Visualizing the Modern Mexican Woman: *Santa* and Cinematic Nation-Building." Hershfield argues that the early sound film *Santa* (1931) maps out an ambiguous response to both the modern city and the modern woman through an examination of the lead character, Santa's, fall into prostitution after her arrival in Mexico City from the countryside. Significantly, it is the linking of the woman's body with new technologies (of the city space and sound cinema) that helps to establish a national identity and national cinema in line with modernization and modernity. Methodologically, Hershfield's essay is noteworthy for its exploration of Mexican cinema with regard to gendered issues of modernity and also for her skillful interweaving of textual analysis and cultural context in her historical account.

Along these lines, but suggesting a poetic tone and structure, Sandy Flitterman-Lewis offers a fascinating juxtaposition of parallel histories with her essay, "Sisters in Rebellion: The Unexpected Kinship of Germaine Dulac and Virginia Woolf." Tracing the lives and deaths of these two feminist icons of the early avant-garde during an era of fascist oppression enables us to understand ways in which all our histories might be linked in collective struggle.

Notes

1. Miriam Hansen, *Babel and Babylon: Spectatorship in American Silent Film* (Cambridge: Harvard Press, 1991); Shelley Stamp, *Movie-Struck Girls: Women and Motion Picture Culture after the Nickelodeon* (Princeton: Princeton University Press, 2000).

2. Janc Gaines, "Of Cabbages and Authors," in *A Feminist Reader in Early Cinema,* ed. Jennifer M. Bean and Diane Negra (Durham, NC: Duke University Press, 2002), 105. Gaines here notes Guy-Blaché's and Notari's parallel "opportunities" and cites Guiliana Bruno's important book, *Streetwalking on a Ruined Map: Cultural Theory and the City Films of Elvira Notari* (Princeton: Princeton University Press, 1993).

3. Cari Beauchamp, *Without Lying Down: Frances Marion and the Powerful Women of Early Hollywood* (New York: Scribner, 1997).

4. Hansen, *Babel and Babylon,* 116–17.

5. Jennifer M. Bean, "Technologies of Early Stardom and the Extraordinary Body," in Bean and Negra, *A Feminist Reader,* 404–43 ; Vicki Callahan, *Zones of Anxiety: Movement, Musidora, and the Crime Serials of Louis Feuillade* (Detroit: Wayne State University Press, 2005).

6. Anne Friedberg, *Window Shopping: Cinema and the Postmodern* (Berkeley: University of California Press, 1993).

7. Judith Mayne, "Uncovering the Female Body," in *Before Hollywood: Turn-of-the-Century Film from American Archives,* ed. Jay Leyda (Manchester, VT: Hudson Hills Press, 1987), 66–67.

8. Although Judith Mayne's "Uncovering the Female Body" (mentioned in the previous note) and Tom Gunning's work on "attractions" (see his "The Cinema of

Attractions: Early Film, Its Spectator, and the Avant-Garde," in *Early Cinema: Space Frame Narrative,* ed. Thomas Elsaesser and Adam Barker [Berkeley: University of California Press, 1990], 56–62) proceed from different frameworks, this implication can be drawn from both works, although Mayne would no doubt argue that gendered vision has not been vanquished (in either its early or classical forms) as much as exposed in all its contradictions.

9. Frederick Van Vranken, "Women's Work in Motion Pictures," *Motion Picture Magazine,* August 1923, 28–29, 89–90 (cited in Muscio, "Clara, Ouida, Beulah, et. al.: Women Screenwriters in American Silent Cinema," this volume).

Further Reading

Higashi, Sumiko. *Cecil B. DeMille and American Culture: The Silent Era.* Berkeley: University of California Press, 1994.

Kirby, Lynne. *Parallel Tracks: The Railroad and Silent Cinema.* Durham, NC: Duke University Press, 1997.

McMahan, Alison. *Alice Guy-Blaché: Lost Visionary of the Cinema.* New York: Continuum, 2002.

Rabinovitz, Lauren. *For the Love of Pleasure: Women, Movies, and Culture in Turn-of the-Century Chicago.* New Brunswick: Rutgers University Press, 1998.

Singer, Ben. "Female Power in the Serial Queen Melodrama: The Etiology of an Anomaly." *Camera Obscura* 22 (January 1990): 91–129.

Slide, Anthony. *Early Women Directors.* New York: A. S. Barnes, 1977.

Staiger, Janet. *Bad Women: Regulating Sexuality in Early American Cinema.* Minneapolis: University of Minnesota Press, 1995.

Sumiko Higashi

Chapter 12

Vitagraph Stardom
Constructing Personalities for "New" Middle-Class Consumption

> Motion picture players must be actors with . . . personality.
> —J. Stuart Blackton

> The situation of the new middle class . . . may be seen as symptom and symbol of modern society as a whole.
> —C. Wright Mills

Answering a query from a curious fan identified as J. M. in New York in 1911, the editors of *Motion Picture Story Magazine* state, "Maurice Costello does not 'hire out' for Vitagraph nights. He is very courteous in complying with requests for public appearances, but he receives no fee for his work." Apparently, J. M., most likely female, wished to see her idol in person. She was not alone. Several personal appearances by Florence Turner, the Vitagraph Girl, had earlier resulted in mob scenes at local theaters in the Northeast. Although her spectacular but brief ascent as a star began to stall in 1912, she remained an attraction. When she appeared that spring at the People's Theatre in Portland, Oregon, "the house was crowded to the doors and hundreds were turned away."[1] Caught unawares by the rise of stars equivalent to luminaries on the theatrical and operatic stage, early film producers began to understand the phenomenon of stardom. An example is *The Picture Idol* (1912), a Vitagraph one-reeler starring Maurice Costello, that is a self-reflexive text about the construction of both stars and fans. As such, it is informative not only about product differentiation and audience reception but also the larger sociohistoric context.

During the early twentieth century, the American middle class was undergoing a historic transformation in composition and ethos that was signified by the emergence of stars. Decidedly not bourgeoisie, who were the respectable middle class? Why were their cultural values being eclipsed? What was the relationship between the rise of celebrity and a changing social structure rooted in urban demographics? Contrary to a Marxist definition of workers in terms of mode of production, American social historians stress social and cultural experience basic to the middle class: family life, education, associations, residence, nonmanual labor, and consumption.[2] Class differences were not only marked but entrenched. Yet the expanding white-collar labor force that worked in corporate America was becoming less homogeneous and more stratified. Consumption, as signified by stars, became the most visible mark of success for the striving "new" middle class and involved not only acquiring goods but transforming selves.

Changing demographics that resulted in a salaried "new" middle class, in contrast to an independent, propertied "old" middle class, required a corresponding shift in modes of self-presentation. Put another way, the accelerating movement from a producer to a consumer economy transformed self-making, as Warren Susman argues, in the first decade of the twentieth century. Signifying the respectable middle class was a model, namely the nineteenth-century concept of character based on self-discipline that was essential to preserving social order and personal morality. Such a prudent and upright individual, however, was not in sync with an evolving consumer economy. Changes in self-making related to consumption as an index of class, therefore, was an undeniable sign of the times. Contrary to the emphasis on character as rooted in ethics, self-restraint, and civic duty, the modern personality was vibrant and attractive.[3] A performer like stage and screen stars, such a personality embraced consumption and risked self-commodification to define the self in a fluid and mobile society. As prototypes, then, stars illustrated the social dynamic and moral issues underlying a consumer culture focused on celebrity.

A transformation in self-making was opportune for middle-class women at a time when Victorian female culture, a homosocial world in which "men made but a shadowy appearance," gave way to mixed-sex leisure and companionate marriage. Contrary to stereotypes, the social construction of gender in the nineteenth century may have produced more, not less, freedom for women. Strong kinship and friendship ties that diminished emotional commitment to marriage or led to Boston marriages among women were common. Self-making in a consumer society, on the other

hand, resulted in greater objectification of females in heterosexual relations.[4] Yet women were now poised to become personalities in ways that
contrasted with previous constraints in self-definition. Appearing as "New
Women" in downtown shopping districts like the Ladies' Mile in Manhattan, they became modern consumers.[5] Predictably, female consumption
became a means of self-making as spectacle in heterosexual romance. As
for working- and lower middle-class women without disposable incomes,
they too redefined themselves by identifying with stars. At the very least,
they consumed images weighted with symbolism at neighborhood venues. Signifying the exchange value of film, especially for moviegoers at the
lower end of the social spectrum, stars were box-office attractions that fans
transformed into objects of commodity fetishism.[6] A troubling portent,
the commodification of self in relation to fetishized others became the basis of social relations in modern urban America.

Stardom as Commodity Fetishism: The Picture Idol

The Picture Idol shows that studios and trade journals were aware of the
contradictions involved in both constructing a star's persona and in a fan's
idolatrous reception. Maurice Costello, a veteran of theatrical stock companies who became Vitagraph's first male star, plays himself. Worshipped
by a schoolgirl named Bertha (Clara Kimball Young), he is the focus of
her entire existence. Although movie fans were not then overwhelmingly
female, spectatorship, like consumption, was construed as irrational so that
fans were characterized in terms of gender. Indeed, *The Picture Idol* illustrates the film studio's role in constructing romance as an obsession for
girls no longer defined by Victorian homosocial culture. Bertha lacks close
relations with her mother, teachers, and friends and is, instead, obsessed
with celebrity. During the screening of Costello's latest film, she sits in
rapt admiration in the front row across the aisle from an acquaintance.
A view of the projection booth window in the rear calls attention to the
cinematic apparatus constructing stardom. A reverse angle shot shows the
actor on screen as he engages in melodramatic heroics. Although editing
reinforces the distance between stalwart star and awestruck fan, their paths
frequently cross in ways that seem contrived. Contrary to the precondi-
tions for stardom articulated by Richard Dyer, Bertha and Costello inhabit
a space approximating a small town rather than a large-scale urban grid.[7]
As she walks to school, the infatuated girl notices her idol on the sidewalk,

follows him home, and sends him flowers. All her repressed adolescent sexual energy is focused on Costello.

More significant than physical proximity is the fact that Bertha and Costello are members of a homogeneous social world that is comfortably middle-class. At the beginning of the film, a shot of a woman emerging from the theater, which predates sumptuous movie palaces, shows her wearing a fur stole. She is far from slumming, however. As evident inside the theater, the movie audience is formally dressed. Any hint of the reality of workers and immigrants seeking cheap amusement in crowded storefront nickelodeons has been erased.[8] The film thus rewrites the social origins of early film reception and, in keeping with Vitagraph's middlebrow pretensions, represents the medium as a middle-class product. Celebrity status signified by conspicuous, upper-class consumption is also downplayed. As a character, Costello is well dressed and lives in a comfortable home, but he is not ensconced in a mansion behind walls. An actor in his thirties with a receding hairline, he even demystifies stardom and seems rather ordinary. Indeed, he willingly participates in a scheme drawn up by Bertha's worried father (Charles Eldridge), who calls on him to propose a scene to discredit his persona.[9]

A subsequent dinner guest in Bertha's home, Costello purposely displays appalling table manners as uniformed servants wait on him. When the schoolgirl persists in clinging to her romantic image, an invitation to his house forces her to confront the shocking "reality" of his wife and four small children. Actually, Costello's "wife" is an amused male acquaintance in drag. Chastened, Bertha tears up the photo of her cherished idol and will presumably accept a proper suitor. Destined to become a middle-class wife and mother—a fate ridiculed by the actor in drag—the young girl finally submits to the social constraint of gender roles. She had chased Costello with singular determination, but her idol helped put her back in her place. Victimized by his many guises, she is manipulated by fetishized images and so is unable to interpret their meanings. Starstruck or bound for conventional marriage, Bertha is unable to realize her own identity as a young girl on the verge of womanhood.

Although Bertha is cured of her fetishistic behavior, "real" fans may have become even more curious about Costello's private life. Appearing with an actor in drag raised issues about masculinity and sexual identity that were only humorously addressed. According to an article titled "A Trip to Vitagraphville," published a couple of years later, Costello himself enjoyed appearing in drag: "He had a lot of fun not long ago when he impersonated a sweet young girl in one of the pictures they took down at Brighton Beach."[10] What these drag appearances amounted to, at a time when spectators had minimal information about stars, was a big tease. Rather than satisfying the curiosity of fans, a film that exploited a star's persona intensified queries. According to a brief review of *The Picture Idol* that questions stargazing, such a text might be questionable: "the film affords him [Costello] an opportunity to cure by mental suggestion at least some of his devoted admirers. . . . Of course, the idol worshippers who see the picture will easily excuse Mr. Costello, on the ground that it would be impossible for him to be that sort of man in real life, so if it were his intention to cure his devotees, it is, perhaps a very deep psychological question as to what the exact result will be."[11]

A spectator's obsession with a screen image was, however, not an individual aberration but a cultural development signifying a profound change in social relations. Stardom as a widespread form of commodity fetishism signified the end of small-town values and the subsequent estrangement of human beings in an industrial order. *The Picture Idol* mitigates this transformation by showcasing its star in a small-town milieu. But under consumer capitalism, social relations would eventually be subject to reification so that, in the words of Georg Lukács, "a relation between people takes on the character of a thing."[12] When personality displaced character as the basis for self-making in urban life, human beings and relationships became commodities subject to market forces. Adherence to ethical precepts as a cornerstone of small-town life no longer determined either self-worth or public recognition. Appearances were more important because the modern personality was based on image. Women were especially vulnerable because they were commodified as spectacle in heterosexual romance, while losing the supportive homosocial ties of Victorian female culture. Unfortunately, appearances could be deceptive. The respectable middle class had codified behavior at social rituals as an index of both character and breeding. But they too grappled with appearances because the decline of referentiality in an urban world of strangers undermined conventional ties. Within the unstable semiotic context of the city, the curiosity of fans about stars was an attempt to gain currency in their quest for reliable information. Stars, on the other hand, exploited the exchange value of their personas. As Epes Winthrop Sargent observed, "personality is the chief asset of the player."[13] According to *Motion Picture News*'s history of Vitagraph, the result could be unpleasant: "Fan worship of Florence Turner and Maurice Costello had

swept over the world of picture goers; and it was inevitable that this idol-
izing should bring out emotional instability in stars, big and little, who
might have remained soberly untemperamental if their bankrolls had not
skyrocketed."[14] Apparently, increased market value, a sign of reification,
led to irrationality both among celebrities who profited and fans who paid
for tickets.

Discourse on stardom as commodity fetishism was still being codified
during this transitional period in social and film history, as signified by Bertha's access to Costello and the rapidity of her cure in *The Picture Idol.* Also
indeterminate was the gender of the movie fan, though idolatry meant a
young starstruck female in Vitagraph's film. Bertha's scheme to investigate
a star's identity, however, was not atypical. As Richard DeCordova argues,
essential to a discourse on stars after 1909 was their identification. When
the focus shifted a few years later to scrutiny about their private lives, such
personalities evolved into stars.[15] According to this (overly) schematic time
frame, Costello was not yet a full-fledged movie star. But even the scant
publicity about his private life attests that the components of stardom were
already in place. Spectator interest about the identity and lives of players
implied a curiosity that could not be sated. Acknowledgment of performers' names by all the studios except Biograph only served to intensify such
questioning. As evidenced by trade journals like *Moving Picture World* and
the first fan magazine, *Motion Picture Story Magazine,* industry attempts
to manipulate reception was often countered by obsessive fans influencing
the trajectory of stardom. As Epes Winthrop Sargent acknowledged, "the
manager can only avail himself of the advantages derived from the exploitation of personality since the situation has run away from him."[16]

Fans presumably did not read trade journals, but exhibitors courting
their business certainly did. According to *Motography:* "Vitagaph measures
the public better than any other maker . . . . And Vitagraph hasn't shown
any foolish aversion to featuring their players. Maurice Costello and Florence Turner are the best known names among the actor folks today, simply
because they have been known for so long. . . . Now all the companies
are featuring their players, except Biograph."[17] A few months earlier, *Moving Picture World* had featured a photograph of Maurice Costello under
the caption "Picture Personalities." A brief comment stresses "the interest
which the public is taking in the personalities of the leading moving picture actors and actresses seen on the screen." Cited as a player "coming into
his own," Costello, the journal asserts, has been proving that an actor can
be as popular as an actress: "Just as much interest attaches to the leading

man of a moving picture company amongst the fair sex, as attaches to the personality of an actress amongst men."[18] Although this comment typically construes fandom in terms of heterosexual romance, like Bertha's obsession in *The Picture Idol,* trade papers did not then construct the movie fan as an infatuated female. And neither did the first fan magazines.

In Search of Maurice Costello:
Fandom in Motion Picture Story Magazine

Motion Picture Story Magazine (hereafter *MPSM*) was the brainchild of J. Stuart Blackton (Jimmy), cofounder of American Vitagraph, and Eugene V. Brewster, later publisher of *Motion Picture Classic.*[19] A product of the Motion Picture Publishing Company in Brooklyn, site of Vitragraph's Flatbush studio, the magazine cost fifteen cents per issue or $1.50 for an annual subscription. The first issue, published in February 1911, features an editorial with middlebrow pretensions and illustrated short story versions of the "very best" photoplays. Among the sections is a photo gallery titled "Personalities of the Picture Players" that, significantly, would be moved from back to front and expanded in later issues. Singled out for a brief write-up in the issue is Maurice Costello. A description of his stage and film career stresses "the impress of genius" and enumerates his notable roles in intertextual works like *Orestes, Electra, St. Elmo,* and the forthcoming *A Tale of Two Cities.* Such a resume, however, would fail to satisfy the curiosity of devotees like Bertha.[20] Indeed, the "will to knowledge" among fans, still undifferentiated in terms of gender, led to increased focus on stardom and passive forms of spectatorship that would characterize females in the 1920s.

During the first few months of its publication, inquisitive fans bombarded *MPSM* with so many queries that the publisher introduced a department titled "Answers to Inquiries." As the Inquiry Editor himself acknowledged, "when Mr. Blackton suggested that we take over a department for questioners, we were inclined to scoff at the suggestion that such a department would be of interest to the readers." But a deluge of letters prompted him to establish guidelines. Presumably, questions regarding the technology of the film business were written by curious males. But both female and male readers—the latter only somewhat outnumbered—made inquiries about stars. Some correspondents, like Flossie C. P., wore out their welcome by sending in several queries for each issue: "You've overrun your allowance by two letters." Also undesirable were questions about

Maurice Costello, Vita-
graph's first male star, became famous in one-reelers
and won *Motion Picture
Story Magazine*'s first popularity contest.

the private lives of stars. Sounding emphatic, the editors stated in August 1911, "Under no circumstances can we give the personal addresses of any of the players." But in the same issue they informed J. M. that Costello's "studio name is 'Dimples.' We do not know his age, but he is still in his early thirties." *Moving Picture World* reported a Costello appearance, thronged with fans, at the Fulton Auditorium in Brooklyn in 1910. Another fan was informed in December 1911, "We do not know whether the Vitagraph players work under 'real' or stage names, but we do know that Maurice Costello uses his own name in the pictures. He is of French parentage [they mistakenly add]." Still plagued by fans, the editors stated firmly in October 1911, "No matrimonial information is supplied." Also, they informed more than one fan that, contrary to stories recalling similar false gossip about the death of Florence Lawrence, the Biograph Girl, "Mr. Costello is alive—very much so."[21] In March 1912, the editors repeated their policy to alert pesky readers: "This department is for the answering of general interest only. Involved technical questions will not be answered [a statement alluding to male fans]. Information as to the matrimonial alliances of the players and other purely personal matters will not be answered. Questions

271

concerning the marriages of players will be completely ignored. . . . No questions can be answered relating to the identity of the Biograph players."[22] Accordingly, a transgressing fan is lectured: "You're not only asking matrimonial questions, but you are on forbidden grounds." Yet in April 1912 the editors responded: "The handsome man is Maurice Costello and as there is a Mrs. Costello, he probably would not be interested in an 'heiress of millions' who breathes her love in post cards." A piece published much later even describes Costello's awkward marriage proposal: "he blubbered, fluttered, flustered and otherwise made himself conspicuous by his lack of speech." Brief data about Costello's two daughters appeared in the magazine in February 1913: "Yes, Helen Costello [who appeared with him in some films] is about six, and Delores [who would also have a screen career and marry John Barrymore] is about twelve." As these examples show, fans clamored for details about the private lives of stars but were given minimal information. A line about Costello in the *Toledo Times* in September 1914 attests that biographical data was indeed scarce: "Sorry to relate (this for the girls) he was married to Miss May Treasham, a nonprofessional, and has two lovely little girls."[23] Significantly, what began in *MPSM* as a brief section to deal with queries had expanded to twenty-five single-spaced pages by December 1913. Additionally, departments such as "Chats with the Players" and "Greenroom Jottings: Little Whispering Room from Everywhere in Playerdom" informed readers about stars. In March 1914 *MPSM* even dropped the word "story" from its title and became *Motion Picture Magazine*. By that time, the illustrated photoplay stories that had made up most of the content in early days, when middlebrow emphasis was on narrative, had been displaced by coverage of the industry and stardom as well as by increasing ads. The magazine was showing signs of relentless commodification under consumer capitalism.

As Vitagraph's first leading man, Costello was interviewed in "Chats with the Players" in April 1912. Claiming that he is everyman, he enhances reader identification: "I have never gone to college, haven't any favorite flower, never did anything heroic, and know all my neighbors." But he also says, "the more I can get of life in the open, the better I like it, whether it be walking, swimming, motor-boating, or any out-door sport." As popularized by Theodore Roosevelt's pursuit of a strenuous life in an effort to debunk overcivilization, the sportsman's existence was an upper-class privilege. A subsequent focus on Costello's two daughters in "Chats with the Players" in June 1913 shows him on the upholstered leather seat of his roadster, decidedly a big-ticket item.[24] According to the chat: "At their beautiful home in Flatbush the children get all the joys of country life, combined with the advantages of a great city. Every morning, in the summertime, the whole family pile into the big touring-car and are off to the beach. . . . [Yet] the Costellos are nothing if not democratic, and the children attend the public school."[25] Attendance at public schools—still out of reach for many working-class families—stress commonalities. But publicity focused on the star's expensive and materialistic life style. Celebrities represented not only studio product differentiation but also consumer goods signifying success. An article in the *Pittsburgh Leader* reported that when Costello bought "a beautiful home near the [Vitagraph] Brooklyn studio," his "ninety horsepower machine" was so enormous that it did not fit in the pathway "along the side of the house." At the time, the actor had just returned from "Vitagraph's World Tour," a well-publicized trip that involved location shooting at exotic locales.[26] Granted, film stars were not then idols of consumption on the same scale projected in the 1920s. But earlier publicity about famous stage actors and opera singers had already focused on palatial homes, expensive cars, and travel abroad. Stars thus prefigured the consumer durables revolution that transformed the economy after the First World War with the spread of automobiles, rural electrification, and communication.[27]

As a way of measuring fan worship, *MPSM* conducted popularity contests that commodified stars in a marketing ploy to boost circulation. Subscribers had to send in votes on a coupon printed in the magazine (a procedure that prompted one fan to protest against players who had "rich friends") or write an "appreciatory letter or verse." When Costello garnered 430,316 votes to win the first "Popular Player Contest" in June 1912, the editors stated, "We know of no other contest that has created the enthusiasm that this one has created," and prefaced the tally with a verse of their own:

> There is one whom the girls call "Dimples,"
>   A man that we all adore
> The Beau Brummel of the Vitagraph
>   And winner of hearts galore.[28]

Since the landscape of stardom was constantly shifting, especially at a time when one-reelers were being displaced by features, the magazine held successive contests with monthly tallies to prod fans to vote. Girls like Bertha may have been more enthusiastic as male stars became the focus of their attention. But female fans were also fickle. Contest results in 1913 showed that Costello, who won the previous year, had fallen to thirteenth place with 183,422 votes. As a variation, the magazine then launched "The Great Artist Contest" by stating, "a player may be very popular, or very pretty, or very graceful, or very picturesque, and all that without being a great artist." When the results were announced in October 1914, Costello's star had waned slightly further as he won 169,580 votes to rank seventeenth.[29] Declining numbers roughly correspond with the trajectory of his film output: one release in 1909, four in 1910, nineteen in 1911, thirty-one in 1912, thirty in 1913, twenty-four in 1914, eight in 1915, and one in 1916.[30]

Costello's stardom was beginning to wane during the very years when he directed his own films rather than acting under Van Dyke Brooke, the director who introduced him to the screen.[31] According to *Moving Picture World*, "his ability as a player had gained him the promotion to director." An assessment of his own input at Vitagraph was blunt: "Acting is child's play. It's directing that is the grinding work." Yet Costello was aware of the changing nature of acting and stated in an interview in 1912, "Now that we have character parts, much more careful study is required, an ability to express the part distinctly, briefly, truly, and eloquently or with appeal."[32] Despite his awareness of acting requirements, Costello's stardom faded during the transition from one-reelers to features. Stars were beginning to sustain careers in feature-length films enhanced by psychologically motivated characters, technological innovation such as lighting and color, and the evolution of film language.[33] Greater curiosity about their private lives may well have been intensified by feature films' enhancing of spectator identification. Costello's appearance in scores of one-reelers, which expanded to a few two- and three-reelers in 1914–15, was thus a disadvantage. Also, he was handicapped to the extent that the Motion Picture Patents Company, a trust formed in 1909 by nine manufacturers, including Vitagraph, lagged behind independent producers in innovation. Because early stars, like other commodities, symbolized changing values in a shifting social context, their careers were often short-lived. Decidedly on the decline, Costello suffered a nervous breakdown in 1915 and was involved a few years later in violent episodes, including wife battering, that led to arrests.[34] Such scenes were more shocking than demystification in *The Picture Idol* and would have disenchanted fans like Bertha.

A brief consideration of *Photoplay*, a rival fan magazine, results in similar conclusions about fans obsessed with stardom as a commodity form. Unlike *MPSM*, a promotional tool for Vitagraph, *Photoplay* was headquartered in Chicago and championed the independent exchanges rather than the General Film Company, distributor of the Motion Picture Patents Company. Consequently, Maurice Costello was not featured in its pages. But like Blackton's brainchild, *Photoplay* published its first issue in 1911, used a comparable format, and followed a similar trajectory. It featured a "Gallery of Picture Stars"; emphasized "Photoplay Stories" as illustrated narratives; ran regular departments like "Players' Personalities," "The Photoplaywright and His Art," and "The Question Box" (introduced as "Answers to Inquiries"); published articles on the industry; and conducted popularity contests. Similarly, the magazine, in response to fans, began to downplay emphasis on film as narrative in favor of space devoted to stardom and the industry. And that meant a decline as well in pages devoted to readers interested in writing screenplays, especially at a time when studio production was itself subject to streamlining and division of labor (Blackton and his assistants received more than two thousand scripts a week in Vitagraph's early days).[35] The increasing construction of readers as passive spectators identifying with stars thus predated, but also anticipated, the evolution of fandom as a female pastime.

An Index of Middlebrow Culture: Florence Turner as the Vitagraph Girl

Attempts to elevate film to middlebrow, if not highbrow, status by casting stars as artists appealed to the social aspirations of lower middle- and working-class fans as well as studio bosses. A case in point was Florence Turner, a star whose fame preceded Maurice Costello's and whose name was frequently linked with his. She was a former vaudeville performer who deserted the stage for Vitagraph, a promising studio, in 1907. Cofounded in Manhattan a decade earlier by Blackton and Albert E. Smith, Vitagraph initially released *The Spanish Flag Pulled Down* (1898), a reenactment with actuality footage shot in Cuba during the Spanish-American War, and *The Battle of Manila Bay*, also a reenactment.[36] But since production priorities shifted in 1907 from nonfiction subjects like boxing matches, presidential inaugurations, and natural disasters to story films, Blackton was prescient in casting Turner as the Vitagraph Girl.[37] She excelled in both slapstick and melodrama at a starting salary of twelve dollars a week to become "the central figure in Vitagraph photodramas." A recapitulation of her brief career in *Moving Picture World* in 1916 labels her "the first actress to be featured in a photodrama" and "the only player then before the public who was honored by having her name used in connection with the advertising of a picture." Although these claims tend toward hyperbole, Turner was an enormous attraction, especially when she began to make personal appearances on Vitagraph nights in 1910. As *Moving Picture World* commented about the "good-natured, shoving jostling mob" that sought admission to a Jersey City theater where she appeared late that year, "it was an enlightening illustration, or demonstration, of the hold the moving picture itself has on the people."[38] But Turner achieved stardom unexpectedly so that the construction of her persona reveals the larger social context in which the industry sought cultural legitimacy.

As the Vitagraph Girl, Turner was cast in a mold set by Blackton, an English immigrant who had reported for the *New York World* and rein-

Florence Turner, the popular Vitagraph Girl, made personal appearances at theaters during Vitagraph nights and drew throngs of spectators.

vented himself as a "magnate artist." Descended from an impoverished family in Sheffield, he claimed that his father was "a gifted artist and portrait painter" and rewrote his childhood to include attendance at Eton. As an entrepreneur, he had pretensions to middlebrow, if not Arnoldian highbrow, culture and was determined to elevate the status of his product. Avoiding the lowbrow nickelodeon craze, he showed his films on the "Lyceum circuit of clubs, schools, and churches" and in vaudeville theaters. After construction of a glass-enclosed studio in Brooklyn in 1905, Blackton, who was dubbed "a new Belasco," sought to adapt the works of Charles Dickens, Walter Scott, and James Barrie. According to *Moving Picture World,* he "became one of the pioneers in the production of moving pictures and . . . [was] a solid contributor to the evolution of the new art. . . . Without losing sight of . . . business [and] . . . giving due consideration to the fact that he was addressing mixed audiences of more than one nationality, . . . he turned out some exceptional photoplays."[39] As his reputation and wealth grew, so did Blackton's social ambition. Among his acquisitions were a three-story mansion described as "The Palace of a Movie King," an Oyster Bay country estate, and a yacht. After hobnobbing with the Vanderbilts and Roosevelts, Blackton, dubbed Commodore, became a member of the Motor Boat Club of America and the Atlantic Yacht Club. His wife Paula rubbed elbows with socialites in well-publicized fund-raising activities.[40]

Also reinventing herself, Turner claimed a pedigree that exemplified Vitagraph's middlebrow pretensions. A daughter of the studio's wardrobe mistress, she became the descendant of an "artistic, theatrical, and scientific family" of "Spanish-Italian" (also "French-Italian") lineage. She was most likely Italian. Since workers were ethnic immigrants signifying the urban Other, any trace of foreign origin was sanitized and romanticized. According to a *MPSM* interview that took place while she was recovering from exhaustion in California in 1912, the star was related to Joseph M. W. Turner, "the great painter; her father was an artist and her mother played with all the theatrical celebrities of her time. . . . One of her ancestors was the Italian author and scientist, Palmieri." Turner herself wanted "to be known as a great artist" and, in accordance with the moral tenor of the times, "to live so that when she is gone the world will be a little better and happier for her having lived in it." Crafting the star's persona, the interviewer states, "We talked about everything, from the philosophy of Pythagoras down to the best method of cooking Welsh rabbits in a chafing-dish." Yet Turner remains "democratic" and "shakes hands and talks with the urchins and laborers just as she does with the lords and ladies." A similar article in *Moving Picture World* chimes, "There isn't a trace of affectation about her nor the slightest indication of a swelled head. . . . She isn't a bit haughty." A later review of her career in *Motion Picture Classic* refers to the "intellectual element always present in her work" and deems her "an almost typical 'highbrow.'"[41]

At odds with this refined portrait were reports of the star's early studio days that stressed the haphazard nature of filmmaking in its infancy. As Turner recollected in the *MPSM* interview, her first picture was a slapstick comedy, *How to Cure a Cold.* "We began it at ten one morning and finished in time for lunch." She also remembered, "There was a time . . . when I was the whole Vitagraph 'stock' company. Everyone else was an 'extra.'" As for *Francesca da Rimini,* the studio's attempt to elevate films to middlebrow status, she was amused that "all the men . . . dressed up in Italian costumes. They didn't have a thing on properly; they looked more like accidents than courtiers! Albert Smith took the picture. We didn't have a cameraman, and Commodore Blackton took the stills and acted—everybody, including the director, acted." Indeed, *Green Book* credited Turner with being adept behind the camera as well: she is "a smart little business woman. Fresh from her own performance on the stage, she takes command of the office which deals with production matters." "When D. W. Griffith took charge of the Biograph Company," Turner recalled, "Vitagraph had to work as never before." Although the history of Vitagraph was published much later in *Motion Picture News,* it, too, portrayed "the very first screen star" as an actress who "played stellar roles, swept the offices, paid off the help—and received the first fan letter."[42] Such details show that early filmmakers could not seamlessly construct a star's persona as a signifier of middlebrow culture.

Contradictions in portraying the Vitagraph Girl as a star who was a refined artist but engaged in slapdash production were inevitable at this early stage. Blackton's ambitious design, like those of other filmmakers, was influenced by the unanticipated response of fans obsessed with favorite stars. Supposedly, he labeled Turner the Vitagraph Girl in order to prevent her from decamping to another studio, though he had also hired Mabel Normand and Norma Talmadge.[43] Blackton was bold enough to capitalize on the popularity of his stars, but neither he nor his colleague Brewster could anticipate the deluge of fan mail that would greet the publication of *MPSM.* Significantly, this magazine was launched when Turner and Costello were Vitagraph's biggest attractions. Indeed, the two stars were so often featured together that fans wondered if they were married.[44] The fast-paced production of one-reelers that would play for only half a week at most venues did not, however, constitute conditions that ensured lasting stardom. Stars would make films at breakneck pace in weekly attractions and risk becoming overexposed, while facing constant competition from newcomers. As popular cultural commodities rather than signifiers of lasting Arnoldian culture, stars were subject to market conditions that included fickle fans.

Attesting to the rise of the film star as a cultural phenomenon was a popularity contest conducted by the *New York Telegraph* at the end of 1911. Fans for the first time could vote for their favorites on either stage or screen. The result could not have been clearer: "Florence E. Turner Wins First Prize in Popularity Contest. Charming Leading Lady of the Vitagraph Co. Given More than a Quarter of a Million Votes and Leaves All Her Competition Far in the Rear—She Will Receive $200.00 Diamond as the Prize." Capturing 233,590 votes, Turner emerged ahead of Marguerite Snow, with 97,950 votes, and Mary Pickford, with 64,007 votes. Unfortunately, Turner's subsequent yearlong absence from the screen due to exhaustion meant the eclipse of her stardom. When *MPSM* announced the results of its first popularity contest, a national rather than regional competition, in 1912, Costello won an easy victory. Because she went on hiatus to recover from exhaustion, Turner placed eleventh with only 31,925 votes. She tried to resuscitate her career by returning to the vaudeville stage and formed her own production company in England in 1913.[45] But the Vitagraph Girl became a casualty not only of illness but of rapid developments in early film history. She was a commodity whose value had been determined by fans invested in dreams of upward mobility easily signified by newer and brighter stars in the firmament.

In Pursuit of Dreams: The Gender and Social Class of Fan Magazine Readers

As twentieth-century personalities, stars mediated social relations subject to reification in a consumer culture and symbolized the aspirations of countless fans. Most important, they demonstrated that self-improvement and social mobility were possible in urban life. Since *The Picture Idol* renders both star and filmgoer socially homogeneous, a consideration of gender and social class requires a closer look at the implied readers of early fan magazines. *Motion Picture Story Magazine* and *Photoplay* appealed to male and female fans in slightly different social groups that, as a whole, were working- and lower middle-class.[46] According to Anthony Slide, *Photoplay* was initially five cents cheaper, had fewer stories and less-lavish illustrations, and was "much less handsomely printed in smaller types." *Motion Picture Story Magazine,* on the other hand, was Blackton's brainchild. A determined social climber, he shared the outsider status of editors of middlebrow magazines like *Saturday Evening Post* and *Ladies Home Journal* who constructed "a world of illusory power and participation that masked delimited options and prefabricated responses."[47]

As the force behind Vitagraph's policy of filming literary classics, Blackton, together with his editor Brewster, elevated *MPSM* to middlebrow status with short story versions of "Thomas à Becket" as well as "The City Boys."[48] Blackton stressed his background in art and claimed, "I found my training in painting, photography, the study of lighting, literature—indeed every phase of art that at all touches upon motion-picture making—has stood me in good stead."[49] Adopting strategies to refute the lowbrow reputation of films and their spectators, *MPSM* published testimonials that stated, "the one-time prejudice against the much-reviled photoplay is rapidly dying out." "The photoplay furnishes the poorer classes with a great deal of innocent enjoyment . . . [but a] wide variety of . . . individuals . . . patronize the photoplay house. The tired businessman, the harassed physician, the wearied shop girl, the worried mother with two or three children, the alert lawyer."[50]

Perhaps most telling about the social aspirations of fan magazine readers, as well as the materialistic path to respectability they were advised to pursue, were the ads. Addressed to both sexes, ads first appeared sparingly in the back of the publications but later increased and appeared in the front as well. At no time did the editors then engage in sophisticated ad stripping, that is, the practice of interspersing ads among articles to achieve intertexuality rendering content as advertisement. A closer look at ads shows a mixed message with respect to the nature of self-making and social climbing. Parents are warned, for example, against the evil of young girls reading novels and advised to invest in Every Girl's Library, ten volumes of "a carefully compiled selection of literature suitable for . . . immature tastes and tendencies."[51] Such a moralistic tone harkens back to Victorian paternalism and sentimentalism, stresses self-making in terms of character, and reinforces advice literature prescribing expenditure to achieve middle-class refinement.[52] Girls still required moral supervision and protection despite the arrival of the New Woman signifying modernity. A similar ad for adults proclaims the virtues of The Century Plan of Library Building, which includes works by "Dickens, George Eliot, Balzac, Hugo, Washington Irving, Dumas, Eugène Sue, Walter Scott, and Ainsworth Historical Romances." And for readers stricken with wanderlust but without the means to travel, Burton Holmes Travelogues promised five thousand pictures, claiming, "It would cost you $50,000 and many years of your time to take these journeys."[53]

Yet *MPSM* also ran ads for both sexes that reinforced the presentation of self as a modern personality based on performance, appearance, and consumption. Bernarr McFadden, for example, displays his nude upper torso as "The Foremost Author on Health and Body Building" in an ad for physical culture. Copywriting that exploited anxiety about appearance include: "Crystolis: Stops Falling Hair, Dandruff and Itching Scalp, Restores Grey and Faded Hair to Natural Color and Brilliancy"; "Nose Straightened" (an ad for the services of Dr. E. P. Robinson); "Dr. James P. Campbell's Safe Arsenic Complexion Wafers"; "Beautiful Eyes: Eyelashes and Eyebrows Can Also Be Made Beautiful"; and "Don't Be Bald." Products exploiting women's desire to own signifiers of respectable middle-class status include "The Genuine Cut Glass Water Set."[54] Similarly, *Photoplay* advertised an "Elgin 17-Jewel" watch for $9.95, a "Superb Wing Piano Shipped on 4 Weeks Free Trial," and diamonds and watches on credit. Perhaps most expressive of the tension between ads that encouraged building character as opposed to becoming a personality were books advertised in *MPSM: Sexual Knowledge,* a work that "tells all about sex matters; what young men and women, young wives and husbands, and all others need to know," is peddled on the same page as the International Bible House.[55]

Despite the comfortable status of filmgoers in *The Picture Idol* and revisionist film histories asserting middle-class attendance at nickelodeons, the evidence in fan magazines points to working-class and lower middle-class fans.[56] Perhaps more noteworthy are ads for employment rather than products. Significantly, these ads are aimed mostly at men. As William Chafe points out, women in the early twentieth century had few options and worked as domestics, farm laborers, factory operatives, and teachers. After 1910, restructuring of the work force in a consumer economy included their entry into low-paying white-collar jobs, but they remained cheap and marginal labor through the 1920s.[57] Job listings in fan magazines, though addressed to males, do signify a growing culture of consumption. Among the ads in *MPSM* are "The Practical Auto School: Learn to Run and Repair an Auto." A pitch from the Banner Tailoring Department in Chicago asks, "Young man, would you . . . wear a fine tailor-made suit just for showing it to your friends? . . . Perhaps we can offer you a steady job? Write at once and get beautiful samples, styles, and this wonderful offer." Decidedly a sign of the times, another ad encourages readers to "Learn to Write Advertisements. Earn from $25.00 to $100.00 a Week. Taught Thoroughly by Correspondence in Six Months." The International Correspondence School asserts, "You Can Rise to a Position of Power" and become a "Mine Foreman, Concrete Constructor, Civil Engineer, Architectural Draftsman, Electrical Lighting Superintendent, Chemist, Building Contractor, Advertising Man, Stenographer, Bookkeeper, Poultry Farmer."[58] Such a mix of manual and nonmanual occupations, which were then distinct in terms of income, conditions of work, and status, implied a desire for social mobility but limited means and prospects.[59]

Photoplay ran similar ads. La Salle Extension University claims, "You, Who Work for a Living, Will Be Interested [in] This Story! New Jobs Open—Earn from $35 to $200 Weekly as Traffic Managers." The magazine even ran full-page classifieds that included "Help Wanted" aimed at readers interested in becoming signal engineers, song writers, government workers, and salespeople. Under sections labeled "Business Opportunities" and "Agents Wanted," the classifieds advertised "an instructive book" for persons wishing to become money collectors, or learning the craft of silvering mirrors, or making and selling a confection called Barley Crisps for "large profits."[60] Presumably, the latter represented one of the few opportunities existing for female fans in the burgeoning economy.

Fan magazine culture, in sum, provides intriguing evidence of the transformation of self-making after the turn of the century to stress personality rather than character. Signifying modernity, stars provided role models for both sexes because they embodied the physical characteristics and materialistic lifestyle promised by ads. Women could now aspire to equality with men in terms of aspiration, if not status and income, in a modern consumer society. As working- and lower middle-class individuals, movie fans were eager to rise, especially at a time when class structure and relations were being significantly reconfigured. At the lower rungs of a rapidly expanding "new" middle class were white-collar employees subject to proletarianization and thus anxious to acquire cultural capital signifying status.[61]

A significant development, the changing demographics of white-collar workers coincided, not surprisingly, with the rise of middlebrow culture. As Janice Radway argues, such cultural forms, produced by "immigrant entrepreneurs" like Blackton and his successors in the culture industry, lacked the Arnoldian imprimatur of Brahmins wary about commercialization. Indeed, the selling of culture in an "age of mechanical reproduction" signified the end of elite stewardship based on nineteenth-century class relations. Cultural hierarchies, even for genteel readers, were increasingly difficult to sustain, as the very success of the middlebrow meant interpenetration of highbrow and lowbrow. Promoters like Blackton were, moreover, successful in co-opting the sacrosanct language of Arnoldian highbrow culture to elevate and sell their goods. A product of increasing democratization in modern urban life, middlebrow culture thus became a "sign of achievement" and social distinction for the aspiring "new" middle classes. The very success of the middlebrow signified not only "restructuring of the culture industry," but "class fracture" signifying fragmentation of a previously homogeneous middle class.[62] Within this historical context, striving white-collar workers, including women, became the most likely consumers of such middlebrow products as film. And as fans they sought to redefine themselves, like the screen idols who fascinated them, as modern personalities in a culture of consumption.

Notes

Although injuries precluded travel, I thank Eva Warth and Annette Förster for inviting me to speak at the Gender and Silent Cinema conference, organized by the Institute of Media and Re/Presentation and held at the University of Utrecht in October 1999, and for providing me with a copy of *The Picture Idol* and a translation of intertitles, courtesy of Noemia Backer.

1. *Motion Picture Story Magazine* (hereafter cited as *MPSM*), August 1911, 146; *Moving Picture World* (hereafter cited as *MPW*), April 30, 1912, in Florence Turner clipping file, New York Public Library for the Performing Arts, Lincoln Center (hereafter cited as NYPL).

2. Stuart M. Blumin, "The Hypothesis of Middle-Class Formation in Nineteenth-Century America: A Critique and Some Proposals," *American Historical Review* 90 (April 1985): 299–338. See also Stuart M. Blumin, *The Emergence of the Middle Class: Social Experience in the American City, 1760–1900* (Cambridge: Cambridge University Press, 1989); Mary P. Ryan, *Cradle of the Middle Class: The Family in Oneida County, New York, 1790–1865* (Cambridge: Cambridge University Press, 1981); Richard Jenkyns, "The Elusiveness of the Bourgeoisie," *Times Literary Supplement*, August 28, 1998, 9–10.

3. Warren Susman, "'Personality' and the Making of Twentieth-Century Culture," in *Culture as History* (New York: Pantheon, 1984), 277. See also Rob King, "The Kid from 'The Kid': Jackie Coogan and the Consolidation of Child Consumerism," *Velvet Light Trap* 48 (2001): 4–19; Samantha Barbas, *Movie Crazy Fans, Stars*

and the Cult of Celebrity (New York: Palgrave Macmillan, 2001).

4. See Carroll Smith-Rosenberg, *Disorderly Conduct: Visions of Gender in Victorian America* (New York: Alfred A. Knopf, 1985), 53; Kathy Peiss, *Cheap Amusements: Working Women and Leisure in Turn-of-the-Century New York* (Philadelphia: Temple University Press, 1986). See also Sumiko Higashi, "The New Woman and Consumer Culture: Cecil B. DeMille's Sex Comedies," in *A Feminist Reader in Early Cinema,* ed. Jennifer M. Bean and Diane Negra (Durham, NC: Duke University Press, 2002), 298–332.

5. A number of works address the subject of women and consumption. See especially Elaine S. Abelson, *When Ladies Go A-Thieving: Middle-Class Shoplifters in the Department Store* (New York: Oxford University Press, 1989); Susan Porter Benson, *Counter Cultures: Saleswomen, Managers, and Customers in American Department Stores,* 1890–1940 (Urbana: University of Illinois Press, 1986); Peiss, *Cheap Amusements.*

6. Karl Marx, *Capital,* vol. 1, trans. Ben Fowkes (New York: Random House, 1976), chap. 1.

7. Richard Dyer, *Stars* (London: British Film Institute, 1979), 7–8. See also Janet Staiger, "Seeing Stars," in *Stardom: Industry of Desire,* ed. Christine Gledhill (London: Routledge, 1991), 3–16.

8. On nickelodeons and early movie palaces, see Eileen Bowser, *The Transformation of Cinema, 1907–1915* (New York: Scribner's, 1990), chap. 1.

9. Players' names are listed in a *New York Dramatic Mirror* (hereafter cited as *NYDM*) review, February 8, 1911, in Maurice Costello scrapbook, Robinson Locke Collection, NYPL (hereafter cited as RLC, NYPL).

10. "A Trip to Vitagraphville," *Motion Picture Magazine,* n.d. (hereafter cited as *MPM*), in Costello scrapbook, RLC, NYPL.

11. *NYDM,* February 8, 1911, in Costello scrapbook, RLC, NYPL.

12. Georg Lukács, *History and Consciousness: Studies in Marxist Dialectics,* trans. Rodney Livingstone (Cambridge: MIT Press, 1971), 83.

13. See Susman, " 'Personality,' "; Karen Halttunen, *Confidence Men and Painted Women: A Study of Middle-Class Culture in America, 1830–1870* (New Haven: Yale University Press, 1982); John F. Kasson, *Rudeness and Civility: Manners in Nineteenth-Century Urban America* (New York: Hill and Wang, 1990); Epes Winthrop Sargent, "Credit Where Credit Is Due," *MPW,* October 14, 1911, 106–7. See also Smith-Rosenberg, *Disorderly Conduct.*

14. William Basic Courtney, "Colorful Incidents Featured Early Vitagraph Days," *Motion Picture News,* April 4, 1925, 1413 (hereafter cited as *MPN*).

15. Richard DeCordova, *Picture Personalities: The Emergence of the Star System in America* (Urbana: University of Illinois Press, 1990).

16. Sargent, "Credit Where Credit Is Due," 907.

17. "The Old Lady in the Audience," *Motography,* May 1911, 78.

18. *MPW,* December 3, 1910, 1402.

19. See Charles Musser, "American Vitagraph: 1897–1901," *Cinema Journal* 22 (1983): 4–46.

20. "Maurice Costello," *MPSM,* February 1911, 114; Anthony Slide, *Interna-*

tional Film, Radio, and Television Journals (Westport, CT: Greenwood Press, 1985), 383–88. Although Costello faded, publicity included news about his divorce from his first wife in 1927; his brief second marriage, also ending in divorce, to a younger woman in 1939; and his lawsuit against his daughter Dolores, whose marriage to John Barrymore he found objectionable, for nonsupport. Destitute, he spent his last years at the Motion Picture Country House in Los Angeles County and died in 1950. He willed each of his daughters one dollar out of an estate totaling $219.55. See Maurice Costello clipping file, Margaret Herrick Library, Academy of Motion Picture Arts and Sciences, Los Angeles (hereafter cited as AMPAS).

21. *MPSM,* March 1911, 162; *MPSM,* October 1912, 168; *MPSM,* August 1911, 146; *MPW,* November 26, 1910, 1223; *MPSM,* December 1911, 134; *MPSM,* October, 1911, 139; *MPSM,* October 1911, 142. Although most names signify gender, a significant number of writers identified themselves as "New Subscriber," "Curious," "Interested Reader," and so forth.

22. *MPSM,* March 1912, 146.

23. Ibid.; *MPSM,* April 1912, 154; "A Trip to Vitagraphville"; *Toledo Times,* September 6, 1914, in Costello scrapbook, RLC, NYPL.

24. "Chats with the Players," *MPSM,* April 1912, 138.

25. "Chats with the Players," *MPSM,* June 1913, 125.

26. "A Question of Mathematics," *Pittsburgh Leader,* October 25, 1914, in Costello scrapbook, RLC, NYPL; "Vitagraph's World Tour: Maurice Costello Heads Company That Sails from San Francisco for Japan," *NYDM,* December 11, 1913, in Costello scrapbook, RLC, NYPL.

27. "Our Fashion Department," *Theatre Magazine,* December 1910, in Geraldine Farrar scrapbook, RLC, NYPL. An international opera star, Farrar also starred in DeMille's early silents. See Sumiko Higashi, *Cecil B. DeMille and American Culture* (Berkeley: University of California Press, 1994), chap. 1. On the consumer durables revolution, see Martha L. Olney, *Buy Now, Pay Later: Advertising, Credit, and Consumer Durables in the 1920s* (Chapel Hill: University of North Carolina Press, 1991), chaps. 1–2.

28. *MPSM,* May 1912, 144; *MPSM,* June 1912, 139, 146.

29. *MPSM,* October 1913, 109; *MPSM,* October 1914, 128.

30. I compiled these figures by consulting the filmography in Paolo Cherchi Usai, ed., *Vitagraph Co. of America: Il cinema prima di Hollywood* (Pordenone: Studio Tesi, 1987).

31. Van Dyke Brooke's discovery of Maurice Costello, which may or may not be apocryphal, is related in "A Trip to Vitagraphville."

32. "Maurice Costello, Popular Player and Director of the Vitagraph Company," *MPW,* July 11, 1914, in Costello scrapbook, RLC, NYPL; *Movie Pictorial,* July 25, 1914, in Costello scrapbook, RLC, NYPL; "Chats with Players," *MPSM,* April 1912, 139.

33. See Higashi, *Cecil B. DeMille and American Culture.*

34. See note 20 above. Unstable and violent, Costello was arrested for disorderly conduct, threatening his wives with guns, and so forth. "Costello Threat Told in Divorce," *Los Angeles Times,* October 30, 1941, in Costello clipping file, AMPAS;

"Maurice Costello, Idol of Silent Films, Dies," *Los Angeles Times,* October 30, 1950, in Costello clipping file, AMPAS; *Pittsburgh Chronicle Telegraph,* August 8, 1917; *Brooklyn Eagle,* November 25, 1918, in Costello scrapbook, RLC, NYPL; "Colorful Incidents Featured Early Vitagraph Days," *MPN,* April 4, 1925, 1413.

35. "A New Belasco," *Blue Book Magazine,* June 1914, 246, in J. Stuart Blackton clipping file, NYPL.

36. Courtney, "History of Vitagraph," *MPN,* February 14, 1925, 662; *MPN,* February 21, 1925, 793–94. Vitagraph's films of American imperialism included racialized portraits of Chinese, whom Courtney refers to as "Chink" and "Chinaman," in a rendering of the Boxer Rebellion. See *MPN,* March 21, 1915, 1221.

37. Courtney, "History of Vitagraph," *MPN,* March 7, 1925, 996. See also Charles Musser, "The Nickelodeon Era Begins: Establishing the Framework for Hollywood's Mode of Representation," *Framework* 22–23 (1983): 4–11; Charles Musser, "Another Look at the 'Chaser Theory,'" *Studies in Visual Communication* 10 (1984): 24–44.

38. Louis Reeves Harrison, "Studio Saunterings," *MPW,* February 17, 1912, 557; *MPW,* July 1, 1916, in Turner clipping file, NYPL; DeCordova, *Picture Personalities,* 64–67.

39. Courtney, "History of Vitagraph," *MPN,* February 7, 1925, 541; *MPN,* February 14, 1925, 661; *MPN,* March 7, 1925, 995; *MPN,* March 21, 1925, 1222; Courtney, "Art Compromised at Flatbush Says Vitagraph Historian," *MPN,* March 28, 1925, 1313; Harrison, "Studio Saunterings," 537. Beginning March 28, 1925, the "History of Vitagraph" segment was retitled for each installment. See also Musser, "American Vitagraph."

40. "The Palace of a Movie King," *Shadowland,* February 1920, in Blackton clipping file, NYPL; Nina Dorothy Gregory, "Building for the Future," *MPM,* July 1917, in Blackton clipping file, NYPL; Don Dewey, "Man of a Thousand Faces," *American Film,* November 1990, 49. Dewey's undocumented account of Blackton is interesting, if not always accurate.

41. Dewey, "Man of a Thousand Faces," 49; "Florence Turner of the Vitagraph Company," *MPSM,* October 1912, in Turner clipping file, NYPL; "Florence Turner Comes Back," *MPW,* May 18, 1912, 622; "The Return of Florence Turner," *Motion Picture Classic,* February 1919, in Florence Turner scrapbook, RLC, NYPL.

42. "Florence Turner of the Vitagraph Company," *Green Book,* February 1912, in Turner clipping file, NYPL; Courtney, "Art Compromised at Flatbush," *MPN,* March 28, 1925, 1317. See also "Picture Personalities," *MPW,* July 23, 1910, 187.

43. Dewey, "Man of a Thousand Faces," 49.

44. "The Return of Florence Turner."

45. "Miss Turner Goes to California," *MPW,* December 9, 1911, 810; *New York Telegraph,* December 17, 1911, in Turner clipping file, NYPL; *MPSM,* June 1912, 146; *NYDM,* March 12, 1913, in Turner clipping file, NYPL; "Florence Turner Going to England," *MPW,* March 22, 1913, 1225.

46. Kathryn Fuller concludes that *MPSM* was aimed at the middle class but that fan magazine readers were most likely working-class. She does not differentiate, however, between the "old" and "new" middle classes, or consider that the middle classes

were subject to stratification. Based on her computation of data in "Answers to Inquiries," Fuller states that 40 percent of correspondents were male and 60 percent were female. I found that a significant number of writers were identified only by initials or labels such as "Unsigned." See Kathryn Fuller, *At the Picture Show: Small-Town Audiences and the Creation of Movie Fan Culture* (Washington, DC: Smithsonian Institution Press, 1996), chaps. 6–8.

47. Christopher Wilson, "The Rhetoric of Consumption: Mass Market Magazines and the Demise of the Gentle Reader, 1880–1920," in *The Culture of Consumption: Critical Essays in American History, 1880–1980,* ed. Richard Wightman Fox and T. J. Jackson Lears (New York: Pantheon, 1983), 44. Although Wilson does not use the term "middlebrow" to describe the editors and magazines he studies, the label is apt.

48. See William Urrichio and Roberta E. Pearson, *Reframing Culture: The Case of the Vitagraph Quality Films* (Princeton: Princeton University Press, 1993).

49. A. M. Botsford, "Camera, Brush and Pencil," *Photo-Play Journal,* November 1918, in Blackton clipping file, NYPL.

50. *MPSM,* March 1911, 119.

51. *MPSM,* June 1911, 159.

52. See Daniel Horowitz, *The Morality of Spending: Attitudes toward the Consumer Society, 1875–1940* (Baltimore: Johns Hopkins University Press, 1985), chap. 6.

53. *MPSM,* March 1911, 126, 130.

54. *MPSM,* July 1911, n.p.; *MPSM,* March 1912, 161, 165; *MPSM,* July 1912, 165.

55. *Photoplay,* October 1913, 106, 102; *Photoplay,* November 1913, 125; *MPSM,* February 1914, n.p.

56. See Sumiko Higashi, "Dialogue: Manhattan's Nickelodeons," Robert C. Allen, "Manhattan Myopia; or Oh! Iowa," and Ben Singer, "New York Just Like I Pictured It . . ." in *Cinema Journal* 35 (1966): 72–128. See also, Higashi, *Cecil B. DeMille and American Culture.* As I argue in *Cinema Journal,* film scholars debating the social composition of early film audiences have not defined the term "middle class." Contrary to the revisionists, I agree with Singer (who, with Allen in the dialogue on Manhattan nickelodeons, does debate definitions of class) that early film audiences were working class and, if middle class, belonged to its lower ranks. Unlike Singer, I would not lump these two social groups together. Although lower middle-class white-collar workers were subject to proletarianization, the divide between manual and nonmanual workers was still meaningful in the first two decades of the twentieth century. See also Musser, "The Nickelodeon Era Begins." Musser concludes in a schematic argument that films expressed the values of the old middle class before 1907; after that date, when story films become dominant, films expressed the values of the new middle class. See also Jennifer Parchesky, "Lois Weber's *The Blot:* Rewriting Melodrama, Reproducing the Middle Class," *Cinema Journal* 39 (1999): 23–53. Parchesky contrasts a respectable but impecunious middle-class family with prosperous working-class neighbors. But the Olsens, in terms of ethnicity and commodities, represent an ambiguous social group that in some ways is "new" middle rather than working class. After all, Mr. Olsen can afford an automobile.

57. See William H. Chafe, *The American Woman: Her Changing Social, Economic, and Political Roles, 1920–1970* (New York: Oxford University Press, 1972).

58. *MPSM,* March 1912, 163; *MPSM,* January 1913, l67; *MPSM,* July 1911, n.p.; *MPSM,* April 1912, 147.

59. See Blumin, "The Hypothesis of Middle-Class Formation."

60. *Photoplay,* August 1913, 130; *Photoplay,* September 1912, 110; *Photoplay,* July 1913, 8.

61. See Blumin, *Emergence of the Middle Class;* C. Wright Mills, *White Collar: The American Middle Classes* (New York: Oxford University Press, 1951), chap. 4; Harry Braverman, *Labor and Monopoly Capital: The Degradation of Work in the Twentieth Century* (New York: Monthly Review Press, 1971), chap. 18. Significantly, Mills pluralizes the term "middle class."

62. Janice Radway, "The Scandal of the Middlebrow: The Book-of-the-Month Club, Class Fracture, and Cultural Authority," *South Atlantic Quarterly* 89 (1990): 726–27, 733. See also Janice Radway, *A Feeling for Books: The Book-of-the Month Club, Literary Taste, and Middle-Class Desire* (Chapel Hill: University of North Caroline Press, 1997); Joan Shelley Rubin, *The Making of Middlebrow Culture* (Chapel Hill: University of North Carolina Press, 1992). Although Radway and Rubin focus more on production than reception, their interpretations differ. Rubin does not investigate class structure and stresses character versus personality in self-making as a genteel tradition rewritten for middlebrow consumption. Radway addresses the issue of class reorganization in a consumer society and stresses the "fracturing" of cultural stewardship in constructing middlebrow culture. She does not use the term "new" middle class, but the work of sociologists like C. Wright Mills is relevant to her study. See also Lawrence W. Levine, *Highbrow/Lowbrow: The Emergence of Cultural Hierarchy in America* (Cambridge: Harvard University Press, 1988).

Clara, Ouida, Beulah, et. al.

Women Screenwriters in American Silent Cinema

In the United States between 1915 and 1930, "the industry's leading scenarists were[,] by large majority, women."[1] "From the end of the century
to the mid-Twenties, women outnumbered men in the screen writing trade
ten to one."[2] These women writers wrote more than one-third (at least) of
American silent films, and at times they were very successful professionals,
holding key positions within the production process. Yet, there seems to be
almost no trace of this phenomenon in film historiography.[3] The history of
American silent cinema is marked by a strong presence of women also in
other areas of film work such as editing, but to ignore the contributions of
so many women to such an important phase of filmmaking as screenwriting erases a crucial historical fact from our discussions of this period, not
only with respect to gender issues, but also with regard to a larger cultural
understanding of the time.

I think it is important to present the women screenwriters from this
era as a collective group, and I want to try to avoid the traditional mapping out of a series of discrete careers-biographies. I also want to forgo a
hierarchical positioning of "author" writers, of masters, as opposed to professionals, to smaller figures, as in traditional film historiography devoted
to directors. It seems to me more important to establish the overall impact
of this group of women on filmmaking and on the culture of the 1920s,
obviously without ever losing sight of their individual traits, and of the historical specificity of each experience. My objective is to provide a detailed
historical account that encourages the creation of accurate portraits of each
woman at work, but within a collective fresco.

The picture I am now drawing of these women at work is closer to a

289

partially restored mosaic than to the detailed fresco I was hoping for, but the little pieces, taken together, offer extraordinary insights in the history of American silent cinema, and in the key contribution women gave to its making. The work of women screenwriters in the silent period has important historical implications that go beyond the terrain of cinema proper and drastically revises the assumption that women were excluded from important roles in the broader cultural industry at that time. On the contrary, women were crucial in the development of the film medium at its very core during the very phase in which the screen learned to express itself, and they played an essential role in the rise of narrative cinema.

The prominent women writers during this period were Clara Beranger, Ouida Bergere, Adele Buffington, Lenore Coffee, Sada Cowan, Beulah Marie Dix, Marion Fairfax, Dorothy Farnum, Agnes Christine Johnston, Sonya Levien, Anita Loos, Josephine Lovett, Jeanie Macpherson, Frances Marion, June Mathis, Bess Meredyth, Lorna Moon, Jane Murfin, Adela Rogers St. Johns, Olga Printzlau, Margaret Turnbull, Gladys Unger, and Eve Unsell. With this list we have a little more than twenty women, who wrote more than two thousand films. Among them was Frances Marion, who is credited for 325 films, including some of the best roles for Mary Pickford, Marie Dressler, Lillian Gish, and for almost every star of her times, and who received two Academy Awards. There was also Anita Loos, the witty author of *Gentlemen Prefer Blondes,* who started writing for Griffith, then "developed" Douglas Fairbanks, the Talmadge sisters, and Jean Harlow in the 1930s. June Mathis is remembered today for her "cutting" of Stroheim's *Greed,* but she also helped produce the film, "discovered" Valentino, and planned *Ben Hur;* just to suggest her importance to the studio, Sam Goldwyn bought an insurance policy for Mathis for one million dollars. Marion Fairfax created the first canine star, Strongheart, and had her own production company, making adventure films. Jeanie Macpherson wrote almost all the films by Cecil B. DeMille and is responsible for their slight sadomasochistic eroticism; Olga Printzlau and Clara Beranger wrote for the other deMille, William; Clara eventually married him. Sonya Levien, Jane Murfin, Lenore Coffee, and Josephine Lovett each had prominent careers that endured into the sound era as well.

The Work of the Silent Screenwriter

To study the work of screenwriters—trying to establish the relation between the script and the resulting film, and the individual contributions among the several hands that might have worked on it—is always a difficult task. For example, it is very hard to find scripts in the original form, especially for silent cinema. In this case, a further difficulty is the scarce knowledge of the division of labor in reference to writing in the silent period. Looking at the available materials, one realizes that since around 1915, screenwriting had already become a specialized phase of work in filmmaking. The activity of a screenwriter covered the entire process of production. Screenwriters "developed projects": that is, they wrote stories and scripts for stars or for specific production trends. The director was assigned to the project later, and worked on the film mostly in the shooting, quite rarely on editing. On the contrary, screenwriters did not end their work on a film when finishing the script, but often stayed on the set to write the lines the actors had to articulate, which were not going to be written as titles but read from their lips.

A screenwriter writing titles for a film—a titlist—worked both on the script and during editing, when films could be modified and adapted by the insertion of a title that could solve narrative problems or smooth the rhythm. "Titlists" such as Anita Loos greatly contributed to the films they wrote through irony and verbal jokes inserted in the titles; as in the case of the modern social satires Loos wrote for Douglas Fairbanks, for example *His Picture in the Papers,* and *American Aristocracy.* As Gary Carey states: "She was the first practitioner of the wisecrack for the screen. . . . At a time when the film had not yet found its voice, she single-handedly introduced verbal humor, with special attention to the national argot that was then evolving, and made the printed subtitle as ubiquitous as the photographic image."[4]

The silent screenwriter was not at all limited to the narrative construction of the film, which at that early time was, in itself, an important task. The very term often used to define a script—continuity—referred to the different stages in the writing of the film, and to the role of the script in editing. In the production of American silent cinema, screenwriters had a more articulated function than directors. This is not to claim that they were the "authors" of the films they wrote; although this was the case at times, it is not the point here. Their work and presence does emphasize, however, a production model based on the story-star relation, which constitutes a strong feature of Hollywood cinema, and in which they played a crucial role. Cary Beauchamp's work on Frances Marion documents this relationship between writers and stars in detail, as most screenwriters' autobiographies confirm.[5] By reading their contracts we discover also that many of them were in charge of writing the publicity material for the film, which implies a continuing relation with the audience in reference to a film, though mostly conducted in fan magazines, through novelizations, and in other forms of advertising.

Revising film historiography research on the actual work of screenwriting allows us to reformulate the division of labor on the set, which, at this stage, was not centered on the director but rather was constituted by the relationship between screenwriter and producer. It was this partnership that controlled the whole process of production, from the story to the editing. Not only were writers consistently present in the process of film production, but also at times they held a position of power in the company, very close to that of a producer. This is the case of June Mathis or Frances Marion, who not only were in charge of writing material for specific stars but had their say in casting (Marion created the film career of Marie Dressler) or in picking directors (as Mathis did for *The Four Horsemen of the Apocalypse*, where she choose Rex Ingram and adapted the script in order to valorize Valentino).

Women as Screenwriters

Using *Photoplay* as a source, we learn that the writer Marion Fairfax was considered "one of the few women producers in the business . . . Miss Fairfax has a rare combination of intelligence, judgment and charm. And her 'picture sense' is so accurate that even the wisest men in the business are willing to bank good money on her decisions."[6] In between the lines it is easy to detect the patronizing attitude of the fan magazine in reference to her gender, as confirmed by other observations in the article, which emphasize her charm and intuition, typical feminine qualities, and stress that, "Marion Fairfax has the gift of predicting success. No wonder she's popular!" In addition to presenting useful biographical data, the article also offers us interesting insights about the writer's activity: "But her real genius, and her real niche in motion pictures, lies in her critical and editorial powers on the other fellow's pictures. There are editors who possess that gift about authors, who can't write a lick themselves . . . She will walk into a projection room, look at a picture, and somehow tabulate its faults, virtues, chances of popularity, artistic value and box office earnings." This observation confirms the presence of the writer throughout the production process, giving a denser meaning to the concept of "continuity writer" and correcting our expectations about the division of labor on the sets. All the same, the author of the *Photoplay* article cannot restrain himself from explaining Fairfax's qualities in gendered terms:

I decided that it was because she had the most logical mind I had ever encountered. Which she vehemently denies. I suppose if I had said it was because she had such pretty curly hair (which she has) or such lovely big brown eyes (ditto) everything would have been all right. But, though she was one of America's successful playwrights, and has been editorial director of a huge producing company like First National, and with Sam Rork is now producing pictures herself, Marion Fairfax is so essentially feminine that she objects violently when being told she has a logical mind.[7]

This quote is just one example of the generic stereotypes circulating in the fan magazines about these women, in the attempt to highlight their feminine qualities as a sort of corrective to the image of intellectual power they expressed.

In *Here Are Ladies!* from the *Photoplay* issue of October 1920, five writers appear in a photo spread, as a clear evidence of their beauty, with the caption: "Stars seen on the screen in name only. Isn't it a shame their faces never get a chance?" They are Jane Murfin, Frances Marion, Anita Loos, Ouida Bergere, and Clara Beranger, who are indeed beautiful ladies, wearing hats or furs in these pictures and looking as glamorous as any star. In reference to Beranger the caption reads: "Clara Beranger writes for Paramount. She is also the co-author of a successful Broadway play. Besides turning out several stories a week, Miss Beranger finds time to be a successful wife and mother. People are always mistaking her for her daughter's slightly-older sister." One can detect the work of literary and Hollywood agents, but it is evident that the proposed image is both that of the successful professional and of the conventional woman, whose beauty is not exploited in order to become a star but within marriage and family. This implicit double standard (they have to be good in their work but also as mothers and wives) is always present in the public discourse on them, but also interiorized by them. Even Anita Loos, who could claim legitimate literary fame and intellectual frequenting, enriches her autobiographies with detailed descriptions of the clothes she would make for herself (not just drawing them, but literally sewing them), and of such frivolous interests as hairdos and makeups, for instance, her famous visits at Coty, in Paris, according to the Lorelei-like character she had created for herself after the success of *Gentlemen Prefer Blondes*.[8]

Another item from *Photoplay* titled "How Twelve Famous Women Scenario Writers Succeeded in this Profession of Unlimited Opportunity and Reward," again accompanied by individual photos, makes explicit the overall view of them as a group:

All of them normal, regular women. Not temperamental "artistes," not short haired advanced feminists, not faddists. Just regular women of good education and adaptability who have caught the trick of writing and understand the picture mind. These twelve women are essentially the feminine brains of the motion picture business, making good equally with men. The field of scenario writing is unique in its possibilities for women. Several of the twelve writers here pictured have earned as a high as a half million a year, and most of them earn from five hundred to a thousand a week.[9]

The twelvs writers featured are Anita Loos, Frances Marion, Ouida Bergere, June Mathis, Olga Printzlau, Margaret Turnball, Clara Beranger, Jane Murfin, Beulah Marie Dix, Marion Fairfax, Eve Unsell, and Sada Cowan. In a way the fan magazine seems both to promote the writing profession for women and to disclaim misconceptions about women in intellectual work: in this case "not short haired advanced feminists, but exquisite 'regular women.'"

Another interesting article, "Women's Work in Motion Pictures," further problematizes the gender issue:

This modern female of the species, following the laws of differentiation and conformity, has perfectly adapted herself to present-day conditions; and in the process she has evolved a sturdy resistance to both physical and psychic shock. But—above all—she has developed an active, competent brain with a marked capacity for generating ideas. She has cultivated commercial talents; she has acquired creative ability; she has mastered various learned professions; and she has become self-supporting. In short, she has met men on equal footing, and has taken her place among the foremost constructive workers of the world.[10]

Women have brains and muscles, then. This still seems to come as a surprise, despite fifty years of women working in factories, and as many years of writing best-selling popular fiction. Pointing to this massive presence of women in the field of sentimental literature, and the predominance of their taste and vision in the culture of the time, Ann Douglas defined

American Victorian literature in terms of "feminization"; but this concept has yet to penetrate the historiography of early cinema.[11]

Though in my view it would be improper to project an explicit feminist agenda onto these screenwriters' work, it is however necessary to take a gendered approach. The work of women screenwriters in silent cinema is an exceptional cultural phenomenon, because they were in charge of producing dominant ideology for the dominant mass-culture medium of the time—cinema. Thus the gender/silent cinema connection is very productive both in terms of historiography and in terms of feminist theory; but with a caution: one should be careful not to attribute excessive value to the statements about gender these writers might make or that they are subjected to, and inspect instead their biographies, their actual behaviors and choices.

One of the women more inclined to represent herself as fastidious about feminine attributes is Beulah Marie Dix, and yet one could not at all describe her as a "feminist." Before entering the film world, Dix wrote successful dramas, children's stories, and historical novels. In *Script Girls,* Lizzie Francke presents her as a vivacious adolescent who liked to think of herself as a boy, wrote a pacifist novel, was a child prodigy who went to college, graduated *summa cum laude,* and was the first woman to win the Sohier's literary prize.[12] Francke derives this information from the autobiography of Dix's daughter, Evelyn Scott, *Hollywood: When Silents Were Golden,* where we learn that Beulah went to college at Radcliffe (then an annex to Harvard) at a time when college education was not at all common for women.[13]

In 1916 Dix visited Hollywood as a guest of Beatrice deMille, her theatrical agent, and met the deMilles, and the Eastern elite on the West Coast. Given the difficulties the war had imposed on her German-born husband as a provider, she accepted work in the Lasky's Scenario Department. In order not to give the impression of "selling out" to Hollywood, she stated: "If I stay, I work only with William deMille, who is a dramatist of equal standing with myself, so I lose no professional prestige." To explain her position, her daughter writes: "Few other published authors were at work in Hollywood in 1916. They might sell the movies a short story or a play . . . or they might drop in for a look. Somerset Maugham dropped in and it was Mother who was called on to develop an idea of his. But they didn't *live* there. Now we did." Actually, notwithstanding Dix's statement, she wrote only one film for William (the quite minor *The Ghost House*), and instead worked regularly with Cecil B. DeMille because she was an expert in historical fiction and Cecil was more inclined to this type of production than William. Perhaps she was also more attracted by the glamour of his sets (and the money circulating in his productions); the scale of William's films, mostly intimate comedy-dramas set in contemporary times, was actually smaller.

Among the screenwriters I examined, Beulah Dix is one of the few to make explicit her problematic attitudes in the choice between work and family, and to impose her status in the family's hierarchy. For example, it was her move to Hollywood that caused the family's transfer in California. In 1919, her husband, George H. Fleebe, became, not by chance, vice president of DeMille's Mercury Aviation, following a pattern by which these women were often promoters of their husbands in their professional lives, and not vice versa. As Dix's daughter notes: "The realities that we sometimes had to eat, that the book business [George ran] in Boston hadn't guaranteed us this, and that switching careers, for father, hadn't yet assured our family economy, were never touched. In fact, there was seldom any mention of my father's name." Dix was not a traditional housewife indeed; and as the daughter adds: "She held to a solemn belief that a woman shouldn't try to mix housekeeping and career. 'You cannot do two things at once,' she would repeat."

Dix was an independent woman, working hard to make a position for herself in this new activity, and keeping very busy. From her daughter's account we learn about the complex activities a screenwriter might be doing, before the studio system was at place with its strict divisions of labor:

Mother also worked on set and costume breakdowns for her films and on the choice of cast. She found it exhilarating. It was a year or more before she stopped to catch her breath among so many jobs, and noted down that people at Lasky worked so hard she had begun to believe in unions! After a few upheavals and strikes, jobs did become defined and separated . . . [obviously much later] Experts moved in and Mother left the cutting room. Of course she still went on the set and no one got more pleasure out of this than she, especially if there was a lot of action—best of all, if it was her own.

In fact, in her interview with Brownlow, Dix stated: "One learned quite quickly what could and couldn't be done with a camera . . . Anybody on the set did anything he or she was called upon to do. I've walked on as an extra, I've tended lights—and anybody not doing anything else wrote down the director's notes on the script. I also spent a good deal of time in the cutting room."[14]

From a professional point of view, in her career as a screenwriter she wrote original stories for films such as *The Call of the East* for Sessue Hayakawa, *Feet of Clay, The Road to Yesterday,* and other of Cecil B. DeMille's films, often together with Jeanie Macpherson. Most of all, she had an important influence on him in the use of historical flashbacks, which she had first used in the play *Road to Yesterday,* written together with Evelyn Greenleaf Sutherland in 1906. This narrative expedient had a crucial impact on silent cinema because of its metaphorical implications: "The biblical spectacle that opens *Ten Commandments.* . . . is designed to amaze and fill the eye with spectacle, but it also grounds the modern story by suggesting that the problems of the present are eternal human conflicts fought in all times by all people."[15]

Dix saw herself as a competent professional, and a cultivated writer, who was expanding the cultural scope of cinema. Therefore, she strongly resented being treated as a *woman* writer: "The money men kept seeing her gift for violence, as in *The Cost of Hatred,* and trying not to believe it. Surely a woman named Beulah Marie Dix would want to write for a star named Mary Miles Minter? Mother puffed her cigarette. She was assigned to work for one of the unique actors of that time, Sessue Hayakawa." Dix confessed to smoking "in order to look as busy and wise during silences at story conferences as men lighting up their cigarettes or knocking out their pipes." At work she often wore "corduroy skirt, a blouse with an orange tie, a leather jacket and boots." It was not only through the way she dressed that she posed like a man: she was conscious of being the main provider in the family, and engaged in colorful styles and attitudes to make a point about who was in charge.

Dix was more an individualist than a feminist, and did not care much about her fellow writers and friends in the intellectual circles—in fact, at the Lasky studio she never got too close to her colleague Marion Fairfax, who was a smart professional but could not boast a college education like hers. Her daughter confirms her low opinion about the other women screenwriters of the time: "As to her colleagues, she never much cared for writers as a group. She found many of the men finicky intellectuals and many of the women fools, if often clever fools, what later would be termed phonies—women who coquetted and connived and plagiarized to success . . . They traded on their relationship with men (all right in history, she felt, but not in art!) or they even advertised." Dix even put down Jeanie

Macpherson for buying into Cecil's attitude toward her. Dix's daughter writes:

Of all the women scenarists, we saw most of Jeanie Macpherson, who was credited with the majority of Uncle Cecil's scripts. Mother never really thought of her as a *writer,* but as an exceptional collaborator for an exceptional man. Uncle Cecil, with his past experience in writing and acting and his unsurpassed showmanship, knew not only what he required in every story he directed, but in every scene. Jeanie had a genius for putting this on paper.

In my analysis of the scripts and of the variations in themes when Jeanie was or was not writing for Cecil B. DeMille, the opposite seems to happen: Macpherson was a crucial element in the team, contributing personally to each film she wrote for the director, especially in the construction of passionate heroines, who are however inclined to look for a man able to dominate them.

Between Work and Family

Even the most innovative women in this group were not early "feminists," that is, they were not aware of, let alone motivated by, the issues today associated with women's rights. They were able to achieve important positions on the professional level, but not without contradictions. Their biographies reveal their originality, their restless search for a balance between love and family life on one hand, and tough work in Hollywood on the other, between creativity and domesticity. Contradictions indeed dominate both the films they wrote and their lives, where they seem to create a gallery of very different possibilities, from the educated, young upper-class writer to the young working women in show business. Many of them were very good-looking young women, who started their careers as actresses. Frances Marion had two husbands before going to Hollywood at the age of twenty-three, but this biographical information was never presented in the fan press, probably because such behavior was considered more "appropriate" and expected for a star, not for a woman writer. Most of them tend to coordinate if not subordinate work to marriage, films to children. Anita Loos wrote the gold-digger's saga *Gentlemen Prefer Blondes,* but she sacrificed part of her professional recognition in favor of her mediocre husband, John Emerson, and probably she was an abused wife. Sonya Levien studied law, was a reformist in the ghettos, then worked for Theodore Roosevelt at

Metropolitan Magazine and published short stories in many magazines, but when the studios invited her to move to Hollywood, she refused until they offered a job to her husband. Jeanie Macpherson was able to fly her own plane but lived most of her professional life in the shadow of DeMille, to the point that she was often considered as his friend more than his collaborator. Clara Beranger silently stood by William deMille as a collaborator first, and as a wife later, accepting his lovers, and even an illegitimate son, and finding a way out of his creative crisis at the coming of sound. William's daughter, Agnes deMille, painfully remembers this period:

Clara swallowed her pride and went to Cecil to beg for help, saying that she did not think it becoming that he should permit his only brother to suffer for lack of work and lack of money and he must find a way to give him some paying job worthy of his considerable talents. It cost her a great deal in humiliation to do this . . . Clara then arranged for Pop to be dean of drama at the University of Southern California. She also assumed the major portion of his living expenses. Not all of them; Father took pride in stressing this point to me.[16]

Strangely enough, the lives of these women writers resembled the apparently contrived dramas they were writing. Powerful and professional as they might have been, their family life was often either quite traditional in roles, or full of secret dramas.

In addition to making a great contribution to film history, the work of these screenwriters had an impact on society in general in the 1920s. These women played an essential role in the modernization of society, both through their own presence in the film industry, in a very peculiar, and visible, work market, and through the type of stories they wrote. The variety of themes and issues of the films they wrote is quite impressive, and while not at all limited to women's interests, their films do deal with a broad range of issues relevant to the feminine sensibility.

Let's consider for instance Olga Printzlau's writing career. In the second decade of the 1900s she wrote some effective immigration dramas, like *John Needham's Double* (dir. Lois Weber and Phillips Smalley, 1916), *The City of Tears* (dir. Elsie Jane Wilson, 1918), and *One More American* (dir. William deMille, 1918). At the Lasky studio, for two years she wrote all of William deMille's films, including some of his most famous titles, such as *Peg o' My Heart* (1919), a comedy-drama about class differences in Great Britain; *Jack Straw* (1920), an adaptation from Maugham's comedy that played again on mistaken identities and class differences; and *Conrad in*

Quest of His Youth (1920), which was particularly appreciated by critics.

All these films deal with romance and yet they address both social issues and topics questions, such as age, aging, and maturity, that were usually avoided. For example, in *Prince Chap* (1920) a painter adopts a little orphan girl and later marries her. Other films of the times, like *Lazybones,* written by Frances Marion, or some scripts by Agnes Christine Johnston, including the prototypical *Daddy Longlegs* (dir. Marshall Neilan, 1919) for Mary Pickford, also proposed these "unexpected" romances between tutors and quasi-daughters. These plots should call our attention to the changing views of age-difference in reference to marriage and romance, but also to these early perceptions of the emotional tensions within the bourgeois family, embedded in these Freudian plots. In fact the very repetition of the melodramatic narratives of so many of these films hides obsessive recurrences of unsolved sociocultural conflicts. It is not surprising that women would be writing these materials.

As did most of her colleagues, in her stories for the deMilles, Printzlau often dealt with married couples and with their troubles; for instance, she is credited (together with Sada Cowan) for the script of *Why Change Your Wife* (1920) written for Cecil B. DeMille. Printzlau also is credited for two marriage romances with Jack Holt, Conrad Nagel, and Lois Wilson, directed by William deMille: *Midsummer Madness* (1921), in which two couples exchange partners and the man discovers how dangerous it can be to neglect one's wife when a woman is "saved" by the sight of the picture of their daughter, and *Lost Romance* (1921), where two men are in love with the same woman but the married couple is kept together by a child. On one hand, these stories exemplify the ideological work these women writers did in support of *companionate marriage*—the reformulation of the institution of marriage, with the added benefit of sentimental attachment, that was typical of the times. But on the other hand, one wonders about the possible personal autobiographical references buried in these plots, especially when one recalls that Olga not only wrote for William deMille but also had an affair with him, all the while being married and having a daughter. Autobiographical references could also be at play in the last film she wrote for William deMille, breaking up their fruitful collaboration after *What Every Woman Knows* (1921), with Lois Wilson and Nagel. In the film, a man makes a political career with the help of his wife, who is responsible for writing jokes in his speeches. He is about to betray her for Lady Sybil, but after having written "an unimpressive speech," he realizes "her devotion and the degree to which he owes her his position."

Most probably, the director deMille did *not* realize how much he owed his success to the woman writing his films, and this might be one of the reasons why the collaboration between him and Printzlau was interrupted. Studying William deMille's filmography, it can be easily argued that the transition toward a naturalistic style of mise-en-scène, a growing attention for daily life and for interpersonal, intimate relations, coincides with his work with Printzlau. After their collaboration was interrupted, a small item on *The Morning Telegraph* reads: "Olga Printzlau will take time from her work on the adaptation of 'Sacrifice' . . . to eat her Christmas turkey with her small daughter Virginia, who came down from school at Glendora to spend the holidays. 'Sacrifice' is to be a Paramount special."[17]

Away from William deMille, her married life takes again a new prominence; as in the films she was writing for him. Given the contract work screenwriters were committed to at that time within the tight, and often prolonged, relations developing between directors and writers, a change in a collaboration, or a hole in a filmography, can become a very significant sign of complex personal situations.[18] This microhistorical reading of Printzlau's filmography points to the bifurcation between the mechanical data of these writers' often successful careers, and the discontinuities in their personal lives. If one only read what the fan magazines reported about them, these women writers would seem to have lived very traditional married lives. On the contrary, one can discover that William deMille was involved in a complex romance with his women screenwriters: Olga, his collaborator and lover; Clara, his colleague in the mature period and his second wife; and Lorna, the mother of his son—all were writers for him. But this scandal, involving such a prominent show business family and these women writers, could never become public. It is as if what was possible for a star, in terms of behavior, would be unacceptable for a woman writer. Reading these women's biographies is therefore a continuous surprise: their transgressive behaviors, their affairs, their independence, revealed in their biographies and autobiographies, is regularly underplayed, in the public discourse conducted by the fan magazines about them, in favor of a normalized representation of them as good professionals *and* solid wives, as if one implied the other.

While all of these women writers were both economically independent and married, and even though they often married actors or directors,[19] they generally retained their maiden names. It seems to me a clear position—a statement about their professional pride—and yet their choice to get married was apparently within traditional roles. However, even though many of them ended up gaining both more money and more power than their husbands, they always kept a low profile in this respect, and often accepted difficult situations with an outstanding self-sacrificing spirit.

Women Writers and Modernity

The cultural interpretation of the role played by these women writers necessitates a reconsideration of their contribution to the modernization of society, within the historical context of the 1920s. During this period the United States, still predominantly rural, faced a quick process of industrialization. Small enterprise was crushed by Big Business; as Warren Susman argues, this was a time of struggle between WASP/production-oriented America and a multicultural/consumption-oriented society. The history of American society in the 1920s is the history of the process of Americanization and standardization, and of the transformation of the role of women in modernization. The mass media, especially cinema, played a key role in social change, but the fact that women were so prominent in writing (and interpreting) films has not yet really been evaluated.

It should be emphasized that these women screenwriters do not specialize in "women films" but instead write all types of movies: westerns, historical super spectacles, comedies, and melodramas set in high society as well as in the slums. Marion Fairfax's company mostly made animal pictures, an adventure genre usually associated with masculinity. Frances Marion wrote all of the eleven westerns for her husband Fred Thomson under a pseudonym (Frank Clifton). However, as noted, women screenwriters also excelled in writing about family relations or love stories or in adding sentimental elements to a narrative. Working on the same line traced by their colleagues in popular sentimental literature, women developed the concept of companionate marriage in the movies too. They thus established an apparently new, and more attractive feature within marriage, thereby accomplishing an important ideological task, that of reshaping this social institution when the vast possibilities of economic autonomy for women might have endangered it. For instance, Jeanie Macpherson wrote the cycle of marital comedies for Cecil B. DeMille (*Old Wives for New, Don't Change Your Husband, Male and Female,* and *The Affairs of Anatol*) that, according to *Screening Out the Past,* constitute the "internal domestic revitalization" of marriage, achieved by "bringing passion into the bonds the Bible has lain down."[20] Olga Printzlau worked in a similar way with the other deMille. These women wrote a great number of films that had at their core marriage and family, but often also discussed affective needs and gender roles.

In terms of gender, through their work, they elaborate the modernization of American mentality from Victorianism to the flapper. For example, June Mathis, with her self-sacrificing heroine of *The Day of Faith* (1923, starring Eleanor Boardman) and the smart girl of *Classified* (1925, starring Corinne Griffith); and Agnes Christine Johnston with *Lovey Mary* and *How Could You, Caroline?* (both films starring Bessie Love), were writers quite efficient in portraying characters—Victorian angels and modern girls—as two aspects of feminine behavior. Yet it was the flapper, played by a young Joan Crawford in *Our Dancing Daughters* and *Our Modern Maidens,* both of which were written by Josephine Lovett, or the Girl played by Clara Bow in *It!* from the manifesto of flapper culture by Elinor Glyn that conquered the collective imaginary.[21]

From a thematic point of view, the work of these writers merges the prevailing presence of the modern woman with the nostalgia for Victorian values. This is particularly evident in the self-sacrificing feminine characters written by Mathis, who function as the mechanism of transformation for the behaviors of all the other characters in the films. Jeanie Macpherson's work oscillates between conservatism and Nietzschean philosophy and the erotic—and, at times, perverted—atmospheres in comedies and melodramas directed by Cecil B. DeMille.

In general, the movies teach us how to kiss, smoke, drive, use make up, and seduce. The beginning of *What Price Hollywood,* written by Marion, where the young waitress copies the make-up of Hollywood stars in front of the mirror, is really exemplary, almost a theoretical essay, in this respect; as is the imitation of famous Hollywood stars in *The Patsy,* written by Agnes Christine Johnston and played by ZaSu Pitts. These writers take their heroines into modernity, accomplishing indeed a complex cultural task, while addressing the myriad questions instigated by the new customs.

Anita Loos played a key role in this direction: in the 1910s she used a language that had the freshness of the absolute present, creating an incredible dynamism between the mercurial Douglas Fairbanks and the irony about the fashions, the "crazes" that the civilization of mass consumption was proposing. For the attention she showed toward women's behaviors, and their fashion in the 1920s, Loos has even been defined a "beauty expert."[22] As the creator of the Lorelei of *Gentlemen Prefer Blondes,* the prototype of the gold digger, she authored the sexually most liberated heroine of the times, a woman who knew how to outwit men, by looking simple-minded, and getting both love and diamonds. The films written by Loos produce a sense of vitality and transgression that makes them emblematic of the Jazz Age: of modernity.

Toward the end of the 1920s, flappers and gold diggers with their bobbed or dyed hair seemed to triumph over the naïve Victorian angels, with their fair curls and big eyes, but also over the New Women, engaged in social reform. According to Nancy Cott, in the 1920s, "the feminist defiance of the sexual division of labor was swept under the rug. Hollywood movies carried a celluloid image worth thousand of words, with the message that private intimacy equaled freedom and the plush of an expensive car capped the search for a good life. These adaptations disarmed the challenges of feminism in the guise of enacting them . . . The culture of modernity and urbanity absorbed the challenges of feminism and re-presented them in the form of the modern American woman."[23] What Cott does not analyze is that the elaboration of the entire operation was not in the hands of a patriarchal elite, but of a great number of women screenwriters. These women had the task, following Gramsci, of efficiently producing hegemony. Yet, in this case, efficiency was not guaranteed by a mechanical functioning of their cultural work or a streamlined production of messages; instead, it rested on contradiction.

In this respect, the biographies of these women are important, because they are narrated by the fan magazines, thus becoming a public discourse on them in more general terms, as we have seen, stressing their beauty and their success, or their intuition, more than their intelligence, or efficiency, presenting them as mothers and wives, not as the independent creatures they often were. Women writers represented an alternative lifestyle to that of the divas; therefore, fan magazines presented their pictures as evidence that they were not dangerous bespectacled ladies but good looking girls, as was Jeanie Macpherson in her pilot outfit, or Anita Loos with her bobbed hair; or nice married women, as was Agnes Christine Johnson at the typewriter surrounded by her three kids.

These writers created a variety of women's roles, from socially conscious movies dealing with progressive social issues to melodramas of sacrifice and repression. June Mathis, for example, created very active roles for Mabel Taliaferro in the 1910s, but also the self-sacrificing heroines (and yet spiritually strong characters) opposite to Valentino in *The Four Horsemen,* or *The Conquering Power.* Clara Beranger very vividly depicted the bitter loneliness of the spinster in *Miss Lulu Bett* (dir. William deMille, 1921).

Agnes Christine Johnson wrote one of the few good comedy roles Marion Davies was allowed to play, in *Show People* (dir. King Vidor, 1928), and films such as *The Man and the Moment* (dir. George Fitzmaurice, 1929), where the heroine flies her own plane, and gets married only to escape her stern guardian. Sonya Levien wrote scripts on immigrant life, centered on women such as *Salomé of the Tenements* (dir. Sidney Olcott, 1925) and the ethnic farce *Princess of Hoboken* (dir. Allan Dale, 1927), but also *Trial Marriage* (dir. Erle Kenton, 1928), a society drama about a "contract marriage."

In fact, contradiction emerges also between style and content in these women's films: at times when arguing for social change, their purpose is at odds with the tone of their stories—too much sentimentality in the "New Women" films, too much suffering and defeat in melodramas. Thus, when they practice Victorian culture, that is, in melodrama, in my view they actually undermine it; while they are at their best in comedies and action films—with movement, lightness, and flappers. And yet, throughout the decade, they continued writing both types of films. The very presence at that time of a genre defined "comedy-drama" emphasizes the difficulty in representing society and its problems without seeming in "contradiction."

These writers do not propose univocal ideological messages. In relation to the middle class, they allow both for the survival of Victorian residues and for modernization. With respect to the turbulent lower classes, they encourage identification with ideals of social mobility and with the new culture of consumption, but they still represent class tensions in slum dramas. Their ideological work is articulated by their different personalities, derived from different sociocultural backgrounds and their quite diverse characters. These writers do not perform a single cultural task; rather, they cover a series of contradictory necessities in a society at a moment of transformation of its collective mentality.

The Writing Profession

To record the role of these writers is necessary from a historiographic point of view, but it is also necessary to attempt a historical explanation of the presence of all these women in film writing in the silent period. When these women entered the field of film production, cinema was considered a low practice. This explains why they were allowed to enter it in the first place, and why they were given so much space (and power)—because of the absence (or scarce motivation) of the representatives of higher forms of culture, namely, theater and literature. At the same time, women writers had already firmly established their position in popular literature, supplying an important precedent in cultural work, and a bridging experience in another area of narrative construction. In fact, most of these women screenwriters also published short stories or novels in installments in various magazines.

As we noticed, however, even if these women held positions of power and made crucial decisions about the films they wrote, their activity has not registered as a historical phenomenon, let alone as a revolutionary or antagonistic presence in the studio system. In fact, they do not seem to be threatening at all to the very patriarchal production system of the film industry in the silent period, because they are co-operative, very useful, and "organic" to that system. They perfectly functioned for this stage of the division of labor within the studio system, because of their generosity, cooperative spirit, and for their typical feminine ability to know a little bit of everything, and be able to do several things at one time, as their complex filmographies amply demonstrate. They could be close to the stars, often assisting them in more than their professional lives, as June Mathis did with Valentino, or Frances Marion with young Mary Pickford. They got along with difficult moguls such as Irving Thalberg, who took away the script of a project for Jean Harlow, *Red-Headed Woman,* from an unmotivated Francis Scott Fitzgerald and assigned it instead to the professionally efficient Anita Loos. Thus their very feminine qualities made them "organic" to this mode of production, still in between family management and modern capitalism. Despite the strong sense of solidarity among the writers, which often encouraged them to collaborate in the same projects, they do not appear as a gendered front. The narratives of the films they wrote, the vision of the world they communicated, their very biographies do not signal a strong antagonistic discourse, a "culture of resistance," a "hidden voice," as feminist criticism would say. But through their work and their experiences, they helped shape the culture of modernity and give voice to the contradictions modernity raised.

It is however difficult to explain in historical terms the sad ending of the story: both the historical erasing of their work in film historiography and the actual disappearance of these women from the sets in the 1930s. In my opinion, with the introduction of sound probably some of these writers did not want to learn the new tricks of the business, because they were not that young any more. A more determining issue is that the studios were developing into more complex industrial structures, with a hierarchical division of labor and increasing power for producers. This changed the nature of the collaborative relation of writer/producer into a power struggle. The construction of Writers' Buildings in the studio lots and the new schedules of work from eight to five probably were not too appealing to these writers, who were used to working at home. Most of all, their feminine quality was represented in their ability to cooperate in a team, to do a little bit of everything, and thus, they did not fit too well in a rigidly specialized schema of work.

Notes

1. Richard Corliss, *The Hollywood Screenwriters* (New York: Avon, 1970), 39.

2. Ally Acker, *Reel Women: Pioneers of the Cinema, 1896 to the Present* (New York: Continuum, 1991), 155.

3. There are only a few books that deal with women screenwriters of the silent period, and then only in sections; see Richard Corliss, *The Hollywood Screenwriters* (1970), Marsha McCreadie, *The Women Who Write the Movies* (1994), Ally Acker, *Reel Women: Pioneers of the Cinema, 1896 to the Present* (1991), and Lizzie Francke, *Script Girls: Women Screenwriters in Hollywood* (1994). Most of these books are based on secondary research on the literature, and it is not uncommon to encounter mistakes, big and small, in them.

4. On the writing of intertitles, see Giuliana Muscio, *Le didascalie di Anita Loos,* in *Scrittura e immagine: Le didascalie nel cinema muto,* ed. F. Pitassio and L. Quaresima (Udine: La Tipografica, 1998): 381–92; and Gary Carey, "Written on the Screen: Anita Loos," *Film Comment* 6.4 (1970–71): 50–55, reprinted as "Prehistory: Anita Loos," in Corliss, *Hollywood Screenwriters,* 37–50. See also Cari Beauchamp and Mary Anita Loos, eds., *Anita Loos Rediscovered: Film Treatments and Fiction by Anita Loos, Creator of* Gentleman Prefer Blondes (Berkeley: University of California Press, 2003).

5. See Cari Beauchamp, *Without Lying Down: Frances Marion and the Powerful Women of Early Hollywood* (Riverside, NJ: Scribner, 1997); Larry Ceplair, *A Great Lady: A Life of the Screenwriter Sonya Levien* (Lanham, MD: Scarecrow Press, 1996); and the autobiography of Frederica Sagor Maas, *The Shocking Miss Pilgrim: A Writer in Early Hollywood* (Lexington: University Press of Kentucky, 1999). Interesting interviews with screenwriters in general can be found in the three volumes of Patrick McGilligan's *Backstory: Interviews with Screenwriters* (Berkeley: University of California Press, 1986, 1997).

6. Ivan St. Johns, "Second Sight," *Photoplay,* August 1926, 76, 127.

7. St. Johns, "Second Sight."

8. Anita Loos, *Cast of Thousands* (New York: Grosset and Dunlap, 1977); *A Girl Like I* (New York: Viking Press, 1966); *Kiss Hollywood Good-By* (New York: Viking Press, 1974).

9. "How Twelve Famous Women Scenario Writers Succeeded in this Profession of Unlimited Opportunity and Reward," *Photoplay,* August 1923, 91–93.

10. Frederick Van Vranken, "Women's Work in Motion Pictures," *Motion Picture Magazine,* August 1923, 28–29, 89–90.

11. Ann Douglas, *The Feminization of America* (New York: Anchor Books, 1977).

12. Lizzie Francke, *Script Girls: Women Screenwriters in Hollywood* (London: BFI, 1994), 23.

13. Evelyn Scott, *Hollywood: When Silents Were Golden* (New York: McGraw Hill, 1972). All of the following quotations in this section regarding Dix, unless otherwise noted, are taken from Scott's book.

14. Kevin Brownlow, *The Parade's Gone By* (Berkeley: University of California Press, 1968), 276.

15. Paolo Cherchi Usai and Lorenzo Codelli, *L'Eredità DeMille* (Pordenone, Italy: Le Giornate del Cinema Muto, 1991), 288.

16. Cherchi Usai and Codelli, *L'Eredità DeMille,* 174–75.

17. *Morning Telegraph,* December 18, 1921.

18. Afterward, Printzlau's career did not develop much, even though she wrote the adaptation of Edith Wharton's *The Age of Innocence* at Warners (dir. Wesley Ruggles, 1924), *Butterfly* (dir. Clarence Brown, 1924, Universal) with Laura La Plante and Cesare Gravina, and a *Camille* for Norma Talmadge (dir. Niblo, 1927). After the introduction of sound, she wrote *Hearts of Humanity* (dir. Christy Cabanne), a minor film set again in an immigrant environment. The best titles in her filmography, as a group, are the ones she wrote for William deMille. Her career ends in 1933 with *Marriage on Approval* (dir. Howard Higgin), a minor production, and *Broken Dreams* (dir. Vignola) at Monogram. She was forty-two when she ceased writing, and she died in 1962 at age seventy—her career stoppage a historiographic mystery yet unsolved.

19. For instance, Ouida Bergere first married the director George Fitzmaurice, and later the actor Basil Rathbone.

20. Lary May, *Screening Out the Past: The Birth of Mass Culture and the Motion Picture Industry* (New York: Oxford University Press, 1980), 209.

21. "The flapper, with her aura of self-indulgence and independence, came to personify the 'point of view' of her generation . . . Temptress and challenger, she was also a consumer, an omnipresent advertisement for clothing, tobacco, and beauty product industries . . . The young woman growing up in the 1920s was more likely to be influenced by national culture, by the media, and by her peers. Two particular influences, the campus and the movies, helped to fuse the new morality with traditional roles." Nancy Woloch, *Women and the American Experience* (New York: McGraw Hill, 2005), 382–83, 402–3. In fact, while the family, the neighborhood, and the ethnic community have lost cohesion, the new urban generations spend most of their time with their peers.

22. Jean Marie Lutes, "Authoring *Gentlemen Prefer Blondes:* Mass-Market Beauty Culture and the Makeup of Writers," *Prospects* 23 (1998): 431–60.

23. Nancy Cott, "The Modern Woman of the 1920s," in *A History of Women in the West,* ed. Francoise Thebaud (Cambridge: Harvard University Press, 1994), 90.

Making More than a Spectacle of Themselves

Creating the Militant Suffragette in *Votes for Women*

If there is one thing that feminist historians have made quite clear, it is that archival "evidence" must be contextualized in order for its cultural significance to become apparent. Women's diaries, for instance, were once thought to be unworthy of study and now are at the core of many historical research projects. In the case of films made by and about the woman suffrage movement, contextualizing the films and the archival "evidence" of their reception is crucial if we are to appreciate the ways in which these films challenged emerging forms of patriarchal desire in American cinema. In this essay, I re-frame one film made by a New York City–based militant suffrage organization in 1913. *Votes for Women* was made at the Edison studios as part of Edison's mid-1910s experiments with sound film known as the kinetophone. Archival "evidence" such as newspaper accounts of the film's production and reception tell the story of a cinematic flop. However, when re-contextualized within the militant politics and practices of the suffrage organization depicted in the film, it becomes clear that the film's "failure" was in fact its greatest success. It agitated audiences as means to promote women's right to vote.

Failed Spectacle or Suffragitprop?

A March 20, 1913, article in the *New York Times* announced an event that would, in the reporter's opinion, have long-term historical significance for the American woman suffrage movement and the future of the film industry:

In the year 2013 the world will know that the suffragists of 1913 could make five good suffrage speeches in five minutes. Suffragists went to the Edison Studios yesterday morning to act and talk before the moving and talking picture machine. . . . The meeting began at the sound of the cocoanut [*sic*]—a couple of cocoanut [*sic*] shells clapped together—and each time the women came out on time in their minute speeches. What interested the moving picture men in charge of the work was that, while the women kept to the time limit, their speeches were so far impromptu that they never gave them twice alike.[1]

Only a little over two weeks later, the Edison kinetophone, *Votes for Women,* premiered in the Fifth Avenue vaudeville theater, where it once again was identified as a generator of historical significance. The headline in *Variety* read: "The Last of 'The Talkers' with This Week's Series: 'Suffragette' Subject Hooted, Jeered and Hissed Wherever Shown. Only Instance of Rowdyism at Fifth Avenue Created by 'Edison Talking Picture' Monday." The suffragette kinetophone did more than generate rowdyism at the theaters where it was screened. It also, according to the article, was a critical component in the pending downfall of the 1910s experiment in sound film:

The boys upstairs [at the Fifth Avenue theater] came prepared to break up the show if the Talkers were again put on the sheet. They happened to have a very good excuse through a "Suffragette" subject. Those from above were joined by the occupants of orchestra seats in hissing the film. The same "Talker" is reported to have caused a disturbance wherever shown Monday. . . . It is believed this week's exhibition of the Edison Talker has sounded its finish. There wouldn't be a chance of a manager from Bayside, Long Island, falling for the Edison flop after this.[2]

In the estimation of these reporters, *Votes for Women* was historical in three ways. First, there was simply the competent use of new technology by women. Thomas Edison first conceived the kinetophone in 1887 as a combination of a phonograph with a film projector, creating synchronized sound motion pictures. However, the technology was not put to use until 1911, when Edison's staff developed an amplification technique that allowed the phonograph recorder to pick up sounds from distances greater than twenty feet. The first kinetophone films were released in 1913 in vaudeville houses rather than motion picture theaters, presenting them more as feats of technology than extensions of cinematic realism. A 1914 advertisement at the Lyceum Theatre in Riverhead, Long Island, described the kinetophone as "The Eighth Wonder of the World." And the films are not described as filmic attractions per se. Rather, the "stars" of the talking pictures are listed as subjects presented through the technology: "Introducing: John J. McGraw, Manager New York Giants; Van & Schenk, Pennant Winners of Songland; Seymour, Dempsey and Seymour, Monarchs of Music, Mirth and Melody."[3] As with the other kinetophones, the suffragette kinetophone functioned as a technological attraction. Thus, the *New York Times* reporter's analysis of the value of *Votes for Women* as a document that "the suffragists of 1913 could make five good suffrage speeches in five minutes" was quite in line with the general uptake of the kinetophone.

This leads to the second significant aspect of the film as identified by these reporters—*Votes for Women* was a historical document. The women's ability to master the technology was paralleled to their ability to present their political ideas coherently and concisely. The kinetophone documented the public speaking skills of the suffragettes, both for their contemporary viewers and for those of us viewing it decades later. Five suffragettes presented speeches from the "headquarters" of the Women's Political Union (WPU), a suffrage organization located in New York City. One at a time, they step forward from the group of banner-waving suffragettes to argue for women's right to vote by directly addressing the audience. They demonstrate their own approval of their speaking skills by welcoming each speaker back into the fold with warm applause. However, as the second reporter indicates, when *Votes for Women* moved out of the production studio and into the theater, the suffragettes' mastery of the technology and public speaking flopped. The intended documentary spectacle failed to fulfill the desires of the male spectators described in the *Variety* article. It equally failed to serve as a long-term historical document; *Votes for Women* went missing shortly after it appeared.[4]

The third historical role of the film, then, was its role in the ultimate downfall of the kinetophone sound experiment. The kinetophone in general was failing at the box office by the time the suffragette piece was released. However, it was *Votes for Women* that led to more than mere boredom in the theaters. When the suffragettes hit the screen, talking to their audience about votes for women, the "boys upstairs" spoke back. Against what Judith Mayne, Miriam Hansen, and others have shown to be the drive of the emerging dominant spectatorship of classical Hollywood cinema that positioned women as spectacles of desire for male consumption, *Votes for Women* broke these gender relationships between the screen subject and male viewer.[5] Furthermore, by utilizing the documentary mode of direct address, it broke the spectator/spectacle relationship by endowing women with a voice directed to the viewing public. Through direct address, the suffragettes spoke of votes for women within an intersubjective mode that demanded a response to their claim. In breaking these norms, *Votes for Women* broke the future of Edison's cinematic innovation.

For all intents and purposes, *Votes for Women* was a complete flop that if evaluated for its historical significance through these two articles could be seen as having had a negative impact on the progress of technology, cinema, and the woman suffrage movement. At best, it seems like an interesting yet isolated engagement with cinema—a footnote in the historical record of cinema history. Instead, when framed within the set of urban political strategies employed by the suffrage organization that cosponsored the production with Edison Studios—the WPU—we can see that *Votes for Women* embodied the organization's efforts to agitate people (particularly men) and challenge traditional notions of femininity. *Votes for Women* represents an early effort by American women to harness the power of cinema to advance a social movement.

Indeed, long before feminist filmmakers began to document the perils of patriarchy in the late twentieth century, suffragettes saw cinema as a vehicle for social movement. They recognized cinema as a powerful force capable of reshaping social relations, in particular in its role in creating modern, visually defined versions of history. The suffragettes' engagement with cinema at the turn of the twentieth century was part of a wider engagement with modern visual culture. Consider some of the now legendary images of the suffrage movement: ladies in white marching down New York City's Fifth Avenue, Inez Milholland leading the first national suffrage parade dressed as the suffrage "herald" atop a white horse, silent females staring into cameras as they formed the first-ever pickets in front of the White House, photos of Susan B. Anthony in her black dress with a white lace collar looking into the distance through her wire-rim glasses. Through posters, plays, pageants, and more, the American woman suffrage movement circulated such images to mass audiences, presenting the women in these images as historical figures within the modern public sphere. Cinema was central to this use of modern visual culture as an organizing tool. Suffragists produced and distributed several feature-length films, experimented with innovations of early cinema, and even transformed theaters into mock voting stations.

Suffrage organizations were key producers of visual culture during this era. They helped shape the modern urban landscape through various organizing tactics, including parades, pageants, bazaars, pickets, and open-air speeches. These efforts translated into their engagement with cinema to forward their movement. *Votes for Women* is one among several cinematic projects produced by the suffrage movement in the 1910s as a means to advance its cause. By examining it within the broader terrain of suffrage organizing, I will show that women of the era both challenged and mobilized the objectifying aspects of modern visual culture to stake their claim to the vote.

Most film histories, sometimes even feminist ones, tend to end on the same sad note. With the emergence and solidification of the narrative forms of classical Hollywood cinema through the late 1910s and into the 1920s, women's position as spectacle became central to the medium and a patriarchal mode of representation has dominated cinema ever since. In these versions of cinematic history, women are at best able to negotiate or mediate objectification within the cinema, never experiencing desire free of patriarchy. These histories are, however, missing a critical element. By looking at the suffrage context, we see that the kinetophone was more than merely a historical footnote. It is a historical landmark that—along with the other cinematic projects of the suffrage movement—requires us to redefine the field of feminist film to include work from the first-wave woman's movement. It also requires us to reconsider the teleology of cinematic history more generally to see that from the earliest years of cinema, women challenged its patriarchal tendencies.

Presenting the Militant Suffragette: The Visual Cultural Strategies of the Women's Political Union

The WPU fostered a militant approach to organizing for the vote, which was in sharp contrast with the more mainstream suffrage campaigns. Suffrage campaigns mounted on the national level by the National American Woman Suffrage Association (NAWSA) and the local level by the Woman Suffrage Party of New York aligned the modern suffrage movement with Victorian ideals of domesticity and motherhood. Such organizations argued that women's right to vote lay in the activity of "civic housekeeping"—just as women cleaned up the home and nurtured the family, so too they cleaned up government corruption and advocated a social welfare system to support society as a whole.[6] A cartoon from the *Chicago Herald* titled "'Cleaning Up'—In Politics" aptly envisioned this civic housekeeping notion by showing women carrying brooms and dusters as they ostensibly march into the public sphere to clean up municipal corruption.[7]

The WPU challenged such traditional notions of femininity through militant tactics that included large-scale parades, street speaking, and take-overs of spaces traditionally defined as male-dominated spaces. WPU suffragettes[8] presented themselves as spectacles to the urban populace. They drew in spectators by their bold public acts and then spoke to them about woman suffrage, thus equating the image of women in public space with women's right to vote. Rather than an extension of Victorian ideals of female domesticity, the WPU's militancy presented women's right to vote as based in their very public roles as wage earners in the economy of the modern public sphere.

To elaborate, as the suffrage movement grew out of the 1800s and into the 1900s, new political ideologies began to influence younger suffrage leaders. In New York, the labor movement was transforming class relations inside of organizations dedicated to reform. By 1903, when the Women's Trade Union League (WTUL) was formed, elite and working-class women were working in coalition to build trade unions as a means to battle exploitation in the workplace. The WTUL provided for New York women activists an arena in which to debate and develop alliances between elite and working-class notions of women's rights and emerging forms of feminism. And in the process, suffrage leaders such as Harriot Stanton Blatch and labor leaders such as Leonora O'Reilly and Rose Schneiderman came to share an understanding that organized labor and women's enfranchisement were deeply connected.[9] At the 1906 suffrage convention, the WTUL formally declared that the vote was integral to the efforts of working women to improve their conditions, and in New York, Blatch called upon the existing suffrage groups to shift their elite positions in relation to working-class women. The existing suffrage groups failed to change their policies and strategies, and in 1907 Blatch declared the formation of the Equality League of Self-Supporting Women (which later became the Women's Political Union) to develop new suffrage movement strategies based on ideals of women's economic independence.[10]

The fundamental shift made by the Equality League was to emphasize work—from industrial to professional labor—as the common factor binding the group's effort to gain suffrage. Furthermore, to ensure full participation of women across class backgrounds, the Equality League abolished the traditional organizational practice of membership fees and built close associations with the WTUL and a range of trade unions. This emphasis on labor as the binding force among women in the Equality League represents an extraordinary shift in political ideology in the American suffrage movement. By embracing women's productive labor in the workforce, the Equality League also embraced a dramatic shift in the modern public sphere and women's place within it. The Equality League argued that women were critical participants in the new urban environment and industrial capitalism; they were participants in the formation of the modern public sphere, and therefore should have full participatory rights, including the right to vote.

Placing woman suffrage as an issue fully inside the public sphere rather than as an extension of women's domestic role required major shifts in organizing practices. Specifically, the challenge facing the Equality League was to make visible the role of women as equal laborers in the new industrial and consumer economies. To do so, the Equality League modeled their movement tactics on a combination of American labor and British suffrage movement forms of "militancy." For years, women members of the American labor movement had participated in open-air speeches and labor parades to demonstrate public resistance to unfair employment practices. In the British suffrage movement, militant strategies had come to the fore a decade earlier, and by the time the Equality League formed, British suffragettes were being arrested for their actions that included tactics ranging from parades to bombing public institutions.[11] The Equality League introduced tactics from the Women's Social and Political Union of England (WSPU) into their movement campaigns, first through open-air meetings and later through large-scale parades. These tactics produced two significant and intertwined results. First, the Equality League was able to gain publicity for the movement, and second, the tactics generated public discourse about new forms of femininity. As Ellen Carol DuBois describes it: "Militant tactics broke through the 'press boycott' by violating standards of respectable femininity, making the cause newsworthy, and embracing the subsequent ridicule and attention."[12]

The Equality League embraced the ridicule that came with contemporary militancy and attempted to harness it into an intersubjective framework in which the suffragists might engage with the public inside of the terms of the public sphere. For example, in 1911, the WPU (by this time the Equality League had been renamed the WPU) launched the *Votes for Women Broadside,* a newspaper that members sold for two cents on the streets of New York City. In an interview with the *New York Times,* they explained that they used the term "broadside" to invoke the nineteenth-century use of the term to describe papers that promoted a political party's interests. However, the broadside's content was second in tactical significance to the act of distributing it in public.[13] On the first day, the WPU sent women in delegations to different business districts. The *New York Times* covered the activities on Wall Street, describing the suffragettes as invading the "tumultuous sea" of Wall Street, where they "straightaway became centres of seething crowds and joyous shouts which precluded the necessity of feminine efforts."[14]

The broadside was one of a host of activities that the WPU undertook to equate women's right to vote with women's entry into the public sphere. In such efforts, the public embodiment was half, if not more, of the argument. In this case, the WPU capitalized on the spectacle of women undertaking a traditionally "male" activity—selling newspapers. Moreover, they did so in the heart of what was perceived as a male-only space—the center of the financial district. In this space, the spectacle they generated was the result of usurping gender norms based on Victorian notions of both public space and labor. "Respectable women" were not meant to occupy public space or labor outside of the household, let alone produce discourse for public consumption.

The WPU overturned multiple gender norms at once in order to form their spectacle, which was offered up not only to the male spectators in the financial district but to those reading the popular press as well. The *New York Times* headline proclaimed, "'Broadside' Fired in Wall Street; Suffragists Pull the Trigger That Sets the 'Votes for Women' Publication Going; Camera Squad Gets Them; Small Boys Join in the Fun and Help Cry the Wares—Brokers Take Kindly to the Invasion." In language that invokes the sense of an assault, the headline and article illustrate the multiple levels at which the suffrage spectacle operated. The suffragists are described as invaders who became the center of attention. And while the businessmen and boys who viewed the event are described in "receptive" terms, the press itself is described as aggressively managing the spectacle by "getting them" photographed. The article interprets for the reader the spectacle and provides three possible forms of spectatorship—idle fascination, juvenile interaction with a comedic spectacle, or police-like control of an out-of-control, dangerous spectacle. Further in the article, the reporter describes the preparations for the event back at the headquarters and along the way to Wall Street in terms that undermine the more aggressive aspects of the spectacle indicated by the title by invoking theatrical spectacles of the sexualized female body. The reporter relates that the suffragettes lined up outside their headquarters "like a Florodora sextet, with the newsbags all to the front to have their first pictures taken." Confusion ensued as they made their way from their musical line up to the subway. The suffragettes headed for the wrong subway station, one that would have landed them in Harlem instead of the Stock Exchange. Realizing their mistake, they rushed back across the street, "holding up three street cars, six automobiles, and two trucks." The spectacle is taken in by those on the sidewalk, who, the reporter tells us, "held themselves at sight of the gay little newsbags."[15]

The article's narrative disempowers the suffrage spectacle by enveloping the women's actions in images of bumbling, absent-minded women who were only *acting* the part of militant suffragettes, not really challenging the norms of the public sphere. Indeed, the article instructs the reader how to view such a spectacle. It provides a model of spectatorship that could reinforce, rather than reconfigure, existing gender norms. Susan Glenn describes the conundrum: "Suffragists faced a special challenge in contending with the concept of the militant activist. A label for deviant femininity, it connoted a package of incongruent associations which included masculinity and shrieking, virago-like female hysteria."[16]

To counter such discursive containments of militant activities, the Equality League attempted to frame their demonstrations as planned, structured events in which the participants embodied the modern notion of rational citizenship. The Equality League's first large-scale public event—a suffrage parade to protest the New York State Legislature's continued failure to take action in support of suffrage—demonstrates how they attempted to advance their use of spectacle beyond mere attention-getting to a means of transforming reception and interpretation of their actions. As Blatch describes the parade in her memoirs, the initial plan was to enlist the participation of all New York City suffrage organizations to march along Fifth Avenue. However, as members of other suffrage organizations were informed of the plan, many either refused to participate or agreed to only if they could ride in automobiles instead of marching. According to Blatch, the initial plan for the march made Alva Belmont, a member of the elite Vanderbilt family, "furious"; she would curiously fall ill on the day of the parade, as did Carrie Chapman Catt, the leader of the more conservative New York Woman Suffrage Party and later president of NAWSA. Both were unable to participate. Anna Howard Shaw, then president of NAWSA, expressed doubts as to the necessity of "so radical a demonstration" but agreed to march and then rode in an automobile. Both the New York State Suffrage Association and NAWSA made organizational statements to the effect that "a parade would set suffrage back fifty years."[17]

The parade was a success in that the media covered it. However, the Equality League considered the overall demonstration less than a complete success because of the mode of presentation. As Blatch describes the organizational sentiment: "riding in a car did not demonstrate courage; it did not show discipline; it did not give any idea of numbers of 'marchers;' it would not show year-by-year growth in adherents."[18] The Equality League's goal with the parade was not to further public images of suffragists as "respectable" women looking to fulfill the civic housekeeping role. They wished to disrupt such images and present women as organized, rational, equal members of society entitled to full citizenship.

To achieve this goal, the Equality League reformulated its relationship to the rest of the New York suffrage movement. The group changed its name to the Women's Political Union to define its relationship to the public sphere and to evoke its ties to the labor movement and trade unions.[19] They also determined that they would be the arbiters for all future parades and created a set of standards for participation in such parades, including that all participants must march and, if necessary, should take classes at WPU headquarters on how to march in public.[20] Through such public actions as parades, the WPU became the leading militant suffrage organization in New York City and began to transform the public image of the movement and its members by turning female spectacle into a feminist practice.

From Street to Stage to Screen: Suffrage Spectacle and Converging Fields of Reception

The WPU's investment in a political economy argument for the vote required first and foremost an investment in image production to change the dominant cultural understandings of both women's place in the political economy and of the suffrage movement's claim to the vote. For the WPU, further advancing use of the modern female spectacle in its various forms in the street, stage, and cinema was the key to accomplishing this task. Glenn describes the potential of this strategy, using a powerful analogy:

As politics and theater became zones of cultural convergence, the perceptual effect was similar to that produced by the machine known as the stereopticon—a popular device of the late nineteenth and early twentieth century's which created

318

a dissolving view from two discrete images. The result was that in the popular imagination two pictures of female spectacle began to blend and merge as the eye of the spectator pulled them together, building image on image. As a consequence, images of the female activist and suffragist were layered with aspects of the stage, and the representations of women in the theater were refracted through the changing nature of women's off-stage behavior.[21]

Activists and actresses formed a shared field of reception that hinged on the use and deployment of female spectacle. Glenn describes the interrelationship as dependent on the spectator's experience of the two forms of female spectacle, which she terms activist and theatrical spectacle: "the eye of the spectator pulled them together."[22] As the site of convergence, the spectator also became the site of contestation as activists (in this case, suffragettes) used female spectacle for very different purposes than fulfilling desires based on sexual objectification of women's bodies. Indeed, activist spectacle used the visual display of women in public space in order to draw a crowd that they would then reengage in an intersubjective, rather than subjective, mode.

As an intersubjective act, such spectacle produced an audience response that was often quite aggressive. Street demonstrations were often described as warlike scenes, with such verbs as "attack," "invade," and "defeat" marking reporters' accounts of suffrage activities and "block" and "stop" describing the milder responses of crowds. For example, when a group of suffragettes attempted to give open-air speeches in Harlem in 1908, the *New York Times* described the scene as follows: "The Suffragettes attacked Harlem last night, and were defeated after a sharp encounter. The battle waged from 125th Street and Seventh Avenue up the avenue to 126th Street and back again, and in the end the Suffragettes were not only defeated; they were routed."[23]

Glenn argues that the reason suffrage spectacles often turned violent lay in the very same power that suffragettes were attempting to harness. By drawing on the structures of desire surrounding stage and cinematic spectacles, the suffragettes faced unfulfilled expectations and desires that were in turn replaced with frustration and anger. In short, such violence signified a dramatic shift in the perception of women occupying public space—from object to be looked at to subject demanding to be engaged with.[24]

When the WPU made the move from street spectacle to cinematic spectacle, they encountered similar challenges to redirecting desires. In

Votes for Women, WPU suffragettes directly addressed their audience and challenged the conditions of the reception of women onscreen by bringing voice to their bodies. The suffragettes face the camera in proscenium staging, giving the appearance of a campaign rally. One at a time, five suffragettes step forward from their ranks to address the audience and then return to the fold of their fellow suffragettes, who clap wildly in appreciation of their brief speeches. However, as the newspaper coverage describes, the audience did not follow the example of the onscreen audience.

As in the street demonstrations, the "failure" of the suffragettes in the kinetophone to "entertain" can be seen as a significant victory in the realm of consciousness. Whether or not the audience listened, the response signifies recognition of a transformation in female spectacle. If, as Glenn describes it, politics and theater became zones of cultural convergence and the images of stage and street began to merge in the minds of spectators, then this is a case in which the zone of politics usurped that of the theater.[25]

Votes for Women was released during the formative years of cinema, when codes were still congealing and the conventions of realism remained flexible. Arguably, the notion that direct address in the suffrage kinetophone was radical is difficult to assert. For a textual form to be challenging, it requires a coherent, dominant set of practices to challenge. However, as discussed at the opening of this essay, kinetophones were framed for their audiences as technological innovations. They were presented as pure spectacle, creating a field of audience expectations based on the notion that on the screen would be objects for desirous consumption. The relationship of sound to image in the kinetophone was presented as augmenting spectacle, not challenging it. When the suffragettes of *Votes for Women* spoke about their cause, the words disrupted the emerging forms of desire associated with cinematic spectacle and produced an intersubjective mode of spectatorship.

In addition, direct address did have precedence in relation to other suffrage practices of the era. Led by Maud Mallone, New York City suffragettes began "intruding" in political meetings several years earlier, demanding that politicians state their positions on suffrage. Similar to responses to street demonstrations, the crowds at political meetings attempted to silence Mallone. When that did not work, she was arrested. In addition, nearly two years before the release of the kinetophone, suffragettes had begun to challenge spectators in New York City's theaters. An article in the January 24, 1911 edition of the *New York Times* describes suffragettes' efforts to challenge spectatorship. Titled "A New Suffragette Device," the article states:

In one of New York's multitudinous theatres far uptown, the other night a burlesque suffragette appeared on the stage. She wore a man's coat and a divided skirt and was a droll object. Three suffragettes in the balcony interrupted the show. "Look at us," they cried to the audience, "we are real suffragettes. Do we look like her?" They did not look like her, but they were more vociferous. They spoiled the performer's "turn" for the sake of their cause, and changed the character of the entertainment temporarily. For the time being it was a suffragist meeting. They are "looking up the performer's route" and propose to follow her about "queering" her turn. They will have to overcome the settled objection of American audiences to disturbances in the theatre. Hissing is not liked here, even when a performance deserves it.

But the novelty of the idea is startling. Once in a great while somebody interrupts a play to protest against some sentiment expressed in it. . . . But generally the audible objector in the theatre is a crazy man. These suffragettes are not crazy. They are suffragettes.[26]

The suffragettes' "new device" to contest antisuffrage images—here on stage, the sister of cinema—was an odd form of direct address. By standing up as part of the audience to address the audience, the suffragettes invoked a notion of realism to challenge a comedic, antisuffrage portrayal of the members of their movement.[27] They disrupted the flow of the performance by staging a performance of their own. Invoking their status as fellow spectators and their status as "real" suffragettes, they forced the audience to see them not as burlesque, "droll objects," but as subjects speaking from experience. Indeed, as the reporter notes, "They did not look like her, but they were more vociferous." Their speech act transformed the space of the theater from one of entertainment based on a gendered spectacle to a social space of thought interchange—"a suffragist meeting."

It is this very transformation of the theatrical experience that *Votes for Women* took part in. It invoked the other aspect of cinema—its function as a public space—to transform the spectacular experience to an intersubjective experience. However, like the street demonstrations, it could not manage the desires it wished to transform. The audience's desire for titillating female spectacle provoked an angry response to that which denied that desire. Hence, as the *New York Times* article at the opening of this section described it, *Votes for Women* "caused a disturbance wherever shown."

In fact, even the suffragettes who participated in the kinetophone experienced the same agitated spectatorship. The *New York Tribune* reported that following the screening of *Votes for Women* at the Colonial Theatre, the participants demanded it be taken out of circulation, describing their response in similar terms as that of the audience at the Fifth Avenue Theatre. The reporter explained that the "suffragists say it makes them homely," an opinion shared by the vaudeville audience that, through their heckling, expressed a "general opinion that these women were not good lookers enough to deserve a man's vote."[28] The reporter went on to describe the suffragettes' experience as one of incongruence between what they "saw in the mirror" at home as to what they saw on the screen at the theater. Mrs. Frances Maule Bjorkman, with "eyes goggling with indignation," claimed that she shall never "forget my emotion . . . when that talking moving abomination began to work." Watching the kinetophone took on surreal dimensions for Mrs. Bjorkman, who explained that "as the different women got up to speak they went up and up and up till they looked about twenty feet tall." By the close of the film, she aligned herself with the male hecklers, exclaiming, "My! I don't wonder the men jeered. And now they'll probably go to their graves thinking that suffragists really look like that."[29]

The suffragettes' experience evokes the grotesque. Indeed, in her study of the female grotesque, Mary Russo points to a number of "types" of the female grotesque throughout the ages, including the "shrieking sisterhood" of the suffragettes, reminding us that the grotesque has often been associated with women's social movements.[30] This instance of the grotesque in a cinematic experience provides an interesting opportunity to examine how this common association between the grotesque and women's movements develops. Specifically, the incongruence between what the suffragette "saw in the mirror" and what she saw on screen is reminiscent of the uncanny experience of the grotesque. In its broadest sense, the uncanny evokes notions of the supernatural—something that is at once familiar yet beyond the realm of the "natural." Freud and others have theorized the experience of the uncanny as a return of the repressed, where the repressed can take a psychical, social, or cultural form, depending on the theoretical framework espoused.[31] The form and experience of the uncanny come together inside the grotesque, which is a profoundly visual domain that marries image with viewer.

Mrs. Bjorkman's uncanny experience of herself as the monstrous image that went "up and up and up" on-screen is informed by the context of her viewing experience. Surrounded by a jeering crowd of men made her "eyes goggle with indignation" at her own image. She is alienated from her image, not able to coordinate it with the image of herself that she saw at home in the mirror that morning. Indeed, she saw herself as society's repressed, which is precisely what the militant acts intended. However, rather than embracing the repressed, the audience rejected it as the grotesque, leading Mrs. Bjorkman to turn her back on her own militant acts to reassert normative femininity and affirm the audience's reaction: "I don't wonder the men jeered. And now they'll probably go to their graves thinking that suffragists really look like that."

Unlike the Bakhtinian ideal of the grotesque as a powerful mode for social transformation,[32] the newspaper coverage of *Votes for Women* reinforces a notion of the abject that is associated with the outcome of horror movies—the monster is killed in the end. In the opinion of the reporter covering the suffragettes' response, the result of the kinetophone seemed to be that it not only "sounded the finish" for the sound experiment, it also foreclosed an alliance between suffrage and cinema. The reporter claimed, "Anybody who wants to see and hear a suffrage meeting will have to go to a real one now. They won't get it in a moving picture show."[33]

Indeed, taking the journalistic accounts at face value, it seems that *Votes for Women* was retrograde to the movement. However, when framed inside of the militant tactics of the WPU, *Votes for Women* can be seen as quite a profound endeavor by women to mobilize cinematic spectacle. On one side, the rejection of the film itself and the new technology on a whole can be seen as patriarchy reasserting itself by rejecting challenges to the visual pleasure of gendered spectacle. One might understand *Votes for Women* as merely a break within the progress of cinema and suffrage. However, if one considers the relationship of *Votes for Women* to the progress of cinema and suffrage on the level of transforming consciousness, lines of historical continuity begin to form and the "break" can be seen as perhaps the very effect of such transformations becoming apparent in public discourse. For example, in 1908, following the early demonstrations and parades by the WPU when it was still the Equality League, Blatch related how militant activities were transforming public consciousness about suffrage:

Our method of spreading information, being new, arrested public attention, and in that way helped to make our cause known. The value of publicity, or, rather, the harm of lack of it, has been brought home to us in many ways. For instance, in answer to a letter asking a candidate at the recent election of his views on woman suffrage came a reply urging that he must have time to consider the question, as it was "a brand new proposition in the State of New York." Our ancient movement, gently agitated in quiet meetings of friends, had become respectable and unknown. More wide-awake methods brought it to notice, and made the movement itself appear "brand new."[34]

The militant suffragette looked and spoke directly within public space, agitating audiences and making them aware of women's full participation within the public sphere. The result was that the militant suffragette appeared as a "new" figure within the American political landscape and woman suffrage looked like a "new" claim to the public sphere. Making more than a spectacle of themselves, the militant suffragettes of *Votes for Women* harnessed the power of cinema to assert their right to the vote and effect transformations in consciousness among viewers, whether they liked it or not.

Footnotes and Landmarks: Reshaping Cinema History

It is ironic that suffrage filmmaking is considered, at best, a footnote in the history of feminist film, for the very purpose of this work was to use cinema to rewrite/reimage history as one that included women as equal members of the public sphere. Recognizing visual culture as the dominant medium of historical record for the twentieth century, suffrage films were intended to fulfill the mandate that Blatch, leader of the WPU, described in adversarial, yet religious language: "The enemy must be converted through his eyes."[35] And yet, almost a century later, historical friends of the suffrage movement have not included these efforts by women to use cinema as a tool of social change in the history of feminist filmmaking.[36]

The kinetophone described here is just one of a number of films and cinematic experiments that suffragists undertook in an effort to advance their movement. Along with the suffragists, members of other women-led movements also used cinema in its early years. For example, the birth control and women's labor movements used cinema to organize for their causes, while members of the settlement house movement (a predominantly female-led movement) used cinema as a vehicle to attract immigrant youth to their settlements.[37]

These works deserve to be studied as early feminist films. Indeed, feminists should claim these works as some of the first attempts by anyone to use cinema to advance social movements. By embracing these works as part of feminist film history, we can re-envision the relationship between feminism and film more generally. For, as in the case of the kinetophone, it is clear that feminists engaged with the patriarchal tendencies of cinema from the outset—both challenging and harnessing these tendencies for their own gain. These works are much more than history's footnotes; they are landmarks in the history of feminist film.

However, it is not enough to simply generate a list of films made by women as part of social movements. We must examine the works within the context of the organizations and movements that created and distributed them. We must study them as organizing tools. This allows us to do more than merely reclaim historical documents; it allows us to reshape cinematic history and expand our theories of feminism and cinema. In the case of the kinetophone, it allows us to expand theories of female spectacle, early cinema, and urban culture that have been central to the recent studies of women and the silent-screen era. The kinetophone—when examined in the context of the WPU's broader organizing efforts—illustrates how suffrage organizations transformed female spectacle from objectification to intersubjective engagement.

By employing historiographic methodologies that ground such films within the movements and organizations that produced them, feminist film historians can reshape the landscape of cinema history. This reshaping should not assume the same outcomes that inform prior feminist histories; we should not assume that the history of cinema is driven strictly by patriarchal desires. By reclaiming such films as feminist historical landmarks, we will be able to envision a history in which feminist desires have always been at the core of cinema.

Notes

1. "Suffragettes Pose," *New York Times,* March 20, 1913.

2. "The Last of 'The Talkers' with This Week's Series: 'Suffragette' Subject Hooted, Jeered and Hissed Wherever Shown. Only Instance of Rowdyism at Fifth Avenue Created by 'Edison Talking Picture' Monday," *Variety,* April 11, 1913.

3. Art Shifrin, "The Trouble with the Kinetophone," *American Cinematographer* (September 1983): 53.

4. The film reel was found by the Library of Congress and is now available for screening. The sound reel, however, remains missing.

5. See Judith Mayne, *Woman at the Keyhole: Feminism and Cinema* (Bloomington: Indiana University Press, 1990); and Miriam Hansen, *Babel and Babylon: Spectatorship and American Silent Film* (Cambridge: Harvard University Press, 1991).

6. For more on the civic housekeeping model of suffrage organizing, see the biography of Ruth Hannah McCormick, leader of NAWSA's Congressional Com-

mittee in the mid-1910s. Under her leadership, NAWSA advanced the civic house-keeping argument for suffrage to the national level. See Kristie Miller, *Ruth Hannah McCormick: A Life in Politics, 1880–1944* (Albuquerque: University of New Mexico Press, 1992). For more on how the civic housekeeping argument advanced New York City suffrage organizing, see Ronald Schaffer, "The New York City Woman Suffrage Party, 1909–1919," *New York History* 43.3 (1962): 269–87. Shelley Stamp provides an excellent summary of how the civic housekeeping argument fueled the narratives of two nationally distributed suffrage films in her book *Movie-Struck Girls: Women and Motion Picture Culture after the Nickelodeon* (Princeton: Princeton University Press, 2000).

7. "'Cleaning Up'—In Politics," *Chicago Herald,* July 11, 1914.

8. At different points in this essay, I refer to members of the suffrage movement as "suffragettes" and "suffragists." I use the term "suffragists" when discussing the movement and its members in a broad sense, as this was the general term used by members across the country. I use "suffragette" when referring to members of the WPU because they specifically invoked this term as part of their militant activities. In the United States, the term "suffragette" was generally used in a derogatory sense by antisuffragists. The WPU used the term to harness and redirect such hostilities toward the movement as well as align itself with the British Women's Social and Political Union, a militant organization that also used the term "suffragette" to refer to its members.

9. Ellen Carol Dubois, "Working Women, Class Relations, and Suffrage Mil-itance," in *Woman Suffrage and Women's Rights* (New York: New York University Press, 1998), 190.

10. For additional information on the history of the Equality League of Self-Supporting Women/Women's Political Union, see Dubois, "Working Women," and Dubois, *Harriot Stanton Blatch and the Winning of Woman Suffrage* (New Haven: Yale University Press, 1997).

11. Lisa Tickner provides an excellent collection of the imagery of British suf-frage militancy in her *The Spectacle of Women: Imagery of the Suffrage Campaign, 1907–1914* (Chicago: University of Chicago Press, 1988). For a description of how the WPU formed alliances with militant British suffrage organizations, see Blatch's autobiography written with Alma Lutz, *Challenging Years: The Memoirs of Harriot Stanton Blatch* (New York: G. P. Putnam's Sons, 1940).

12. Dubois, "Working Women," 198.

13. "New Newspaper Out To-day," *New York Times,* January 21, 1911.

14. "'Broadside' Fired in Wall Street; Suffragists Pull the Trigger That Sets the 'Votes for Women' Publication Going; Camera Squad Gets Them; Small Boys Join in the Fun and Help Cry the Wares—Brokers Take Kindly to the Invasion," *New York Times,* January 22, 1911.

15. Ibid.

16. Susan Glenn, *Female Spectacle: The Theatrical Roots of Modern Feminism* (Cambridge: Harvard University Press, 2000), 133.

17. Blatch and Lutz, *Challenging Years,* 129.

18. Ibid., 132.

19. The new name also evoked the British militant organization, the Women's Social and Political Union (WSPU), which had by this point gained worldwide publicity for its militant activities.

20. Blatch and Lutz, *Challenging Years,* 132.

21. Glenn, *Female Spectacle,* 128.

22. Ibid.

23. "Harlemites Hoot the Suffragettes; Street Crowd Stops Their Speaking and Mrs. Wells Shakes her Fist in Anger," *New York Times,* April 28, 1908. In an article that appeared later in the month, Mrs. Borrman Wells, one of the organizers of the event, complained that she and Blatch were both kicked and thrown down at the meeting and demanded additional police presence at future events. She also complained that reports of the event misrepresented the demonstration, explaining, "We were not driven away. We held the meeting for two hours, and I announced the coming meeting on three different corners of the street." "Suffragettes Protest," *New York Times,* April 30, 1908.

24. Indeed, it is interesting to note that in many of the street confrontations, the outcome was described in terms of silencing the suffragists. Covering a demonstration at 125th Street in Harlem three years earlier, the article "Harlemites Hoot the Suffragettes" described the defeat of Mrs. Wells as follows: "There were catcalls and yells. Mrs. Wells could not make herself heard and she ceased speaking until there was a lull. By this time she was angry, and indignantly told the crowd that never before had she been submitted to such treatment. The crowd laughed her silent again and at last Mrs. Wells appealed to Policeman Bayer" ("Harlemites Hoot the Suffragettes," *New York Times,* April 28, 1908.

26. "A New Suffragette Device," *New York Times,* January 24, 1911.

27. In cinema, comedic antisuffrage portrayals of the movement and its members formed part of what Martin Norden describes as a "one cycle" genre. Comedic suffrage travesties made fun of women's efforts to move outside of the Victorian roles as mother, wife, and caregiver, often by presenting cross-dressing men as bumbling suffragists or creating narratives in which suffragists cause social chaos only to be returned to the Victorian fold at the end. For more on these films, see Martin F. Norden, "'A Good Travesty upon the Suffragette Movement': Women's Suffrage Films as Genre," *Journal of Popular Film & Television* 13.4 (1986): 172. Also see Stamp, *Movie-Struck Girls,* and Kay Sloan, *The Loud Silents: Origins of the Social Problem Film* (Urbana: University of Illinois Press, 1988).

28. "'Cause' Film Must Go," *New York Tribune,* April 10, 1913.

29. Ibid.

30. Mary Russo, *The Female Grotesque: Risk, Excess, and Modernity* (New York: Routledge, 1995), 14.

31. For a discussion of Freud's concept of the uncanny in relation to feminist cultural theory, see the work of Russo.

32. See Michael Bakhtin, *Rabelais and His World,* trans. H. Iswolsky (Cambridge: MIT Press, 1968).

33. "'Cause' Film Must Go."

34. "Women Who Want the Ballot Give Their Reasons," *New York Times,* No-

vember 8, 1908.

35. Blatch and Lutz, *Challenging Years,* 180.

36. Only three other works have attempted to historicize the suffrage films, with Shelley Stamp's 2000 study being the only one that envisions them from a feminist standpoint. However, none of them discuss the kinetophone in detail. See Norden, "'A Good Travesty upon the Suffragette Movement'"; Sloan, *The Loud Silents;* Stamp, *Movie-Struck Girls.*

37. See Sloan, *The Loud Silents,* and Martin Norden, "'You're a Woman—Won't You Help Me?': An Analysis of Margaret Sanger's Birth Control," paper delivered at the Women and the Silent Screen Congress, Santa Cruz, California, November 2001. See also the writings of Jane Addams on the role of cinema in organizing youth: Jane Addams, *The Spirit of Youth and the City Streets* [1909] (Urbana: University of Illinois Press, 1972); Jane Addams, *Twenty Years at Hull House* (Urbana: University of Illinois Press, 1990). J. A. Lindstrom provides a useful overview of the Progressive Era organizers' use of cinema in "'Almost Worse than the Restrictive Measures': Chicago Reformers and the Nickelodeons," *Cinema Journal* 39.1 (1999): 90–112.

Joanne Hershfield

Visualizing the Modern Mexican Woman

Santa and Cinematic Nation-Building

Santa (1931), one of the first successful Mexican sound films released during the transformation from silent to sound cinema in Mexico, was adapted from a popular novel of the same name published in 1902 by the Mexican writer Federico Gamboa. Directed by the Spanish émigré Antonio Moreno and starring Lupita Tovar, the film was the second film adaptation of Gamboa's novel. (An earlier version, directed by Luis G. Peredo and starring Elena Sánchez Valenzuela, was released in 1918 and enjoyed popular and critical success.) The book and both of the films narrate the tragedy of a young peasant girl named Santa who is seduced and abandoned by a handsome soldier. When her older brothers discover her affair, she is banished from her village home and escapes to Mexico City and turns to prostitution to support herself.

Like many writers of his generation, Gamboa was influenced by French literary naturalism, represented by the work of Emile Zola (who coined the term "naturalism" to distinguish his style of writing from nineteenth-century Romanticism).[1] Naturalist writers distinguished their work from that of literary realism by characterizing the genre as, above all, "scientific." Influenced by social Darwinism and scientific determinism, Zola, Guy de Maupassant, and others believed in the determinacy of heredity and environment in the formation of social identity and, rejecting the romantic notion of free will, saw individuals as products of historical circumstances. These authors focused on the underclasses, situating their stories in the slums and barrios of urban cities caught up in the forward march of modernity and modern industrial capitalism. Their characters were not fully developed psychological characters but "specimens" or types that represented classes or categories of society, molded not by their own moral or rational qualities but by these particular urban social settings into which they were inserted.[2]

While Gamboa drew from the aesthetics and ideals of French literary practices, his novel was unquestionably a commentary on contemporary concerns specific to the emergence of a "modern" Mexico during the reign of Porfirio Díaz, a period known as the Porfiriato (1896–1910). Gamboa situated his narrative in the slums of Mexico City and supposedly based the character of Santa on a Mexico City prostitute named María Villa, known as "La Chiquita," who became a prostitute at age thirteen and was tried for the murder of another prostitute, "La Malagueña," in 1897.[3] Similarly, although Moreno's *Santa* was based on the 1902 novel, his film that narrates the fictional journey of a young girl from her rural home to Mexico City, and her entry into the economic sphere through prostitution, speaks to its contemporary audience: the population of Mexico City during the post-Revolutionary decade of the 1920s.

Santa's journey emulated the massive post-Revolutionary migration of Mexico's rural population to the modern city, the insertion of peasant workers into the machinery of modern commerce, the expanded penetration of women into the public economic sphere in the 1920s, and the growth of prostitution that accompanied rapid urbanization. In 1905 there were 11,554 legally registered prostitutes in Mexico City, a figure that equaled about 3 percent of the total population.[4] After 1910, the number of prostitutes increased dramatically because of the economic and social devastation caused by war and the migration of large numbers of unskilled rural peasants to the cities in search of work. And by the 1920s, prostitution "occupied vast sectors of downtown Mexico City," instigating widespread public concern. In fact, a few years before the release of Moreno's film, an anti–venereal disease film produced for the state public health agency by an American production company was screened in downtown theaters for Mexican audiences. Titled *The End of the Road,* the film depicted shocking images of bodies afflicted by untreated syphilis and gonorrhea, and suggested that prostitution was the main culprit.[5]

While Moreno's film is about prostitution in post-Revolutionary Mexico City, it is also about the interrelationships among film technology, the female body, and urban space at a particular "in-between" moment in Mexican history. Elizabeth Grosz situates the city as a space "midway between the village and the state" and sees the body as a "hinge between the population and the individual." For her, these two metaphors offer a way of thinking about bodies and cities that takes into consideration the complex social determinates that contribute to the complexity of this particular relation. Instead of conceiving of the city as a "reflection, projection, or product" of pre-existent bodies, or envisioning bodies and cities as "analogues" that parallel and reflect each other, Grosz theorizes a "two-way linkage" that presupposes bodies and cities as "assemblages or collections of parts. . . . a series of disparate flows, energies, events or entities, and spaces, brought together or drawn apart in more or less temporary alignments." The city is conceived of as "one particular ingredient in the social construction of the body" while the body "transforms, re-inscribes the urban landscape according to its changing . . . needs."[6]

While there has certainly been disagreement as to the exact time frame of modernity, there is consensus that it was a historical period qualitatively different from preceding periods, and that it was marked by profound and long-term changes in economic, political, technological, and cultural domains. This process was a gradual, uneven, and often incomplete shift from a traditional, religious view of the world to a more secular one. Most significantly, modernity is linked to the rise of industrial capitalism, the invocation of scientific analysis, rationality, and material progress, and the proliferation of the "masses" and their attendant public spectacles.

Cinema, especially in its classical form, is the modern apparatus that has most effectively portrayed this reciprocal relation through a number of different conventions. First, classical cinema focused on individual characters that inhabited and interacted with the cinematic city in explicit ways. Second, cinematic spaces were conventionalized by the actions of specific characters within spaces specifically coded with certain social functions: domestic spaces, public spaces, political spaces, ritual spaces, and national spaces. Third, spaces were also gendered in relation to the bodies that occupied them in particular ways. Finally, in certain historical contexts, national cinemas worked to construct and authenticate the relation between nationalized spaces and nationalized bodies. *Santa* offers a particularly vivid example of Grosz's thesis about the relationship between bodies and spaces in a specific sociohistorical context. It is this intersection of the history of cinema, the history of Mexico, and the history of the female body that the following essay will focus on.

At the turn of the century, Mexico City enjoyed the reputation of being a modern, cosmopolitan, European-style urban center, even though, as Pablo Piccato observes, the façade of Porfirian Mexico City as an elegant and peaceful cosmopolitan city was only "the precarious result of a ne-

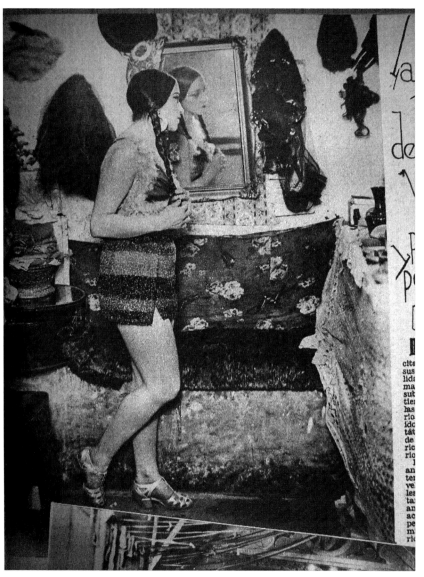

"An Urban Prostitute in the Space of Mexican Modernity" (*Ilustrado,* Mexico City, July 25, 1929, p. 23).

gotiation between the regime's projects of urban modernization and the everyday practices of the majority of the urban population."[7] This fragile alliance was ultimately severed by the violent civil war known as the Mexican Revolution (1911–17). The history of twentieth-century modernity in Mexico is unarguably tied to the massive social, cultural, and economic upheaval brought about by this unrelenting seven-year span of hostilities and its aftermath.

Following the military phase of the Revolution was a two-decade period in which successive post-Revolutionary Mexican administrations promoted their versions of a nationalist campaign intended to mold a modern nation and a coherent national identity; this came to be known as *mexicanidad*.[8] As many scholars of Mexican history have noted, despite large-scale social and economic transformations, the shift from the pre-Revolutionary Porfirian regime (1898–1910) to post-Revolutionary nationalism cannot be categorized as a movement from tradition to modernity. Instead, this period may be understood as an example of an accelerated shift from one kind of modernizing project to another that was concerned with social, economic, and cultural modernization.[9]

The population of Mexico's capital in 1895 when Díaz came to power was 329,774. By 1921 it had doubled, primarily because of the migration of inhabitants from rural areas into the city center. Piccato notes that "migration to Mexico City also distinguished itself from that of other areas of the country in that the sex ratio favored women" so that by 1930 women made up more than 55 percent of the city's population. As a consequence, there were more opportunities for women to work outside the home, and almost 50 percent of women were employed doing needlework, cigar making, domestic work, laundry, and concierge work, while many others worked in brothels, dance halls, and on the street as prostitutes.[10]

As has happened in other historical contexts, modernity in Mexico was marked by debate and anxiety concerning the rapidly changing role of women in the home and in social and economic spaces, and it is not surprising that the "problem" of women, especially their sexuality, was of major concern to Mexican (male) public intellectuals.[11] Journalists and public figures held forth on the shifting terrain of gender roles and relations, discussing such issues as the family, domesticity, maternity, child rearing, work, fashion, and sexuality. The titles of their articles included: "Women and International Peace," "Feminism, Long Live the Small Differences," "The Mexican Woman Who Murders," "The Mother as Educational Factor," "Women Who Work and Men Who Don't Work," and "In Spite of the Great Parisienne Models, Our Women Continue to Prefer New York's Confections." At the same time, the popular media paid as much attention to the "other" Mexican woman as it did to wives and mothers with stories and editorials about "*la trata de blancas*" (literally, white slavery), the term used for prostitution in Mexico during the 1920s and 1930s.

A number of critics have noted that in many nineteenth- and early twentieth-century national literary and cinematic practices, the urban prostitute signified social anxieties connected to modernity and the modern city. She was a popular and recurrent character in French naturalist writing as evidenced by Zola's Nana and appeared regularly in nineteenth- and early twentieth-century Mexican literature and film. Just a few years after Moreno's film was released, another film, *La mujer del puerto* (*Woman of the Port*, dir. Arcady Boytler, 1933), based on a story by the naturalist French author Guy de Maupassant, reprised Santa's story of a good woman forced into prostitution.

Interviews with prostitutes in the 1920s revealed that, like Santa, most had migrated to Mexico City from rural areas in search of work and that, generally, their reasons for becoming prostitutes were similar to those of Santa: lack of education, limited work opportunities, family problems, and failed romance. Many, however, chose prostitution because it was more lucrative than other economic opportunities available to women and provided a degree of independence not available in those forms of employment.[12] Indeed, this ambiguity around moral versus economic imperatives was reflective of contemporary public discourse around prostitution in post-Revolutionary Mexico. If prostitution in Mexico in the 1920s and 1930s was condemned as a moral problem, it was also accepted as a necessary social and economic practice. In 1926 the federal government introduced the *Reglamento para el ejercicio de la prostitución* (Regulation for the Practice of Prostitution), which required the "registration, inspection, and surveillance of sexually active prostitutes." As Katherine Bliss notes, while the particulars of this regulation were "based on the modern science of hygiene," its ideology was grounded in conservative religious beliefs that tolerated male promiscuity as "natural" while holding female prostitutes responsible for moral degeneration.[13] Signifying a "feminization of syphilis," prostitutes "became the main target" of prosecution."[14]

At the same time, if the decision to produce another adaptation of Gamboa's novel might have been linked to the visibility of prostitution in public discourse, it was also part of a calculated response on the part of the Mexican film industry to define a Mexican national cinema and to reclaim its domestic audience from Hollywood: in other words, the release of *Santa* was intended to jump-start a failing film industry. Although a viable studio system emerged in Mexico at the end of armed conflict in 1917, by 1924, the production of feature-length narrative films declined to an alarming level (an average of one film per year). Mexican filmmakers could not keep up with the audience's demand for an endless and varied supply of films. Neither could they compete with a booming United States film industry that was already looking to expand its global reach.

While the administration of President Alvaro Obregón (1920–24) lent its patronage to other cultural practices such as painting and crafts, filmmakers did not enjoy the same kind or level of support. Although Obregón did make some attempt to stabilize the film industry, he exhibited little interest in taking an active part in its economic, ideological, or aesthetic development. According to the historian Federico Dávalos Orozco, "at best, the state conceived of the cinema as a useful pedagogical tool for mass education."[15] Although more than a hundred silent features and documentaries had been produced in Mexico between 1898 and 1928, by 1928, 90 percent of all films exhibited throughout Mexico (as well as in the rest of Latin America) were produced in the United States.

Ultimately, it was the introduction of sound and the ensuing development of well-equipped film production studios in the 1930s bankrolled by private investment, government loans, and U.S. money that fostered the expansion of the Mexican film industry and gave filmmakers a chance to develop an economically viable national cinematic vision. Initially, Hollywood attempted to retain its Mexican and Latin American audience base through the production of Spanish-language films—basically, Hollywood films produced in Spanish with Mexican, Spanish, and Latin American actors and, sometimes, Spanish-speaking directors such as Ramón Novarro and Gilbert Roland. Mexican audiences, however, rejected these films because of their mix of Andalusian, Cuban, Chilean, Argentinean, and Mexican accents. According to one editorial, "El patriotismo y el cine" (Patriotism and the cinema) in the Mexico City daily newspaper *Excelsior* (January 30, 1930), Mexico "was in the middle of a struggle in, with, for, without, of, against, about the vitaphone," and this struggle was in no small way dependent on language.

Mexican studios responded by producing sound films that, while following the dominant Hollywood aesthetic, drew on Mexican stories and history and contemporary Mexican life, employed Mexican actors, and included Mexican popular music. By 1932, Mexican films were again attracting a respectable share of the domestic audience, and suddenly, there was a large-enough market to sustain an industry that was dependent on box-office receipts. Journalists and intellectuals were calling on filmmakers to use the opportunity to create a national cinema. When it was apparent that work was available in Mexico, Mexican actors and technicians working in Hollywood returned to their native country, bringing with them the skills and cinematic conventions they'd learned and providing a ready-made technical and artistic force for the reemerging cinema industry. In fact *Santa's* director, Antonio Moreno, began his career as a child actor in Hollywood in 1912 after immigrating to the United States from Spain with his family.[16]

Approximately ten feature films, as well as numerous shorts and news-reels, were produced in Mexico between 1929 and 1930; these were accompanied by various kinds of synchronized sound. Some of these films adapted Mexican novels, dealt with Mexican historical events, or borrowed their stories from current events of the times. Others were unabashedly Mexican versions of Hollywood films. These early films, however, met with little success, primarily because of the inferior sound systems Mexican filmmakers used. *Santa* was the first Mexican sound film to use a superior optical sound system invented by Joselito and Roberto Rodríguez, Mexican filmmakers working in Hollywood. While its success was, in part, due to its allegiance to the "Hollywood" aesthetic, the film was also specifically Mexican: it was based on a well-known and popular Mexican novel, and it featured popular Mexican actors such as Lupita Tovar, who had made her name in Hollywood and returned specifically to star in Moreno's film; Mimi Derba in the role of the brothel madam, Elvira; and Carlos Orellana as Hipólito, the blind piano player who loves and protects Santa. Finally, it introduced the music of the Mexico composer Augustín Lara, who would go on to become one of the most beloved composers of popular music in Mexican cinema.

Mexican producers and directors of the 1930s immediately realized that box-office success depended on a loyal public and that this public was, first and foremost, interested primarily in being entertained by genres, stories, and stars they recognized as "Mexican." Additionally, as Carlos Monsiváis points out, the public looked to their cinema to "explain how to survive in a bewildering age of modernization . . . to find and experience entertainment, family unity, honour, 'permissible' sexuality . . . and to understand how they belonged to the nation."[17] It wasn't that films were specifically formulated as educational tools or that the film industry evolved as a cultural arm of official propaganda. The state did provide some funding to producers in the form of loans but did not mandate film content. The Mexican film industry was primarily a private venture that enjoyed, off and on, government support. Instead, the films the audiences responded to portrayed and narrated the complexities of their lives, of their world transformed. Ultimately, then, *Santa* spoke to people grappling with three decades of profound social and economic upheavals that had resulted in the massive urbanization of a predominantly rural population. Mexico City had become a much different place than it had been during the Porfiriato, and similarly, the Mexican citizen was a much different subject than she had been at the turn of the century.[18]

The transition from the film's prologue, which is set in the rural village of Chimalistac, to the sequence that establishes Santa's arrival in Mexico City and her entrance into the space of modernity marks this difference both visually and aurally. The deliberate juxtaposition of the ordered, uncluttered, immobile "premodern" rural landscape with the scene of modern urban life marked by a visual and aural intensity, an overabundance of stimuli, and a formless and crowded discontinuity reinforces this observation. The film's introduction to the city presents the idea that urban modernity was "overstimulating" to millions of rural migrants who poured into Mexico City during the first few decades of the new century. Indeed, the contrast between the sounds of Santa's rural village and the sounds of Mexico City are emphasized in the initial transition between the rural and urban space.

Moreover, the female body is used to visualize this transformation, which is marked by a fade-to-black from an image of Santa lying in the dust of Chimalistac as her lover rides off with his troops, and fade-up to a montage of "technologies of amusement"—a spinning game wheel, a Ferris wheel, and a merry-go-round. The optical effect itself serves as a metaphor for historical, social, and cinematic change. Through the optical technology of the modern cinema, Santa's body is aligned with the mechanical body that is representative of modern life: both woman and the cinema become modern, and she is thus the signifier of change and transformation. In addition, the use of a static camera and immobile framing in the prologue is replaced by a moving camera and mobile composition, while the melodramatic acting style of silent film gives way to a more realist method. As the film fades up from black, a sequence of documentary style footage shot with a handheld, moving camera reveals the crowd of modern life moving as one body through a bustling urban marketplace, a symbol of commodified modern space. We can begin to make out that this crowd is composed of individuals: some are clothed in modern dress, others wear the traditional clothing of their village; women with bobbed hair and cloche hats mingle with those adorned in long braids tied with ribbons; and men in suits rub shoulders with Indians in the peasant's "uniform" of white pants and shirt. It is an image of the modern, post-Revolutionary Mexican nation that is made up of new and old, middle-class and working-class, traditional and contemporary modes of being.

According to Ben Singer, classical cinematic scenes of crowds convey an image of modern life in which a "sense of disorder and fragmentation was heightened by a new level of social heterogeneity as far-flung immigrant groups poured into the cities and women enjoyed greater freedom to circulate unchaperoned in public."[19] This particular sequence, through its documentary-style camera work and editing, communicates such an image, highlighting images of men and women, upper and lower classes, tradition and modernity, all mingling in a common public place and highlighting the heterogeneity of modern Mexico that was the lynchpin of Mexican post-Revolutionary national identity. Traces of the traditional are evident in the city: musicians in traditional costumes mingle with men in zoot suits; Indian women sell native handicrafts to fashionably dressed young girls.

This scene, a depiction of the "ultimate" urban experience, also emphasizes the "sensational" aspect of modern urban life or, more precisely, the overload of sensory stimulus, both visual and aural, that modern citizens are exposed to. The camera's point of view simulates what it is like to move through a mass of bodies that moves as if it is a single giant organism. The camera glances here and there at the mix of social characters brought together in the modern city: Indians, farmers, modern women in French cloche hats and short dresses, and businessmen in two-piece suits. Finally, the camera rests on Santa's face in this crowd. Her expression of shock and wonder mirrors the emotions that many rural migrants to the city must have felt on their first encounter with the "intensity and discontinuity" of modernity, and thus this scene would be quite familiar to Mexican film audiences, many of whom, as has been noted earlier, were also new arrivals to the city.

Significantly, in this introduction to the city it is cinema's newest "modern" technology that is highlighted as we are bombarded by a cacophony of sounds: voices, the whir of machines, and snatches of traditional and modern popular music. This acoustic montage reinforces the barrage of images that assail Santa and the cinema audience. What is presented on screen is a visual and aural representation of the dissonance of modernity. One scene in particular illustrates the film industries' deliberate strategy regarding the introduction of sound as a central aesthetic element of modern cinema. The opening shot in this scene is a close-up of an RCA Victor radio that is playing a popular Augustín Lara composition. The camera dollies back to reveal Santa dancing in her bedroom, and Hipólito, the blind piano player who is in love with her, enters the room and waits for the music to finish. While the scene does contribute to the narrative's imperative—it demonstrates Hipólito's love for the beautiful and unattainable Santa—it functions primarily to showcase the new technology of sound by making a radio and its music the central character of the scene.

What is most interesting, however, is the way in which the scene explicitly links the body of modern technology—the radio—to Santa's body.[20] As the song plays, the scene cuts back and forth between the radio and Santa: both the radio and Santa "perform" for the camera. Hipólito can't see Santa; the performances—by both the radio and Santa—are addressed to the cinema audience. This link suggests that these two bodies are not distinct but are actually different manifestations or parts of a larger social construction—that of a "modern sensibility" both embodied and aural. This reading is made more obvious if we consider that fact that this scene was not included in Gamboa's 1903 novel as radio was not yet part of Mexican daily life.[21]

It is apparent that both scenes are generally "about" the modern Mexican woman. In the marketplace scene, the camera focuses on women: groups of modern young women dressed in the latest fashions stroll arm in arm through the market; an Indian woman sells hand-made crafts from her village; another young woman, wrapped around her lover, drops her handkerchief. Women in this scene are free to wander the domain of public space with or without the companionship of men. They are represented as both producers and consumers—vital members of the new Mexican economy. In fact, it is in this marketplace that Santa makes the critical connection with Señora Elvira, the brothel madam, that will allow her to remove herself from a place in which she is an observer of modernity—an outsider—and insert herself into the commercial flow of the modern Mexican economy as a high-class prostitute.

Prostitution and the prostitute have been popular tropes of modernity across national literatures and cinemas. Yinghin Zhang, for example, describes "three major textual modes in the public discourse on prostitution" in China. The first of these is the "informative, journalistic mode," which presents itself as primarily descriptive of a "natural" everyday practice. The second is the "appreciative, hedonistic mode," in which "prostitution is imagined as a fantastic cultural realm, an exquisite artistic form, and a fountain of nostalgia." Finally, the "castigatory, moralistic mode" situates itself as a moralistic intervention and "links prostitution to issues of national concern." In his analysis of six Chinese films about prostitution from the 1930s, Zhang finds that the films generally adopted this third mode of representation.[22] Classical Mexican cinema also relied on this third textual mode, which corresponds most closely with the prevailing public discourse in Mexico about prostitution, as has been noted earlier. At the same time, this discourse was complicated by competing and intersecting conversations connected to women's social and economic emancipation and to changing social structures.

For example, the brothel in *Santa* is portrayed as a modern social space that functions both as a public commercial space and as a private domestic space. Business is transacted between the prostitutes and their clients, but at the same time, the brothel is where the young women live: it is their home; it houses their new "family"; the madam is a new figure that functions as both mother and father; the prostitutes are her sisters. In the same way, the modern Mexican nation is both public and private: it is home and marketplace; the nation-state is the new father and the new mother; previously diverse ethnic and linguistic groups are now united as "Mexicans."

We are introduced to brothel life through another montage of images and sound. This montage is presented in the same manner as the marketplace scene, characterized by documentary-style footage, hand-held wideshots, and moving camera. In the first tracking shot, the camera comes to rest on Santa. Her body is folded in on itself, her face and eyes are cast down, she looks at no one. In the next scene, Santa now appears more comfortable in the space and more modern: instead of crouching in a corner chair, she moves confidently through the room; her long braids are gone and she sports a stylish short bob; her cotton dress and colored ribbons have been replaced by a silky evening dress and dangling earrings; she looks outward, makes eye contact with the customers, and moves about in a free and self-assured manner. And, once more, sound is emphasized as a defining trope of modern life and modern cinema: Hipólito performs another Lara composition; a different man serenades the room with a classical Flamenco piece; and an American band plays popular jazz for Santa and her friends.

The final scene of the film situates film sound in relation to another modern trope: that of science and medicine. Santa's ascendancy to the role of the successful high-class prostitute who enjoys momentary fame, fortune, and the adulation of handsome and wealthy men is followed by the story of her fall from grace. Hipólito finds her in a seedy room in one of the poorest areas of the city, dying from the effects of poverty, alcoholism, and an unnamed disease and convinces a respected doctor to perform life-saving surgery. As Hipólito and his son wait in the hospital foyer, the doctor and his medical team attend to Santa in the operating auditorium. Again, it is sound that is emphasized in this scene: we hear the clanking of metal instruments, the shuffling of doctors' and nurses' feet, the reverberation of Santa's breathing, and the ticking clock that signifies her life. Finally, Santa's death is marked by the absence of sound when we no longer hear her breath.

As Richard Maltby has noted, "the sound 'revolution' proposed no simple break with the cinema of the past." Speaking about Hollywood film, Maltby suggests that while the industry did engage in some stylistic experimentation, its primary strategy was to adapt silent film conventions to the new technology.[23] Such a view rejects the notion that a period of film production can be defined by a single mode of film practice. During any particular moment of transition, filmmakers use the technical, stylistic, and narrative tools at hand while adapting them to suit generic, industrial, and authorial preferences. In any case, the first films released as sound films can thus be seen as "in-between" silent and sound films, as studios and directors explored aesthetic possibilities as well as problems. *Santa* is exemplary in its employment of both conventional silent cinema practices and newer, experimental strategies associated with the introduction of sound. The film uses the new technology of film sound to foreground the relations among film technology, the female body, and post-Revolutionary Mexican urban space.

Moreno's *Santa* has been read as a specific critique of a post-Revolutionary nationalism that promoted industrialization and urbanization and encouraged women to abandon the safety of the home and the church. According to Federico Dávalos Orozco, for example, the film "follows the life of the protagonist from her upbringing in a sort of idyllic paradise . . . to Hell, which is represented by the modern city and the brothel."[24] I have argued, however, that the film paints a more ambiguous picture of women's life in modern Mexico City. This ambiguity is due, in part, to the conflict between an economic imperative to sell theater tickets and promote modernity and a socially proscribed moral obligation to condemn prostitution.

I have argued that the 1931 version of *Santa* functions as a "transitional" film in a number of visual, narrative, thematic, and formal aspects: the film was situated "in-between" silent cinema and sound cinema; it was released during a transformative moment in Mexican history "in-between" tradition and modernity; and its representation of female characters was situated "in-between" older and newer ideologies of femininity. Because of this in-betweenness, *Santa* is an exemplary illustration of ways in which Mexican rural culture participated in the shaping of a new urban culture, and older notions of femininity and female sexuality lingered and shaped new understandings. Ultimately, *Santa* visualizes the conflicts and ambiguities that arose in the response to the emergence of new social formations in the midst of older ones.

Notes

1. American authors writing in the 1890s who were influenced by French naturalism include Jack London, Stephen Crane, Frank Norris, and Theodore Dreiser. In Great Britain, Charles Dickens's writings evidence a naturalist influence.

2. Parallel movements in theater and the visual arts in France focused on natural settings, stories, and acting styles. Painters like Gustave Courbet and directors such as André Antoine in France and Freie Bühne in Germany utilized naturalist themes and styles.

3. Robert Buffington and Pablo Piccato, "Tales of Two Women: The Narrative Construal of Porfirian Reality," *The Americas* 55.3 (1999): 391–424.

4. Frederick C. Turner, *The Dynamic of Mexican Nationalism* (Chapel Hill: University of North Carolina Press, 1968).

5. Katherine Bliss, *Compromised Positions: Prostitution, Public Health, and Gender Politics in Revolutionary Mexico City* (University Park: Pennsylvania State University Press, 2001), 186.

6. Elizabeth Grosz, "Bodies-Cities," in *Sexuality and Space*, ed. Beatriz Colomina (New York: Princeton Architectural Press, 1992): 244–49. Grosz criticizes these two dominant (and in her estimation inadequate) views of the link between bodies and cities, which she defines as causal and representational. In the first view, bodies are the "cause and motivation" for the configuration of cities. Grosz denounces this view because it reinforces a philosophical split between body and mind, subordinating the first to the second, and because it "posits a one-way relation" between bodies and cities. Grosz condemns the second model—often represented through the metaphor of the "body-politic"—because it justifies and naturalizes the dominant hegemonic social organization, and because it "relies on a fundamental opposition between nature and culture . . . [in which] . . . culture is a supercession and perfection of nature" (245–47).

7. Pablo Piccato, *City of Suspects: Crime in Mexico City, 1900–1930* (Durham, NC: Duke University Press, 2001), 17.

8. *Mexicanidad* was formed through a set of discourses, stereotypes, myths, and histories that were represented through state-controlled public education and through numerous official cultural projects that included the painting of huge murals in public places and the building of monuments to Revolutionary heroes. At the same time, popular culture in the form of radio, recorded music, illustrated magazines, comic books, and the cinema blanketed the nation with images of a modern Mexico that were not always in agreement with the state's vision. This was, in part, owing to Mexico's place in the global network of economic and cultural relations and to the flow of popular culture across national borders.

9. Tenorio-Trillo finds that during the Porfiriato, "nationalism as a global, coherent, comprehensive reshaping of the country's image was managed by elites." Mauricio Tenorio-Trillo, *Mexico at the World's Fairs: Crafting a Modern Nation* (Berkeley: University of California Press, 1996), 17. Conversely, Alan Knight argues that after the Revolution, the "forces of private and foreign investment, urbanization, and population growth" shaped popular culture in ways that were not foreseen by the state. Alan Knight, "Revolutionary Project, Recalcitrant People: Popular Culture and the Mexican Revolution," in *The Revolutionary Process in Mexico: Essays on Political and Social Change, 1880–1940,* ed. Jaime Rodriquez (Los Angeles: UCLA Latin American Center Publications, 1990), 254–58.

10. Piccato, *City of Suspects,* 21–29. Before 1930 many women labored in the fields, did piecework for local businessmen, worked in low-wage manufacturing jobs, and were teachers. And under the direction of government-educated school teachers from the cities, rural Indian women were in the vanguard of local village reforms in the areas of sanitation, public health, alcohol abuse, and cultural reconstruction. In addition, women had been actively involved in the armed revolutionary struggle as *soldaderas,* or female soldiers, as cooks, and as nurses. For discussions of the *soldadera,* see Ilene V. O'Malley, *The Myth of the Revolution: Hero Cults and the Institutionalization of the Mexican State, 1920–1940* (New York: Greenwood Press, 1986); and Elizabeth Salas, *Soldaderas in the Mexican Military: Myth and History* (Austin: University of Texas Press, 1990).

11. Elizabeth Wilson has argued that the "sophisticated urban consciousness" that emerged in the early twentieth century among artists and intellectuals "was an essentially male consciousness." She writes that one of the "major preoccupations" of this male consciousness had to do with nontraditional explorations of sexuality and that this preoccupation "made women's very presence in cities a problem." See her *The Sphinx in the City: Urban Life, the Control of Disorder, and Women* (Berkeley: University of California Press, 1992), 5.

12. Cristina Rivera-Garza quotes various letters written by prostitutes in jail to local officials: "We used to be factory workers and rural laborers, but factories have closed and activities in the field have stalled. We believed that 70% of us were forced to lead this life out of necessity, and only 30% chose it because of personal proclivity to vice." See Cristina Rivera-Garza, "The Criminalization of the Syphilitic Body: Prostitutes, Health Crimes, and Society in Mexico City, 1867–1930," in *Crime and*

Punishment in Latin America: Law and Society since Late Colonial Times, ed. Ricardo D. Salvatore, Carlos Aguirre, and Gilbert Joseph (Durham, NC: Duke University Press, 2001), 173.

13. Bliss, *Compromised Positions,* 3. Bliss argues that "redemption" for the subaltern classes was a prevalent theme in immediate post-Revolutionary politics and that prostitutes "were overwhelmingly invoked as those citizens most deserving of 'moral uplift' and a second chance" (5).

14. Rivera-Garza, "Criminalization of the Syphilitic Body," 170.

15. Federico Dávalos Orozco, "The Birth of the Film Industry and the Emergence of Sound," in *Mexico's Cinema: A Century of Film and Filmmakers,* ed. Joanne Hershfield and David R. Maciel (Wilmington, DE: Scholarly Resources, 1999), 18.

16. Dávalos Orozco, *Albores del cine Mexicano* (Mexico City: Editorial Clío Libros y Videos, 1996), 65.

17. Carlos Monsiváis, "Mythologies," in *Mexican Cinema,* ed. Paulo Antonio Paranaguá, trans. Ana M. López (London: BFI, 1995), 117–18.

18. Piccato, *City of Suspects,* 21.

19. Ben Singer, *Melodrama and Modernity: Early Sensational Cinema and Its Contexts* (New York: Columbia University Press, 2001), 61.

20. Both RCA and Philco, American producers and distributors of radios in Mexico in the 1930s, advertised extensively in the Mexican mass media. I found two ads in particular in popular weekly magazines—one for RCA Victor 1939 (in *Todo,* 1939) and another for Philco's 1939 model (in *Hoy,* April 8, 1939)—that both featured women in evening gowns promoting new radio models.

21. The first commercial radio station, CYL, was launched in 1923 in partnership with the Mexico City newspaper *El Universal.* Joy Elizabeth Hayes, *Radio Nation: Communication, Popular Culture, and Nationalism in Mexico, 1920–1950* (Tucson: University of Arizona Press, 2000), 30.

22. Yingjin Zhang. "Prostitution and Urban Imagination: Negotiating the Public and the Private in Chinese Films of the 1930s," in *Cinema and Urban Culture in Shanghai, 1922–1943,* ed. Yingjin Zhang (Stanford: Stanford University Press, 1999), 164–65.

23. Richard Maltby and Ian Craven, *Hollywood Cinema* (Oxford: Blackwell, 1995).

24. Dávalos Orozco, "Birth of the Film Industry," 19.

Sisters in Rebellion

The Unexpected Kinship of Germaine Dulac and Virginia Woolf

At some point during the last decade of the twentieth century I learned that the Tavistock Hotel, where I'd stay when in London, had been built on the site of what used to be the Hogarth Press, at Virginia and Leonard Woolf's Bloomsbury home before it was obliterated during the bombing of World War II. This was one reason that Woolf was writing what turned out to be her final novel at Monk's House in the Sussex countryside, a train ride away from the chaos and destruction of London. A few years into the following century, I researched Germaine Dulac's last address in Paris, the place where she'd conceived her final projects and where her life had ended; it was in a beautiful section of the seventeenth arrondissement, within walking distance of the tranquil nineteenth-century Parc Monceau and bordering the Quartier de l'Europe made famous by the Impressionist painters who lived and worked there. Two found addresses, one from the archive of personal experience, the other from a more formal repository of cinematic memory (the Bibliothèque du Film), initiated a unique kind of mental flânerie that produced some unforeseen revelations. For the addresses of these two highly productive and relatively celebrated women evoked a set of questions about the lesser-known, personal aspects of their lives, questions that enhanced my understanding of each woman's artistic practice while they opened new arenas of possible connection.

What, I wondered, were they thinking and doing in their most private and intimate moments at this point in their lives? Did they always have some project or other to engage their energies as they lived the great events of their time? And what of the social and political upheavals that gave context to their deaths? What impact did such global events have on the lives and deaths of these two intensely creative yet highly sensitive women, women who expressed their personal visions in the public arena with such grace, commitment, and originality? I had very public documentary evidence—novels for Woolf, films for Dulac—and the endless creative musings of both to work with. I also had official archives (the Fonds Colson Malleville at the Bibliothèque du film, deposited by Dulac's partner Marie-Anne Colson-Malleville) and unofficial ones (Woolf's diaries and journals, now public record) to peruse. But what I didn't expect was that the intuitive affinity and random association of locations that had encouraged me to consider these women side by side would yield, through this circuitous route of documents, textual analysis, and the juxtaposition of two diverse but suggestively related artistic talents, such exciting parallels and unexpected relations. So let us begin with some formal documentation of the attested public facts.

Charles Ford's 1968 booklet on Germaine Dulac (*Anthologie du Cinéma* 31, part of which I translated for *Women and Film* in 1974) holds a privileged place in the study of women's cinematic authorship, for it is the first acknowledgment in print (and in monograph form) of Dulac's central and enduring place in the history of film. Dulac's sudden death in 1942 at the age of fifty-nine owing to "undisclosed causes," put an end to her rich and varied career at a time when her cinematic experimentation had long been superceded by a return to the feminist and socialist activism that had characterized her precinematic journalism. Having completed her most adventurous and abstract phase of filmmaking with the exquisitely evocative, Debussy-inspired lyricism of *Arabesque (Etude cinégraphique sur une arabesque)* in 1929, Dulac turned her attention to documentary and its concomitant socially relevant activities. According to Siân Reynolds's introduction to three translated Dulac articles from the 1930s, Germaine Dulac formed a small production company, France-Actualités (associated with Gaumont but editorially independent), which made documentaries and newsreels between 1932 and 1935.[1] In 1936 she was closely involved with the Popular Front, whose election of Léon Blum, a socialist and Jewish prime minister, belied the climate of right-wing racial hatred seething just beneath the surface of the populist electoral victory. Dulac worked with Popular Front cultural groups, combining her spirited appreciation for the cinema audience with the progressive social politics that inspired a generation.

In Ford's monograph, tucked between sections titled "Dernières réalisations, Activités multiples" and "Testament spirituel," there is a section under the rubric "Fin de carrière," where he describes the curious set of difficulties surrounding the publication of Germaine Dulac's obituary:

[Dulac continued to work on projects despite poor health.] Only the occupation of Paris and the installation of the Propagandastaffel put an end to these activities. Relegated to the sidelines by the invasion and undermined by its forced inaction, she wouldn't give up, and her friends knew that, up to the last day of her life, she was interested in everything that had to do with the art of the moving image. Near the end of July . . . Germaine Dulac died, just a few months before her sixtieth birthday. Out of all the press, only a single publication in the Free Zone, *La Revue de L'Ecran* (which came out of Marseilles) printed an obituary, for which it was necessary, moreover, to extract an authorization from the Vichy censors. Bothered by her nonconformist ideas, disturbed by her impure origins, the censors had rejected Dulac's obituary, which only appeared three weeks late, after strenuous protest by the editor in chief. Even in death, Germaine Dulac still seemed dangerous.[2]

Perhaps even more intriguing than Ford's speculation on the reasons for this censorship is the exact date of Dulac's death in Paris—July 19, 1942—and the broader sociohistorical circumstances that contextualize it. Just two days earlier, on July 16–17, the City of Light was witness to one of the darkest moments in its history, the mass roundups and deportations associated with the Vélodrôme d'Hiver (the Winter Cycling Stadium). These two days inaugurated what is now understood as Occupation France's "War against Women and Children," a focused persecution that occurred in both Nazi-occupied northern France and its tragically misnamed southern counterpart, Free France, otherwise known as Vichy.[3] The debacle took place a mere six months after Wansee (where the Final Solution determining how Europe's Jews were to be exterminated was developed), and it involved the roundup, detainment, and subsequent deporation to Auschwitz of nearly 13,000 Jewish men, women, and children (mostly the latter two), who were held for days after having been seized from their homes, hiding places, and the streets of Paris. All were deported; only about two hundred people ever returned. Now known simply as the "Vél d'Hiv," the event was originally referred to by its French coordinators as "Operation Spring Wind" and would later be called, by historians, the "Massacre of the Innocents."

The horrifying reason for this latter assignation is actually very simple: networks informing immigrant Jews of the roundups began almost immediately after the Nazis arrived in Paris in June 1940; they allowed foreign men to hide until each threat had dissipated. Although warnings in Yiddish had been posted in the Jewish community suggesting that all Jews were in danger, the belief that only males were considered a threat, and thus that only men were being sought, was pervasive. Word of the mid-July roundups (which were strategically rescheduled to avoid Bastille Day), therefore, warned the men to go into hiding until the sweep was over; women and children would simply remain in their homes. But French police, eager to fill their quotas, took anyone they could. Thus it was that for two chaotic days, busloads of terrified families—ordinary Parisians except for the fact that they were Jewish or suspected of being so—crisscrossed the city on their way to the central dumping site in the fifteenth arrondissement, within view of the Eiffel Tower and home to one of the most popular national pastimes in French history, bicycle racing. Sudden heart attacks were common; so were suicides, as women and men seeing no possibility of escape sought to put an end to the suffering before it began in earnest. Some women left their children with strangers for safekeeping. Others tried perilous and impromptu means of escape, with varied success depending largely on luck. At any rate, the moment of Dulac's death was marked by an atmosphere of utter terror throughout Paris that wreaked havoc on even the most accomplished and stable personalities.

Skeptics following my line of speculation will certainly point out that Germaine Dulac was not Jewish, or that she had no particular reason to be inclined toward panic and despair in such circumstances—which, given the obvious reality of those marked for deportation, had absolutely nothing to do with her. However, according to Evelyn Ehrlich, whose magisterial work on French filmmaking under the German Occupation, *Cinema of Paradox,* remains the only book in English on the topic, Dulac had in fact been arrested for precisely such cause:

In September 1941, the Filmprüfstelle compiled two lists, for internal use, of Jewish and non-Jewish proscribed personnel (R141/F1025–1029). The first was a list of "non-Jewish filmworkers" whose films were not to be allowed exhibition [and included such names as Marlene Dietrich, Charles Boyer and Joris Ivens]. The second list was of French Jews in the film industry, and oddly overlapped the first list. Director Germaine Dulac was on both lists, identified as a Jew and a Communist. She managed to prove to the Germans' satisfaction that she was neither.[4]

I maintain that it is no coincidence that, less than ten months after these lists were compiled, an English language news source could simply print: "[Paris, July 19, 1942] Germaine Dulac, the avant-garde director and cinema theorist, died unexpectedly during the night." Let's not belabor the point; Dulac's feminist and socialist activities in the decade preceding the invasion, her militant tracts calling for film workers' unity, and her uncompromising stance on artistic responsibility in the face of fascism all made her a logical candidate for Nazi persecution. That this persecution manifested itself in a particularly hateful—and anti-Semitic—way in the few days immediately preceding her sudden death makes the timing, it seems to me, more than coincidental.

Germaine Dulac wasn't a Jew, but Virginia Woolf's husband Leonard was. Naively romantic notions of her suicide aside, Woolf's drowning in the River Ouse was in no small part occasioned by the same very real terror that permeated Dulac's world at the end of her life. Woolf explains in diary entries from 1940 how she and Leonard discussed the possibility of the Nazis invading England:

[Monday 13 May] Apple blossom snowing in the garden. Churchill exhorting all men to stand together. . . . So my little moment of peace comes in a yawning hollow. But though L. says he has petrol in the garage for suicide should Hitler win, we go on. It's the vastness, and the smallness, that make this possible.

[Tuesday 14 May] War war—a great battle—this hot day, with the blossom on the grass. A plane goes over—

[Wednesday 15 May] Behind that the strain: this morning we discussed suicide if Hitler lands. Jews beaten up. What point in waiting? Better shut the garage doors. This a sensible, rather matter of fact talk. A thunderous hot day. Dutch laid down arms last night. The great battle now raging. . . . On the other hand— No, I don't want the garage to see the end of me. I've a wish for ten years more, and to write my book which as usual darts into my brain. . . . This idea struck me: the army is the body: I am the brain. Thinking is my fighting.

And in another entry, a short time later, Woolf writes, "I reflect: capitulation will mean all Jews to be given up. Concentration camps."[5]

The struggle is clear; faced with the impossible evil engulfing everything around her, yet indomitably believing in writing as salvation, Woolf found herself jostled between the extremes of human feeling. If we are to take Woolf's action of March 28, 1941, pockets filled with stones and a chorus of birds chanting in Greek, in any sort of context other than the cliché of melodramatic self-destruction, we must acknowledge the pressure of these kinds of persecutorial events in the Nazi era. For a writer like Woolf, so attuned to the intricate meanderings of both mind and soul, and so committed to the shared dialogue of friends in art and culture, the possibility that all could be overwhelmed by the goose-stepping urge to annihilate would have been too much. Added to that the many years of antiwar polemical writing, the work of intense mourning and questioning brought on by the death of her nephew Julian in the Spanish Civil War—and the parallel between the lives and deaths of Dulac and Woolf seems more than striking.

And now it is to the writing of the 1930s that I turn for an even stronger connection binding these two women, both of them exact contemporaries born in 1882, each of whose life ended just before the age of sixty in the midst of the turmoil of World War II. Dulac spent the decade of the 1930s in energetic promotion of the collective ideals of the Popular Front, and although she made only one or two films, her newsreel work, her activism, her writing, and her lecturing were as prolific as ever. She was highly visible on the international film education scene, calling for the cinema's place in the struggle for social justice and for general enlightenment through the art of film. At about the same time that Dulac was working on these projects, Woolf produced her second major work of nonfiction, *Three Guineas* (1938). This book established her as (according to the critic Mark Hussey) "a significant voice in the cause of pacifism,"[6] but more important, it posited a feminist vision of human interconnectedness in its critique of patriarchal bellicosity. In preparation for its writing, Woolf compiled three full notebooks of news clippings, thus matching in an almost uncanny way, the news-event activity that was at the heart of Dulac's work at that time. The last note on this amalgam of texts and documents, philosophy and history, poetry and reportage, is taken from Georges Sand, one of Woolf's "forgotten women":

All existences are interdependent, and every human being who considers himself in isolation, without connection to others, is nothing but a riddle to be figured out. . . . Individuality alone has neither significance nor importance. An individual takes on meaning only to the extent that he is part of life in general, an individual in concert with one's fellow-beings, and it is by this process that one becomes a part of history.[7]

If there is a cinematic form that can be associated with Germaine Dulac's work of the 1930s, it is the newsreel. In fact, both of her films from this period, the 1935 film about contemporary history, *Le Cinéma au service de l'Histoire,* and the eleven-minute fiction film produced by the group "Mai 36" titled *Retour à la vie* (1936), use extensive documentary footage. Likewise, Dulac's writing and lecturing during this time are about the social uses of the newsreel, combining her typical respect for the audience's intelligence with an acute awareness of the political effectiveness of observational cinema. As she wrote in a projected book on the cinema, "Newsreels are the history of an age, which the film-maker and his or her lens record, day in day out. The news item is the irrefutable, lived document that any given year bequeaths to the next. An event recorded today, the importance of which has not immediately been grasped, may appear at a later date in the fullness of its significance, and in all its immediacy of movement, for later generations who will know how to judge it."[8]

If there is an ideological and theoretical thread in Dulac's work at this time, it is socialist feminism, for all of this work was grounded in specific, concrete political activity. She presented papers at international congresses sponsored by the Conseil International des Femmes (at one point she was president of the film section) and by the Conseil National des Femmes Françaises; she wrote for the Leftist journals *Le Populaire* and *Le Travailleur du Film* and was active in trade unions (president of the filmmakers section of the Syndicat des Techniciens de la Production Cinématographique from 1938 until her death). In addition, Dulac was actively involved in collective projects typical of Popular Front cultural production. According to Ginette Vincendeau, "[The] Popular Front unleashed a ferment of cultural experiment as intellectuals and artists poured into the political arena. Newsreels, documentaries and propaganda films were made in an extraordinary burst of activity and enthusiasm, especially at the cooperative Ciné-Liberté."[9] Germaine Dulac, listed as a member of this group by Louis Aragon in the Communist weekly *Regards,* embraced this opportunity for collective film work with her typical energy and imagination.[10] As the Popular Front's most successful attempt to join film production with political activism,[11] Ciné-Liberté provided Dulac with the perfect arena in which to blend cinematic experimentation and political commitment, allowing the documentation of objective reality to create a radical new cinematic form for popular audiences.

Dulac's more enduring connection in the 1930s, however, was to the film section of the "Mai 36" group, which produced her short film *Retour à la vie.* Dulac had originally joined the Alliance du Cinéma Indépendent, a cultural forum open to film workers and professionals that became the film unit of the Maisons de la Culture, before finding a more suitable structure in Mai 36. *Retour à la vie* was largely misunderstood by the critics, who did not appreciate Dulac's effort to use documentary footage in an expressive, metaphoric way ("Do you take us for morons?"[12]), and they failed to grasp the film's radical innovation: it is a daughter (who also happens to be a mother) who articulates the progressive social argument of unity and optimism of the masses.

Eventually, Dulac turned to other modes of collective film production and distribution, and by the end of the decade she became the vice president of the film cooperative Les Artisans du Cinéma, and the artistic director (along with Jean Zay, who had been the Popular Front Education Minister)[13] of the film production company Les Diffusions Modernes, a position she held until the end of her life. The spirit of the Popular Front, with its combination of intellectuals, artists, and workers all joined in the struggle to create new cultural forms that would directly move and educate the public, never left Dulac. Whether she was making films, lecturing, doing collective work, or agitating for her most recent cinematic love, the newsreel, Dulac always grounded herself in daily life: "If only you knew how much constant contact with ordinary people, living their lives, suffering, working, loving normally can change the perspective of a film director used to facing more or less fictional characters. In a filmed report, all is real, not deformed by the imagination or theoretical reasoning."[14] It can only be surmised to what extent the involuntary removal from this vitality affected Dulac in the last months of her life.

Something of the spirit of these words of Dulac's (as well as the devastating pressure of current events that subsequently tempered it) resonates with the writing of Virginia Woolf, and with the humanistic passion for the documented detail at the core of both her antiwar polemic, *Three Guineas,* and her modernist epic novel *Between the Acts* (1941), completed before she died and published posthumously. In the latter, it is the very "ordinary people, living their lives" that provides continuity and affirmation in a world torn to pieces by violence, chaos, and despair. The novel's setting closely resembles the village of Rodmell in Sussex, where the Woolfs' home, Monk's House, was located; its action involves the staging of a pageant representing a satirical version of England's history, with the villagers as both actors and audience. The novel is a richly heterogeneous texture of disparate voices—the daily sounds of war (the zoom of planes), the chatter of public media (newspapers, loudspeakers), the claims of art and history (the pageant and performances), and common conversation (snatches of dialogue in suspension)—all intertwine in polyphonous, dissonant music. In a diary entry when she began the novel (in 1938), Woolf stated that she wanted to discuss "all lit. . . . in connection with real little incongruous living humor," intending to "reject 'I' in favor of 'We'" and present a "rambling capricious but somehow unified whole."[15] This desire for unity from fragmentation is very similar to Dulac's concern in organizing newsreels: "[Newsreels] are shown all over the world. . . . This is another example in which the cinema binds together the scattered forces of humanity and coordinates them into a single current. . . . From familiarity to understanding, and from understanding to friendship, is but a step."[16]

The momentary yet affirming unity in *Between the Acts* takes on a philosophical and social dimension (again, Dulac comes to mind) in Katherine Hill-Miller's assessment: "Monk's House and the villagers of Rodmell represented the continuity of human history—the idea that human history endured in the lives of the obscure, and that any single life gained significance by connecting itself to that unconscious pageant."[17] But this is a fragile unity, almost ephemeral, a hopeful dream among the shards and fragments of a world wrenched by war, pillaged by violence. Near the end of the novel, as the pageant closes in "Present Time" with a visual cacophony of reflecting shards, a harmonious vision of shared understanding emerges. After a sudden storm, the gramophone's music provides a backdrop for this collective realization, just before the shattering drone of military aircraft pierces the sky ("The word was cut in two. A zoom severed it"):

Like quicksilver sliding, filings magnetized, the distracted united. The tune began; the first note meant a second; the second a third. . . . The whole population of the mind's immeasurable profundity came flocking; from the unprotected, the unskinned; and dawn rose; and azure; from chaos and cacophony measure; but not the melody of surface sound alone controlled it; but also the warring battle-plumed warriors straining asunder . . . recalled from the edge of appalling crevasses; they crashed; solved; united.[18]

In contrast to the narrative multivalence of *Between the Acts, Three Guineas* is a carefully reasoned polemical essay on the relations between women and war in the form of a letter to a barrister who has asked how war might be prevented. It is a dense and complex text that elaborates, in the course of an argument punctuated with drafts of letters, requests, and documented historical facts, on the symbiosis of patriarchy, militarism, and fascism. Early on, Woolf asserts that her view on women and war is established "from the bridge which connects the private house with the world of public life," a bridge that "suggests that the public and the private worlds are inseparably connected; that the tyrannies and servilities of the one are the tyrannies and servilities of the other."[19] In a brilliant assessment of Woolf's structures of opposition and rhythms of alternation, the dialectics of fragmentation and unity, the literary scholar Patricia Laurence states:

The juxtaposition of newspaper articles in the notebooks and *Three Guineas* is deconstructed into gliding displacements of the war front and the home front, the public and the private, men and women, the rape of women and the rape of lands, the voice of the reporter and the voice of the artist in *Between the Acts.* . . . The trope of ruined houses—the dislocated relationships, . . . the rape of the young girl by British soldiers, . . . and the destruction of war—are presented in a fugue: the sounds of daily life, the gramophone, the daily paper, the airplanes. All become part of a polyphony that M. M. Bakhtin might describe as "a diversity of social speech types . . . and a diversity of individual voices, artistically organized."[20]

Virginia Woolf cleverly situates her antiwar polemic in *Three Guineas* in the context of an optimistic assessment. "There is that marvelous, perpetually renewed, and as yet largely untapped aid to the understanding of human motives which is provided in our age by biography and autobiography. Also there is the daily paper, history in the raw. There is thus no longer any reason to be confined to the minute span of actual experience which is still, for us, so narrow, so circumscribed. We can supplement it by looking at the picture of the lives of others."[21] Utopian to be sure, but this optimism about the media's progressive capability can also be found in Dulac, whose comments about the newsreel were also written in the 1930s:

[This] kind of cinema is the great modern educator of society. It brings together the most diverse intelligences, the most varied races. . . . It can show every cinemagoer the intimate details of the life in foreign countries and the human beings behind the official face of historical tradition. . . . [The] newsreel reveals the kind of truth about life everywhere which cannot be gained from books. . . . Classes and races meet in the cinema without intermediaries. Emotions, gestures, joy—humanity rises above its individual characteristics: as the sight of other human beings brings understanding, it helps to destroy hostility.[22]

Yet, sadly for both women, the inexorable volatility and violence of wartime short-circuited the optimism expressed.

In the epilogue to the second edition of *To Desire Differently* I expand on a comparison that had always intrigued me: an affinity of perspective and feeling between Germaine Dulac's abstract film poems of the late 1920s and Virginia Woolf's subjective interior monologues.[23] At that time I validated the textual kinship through close comparative readings and went no further. Today, almost a decade since that epilogue was written, it is to the period after the 1920s—Dulac's and Woolf's work of the 1930s and their subsequent untimely deaths—that I turn to unite them as defiant female rebels amid the horrors of World War II. Visionary sisters, Dulac and Woolf, they dared to dream of a social whole in which feminist values of mutual respect and the inspired celebration of human potential could survive the ravages of patriarchal war. The fact that this war inevitably defeated them both merely defers the dream, it does not destroy it. We have their legacies in word and image, and we also have their challenge.

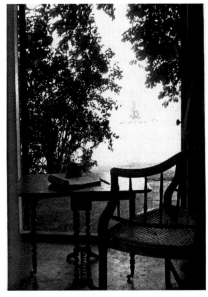

Left: "Homage to Germaine Dulac: in Paris, July 1942" (Sandy Flitterman-Lewis, 1977). *Right:* "View From Virginia Woolf's Study in Monk's House, circa 1941" (Gisèle Freund, 1966).

Notes

1. Siân Reynolds, "Germaine Dulac and Newsreel: 3 Articles, Introduction," *Screening the Past* 12 (2001): 1, http://www.latrobe.edu.au/screeningthepast.

2. Charles Ford, *Germaine Dulac, Anthologie du Cinéma* 31 (Paris, 1968), 41. Excerpt translated by the author of this essay.

3. At the outset of the Occupation, France was a divided country. Northern France was occupied by the Nazis from June 1940 until the end of the war. The "official" French government moved south to Vichy, operating independently (with its own anti-Semitic laws and statutes) until November 11, 1942, when all of France became Nazi-occupied. I use the term "Occupation France" to incorporate Vichy into the overall historical ethos—as opposed to "Occupied France," which fuels the mistaken attribution of evil to the Germans alone.

4. Evelyn Ehrlich, *Cinema of Paradox: French Filmmaking under the German Occupation* (New York: Columbia University Press, 1985), 58. The fact of the arrest was pointed out to the author of this essay in conversation.

5. Virginia Woolf, *A Moment's Liberty (The Shorter Diary)* (New York: Harcourt Brace, 1990), 476–77; Anne Oliver Bell, ed., *The Diary of Virginia Woolf, Vol. 5: 1936–1941* (San Diego, CA: Harcourt/Harvest Books, 1985), 292. Both Virginia and Leonard knew that the Gestapo had an arrest list for Great Britain. Although the names were unknown, it was assumed that, in addition to Leonard's being Jewish, their leftist leanings and publishing connections would have almost certainly included them. In fact, both "Leonard Woolf, Schriftsteller" and "Virginia Woolf, Schriftstellerin" were on the Gestapo list, along with their friends Harold Nicholson and Lytton Strachey, as well as Sigmund Freud. See Katherine Hill-Miller, *From the Lighthouse to Monk's House: A Guide to Virginia Woolf's Literary Landscapes* (London: Gerald Duckworth, 2001), 252.

6. Mark Hussey, *Virginia Woolf A to Z: The Essential Reference to Her Life and Writings* (Oxford: Oxford University Press, 1995), 285.

7. Georges Sand, *Histoire de ma vie*, 240–41, quoted by Virginia Woolf in *Three Guineas* (Oxford: Harcourt Brace, 1938), 188.

8. Germaine Dulac, "Cinema at the Service of History: The Role of Newsreels," chapter of a projected book, Fonds Malleville, GD 1371, Bibliothèque du Film (hereafter BiFi) archives, Paris. In Reynolds, "Germaine Dulac and Newsreel."

9. Ginette Vincendeau, *The Companion to French Cinema* (London: Cassells, 1996), 119.

10. Ciné-Liberté, a militant cultural action group begun in early 1936, stated its aims to *Comoedia*: "A true cooperative of film workers, technicians and actors, united in a single purpose, that of making popular news-reels, documentaries and fiction films" whose aims are: 1) the abolition of censorship; 2) distribution of "popular" films; 3) the promotion of truly revolutionary film education; 4) a "clean-up" of the French film industry's financial chaos. *Comoedia* July 14, 1936, cited by Pascal Ory in "De Ciné-Liberté à 'La Marseillaise': Hopes and Limitations of a Liberated Cinema (1936–1938)," *La Vie ets à nous: French Cinema of the Popular Front, 1935–1938*, ed. Ginette Vincendeau and Keith Reader (London: BFI, 1986).

11. "A daring experiment to try to reconcile militant cultural action with an equally militant and collective form of artistic creation" says Ory in "De Ciné-Liberté à 'La Marseillaise,'" 31.

12. *Comoedia* August 8, 1936.

13. "To the anti-Jewish press, Zay was the man who had corrupted French youth as the Popular Front's Minister of Education." See Paul Webster, *Pétain's Crime* (London: Macmillan, 1990), 40, 42, 43–44.

14. Qtd. in Reynolds, "Germaine Dulac and Newsreel: 3 Articles, Introduction," 3.

15. Qtd. in Hussey, *Virginia Woolf A to Z,* 27.

16. Dulac, "Cinema at the Service of History."

17. Hill-Miller, *From the Lighthouse to Monk's House,* 250.

18. Virginia Woolf, *Between the Acts,* Harvest ed. (London: Harcourt, 1970), 193, 189.

19. Woolf, *Three Guineas,* 18, 142.

20. Patricia Laurence, "The Facts and Fugue of War," in *Virginia Woolf and War: Fiction, Reality and Myth,* ed. Mark Hussey (Syracuse: Syracuse University Press, 1991), 245.

21. Woolf, *Three Guineas,* 7.

22. Germaine Dulac, "The Educational and Social Value of the Newsreel," Fonds Malleville, GD 1298, BiFi archives. Originally published in *Revue internationale du cinéma éducateur* (International review of educational cinematography) (August 1934): 545–50. Translation by Siân Reynolds, in Reynolds, "Germaine Dulac and Newsreel." The optimism of this article reflects the national spirit just before the Popular Front victory. By 1941 Dulac's enthusiasm had dwindled significantly. However, the core of the idea, respect for the human family, remained intact.

23. Sandy Flitterman-Lewis, *To Desire Differently: Feminism and the French Cinema,* 2nd ed. (New York: Columbia University Press, 1996).

Part 4

CONSTRUCTING A (POST)FEMINIST FUTURE

I have placed parenthesis around "post" in the title of part 4 in an effort to get a visual grip on and around a term that has much vexed contemporary discussions of the women's movement. The "post" of postfeminism functions as a type of shadow presence for a variety of debates that circulate around this ongoing political engagement directed toward an international critique of patriarchy. In many ways, the very appearance of this shadow speaks to a certain measure of feminism's success and its entry into a larger political discourse. At the same time, however, the shadow designates another side to the feminist "success" story, one that points toward issues unresolved and blind spots still in place, particularly those concerning inequities based on race, class, ethnicity, and sexuality.

It is perhaps most useful to see postfeminism as a range of discourses that began to emerge in the 1980s, although, as Sarah Projansky has argued, iterations of postfeminist views can be traced as far back as the 1920s (after the gains of the women's suffrage movement).[1] For Projansky, "post" is a response to, or especially a reaction against, feminist agendas. Here I would agree with her assessment: if we set aside the notion that all such postfeminist "reactions" assume that feminism is no longer needed and is therefore something reactionary and dangerous. Such an assumption would presume that feminism itself was a stable and an always-progressive enterprise, a premise highly suspect, to say the least.

Chris Holmlund notes in a *Cinema Journal* essay that the discourse of postfeminism is wide-ranging and often contradictory, encompassing everything from

a) "chick feminism"—in the main a variant of a backlash against feminism—to
b) riot grrls or Third Wave proponents (the supposed next generation of feminists) to c) academic types with an affinity for a range of contemporary critical
theory (e.g., post-structural, post-colonial, post-modern, queer theory).[2]

Holmlund's remarks seem particularly appropriate in certain international
contexts where the term "postfeminism" seems less troubling and is often
the preferred designation. For Ann Brooks, the "post" of postfeminism
functions as it does in other important parallel contexts, namely, as a critique of an ongoing discourse (as in postcolonialism or postmodernism).
Here, postfeminism is not only a critique of patriarchy but also of "hegemonic feminism," that is, a feminism that works toward universalizing or
essentializing categories that erase differences among women.[3] For example, liberal humanist notions of "equality" prominent in earlier feminist
agendas often deflect discussions of the precise historical, economic, and
cultural conditions under which such terms might in fact be viable (by
assuming that suffrage or an open-admission policy would be in effect a
sufficient condition of equality).[4] However, as Amelia Jones has noted, the
alignment of postfeminism with the other "posts" has produced, within
at least an arts and visual culture discourse, a certain flattening out of the
critique of patriarchy, resulting in a vagueness and imprecision that in effect renders feminism simply another methodological turn (among many
other related turns), rather than a political force.[5] In any event, the current
divide on whether the emergence of postfeminism is a positive or negative
development invokes the old 1970s-era divide between Anglo-American
pragmatists and continental feminist theorists about whether feminists
should focus their energies on examining "real" women or investigating
the structures of the "feminine."

  While postfeminism may inspire contradictory definitions, there
seems to be little doubt about the way in which the mainstream media
has invoked the category. In this instance, the word "post" takes on the
most obvious and banal meaning of "life after" feminism. Feminism's
"death" or obsolescence is now attributed to everything from the end of sex
discrimination to young women's renewed embrace of the maternal and
domestic space (and the implied rejection of work outside of the home).
Clearly ignored by the popular press in the latter is the privileged position
of those who have the luxury of making such choices. Indeed, the rhetoric
of "choice" saturates the terms of the current popular debate regarding
feminism, at once coopting a crucial term from the abortion rights move-

ment and presenting a range of options, from employment to consumer purchases, as equivalent selections.[6] The reduction of feminism's human rights agenda to a kind of shopping spree has been labeled by critics as "lifestyle feminism" or "commodity feminism."[7]

It is no wonder, then, that a new generation of feminists has looked for strategies to combat the media's assault on both past political achievements and future goals. The notion of a "Third Wave" in feminist activism was an effort to provide a bridge to past history as well as an acknowledgment that conditions for contemporary women have changed. For some, the Third Wave is both an attempt to address historical gaps in the feminist agenda and to acknowledge and self-consciously reflect on the ever-increasing importance of media texts as a central site of cultural knowledge and communication.[8] However, for others, the "Third Wave" simply replays and repeats deep-seated problems within the movement, especially heterosexism and racism. Kimberly Springer notes that indeed the very designation of a "Third Wave" participates in the same sort of erasure of African American women's struggles that occurred in the first two "waves," particularly given that the wave metaphor is typically organized around two eras associated with white middle-class women (i.e., the suffrage movement and 1970s women's liberation). These prior two "waves" obscure or at times deny the specific historical conditions of women of color as well as their efforts in the abolitionist and civil rights movements, which served as important foundations for the later political agendas.[9]

In putting together this collection, I do not expect to resolve the difficulties of terminology that exist in contemporary feminism; that is, I do not intend to resolve whether feminists should, once and for all, adopt a single label, whether "Third Wave," "postfeminism," or even "Feminism 3.0," the term I use in the introduction to this work. However, the essays in this section present a range of responses to and around the discourse of postfeminism. The first essay by Michele Schreiber investigates the many contradictions central to contemporary representations of romance, especially the oft-shifting, inconsistent, and at times nonsensical notions of "choice" that pervade the genre. Intriguingly, Schreiber points toward the self-conscious use of references across media as a means of engaging with these challenges. The media cross talk, which traverses not only formats but also generations, becomes a kind of shared language and communal space for women.

This exchange across media platforms, indicative of our era of media convergence, continues in the collection's final essays, by Anna Everett and

Soyoung Kim, respectively, and in my interview with Lynn Hershman Leeson. Significantly, all of these chapters point toward very practical political enterprises, in particular to the use of new media as organizing spaces for those challenging hegemonic structures. Everett examines the potential of new media to push feminist dialogue beyond the gridlock of generational and racial divides, especially the ways in which cyber culture is facilitating new organizing tools for political ends. Kim, opening the theory/practice investigation to global concerns, proposes for us a notion of "trans-cinema." "Trans-cinema" rather than "transnational" cinema includes not only cinema but a variety of media forms that require us to rethink the very definitions of cinema, spectatorship, and the "public sphere."

The intervention across media, and as the transformation of public space into a feminist performative site have been central elements in Lynn Hershman Leeson's long creative career. The final chapter in this work features an interview with this pioneering artist whose work explores technology and interactive media. In Hershman Leeson's ideas we see not only new possibilities for the archive but also how truly vital it is for feminists to claim the tools of historical writing. Hershman Leeson's work makes clear that we are always surrounded by "remains," "artifacts" of the past that shape who we are today and point us toward what our possibilities might be. The assembly and narratives assigned to these remains are there for us to claim, especially now in the digital era, which foregrounds the mutability of material and provides new venues for communication and collaboration.

The essays in this section provide a reminder of the "deep-time" archaeological approach needed for a feminist cinema and media history. The links between 1970s and contemporary feminist theory, history, and practice must be constantly renewed, reclaimed, and reassembled, lest amnesia and nostalgia settle in. In the final analysis, this endeavor, this kind of "writing"—which brings together the past, present, and future, the critical and the creative, and opens up new conversations for feminist engagement—is as much about *making* history as it is recording it.

Notes

Many thanks to Michele Schreiber and Suzanne Leonard for their suggestions of readings in this area and for many engaging hours of discussion on the (post)feminist future.

1. Sarah Projansky, *Watching Rape: Film and Television in a Postfeminist Culture* (New York: New York University Press, 2001), 88.

2. Chris Holmlund, "Postfeminism from A to G," in "In Focus: Postfeminism and Contemporary Media Studies," special section of articles edited by Yvonne Tasker and Diane Negra in *Cinema Journal* 44.2 (2005): 107–32 (the issue contains related essays by Charlotte Brunsdon, Chris Holmlund, Linda Mizejewski, and Justine Ashby).

3. Ann Brooks, *Postfeminisms: Feminism, Cultural Theory, and Cultural Forms* (London: Routledge, 1997), 1–4.

4. Sarah Gamble, "Postfeminism," in *The Routledge Critical Dictionary of Feminism and Post-Feminism,* ed. Sarah Gamble (Routledge: London, 2000), 50.

5. Amelia Jones, "Feminism, Incorporated: Reading 'Postfeminism' in an Anti-Feminist Age," in *The Feminism and Visual Culture Reader,* ed. Amelia Jones (Routledge: London, 2003), 321–22.

6. Projansky, *Watching Rape,* 78.

7. Ibid., 80; Yvonne Tasker and Diane Negra, "Postfeminism and Contemporary Media Studies," *Cinema Journal* 44.2 (2005): 107.

8. Amber E. Kinser, "Negotiating Spaces For/Through Third Wave Feminism," *NWSA Journal* 16.3 (2004): 135–36.

9. Kimberly Springer, "Third Wave Black Feminism?" *Signs* 27.4 (2002): 1061–62.

Further Reading

Faludi, Susan. *Backlash: The Undeclared War against American Women.* New York: Crown, 1991.

Lotz, Amanda. "Postfeminist Television Criticism: Rehabilitating Critical Terms and Identifying Postfeminist Attributes." *Feminist Media Studies* 1.1 (2001): 105–21.

Modleski, Tania. *Feminism without Women: Culture and Criticism in a "Postfeminist" Age.* New York: Routledge, 1991.

Morgan, Joan. *When the Chickenheads Come Home to Roost: My Life as a Hip-Hop Feminist.* New York: Simon and Schuster, 1999.

Probyn, Elspeth. "Choosing Choice: Images of Sexuality and 'Choiceoisie' in Popular Culture," in *Negotiating at the Margins: The Gendered Discourses of Power and Resistance,* ed. Sue Fisher and Kathy Davis, 278–94. New Brunswick: Rutgers University Press, 1993.

Walker, Rebecca. *To Be Real: Telling the Truth and Changing the Face of Feminism.* New York: Anchor, 1995.

Wolf, Naomi. *Fire with Fire: The New Female Power and How It Will Change the Twenty-First Century.* New York: Random House, 1993.

Yaszek, Lisa. "I'll Be Postfeminist in a Postpatriarchy, or, Can We Really Imagine Life after Feminism," electronic book review, http://www.electronicbookreview.com/thread/writingpostfeminism/(fem)sci-fi.

"Misty Water-Colored Memories
of the Way We Were . . ."

Postfeminist Nostalgia in Contemporary Romance Narratives

Katie, the female protagonist played by Barbra Streisand in the 1973 romance film *The Way We Were,* is presumably the subject speaking the lines from the film's theme song, from which this article takes its title. The lyrics to the song express ambivalence about the role that time plays in the process of making sense of romance and suggest that events from the past—in the case of this film, a romance from the past—can only be seen via hazy memories that obscure the clarity of the events as they actually occurred and diminish the intensity of the emotion that accompanied them. The song goes on to question, "Could it be that it was all so simple then, or has time rewritten every line?" which suggests a muddled distinction between recalling the past as it really happened, and the sort of revisionism inherent in recollection that transforms the historical and personal past to fit one's own present subjectivity.

The setting of *The Way We Were* in the oft-romanticized World War II and postwar era, the film's basic flashback structure, and the lyrics of its prescient theme song are examples of how issues of temporality, history, and subjectivity often become inextricably intertwined in romance texts. In fact, since the release of *The Way We Were* in 1973, a subgenre of contemporary film and television romance texts has emerged in which "timelessness" is no longer just a thematic element but serves an increasingly prominent and explicit narrative function. Some groups of texts of this type include the "what if" narrative, such as *The Family Man* (dir. Ratner, 2000) and *Me Myself I* (dir. Karmel, 1999); the forking-path narrative, such as *Sliding Doors* (dir. Howitt, 1998) and *Groundhog Day* (dir. Ramis, 1993); and the "time travel as matchmaker" narrative, such as *Somewhere in Time* (dir. Szwarc, 1980) *Kate and Leopold* (dir. Mangold, 2001), *The Lake House* (dir. Agresti, 2006), and *The Time Traveler's Wife* (dir. Schwentke, 2009). Here I will focus on another of these groups of temporally engaged romance texts—the nostalgia narrative, which is a contemporary text that features characters who revere a classic fictional romance text and seek within it insight into their present-day romantic trials and tribulations.

I will argue that in the texts *Sex and the City*—specifically the final episode from the series' second season titled "Ex and the City"—and the film *Sleepless in Seattle* (dir. Ephron, 1993), nostalgia is representative of a broader postfeminist cultural trend—seen in other media forms and neoconservative "feminist" writing—in which the reflection on, or imitation of, the prefeminist period (both real and fictional) is implicitly (and often explicitly) encouraged as a means of resolving complex postfeminist quandaries, specifically those related to female identity and romantic relationships. Both texts illustrate how nostalgia functions as a sort of therapeutic discourse through which women, individually and collectively, negotiate their ambivalence about their role in contemporary culture—wanting to be autonomous, professionally successful, and economically independent individuals while at the same time desiring traditional love narratives in which their identity becomes subsumed by the promise of heterosexual coupling and marriage.

The nostalgia of the female characters in *Sex* and *Sleepless* reveals how much women's roles and courtship rituals have changed over the course of recent history (in the case of these two texts—since the World War II and postwar period) and imply that inherent in women's postfeminist identity is an impulse to reconcile the past, present, and future simultaneously. However, the fact that nostalgia here is completely disconnected from a genuine recollection of, or longing for, the actual, lived historical past (and its accompanying sociopolitical ramifications) but rather is predicated on a desire for the seemingly purer, tidily packaged vision of romantic relationships represented in fictional texts produced in, and/or depicting, past historical periods, is suggestive of a collapse of boundaries between fiction and reality, subjectivity and objectivity.

I will explore how the language of nostalgia in these two texts is a way of understanding postfeminist culture's conflation of the history and politics of feminism with fictional discourses. Two main areas will be addressed. First, I will consider how nostalgia allows women (both inside and outside of the text) to fulfill their desire to "have it both ways"—

to long for the unapologetic traditionalism of romance of a prefeminist past while still remaining in the more progressive present—without any negative repercussions. Second, I will discuss how nostalgia establishes a collective "we" among women, creating a communal language that they can use, both individually and collectively, to navigate the complicated postfeminist cultural and political terrain and perhaps, more important, to communicate with one another. There is some question as to whether its ability to link women with other women within a sort of community that effectively excludes men gives postfeminist nostalgia the potential to take on an empowering political dimension, or if the constraint of its fictional conduit negates this promise.[1]

Romance and Postfeminism

The evolution from feminism to postfeminism occurred upon the emergence of two divergent political and cultural trends: first, the neoconservative political climate that accompanied the Reagan administration, and second, the gradual mainstream acceptance of the feminist and the gay rights movements. In *Moving the Mountain: The Women's Movement in America since 1960,* Flora Davis attributes the rise of the new right and the war on feminism to the election of Ronald Reagan in 1980.[2] And, as Jane Feuer contends, "Under Reaganism, there was a sense in which just about every social group was 'subordinate' to a dominant white conservative male power block."[3] The simultaneous presence of these forces in opposition began to effect a cultural trend toward traditional values that not only detrimentally affected policy decisions with regard to women's rights but also influenced the larger perception of feminism's importance to American women.

To many people, the death of the Equal Rights Amendment, which had become the central issue of the movement in the 1970s, signaled the defeat of mainstream feminism; there was also a increasingly palpable sense, perpetuated by the news media, that feminism's job was "done," that it had achieved all of its goals. As a result of these factors, what was previously a movement that called for rallying around a central political project became so broad in its relation to political and social issues that its meaning in the mainstream was lost as people slowly began to appropriate feminism to serve their own interests. While Susan Faludi's 1991 treatise *Backlash* was perceived to give a voice to this new "phase" of feminism, postfeminism has many definitions, which is a product of the very conflicted sociopolitical climate within which it surfaced.[4]

One of these definitions distinguishes postfeminism from feminism in terms of historical time, as merely marking the time period immediately following the second wave feminism of the 1970s. This notion of moving forward and trying to find ways of making political feminism meaningful for younger generations is generally referred to as third wave feminism and is best exemplified by The Third Wave Foundation (started by Rebecca Walker), and Jennifer Baumgardner and Amy Richards's book *Manifesta: Young Women, Feminism, and the Future.* A second definition, best illustrated by Tania Modleski in her book *Feminism without Women,* marks a shift in academic theory that occurred alongside postmodernism and postcolonialism. Postfeminism's most common definition is as a state of mind that renders the political activism of 1970s second wave feminism as irrelevant or unnecessary. This "movement" away from a collective of women toward the individual woman effectively reverses the 1970s feminist mantra—the personal is political. With postfeminism, the political is personal, and all decisions result from what is best for individual women. This has resulted in postfeminism's other moniker—"me" feminism.

Postfeminism is seen as "me" feminism because its loose framework enables women to pick and choose the aspects of second wave feminism that work within the context of their life choices, while simultaneously appropriating the pre–second wave traditions that suit them as well. In other words, postfeminism can be interpreted as a sort of permanent state of limbo wherein the concept of choice is celebrated so broadly that pre–second wave traditional views share equal footing with second wave views. In other words, in this sort of open playing field of postfeminism, feminism has become hazily defined. In some contexts, it is a foundation that has enabled women to make revolutionary and progressive choices. In others, it is seen as a sort of cautionary tale and a foundation upon which one can reflect on what has been lost.

Regardless of how one chooses to define feminism within a political context, there is undeniable evidence of a shift in the social and cultural position of women since the Second Wave of the 1970s. Since then women have, in increasing numbers, devoted their early adult lives—their twenties and thirties—to making progress in their careers, while waiting until later in life to get married and have children or, more radically to some, choosing to stay single and never marry. A *Time* magazine study showed that in the year 2000, more than 40 percent of all adult females were single, significantly higher than the 10 percent in 1960. And in contrast to 1963, when 83 percent of women aged 25 to 55 were married, in 1997 the number of married women in this age range had dropped to 65 percent. In response to these figures, the University of Chicago sociologist Linda Waite remarked, "Are you kidding? An 18 percent to 20 percent point change? This is huge."[5]

These statistics imply that if and when contemporary women seek romantic relationships they are, for the first time in history, entering into them on a playing field somewhat level with that of their male counterparts.[6] Since they have devoted a comparable amount of time to building their careers, as men have, most women do not have to enter into a relationship or marriage solely for economic reasons. In addition, our culture no longer dictates that female sexual exploration should be confined to marriage; therefore, women no longer need it as a protective shield against social ostracism. Since social and economic circumstances have made it so women don't really "need" marriage, questions arise as to why women still seek it out. In this regard, the contemporary romance narrative possesses a dramatically different discourse from its predecessors in that it explicitly calls attention to the divide between "need" and "want." Women don't really need romance or marriage; however, they still desire it, despite the fact that they recognize its limitations.

Contemporary romance narratives mirror this state of limbo, wavering between a faithful adherence to the Caucasian, heterosexist attributes of traditional romance narrative structures, and the more progressive attitudes toward romance that have resulted from feminism and other contemporary political and social movements, such as those for gay rights and civil rights—and perhaps most important, the rising divorce rate. The plot structures of contemporary texts almost always follow the model of the classic Hollywood romance texts that they imitate—attractive heterosexual protagonists "meet cute," fall in love unsuspectingly, face conflict, separate, and then reunite and admit and/or consummate their love. (In television, this process may be prolonged over the course of an episode, a series of episodes, or the entire run of the show, and is often repeated more than once with the same couple.) However, where contemporary texts differ from their classic counterparts is in regard to their often-explicit level of self-consciousness about the ramifications of this narrative structure for the contemporary women who repeatedly serve as their protagonists.

Most contemporary romance texts feature women who are single (or in unsatisfying relationships) and professionally accomplished. However successful the text may deem this lifestyle, the women are generally depicted as emotionally and psychologically unfulfilled, and missing an unidentified "something." Despite the fact that these female characters explicitly voice their doubts about romance as a viable path for their lives and are openly ambivalent about the "needing" versus "wanting" dilemma, romance is still ultimately presented as a much-needed and much-desired salve for their weary and injured psyche. Consequently, the heterosexual romantic coupling that inevitably takes place at the end of contemporary romance texts not only represents a satisfying conclusion to a linear narrative structure but can be read as providing an individual (on the part of the fictional female protagonist) and, by extension, collective (on the part of the female audience) sensation of contentment and relief that the woman (or women) can finally, as a popular film of the 1990s put it, "exhale."

In this regard, contemporary romance texts are a truly illuminating lens through which postfeminist discourses are revealed. By representing an accomplished contemporary female whose problems with her professional and personal life are easy for the female spectator to identify with, and then presenting what is seemingly a perfect solution for her dissatisfaction—a romantic relationship—film and television romance texts package the real anxiety that surrounds the concept of choice in contemporary postfeminist culture in a way that is glamorous, and filled with high-budget production design and costumes. If we read the contemporary female protagonist's struggles with her career and her independence as progressive, and the love story as traditional, then it is safe to say that the contemporary romance narrative fulfills the desire of the contemporary female spectator to have it all ways. However, not surprisingly, the resolution of individual texts is tenuous at best, as the tension raised by these narratives—between succumbing to the myth of romance and resisting it, and between traditional and progressive notions of women in relation to feminism, femininity, sexuality, marriage, motherhood, professionalism, and domesticity—linger on to be negotiated again and again in other film and television texts, as well as in the wider cultural discourse on the position of real women.

When taking into account the postfeminist cultural climate, it is no surprise that nostalgia has emerged as one of its most pervasive discourses, as its definition is based in the transcendence of concrete historical, or, as in the case of "Ex and the City" and *Sleepless in Seattle,* textual time. In fact, the explicit encouragement of women to look backward to the seemingly "simple" romantic rituals of a past historical time in order to gain valuable insight into the complicated rituals of the present has been a mainstay of countless contemporary media texts, across a wide spectrum of genres. Two of the most notable examples are self-help books, such as Ellen Fein and Sherrie Schneider's *The Rules,* and neoconservative feminist books, such as Danielle Crittenden's *What Our Mothers Didn't Tell Us.* Both texts rely on the same basic premise, which is that in order to undo feminism's wrongs and consequently gain more personal happiness, contemporary women should look to the past and, both individually and collectively, import prefeminist romantic ideals into the present.

Ellen Fein and Sherrie Schneider's *The Rules* argues that because women have been so preoccupied with professional success, they have abandoned the more traditionally feminine side of their nature, mistakenly using their (aggressive) business savvy rather than their (passive) innate femininity in their pursuit of romantic relationships. As the front cover of the book alleges, if women are to "catch the heart of Mr. Right" they must follow the "time-tested" rules that come from generations of women who understand how to effectively play hard to get. As the authors highlight in their introduction,

Modern women aren't to talk loudly about wanting to get married. We had grown up dreaming about being the president of the company, not the wife of the president. So, we quietly passed *The Rules* on from friend to friend, somewhat embarrassed because they seemed so, well, '50s. Still we had to face it: as much as we loved being powerful in business, for most of us, that just wasn't enough . . . Deep inside, if the truth be told, we really wanted to get married—the romance, the gown, the flowers, the presents, the honeymoon—the whole package. We didn't want to give up our liberation, but neither did we want to come home to empty apartments. . . . We needed *The Rules!* Nineties women simply have not been schooled in the basics—*The Rules* of finding a husband or at least being very popular with men.[7]

It is interesting that the authors specifically mention and express some degree of ambivalence about the basis of *The Rules* in a 1950s cultural mentality in which society dictated the appropriate behavior for women who wished to be married. However, Fein and Schneider willingly ignore the feminist-inspired voices inside their heads that might motivate them to resist traditionally gendered romance structures in exchange for a whole-hearted prefeminist acquiescence to them. In fact, Fein and Schneider recommend that women take their professional acumen and put it to good use, calculatedly assuming a retrograde position in courtship rituals by being elusive and playing hard to get. In other words, they should be aggressively passive—effectively appropriating prefeminist and postfeminist behavior at the same time.

In neoconservative Danielle Crittenden's *What Our Mothers Didn't Tell Us,* the most pointed critiques are aimed at the effects that the feminist movement has had on women's sexual behavior. She argues that women's sexual availability has taught men that they can simply move from woman to woman, receiving the sexual satisfaction they seek without any commitment. Crittenden's solution is to turn back the clock on how women enter sexual relationships:

Our grandmothers might have led more sheltered sex lives, but they also controlled what amounted to a sexual cartel: setting a high price for sexual involvement and punishing both men and women if they broke the agreement (either by forcing them into marriage or by ostracizing them from respectable company). Sexual rules create female solidarity among women. If men feel that they can flit from woman to woman they will. They will enjoy our ready availability and exploit it to their advantage. But if women *as a group* cease to be readily available—if they begin to demand commitment (and real commitment, as in marriage) in exchange for sex—market conditions will shift in favor of women.[8]

Crittenden turns to film and TV texts for evidence of the inferiority of the contemporary woman's way of navigating her sexuality and the superiority of pre–sexual revolution courtship rituals. For instance, she cites her friend's reaction to the 1995 adaptation of Jane Austen's *Emma:* "There are no more Mr. Knightleys!" she said, suggesting that contemporary men do not observe the same standards of social interaction as they did in the period of Austen's novel. In response, Crittenden said, there are "no more Emma Woodhouses either," implying that women have as much responsibility for the breakdown of rules governing courtship as do men.[9] The idealized characters in the Austen adaptation are held in stark contrast to what Crittenden refers to as *"unglamorous* [her italics] single, thirtyish female characters neurotically brooding about their thwarted love lives" seen in prime time television. She continues, "To the lonely urban women, the times before the sexual revolution suddenly do not look so bad."[10]

Both *The Rules* and *What Our Mothers Didn't Tell Us* participate in a form of postfeminist nostalgia that explicitly condemns the advancements of feminism, encouraging women to do their part in transforming contemporary courtship rituals to mirror those of past generations. While, as we will see in examining the texts more closely, the nostalgia engaged by "Ex and the City" and *Sleepless in Seattle* offers a decidedly less explicitly judgmental commentary on the difference between the past and the present, all of these texts allude to the significant role that our cultural conception of the past plays in the formation of contemporary women's identity and the degree to which our collective memory and language is entirely mediated through fiction. Even Crittenden, who is attempting to shake women out of their delusions regarding feminism, relies on ideas about romance that are channeled through not one, but two fictional lenses—the fictional novel *Emma* and its film adaptation. And, she makes her point by contrasting this "pure" vision of romantic courtship with another fictional text that features unglamorous (read: feminist) single women—quite obviously, *Sex and the City*.

The nostalgia for the romance in *The Way We Were* demonstrated in *Sex and the City* is exclusive to a single episode and certainly not representative of the narrative style of the entire series. However, this episode effectively represents the unifying role that nostalgia can play even in a text that has been discussed extensively with regard to its progressive representation of women who are less than idealistic about romance as a life choice. *Sleepless* takes the unifying function of nostalgia one step further both by imitating the plot structure of *An Affair to Remember* and presenting the female characters' nostalgia for the romance represented in the film as a way of life. While nostalgia empowers Annie and Becky (and the other female spectators presented throughout the film) to fluidly move in and out of textual and historical time, allowing them multiple subject positions, their preoccupation with the classic film, as well as other types of romance narratives presented in the film, effectively erases their agency in the contemporary time period of *Sleepless*. Their nostalgia, in fact, situates them as examples of, rather than participants in, the film's politically charged discourses.

Sex and the City *and* The Way We Were

Sex and the City's six-year run on HBO and its 2008 film adaptation have been regularly discussed within the context of postfeminism, not only because of its popularity among women in their twenties and thirties who have felt both the negative and positive repercussions of second wave feminism, but also because it demonstrates a dramatic shift in the way television represented female characters and addressed female spectators. While producing the same kind of active (female) fan base as previous shows created for a female audience throughout television history, such as daytime soap operas and nighttime dramas, as well as previous hit "feminist" sitcoms like *The Mary Tyler Moore Show* and *Murphy Brown*, *Sex and the City* addresses the specific types of problems and challenges that face young, professional, unmarried women.

The series' use of film as opposed to video enables *Sex and the City* to clearly foreground the "I," as the show revolves around the subjectivity of Carrie, its central female character and narrator. Although *Sex* also focuses on the relationships of the other three characters, the viewer is most closely aligned with Carrie's point of view and inner thought processes. Carrie maintains a voiceover throughout every episode, not only speaking her own thoughts but also assuming to have knowledge of the thoughts of her friends. In fact, the theme of every show is mirrored by, and often aptly summarized in, the column that Carrie writes in that episode. What is particularly interesting about *Sex*'s emphasis on subjectivity is its reflection of postfeminism as "me" feminism. Despite the fact that the show is set in expansive Manhattan, its closed textual environment fails to present the female characters as part of a larger community of women or even as really needing anyone other than those who happen to enter their insular world (as many critics have noted, people of color are almost entirely absent from the Manhattan in which the women reside). Despite, or perhaps because of, this textual environment, *Sex*'s four main characters have been "read" by the media as representations of all possible variations on femininity and female roles. Carrie is cute, agreeable, and playful; Miranda is cynical and judgmental; Charlotte is traditional, demure, and naïve; and Samantha is bold and adventurous.

It is the skillful construction of these female characters and their universally identifiable qualities that fosters a sense of community among female spectators who recognize themselves in one or more of them. The show's creator and producer Darren Star professes that all of the scenarios depicted in the show are based on the real-life experiences of female friends and staff writers, and therefore the plots have a distinctly identifiable quality about them.[11] However, it is evidence of the postfeminist era that this female-to-female identification is channeled through fictional characters rather than taking place among a real community of women.

The show's ability to blur the lines between reality and fiction was nowhere more evident than in the August 28, 2000, cover story of *Time* magazine, "Who Needs a Husband?" which featured a picture of the *Sex and the City* cast. Two articles accompanied the cover story, one of which discussed the difficult but empowering decision that many women make to forgo marriage and live a single life well into their late thirties and forties, and often permanently. The second of the two articles, titled "Waiting for Prince Charming," discussed the relevance of *Sex* as a "pop-culture icon."[12] The latter article's author, James Poniewozik, attempted to understand the manner in which *Sex and the City* tapped into the way in which women really think in its avoidance of "p.c. feminism and love-conquers-all romanticism." The show's realistic depiction of female interaction was at the core of many of the articles written about it. One critic in the *Los Angeles Times* wrote, "It is arguably the first show to feature characters who talk the way real women do," and a *New Yorker* critic stated "It's thrilling because you finally feel like you're watching real people talk about their real lives."[13]

In order to prove the show's ability to reflect women's experiences accurately, the *New York Times* sent a reporter to venture into the suburbs of Atlanta to uncover *Sex*'s popularity in a geographical location far removed from the show's Manhattan setting. It was revealed that *Sex*'s realistic dialogue and portrayal of female camaraderie was universally understood among women, regardless of the difference in geography. One Atlanta woman remarked, "I feel like they really are saying what we're all thinking," and another says, "I love that on the show they talk about men the way that men talk about women. It turns the tables and I like to think of how I can do that in my own life."[14]

The level of identification between *Sex and the City*'s female audience and the scenarios depicted in the show are mirrored in the episode "Ex and the City," which is the final episode of the series' second season. Carrie, Miranda, Charlotte, and Samantha are sitting at a café commiserating about the upcoming marriage of Carrie's ex-boyfriend, Mr. Big. As the women meet for cocktails, Carrie is avoiding the engagement party, which is being held six blocks away at the Plaza Hotel. She cannot accept the fact that Mr. Big, a consummate bachelor who had avoided making a commitment to her, has now chosen to marry a much younger woman with whom he had a whirlwind courtship. In an attempt to help Carrie with her predicament, Miranda offers Carrie a one-word answer—"Hubble." Carrie immediately takes this in and in a moment of understanding confirms Miranda's statement by replying, "Oh my God, Hubble! . . . It is! It is soooo Hubble!" As the scene soon reveals, Hubble is the character played by Robert Redford in the 1973 film *The Way We Were*, who, as Miranda explains it to Samantha, "is deeply in love with Katie but he can't be with her because she is complicated and has wild, curly hair." (Samantha, the most male-associated of the group, has never seen what she describes as the "chick flick.")

Carrie claims that just as Hubble never understood Katie, Mr. Big never truly understood her. This provides her with a sense of peace and gives her the courage she needs to attend the party. In the scene immediately following, Carrie goes to the Plaza Hotel (also the site of the final scene of *The Way We Were*) to attend the last minutes of the engagement party. Upon being confronted by Mr. Big outside of the hotel, Carrie proceeds to reenact the final scene of *The Way We Were* when she recites the line: "Your girl is lovely, Hubble." Mr. Big replies, "I don't get it," to which Carrie responds, summing up the crux of their relationship problems, by saying, "No, and you never did."

Carrie (Sarah Jessica Parker) reenacts the final scene of *The Way We Were* in the last episode of *Sex and the City*'s second season.

The implication of this exchange between Carrie and Big is that he cannot "get" her because he doesn't understand the coded language that she is speaking. He does not recognize that she is quoting literally and figuratively a famous romance text, nor does he recognize the implication of her reenactment of *The Way We Were* and how it relates to their current predicament. However, the text assumes that the spectator of this episode is fully aware of the context of Carrie's reference, not just because *The Way We Were* has been introduced in the preceding scene but because there is an assumption that *Sex and the City*'s female community of spectators are already familiar with the plot and pivotal moments of the classic film. Therefore, the nostalgia for *The Way We Were* presented in this scene serves to forge a bond and a level of understanding between women both within and outside of *Sex and the City*'s textual environment. Carrie's ability to circumvent Mr. Big's continued power over her emotions by speaking this nostalgia-infused language, which she knows he has no access to, creates a sense of victory, both for her and *Sex*'s female audience.

This episode not only highlights the manner in which women's shared, collective language can divide them from men but also the significant role that film and television spectatorship plays in the formulation of this language. When Carrie and her friends discuss *The Way We Were,* they are not only talking about the plot of the film but also their collective memory of watching the text, despite the fact that they did not necessarily engage in this activity together. It is implied that the audience of women watching *Sex and the City* are being cued to take part in the same type of recollection, and therefore they have two degrees of textual identification—that in response to *Sex and the City,* and another in response to *The Way We Were.* Like the discussion of the theme song from *The Way We Were* that began this article, *Sex and the City*'s nostalgia renders this recollection as a pleasurable space that unites a "we," which, in this case, consists not only of *Sex*'s contemporary female spectators but also of the women of the 1970s (when *The Way We Were* was made), the 1940s, and the 1950s (the period depicted in the film).

Sleepless in Seattle *and* An Affair to Remember

One of many reexaminations of the 1939 film *Love Affair,* faithfully remade twice in Leo McCarey's 1954 *An Affair to Remember* and Caron's 1994's *Love Affair,* Nora Ephron's *Sleepless in Seattle* (1993) is an exemplary case study of the nostalgia romance text. Its place within this long lineage of remakes both highlights its built-in self-referential tone, and is evidence of contemporary media's tendency to consistently revisit and recycle the same traditional narrative. *Sleepless* is essentially about the state of male-female relationships in the 1990s, and it presents its female protagonists, Annie (Meg Ryan) and Becky (Rosie O'Donnell), as actively seeking their soul mates. They wonder aloud if such people exist or if their consistent spectatorship of classic romance films has merely led them to believe that "he" is out there. In the process of engaging with the reality of their own historical time, in which romance is seen as a lost cause, the film and its characters turn to *An Affair to Remember* as a representation of the past—and a purer vision of what romance *could* and *should* be.

An Affair to Remember is regularly cited as one of the most classic romance texts in American film history and was ranked number five on the American Film Institute's "100 Years, 100 Passions" list. The plot features Nickie (Cary Grant) and Terry (Deborah Kerr), who meet on a cruise ship. Although they are both involved with other people (both conspicuously absent), they fall in love. As the boat docks at their destination—New York Harbor—they decide to end their respective relationships and to reunite on the top of the Empire State Building on Valentine's Day. When the day finally comes, Terry is so overcome with anticipation on her way to meet Nickie that she focuses her attention upward to the top of the Empire State Building, and doesn't see an oncoming taxicab, which hits her. The accident paralyzes her from the waist down. Nickie interprets her absence as a betrayal, and with his sense of pride devastated, he returns to his life without contacting Terry to see what became of her. Terry is ashamed of her disability and also refrains from contacting Nickie, never knowing if he, in fact, showed up for their reunion. Eventually, through a convoluted turn of events, Nickie realizes what has happened and rushes to Terry's apartment, and the two reconcile in a very emotional, cathartic concluding scene.

Affair fits perfectly into Steve Neale's characterization of romance as an inherently temporal form. In his article "Melodrama and Tears," Neale argues that romance films engage in a particularly complex interaction with their spectators, granting privileged knowledge of the couple's destiny to be together. The inability for the characters to communicate their true feelings to each other causes the spectator to have a profound investment in the eventual outcome for the couple and, in turn, the film. The structure of the romantic melodrama text, as Neale points out, is based on the failure of points-of-view—either "moral or ideological opinion or position of judgment," or "function of access to narrative 'facts'"—to match or correspond.[15] Therefore, the film is based around the prolongation of the time that it takes for the characters' knowledge to align with the knowledge of the spectator. However, he argues, this alignment often comes too late, causing the spectator to experience a sense of loss, often leading to tears.

For Neale the tears do not necessarily only accompany a spectator's feeling of loss in response to a missed opportunity for fulfillment but also indicate a desire for the future fulfillment of what has been lost in the present. He contends: "If they are over at this time, in this particular film, the wish and its fantasy are not themselves lost, destroyed forever; they are shown as capable of fulfillment; they can hence be re-engaged, re-articulated, perhaps finally fulfilled in the next film, the next melodrama (or the next episode of a soap opera)."[16]

As Neale aptly sums up, the temporality inherent within the individual romance text is not contained within its diegetic confines but is dependent on the spectator for its effect. The extratextual reach of this interaction is also apparent in the ongoing desire produced by the romance narrative itself, which the individual text lacks the ability to fulfill on its own.

Sleepless in Seattle picks up on the sense of anticipation and desire generated by *An Affair,* both in its homage to the film's plot structure and in its reverence of the desire generated by the temporality of its romance. In fact, the desire for the romance narrative is sustained for *Sleepless*'s entire plot, as the two lovers don't actually meet until the last scene of the film. The film is about Sam (Tom Hanks), a recent widower with a young son, Jonah, and Annie (Meg Ryan), a journalist who is engaged to the sweet but dull associate publisher of the newspaper for which she works. The main impetus for action within the plot of the film is a phone call placed by Sam's son, Jonah, to a radio show, expressing his concern for his grieving widower father, and his desire to see him start a new relationship. The response to the sensitivity portrayed by Sam in his discussion with the radio psychologist assumes epic proportions, resulting in thousands of letters from women who would like to get to know Sam.

This phone call to the radio show also captures the attention of Annie, who becomes obsessed with the idea of Sam and the possibility that he could be her soul mate. She is encouraged by her sidekick friend Becky to pretend to write a newspaper story about Sam's call to the radio show in order to investigate him. After receiving a letter from Annie (which she initially threw away but Becky later sent), Jonah becomes convinced that she is the right person for his father and, in the face of his father's hesitancy, goes to New York on Valentine's Day to meet Annie at the top of the Empire State Building per her request. Sam chases after Jonah and eventually meets up with Annie, and the two immediately recognize the "magic" between them as soul mates.

Sleepless distinguishes itself from the 1994 *Love Affair* remake not only by refusing to directly imitate the story or use any variation of the *Love Affair* title but also by suggesting that to be truly contemporary, it must be self-conscious of its own participation in a broader lineage of films and the larger role that such films play in social and historical discourses. The film is not just about romance but about women watching women watch romance and the ramifications of this watching on the romantic "psyches" of both men and women. In fact, the film assumes that everyone is connected through his or her spectatorship of media texts.

Similar to the nostalgia depicted in *Sex and the City,* the deeply felt connection between the female characters in *Sleepless* and *An Affair to Remember* has less to do with their experience of the plot of the film than with their experience as spectators watching the film, and the emotional catharsis this spectatorship grants them. Whether *Affair* has been watched once in the past and needs to be recalled from memory, or has been watched over and over again on a daily or weekly basis, all women in *Sleepless* are familiar with the film. And, like the discussion in *Sex and the City,* this is not only the basis for a sense of solidarity among the women in the film, who claim that "men never get the movie," but also a foundation for solidarity with the female spectators of *Sleepless,* who identify not only with their onscreen counterparts but also with their counterparts' identification of another set of onscreen counterparts in *Affair.* Just as Carrie's reference to *The Way We Were* excluded Mr. Big, *Sleepless's* romance discourse also excludes men. However, in this case they are outsiders by choice, as they consistently belittle the female characters' preoccupation with romance. In fact, as a mocking response to his sister's tear-filled recollection of a scene from *An Affair to Remember,* Sam and his brother-in-law describe their relationship with the classic film *The Dirty Dozen,* making comically evident that as male spectators, their recollections are dependent entirely on the film's plot and action rather than on any real emotional response.

This distinction is important as it serves to highlight *Sleepless's* implicit proposition that media spectatorship plays an important role in informing one's position in relation to broader historical discourses. While romance texts and other theoretically designated women's genres, like the melodrama and women's film, have always been seen as implicitly—if not explicitly—engaging women's relationship to larger political, social, and ideological issues, *Sleepless in Seattle* transparently discusses such matters, making overt mention of the state of contemporary male-female relations, the changing nature of femininity and masculinity, and the influence of feminism. While women dominate *Sleepless*'s narrative, their investment in the historical time of the past—in *An Affair*—actually diminishes their ability to maintain a powerful sense of agency in their own historical present. While the male characters are able to make distinctions between the past and the present, action and emotion, they are thus represented as having a more objective, and ultimately more stable, position in the film. The male dominance over the film's discourse about its own historical and political present time creates a set of oppositions placing men on the side of reality and objectivity and women on the side of fantasy and subjectivity.

Several scenes demonstrate the frequency with which the male characters in *Sleepless* spout generalizations about gender positioning in the 1990s: "Every man in America saw *Fatal Attraction* and it scared the hell out of them"; only "desperate, rapacious, and love-starved" women are forced to call into radio talk shows in their search for a husband; and "A woman over the age of forty is more likely to be killed by a terrorist than find a husband." These comments are delivered as comedic asides, which seemingly diffuses their offensiveness, but they also construct an image of women that falls completely in line with the backlash mentality that is combated by Faludi's *Backlash,* which is obviously the unnamed book being referenced in the film. All of the contentions that they make about "women" are, on some level, a dismissal of the female dependence on fantasy and ideas about life that are overly associated with the past. For *Sleepless*'s female characters, this seemingly logical account of contemporary reality is of very little interest. Annie and Becky are successful journalists, which assumes that they are well educated and fairly intelligent, yet while they are well versed in their knowledge of romance film and television, they lack the ability to counter any of the male-designated logic with an intelligent argument. Even when Annie tries her best to deflate the "terrorist statistic" by making vague mention of *Backlash,* her argument quickly loses steam, perhaps because, just as her male work colleagues suggest, she didn't read the book all the way through.

The only topic about which all of the women in the film speak with passion is romance, particularly as it is portrayed in *An Affair.* In fact, the world of *An Affair* (meaning not just the film itself, but the mode of spectatorship that the film elicits), is represented as a welcome and necessary refuge for women from the harsh and real social and political world as presented by the men. While the men doggedly try to sustain the distinction between *Affair*'s past textual and historical space and the space of the contemporary present, the women invite the collapse of boundaries and find pleasure in moving in and out of these metaphorical spaces. However, it seems that the more they attempt to bring their conception of romance as depicted in *An Affair* into the world of the present, the more it is deflated by the logic of men, and hence the more they need to return to the text as a safe haven of temporal and historical limbo.

Both *Sex and the City* and *Sleepless in Seattle* serve as unifying forces in creating communities of women who share a discourse on the notion of romance. In addition, the nostalgia that these texts engage in fosters a fluid spectatorship that allows these female viewers to transcend historical time and assume different subject positions, an act that is seemingly empowering. However, it is questionable what nostalgia can offer women other than the opportunity to renounce, however temporarily or metaphorically, their place in social and political history. As Jackie Stacey and Lynne Pearce point out in the introduction to the anthology *Romance Revisited*, "So many books and films have shown, desire for 'another' . . . is often symptomatic of discontent with ourselves and our way of life, and a recognition of this can sometimes provide the catalyst for transformation and change."[17] It is possible to read the nostalgia in *Sex and the City* and *Sleepless in Seattle* as a manifestation of this desiring—whether it is the desire for another person, another life, or another time, and to see this desiring is symptomatic of a larger discontent within the texts' historical present. However, in their reflection of the pitfalls in the struggle to define the contemporary present in a way that addresses women's complexities, these texts reinforce a sense of community among women who find commonality through their very contradictory and confused wants and needs in their personal and professional lives.

It is disturbing that the cost of this community is in the renouncement of a solid place in one's own historical and political present, and the submission to "truth" and "reality" as represented in a classic fictional text. This breakdown of distinctions might be the clearest way to define a seemingly indefinable era of postfeminism. Sarah Gamble speaks to this issue in her piece on postfeminism in the *Routledge Critical Dictionary of Feminism and Post-Feminism*:

The source of such confusion, for post-feminism as much as for post-modernism, is at least partially due to the semantic uncertainty generated by the prefix. Turning again to the *Concise Oxford Dictionary,* "post" is defined as "after in time or order," but not as denoting rejection. Yet many feminists argue strongly that postfeminism constitutes precisely that—a betrayal of a history of feminist struggle, and rejection of all it has gained . . . but it is possible to argue that the prefix "post" does not necessarily always direct us back to where we've come. Instead, its trajectory is bewilderingly uncertain, since while it can certainly be interpreted as suggestive of a relapse *back* to a former set of ideological beliefs, it can also be read as indicating the *continuation* of the originating term's aims and ideologies, albeit on a different level.[18]

While, as Gamble states, the trajectory of postfeminism is bewilderingly uncertain, as long as this uncertain temporality remains satisfying and women continue to find pleasure in the simultaneous embrace and disavowal of time, contemporary fiction texts will undoubtedly continue to foreground nostalgia as a way of representing the ambivalence that pervades this era.

Notes

1. It is clear that this discussion of the postfeminist nostalgia romance text departs from previous definitions of nostalgia in film and television scholarship, specifically Frederic Jameson's definition of the nostalgia film in his essay "Post-Modernism and Consumer Society." Jameson defines two types of nostalgia films, first: "films about the past and/or about specific generational moments of that past," as in *American Graffiti,* and second, films such as *Raiders of the Lost Ark,* which, "reinventing the feel and shape of characteristic art objects of an older period, seek to reawaken a sense of the past associated with those objects." While nostalgia romance texts like *Sleepless in Seattle* and *Sex and the City* aim to elicit an emotional response by conjuring an idea of the past, they depart from Jameson's definition in two ways. First, these texts are not set in the past but in the contemporary era of their own production. This setting within the contemporary postfeminist period of the 1990s is instrumental in providing the motivation for the characters' want and/or need to reflect on the past. Second, the nostalgia romance text is not nostalgic for a past historical time per se, but for the "idea" of that historical time as it is represented in another fictional text, and is reverential to the classic text's narrative and/or its values. In other words, in these film and television texts, what comes to be known as the past is even further removed from a concrete sense of history. Having been channeled through Hollywood fiction, the memories are more subjective and "water-colored" than usual. See Frederic Jameson, "Post-Modernism and Consumer Society," in *Movies and Mass Culture,* ed. John Belton (New Brunswick: Rutgers University Press, 1996), 190–92.

2. Flora Davis, *Moving the Mountain: The Women's Movement in America since*

1960 (Champaign-Urbana: University of Illinois Press, 1999), 432.

3. Jane Feuer, *Seeing through the Eighties: Television and Reaganism* (Durham, NC: Duke University Press, 1995), 5.

4. Other works that list the various stages and incarnations of postfeminism include Diane Negra, *What a Girl Wants? Fantasizing the Reclamation of Self in Postfeminism* (New York: Routledge, 2008); Yvonne Tasker and Diane Negra, eds., *Interrogating Postfeminism: Gender and the Politics of Popular Culture* (Raleigh, NC: Duke University Press, 2007); Sarah Projansky, *Watching Rape: Film and Television in Postfeminist Culture* (New York: New York University Press, 2001); Chris Holmlund, "Postfeminism from A to G," *Cinema Journal* 44:2 (2005) 116–21; Sarah Gamble, ed. *The Routledge Critical Dictionary of Feminism and Post-feminism* (New York: Routledge, 2000); and Ann Brooks, *Postfeminisms: Feminism, Cultural Theory, and Cultural Forms* (New York: Routledge, 1997).

5. Gina Bellafante, "Feminism: It's All about Me," *Time,* June 28, 1998, http://www.time.com/time/archive/preview/0,10987,988616,00.html.

6. The playing field isn't quite level yet. The U.S. Women's Bureau and the National Committee on Pay Equity showed that as of 2004, women still earned only 76.5 cents for every one dollar earned by men.

7. Ellen Fein and Sherrie Schneider, *The Rules: Time-tested Secrets for Capturing the Heart of Mr. Right* (New York: Warner Books, 1995), 2.

8. Danielle Crittenden, *What Our Mothers Didn't Tell Us: Why Happiness Eludes the Modern Woman* (New York: Touchstone, 1999), 35.

9. Ibid., 40.

10. Ibid., 39.

11. Tim Cornwell, "Is It Just Dirty Talk for Girls?" *Times* (London), January 15, 1999.

12. James Poniewozik, "Waiting for Prince Charming," *Time*, July 28, 2000, 50–51.

13. Mimi Avins, "Let's Talk about 'Sex': They Sure Do." *Los Angeles Times,* June 5, 1999; Nancy Franklin, "Sex and the Single Girl," *New Yorker,* July 6, 1998, 74.

14. Nancy Hass, "*Sex* Sells, in the City and Elsewhere," *New York Times,* July 11, 1999.

15. Steve Neale, "Melodrama and Tears," *Screen* 27:6 (1986): 8.

16. Ibid., 21.

17. Jackie Stacey and Lynne Pearce, "The Heart of the Matter: Feminists Revisit Romance," in *Romance Revisited,* ed. Jackie Stacey and Lynne Pearce (New York: New York University Press, 1995), 13.

18. Sarah Gamble, "Post-Feminism," in *The Routledge Critical Dictionary of Feminism and Post-Feminism,* ed. Sarah Gamble (New York: Routledge, 1999), 44.

On Cyberfeminism and Cyberwomanism

High-Tech Mediations of Feminism's Discontents

By the year 2000, an important survey of the so-called gender divide in Internet usage concluded that for the first time, the number of U.S. women online equaled that of their male counterparts.[1] A year later, it was reported that American women even outpaced men in online participation. However, it should not be surprising that globally the percentage of women online remains low.[2] The good news–bad news scenario represented by this empirical data got me thinking about certain qualitative aspects of women's changing position within new media environments and within feminism's changing paradigms. Clearly, such formidable technological and cultural changes are transforming women's roles in all spheres of public and private life, locally and globally, as well as inside and outside the academy. With the striking emergence of the new media-based cyberfeminist movement among women from all walks of life, it seems imperative to look beyond the statistics to appreciate the magnitude of these transformations.

Is Digital Sisterhood Powerful?

In many ways contemporary cyberfeminism's interventions in the masculinist domain of digital and new media culture reenacts the 1970s feminist "break-ins" to the masculine traditions and foundations of film studies at its crucial moment of academic institutionalization. However, there are some fundamental questions to ponder along with my construction of this particular discursive feminist continuum. One question is: How might an interrogation of certain cyberfeminist practices, presumptions, and prescriptions serve an avowed feminist agenda today, especially when today's powerful antifeminist backlash, as Susan Faludi has observed, blinds some women to the realization that indeed the struggle continues? Second, given the largely utopian view of posthuman subjectivity in digital cultures, how might a reconsideration of this seductive notion strengthen some of cyberfeminism's significant accomplishments? This is an especially important question for resolving feminism's persistent racial problematic. I acknowledge from the start that this brief discussion will pose more questions than I am prepared to answer. I am especially mindful of the perils of such a rhetorical move after reviewing the heated 1998 debate about feminism's discontents as articulated in Susan Gubar's infamous "What Ails Feminist Criticism?" and Robyn Wiegman's pointed reply, "What Ails Feminist Criticism? A Second Opinion," which appeared in the journal *Critical Inquiry* in 1988–99.[3] Still, I believe our commitment to feminist work, and the increasing technologization of our lives, demands our responsiveness to these issues. A third question I would pose is this: What should feminism say about the leveraging of gender equity on military battlefields, where high-tech enabled women warriors from the West become glorified agents and powerful symbols of oppression against other women around the globe?

Coming to Terms with Our Isms

On April 18, 2002, Oprah Winfrey convened a meeting between popular representatives of second-wave and third-wave feminisms for her syndicated TV show. The show combined live and taped interviews with Gloria Steinem, Naomi Wolf, Faye Wattelton, Jennifer Baumgardner, Rebecca Walker (Alice Walker's daughter), Susanne Braun Levine, and Ariel Hyatt, among others. Winfrey opened the show by promising "a revealing look at what younger women think about older women. From tensions in the workplace, to their views on sex and marriage . . . younger women tell feminism's warriors what they really think." She delivered on that promise as the discussion was frank, genial and confrontational, and informative. Still, I was uncomfortable with the show's neat demarcation of differences between the feminists primarily along generational lines, and especially in terms of mother-daughter tensions.

Adhering to a familiar generation-gap model of conflict between parent versus child, second-wave feminists on the show chastised third-wave feminists for their apparent ingratitude and unearned sense of entitlement. Not to be outdone, third-wave feminists countered with charges of their own. For them the conflict centered on second-wave feminists' seeming failure to relinquish power and to recognize the changed realities and contemporary rules of engagement in the new gender wars.

Among some of the show participants' more interesting charges and countercharges that reflect mainstream culture's discomfiture with and alienation from feminism's politics of gender equity were: "You ruined men." "They let men off the hook." "My mother's generation put themselves before their families and children." "We were forced to make a choice between family and work. We had to compartmentalize—all we want to hear from them is, thanks." "Younger women want to make [in salaries] what older women make without putting in the time." "Those women gave up so much to make things happen. My generation is so afraid of the word 'feminists.'" "I can't put into words how much I owe them. What I don't admire is that Baby Boomer women don't reach back, they don't want to help . . . [and] that relentless pursuit of youth—I wish they could grow old gracefully." "We are going to be in the workplace for a long time, we've got to figure out ways of working together." "Don't hate me because I am confident—every choice we make is seen as a rejection if we don't follow what they did. The mother-daughter thing is nagging. You have a responsibility to find out what our lives are like." "We fought like crazy for the maternity leave. Younger women say, 'I don't think I want to go back after having a baby.' We say, 'How can you do that after all we sacrificed?'" "We have to keep talking. The conversation has begun today. We take the initiative today." These utterances from Gen-Xers and Baby Boomers (as the show dubbed them) do not need generational attribution, as they seem to articulate quite clearly each woman's respective locations. However, it seems appropriate to associate the final quotes that I want to share with their respective speakers because I think they go far as a sort of reconciliation salve for "what ails feminism."

Some of Gloria Steinem's and Naomi Wolf's remarks seem particularly suited to concluding this summary of the *Oprah Winfrey Show* episode I have been discussing. According to Steinem, "A woman in her twenties and thirties and I are in parallel universes. We have an awful lot to learn from one another. Younger women say they don't feel strong enough to be feminists. This makes me extremely sad. I can learn a lot from them, and they can learn a lot from me." Naomi Wolf adds, "We should not blame each other for things that are not our fault. Each of us should learn the appropriate strategies for coping. Older women need to relax, have fun. Younger women can learn seriousness strategies." As expected, the show ended on a conciliatory note with these women pledging a new beginning for Gen-Xers and Baby Boomer feminists, one based on mutual respect.

As I reflected on this rare and serious televisual encounter with feminism's intergenerational schisms for a mass audience, I thought it would make a perfect object of analysis for my teaching and research. When I mentioned to my colleague Kathleen McHugh that I was going to write about the show's focus on intergenerational conflicts between second- and third-wave feminists, and similarities to earlier fissures within feminism along race and class lines, she alerted me to the "What Ails Feminist Criticism" debate between Susan Gubar and Robyn Wiegman mentioned earlier. Before delving into a brief comparison of feminism's internecine battles as reflected on the *Oprah Winfrey Show* and in *Critical Inquiry*, it seems necessary to explain this line of inquiry in my concern with the intersection of feminist practices and digital media.

For one thing, the Internet's ability to proliferate channels of discourse on a global scale has served to reinvigorate and amplify feminist liberation struggles on multiple fronts (i.e., political, economic, national, cultural, spiritual, and sexual). Thus, I see the recurrence of passionate debates within feminism not as evidence of its eminent demise or feared irrelevance, but rather as evidence of its incredible resilience, elasticity, growth potential, and, most important, its undeniable use value (to borrow a beleaguered Marxist trope). To be blunt, people only debate and battle over what they care about. While as feminists we care differently, often due to our situated knowledges and vexing experiences within destructive race, class, and religious hierarchies, we still care.

Second, we must recognize the needs of different women to practice feminism differently, because societal divisions result in regimes of power that oppress different women differently. It is not enough to argue for feminism's tolerance of women's fundamental differences, rather, it is imperative that feminism respect and value those differences and see them as strengths. Otherwise, as history teaches us, the tenuous bracketing or subordination of differences in oppositional political struggles ultimately destroys the collective efforts of a diverse coalition. Feminism must resist replicating, for example, those Marxist responses to class oppression that bracketed both the so-called woman question and the Negro question in the class struggle. My question, then, is what is to be gained when white feminism's response to gender oppression is to bracket the "race question," and black feminism's response to racial oppression is to bracket the "gender question," albeit to a lesser degree? Will young women today respond to age and "antifun" oppression by bracketing both of the above? The flippant tone of my latter remarks reflects my own frustration with all of feminisms' discontent with what Vivian Sobchack calls "the persistence of history," a persistent historical masculinist oppression, which we must resist displacing onto ourselves. This train of thought leads to my enthusiasm about feminism's encounter with digital media, which I will discuss later. First, I want to return briefly to the feminist debate published in *Critical Inquiry* as it relates to the *Oprah Winfrey* television broadcast I just discussed.

The *Oprah Winfrey Show*'s convening of prominent feminists in mainstream society represents a televisual milestone. I believe this was the first time that broadcast television devoted an entire show to a serious treatment of feminism between older and younger women. At this writing and to my knowledge, not even cable television's Oxygen Network (renamed the Oxygen Media Network) nor the Lifetime Movie Network, which specifically targets women viewers, have done so. Whereas I found aspects of the *Oprah Winfrey Show*'s feminist debate surprising at some points and annoying at others, because of some of the women's specific generational complaints, I found the feminist debate in *Critical Inquiry* (*CI*) between Susan Gubar and Robyn Wiegman downright shocking upon reading some of Gubar's racialized complaints. Thus, I greatly appreciated Wiegman's measured and intellectually generous response.[4] It reframed the debate in terms that were sympathetic yet unswayed, pointed yet not picky, and most of all, it was dissenting without being dissembling. As an African American scholar, feminist, womanist, and technophile, I could at least engage with Gubar's fears and frustrations because of Wiegman's recontextualizations.

Although both of these contemporary debates (the *CI* articles and the *Oprah Winfrey Show*) manifest feminism's ongoing susceptibility to nagging historical identity politics and frustrating "isms" (i.e., racism, classism, and ageism), I am not sure which of these murderous isms disturbs me most. However, as much as I want to excerpt more from Gubar and Wiegman for comparative symmetry with my excerpts from the *Oprah Winfrey Show,* the *CI* feminist debate can be easily accessed in print and on the Internet. The fact is that I gained access to the *CI* publication of both Gubar and Wiegman's entire essays by downloading them from the Internet. Given the focus of my discussion, clearly this is no minor point.

Gubar begins "What Ails Feminist Criticism" by explaining her rationale for lowering "the metaphorical decibels" of her essay's original title, "Who Killed Feminist Criticism." Among her motivations for switching the metaphors "from death to disease" to convey her "apprehension about the state of feminist literary criticism" are: (1) the blunting of criticism that her project expressed "a femicidal fury at the critical daughters supplanting their predecessors," and (2) that it might be construed as supporting the racist and homophobic backlash directed against all feminists.[5] Yet any fair, critical engagement with "the disorders [Gubar's own] idioms inculcate" reveals that her essay, arguably, does precisely what she claims it does not, and that is to blame feminisms' putative ills on notable feminist scholars of "African American, postcolonial and poststructuralists studies." To avoid this trap of misconstrual or misrepresentation of Gubar's position, let me recommend that you read or reread her argument for yourself. She writes:

"What Ails Feminist Criticism?"—in one diagnostic phrase summing up the net effect of the rhetorics of dissension, I could call the problem a bad case of critical anorexia, for racialized identity politics made the word "women" slim down to stand only for a very particularized kind of woman, whereas poststucturalists obliged the term to disappear altogether. How paradoxical that during the time of feminist criticism's successful institutionalization in many academic fields it seems to be suffering from a sickness that can end in suicide.[6]

I share Robyn Wiegman's less apocalyptic assessment of academic feminism's fecund rhetorics of dissension. As Wiegman correctly points out, Gubar's lament is symptomatic of some feminists' desires to police what they consider feminism's wayward reproducibility. "This issue of reproduction," Wiegman states, "is absolutely central to the tensions and anxieties that now accompany academic feminism, provoking further questions that carry deep generational weight: 'which feminism will be reproduced? by whom? and with what (indeed, whose) historical memory?'" More directly, and of central importance to the rest of my discussion, she makes the following point:

When "What Ails Feminist Criticism?" refuses theory and critiques the centrality of racial and national thought to academic feminism's project, it circumscribes what feminism is allowed to know. . . . Feminism . . . must resist the impulse to reproduce only what it thinks it already knows. It must challenge the compulsion to repeat. This kind of feminism is one that cannot be owned; its rearticulation does not mean that it has suffered and grown weak. Rather, it is a feminism that can be radically refunctioned in the present.[7]

Wiegman's cogent and fair recontextualization of the tensions and anxieties attendant on feminism's mutabilities and transformations, as expressed in Gubar's essay, segues perfectly to my own discussion of feminism's rearticulations in new digital domains. For it is Wiegman's forward-looking embrace of feminism's reproductive capacity to engender "new ways of knowing and new knowing subjects," and not Gubar's nostalgic privileging of feminism's idealized Edenic past, that speaks to the changing realities of and emancipatory possibilities for feminist praxis in new media culture's growing hegemonic configurations.

I realize that the Gubar and Wiegman debate is specifically concerned with feminist literary criticism, and my own specializations are in film, television, and new media criticism. But my personal investment in the perpetuation of feminism's health, to borrow Gubar's metaphor, runs deep. Since feminist literary and media criticism share mutual histories and intellectual influences, one might say, to strain Gubar's sickness metaphor a bit, when feminist literary criticism coughs, feminist media criticism catches a cold. By this logic, I am arguing that feminism's present reproductions, new knowledges, and new subjectivities in new media culture are timely remedies for some of its historic ailments.

Cyberfeminism(s) in a Postfeminist Age? New Media's Digital Daughters

It is interesting that the second-wave feminist Susan Gubar and the third-wave or Gen-X feminist Naomi Wolf call on feminists in each camp to develop or rekindle their senses of humor. Rosi Braidotti puts it best when she says, "Cyberfeminism needs to cultivate a culture of joy and affirmation. Feminist women have a long history of dancing through a variety of potentially lethal mine-fields in their pursuit of socio-symbolic justice."[8] Indeed, the Internet, especially, has been and continues to be a viable space for the recovery of feminist mirth, pleasure, joy, and deadly seriousness. Over the years, the unregulated, nonhierarchical democratic ethos of the Internet and other new media technologies have proved most accommodating in this regard. Experience with de rigueur flame wars, personal rants, and hyperbolic manifestoes have habituated new media users to more confrontational discursive protocols. The well-known comedic nostrum that holds "No one knows you're a dog in cyberspace" powerfully evokes this seductive and utopian vision of the Internet as a level playing field.

The significance of all this for contemporary feminism has been nothing short of phenomenal as women from different walks of life are no longer compelled to compete against themselves for marginal access to male-dominated structures of the idealized Habermassian public sphere. Instead, the Internet and other new media technologies have made it possible for feminists from different racial, educational, generational, national, economic, and sexual orientation backgrounds to advance their often-divergent agendas. Thus, at the height of mainstream media proclamations of the arrival of a new postfeminist age during the 1990s, feminism's various "counterpublics" (to borrow Nancy Fraser's terminology) and cyberspace became fruitfully conjoined. As Faith Wilding characterizes it, "Linking the terms 'cyber' and 'feminism' creates a crucial new formation in the history of feminism(s) and of the e-media. Each part of the term necessarily modifies the meaning of the other."[9] Accordingly, this precondition of mutual modification had engendered a new affirmative space for new modes of feminist activism. By the mid-1990s, cyberfeminists and cyberwomanists had begun their anarchic keystroke encroachments on the Net's perceived and actual gender gap and its concomitant cult of masculinity. Young, privileged white women who grew up with personal computers in their homes and school, and underprivileged, urban black women who gained computer skills in the workplace used their varied computer literacies to modify their individual group conditions on and off-line.

As both movements made their dramatic entrances on the stage of our new information society, few were prepared for their far-reaching consequences. The significant year, for my purposes, was 1997, which was an amazingly productive year for women confronting their often-contradictory positions of "working with new technologies and feminist politics."[10] This year saw the incredible confluence of women's groundbreaking productivity and involvement in digital media technologies across theoretical, critical, and activist spheres of feminist influence. And despite technology's gender gap and racialized digital divide rhetorics, black and white women's technophilia would not be denied at this point. Consider the First Cyberfeminist International (organized primarily by white women) as part of the Hybrid Workspace at Documenta X in Kassel, Germany; the formation of the Million Woman March organization in Philadelphia, Pennsylvania (organized predominantly by black women); and the appearance of numerous important new media books published by women. Among the books were: Sadie Plant's *Zeros + Ones: Digital Women + the New Technoculture,* Sherry Turkel's *Life on the Screen: Identity in the Age of the Internet,* J. C. Herz's *Joystick Nation: How Videogames Ate Our Quarters, Won Our Hearts, and*

Rewired Our Minds, and Leslie Heywood and Jennifer Drake's anthology *Third Wave Agenda: Being Feminist, Doing Feminism.*

It is also instructive to see the First Cyberfeminist International and Million Woman March face-to-face gatherings as modifications of the hyped and privileged discourses of the posthuman condition, as both recuperate a politics of embodiment and real-life conflict against digital culture's disembodied and depoliticized consensual hallucination. In what remains of my discussion, I want to focus briefly on lessons to be learned from the First Cyberfeminist International and the Million Woman March's cyberwomanist activism at that historical moment, and especially now, as women's global participation in the information society grows and develops. What I find useful about considering these two cases in tandem is how they expand feminisms' influence on the Internet, while providing useful and significantly different models of politically engaged feminist praxis.

Cyberfeminism and Cyberwomanism: Reconstructing Feminism in Digital Spaces

When the First Cyberfeminist International (FCI) convened in Kassel, Germany, from September 20–28, 1997, a continent away in Philadelphia, Pennsylvania, the Million Women March (MWM) organizers were finalizing the details of their march and convention planned for October 24–25, 1997. Both groups had undertaken formidable feminist projects that required computer technology for their successful organization and implementation; in the course of the two events, this technology functioned simultaneously to highlight and erode what Jennifer Brayton terms "the patriarchal structuring of technology as a masculine space alienating to women."[11] In fact, once there, these women did not find technologized space forbidding at all. Rather, the Net's combination of speech and writing via IRCs (Internet relay chat), bulletin boards, listservs, and other social media were quite conducive to traditional modes and patterns of women's communicative cultures. But where the FCI met to consider how cyberfeminists might "organize to work for a feminist political and cultural environment on the Net," the MWM met "to develop an assertive and aggressive movement" for resolving devastating problems affecting the black community in real life.[12]

For the cyberfeminists, cyberspace itself was the primary problem, and for the cyberwomanists, cyberspace became a primary solution. Cyberspace was a solution for the MWM's publicity vacuum caused by mainstream media disinterest in the yearlong planning campaign for a political march "implemented by Black Women who interact on grassroots and global levels."[13] Referring to the mobilization power of the Internet just days after the March, one MWM organizer commented, "We also found that we don't need the mainstream media to publicize or endorse our events [or] ourselves." The cyberwomanists had deployed the Net as an oppositional technology of power, to borrow Chela Sandoval's phrase.[14] Alternatively, cyberspace itself was a problem for the former group because, as one cyberfeminist expresses it, "I am sick and tired of Virtual Reality technology and cyberspace being toys for the boys . . . I, as one of the riot girls, of the bad girls, want my own imaginary, my own projected self."[15] Certainly the cyberfeminists at Documenta X came together with new imaginings of and projections for women's embodied and disembodied computerized relations. As one FCI participant informant, Faith Wilding, reminds us, "the personal computer is the political computer," an important factor that becomes increasingly clear when we stop to consider that many people today rely on the Net for most of their news and information. This is particularly true for those seeking alternatives to the corporate media industries.

The FCI at Kassel was notable for its apparent redeployment of second-wave feminism's consciousness raising encounters but repurposed for the contemporary realities of "wired women" (Wilding's term). Wilding informs us that at FCI there were simultaneous virtual (online, faxes) and face-to-face interactions in the form of hands-on workshops, public lectures, discussions, and presentations in which more than thirty women from nearly ten countries, and "from different economic, ethnic, professional, and political backgrounds" participated. What I found particularly interesting was Wilding's report that these women attempted "to define cyberfeminism by refusal." So, those women who "called themselves cyberfeminist" refused its definition because they feared repeating some of feminism's earlier mistakes. But, as Wilding points out, "While cyberfeminists want to avoid the damaging mistakes of exclusion, lesbophobia, political correctness, and racism, which sometimes were a part of past feminist thinking, the knowledge, experience, and feminist analysis and strategies accumulated thus far are crucial for carrying their work forward now."

One promising outcome of the FCI was the agreement to pursue further work and research to make cyberfeminism more visible to diverse women using technology. They argued for creating a cyberfeminist search engine to link feminist websites across the globe; "forming coalitions with female technologists, programmers, scientists and hacks to link feminist Net theory, content and practice with technological research and invention; and addressing traditional gender constructions and biases built into technology."[16] Wilding's report on FCI is quite instructive. She brooks no compromise with what she sees as some of cyberfeminism's weaknesses, among which she stresses its lack of historical knowledge of feminism's past and philosophies, its utopianism. This is a charge leveled especially at the bad grrrls on the Net—summed up as a cybergrrrl-ism, itself defined by " 'an anything you wanna be and do in cyberspace is cool' attitude," and a "somewhat anti-theory attitude." Ultimately, though, and in different ways, Wilding, Braidotti, Plant, and others recognize cyberfeminism's potential as "a promising new wave of feminist practice that can contest technologically complex territories and chart new ground for women." Despite Wilding's penchant for *telling* (rather than suggesting or recommending) younger women what to do to be effective cyberfeminists, I am convinced that these exchanges between cyberfeminists, cybergrrrls, and nonwired women are extremely exciting and beneficial. For one thing, older feminists are encouraged to reconceptualize their relationships to their younger digital sisters, daughters, and cousins. The obverse holds for younger feminists as well. This is a good thing. For even as older feminists *tell* younger feminists how to do feminist history and philosophy, younger feminists can *tell* older feminists how to do cyberfeminist art, hactivism, and technological wizardry. Finally, we can move beyond some false or socially engineered generational barriers, develop mutual respect, and ultimately get over the "nagging mother-daughter thing." By the same token, I believe the cyberwomanists of the Million Woman March (MWM) suggest new subjectivities and new knowledges for feminism in terms of race at the interface.

When the organizers of the MWM mobilized upward of a million and a half people (mostly black women) to march on Philadelphia in October 1997, few outside the group expected such a success. Demonstrating the power of the Net as an organizational power that rivals (even surpasses) mainstream media, the MWM generated a financial return for the city of Philadelphia in the amount of $21.7 million.[17] Surprisingly, this amazing feat was accomplished by two local women, Phile Chionesu and Asia Coney, who modeled the MWM after the Million Man March (MMM) that occurred two years earlier. Like the MMM, the women used the Internet to promote and publicize their event. Unlike the MMM, the MWM did not have high-profile organizers to generate mass interest in or mass publicity for their cause. Instead, these grassroots women set up a network of websites, including one national (or official) site and several regional ones in big cities across the country to publicize the twelve-point platform of the organization. They also posted their mission statement, and provided information about pre-march workshops, accommodations and transportation logistics, and the program of speakers and artists.

That these women produced this unanticipated historic phenomenon is doubly remarkable since it occurred at the height of the digital divide's disabling rhetoric that positioned black people in general, and black women especially, as casualties of the information revolution—a new permanent underclass of the information economy. But the women found a way around this limitation and enacted their stealth cyberwomanist activism to everybody's astonishment, for they did use the master's tools to tear down barriers to mass publicity for their cause. It is true that many women did not have computers at home, but those who did engaged in a bit of what Michel de Certeau calls "making-do" or *la perruque*. For example, at work the MWM cyberwomanist office workers downloaded march organizers' directives from the official website and made Xerox copies for their computerless counterparts, thus disguising their march work as work for the boss. The MWM Webmaster, Ken Anderson, told how black women office workers pulled it off and galvanized hundreds of thousands. He said: "While I was at the March, Sisters walked up to me . . . and told me that they would not have heard about the March without the website. I have heard from at least 30 Sisters who printed out the entire website and shared it with friends, neighbors, and co-workers who weren't online yet. This is very flattering, and I appreciate every Sister's attention to and use of the website."[18]

This is significant as Anderson makes us privy to something truly amazing in black women's tactics of "making do." By making virtual computers available to black women who "weren't online yet," MWM supporters with access to the Net, either through their jobs or in-home Internet Service Providers (ISPs), effectively transformed low-tech, sixties-era mimeograph activism into high-tech, new-millennial digital news and information flows. In fact, since "huge numbers of female employees occupy clerical jobs that use computers for processing payroll, word-processing, conducting inventory, sales, and airline reservations—more than 16 million held such positions in the United States in 1993,"[19] it is surprising that it took the MWM to actualize this enormous potential. In a turn on the usual racial hierarchy of feminism, these black feminists were at the forefront of cyberactivism, which inspired their white counterparts who later organized the Million Mom March for gun control. What is exciting and promising here is that these MWM cyberwomanist organizers utilized cyberspace to enlist support for their platform issues, which included bringing about "a probe into the CIA's participation and its relationship to the influx of drugs into the African American community," the rehabilitation of "Black women upon leaving the penal system," the examining of "Human Rights violations of Africans in the Americas and their effects," the cessation of "gentrification of our neighborhoods," and the "reclaiming of our elders' rights."[20] In sum, the MWM posted this rationale for the March's raison d'être: "For the day and the time for Black women (African Women) has come, and the time for self-destruction, injustice, racism, and all such practices put to [an] end."[21] The sistahs of the MWM recognized the value of new technologies to further their own agendas and promote their brand of activism that did not require choosing which liberation struggle to fight first, gender or race oppression.

This promise does not mitigate against the reality of counterproductive, hegemonic sexism, classism, racism, and homophobia that dominates the Web and other new media platforms. At the same time, these inroads cannot be minimized and, as particularly illustrated in the case of the Million Woman March, these virtual Web presences do not supplant face-to-face activisms and creativity; most significantly, they function as phenomenal augmentations. Yes, patriarchy is alive and well online, as in real life. Nonetheless, cyberfeminism and cyberwomanism are also alive, well, and destined to grow in number and influence as women increasingly outpace men in Internet participation. There should be little doubt that women were active in mobilizing large numbers of antiwar protests in the recent global resistance to the Bush/Cheney administration's Iraqi Freedom war.

It seems to me that the next urgent question for feminists, cyberfeminists, cyberwomanists, womanists, and cybergrrrls is: What can we as a collective do to address the next big threat to all manner of feminisms—the emergence of New Women Warriors in service to neo-imperialist nations? Talk about "killing feminism"—quite literally, this is what the most potent new signifier of female equity and agency represents; an alarming coalition of poor, working-class, multiracial, multinational women are dying for their right to kill other women. For all we have discussed, it seems to me that this latest new economy, new millennial development, is what really ails feminism!

Notes

This essay has been adapted from "Double Click: The Million Woman March on Television and the Internet," in *Television after TV: Essays on a Medium in Transition*, ed. Lynn Spigel and Jan Olsson (Durham, NC: Duke University Press, 2004), 224–41; and from my recently published book, *Digital Diaspora: A Race for Cyberspace* (Albany: State University of New York Press, 2009).

1. Debra Donston provides further details and implications of the Media Metrix and Jupiter Communications' study, which is titled "It's a Woman's World Wide Web." Donston, "When Worlds Collide," http://www.zdnetindia.com/print.html?IElementd=2697.

2. Michael Pastore considers the gender gap in global terms. See Pastore, "Gender Split Nearly Even by 2001," http://cyberatlas.internet.com/bit_pictmographics/print/0,,5901_150111,00.html.

3. I thank Kathleen McHugh for informing me about this debate in literary circles.

4. Robyn Wiegman acknowledges that her familiarity with and dissension from some of Gubar's positions were the result of her serving as a reader of the manuscript. See Robyn Wiegman, "What Ails Feminist Criticism? A Second Opinion," *Critical Inquiry* 25 (Winter 1999), http://criticalinquiry.uchicago.edu/issues/v25/wiegman1.html.

5. Susan Gubar, "What Ails Feminist Criticism?" *Critical Inquiry* 24.4 (1998), 878–902, http://criticalinquiry.uchicago.edu/issues/v24/gubar1.html.

6. Gubar, "What Ails Feminist Criticism?"

7. Wiegman, "What Ails Feminist Criticism? A Second Opinion."

8. See Rosi Braidotti's discussion of cyberfeminist and cybergrrrl's politics of parody in "Cyberfeminism with a Difference," http://www.let.uu.nl/womens_studies.rosi/cyberfem.htm.

9. This quote comes from Faith Wilding's report on the First Cyberfeminist International. The full text of Wilding's article, "Where Is Feminism in Cyberfeminism?" is available at http://www.obn.org/cfundef/faith_def.html.

10. Wilding, "Where Is Feminism in Cyberfeminism."

11. Jennifer Brayton, "Cyberfeminism as New Theory," http://www.unb.ca/web/PAR-L/win/cyberfem.htm.

12. Wilding, "Where Is Feminism in Cyberfeminism?"; The "Million Woman March Mission Statement," originally at http://members.aol.com/lilbitz/mission.html, can now be found at the website "Tribute in Honor of: The Million Woman March," http://www.geocities.com/ifamathink.

13. "Million Woman March Mission Statement."

14. Chela Sandoval, "New Sciences: Cyborg Feminism and the Methodology of the Oppressed," in *The Cybercultures Reader,* ed. David Bell and Barbara M. Kennedy (London: Routledge, 2000), 374–87.

15. Quoted in Braidotti, "Feminism with a Difference."

16. Wilding, "Where Is Feminism in Cyberfeminism?"

17. "Successful Million Woman March Generates $21.7 Million," June 3, 1998, http://www.afamnet.com/NationalPage/frontpage/ 110597_million.htm.

18. Ken Anderson, e-mail to author, October 30, 1997.

19. Ellen Seiter, "Television and the Internet," in *Electronic Media and Technoculture,* ed. John T. Caldwell (New Brunswick: Rutgers University Press, 2000), 227–43.

20. The full text of the Million Woman March "Platform Issues" can be found on one of the main sites of the now-enlarged organization. Go to http://members.aol.com/lilbitz/platform.htm.

21. See "Million Woman March Mission Statement." Further details of the Million Woman March can be found at Tribute in Honor of: The Million Woman March, http://www.geocities.com/ifamathink.

Soyoung Kim

Chapter 19

The Birth of the Local Feminist Sphere in the Global Era

Yeoseongjang and "Trans-cinema"

My approach to the principal question that inspired this anthology, namely, the invitation to think about feminism and a cinema archive, is rather complex and may at first seem somewhat oblique. An archive is typically an extension of a canon. I am interested in what is excluded from the canon, and what exceeds archival conservation. My focus includes not only films but their audiences; not only texts but contexts; not only objects but events. In this essay I will adopt and adapt two terms from other contexts as a means of reframing an understanding of Korean cinema history and intervening in that history. I will use *"yeoseongjang"* and "trans-cinema" to identify specific counterstrategies deployed within feminist cultural-political practices. Furthermore, I propose this use of these terms as another counterstrategic response to the operations of legitimation, delegitimation, and exclusion that permeate dominant discourses, institutional practices, and habits of signification underlying the formation of canons and archives, cinematic and otherwise. In particular, *yeoseongjang* and "trans-cinema" will articulate modes of cultural production as alternatives to the Korean blockbuster, often by reinhabiting the various digital communication devices most closely identified with the global capitalism essential to the blockbuster's hegemony.

In one sense, my essay responds to a marked proliferation of disparate forms of feminist production in South Korea. Feminist websites in particular provide an interesting case of activism in the way they are linked to both existing and newly formed feminist publishing houses, street protests, performances, and women's film festivals.

399

Key Terms: Yeonseongjang
("Woman's Funeral"/"Woman's Sphere") and Trans-cinema

On January 29, 2002, a fire broke out in a bordello in the city of Kunsan. Since the building was designed to confine the women to sexual slavery, it had no exits, and fourteen sex workers died with no way of escape. On February 8, various women's groups held a ritual funeral at the site of the tragedy. On the same day, other women's groups and their supporters organized a funeral protest on the street in front of the police headquarters in Seoul. These public ceremonies became known as a *yeoseongjang*, which literally means "women's funeral." I would like to exploit a peculiarity of the use of Sino-Korean terms here, to note that *jang*, meaning "funeral," is a homonym with *jang*, meaning "space" or "sphere." Thus, in adopting the term *yeoseongjang*, I am also adapting it to include both the meanings of "women's funeral" and "women's sphere." This doubled meaning not only serves new purposes but also highlights important aspects of the events from which I have taken the term. The funerals conducted in Kunsan and Seoul did not merely mourn the deaths of women but also insistently affirmed the value of their lives. The dual affective and political expressions of mourning and affirmation are essential to the counterstrategies I will examine and propose herein. My discontent with a historically gendered and Eurocentric notion of the public sphere propels me to move toward *yeoseongjang*, a concept that I suggest is closer to the notion of *political society* than that of the public sphere. Hence, I invite the tearful scenes of women's public funeral.

Yeoseongjang can encompass many aspects of feminist rereading of cinematic production, reception, and dissemination. In the late 1950s and early 1960s, the matinees brought women into the theaters to watch melodramas; this gave them time away from their duties as daughters, sisters, wives, and mothers. Women also produced documentaries that were forms of activism: demands for the redress of injustices and a positive entry into the historical record as well as for modes of networking and community formation.[1] Women's film festivals are yet another example of a cinema-centered *yeoseonjang*.

Digital communications have revolutionized concepts of space, and thus have also enabled new venues for a "women's sphere," or *yeoseongjang*. "Trans-cinema" encourages experiments in adapting these media for alternative venues and multifaceted forms of activism. To help situate *yeoseongjang* and trans-cinema within profoundly local scenes that are penetrated by elements of globalization, I turn to two formations against which they constitute versatile responses, namely, Korean "blockbuster" culture and the digital mediascape of global capital.

The Korean Blockbuster Culture: A Brief History

A synopsis of the emergence and consolidation of the Korean blockbuster film since the end of the twentieth century reveals a history of obsessive exclusions. *Shiri* (dir. Kang Je-gyu, 1999) is a five-million-dollar suspense film about a terrorist plot enacted by a North Korean band of renegade spies in Seoul. Its production values and special effects were modeled to some extent on the American blockbuster, and the film became the most successful box-office draw in Korean history, outgrossing even *Titanic.* The success of *Shiri* drew the interest of venture capitalists to the film industry and was a contributing factor in stimulating other companies to sell Korean films on the international market.

In 2000, another blockbuster about the North-South division of Korea, *Joint Security Area* (dir. Park Chon-wook), would break the record set by *Shiri* and make more inroads into the international film market. *Joint Security Area*'s take at the box office would in turn be broken in 2001 by *Chingu, Friends* (dir. Kwak Kyung-taek), a film about four young men who grew up together in Pusan, three of them falling into organized crime.

The production budgets grew even larger, the spectacle more sweeping, and the universe more insistently and myopically male in 2003–4. *Silmido* (dir. Kang Woo-suk, 2003) is an eight-million-dollar epic version of an actual incident that occurred during the Pak Chong-hee administration. A group of men were imprisoned on the island of Silmido and forced to undergo brutal military training for nearly three years, which was to prepare them to assassinate the North Korean president. A change in the political climate led the South Korean government to scrap the plan and dispose of the men. The film itself disposes of all women. The sole woman in the film is a silent female who appears, only to be raped by two men that the film portrays sympathetically. The film's ticket sales and related profits reportedly soared to three hundred million dollars.[2]

Silmido's remarkable success was surpassed by *Taegukki* (dir. Kang Je-gyu, 2004), another Korean War film reducing the scope of the politics and tragedy to the melodramatic love of an older brother for his younger sibling. *Shiri* helped Kang raise the 12.8 million dollar budget to make this film, and his production company's ties with distributors got the film placed on 450 screens throughout Korea. *Taegukki* also did well in Japan, and perhaps because of the current political climate, it enjoyed a reception in the United States almost unheard of for a foreign-language film.

The Symptoms and Significance of the Blockbuster Phenomenon

As the Korean version of the blockbuster hits the box office, at home and in parts of Asia, a certain desire brews at the heart of a Korean film industry that has been bombarded by venture capital. Reclaiming its a position as something in-between the Hollywood, the Asian, and the Korean cinema industries, the South Korean film industry has begun producing block-busters that desperately seek ways in which an internal cultural incom-mensurability makes its peace within the optical and aural unconscious of its imagined audience. In one sense, it is not a surprise that the existence of such an audience largely depends on the technological mobilization of digital effects, on promotion and marketing systems, and on saturation booking. But this aspect alone cannot sustain the larger *cultural* ambitions of the blockbuster movie industry, which aspires to square its Asian aspirations and global markets with the excess of a guarded nationalism.

Obviously, the South Korean blockbuster is a compromise between foreign forms and local materials, a compromise itself often staged on a grand scale. These blockbusters offer both a voluntary mimicry of, as well as imagined resistance to, large Hollywood productions, playing off the various logics of both identity and difference in the global culture industry. Backed by the Korean nation-state and its national culture, the South Korean blockbuster presents itself as the cultural difference opposing the homogenizing tendencies of Hollywood. But it is an opposition between what Jameson once called "the Identity of identity and nonidentity,"[3] and as such, the blockbuster in the South Korean mode incarnates a contradiction.

In the recent book *Hankukhyong blockbuster: Atlantis hokun America* (Blockbuster in Korean Mode: America or Atlantis), film critics and scholars noted the huge impact of recent popular cinema on society.[4] The effects range from redefinitions of the very role of cultural nationalism and globalization to the new configurations of morality, desire, and everydayness. The local film weekly, *Cine-21*, estimates that 40 percent of the domestic market is dominated by Korean film.[5]

The key issue that local blockbusters bring to the fore is not so much in the actual monetary profit they generate as in the investment they show in national cultural value. These investments go alongside a consistent emphasis, on the part of the government, since the 1990s, on the virtues of the movie industry itself as something of an exemplary smog-free, postindustrial sector; this sits well with blockbuster's new purpose in the popular imagination. Notwithstanding the often outrageous marketing fees and ticket sales, the film industry as a whole in the year of 2001 made profits that were only equivalent to those of a medium-size corporation. Nevertheless, what the film industry in its blockbuster mode displays and informs are the popular imaginings of the working of finance capital and mass investment culture. The "Netizen Fund" set up on the Internet by film companies to solicit funding for film projects in progress finds enthusiastic investors, often with such volume of usage that people complain about accessibility. Both the blockbuster movies and the related dissemination of blockbuster culture appear to announce a cultural era of investment that clearly plays a critical role in strengthening the hegemonic dominance of finance capital. This cultural intervention links the perceived interests of tens of millions of workers to its own by embedding "investor practices" into their everyday lives and by offering them the appearance of a stake within a neoliberal order.[6]

Beyond the blockbuster phenomenon found in multiplexes, there has been the parallel proliferation of other venues and formats for the cinema. Apart from the three international film festivals in the cities of Pusan, Puchon, and Jeonju, we now see a range of alternative festivals (which I will explore later) that focus on such topics as women, queer studies, labor, and human rights, all managing to carve out a distinct audience. In addition, some filmmakers have turned to digital video, which is easily transferable to streaming technology on the Internet; this shift in format parallels the emphasis that activists and intellectuals have placed on the Internet as an alternative public sphere. Access to DSL service is both easy and cheap (approximately fifteen dollars a month per household), both at home and outside (less than one dollar per hour at PC lounges). This kind of public access has introduced two independent but related phenomena into the home. On the one hand, we see the popularization of cybertrading and stock investment, and on the other, the formation of a new kind of public sphere that is sometimes claimed, perhaps hastily, as cyberdemocracy (http://soback.kornet.nm.kr/~wipaik).

403

Glimpsing the possibilities of constructing a new critical space, most militant independent film and video groups, many of whom were connected to and have grown out of the labor and people's movements of the 1980s, have created websites on which both demo versions and full-length documentaries are freely available. Recently, the female workers' network (http://www.kwwnet.org) has been showing *I Dream of Tomorrow* (dir. Nanun Nalmada Naeilul Ggumggunda, 2001), a documentary on employment after the International Monetary Fund (IMF) crisis. *I Dream of Tomorrow* claims that seven out of ten female workers are now employed as irregular and flexible labor without any benefits. In the context of Internet-based cinema, *Patriotic Games* (http://www.redsnowman.com) is a forceful attack on nationalism. This is a taboo subject even among the progressive intellectuals of 1980s, not only because of the National Security Law, but also because it reflects on the postcolonial and neoimperial impact of Japan and America. The makers of *Patriotic Games* have claimed the Internet as a distinctive space for their countercinema. They refuse to sell their works on video and have very limited public screenings outside this venue.

Trans-cinema

Taking a cue from the proliferation of digital cinema vis-à-vis new modes of activism, I propose a notion of "trans-cinema," or a cinema that should, I suggest, be attentive to the transformation of its production, distribution, and reception modes as shown by independent digital filmmaking and its availability on the Internet. Trans-cinema proposes that digital and internet cinema, LCD screens (installed in subways, taxis, and buses), and gigantic electrified display boards (called *chonkwangpan* in Korean) should be seen as spaces into which cinema theories and criticism should intervene. The gigantic screens in downtown of Seoul exist as a phantasmatic space permeating and simultaneously constructing the everydayness of the city.

By conceptually framing this new space as trans-cinema, one could further claim that it should not be used exclusively as advertisement space, and indeed that such space should be opened up to issues concerning the public. Unlike the individual or family viewing that marks TV viewership, the big monitors installed on the walls of tall buildings inevitably involve collective and temporary watching. People in transit get a glimpse of electric displays showing movie trailers, advertisements, and news. Gigantic images looming on the walls of buildings certainly create *Blade Runner–*

type effects that bring differing registers of temporality and spatiality to existing urban space. In a word, a heterotopia is being constantly invented in such space.

Media City Seoul 2000 used these electronic display boards to present experimental images by twenty-five media artists, including Namjun Paik. It was titled the "Clip City" project under the section of City Vision. To watch a one-minute clip of experimental images in the midst of the usual commercials was an eye-opening experience. The tone of festivity around the project was, however, suddenly changed when Song Ilkon's video *Flush* appeared among the abstract and experimental images on forty-three monumental electronic boards (http://www.nkino.com/moviedom/online_sig. asp). The one-minute video captures a sequence in which a teenage girl delivers a baby and then flushes it down a toilet. *Flush* soon disappeared from the Clip City project, but the video served as a striking example of the experimental and political possibilities of the electronic display boards, or *chonkwangpan,* as spaces for public art.

The social disaster assumes titanic proportions in the *chonkwangpan.* It was almost an apocalyptic experience to watch on the electronic display boards the collapse of the Songsu bridge and the Sampung department store (both icons of successful modernity), which claimed thousands of lives. The female body in *Flush* and the fractured modernity epitomized by the fall of modern monuments challenged the viewers of the *chonkwangpan.* As an exemplary icon of Marc Augé's supermodern non-place or of Manuel Castells's postindustrial space in flow, *chonkwangpan* disrupts the demarcations among cinema, television, and billboards, while also blurring the lines between public art, commercials, and public announcements.[7] In terms of collective spectatorship, *chonkwangpan* resembles the cinema, yet it is also akin to the content of television (composed as it is of commercials, news, and public announcements). The City Vision/Clip City project enabled, within the public sphere, a space in which a communicative and artistic dimension could be articulated. *Chonkwangpan* is trans-cinema and public TV that expands existing notions of both cinema and television.

A marked transformation in the way people perceived these mushrooming electronic billboards was demonstrated by the public transmission of the 2002 World Cup. The billboard in front of the City Hall momentarily served as public cinema and a street TV contingent upon a collective spectatorship. The supporters of the Korean football team known as the "Red Devils" mobilized almost a whole nation to "be the reds." While in Japan public gatherings are not allowed around these billboards, the case was quite different in South Korea: the City Hall was turned into a public space that was a liberation zone where millions flocked together to watch the World Cup games. Many were reminded of the massive protests in the late 1980s in this same space. This memory brought forth an uncanny superimposition of the political upon the mass gatherings of the World Cup. The layers of events and historical memories inscribed in *chonkwangpan* await a name other than that of pure advertising. I suggest trans-cinema. Rather than a premature and sensational celebration of the "death of cinema" into its high-tech corporate versions, trans-cinema is an endeavor to locate and theorize an emergent spectatorship and mode of production. It becomes, then, a form of theory and practice that can potentially unsettle the dominant interpellation of cinemas as either national or transnational.

The construction of a critical constellation around trans-cinema would contribute to the effort to stimulate new comparative work in film studies. Just as the theoretical construction of the alternative public sphere in early cinema was proposed within the context of *industrial* capitalism by Miriam Hansen,[8] so today there is a need to imagine the (cinematic) alternative public sphere within the context of *transnational* capitalism. Yet trans-cinema is a curious entity, an unstable mixture. It cuts across film and digital technology and challenges the normative process of spectatorship that followed the institutionalization of cinema. As a critique of and successor to the pairing of world cinema with national cinemas, it proposes the need to rethink the constellations of the local cinemas in the era of transnational capitalism. As such, trans-cinema, unlike trans*national* cinema, is also recognition of and a response to the increasing rate of, for instance, inter-Asia cultural traffics that include local blockbuster movies (Hong Kong, China, India, and South Korea) and art-house cinema (Taiwanese and Iranian cinema). Inter-Asian blockbusters in particular should provide an opportunity for revisiting the Hollywood-type global culture industry formations and allow a rethinking of the way in which local or subglobal (regional) circuits are simultaneously dearticulated and rearticulated. The genealogy of the cinematic apparatus as we know it is embedded in the culture of industrial capitalism. One might need to redefine this apparatus in relation to a shifting political economy and its transformation into a global space. In order to articulate the cinematic apparatus in relation to a public sphere that encounters radically shifting socioeconomic, political, and cultural conditions, it becomes very clear that one should note both the persistence of diverse constituencies as well as the emergence of new ones in cinematically aided "public spheres."

Trans-Nationalization of Women
in the Blockbuster Culture

As South Korea is exposed to a powerful global gaze and in turn mimics this gaze in its desire to be a player in Asia, anxiety and desire explode within the Korean blockbuster in unexpected ways, which in turn shape new possibilities for the public sphere(s). As one gesture toward the global market, the makers of the Korean blockbuster turned to a strategy of multinationalizing their women characters. Paralleling the rise of a local popular culture known as the Korean Wave (*hanryu,* composed mainly of TV drama, music, and fashion) now hitting other parts of Asia, *Shiri* features a North Korean woman as an espionage agent (code name Hydra). *Joint Security Area* (*JSA*) employs a Swiss-Korean woman as an inspector to resolve a murder mystery at the JSA. *Failan* casts a Hong Kong actress to play a Chinese migrant worker in Korea. The actress Zhang Ziyi (a heroine in *Crouching Tiger, Hidden Dragon*) plays the Ming Princess Musa in *Warrior*. The heroine of *Pichonmu* (*Flying Heaven Martial Arts*) is cast as a Mongolian.

Such characterization of women is unprecedented. From the mid-1950s, South Korean films sustained themselves largely through representing women as tropes of trauma around modernity and the postcolonial condition. These included *Madame Freedom* (1955), *Bitter But Once Again* (1968), *Petal* (1996), and *Sopyonjae* (1993). Now, however, when South Korean blockbusters feature women in central roles, they are usually associated with gangsters or sci-fi/horror monsters. Recent examples include *A Wife of a Gangster* (*Chopok Manura*), *The Moonlight in Shilla* (*Shillaui Dalbam*), and *Soul Guardians* (*Toimarok*).

The disappearance of South Korean women from the films and their displacement into these new characters is problematic, especially in circumstances where the identity of a fraternal collective is being reconstituted around notions of a global citizenship. At the representational level, it appears that such a global citizenship now excludes South Korean women. The films mentioned in the previous paragraph reveal a newly forming nationalism in conjunction with globalization. To create a global façade, these films appear to suggest that it is necessary to make local women invisible. Predictably, the vanishing of South Korean women characters is offset by a new consolidation of homosocial bonding among men. Even when the Chinese migrant female labor is invoked in *Failan* (2001), it is in the form of the archetypal innocent and sacrificing woman that was common in the film and the literature of the 1970s, a period of condensed industrialization. The presumed virtue of this archetype, which present-day South Korean women have allegedly lost, is now projected on a woman from a less globalized sector. As images of South Korean women disappear, women of other nationalities are summoned to evoke nostalgic representations of gender and culture.

Relegating South Korean women to the realm of the invisible, blockbusters often feature such male-dominant groups as the army, the Korean Central Intelligence Agency, and the world of organized crime in an attempt to foreground homosocial relations. The relationship among men in these groups simply becomes opaque to female characters. For example, Sophie Chang (Yi Yeong-ae), a Swiss-Korean heroine in *Joint Security Area* (*JSA*), is dispatched by the Neutral Nations Supervisory Commission as an investigator to unravel the mystery around the murders of two North Korean soldiers on the North Korean side of the Demilitarized Zone (DMZ). The situation becomes impenetrable to Sophie. Her investigator's "look" is constantly denied agency, presumably because the murder and its concealment are provoked, sustained, and empowered by a brotherhood based on an ethnic nationalism that transcends the different ideologies along the line of the cold war. Sophie, in desperation, tries to connect to this situation via her deceased father, who served in the Korean War but had defected to Switzerland after being detained in the war prisoners' camp. Her father's photograph now alludes to the complexities of a modern history ravaged by the cold war, division, and migration. But it does not really enable her to solve the cover-up of the murders among North and South Korean soldiers. Her expertise in international law (she is a Zurich law school graduate) does not help, nor does her ethnicity as half Korean.

What the impenetrability and opacity of male bonding in blockbusters suggest is quite evident. However, the brotherhood of nationalism is not destined to find a secure space of its own under a global gaze that demands transparency. This sense of the impossibility of reconstructing a nationalist male space is both a cause and a consequence of the endless remaking of blockbusters. The disappearance of images of South Korean women constitutes a new globalized national discourse. The orchestration of transparency and impenetrability bitterly resounds in the global and the national arena and increasingly stages an orchestra without women players—a retreat from gender politics indeed. This retreat does not stop, however, at the level of representation. In addition to the South Korean government's official declaration of the collapse of public intellectuals and

their replacement with twenty- or thirty-something young venture capitalists as the "new intellectuals," feminist intervention in a public sphere
attuned to a concept of a globalized national is doubly denied.

In this milieu, the feminist journal *Yo/Song I-lon* (Feminist theory,
2001) declares the present government of South Korea to be a zombie that
incorporates the remnants of an earlier military regime that took pride in
presenting itself as an authoritarian father. As the dominant media and
blockbuster films register the absence of local women and the mobilization
of other Asian women for reasons of both economy and nostalgia, there
arises a dire need to cope with this situation through a feminist cultural
politics. Neither international nor local feminism can provide a sufficient
analysis of conditions in which both the transnational and the national
are structured within the relations of competitive dominance (even as they
often equally function in complicity). These conditions debilitate liminal
subject positions, which the abstract promises of triumphal globalization
do not address in terms of everyday experience. Without taking a position
similar either to statist or liberal feminism, an emergent feminist articulation needs be attentive to locally specific but globally resistant issues.

Film Festivals and Local Female Labor

Toward the late 1990s, the need for a new direction in a social movement
that no longer appeared grounded in the proletarian class perspective of
the 1980s' labor movement became evident. Groups composed of feminists, gay and lesbian activists, some members of youth subcultures, and
civil activists, in alliance with student protestors, have initiated film festivals as public platforms from which to address their rights and concerns.
The desire to be represented or recognized in public prevails in many such
festivals. It seems that diverse festivals have not only become a space of
negotiation among different forces, but also form a cultural practice that
links audiences to the specific agendas raised by new identities, subject positions, and newly proliferating nongovernmental organizations (NGOs).

Generally speaking, the film festivals can be classified into three categories. First, there are those events that developed from a coalition of
the state, local governments, corporations, and specialists equipped with
film expertise, as exemplified by the Pusan International Film Festival, the
Puchon International Fantastic Film Festival, and the Jeonju International
Film Festival. Second, there are corporate-sponsored film festivals such as
Q channel Documentary Film and Video Festival and Nices Film Festi-

val (a festival of short films; it closed in 1999). Third, both new and old activist groups organize festivals. This last group of organizers is relatively autonomous from the state and the corporate sector. Therefore, it provides an interesting example of how the new social movement of the 1990s is taking tentative steps away from the preceding 1980s social movement that centered on labor movements.

In the third, or activist, category, the discourses of the 1980s and 1990s are simultaneously operative. The similarities and continuities as well as the differences and ruptures between the two periods become visible when the different film festivals are examined closely. Also, through the politics of these festivals, the notion of identity politics and the possible formation of alternative public spheres may be tested against the claims for civil society put forth by the Kim Yongsam and Kim Daejung governments and the mainstream media. So far, the third category has included the Women's Film Festival in Seoul, the Queer Film Festival, and the Human Rights Watch Festival (organized by an ex-political prisoner previously jailed for violation of the National Security Law), and the Independent Film Festival (held by young filmmakers), as well as various other small-scale and perennial festivals that take place on college campuses, in cinemas, vidéothèques, and so forth.

The way in which the three categories of film festivals operate may be viewed as an index to the new contours of cultural specificity in the 1990s. The notion of the public sphere and the alternative public spheres within which each film festival is located (or dislocated) has to be taken into consideration vis-à-vis the inauguration of the civil government, the retreat of the labor movement as the privileged force of social change, and the concomitant endeavor to find new agencies for social change. Around the same period, the discourse on nationalism has been remobilized, both with and against the official discourse of *Saegaehwa* (or, "globalization" in Korean in the late 1990s). The various film festivals are indeed public spaces working through a complex structure of articulation. These public spaces tend to operate in a strategic way so as to render the festival occasion a cultural and political site of ongoing recognition, negotiation, and contest. The banning of the Queer Film Festival and Human Rights Watch Film Festival explicitly illuminates the pressure points in the hegemonic order. The whole process of organizing, exhibiting, and banning film festivals reveals blockages and points of compromise, as well as possible directions for alternative or oppositional platforms.[9]

With the removal of the official ban on the above festivals in 1998, the festivals continued to pursue the issues that they initially raised. However, there was one deeply problematic incident that concerned internalized censorship and female local labor in the global era. The documentary *Pab, Ggot, Yang* (*Food, Flower, and Scapegoat*) dealt with the protest of female workers at the Hyundai car factory in the city of Ulsan after the IMF crisis provoked a restructuring of the plant. The women workers, most of who were cooks and kitchen aides at the canteen, were the first to be laid off after a strike. During the strike, male workers described their female colleagues as "flowers" because they provided food. However, the labor union did not give substantive support when the female workers lost their jobs; instead, the women became scapegoats. This is a story rarely told even by the progressive media. *Pab, Ggot, Yang* (2000), made by the woman filmmaker Im Inae with her group Labour Reporters' Network, encountered difficulties during its release. Ulsan is a heavy industry city and a home of Hyundai. In the 1980s, the labor struggle at Hyundai was often depicted as a David and Goliath fight. After the crisis, Hyundai, like other *chaebols* (multinational corporations), was forced by the IMF to restructure its system. The multinational corporation, heavily backed by the state, was to disintegrate under pressures from global capital.

Pab, Ggot, Yang was made in this immediate post-IMF period, and as part of the Human Rights Watch Film Festival the film soon began to tour the country. The city of Ulsan, which had its own Human Rights Watch film festival, refused to include *Pab, Ggot, Yang* in the program, saying that it would antagonize the people of Ulsan. The exclusion of the film led to protests on the Internet site jinbo.net (Progressive net), and others viewed this censorship as not only a violation of freedom of expression, but also an obvious repression of the female labor issue.

The incident broke open the long-overdue gender-and-class related problems within the allegedly progressive movement sector, and it demonstrated quite clearly that control of female labor continues to be an issue. Neither the labor union nor the festival committee, both composed of local activists and intellectuals in Ulsan, viewed the women's labor issue as crucial to their agenda. One of the labor activists in Ulsan noted that the public screening of this kind of documentary would put the upcoming labor-capital negotiation in jeopardy. The fact that the emergent underclass is heavily marked by gender mirrors the troublesome erasure of images of South Korean women in some blockbusters, a situation that upsets festival and Internet communities.

Intriguingly, the filmmaker of *Pab, Ggot, Yang* declares to audiences that hers is not a film. She obviously seeks to exclude her work from the ways in which "film" is made, viewed, and presented. She has also expressed reservations about showing this work in existing exhibition venues, including film festivals. In the end, she preferred to show it in segments on the Internet (http://larnet.jinbo.net/movie.html). However, the question remains—if it cannot be named as a film and if it cannot be circulated in the usual film exhibition venues, what then is it?

Links: Formation of a Feminist Sphere

Since the late 1990s, there have been increasing numbers of feminist publications and activities centered on the Internet. If one enters the word "feminism" in a search engine, one gets many hits. These range from lesbian sites to female labor organization sites. In feminist cultural politics, they exist along with feminist presses like *Ttohanui Munhwa* (Alternative culture), *Yoyon* (Women's studies), *Asian Women Studies, Feminism Studies,* and webzines—notably, *Onninae* (Sisters) and *Dalnara Ttalsepo* (Moon Daughter cell). It appears that a relatively autonomous and radical (virtual) space is in the process of being formed, one that (in)voluntarily puts a distance between itself and the state and the economy. Is it not a truism now that, even as critique, the notion of the public sphere is deeply entrenched in the idealization and the rationalization of the bourgeois? Moreover, is it not also true that one of the feminist critiques of the Habermasian public sphere is that it notoriously excludes women's dissident subjectivities and nonnormative sexualities?[10]

Not dissimilar to the ideas of modernity and the universal, the public sphere continues to be a quite contentious concept, especially when it shifts its locale to the non-West, or to the "rest of the world." Once the notion is evoked in the non-Western context, it immediately invites controversy. For instance, the Korean historian Choi Kapsu argues that Europe, in comparison with China, lags behind in the formation of the state. In the midst of a relatively delayed political process, the European notion of the public sphere emerged as a mediator between the civil society and the state. Hence, the European idea of a public sphere betrays itself as a particular case rather than a universal one, thus contradicting its own claim to universality.[11]

The Chinese scholar Wang Hui reminds us of the vision of Lu Xun, whose critique of the nation-state and industrialization is inspired by the world of ghosts in folklore, one that contains both affection and horror. Instead of evoking Confucian civilization in East Asia, Lu Xun sees the modern in an entirely new mode. He asserts the persistence of the living world of the subaltern class, despite the violence of the modern state, in invoking the realm of ghosts, which refuses to be reducible. It is the realm of affect that defies the logic of modernization. Wang Hui's evocation of Lu Xun's world of ghosts as the repressed but nevertheless persistent vision of the subaltern is an intriguing one. Instead of expelling it to the realm of superstition, one can learn something from defining the world of ghosts alongside a subaltern class rendered invisible and inarticulate by the ruling elite. In other writing, Wang Hui evokes the last days of Lu Xun to illustrate the scene in which Lu Xun envisions himself as a female ghost (Nu Diao) in red.[12]

The male author's identification with and affective investment in the female ghost is illuminating in the sense that Nu Diao belongs to the penumbrae, the possible dwelling place of the "nonsubject" that is positioned in the hierarchized modes of existence as "substance," "shadow," and "penumbrae."[13] In this schema, subject positions such as the courtesan, the maid, and the concubine belong to the penumbrae, the shadow of a shadow.[14] Lu Xun's Nu Diao also slips into the penumbrae with her vengeance and bitterness. The theoretical rereading of the hierarchized living space as "substance," "shadow," and "penumbrae" renders visible what the notion of the public sphere excludes.[15]

Lu Xun's storytelling of a disenchanted world of ghosts in the midst of modernization has some resonance with a mode of storytelling that Partha Chatterjee calls for when he quotes an epitaph that the Urdu writer Saadat Hassan Manto wrote for himself. Chatterjee reads into it the desire for a storytelling mode that deals with the complicated relationship of modernity to democracy and the role of the violence of the modern state. This storytelling renders political society legible, as a site where the specter of pure politics haunts, and thereby, the certainties of civil social norms and constitutional proprieties are challenged.[16] Thus, as Manto writes, "those who dream of building the new democratic society must aspire to be greater storywriters than god."[17]

Taking up the constellation of political society, Kuan-Hsing Chen throws it into relief by criticizing the binary framework of state and civil society. As a transient mediating space between state and civil society, political society provides a space for the subaltern to rethink the notion of the political. In the Taiwanese case, it is the popular democracy line that shares

a sort of elective affinity with political society. Translating Partha Chatterjee's influential proposition of political society into an East Asian context
and one addressing Taiwan in particular, Chen suggests that political society not only mediates the state and civil society, but also *min-jian* (roughly,
a folk, people, or commoner society—*jian* means in-between and space).
Here *min-jian* is the space that has allowed the commoners to survive, so
that no radical break could be brought about by the violence of modernizing state and civil society.[18]

These are issues and subject positions that require a theorization of an
uncertain zone of political society, *min-jian* and *yeoseongjang:* nonunion-
ized female casual labor, sex workers, and the public memorial ceremony
named as women's funeral (*yeoseongjang*). All of these certainly demand to
be re-viewed within a perspective distinct from the trinity of state, civil
society, and public sphere. Female casual labor was originally dismissed
as "illegitimate" even by the labor unions, as is vividly captured in the
documentary *Pab, Ggot, Yang.* Issues concerning sex work do not enter the
realm of civil society and public sphere in the South Korean context unless
it is the U.S. military–related sex industry.

Just like the concept of the forked tongue used in the postcolonial
context, one needs to be strategically dexterous with the use and promise
of the public sphere. It has constantly, historically, made gestures toward
including the sector of the excluded. Because of its hopelessly unattainable
ideal, it accidentally redraws a map even though there is a limit. Being
wary of contingent opening in its true sense of the *Offentlichkeit,* or public
sphere, but certainly not being dependent upon it, one needs to make an
"event" out of the contingent and accidental opening of an episodic public
sphere. Film festivals like the Women's Film Festival in Seoul, the Queer
Film Festival, the Labor Film Festival, and the Human Rights Film Festival
are instances of such events. But at the same time, attention must be drawn
to the way in which normative notions of the public sphere cannot deal
with the persistence and transformation of political society, *min-jian* and
yeoseongjang. Thus it is that one needs frameworks that are attentive to the
in-between and emergent movement.

Conclusion

As I noted in the beginning of this essay, there have been women's funerals (*yeoseongjang*) organized by different groups of women. The organizers

argue that the history of *yeoseongjang* dates back to an incident in 1979 involving the YH Company, which is recorded as one of the crucial labor uprisings against a multinational corporation. Female workers went naked during the strike in defense against the police and gangsters that were privately hired by the YH Company. The women's leader, Kim Kyongsuk, was found dead in the midst of the violent suppression of the strike. Her fellow workers held her funeral in secret. Now, the organizer of *yeoseongjang* for sex workers has chosen to trace its origin to the funeral held for Kim Kyongsuk by her fellow workers.

The two meanings of *yeoseongjang* (women's sphere, women's funeral) evoke death, friendship, and resistance and betray the accidental coming together of different elements of the female public sphere. The public ritual for sex workers in the streets marks a new chapter for the women's movement in South Korea, as the *Women's Weekly News (yosongshinmun)* reported. First, it implicitly challenges a dominant form of ritual conducted in the Confucian way, one that excludes women as key participants in the process. Second, it is an open acknowledgment of a certain sector of sex workers who are rendered largely invisible in the public sphere. However, this protest must shift arenas if effective change is to be made. Organizers must call upon the state and the legal system to tackle the laws concerning reparation and prostitution. Is such a move similar to the liberal reformism undertaken by such groups as NOW (the National Organization for Women) in the United States? Or, are these politics specific to the South Korean context?

Trans-cinema is a cinema in *translation* and in *transition*. What *Pab, Ggot, Yang* and other works like it have is an afterlife, even after they have been barred from entering the progressive public space. This afterlife has much to do with their dissemination on the Internet and with the support they gain there. Nevertheless, the critical constellation of trans-cinema, I think, is yet to come.

Notes

This is a substantive revision of the essay of the same title that appeared in *Inter-Asia Cultural Studies* 4.1 (2003): 10–24. I thank Chris Berry, Kim Eunshil, Kang Myung-Koo, and Yoshimi Shunya for their kind invitations to present this material. Because of their encouragement, this paper itself becomes a trans-Asia project. My thanks also go to Naifei Ding, Kuan-Hsing Chen, Ashish Rajadhyaksha, and Earl Jackson Jr. for their suggestions.

1. For more on this context, see Soyoung Kim, "Question of Woman's Film: The Maid, Madame Freedom, and Women," in *South Korean Golden Age Melodrama,* ed. Kathleen McHugh and Nancy Abelman (Detroit: Wayne State University Press, 2005), 185–200.

2. The financial statistics are taken from the Korean Film Commission (KOFIC) reports on the Korean film industry.

3. Fredric Jameson, "Notes on Globalization as a Philosophical Issue," in *The Cultures of Globalization,* ed. Fredric Jameson and Masao Miyoshi (Durham, NC: Duke University Press, 1998), 76.

4. Soyoung Kim et al., *Hankukhyong blockbuster: Atlantis hokun America* (Blockbuster in Korean mode: America or Atlantis) (Seoul: Hyonshilmunhwayongu, 2001).

5. *Cine-21,* August 17, 2001.

6. Adams Harmes, "Mass Investment Culture," *New Left Review* 9 (May–June 2001): 103–24.

7. Marc Augé, *Non-Places: Introduction to an Anthropology of Supermodernity,* trans. John Howe (London: Verso, 1995); Manuel Castells, *The Rise of the Network Society* (London: Blackwell, 2000), 440–41.

8. Miriam Hansen, *Babel and Babylon: Spectatorship in American Silent Film* (Cambridge: Harvard University Press, 1991), 5–20.

9. Soyoung Kim, "Cinemania, Cinephilia and the Identity Question," *UTS Review* 4.2 (1998): 174–87.

10. Iris Marion Young, "Impartiality and the Civic Public," in *Feminism as Critique,* ed. Seyla Benhabib (Minneapolis: University of Minnesota Press, 1987), 67.

11. Kapsu Choi, "The Public-ness and Public Sphere in the West," *Jinbo Pyonglon* (Radical review) 9 (2001): 17–37.

12. Wang Hui, *Resistance and Despair: The Literary World of Lu Xun* (Shanghai: Shanghai People's Publishing, 1999), 18–38. I thank Wang Hui for alerting me to this book. I also thank Lee Jung-Koo for translating this passage in Chinese to Korean for me.

13. Jen Peng Liu, "The Disposition of Hierarchy and the Late Qing Discourse of Gender Equality," *Inter-Asia Cultural Studies* 2.1 (2001): 71–72.

14. Naifei Ding and Jen-Peng Liu, "Penumbrae ask shadow (II): crocodile skin, lesbian stuffing, Qiu Mialjin's half man half-horse," presented at the third International Crossroads in Cultural Studies Conference, June 21–25, 2000, Birmingham, United Kingdom.

15. I am particularly interested in Lu Xun's perspective since it illuminates my own reading of horror cinema with female ghosts in 1960s South Korea, when state-led modernization took place with full force. In relation to horror cinema, modernization, and female ghosts, please refer to my book *Specters of Modernity: Fantastic Korean Cinema* (Seoul: Ssiat, 2000), which tries a diagnostic reading of modernity and gender.

16. For an articulation of cinema and political society, see Ashish Rajadhyaksha's essay "Bollywoodisation," *Inter-Asia Cultural Studies* 3.1 (2002): 25–39.

17. Partha Chatterjee, "Democracy and the Violence of the State: A Political Ne-

gotiation of Death," *Inter-Asia Cultural Studies* 2.1 (2001): 20.

18. Kuan-Hsing Chen, "Civil Society and Min Jian: On Political Society and Popular Democracy," paper delivered at the Pre-ICA conference in Tokyo, July 2002, organized by Yoshimi Sunya and Kang Myung-Koo.

Vicki Callahan

Chapter 20

The Future of the Archive

An Interview with Lynn Hershman Leeson

As I was working on revisions for this collection, I fortuitously came upon a presentation from the 2007 SIGGRAPH conference by Henrik Bennetsen, the project manager and developer for *Life Squared,* a virtual archive in *Second Life* of the artist Lynn Hershman Leeson's work. *Life Squared* is an online venture produced in collaboration with Hershman Leeson and the Stanford Humanities Lab, and serves here as a fitting conclusion to *Reclaiming the Archive,* as it is as much about the future of the archive as it is about a record of an artistic career. The Hershman Leeson archive is an exemplary space for feminist historians to explore, as it contains crucial documents and traces from the career of a multimedia/performance artist whose work for the last thirty-plus years has featured a thorough and ongoing examination of issues around the intersections of identity, image making/viewing, and technology. Moreover, *Life Squared* offers to feminist historians another important lesson in that it provides a new model for *writing* history.

The Hershman Leeson *Second Life* archive enacts, and indeed *visualizes,* a feminist historical project by taking received, found, and discarded materials and reexamining them with an eye toward what has been previously marginalized, overlooked, or even erased. Certainly, an attention to speaking, seeing, and writing that which has been left out or unseen is central throughout the artist's career. As Hershman Leeson notes, "I like to pull forward the things we've always thought should be invisible and make that a part of the communication structure, in fact the whole nature of the work. So, the invisible becomes the aesthetic itself. Because by the revealing process, we reveal meaning."[1] The *Life Squared* archive is particularly instructive for our purposes as contemporary feminist historians since it takes this component of Hershman Leeson's work and moves explicitly into the digital domain. While the artist has long been a new media pioneer, the archive's link between counternarratives, digital technology, and historical "writing" helps us to visualize the larger issues at stake for feminism, film history, and future expanded cinema/writing.

Hershman Leeson's work has consistently explored the relationship between images and identity, but always there is an attention in her work to the "two-way mirror" of the image, that is, to the idea that we are both created by and creating images and our identity.[2] Regardless of the format, whether video such as *The Electronic Diaries* (1986–89), interactive installations such as *Deep Contact* (1984–89), or net art such as *The Dollie Clones* (1995–98), Hershman Leeson invokes a feminist return of the gaze, thereby destabilizing any "essential" identity found in our images of gender. Not only is the location or stability of identity put into question, but the veracity of the image is itself destabilized. For example, the short video "Commercial for Lynn Hershman" (1978) begins with the artist entering the frame and immediately announcing that Lynn Hershman could not be present for the taping—a commentary about the invisibility of women artists and an admonition against our belief that an image can produce an essential truth about anyone. In the case of Roberta Breitmore (1974–78), "a simulated person who interacts with real life in real time," the investigation of identity is carried out through Hershman's live performances as Breitmore and a variety of "artifacts" that serve as a trail of information: drawings, photographs, comics, letters, and assorted documents.[3] But even here, Hershman's performances at times feature a "double," or "Roberta multiples" who are all present at the same event.

Yet for all the dispersed, dislocated, and disclaimed "I"s that circulate in Hershman Leeson's work, it would be a mistake to read her work as an absence of individual identity or efficacy. As the artist notes, "the pursuit of autonomy became my life's work. Eventually, through persistence and vigilance, I became my own witness and my own private 'I.'"[4] Autonomy is in this case about the *possibilities* for the "I," for an identity that is open and not fixed by institutional and representational forms. Technology becomes for Hershman Leeson the site that both shuts down and liberates these forms and thus a prime motivation for her ongoing experimentation in her work with diverse and innovative tools. As she notes, "I love to work with technologies as they are being invented, or even before anyone else has used them, because they have no history. How one uses these new possibilities can shape the future."[5]

The facility with and our right to understand the workings of technology in our daily lives is the subject of Hershman Leeson's film *Strange Culture* (2007), a documentary on the government's prosecution of Steve Kurtz of the Critical Art Ensemble (CAE) as a "bioterrorist" following an investigation into his wife's tragic and (later learned) unrelated death from heart failure.[6] Using a variety of documentary forms (docudrama reenactments; original media coverage; graphic novel illustrations; interviews with Kurtz, other CAE artists, and other participants in the events), the hybrid format both allows for material to be included that might otherwise be censored and highlights the way representational forms, often by their mere consistency, produces an interpretation and authenticity. Although the government's case—dismissed in 2008—by itself reads like a Franz Kafka novel, *Strange Culture*'s shifting narrative and visual strategies underscore the surreal nightmare that is Kurtz's everyday reality.[7]

Given Hershman Leeson's attention to politics at both a macro and a micro level—the politics of institutions and the politics of identity—it is appropriate that one of her works in progress is a documentary on feminist artists, titled *Women Art Revolution*. As she notes in the following interview, beyond documenting the principal women artists of the last forty years, one of the goals of the work is to make clear the strong links between the social justice movements and feminist art and activism in the 1960s and 1970s.[8]

In a sense, *Women Art Revolution* parallels the *Life Squared* archive in that it takes the artifacts from the feminist past and rewrites history for future generations to see pathways yet to be explored. The *Life Squared* project is indicative of what Michael Shanks calls "a new archival era" or "Archive 3.0," by which he means new spaces of enhanced collaboration, interactive sites of "personal affective engagement," where documentation is not a record as much as a "performative."[9] I would understand his use of performative here to reference the viewer's active participation as well as this new archive's mutability, its space as a place of becoming.

One area of *Life Squared* serves as a new media gallery space with photographs and related documents from the Roberta Breitmore series and Hershman's Dante Hotel installation (1973–74) hanging on virtual walls. The images morph into a series of pictures within each "frame," and nearby assorted screens feature clips by Hershman and Shanks discussing the larger archival project at work. But even in its "first life" the Dante Hotel installation is best described as a kind of interactive archive, a hotel room in San Francisco, left open twenty-four hours a day (for nine months), where visitors could see the artifacts left by fictional characters inhabiting the room, the remains including wax figures, audiotapes, and assorted personal effects, as well as materials left by the viewers/visitors to the space.

A second area of *Life Squared* pushes interactivity even further—your avatar can explore a 3-D reproduction of the hotel after meeting a receptionist, signing in, and getting the key. Nearby, a chatbot named Dante engages you in a conversation and song.[10] In yet another part of the space, one finds a "theater" where *Strange Culture* was simultaneously streamed from the Sundance Film Festival to the *Second Life* venue with the filmmaker fielding a discussion from both spaces. A separate gallery space doubles or reproduces a recent Montreal Museum of Fine Arts show, which featured Hershsman Leeson's work and incorporated a live link back to the *Second Life* site.[11] As always, the viewer/audience plays an important role and leaves a "mark"—a notion visualized in the space by a "documentation" of visitors with a colored trail of their individual movements.

As Hershman Leeson states regarding *Life Squared:* "You're able to see the evidence being looked at and to look inside and watch somebody else discovering the evidence and recreate endless narratives, as they re-pattern the same information and create yet another trail of how it's being seen, re-seen, recomposed, remixed, so that there are an infinite number of ways you can perceive it."[12] *Life Squared* thus not only takes history digital but, I would argue, pushes it to a logical feminist conclusion, a collaborative space for the artist and spectator that opens up an array of possibilities and inspires us as we move toward the future.

Interview

VICKI CALLAHAN: In looking at your career, it is clear there are long-standing feminist objectives in your work. What is especially of interest is that there consistently has been in place a critique of the media, but one which moves beyond a reductive exposé of negative images of women in the media. Rather, from the beginning, your work poses a kind of historical project with attention to the documentation of the "traces" of gender and identity in our culture. In other words, this is a much different kind of feminist project than some of the early feminist work on representation as a simple reflective model.

LYNN HERSHMAN LEESON: Well, I think one thing you can say is that my work is a lot about evidence. I mean you can construct evidence from things that are left around people, the fictional person I made in the seventies [Roberta Breitmore] was defined by the evidence that existed. It was real evidence even though she wasn't real. But therefore she had a real history where I didn't. She could get credit cards and I couldn't, for instance. And in my latest film [*Strange Culture*], Steve Kurtz is also about evidence and what the media does to manipulate evidence, how the media often creates a different identity for who we are. From the point of feminism, how the media creates the altered, inaccessible portrait of what would define us as being appropriate for society. Most people don't fit into that stereotype. You know, it's kind of in the way James Baldwin talks about the ingestion in a sense of a projection media puts on you that is impossible or negative. Which is extremely destructive.

VC: The word "evidence" is perfect. You are both setting in place and stirring around the artifacts of everyday life and then documenting this activity at the same time. I was struck by the way in which your work becomes a kind of demonstration of how to *use* media. Thus, we have not only traces or artifacts in the construction of identity but, again, a feminist *activist* project about writing with media. You provide an instruction in your work of "here is the way media works; here is what it does; these are the kinds of images that we get, how they shape us, and how we might shape *them* and in turn control our own 'identity.'" From the beginning, you're already turning around a "criticism" of "bad" images and instead showing us through performance how to use the tools differently.

LHL: It's absolutely about using the media against itself in a way of personal empowerment. Taking what is already a given, inserting yourself in it, and shifting the location so that you become in control, and all the work is about that.

VC: You mention the issue of control, which brings me to a concern throughout all your work and which you have written about, which is the pursuit of autonomy. This seems to be a fairly specialized notion of autonomy since there is not a "self" presented to us in your work in the sense of a fixed self. There is the 1978 video, "Commercial for Lynn Hershman," where you are performing as "Lynn Hershman" while saying that Lynn herself could not be there for the interview. It is both a very fluid take on identify as well as a commentary on questions of the female artist's invisibility, and a rather contemporary notion consistent with what's happening in feminist work today.

LHL: Right, although when I did it thirty-five to forty years ago, I was considered crazy.

VC: How do you see yourself in relationship to contemporary feminism?

LHL: I don't put myself into different categories. I just do what I do—it would depend upon whom you are talking about. I just had a retrospective in the UK, and Amelia Jones was in conversation with me after *Strange Culture,* which she thought was a feminist film. She took the idea of evidence from the film, the idea of political activism, the idea of not waiting; all these are core feminist strategies.

VC: There is a kind of pedagogy, or again, demonstration in your work, which seems to be about the workings of narrative. Perhaps that is one reason Amelia Jones describes this as a feminist project, because of the way *Strange Culture* uses these different levels, strategies, to relay the narrative.

LHL: Well, yeah, and I kind of fracture it and work outside the normal frame. I'm letting the seams show, so to speak. Hollywood films, they keep the seams really well creased, you know, invisible, and this is just like we're using the frayed edges and whatever is there. Of course, you know, it's all we had; all we had were frayed edges.

VC: You have so much going on right now. You have the *Second Life* archive project, but then also have recently premiered *Strange Culture,* and then there's the documentary you are working on, a history of feminist art: *Women Art Revolution.*

LHL: That's what we're doing next. I'm trying to raise money for [*Women Art Revolution*]. I was working on two films simultaneously, and *Strange Culture* was really crucial because somebody's life was at stake; the other is a history that will be there beyond. So, we hope to start editing in January, but I've two hundred hours shot. I've been shooting it since the sixties.

VC: Can you tell me a little more about the project?

LHL: Well, it's the history. Everybody is in it. It's the history as it happened. So, through Judy Chicago, Miriam Shapiro, Faith Ringgold, and Martha Rosler, but I have been shooting it over the years as things happened, you know, just tracking what was going on. Because I knew something was. And it's things that nobody knows about, for example, how the invasion of Cambodia caused the first feminist performance . . . stories that aren't in any books.

I've never gotten a grant. Nobody has ever funded me. I've been turned down seven times by the Rockefeller Foundation, who this year funded mainly men under thirty. I've been turned down probably fifteen times for a Guggenheim. I've never gotten support. So consequently, I've got to work all these different jobs just to do my work. My hope is that we can get some funding and get this film done by next year. The work always gets done, but it's just really hard for me to do it with no support.

VC: The status of women within the arts establishment and with respect to funding, it hasn't really changed. Here we are in a "third-wave era" or "postfeminist world" and sometimes this is a difficult idea to get across to women students as well, that no, the feminist revolution *isn't* done. That why your work has such an important lesson for us regarding feminism and the media today, about the necessity of taking hold of technology, taking hold of new media tools. I'm wondering how that idea is received today when you teach women students? We have these amazing new tools for expression, easier to use and with more access, but I still see so few women students in film, in the digital arts. Have you found ways of connecting with women students to help them sort of get over the technophobias that they might have and to bring more women into this area of work?

LHL: Well, I think it exists. I think it's there. Women invent things. Computer language was invented by Ada Lovelace. Cell phone technology was invented by Hedy Lamarr. Artificial intelligence was invented by Mary Shelley, or rather the first concept of it. Women invent technology. Then when it gets to a point of marketing it, men step in and take pretty much and get the jobs. But women are there, out there inventing it.

VC: To return to the question of history itself, in a *Seed* magazine interview with yourself and Stanford Humanities Lab Director Michael Shanks, there is an interesting discussion of temporality and historical "method." Professor Shanks defines the archaeological project as having a "forensic sensibility," that is, making use of remains or traces of the past to get back to a point of origination. In response, you point to an essentially "digital" perspective to questions of evidence. Here you note that you can never really go back to this moment in the past but with the found materials, as you say, "you can go forward, using them as a context for the future. The trail and remains may be dormant, but they exist waiting to be revived or resurrected." This strikes me as a really dynamic conception of history as remix.

LHL: One thing that I realize, Stanford bought my archive and they wanted to find a way to keep it active, not just put it in a drawer. And so that's why we did the *Second Life* project, which we invented in order to get the materials into the world again. Everything leaves a trail. Nothing ever leaves—it transforms, changes, but the base is there in whatever we create. It is just a matter of recalling it at different times. Duchamp says that maybe we have three ideas in our lifetime, but one idea just keeps camouflaging itself.

VC: The notion of remix in your work seems related to the explorations of narrative we discussed earlier. Again, as I look at your work, I think, it has always been very "digital" in the use of these nonlinear paths.

LHL: Well, I mean, even the things in the seventies were really about leaving trails, narratives, you know, the place over time. So, we always had that architecture that could be filmic.

VC: Who are the major influences for you?

LHL: Oh, Emma Goldman . . . maybe . . . a cross between Man Ray . . . Emma Goldman, and Cézanne. Artists that really bucked the system, and that had an original voice that were not appreciated in their time, that stayed with their original voice despite not being appreciated, and who generally had something political to say about their time, which I think Duchamp and Cézanne did. I think all art that makes a difference is radical. And if it's radical, then it speaks to the politics of the repression of a particular point in history.

VC: How about influences on your use of narrative as well? The narrative strategies you employ are central to demonstrating the fluid, multiple, or rather the nonsystematic quality of identities.

LHL: I have to mention the surrealist André Breton and the idea of creating Nadja, which was kind of a personality that became a city. Also, some of the Polish theater actionists, as for example Jerzy Grotowski, in life coming into the street and finding the narrative where it exists and expanding on reality. When I tried to write a script it never works. You just sort of have to look around the script and figure out what you're talking about.

VC: In coming back to cinema or more cinema based projects, has that been a change where you feel like your work is more narrative focused? Not so much a linear narrative, but a much more script driven work, or do you think it's always sort of been very similar kinds of approaches to script?

LHL: Well, I've had to do scripts, but I don't think I'm a great scriptwriter. But the people won't fund you based on the fact that you tell them you can make it work.

425

VC: There's a kind of hopefulness to your work as well as a playfulness. I am wondering are you hopeful about new technology, and how do you feel about the rhetoric now around new media tools and democracy (as in the YouTube phenomenon)? Are you hopeful in terms of the kinds of political opportunities it potentially raises? *Strange Culture* makes clear that we're at this crucial juncture with regard to who will have access to media tools and how these tools are to be used to distribute information. The effort by the FBI and the justice system to prosecute Steve Kurtz for his artistic practice demonstrates the critical moment we are in with regard to question of who is going to own these new technologies and our right to creative expression.

LHL: Well, I don't think the technology is in itself democratic. Cell phones may be democratic because there are a lot of them in third world countries, where they don't have access to computers—they need to communicate and they are developing really interesting ways of using those tools. But certainly, most people in the world *don't* have access to YouTube, and the people in the U.S. who do have access are still a different demographic. However, it *has* gotten more information into the world. This aspect has been trivialized, like for instance, when we started working *Second Life*, there are seventy thousand people. Now in a year there's six million. The conversation about this growth, though, is trivialized.

VC: This interview will be the finale for a book I am writing, which was inspired by a class I taught on feminist film theory. In the class we read a lot of very early feminist history, infamous writings, nineteenth-century feminists, and then the seventies feminists, which for the students might have seemed like it was from the nineteenth century. So, how do you engage with feminist questions today? How do you do that so it's not fossilized and how do you "animate" feminism today?

LHL: Well, I just animated Roberta in *Second Life*. I think that one has to constantly be vigilant and question inequities in various ways. It just seems that all my work deals with feminist issues in one way, even the ones that don't start out as being a feminist project, but they all do. So, I can't say there's any rule for doing it.

VC: What is the core issue of feminism in your work: is it the question of voices that don't get to be heard? The inequities in the system? Or, is it about making visible traces that we don't necessarily see? Or about the multiplication of narratives?

LHL: I think it's *all* of that. You know, I think that one personality in the

426

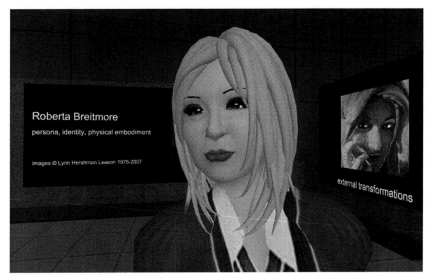

The avatar Roberta Ware (Roberta Breitmore/Lynn Hershman Leeson) tours the *Life Squared* gallery in *Second Life,* one part of the Stanford Humanities Lab online "archive" drawn from Hershman Leeson's diverse artistic career. Courtesy Jeff Aldrich, Stanford Humanities Lab, 2008. Creative Commons license.

twenty-first century is a fractured thing. There's no singular line of it. The mirror's been broken, and yet you have to look at all aspects. It's not enough to be heard; you have to be able to have what you deserve, not just be seen, but be given equity, maybe super equity in every instance. I am just in a show in Montreal right now that opened last week. Men in the show were all selling their work between a hundred thousand to five hundred thousand to a million dollars. I'm not. I did it first. I'm the pioneer in the field. Why isn't my work selling for that much, or at all? I'm the only woman in my gallery. Why is their work valued more than mine? It shouldn't be, and you want to fight to make sure you have that kind of parity on every level. I'm being heard and I'm in all the shows and people invite me to talk all over the place, but the fees are different, the salaries are different, and the sale price is different, and that can't continue.

I've been lucky cause I've had one or two collectors, and the gallery I'm with in New York raised my prices fifteen times what they were selling for. Say they were selling for a dollar; they then sold the stuff for fifteen dollars. Put that price in, and then they started to sell. So, they weren't valued at the low value. I'm going to continue to raise my prices because it worked—and they're still way underrated. They're still maybe 10 percent of what other people in my field are getting. I'm just going to start to value my own work more and I think if you do that then it creates a sense of worth. I think you have to value yourself and value your own work before anybody else will and not accept anything less.

VC: How about future projects?

LHL: The *Women Art Revolution* project, and I have a vampire movie after that—I have to raise money for that too. You know about the *Life Squared* piece in *Second Life,* and I have a new piece called the Global Mind Reader. The Global Mind Reader takes blog tags of different subjects and creates a value system for it. So if you say "greed," then it takes all the blogs from around the world, in the top five dealing with greed or consumerism or Britney Spears, anything. The face just reacts to what's being said. The face reads the blogs and reacts. It's an installation that we're showing for the first time in April [2007].

Author's Note: *Beyond* Life Squared, *Lynn Hershman Leeson's website features more information on these forthcoming projects, especially* Women Art Revolution *and* Strange Culture. *Her website is also an amazing interactive tour through an innovative, diverse, and long-standing feminist artistic career.*[13]

Notes

Many thanks to Lynn Hershan, Jeff Aldrich, and Hennick Bennetsen for their time, energy, and enthusiasm over several discussions—and tours—with me of the *Life Squared* project. I am particularly grateful to both Lynn and Jeff for the use of the beautiful image that accompanies this essay.

1. Michael Shanks and Lynn Hershman Leeson, "The Archaeologist and the Artist Meet Up to Talk about Presence," *Seed,* August 27, 2007, http://seedmagazine.com/news/2007/08/michael_shanks_lynn_hershman_l.php.

2. Lynn Hershman, "The Fantasy beyond Control," on DVD included with *The Art and Films of Lynn Hershman Leeson: Secret Agents, Private I,* ed. Meredith Tromble (Berkeley: University of California Press, 2005), 1.

3. See Hershman Leeson's website for details on Roberta's many lives: http://www.lynnhershman.com (see "Roberta Breitmore" under "Performances/Installations" tab

4. Lynn Hershman Leeson, "Private I: An Investigator's Timeline," in Tromble, *Art and Films,* 14.

5. Ibid., 102.

6. Robert Hirsch, "The Strange Case of Steve Kurtz: Critical Art Ensemble and the Price of Freedom," *Afterimage* May/June 2005, 22.

7. "Case Dropped Against Artist in Terror Case," *New York Times,* April 22, 2008.

8. Inteview with Lynn Hershman Leeson, September 24, 2007, San Francisco, CA.

9. Shanks's discussion can be found as a short video within the Roberta Breitmore gallery (in *Life Squared,* accessed through *Second Life,* http://www.secondlife.com). For more information on the mission and projects of the Stanford Humanities Lab, see http://shl.stanford.edu.

10. I was fortunate to have two separate tours of *Life Squared*'s site guided by those who worked closely on the project. Henrik Bennetsen gave me a early tour while the site was still in progress and access was limited, and Motorato "Moto" Ware, lead virtuality architect at the Stanford Humanities Lab, generously spent time walking me through new parts of the site while providing background information and, most important, introducing me to Dante, the chatbot.

11. *E-art: New Technologies and Contemporary Art: Ten Years of Accomplishments by the Daniel Langlois Foundation,* Montreal Museum of Fine Arts, September 20–December 9, 2007.

12. Shanks and Hershman Leeson, "Archaeologist and Artist."

13. For information on *Women Art Revolution,* see http://www.lynnhershman.com/index.php?main_page=product_info&products_id=6; for *Strange Culture,* see http://www.lynnhershman.com/newprojects.htm.

Contributors

VICKI CALLAHAN is an associate professor and founder of the Conceptual Studies program in the Peck School of the Arts at the University of Wisconsin–Milwaukee, as well as a visiting scholar at the Institute of Multimedia Literacy at the University of Southern California. She is the author of *Zones of Anxiety: Movement, Musidora, and the Crime Serials of Louis Feuilllade* (Wayne State University Press, 2004). Her current research project is focused on the silent film comedienne/director Mabel Normand. She also co-authors with Lina Srivastava http://www.transmedia-activism.com, a resource website for using cross-media platforms for social change.

VICTORIA DUCKETT received her Ph.D. in Critical Studies from UCLA and teaches film history and theory in the Department of Media and Performing Arts, Università Cattolica, Milan. She is completing a book entitled *"A Little Too Much is Enough for Me": Sarah Bernhardt and Silent Cinema* and is editing a special issue of *Nineteenth Century Theatre and Film* which explores the intersections between gender, theater, and early film. Currently, she is a Fellow in the School of Culture and Communication at the University of Melbourne.

ANNA EVERETT is a professor of film, television and new media studies at the University of California at Santa Barbara (UCSB). She has published numerous books and articles including *Returning the Gaze: A Genealogy of Black Film Criticism, 1909–1949* (Duke University Press, 2001); *New Media Theories and Practices of Digitextuality,* edited with John Caldwell (Routledge, 2003); and *Digital Diaspora: A Race for Cyberspace* (SUNY Press, 2009).

SANDY FLITTERMAN-LEWIS is the author of *To Desire Differently: Feminism and the French Cinema,* 2nd ed. (Columbia University Press, 1996) and coauthor of *New Vocabularies in Film Semiotics* (Routledge, 1992). Her current work, *Hidden Voices: Essays on Childhood, the Family, and Anti-Semitism in Occupation France,* comes out of a conference she organized at Columbia University in 1998. She teaches English, cinema studies, and comparative literature and is an associate professor at Rutgers University in New Brunswick, NJ.

Terri Simone Francis is assistant professor in the Film Studies Program and the Department of African American Studies at Yale University. She is the author of several articles on Josephine Baker, and her book analyzing the Parisian's career as a primal site of black American cinema is forthcoming from Indiana University Press. Further research projects concern Jamaica's transnational history with film and experimental expressions in black cinemas.

Joanne Hershfield is professor and chair of women's studies at the University of North Carolina at Chapel Hill. She is the author of *Imagining La Chica Moderna: Women and Visual Culture in Mexico, 1917–1936* (Duke University Press, 2008), *The Invention of Dolores del Rio* (University of Minnesota Press, 2000), and *Mexican Cinema/Mexican Woman, 1940–1950* (University of Arizona Press, 1996).

Sumiko Higashi is professor emerita in the Department of History at SUNY Brockport. She is the author of *Cecil B. DeMille and American Culture: The Silent Era* (University of California Press, 1994) as well as numerous essays on American film history, especially the silent period; women in film and television; and film as historical representation. She is currently working on a study of stardom, femininity, and consumption in the 1950s.

Soyoung Kim teaches in the Department of Film Studies at Korean National University in Seoul. Her publications include *Specters of Modernity: Fantastic Korean Cinema* (Ssiaseul Ppurineun Saramdeul, 2000), *Cinema: Blue Flower in the Land of Technology* (Youlhwadang, 1996), and other books on issues of cinema, modernity, and gender. Her articles have appeared in *Inter-Asia Cultural Studies, Traces, UTS Review, Postcolonial Studies, Shiso* (in Japanese), and *Gendai Shiso* (in Japanese), and she has co-edited the special issue on *Cinema, Culture Industry and Political Societies* for *Inter-Asia Cultural Studies*. Her documentaries on Korean women, including *Women's History Trilogy* (2000–2004), have been screened at Seoul Women's Film Festival, Yamgata international documentary film festival, and Hong Kong International film festival, as well as shown on EBS public channel.

Annette Kuhn is professor of film studies in the School of Languages, Linguistics, and Film at Queen Mary, University of London, and is an editor of the journal *Screen*. Her recently published work includes *An Everyday Magic: Cinema and Cultural Memory* (US title *Dreaming of Fred and Ginger*) (I. B. Tauris; New York University Press, 2002).

Suzanne Leonard is assistant professor of English at Simmons College, where she coordinates the minor in cinema and media studies. She recently published a book-length study of the film *Fatal Attraction* (Wiley-Blackwell, 2009), and her research interests include feminist media studies, film theory, and women's literature.

Laura Mulvey is professor of film and media studies at Birkbeck College, University of London. She is the author of *Visual and Other Pleasures* (Macmillan, 1989;

second edition 2009), *Fetishism and Curiosity* (British Film Institute, 1996), *Citizen Kane* (BFI Classics, British Film Institute, 1996), and *Death 24 x a Second: Stillness and the Moving Image* (Reaktion Books, 2006). She has co-directed six films with Peter Wollen, including *Riddles of the Sphinx* (BFI, 1978) and *Frida Kahlo and Tina Modotti* (Arts Council 1980), and also co-directed, with artist/film-maker Mark Lewis, *Disgraced Monuments* (Channel Four, 1994).

GIULIANA MUSCIO is professor of cinema at the University of Padua, Italy. She received her Ph.D. in critical studies at UCLA. She is author of *Hollywood's New Deal* (Temple University Press, 1996) and of works both in Italian and English on screenwriting, cold war cinema, the 1930s, women screenwriters in American silent cinema, film and history, and film relations between the US and Italy. She has been on the editorial board of *Cinema Journal,* and she was part of the European committee *Changing Media, Changing Europe.*

AYAKO SAITO is a professor in the Department of Art Studies at Meiji Gakuin University in Tokyo, Japan. She has written extensively about the work of such directors as Alfred Hitchcock, Max Ophuls, Fritz Lang, Jean-Luc Godard, and Chantal Akerman, as well as about postwar Japanese cinema and the representation of women. Her studies include "Hitchcock's Trilogy: A Logic of Mise-en-Scène" in *Endless Night: Cinema and Psychoanalysis, Parallel Histories* (University of California Press, 1999) and "Orchestration of Tears: Politics of Crying and Reclaiming Women's Public Sphere" for the online journal *Senses of Cinema* (2003). She also edited *Film and Body/Sexuality* (Shinwasha, 2006) and is the co-author of *Male Bonding: Asian Cinema and Homosociality* (Heibonsha, 2004) and *Fighting Women: Female Action in Japanese Cinema* (Sakuhinsha, 2009).

MICHELE SCHREIBER is an assistant professor of film studies at Emory University. She is the author of *The Cinema of David Fincher: Movies that Scar* (forthcoming from Wallflower Press). She is also completing a book project titled *These Fish Want a Bicycle: Romance in the Post-feminist Media,* which examines the perseverance and increasing ubiquity of the traditional romance narrative in the postfeminist political and cultural landscape.

GENEVIÈVE SELLIER, professor of film studies at the University of Caen in Normandy, France, is the author of *Jean Grémillon, Le cinéma est à vous* (Éditions Méridiens-Klincsieck, 1989), *La Drôle de guerre des sexes 1930–1956* with Noël Burch (Éditions Nathan, 1996), and *La Nouvelle Vague, un cinéma au masculin singulier* (2005), which was translated by Kristin Ross and published in English as *Masculine Singular: French New Wave Cinema* (Duke University Press, 2008). Professor Sellier is a member of the Institut Universitaire de France.

AMY SHORE is director and assistant professor for the Cinema and Screen Studies Program at the State University of New York at Oswego. Her scholarship on suffrage and early cinema has appeared in *Camera Obscura,* and she is currently completing a book-length study of the subject.

JANET STAIGER teaches critical and cultural studies at the University of Texas at Austin. Her most recent books are *Media Reception Studies* (New York University Press, 2005); *Authorship and Cinema,* co-edited with David Gerstner (Routledge, 2003); *Perverse Spectators: The Practices of Film Reception* (New York University Press, 2000); and *Blockbuster TV: Must-See Sitcoms in the Network Era* (New York University Press, 2000).

SHELLEY STAMP is the author of *Movie-Struck Girls: Women and Motion Picture Culture after the Nickelodeon* (Princeton University Press, 2000) and the co-editor of two collections: *American Cinema's Transitional Era: Audiences, Institutions, Practices* with Charlie Keil (University of California Press, 2004) and a special issue of *Film History* on "Women and the Silent Screen" with Amelie Hastie. She is professor of film and digital media at the University of California, Santa Cruz. Her current book project, Lois Weber in Early Hollywood, is supported by a Film Scholars Grant from the Academy of Motion Picture Arts and Sciences.

YVONNE TASKER is professor of film and television studies at the University of East Anglia in Norwich, England. She is the author of various books and articles exploring gender and popular culture, including *Working Girls: Gender and Sexuality in Popular Cinema* (Routledge, 1998) and *The Silence of the Lambs* (BFI, 2002), and is co-editor with Diane Negra of the anthology *Interrogating Postfeminism: Gender and the Politics of Popular Culture* (Duke University Press, 2007). Her latest book, *Soldiers' Stories: Military in Cinema and Television since WWII,* will be published by Duke University Press in 2010.

PATRICIA WHITE is a professor of film and media studies at Swarthmore College. She is the author of *Uninvited: Classical Hollywood Cinema and Lesbian Representability* (Indiana University Press, 1999) and co-author with Timothy Corrigan of *The Film Experience* (Bedford St. Martin's, 2004; second edition 2009). She is a member of the editorial collective of *Camera Obscura* and the board of directors of Women Make Movies. She is working on a book on contemporary global women directors.

Index

Page numbers in italics refer to illustrations

Asaoka, Ruriko, 157
Ascenseur pour l'échafaud (Elevator to the Gallows) (1957), 180
Asian Women Studies, 412
audience: female, in 1920s, 22, 23–24; focus on, 10; new ability to manipulate film with video and DVD, 30. *See also* spectator; spectatorship
Auge, Marc, 405
Austen, Jane, 371
auteurism, 227n5; and contemporary film culture, 216–18; figure of auteur as masculine, 219–20; and focus on director, 215; popular discourse of, and women filmmakers, 214, 216, 226–27; privileging of authored text over context, 213; rewriting of in feminist film studies, 127–29
authorship criticism: biographical, 222; as matter of taste, 217; and romanticized personal vision, 226

Babel and Babylon: Spectatorship in American Silent Film (Hansen), 259
Baby Face (1933), 45–46, 46, 51
Backlash (Faludi), 366, 380
Back Street (1932), 49
Bade, Patrick, 36
Bad Women (Staiger), 52, 55n15
Baker, Josephine, 100, 113–15; characters as product of viewer's fantasy, 115; characters as women not chosen, 116; characters excluded from romance, 115; scary subjectivity, 115
Baldwin, James, 422
Bambara, Toni Cade, 104, 105, 123n10
Bamboozled (2000), 224
Bankhead, Tallulah, 232
Bara, Theda, 33, 40, 41
Bardot, Brigitte, and alienated mass culture, 185–87
Baroncelli, Jacques de, 115
Barriga, Cecilia, 231, 232, 241, 250, 253–54
Barry, Iris, 23
Barrymore, John, 272
Barthes, Roland, 243
The Battle of Algiers (1966), 105

The Battle of Manila Bay, 275
Baudelaire, Charles, 180
Baumgardner, Jennifer, 367, 385
Bean, Jennifer, 2, 260
Beaton, Cecil, 233, 236, 239, 240, 241, 251, 256n28, 257n59
Beauchamp, Cari, 259, 291
Le Beau Serge, 184
Beerbohm, Max, 207
Beery, Noah, Sr., 48
Belleforest, François de, 199
Belmondo, Jean-Paul, 181
Belmont, Alva, 317
Ben Hur (1959), 290
Bennetsen, Henrik, 418
Bennett, Tony, 12
Bennington, Geoff, 12
Beranger, Clara, 290, 293, 294; and William deMille, 299, 301
Bergere, Ouida, 290, 293, 294, 308n19
Bergner, Elisabeth, 61
Bergstrom, Janet, 14n2
Berlant, Lauren, 76
Bernhardt, Sarah, 129; critique of roles available for women on stage, 209; defense of changes to *Hamlet,* 203; famous for thinness, 206; fencing on stage, 206; introduction of standing death, 201, 211n23; involvement in interpretation and presentation of *Hamlet,* 204; as mediator between old and new, 197; "Men's Roles as Played by Women," 208–9; nascent twentieth-century feminism, 204, 209; performative excess, 204; *premier travesti rôle,* 198, 210n11; public criticism of performance of masculinity and youth, 207–8; and shift in concept of female figure, 206; *Tosca,* 197; as Tosca advertising herself in *Hamlet,* 196
Between the Acts (Woolf), 352–53
Bigelow, Kathryn, 213, 214, 218–19; action-oriented films, 218; associated by media with male filmmaker, 222; critical view of as inappropriate, 218–19, 220–21; criticism of her use of genre, 220–21; maverick image tied

of other women screenwriters, 297–98; more individualist than feminist, 297; problematic attitudes in choice between work and family, 296; resented treatment as "woman writer," 297

Doane, Mary Ann, 14n2, 32, 93

The Doctor and the Woman (1918), 133, 147

La Dolce Vita (1960), 186

The Dollie Clones (1995–98) (Hershman Leeson), 419

Don't Change Your Husband (1919), 302

Dottie Gets Spanked (1993), 225

double consciousness, 112–13

double discrimination, 98–99

Douglas, Ann, 294–95

Dove, Billie, 47, 131, 134, 135, 136; with Weber, *136*

Drake, Jennifer, 392

Dreiser, Theodore, 144, 342n1

Dressler, Marie, 68, 290, 292

DuBois, Ellen Carol, 315

Du Bois, W. E. B., 112

Duchamp, Marcel, 425

Duckett, Victoria, 129

Dulac, Germaine, 345; abstract film poems, 355; central place in film history, 346; and film section of "Mai 36" group, 351–52; Nazi persecution, 348–49; optimism about progressive capability of media, 354; organization of newsreels, 353; problems with publication of obituary, 347; production company, 346; work with newsreel, 351; work with Popular Front cultural groups, 346, 350, 351

The Dumb Girl of Portici (1914), 140, 146

Dunbar, Paul Laurence, 123n6

Duncan, Isadora, 236

Dunn, Stephanie, 102

Duras, Marguerite, 181, 187, 190

Durbin, Deanna, 61, 62, 64, 65, 70

Dyer, Richard, 79, 266

early cinema: and breaking down of distinctions between public and private gendered domains, 260;

foregrounding and undermining of "woman as spectacle," 260; and modern woman as key component of consumer culture, 260; women and, 259–60; working-class and lower-middle-class audiences, 287n56

Ebony, 105

Edison, Thomas, 310

Edison Studios, 309, 312

Ehrlich, Evelyn, 348

Eldridge, Charles, 267

The Electronic Diaries (1986–89) (Hershman Leeson), 419

Emma (Austen), 371, 372

The End of the Road, 330

Ephron, Nora, 376

The Epistemology of the Closet (Sedgwick), 242

Epps, Omar, 117

Equality League of Self-Supporting Women, 314–15; change of name, 318; framing of demonstrations on modern rational citizenship, 317; modeled after American labor and British suffrage tactics, 315; and shift in political ideology in suffrage movement, 315; suffrage parade, 317–18

Equal Rights Amendment, 366

essentialism, 160, 227n5

Eternal Sunshine of the Spotless Mind (2004), 225

ethnohistorical studies, 2, 60

Étiévant, Henri, 115

L'Etranger (The Stranger) (Camus), 178

Everett, Anna, 14, 361, 362

"expanded cinema," 5

Failan (2001), 407

Fairbanks, Douglas, 290, 291, 303

Fairfax, Marion, 290, 294, 297; animal pictures, 302; *Photoplay* article on, 292–93

fallen-man narrative, 46–48

fallen woman: comedic approach, 51–52; as desiring subject, 49–52; films of, 42–*44;* rhetoric of in 1800s, 34, 35–36; as sacrificing mother,

fallen woman (*continued*)
49–50; typology of, 42–53; value in
reminding men about remaining in
control, 42; as victimizer, 42, 43, 45–
46; as working-class victim, 43, 45.
See also femme fatale, in early cinema
(1905–33)
Faludi, Susan, 366, 385
The Family Man (2000), 364
Family Secrets (Kuhn), 11
Famous Players-Lasky, 133
fan magazine readers, gender and social
class of, 279–83
fan magazines: ads for employment, 281;
biographies of women screenwriters,
304; construction of readers as passive
spectators, 275; social aspirations of
ads, 280–81; and transformation of
self-making to stress personality rather
than character, 282
Fanon, Frantz: *The Wretched of the Earth*,
105
fans: gender of, 269; homoeroticism
of, 251; and *Motion Picture Story
Magazine* (*MPSM*), 270–75
Farnum, Dorothy, 290
Fausse Alerte (1945), 115
Federated Clubwomen of America, 147
Feet of Clay, 297
Fein, Ellen, 370–71
Fellini, Federico, 186
Felman, Shoshana, 155
female grotesque, 322
Female Masculinity (Halberstam), 249
Femina, 206
feminism: commodity, 361; evolution to
postfeminism, 366–68; lifestyle, 361;
need to respect and value differences
among women, 387–88; on pitfalls of
assuming that one identity category
is sufficient for analysis, 34; racial
problematic, 385, 387; and romantic
mystification, 76; second wave, 367;
socialist, 351; and social justice, 3. *See
also* cyberfeminism
Feminism 3.0, 6, 7n19, 361
Feminism and the Future (Modleski), 367
Feminism Studies, 412

feminist film history, 259; diversity of
approaches, 2; rejection of claims
made by male director for priority over
text, 213; and theorization, 22; turn
to, 2–3, 4
feminist film studies, 1; current emphasis
on historical conditions, 18;
development in Britain, 18–19; early
emphasis on binary opposition of
gaze and spectacle, 18; engagement
with opposition of femininity and
masculinity, 109; failure to consider
race and racial ideologies, 104, 109;
1970s influence on film history
and feminist film theory, 4; and
rewriting authorship, 127–29; search
for feminine aesthetic, 128; tension
between cinema as pleasure and as
oppression, 3
A Feminist Reader in Early Cinema (Bean
and Negra), 2
femme fatale, in early cinema (1905–33),
32–57; choice involved in narrative
resolution, 36–38; choice to enter
exchange system and become
commodity, 32–33; and class status,
42; as fallen woman, 41–42; of film
noir, 53; and genre of narrative, 42;
humanization, 39; as masquerade,
32; moral agency within realm of
individual action, 37; and narrative
about masculinity in relation to
female's actions, 33; narrative value
of in determining masculinity, 53;
and threat of women's place in social
hierarchy, 36
femme fatale, in late 1800s, 36
fencing, popularity among "belles
mondaines" in mid-nineteenth-
century Paris, 205–7
Feuer, Jane, 366
Fields, Gracie, 58–59, 62, 64
film. *See* cinema
Film Comment, Jodie Foster cover, 215
Film Fashionland, 63
film studies. *See* cinema studies; feminist
film studies
Fincher, David, 217

Human Rights Watch Film Festival,
410, 411, 414; Independent Film
Festival, 410; international film
festivals, 403, 409–12; *Media City
Seoul 2000,* 405; nongovernmental
organizations (NGOs), 409; Queer
Film Festival, 410, 414; women's labor
strike, 415; *yeoseongjang,* 399, 414–15.
See also Korean blockbuster
South Korean film industry, 396, 402–3
The Spanish Flag Pulled Down (1898), 275
specificity, and avant-garde theory, 19
spectacle: feminization of, 20; and gaze, 18.
See also woman as spectacle
spectator: absent female, 11; black female,
10; black man, 10; unassimilated,
117–22; women as, 155, 259. *See also*
black woman spectator
spectatorship: and aesthetics of film, 17;
black, 111–12, 118; nonheterosexist,
129; reconstructed, 122
Spheeris, Penelope, 221
Springer, Kimberly, 361
St. Clair, Malcolm, 18
St. Johns, Adela Rogers, 144, 290
Stacey, Jackie, 11, 381
Staiger, Janet, 10–11, 13, 52, 55n15,
60–61
Stamp, Shelley, 128–29, 259, 326n6,
328n36
Stanford Humanities Lab, 424, *427*
Stanwyck, Barbara, 46
Star, Darren, 373
stardom: as commodity fetishism,
266–70; discourses of, and notions of
heteronormativity, 76; phenomenon
of, 264; role in redefinition of self in
consumer culture, 261; role models for
both men and women, 282
*Star Gazing: Hollywood Cinema and Female
Spectatorship* (Stacey), 11
star-maker persona, gendered implications
of, 142
Steichen, Edward, 231, 248
Stein, Gertrude, 250
Steinem, Gloria, 385, 386
stereopticon, 318–19
Stewart, Jacqueline, 111–12, 122

stock investment, online, 403
Stonehouse, Ruth, 147
Strachey, Lytton, 356n5
Strands (1996), 102, 106–9; characters
create alternate logics of their
own, 108; and critically reflexive
spectatorship in black film culture,
110; engagement of beauty culture
and family expectations, 108–9; first-
person voice, 110; and racist, sexist,
and professional expectations of self
and society, 107
Strange Culture (2007), 420, 421, 422,
423, 426
*Stranger than Paradise: Maverick
Filmmakers in Recent American Cinema*
(Andrew), 217
Stravinsky, Igor, 236
Streisand, Barbara, 364
Stroheim, Erich von, 142
Strongheart (canine star), 290
Studlar, Gaylyn, 22
Sugar Town, 222
Summer of Sam (1999), 224
surrealism, 17
Susan Lenox: Her Fall and Rise (1931), 35,
38, 239
Susman, Warren, 265, 302
Sutherland, Evelyn Greenleaf, 297
Swanson, Gloria, 23, 142
Swenson, Karen, 235, 239, 243, 255n24
Swoon (1992), 224, 225–26
Syndicat des Techiciens de la Production
Cinématographique, 351

Tadare (Indulgence), 171
Taegukki (2004), 401–2
Tainted Souls and Painted Faces (Anderson),
34
Taiwan, 414
Taki no Shiraito (The water magician)
(1933), 157
Taliaferro, Mabel, 304
Talmadge, Constance, 23, 290
Talmadge, Norma, 23, 278, 290, 308n18
The Taming of the Shrew (Shakespeare), 87
Taranow, Gerda, 197, 198, 201, 206,
211n23, 211n29, 212n41